Shaping Tomorrow

Unveiling the Potential of AR, VR, and MR in Every Realm

nova
science publishers
www.novapublishers.com

Computer Science, Technology and Applications Series

Building Intelligent Systems for the Future: Mastering the Revolution in Cognitive Computing
Anamika Ahirwar, PhD, Neelesh Jain, PhD, and Sumitha Elayaperumal, PhD
ISBN: 979-8-90134-050-9
eBook ISBN: 979-8-90134-094-3

Smart Decision Systems: Integrating Symbolic AI and Cognitive Heuristics for IOMT
Hemant Kumar Saini, PhD, Christian Kaunert and Bhupinder Singh
ISBN: 979-8-89530-935-3
eBook ISBN: 979-8-89530-993-3

Artificial Intelligence: Policy Perspectives and Global Impacts
Sonja Buckley (Editor)
ISBN: 979-8-89530-859-2
eBook ISBN: 979-8-89530-960-5

Immersive Technologies: The Role of Augmented and Virtual Reality in Civilian and Military Use
Rosalie T. Bryant (Editor)
ISBN: 979-8-89530-796-0
eBook ISBN: 979-8-89530-910-0

Harnessing the Power of IoT-Enabled Machine Learning in Healthcare Applications
Mritunjay Rai, PhD, Ravindra Kumar Yadav, PhD, Neha Goel, PhD and Mahesh Kumar H. Kolekar, PhD
ISBN: 979-8-89530-626-0
eBook ISBN: 979-8-89530-761-8

The Future of Machine Learning with Automation in Engineering
Sandeep Gupta, PhD
ISBN: 979-8-89530-556-0
eBook ISBN: 979-8-89530-607-9

More information about this series can be found at
https://novapublishers.com/product-category/series/computer-science-technology-and-applications/

Prithi Samuel
A. Sathya
Balamurugan Balusamy
Chithirai Pon Selvan
Editors

Shaping Tomorrow

Unveiling the Potential of AR, VR, and MR in Every Realm

nova
science publishers
www.novapublishers.com

DOI: https://doi.org/10.52305/NXRX0883

Library of Congress Cataloging-in-Publication Data

ISBN: 979-8-90134-076-9 (Hardcover)
ISBN: 979-8-90134-179-7 (eBook)

Published by Nova Science Publishers, Inc. † New York

Contents

Chapter 1

Comprehensive Analysis of Immersive Technologies

Kaavya Kanagaraj[*]
M. Kiruthika[†]
and Prithi Samuel[‡]
Department of Computational Intelligence, School of Computing, SRM Institute of Science and Technology, Kattankulathur Campus, Chennai, Tamil Nadu, India

Abstract

Immersive technologies—comprising Virtual Reality (VR), Augmented Reality (AR), Mixed Reality (MR), and Extended Reality (XR)—are transforming how individuals interact with digital content, physical environments, and each other. This chapter comprehensively analyses these technologies, exploring their underlying architectures, interaction paradigms, enabling hardware, and software ecosystems. It delves into immersion's cognitive and experiential aspects, highlighting how multisensory engagement and real-time responsiveness create presence and realism. The chapter also reviews emerging applications across sectors such as education, healthcare, manufacturing, and entertainment, showcasing their impact on productivity, engagement, and decision-making. Key challenges, including technical limitations, data privacy concerns, ethical implications, and the digital divide, are critically examined. Furthermore, the chapter evaluates future trends in immersive media, such as AI-enhanced environments, haptic feedback systems, and cloud-based XR.

Keywords: virtual reality, augmented, mixed reality, extended reality, immersive technologies

1. Introduction

Immersive technologies [1], also known as Extended Reality (XR) technologies, are the next level technologies designed to strengthen or replace real-world experiences with simulated ones. X in eXtended Reality refers to any of the technologies – VR (Virtual Reality), AR

[*] Corresponding Author's Email: kaavyak@srmist.edu.in
[†] Corresponding Author's Email: kiruthim4@srmist.edu.in
[‡] Corresponding Author's Email: drprithisamuel@gmail.com

In: Shaping Tomorrow
Editors: Prithi Samuel, A. Sathya, Balamurugan Balusamy et al.
ISBN: 979-8-90134-076-9

(Augmented Reality) and MR (Mixed Reality), as in Figure 1. These three technologies share most technical qualities, with few differences. In VR, the input devices and head-mounted display units to give the user a sense of real immersion. The display unit covers the user's entire field of view with the display content generated by the computer. Many input devices, such as tracker balls, joysticks, data gloves, etc., allow users to interact with the virtual environment. VR does create a virtual experience with sounds and 3D visuals. VR only provides computer-generated content and not any real-world content [2].

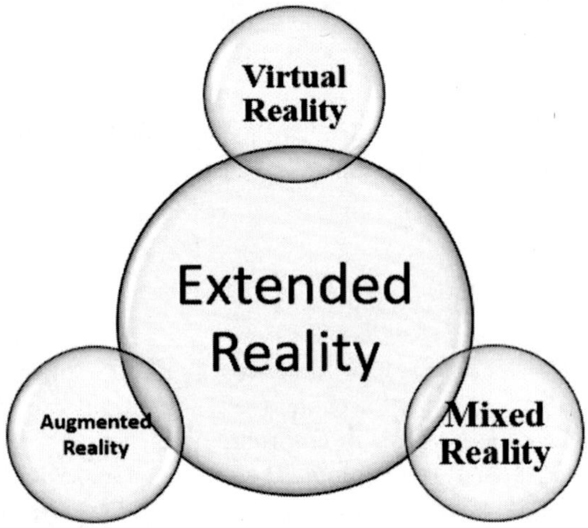

Figure 1. Extended reality.

Table 1. Significant differences between types of VR

Features	Non-immersive VR	Semi-immersive VR	Fully-immersive VR
Level of Immersion	Minimal immersion	Nominal immersion	Maximum immersion
Hardware Requirement	Basic desktops, monitors, and mobile screens for display. Keyboards, mouse and controllers for input.	Advanced 3D graphics modelling. Wrap-around / CAVE screens, head-mounted displays for display: joysticks and motion trackers for input.	HMDs, data gloves, and multi-sensory input devices. Also, users can interact with VR using body gestures and movements.
Level of Interaction	Low	Moderate	High
Expense	Low	Moderate	High
Use cases	Virtual tours and casual video games	Simulations for training	VR gaming, highly sensitive medical training and therapies

Based on the use cases, there are different types of VR such as Non-immersive VR, Semi-immersive VR and Fully immersive VR [3]. Non-immersive VR allows users to interact with the virtual environment using a computer. At the same time, the user will be aware of the real-world surroundings. This type of VR provides very minimal immersion and limited sensory involvement. This is used mainly in simulation-based video games and virtual tours. Semi-immersive VR provides better immersion than Non-immersive VR. However, entirely it does not isolate the user entirely from the real world. Advanced 3D graphics modelling is used. This mostly used in driving simulations for training drivers, educational and industrial simulations. Fully immersive VR provides the highest level of immersion for the user as it completely engages the user in a virtual environment. It employs advanced hardware and multi-sensory systems for high interaction. This type of VR is mainly involved in gaming, VR-based medical training, and immersive healthcare treatments. Table 1 shows the significant differences between the three types of VR.

Augmented Reality [4] enhances/augments the real-world view through virtual objects. In this technology, the generated virtual content overlaps the real-world objects. The virtual content may be 3D images, sounds or any interactive elements. While VR immerses the users into the virtual world, AR enhances the real-world experience by overlaying digital content over the real-world elements. Processors and GPUs are used to process real-world data and position the digital content. AR is implemented using exclusive software development tools such as ARKit, ARCore, Vuforia, etc. To create an immersive augmented experience, AR operates by leveraging various hardware components, sensors, and algorithms to create an immersive augmented expertise [5]. The working of AR software can be summarized as follows:

Hardware components are used in AR to bring in the complete real-world experience. Cameras and sensors are used to capture and detect real-world objects. Global Positioning System (GPS) is used to help in navigation. AR uses an accelerometer, an accelerometer, and a gyroscope to determine the device's orientation and movement and to support aligning digital elements with the physical world. Smartphones, AR glasses or digital tablets render the AR experience.

AR track the position and movement of user's devices with the help of tracking algorithms categorized into marker-based and marker-less methods. These algorithms are further divided into multiple types used to position virtual objects with respect to physical surroundings. This rendering gives the impression that the digital contents are affixed to real places.

AR also uses computer vision (CV) techniques to recognize and realize real world objects. CV identifies the objectsand surfaces multiple landmarks that make activating particular AR content easier over real-world objects.

After capturing the real-world entity, AR software takes up the responsibility to create and impose the digital content in the proper physical-world context. This software is also responsible for picking up the animations or 3D models that seem real for the given context. For instance, this feature is used in Snapchat and Instagram, where the real faces are superimposed with attractive filters, animations and 3D objects.

AR enables users to engage with digital content using voice commands, touchscreens, or gestures. Smooth interaction is possible for users, as they can manipulate virtual objects were real-world objects. For instance, players can engage with other players in real-time or capture virtual creatures by tapping on them on their smartphone screen in augmented reality games like Pokémon GO, which combine the real and virtual worlds.

AR can be differentiated into various types based on the underlying technologies [6]. The different types of AR are as follows:

Marker-Based AR: Also known as recognition-based AR identifies markers or images to trigger an augmented function. Marker-based AR requires a marker to activate an augmentation. Markers are distinct patterns that cameras can easily recognise and process, and are visually independent of the environment around them. These patterns can be paper-based or physical objects in the real world. For example, QR code on specific pages of the book when scanned might be able to display animations or any interactive contents, like quiz, that is relevant to the page's content.

Marker-less AR: No particular markers are required for marker-less AR. Instead, it detects and superimposes digital content onto actual objects and environments using sensors and GPS data. For example, Google Maps AR employs marker-less AR to superimpose navigational instructions / directions on a street's real-time view, directing users to the appropriate location based on their present location.

Location-Based AR: For context-aware or geo-based augmented reality experiences, location-based AR uses the Global Positioning System (GPS) or Real-time Location System (RTLS). GPS data is used in place of physical markers. This is frequently utilized for gaming, travel, and navigation. With the ability to overlay directions onto the actual environment and direct users to their destination, this kind of augmented reality is incredibly helpful when navigating. Additionally, it can show nearby tourist destinations, well-known landmarks, eateries, or fuel refilling stations.

Projection-Based AR: Projection-based AR involves projecting light or images onto physical surfaces, turning them into interactive interfaces or displaying AR content without the need for a screen. Example: Interactive museums can use projection-based AR to bring historical artifacts to life, allowing users to interact with projected content through touch.

Mixed Reality (MR) [7], blends VR and AR with the physical world. Mixed reality programming allows people to interact with virtual elements as if they were real and enable digital objects to interact with real-world environments. Like AR, it enriches the real world by augmenting it with virtual objects. However, the distinction lies in the level of integration. In MR, the virtual objects are not merely overlaid on top of the real world; instead, they are aware of the real world, and even virtual and physical components can interact with one another. The boundary between virtual and physical objects becomes opaque to the user. Because of these characteristics, mixed reality has been used for environmental understanding (like spatial mapping and anchoring), human understanding (includes hand-tracking, eye ball-tracking, and vocal input), locating and positioning of virtual spaces over physical spaces, and collaboration on 3D assets. There are multiple advantages in deploying mixed reality. The design team can utilise MR to build digital twins of the end products that allow them to test challenging concepts/materials, with minimal design cost. MR paves way for people to work together even from a far distance. MR functions with headsets that may be used by the employers to give real-time feedback for the work that is currently done by the employees. Also, the training and development associated with hazardous situations can be done using MR, which reduces the danger that will be encountered during real-time training.

By merging the virtual and real worlds, mixed reality allows for natural and intuitive three-dimensional interactions between people, machines, and their surroundings. This results from advancements in computer vision, graphical interfaces, input methods, audio and visual technologies, and cloud computing. Since we are in the early stages of MR's discovery, it is challenging to create mixed reality experiences successfully. But the possibilities are seamless. The working of mixed reality depends on cloud computing and artificial intelligence. The data generated by the MR device robustis processed and stored in 3D format using robust AI sensors, smart lenses, a GPU and graphics cards. Mixed reality experience highly depends on the end devices' capabilities. These devices can be intelligent eye glasses, gloves, bodysuits, and smartphones. MR headsets, such as Hololens, generate high-fidelity settings to engage users in virtual activities, thus erasing the boundaries between reality and virtual reality. The other devices used by MR are Heads-up display (to project 3D graphics to the user) and a 360-degree Cave Automatic Virtual Environment – CAVE (where a person is encircled by projected screens on all sides, above and below). It is crucial to note that the boundaries between VR, AR and MR are not always clear, and there can be differences in the definitions [8], as in Figure 2.

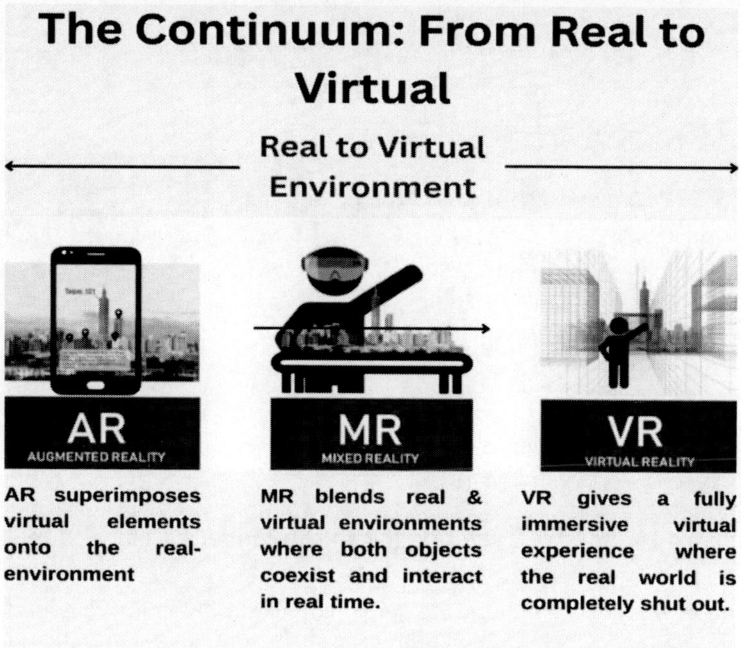

Figure 2. Augmented, mixed and virtual reality.

1.1. Evolution of Immersive Technologies

Immersive technologies have evolved significantly, transforming human interaction with digital environments. The journey began in the 19th century with stereoscopic viewing and early optical illusions, later advancing to mechanical simulators in aviation and military applications [9, 10]. The 1950s saw the creation of Sensorama, an early attempt at multi-sensory VR, followed by the first head-mounted display (HMD) in 1968. In the 1980s, commercial exploration of Immersive technology began where VR gained momentum with NASA's astronaut training simulations and Jaron Lanier's introduction of data gloves. The 1990s saw the rise and fall of VR. The term augmented reality was coined by Tom Caudell in 1994. AR applications develop in many vital areas, including military and medical training. The 2000s paved the way for research and niche applications, and the very first mobile apps based on AR emerged using mobile cameras and GPS. After 2010, many mainstream applications started adopting AR / VR, and this brought mobile AR innovations, notably Google Glass (2012) and Pokémon GO (2016), which popularised augmented reality experiences. Meanwhile, VR has been resurged by consumer headsets like Oculus Rift (2012) and PlayStation VR (2016). Today, AI-powered AR, 5G connectivity, and the AR Cloud enabling real-time, persistent digital overlays, shaping the future of the Metaverse, spatial computing, and neural interfaces. Figure 3 illustrates the key milestones in the evolution of immersive technologies.

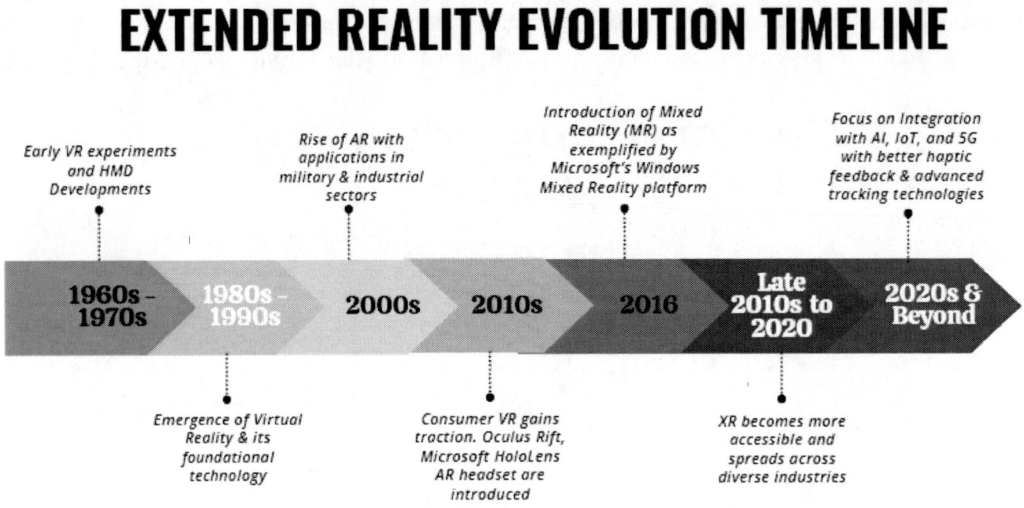

Figure 3. Key milestones in the evolution of extended reality.

1.2. Importance of Immersive Technologies in the Modern Era

Immersive technologies are revolutionising various industries by improving human interaction with digital environments. These technologies allow for interactive learning, real-time simulations, and improved decision-making. VR facilitates therapy and rehabilitation in the healthcare industry, while AR helps with surgeries and healthcare training [11]. Immersion skill development modules and virtual classrooms are beneficial for training and education. Digital twins, assembly line simulations, and AR-driven maintenance are used in manufacturing and Industry 4.0. AR-powered virtual try-ons and interactive advertisements improve consumer interaction in marketing and retail. With XR-based experiences, gaming and entertainment have advanced to new heights, and smart cities use AR for urban planning and navigation. AI, 5G networking, and the Metaverse are all key components of the immersive technology of the future, which will propel remote collaboration, workplace transformation, and incredibly lifelike virtual worlds [12]. These technologies will continue to transform user experiences, productivity, and communication in of fields as they develop.

2. Architectural Framework of Immersive Technologies

Immersive technologies, including Virtual Reality (VR), Augmented Reality (AR), and Mixed Reality (MR), rely on a robust and multi-layered architectural framework that integrates hardware, software, networking, and data processing to create seamless, interactive, and real-time experiences. This framework bridge the gap between the physical and digital worlds, enabling enhanced human-computer interaction across industries such as healthcare, education, manufacturing, retail, and entertainment [13].

At the core of immersive technologies lies the hardware layer, which includes a variety of input and output devices. Display devices, such as VR headsets (Oculus Rift, HTC Vive) and AR smart glasses (Microsoft HoloLens, Magic Leap), provide users with a rich visual experience by overlaying digital content onto the real world or fully immersing them in a virtual environment. Accurate spatial awareness and real-time motion tracking are made possible by sensors and tracking devices such as LiDAR, depth cameras, gyroscopes, and accelerometers. In addition, the haptic devices such as smart body suits and hand gloves often provide intricate feedback, which helps in improving the sense of immersion. Rendering . Thishigh-quality XR demands more computational power, and this requirement is satisfied using high-performance GPUs, CPUs, and dedicated XR processors, which ensure smooth and quality real-time interactions.

Another essential layer is the software layer for rendering the content in real-time, but also for creating effective content. The content that makes use of 3D animations and physics simulations is usually created using game engines such as Unity3D, Unreal Engine, Godot and GameMaker Studio. There are exclusive Software Development Kits like Vuforia [14], Apple's ARKit, Google's ARCore, etc., that support the developers with a variety of tools that are used for incorporating the features of augmented reality into real-time applications. Furthermore, AI-enhanced computer vision algorithms allow seamless interaction between gesture/motion users and virtual content through improved object recognition, gesture/motion monitoring, and understanding of scenarios based on the inputs provided. Additionally, SLAM (Simultaneous Localization and Mapping) technology is essential for spatial mapping, ensuring precise placement of virtual elements within the real-world environment.

The data and connectivity layer facilitates high-speed data transmission and processing, enabling real-time rendering and interaction. Cloud computing plays a vital role by allowing immersive applications to offload computational workloads to cloud servers, reducing the processing burden on local devices. Combined with 5G technology, Edge computing minimizes latency and enables responsive XR experiences, particularly for remote collaboration, smart cities, and IoT-integrated applications. Furthermore, blockchain technology is being explored to ensure data privacy, security, and digital content ownership, particularly in decentralized virtual worlds like the Metaverse.

At the application layer, immersive technologies are being adopted across various industries to enhance productivity, engagement, and decision-making. In healthcare, AR-assisted surgeries and VR-based rehabilitation programs improving patient outcomes by providing real-time guidance and simulated training environments. In education, virtual classrooms and interactive 3D learning modules enable students to engage with complex subjects in an immersive manner. Immersive technologies play a vital role in the manufacturing industry with the help of AR-guided assembly, digital twin-based predictive maintenance, and AR-supported remote assistance. Immersive technologies are widely applied in the retail and e-commerce through live interactive advertisements, AR-based shopping experiences and virtual try-ons. Of all, significant development of immersive technologies can be seen in gaming and entertainment industry through XR-based gaming experiences.

Human-computer interaction is optimised as it forms the core objective of the user experience (UX) layer, which is a key component of this architecture. AI-driven personalization ensures immersive experiences are tailored to each user's preferences, enhancing usability and engagement. Voice control, gesture/motion recognition, and eye tracking are some multimodal interaction methods that provides natural and effortless means for users to interact with virtual world. In addition, features such as haptic feedback, voice assistants, and adaptive interfaces ensure accessibility to physically challenged users, widening the scope of immersive technologies.

Due to the advancements in AI, spatial computing and 5G connectivity, the architectural pillar of immersive technologies is evolving rapidly. These cutting-edge technologies, without doubt, will a user's digital experiences revolutionise the digital experiences of a user by enabling seamless and smooth transitions between the virtual and real world. Immersion technologies will revolutionize several industries, ranging from AR-enhanced architectural design to real-time visualization of architectural plans in smart cities. The framework's future will be more human-centric, AI-driven, and hyperconnected, opening up various opportunities for new innovation in how we communicate, learn, work, and consume digital content.

2.1. Role of Artificial Intelligence in Immersive Technologies

By enabling intelligent interaction, real-time adaptability, and commendable user experience, AI considerably enhances VR, AR, and MR. Natural Language Processing (NLP), object recognition, scene understanding, and adaptive content generation are all driven by AI-powered algorithms, enhancing immersive technologies' responsiveness and intuitiveness [15]. AI has contributed immensely to computer vision, which tracks and identifies faces, objects, and gestures in a natural and realistic environment. This capability is necessary for use in augmented reality applications such as real-time navigation, interactive shopping, and medical imaging. AI-powered Simultaneous Localization and Mapping (SLAM) enhances spatial awareness and lets AR devices accurately locate virtual objects in real environments. By adjusting settings and interactions based on user preference and action, AI-powered virtual reality (VR) analytics enable personalized virtual experiences.

AI enhances human–computer interaction with the help of NLP, voice recognition and emotion detection software. This allows users to communicate freely with immersive technologies by speaking in their own language and showing facial expressions. This evolution is particularly useful in fields like education, customer support, and gaming, where chatbots and virtual assistants based on AI enhance interaction and engagement. AI-based immersive technologies enhance accuracy and patient outcomes in medical care by enabling virtual diagnostics, cognitive therapy, and robot-assisted operations. Deep learning and machine learning (ML) models also assist in developing dynamic and extremely realistic environments. AI is used for procedural content generation, that is capable of creating engaging 3D contents that in turn enhances the flexibility and effectiveness of VR simulations, training, and gaming. AI also optimizes real-time rendering through reduced computational load and graphics optimization, leading to high-fidelity and smooth visual experiences on resource-constrained devices.

AI-powered avatars use motion capture and facial recognition technologies to mimic human gestures and expressions in the Metaverse and remote collaboration, allowing for a completely realistic virtual interaction. Safe, authenticated and customized immersive experiences are further guaranteed by AI-powered security features like biometric authentication and anomaly detection. More realistic, individualized, and effective digital experiences will be made possible by AI's continued role as a driving force behind intelligent automation, improved interactivity, and adaptive learning systems in immersive technologies.

3. Applications Across Industries

Immersion technologies are unquestionably transforming a greater number of industries with improvised decision-making, training, user experiences, and collaboration. Key applications in various sectors of these industries are listed below:

1. Healthcare
   - AR-assisted surgeries: Surgeons use AR overlays to visualize internal organs and critical structures in real time [16].
   - VR-based therapy: Used for pain management, PTSD treatment, and cognitive rehabilitation.
   - Medical training & simulations: Enables realistic surgical simulations for medical students and professionals.
   - Remote consultations: AR-powered telemedicine enhances doctor-patient interactions.

2. Education & Training
   - Immersive learning environments: VR classrooms allow students to explore historical events, scientific concepts, and 3D simulations [17].
   - AR-based textbooks: Interactive AR books and applications make learning more engaging and visual.
   - Corporate training & skill development: VR simulations help employees practice hazardous or complex procedures safely.
   - Language learning & soft skills training: AI-driven VR environments enhance language acquisition and communication skills.

3. Manufacturing & Engineering
   - Digital twins & prototyping: Engineers and designers visualize and test product designs in a virtual environment before physical production.
   - AR-guided assembly & maintenance: AR overlays provide real-time instructions for equipment maintenance and repair [18].
   - Workforce training: VR simulations train workers in hazardous environments without real-world risks.

4. Retail & E-Commerce
   - Virtual try-ons: Customers can try clothing, eyewear, and cosmetics virtually before making a purchase.
   - AR-powered shopping experiences: AR apps allow users to visualize furniture, home decor, and appliances in their own spaces.
   - Personalized shopping: AI-powered AR recommendations enhance customer engagement and decision-making.

5. Real Estate & Architecture
   - Virtual tours of Properties: With VR, tenants and buyers can virtually tour properties. This is a very attractive feature that helps buyers from different countries to visualize the properties.
   - AR-based interior design: AR is used by designers to see how furniture will be arranged and how architecture will change. This guides the customers to invest right and plan their own spaces in a minimal time period.
   - Smart city planning: Urban planners can more effectively design and evaluate infrastructure projects with the aid of immersive simulations. This greatly saves time and money.

6. Entertainment & Gaming
   - VR gaming experiences: Realistic simulations, haptic feedback, and multiplayer interactions are all features of immersive gaming environments.
   - AR-enhanced live events: AR is used in concerts and sports to create engaging fan experiences.
   - 360-degree storytelling: To produce immersive and interactive cinematic experiences, filmmakers utilize virtual reality.

7. Defense & Military
   - Combat training simulations: Virtual reality training improves readiness and decision-making for tactical teams, pilots, and soldiers, which is highly helpful for the militants.
   - Enhanced battlefield awareness: Military personnel can access real-time situational data through AR-enabled helmets and HUDs.
   - Remote-controlled operations: VR-powered robots help with surveillance and bomb diffusion/disposal [19]. This saves Many human lives, and more accurate strategies may be deployed.

8. Tourism & Hospitality
   - Virtual travel experiences: The users are allowed to explore historical sites, monumental museums, and popular landmarks before seeing them in person.
   - AR-guided tours: Interactive AR-based information overlays are available at museums and other tourist locations, to guide the travelers in knowing about the details of each of the places.
   - VR hotel previews: Prior to making a reservation, guests can take virtual tours of the hotel's rooms and facilities.

9. Automotive Industry
   - Virtual reality vehicle prototyping: Car and other automobile manufacturers can design, develop, and test new models in virtual environments.
   - AR-enhanced navigation: AR-enabled HUDs offer safety alerts and real-time driving assistance that ease the job of the navigators.

- Driver training simulators: VR-based simulated driving environment can help the novice drivers to experience a safe driving and hazard perception training experience [20].

10. Workplace & Remote Collaboration
    - Virtual meetings and collaborations: Working teams can collaborate in 3D virtual spaces using platforms like Microsoft Mesh and Meta Horizon Workrooms.
    - AR-powered remote assistance: Using AR overlays, technicians can troubleshoot machinery and equipment in real time, even remotely.
    - Digital workspaces: Remote workers can collaborate in engaging, interactive settings in virtual reality offices.

4. Key Challenges and Limitations

Immersive technologies, such as virtual reality (VR), augmented reality (AR), mixed reality (MR), and extended reality (XR), offer transformational possibilities in fields like education, healthcare, manufacturing, entertainment and many more. They offer interactive and immersive experiences to users, by integrating into physical and digital environments. Yet, immersive technologies encounter a range of issues that prevent their widespread use and smooth contextualization in several applications. We'll discuss these issues in the following section, giving some pointers as to what needs to change to make the most of being immersive.

4.1. Development Costs and Resource Constraints

High production and implementation costs are one of the highest obstacles to the adoption of immersive technologies. Immersion technology production is not simply about general software engineering but requires specific 3D modeling, animation, interaction design, and game engine experience. This in turn requires companies to have access to talent like VR/AR developers, UX designers, and 3D artists, who can be costly to recruit, develop, or train up. And the tools and platforms that are required to develop them — For example, Unity or Unreal Engine; or with licensing for 3D modeling tools like Autodesk Maya or Blender — have steep learning curves and high price tags to boot.

What's more, creating immersive content is time-consuming. Unlike a 2D application, immersive experiences need to be optimized across platforms, tested for interactivity and user comfort, and have a solid back end. This has the consequence that project realization will take longer, and they will have more resource requirements. For startups, universities and organizations in emerging economies, these financial and time costs are impossible to meet. In fields like public education or local government where funds are sparse, expensive aspects mask any potential short-term benefits, causing a hesitancy towards involving themselves with immersive technology development.

4.2. Hardware and Software Obstacles

An equally big hurdle is the hardware and software infrastructure that needs to be in place to deliver immersive experiences. While the tech is now considerably better than it was even a few years ago, the equipment required for most AR or VR still costs several bills, putting it beyond the price that average consumers can afford. Top-of-the-line VR headsets, such as the Meta Quest Pro or HTC Vive Pro, and AR smart glasses like Microsoft HoloLens can cost more than even thousands of dollars [47]. This renders the technology off limits to most users and institutions, particularly in poor regions.

Apart from cost, there are technical constraints in usability. Most VR headsets have the issue of small field of view, low resolution and short battery life that make the VR experience not that immersive. Mobile AR is more accessible but limited by the power and resolution of phone cameras. Moreover, immersive systems generally need powerful computers or cloud-based rendering services which is not available to all users. On the software front, there is a problem of standardization. Key features of AR are not universally standardized, and applications developed for one ecosystem (e.g., Apple's ARKit or Google's ARCore) are often not supported on another ecosystem, resulting in disjoint user experiences and increased development time [48]. End to end interoperability between platforms (EG, oculus, Steam VR, Windows Mixed Reality) also makes generating a seamless cross-platform solution much more difficult.

4.3. Challenges of User Experience

User experience is a key point which could make or break immersive technologies. Although all these immersive applications have pursued novel and interactive experience on the one hand, they have the other on the other side brought many uncomfortable and inconvenient problems. One of the most frequent challenges in VR is motion sickness, or cybersickness. This is due to the discrepancy between the bodily action of the user and the visual feedback received from the headset. Symptoms include dizziness, nausea, headaches and disorientation, and they are frequently aggravated by factors like low refresh rates, lag in head tracking and poorly designed environments.

There's also the physical discomfort of immersive machines to deter people. VR headsets can be clunky and heavy, and thus uncomfortable for long periods of time. It could put a strain on the neck, face or chin, and could cause skin irritation with prolonged use. These ergonomic concerns may have particular effects on children, the elderly, and users with physical limitations.

A second problem is the dearth of inclusive, accessible design. Interactive environments do not usually concern with the development of environments that can be used by special people, as visual, auditory, or mobility impaired users. In consequence, such technologies may be challenging or even impossible to use for persons with disabilities. In order for any immersive technology to become ubiquitous, an approach is needed that values universal design considering various users and scenarios of use.

4.4. Data Privacy and Ethical Considerations

The enriched nature of AR, VR, and MR technologies bring about challenging data privacy, security, and ethical concerns. These systems can capture vast amounts of personal information including biometrics (e.g., eye tracking, heart rate, facial expressions), location and environmental scans, and voice recordings [49]. During immersion additional contextual information can decisively improve personalization and reality of experience; on the other hand, it also raises important issues related to user privacy — in particular, when such data is collected, maintained, extracted or shared without explicit user consent in all the process phases.

In AR settings, it is more common to collect information about what a user can see through devices such as smart glasses or smartphones, which when doing so, will frequently capture other people accidentally or will invade areas of privacy [50]. This raises questions about surveillance, forcing yourself and others to enjoy your rights of privacy in both the public and private spheres. The lack of transparency about the ownership, retention, and use of data are further concerns when it comes to immersive platforms. The vast majority of users do not know what personal or environmental data is collected, how long it is maintained, or who has access to it [51].

Ethical considerations are heightened when incorporating AI into immersive technologies. Social VR platforms see users engaging with AI driven avatars and each other in worlds that are not consistently (or at all) moderated. This leave room for harassment, identity theft or the alteration of attitudes based on hyperrealistic simulations. As these immersive technologies are being adopted into education, therapy, and work contexts in greater numbers, the need to create an ethical and regulatory environment that protects user choice and safety, and dignity has never been greater.

4.5. System Integration

In this approach, the affordances sought are to integrate with legacy contents and to support traditional access methods provided by the Information Retrieval Systems (IRSs) in use within organizations.

For immersive to be a game changer in enterprise and institutional practices, interoperation with current systems and procedures is essential. But it is still a big hurdle. Legacy systems are an important stake-holder in their own right, even more so when they are not able to support real-time 3D rendering, spatial data processing and interactive virtual interfaces again today [52]. Costs for retrofitting such environments for the use of immersive platforms are typically substantial, both in hardware, software and IT resources.

One of the main challenges is the absence of standardisation across the immersive technology field. Contrary to web development or mobile applications, immersive platforms frequently employ proprietary formats, APIs, and development environments, which results in limited portability of content across systems. This splintering results in duplicated work and high development costs that have the solutions tailored for each incompatible pl atform. That means, for example, an app developed for Oculus won't readily work on Microsoft HoloLens or HTC Vive without significant changes.

Table 2. Impact and potential solutions

Challenge Area	Description	Impact	Potential Solutions
Sensitive Data Collection	Immersive systems collect biometric, environmental, and location data.	Risk of data misuse, privacy breaches, and unauthorized surveillance.	Implement transparent data policies and user consent mechanisms.
Lack of Privacy Protections	Devices may capture bystanders or private spaces unintentionally.	Violates privacy norms; legal liabilities in public/private contexts.	Enforce context-aware recording controls; introduce opt-out features.
Ethical Use of AI and Avatars	AI-driven avatars and social VR environments can lead to manipulation or harassment.	Psychological harm, identity misuse, unregulated virtual interactions.	Develop ethical codes, real-time moderation, and user reporting tools.
Lack of Regulatory Standards	No universal ethical or legal frameworks for immersive data governance.	Ambiguity in accountability and user protection.	Establish international standards and compliance protocols.
Legacy System Compatibility	Existing IT infrastructure lacks support for spatial and real-time 3D data.	Integration delays, inefficiencies, and limited scalability.	Upgrade infrastructure or use middleware for backward compatibility.
Fragmented Ecosystem	Lack of standardization across AR/VR platforms and file formats.	Interoperability issues, duplicated development efforts.	Promote industry-wide open standards and cross-platform development tools.
Organizational Resistance	Businesses are hesitant to adopt unfamiliar or "experimental" technologies.	Delays in adoption, missed innovation opportunities.	Demonstrate ROI through pilot projects and provide leadership training.
High Costs of Integration	Upgrading systems, retraining staff, and changing workflows incur high costs.	Financial burden, especially for small and mid-sized enterprises.	Access to government grants, phased adoption strategies, and public-private partnerships.

Organisational reluctance is also a factor constraining the uptake of immersive technologies, in addition to the technical aspects. Some organisations are reluctant to invest in risky systems that remain in the experimental or unproven stage in their operations. Return on investment, long-term maintenance, and vendor lock-in are often cited barriers. Furthermore, introducing immersive technologies usually also involves training of staff and reorganizing workflows and objectives–low-speed tasks that require comprehensive planning and change management. So, successful implementation depends not just on technical architecture, but also visionary leadership, interdisciplinary teamwork, and strong user adoption plans.

Table 2 describes the various challenges, impact and potential solutions in using immersive technologies.

5. Future Directions and Emerging Trends

5.1. AI and Machine Learning Integration

How AI/ML is being used to provide transformative immersion across AR/VR/MR Artificial Intelligence (AI) and Machine Learning (ML) are now playing larger roles, helping to immerse into AR/VR/MR experiences. Smart object recognition, ambient understanding, and adaptive environments within immersive systems are made possible using AI algorithms [53]. For example, AI-powered behavior prediction enables virtual environments to react intelligently to users, making training simulations and virtual assistants more realistic and personalized [54]. Natural Language Processing (NLP) allows for virtual environment-based conversational agents, offering better interaction quality and accessibility to users who speak different languages and/or have different abilities. In addition, reinforcement learning and neural networks are being combined increasingly to dynamically optimize the rendering of the environment, increase the frame rates and lower the latency in the real time, providing a more smooth and responsive perception.

5.2. 5G and Beyond Connectivity Impacts

The deployment of 5G networks is expected to transform immersive technology by allowing much faster data transmission speed and lower latency. 5G, with its high bandwidth and ultra-low latency, supports real-time rendering of complex AR/VR scenes on cloud servers and fast delivery to user devices. This would enable richer, interactive content without overloading the local hardware, decreasing device costs and power. QoS requirements of Remote collaboration, Telemedicine, and real-time multiplayer gaming require multi-Gbps streams of HD immersive content. With increased connectivity, such immersive experiences will become available more widely across geographies (including rural and underserved areas), and will help reduce the digital divide.

5.3. Immersive Systems – Cloud and Edge Computing

Cloud and edge computing are reinventing where and how immersive content is experienced. With those kinds of devices, data processing and rendering can be offloaded to clouds or edge servers, which relieve the computational burden of user-end devices. That's particularly useful for mobile and lightweight AR/VR headsets that may not have the power to render high-fidelity content all on their own [55]. Edge computing improves the responsiveness of immersive applications by moving compute resources closer to the user, thereby reducing latency. Collectively, these technologies enable scalable and low-latency experiences and enable shared virtual environments to be used by multiple users at the same time -- which is essential for industrial training, education and entertainment platforms.

5.4. Metaverse and Unified Immersive Platforms

Metaverse is typically characterized by three words: "virtual reality + open source + blockchain."

The metaverse— an AR, VR and internet-enabled, persistent shared virtual space — has been an emerging vision for the future of digital interaction. Enormous of top technology companies' resources are being poured into creating unified ecosystems that cover communication, work, and creation and are built around free play [56]. The metaverse together a diverse range of immersive experiences into one platform where everything can be interoperable, and users can maintain an identity, economy, and data across all the applications they use. Blockchain and decentralized technology are also under exploration to facilitate secure digital asset ownership and virtual markets. While the metaverse is still in development, the trend towards platform consolidation and avatar persistence is paving the way for smoother transitions through digital worlds.

5.5. Haptic and Sensory Feedback Development

I think the most exciting tech field that immersive media is shaping is haptic and multisensory feedback. Classic immersive systems have primarily focused on visual and audio stimuli. However, new interfaces are being developed that also consider tactile, thermal, pressure, and even olfactory sensations to enhance user sensation [57]. Haptic Gloves, Jackets, and Full-body Suits Haptic gloves, vests and full-body suits are in the works to bring virtual environments to life by linking a user's sense of physical presence to tactile effects throughout the virtual worlds. Such innovations are important within fields like surgical simulation, physical rehabilitation and remote collaboration, which present opportunities for increased performance and realism due to the incorporation of tactile feedback [58]. These technologies are becoming increasingly cost-effective and scalable, and play a role in creating a more natural, immersive digital reality.

5.6. Eco-Friendly Improvements in Immersive Tech

As digital technologies' environmental impact becomes more pressing, there is a growing momentum around a green shift in immersive technologies. Today's AR/VR hardware production is also driven by sustainability principles, from using recyclable energy-saving materials and components, to easier repair and upgrade thanks to modular designs [59]. And in fields like education and remote employment, immersion tech can reduce the physical footprint required to attend meetings or classrooms, which is also great for reducing our carbon footprints. For delivery of immersive content, companies are also investigating green data centers and low energy rendering methods to minimize power consumption. The innovations are all part of a larger trend of marrying technological advancements with environmentally sound practices.

6. Comparative Analysis of Technologies

6.1. VR vs AR: Strengths and Weaknesses

Two of the most talked-about immersive technologies, virtual reality (VR) and augmented reality (AR), each have their advantages and disadvantages. By creating a completely simulated digital environment, virtual reality (VR) transports users to a world where they can engage with things, situations, or people that are completely apart from their real-world surroundings. Because of this, VR is especially well-suited for uses like entertainment, simulations, and virtual training [21]. For instance, VR-powered flight simulators let pilots rehearse operations in a safe setting, and games like Half-Life: Alyx provide previously unheard-of levels of interaction. VR's strength is its unmatched immersion, which allows consumers to concentrate fully on the virtual experience.

VR does have some significant drawbacks, though. One of its main disadvantages is its dependence on specialist hardware, such as headsets, controllers, and motion-tracking systems, which can be costly and unavailable to regular users. Furthermore, virtual reality (VR) isolates users from the outside world, which can be detrimental in group situations. Long-term usability is further restricted by physical side effects such as motion sickness, eye strain, and dizziness. Despite these drawbacks, VR is still a popular technology for industries that need realistic, immersive simulations [22].

AR, on the other hand, lets users engage with both virtual and physical aspects simultaneously by superimposing digital content onto the real world. The most significant benefit of AR is its accessibility; it doesn't require bulky equipment and can be used with smartphones, tablets, and lightweight wearables like AR glasses. AR has been used by sectors like retail, education, and navigation to improve in-person interactions. Customers may visually "place" furniture in their homes using IKEA's augmented reality app, for instance, to ensure that the size and style fit, enhancing the buying experience. Similarly, AR-based learning applications provide pupils with dynamic visuals that enhance their memory of information.

AR does, however, have several drawbacks. Because digital features only overlay reality rather than replace it, augmented reality (AR) delivers a lower level of immersion than virtual reality (VR). Hardware processing power, spatial mapping, lighting, and other environmental elements affect how well AR is implemented. For instance, AR objects could appear shaky on older devices or might not work correctly in low light. Notwithstanding these difficulties, AR is more useful for real-world applications than VR because of its portability and simplicity of usage [23].

In conclusion, AR improves real-world interactions by fusing digital and physical elements, whereas VR is excellent at producing isolated, completely immersive experiences that are perfect for training and enjoyment. The degree of immersion needed and the particular objectives of an application play a significant role in the decision between VR and AR. The comparative analysis of AR, VR and Mixed reality is shown in Table 3 below.

Table 3. Comparative analysis of AR, VR and mixed reality

Feature/Aspect	Virtual Reality (VR)	Augmented Reality (AR)	Mixed Reality (MR)
Definition	Fully immersive digital environment.	Overlays digital content onto the real world.	Combines AR and VR for interaction in real time.
User Interaction	Interacts entirely with virtual elements.	Interacts with real and virtual elements.	Interacts with real-world and virtual objects.
Hardware Requirements	VR headset, controllers, and sensors.	AR-capable devices (smartphones, glasses).	Specialized MR headsets (e.g., HoloLens).
Applications	Gaming, training simulations, virtual tours.	Retail, education, navigation, healthcare.	Industrial design, remote collaboration.
Immersion Level	High; completely replaces real-world view.	Low to moderate; enhances real-world view.	Moderate to high; blends real and virtual.
Cost	Relatively high (due to hardware).	Moderate; accessible via mobile devices.	High; advanced hardware required.
Technological Challenges	Motion sickness, hardware cost.	Accuracy, limited field of view, latency.	Complex development, high computational needs.

6.2. MR and XR: Converging the Real and Digital Worlds

Mixed Reality (MR) and Extended Reality (XR) are the next wave of immersive technology, combining the finest aspects of AR and VR to create hybrid experiences. In addition to superimposing digital content, mixed reality goes beyond augmented reality by allowing real-time interaction with virtual objects in the real environment. Users can manipulate holograms, alter 3D objects, and interact with digital materials like real-world items using MR. For instance, Microsoft's HoloLens allows engineers and architects to see 3D models of structures or machinery by superimposing them on actual surfaces [24]. This facilitates collaboration and allows for design modifications that are impossible with conventional tools.

The design, industrial, and healthcare sectors are among the areas that stand to benefit significantly from MR's ability to combine digital and physical interactions. Using MR technologies, for example, surgeons can see 3D images of organs during procedures, improving precision and reducing risks. Similarly, automakers can shorten time to market and reduce costs by testing and changing vehicle designs in a virtual reality environment instead of using physical prototypes [25].

The more generic umbrella term "extended reality" (XR) encompasses VR, AR, and MR. XR is the combination of immersive technologies to provide a seamless spectrum of experiences from complete immersion (VR) to real-world enhancement (AR) and hybrid interactions (MR). One of XR's advantages is its scalability, which lets businesses and developers tailor experiences to specific needs [26]. For example, XR tools in healthcare enable virtual consultations, telemedicine, and remote surgery via 3D holographic displays. By allowing students to conduct virtual science experiments or travel to historical sites, XR combines the benefits of AR's real-world integration and VR's immersion in education.

MR and XR have revolutionary potential, yet challenges remain that need to be solved. Both methods rely on advanced hardware, geographical mapping, and computing capacity to ensure seamless interactions [27]. Because of their high costs and complicated implementation processes, only major enterprises can use them. Moreover, latency issues and technology limitations may reduce the effectiveness of MR and XR applications. Notwithstanding these challenges, it is projected that further advancements in 5G technology, artificial intelligence, and spatial computing would eliminate them, boosting MR and XR's future usability and accessibility [28].

6.3. Use Case Scenarios by Technology

Immersion technologies have many real-world uses, and depending on their strengths, VR, AR, MR, and XR each perform exceptionally well in particular situations. The various use cases of Immersive Technologies is shown in Figure 4.

6.3.1. VR Use Cases

Training and Simulations: Virtual reality is used in the aviation, military, and healthcare sectors to replicate real-world situations for training. Through virtual reality, students may hone their talents in a safe and regulated setting. For instance, before performing complex procedures on actual patients, medical students practice using virtual reality surgical simulators [29].

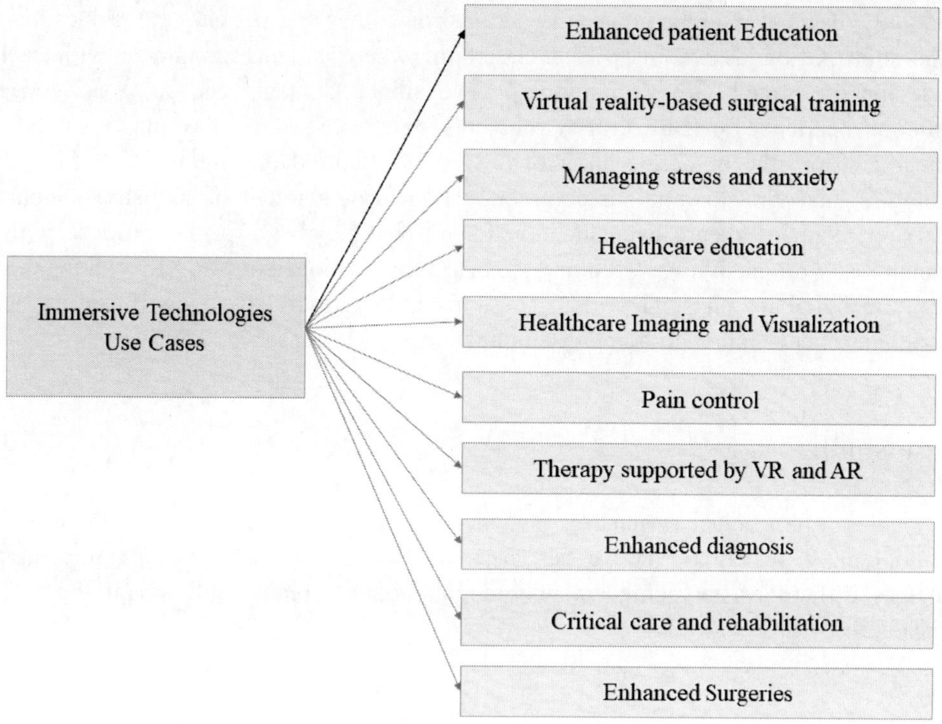

Figure 4. Use cases of immersive technologies.

Gaming & Entertainment: By producing completely immersive and interactive settings, virtual reality (VR) transforms gaming. Realistic experiences are provided by games like Resident Evil VR and Beat Saber, which increase player involvement and enjoyment. Virtual reality is also utilized in virtual tourism, which allows users to go to famous sites and locations from the comfort of their own homes.

6.3.2. AR Use Cases

Retail and Marketing: By providing virtual try-ons and product previews, augmented reality improves the shopping experience. Customers may virtually try on shoes or test out makeup hues with AR apps from companies like Nike and Sephora. This increases customer happiness and lowers return rates [30].

Education and Navigation: By superimposing interactive content on real-world objects, augmented reality enhances learning. For example, AR apps let students understand complicated subjects through immersive visualizations or see the human anatomy in three dimensions. AR-powered navigation apps like Google Maps, which offer real-time instructions and landmarks, make it easier to find your way around new locations.

6.3.3. MR and XR Use Cases

Engineering & Design: MR enables engineers to examine and work with 3D models during the product design process. Automakers like Ford, for example, use MR to test car designs, identify flaws, and make changes before to production [31].

Healthcare: Thanks to XR technologies, surgeons can collaborate during remote surgeries and telemedicine by using virtual 3D models of patients' anatomy. MR enables real-time interaction with these models, improving surgical outcomes and patient care. Education and Collaboration: XR builds dynamic virtual classrooms where students can interact with teachers and classmates through 3D simulations. For example, students can have an engaging educational experience by using XR environments to recreate historical events.

In conclusion, the numerous uses of VR, AR, MR, and XR demonstrate how these technologies have the potential to completely transform a range of industries, including engineering, retail, healthcare, and education. Each technology has a specific purpose, with AR enhancing real-world activities, VR being the best at immersion, and MR/XR bridging the gap between the digital and physical worlds. These technologies will have a significant impact on future advancements in human-computer interaction.

7. Case Studies

Case studies offer actual instances that demonstrate how immersive technology are revolutionizing a variety of industries. These real-world examples highlight the possible advantages, difficulties, and achievements brought about by creative solutions in the fields of healthcare, retail, and education.

7.1. Immersive Technologies in Healthcare

7.1.1. Using VR to Improve Medical Education

Virtual reality (VR) has completely changed medical education by providing realistic simulations allowing professionals and students to perform treatments in a risk-free environment. Platforms like Osso VR and SimX enable surgeons to refine their techniques by using virtual representations of human anatomy. For instance, a Stanford University study revealed that surgeons taught with virtual reality executed procedures 29% more quickly and accurately than those trained with conventional techniques [32]. Additionally, these instruments aid in lowering the learning curve for intricate surgery.

7.1.2. Pain Management and Patient Rehabilitation

VR and other immersive technologies have demonstrated encouraging outcomes in the treatment of pain. For patients receiving therapy, virtual reality distractions like relaxing virtual worlds or engrossing games lessen their sense of pain. For instance, during wound care, burn patients' pain has been effectively reduced by using the "SnowWorld" program [33]. Similarly, by leading stroke patients through repetitive, interactive activities in an entertaining setting, virtual reality rehabilitation programs are aiding in the recovery of motor abilities.

7.1.3. AR for Surgical Precision

Critical uses of augmented reality (AR) have also been discovered in the medical field, particularly in improving surgical accuracy. Surgeons can increase accuracy and lower the chance of mistakes by superimposing 3D images of a patient's anatomy during surgeries using augmented reality systems like Microsoft HoloLens. At Johns Hopkins Hospital, AR was utilized in spinal procedures in 2021 to let doctors see the precise location of implants, which sped up patient rehabilitation [34].

7.2. AR in Retail Success Stories

7.2.1. Enhancing Customer Experience with Virtual Try-Ons

By enabling buyers to virtually try things before buying, augmented reality has completely changed the retail industry. AR has been successfully used by businesses like Sephora and IKEA to increase consumer happiness. IKEA Place is an augmented reality app that lets users see furniture in their homes by superimposing 3D models over their actual surroundings. Users may virtually try makeup with Sephora's Virtual Artist, which significantly increases online sales and customer engagement.

7.2.2. AR-Driven Product Visualization

Augmented reality technology has helped businesses bridge the gap between online and in-store shopping by enhancing product visualization. For example, Nike released the Nike Fit app, which measures customers' feet accurately and recommends the correct shoe size using augmented reality [35]. Thanks to this innovative method, customer satisfaction has increased and return rates have dropped. In a similar vein, luxury brands like Gucci have employed augmented reality to let customers virtually try on shoes and accessories.

7.2.3. Personalized Shopping Experiences

Retailers are increasingly using AR to personalize the shopping experience. For instance, L'Oréal's AR app uses facial recognition to determine skin tone and make product recommendations [36]. This boosts sales while also boosting customer loyalty and trust. Retail success stories demonstrate that augmented reality (AR) is a revolutionary tool for enhancing in-store and online experiences, increasing customer convenience and engagement.

7.3. VR in Education: Real-Life Applications

7.3.1. Immersive Learning Environments

Through the development of immersive, interactive learning environments, virtual reality has significantly advanced education. Through virtual field trips like touring the pyramids of ancient Egypt or going to Mars, platforms like Google Expeditions and Engage VR give students a greater understanding of subjects that are typically only covered in textbooks. For instance, a Washington Leadership Academy pilot program discovered that VR-based history classes improved student interest and memory [37].

7.3.2. Skill Development and Vocational Training

Programs for vocational training that call for practical experience using virtual reality. The automotive and aviation industries use VR simulations to instruct trainees on intricate technology. Boeing, for example, uses virtual reality (VR) simulations to teach technicians how to assemble aeroplane parts, which lowers training costs while increasing safety [38].

education. In nursing education, students can practice diagnosing and treating patients in virtual settings provided by VR systems such as Oxford Medical Simulation.

7.3.3. Special Education and Inclusivity

Special education is one of the most influential areas of education in which virtual reality is used. Students with impairments can learn in environments adapted to meet their needs thanks to virtual reality equipment. For instance, VR apps like as Floreo help kids with autism by teaching them social skills in environments that mimic the real world. Similarly, children with cognitive disabilities can enhance their communication and understanding abilities using immersive storytelling techniques.

7.3.4. Enhancing STEM Education

STEM (science, technology, engineering, and mathematics) courses can be taught quite successfully with virtual reality. Students can perform experiments in virtual science labs without the need for physical resources thanks to platforms like Labster. For instance, learning outcomes were found to have improved by 76% in Danish schools that used Labster's VR simulations [39]. In an interesting, interactive way, students can see engineering models, physics simulations, and molecular structures, which helps them understand difficult ideas.

8. Future Prospects and Trends

8.1. Enhancing Accessibility

Accessibility has emerged as a major area of interest in developing technologies, especially in virtual and augmented reality (VR/AR). As these technologies become more widely used throughout businesses, it is still crucial to make sure that people with disabilities are included. Wider adoption and more egalitarian experiences will be made possible by improved accessibility.

8.1.1. Adaptive Hardware and Software

Adaptive hardware, like controllers with adjustable grips, eye-tracking devices, and gesture recognition for users with mobility problems, is anticipated to be a future development. It is also anticipated that advancements in brain-computer interfaces (BCIs) and voice-command technologies would make VR/AR settings more inclusive. For instance, alternative navigation tools are designed to accommodate users with visual impairments, while speech-to-text technologies are being incorporated to assist those with hearing impairments [40].

8.1.2. Universal Design Principles

Barriers will be lessened by creating virtual experiences using universal accessibility principles. Developers can design systems that meet a variety of user needs by incorporating elements like haptic cues, high contrast images, subtitles, and scalable interfaces. To encourage digital diversity, businesses are progressively integrating Web Content Accessibility Guidelines (WCAG) into their products [41].

8.1.3. Real-World Impact

Improved accessibility has enormous potential benefits for sectors including entertainment, healthcare, and education. While virtual healthcare consultations can provide individualized solutions for patients with mobility limitations, virtual classes with accessible technologies will empower students of all abilities. Similarly, inclusive entertainment systems guarantee equal participation and engagement from all.

8.2. Improving Haptic Feedback Systems

By mimicking tactile sensations, haptic feedback technologies are revolutionizing how people interact with virtual surroundings. Enhancing the realism and precision of haptic feedback will emerge as a key trend in the technology industry as the demand for immersive experiences rises.

8.2.1. Advanced Haptic Technologies

Tactile interactions are being redefined by emerging technologies, such as wearable haptic devices, ultrasonic haptics, and electrostatic actuators. For example, electrostatic actuators simulate the roughness of various materials by producing changing friction on touchscreen panels [42]. Similarly, ultrasonic technologies allow users to “feel” virtual items without making actual contact by creating sensations in midair using sound waves.

8.2.2. Integration with AI and Machine Learning

Real-time adaptive feedback made possible by artificial intelligence (AI) and machine learning improving haptic devices. These technologies provide a smooth experience by anticipating user activities and modifying tactile responses accordingly. AI-powered haptics, for instance, can replicate environmental changes, such as wind resistance or object weight, or the force of objects in virtual reality games [43].

8.2.3. Application in Key Sectors

Gaming and Entertainment: To replicate realistic feedback in video games and increase player engagement and immersion, haptic suits and gloves are being employed more and more.

Healthcare: Surgeons can practice procedures with precise tactile input through medical simulations equipped with cutting-edge haptic devices, which enhance training and surgical results.

Robotics in manufacturing: By enabling operators to “feel” robotic movements in real time, haptic interfaces are transforming remote operations. Precision manufacturing and hazardous situations can both benefit from this.

8.2.4. Challenges and Future Solutions

Enhancing the scalability and affordability of haptic devices is still difficult despite developments. to provide high-fidelity input without sacrificing user comfort, researchers are striving to create lightweight and energy efficient devices. Portability and usefulness will be further improved with the development of wireless and modular haptic systems.

8.3. Increasing Content Diversity

Content diversity in virtual and digital places is essential for long-term user engagement and worldwide acceptance. Diverse, inclusive, and culturally appropriate material will be given priority in future VR/AR, media, and digital platform developments.

8.3.1. Expanding Multicultural Representation

One critical tendency is the production of content that represents a variety of racial, cultural, and socioeconomic identities. As viewers worldwide look for more authentic experiences, content creators are investing in stories that showcase a variety of perspectives. To promote international understanding, VR documentaries and films, for example, depict global cultures, history, and cultural heritage [44].

8.3.2. Customized and Niche Content

Future content trends include hyper-personalized experiences tailored to individual preferences. Algorithms using artificial intelligence (AI) analyze user behavior to deliver entertainment, education, or training that caters to specific interests. Platforms are also producing specialized content, such as VR-based mental health apps, immersive language learning tools, and personalized exercise plans.

8.3.3. Education and Training Applications

Diversity in content is driving innovation in professional education and training. Immersion learning environments allow students to explore subjects like history, art, and science in engaging ways. For example, in STEM education, students can explore physics, chemistry, and engineering concepts through virtual experiments thanks to virtual reality simulations [45].

Workplace Training: In industries including manufacturing, aviation, and emergency response, virtual reality is being used to create training modules that mimic real-world scenarios. Specialized Skills: Virtual platforms are introducing specialized programs like culinary arts, musical instrument practice, and soft skills development to expand learning opportunities.

8.3.4. User-Generated Content

User-generated content (UGC) is another new trend that promotes creativity and variety. Platforms like VR Chat and metaverse ecosystems allow users to create and share virtual worlds, games, and experiences. This creates groups based on shared interests and expands the variety of content that is available.

8.3.5. Ethical Considerations

As content variety increases, it becomes increasingly important to address ethical concerns around prejudice, misinformation, and representation [46]. These issues will be lessened with the use of collaborative frameworks that involve communities, developers, and stakeholders.

Conclusion

By reinventing how people interact with digital surroundings, immersive technologies—which include virtual reality (VR), augmented reality (AR), and mixed reality (MR)—have become potent instruments that are revolutionizing a number of industries. By bridging the gap between the actual and virtual worlds, these technologies provide more realistic, interactive, and captivating experiences. It is clear from a thorough examination of immersive technologies that their uses, advantages, and difficulties offer both substantial potential and difficulties for a variety of industries.

The growing adoption of immersion technologies in sectors such as industry, retail, healthcare, education, and entertainment demonstrates its versatility and promise. Immersion technologies in education encourage experience learning and aid students in better understanding and remembering complex concepts by enabling them to interact with virtual environments. Similar to this, VR and AR are revolutionizing treatment methods in the healthcare sector by assisting with patient care, mental health therapy, and surgical simulators. Significant advancements have also been made in the entertainment industry because to VR and AR apps, which offer immersive narrative, interactive media, and enhanced gaming experiences.

The application of immersion technologies in manufacturing and retail demonstrates their capacity to foster innovation and productivity. Virtual showrooms, augmented reality-enhanced shopping, and digital product development have transformed consumer engagement and reduced production costs. Because immersion technology can simulate real-world scenarios, businesses may speed up operations, train employees in risk-free environments, and make better decisions.

Despite these advantages, challenges remain before immersive technology can be applied extensively. Exorbitant costs, technological limitations, and data security concerns are some of the major challenges. Because developing immersive experiences requires a large investment in technology, software, and content creation, it may be too costly for smaller businesses. Furthermore, privacy issues, ethical considerations, and user health repercussions (including motion sickness and eye strain) necessitate ongoing research and regulation to ensure responsible usage.

From a technological perspective, advancements in hardware, software, and connectivity are critical to enhancing the user experience and increasing access to immersive technology. Developments in areas like 5G, artificial intelligence (AI), and spatial computing are already addressing these problems. Smoother, more realistic immersive experiences are being made possible by faster networks and smarter devices, opening the door for wider industry usage.

As we look to the future, immersive technologies will keep developing and will be crucial in determining how humans and computers interact. The distinction between the actual and virtual worlds may become even more hazy because of their integration with cutting-edge technologies like artificial intelligence (AI), the Internet of Things (IoT), and blockchain. Policymakers, engineers, educators, and companies must work together to overcome current issues and create an ecosystem that encourages creativity, accessibility, and moral use if immersive technologies are to reach their full potential.

To sum up, immersive technologies offer a revolutionary change in how people and organizations engage with the digital environment. Even while there are still obstacles to overcome, there are countless chances to improve connectivity, creativity, and productivity.

The future is full of exciting opportunities to use VR, AR, and MR to improve society and the economy if technology developments continue to propel the creation of immersive experiences. We may rethink what is possible and uncover new facets of the human experience by adopting these technologies in a responsible and inclusive manner.

References

[1] Suh, A. and Prophet, J., 2018. The state of immersive technology research: A literature analysis. *Computers in Human Behavior*, 86, pp. 77–90.

[2] Wohlgenannt, I., Simons, A. and Stieglitz, S., 2020. Virtual reality. *Business & Information Systems Engineering*, 62, pp. 455–461.

[3] Alqahtani, A. S., Daghestani, L. F. and Ibrahim, L. F., 2017. Environments and system types of virtual reality technology in STEM: A survey. *International Journal of Advanced Computer Science and Applications* (IJACSA), 8(6).

[4] Arena, F., Collotta, M., Pau, G. and Termine, F., 2022. An overview of augmented reality. *Computers*, 11(2), p. 28.

[5] Chen, Y., Wang, Q., Chen, H., Song, X., Tang, H. and Tian, M., 2019, June. An overview of augmented reality technology. In *Journal of Physics: Conference Series* (Vol. 1237, No. 2, p. 022082). IOP Publishing.

[6] Peddie, J., 2017. Types of augmented reality. In *Augmented Reality: Where We Will All Live* (pp. 29–46). Cham: Springer International Publishing.

[7] Rokhsaritalemi, S., Sadeghi-Niaraki, A. and Choi, S. M., 2020. A review on mixed reality: Current trends, challenges and prospects. *Applied Sciences*, 10(2), p. 636.

[8] Peddie, J., 2017. Types of augmented reality. In *Augmented Reality: Where We Will All Live* (pp. 29–46). Cham: Springer International Publishing.

[9] Kumawat, V., Dhaked, R., Sharma, L. and Jain, S., 2020. Evolution of immersive technology: Journey of computational reality. *Virtual Reality* (VR), 1, p. 360.

[10] Benaben, F., Congès, A. and Fertier, A., 2025. A prospective vision of the evolution of immersive technologies: Towards a definition of metaverse. *Technovation*, 140, p. 103154.

[11] Ali, S., 2022. The effectiveness of immersive technologies for future professional education. *Futurity Education*, 2(2), pp. 13–21.

[12] Santos, N. M. and Peslak, A., 2022. *Immersive technologies: Benefits, timeframes, and obstacles. Issues in Information Systems*, 23(2).

[13] Fernandes, F. A., Rodrigues, C. S. C., Teixeira, E. N. and Werner, C. M., 2023. Immersive learning frameworks: A systematic literature review. *IEEE Transactions on Learning Technologies*, 16(5), pp. 736–747.

[14] Feigl, T., Porada, A., Steiner, S., Löffler, C., Mutschler, C. and Philippsen, M., 2020, February. Localization Limitations of ARCore, ARKit, and Hololens in Dynamic Large-scale Industry Environments. In *VISIGRAPP* (1: GRAPP) (pp. 307–318).

[15] Partarakis, N. and Zabulis, X., 2024. A review of immersive technologies, knowledge representation, and AI for human-centered digital experiences. *Electronics*, 13(2), p. 269.

[16] Qu, Z., Lau, C. W., Simoff, S. J., Kennedy, P. J., Nguyen, Q. V. and Catchpoole, D. R., 2022. Review of innovative immersive technologies for healthcare applications. *Innovations in Digital Health, Diagnostics, and Biomarkers*, 2(2022), pp. 27–39.

[17] Turan, Z. and Karabey, S.C., 2023. The use of immersive technologies in distance education: A systematic review. *Education and Information Technologies*, 28(12), pp. 16041–16064.

[18] Sekhar, K. C., Ingle, R. B., Banu, E. A., Rinawa, M. L., Prasad, M. M. and Boopathi, S., 2024. Integrating VR and AR for Enhanced Production Systems: Immersive Technologies in Smart Manufacturing. In *Human-Machine Collaboration and Emotional Intelligence in Industry* 5.0 (pp. 90–112). IGI Global.

[19] Duchidze, G. and Zeikidze, V., 2024, October. Development of Immersive Technologies in Military Education. In *International Scientific-Practical Conference* (pp. 318–323). Cham: Springer Nature Switzerland.

[20] Islas Munoz, J. A., Baha, E. and Muratovski, G., 2022. Radically Innovating the Automotive Design Process with Immersive Technologies. In *DS 117: Proceedings of the 24th International Conference on Engineering and Product Design Education* (E&PDE 2022), London South Bank University in London, UK. 8th–9th September 2022.

[21] Gilberto, L. G., Bermejo, F. R., Tommasini, F. C. and García Bauza, C., 2024. Virtual reality audio game for entertainment and sound localization training. *ACM Transactions on Applied Perception*, 22(1), pp. 1–24.

[22] Radu, I. and Schneider, B., 2023. What Can We Learn from Augmented Reality (AR)? Benefits and Drawbacks of AR for Inquiry-Based Learning of Physics. *Proceedings of the 2023 CHI Conference on Human Factors in Computing Systems*, 1–12.

[23] Acevedo, P. and Vergel, R. S., 2024. A Systematic Review of Immersive Virtual Reality in STEM Education. *2024 IEEE International Conference on Engineering, Technology, and Education* (TALE), 1–8.

[24] Zainal, N. H. M. and Omar, N., 2024. The Applications of Augmented Reality (AR) and Virtual Reality (VR) in Teaching Medical and Dentistry Students. *2024 IEEE Conference on e-Learning, e-Management, and e-Services* (IC3e), 1–6.

[25] Vergel, R. S. and Martin-Gomez, A., 2023. A Comparative Evaluation of a Virtual Reality Table and a HoloLens-Based Augmented Reality System for Anatomy Training. *2023 IEEE International Conference on Artificial Intelligence and Virtual Reality* (AIVR), 1–8.

[26] Gans, J. and Nagaraj, A., 2023. *The economics of augmented and virtual reality*. arXiv preprint arXiv:2305.16872.

[27] Zhou, X., Batmaz, A. U., Williams, A. S., Schreiber, D. and Ortega, F. R., 2024, May. I Did Not Notice: A Comparison of Immersive Analytics with Augmented and Virtual Reality. In *Extended Abstracts of the CHI Conference on Human Factors in Computing Systems* (pp. 1–7).

[28] Laha, M., Roy, D., Dutta, S. and Das, G., 2023. AI-assisted Improved Service Provisioning for Low-latency XR over 5G NR. *IEEE Networking Letters*, 6(1), pp. 31–35.

[29] Daling, L. M., Tenbrock, M., Isenhardt, I. and Schlittmeier, S. J., 2023. Assemble it like this! – Is AR- or VR-based training an effective alternative to video-based training in manual assembly? *Applied Ergonomics*, 110, p. 104021.

[30] Lisle, L., Davidson, K., Gitre, E. J., North, C. and Bowman, D. A., 2023. Different realities: a comparison of augmented and virtual reality for the sensemaking process. *Frontiers in Virtual Reality*, 4, p. 1177855.

[31] Naik, A. G. and Reddy, A., 2023. Industrial Trends, Challenges & Opportunities in the field of Augmented & Virtual Reality. *International Journal of Computer Engineering and Technology* (IJCET), 14(2), pp. 1–16.

[32] Mao, R. Q., Lan, L., Kay, J., Lohre, R., Ayeni, O. R. and Goel, D. P., 2021. Immersive virtual reality for surgical training: a systematic review. *Journal of Surgical Research*, 268, pp. 40–58.

[33] Rueda Márquez de la Plata, A., Cruz Franco, P. A. and Ramos Sánchez, J. A., 2023. Applications of Virtual and Augmented Reality Technology to Teaching and Research in Construction. *Sustainability*, 15(12), p. 9628.

[34] Birlo, M., Edwards, P. E., Clarkson, M. and Stoyanov, D., 2022. Utility of optical see-through head mounted displays in augmented reality-assisted surgery: A systematic review. *Medical Image Analysis,* 77, p. 102361.

[35] Chu, C. H., Chen, Y. A., Huang, Y. Y. and Lee, Y. J., 2022. A comparative study of virtual footwear try-on applications in virtual and augmented reality. *Journal of Computing and Information Science in Engineering*, 22(4), p.041004.

[36] Kyaw, N., Gu, M., Croft, E. and Cosgun, A., 2023. Comparing usability of augmented reality and virtual reality for creating virtual bounding boxes. *Applied Sciences*, 13(21), p. 11693.

[37] Wu, J. G., Zhang, D., Lee, S. M. and Xian, J., 2025. Game on! Digital Gaming and Augmented Reality/Virtual Reality in Language Learning. *International Journal of Computer-Assisted Language Learning and Teaching* (IJCALLT), 15(1), pp. 1–15.

[38] Angra, S., Jangra, S., Gulzar, Y., Sharma, B., Singh, G. and Onn, C. W., 2025. Twenty-two years of advancements in augmented and virtual reality: a bibliometric and systematic review. *Frontiers in Computer Science*, 7, p. 1470038.

[39] Bauermeister, T., Janßen, N. and Engler, J. O., 2024. Conventional teaching vs. e-learning: A case study of German undergraduate biology students. *Education and Information Technologies*, pp. 1–17.

[40] Dudley, J., Yin, L., Garaj, V. and Kristensson, P. O., 2023. Inclusive Immersion: a review of efforts to improve accessibility in virtual reality, augmented reality and the metaverse. *Virtual Reality*, 27(4), pp. 2989–3020.

[41] Othman, A., Chemnad, K., Hassanien, A. E., Tlili, A., Zhang, C. Y., Al-Thani, D., et al., 2024. Accessible metaverse: A theoretical framework for accessibility and inclusion in the metaverse. *Multimodal Technologies and Interaction*, 8(3), p. 21.

[42] Rakkolainen, I., Freeman, E., Sand, A., Raisamo, R. and Brewster, S., 2020. A survey of mid-air ultrasound haptics and its applications. *IEEE Transactions on Haptics*, 14(1), pp. 2–19.

[43] Sung, Y., Kim, R., Song, K. W., Shao, Y. and Yoon, S. H., 2024. Hapticpilot: Authoring in-situ hand posture-adaptive vibrotactile feedback for virtual reality. Proceedings of the ACM on Interactive, *Mobile, Wearable and Ubiquitous Technologies*, 7(4), pp. 1–28.

[44] Li, C., Kon, A. L. L. and Ip, H. H. S., 2022. Use virtual reality to enhance intercultural sensitivity. *IEEE Transactions on Visualization and Computer Graphics,* 28(11), pp.3673–3683.

[45] Yang, C. et al., 2024. The impact of virtual reality on practical skills in science and engineering education: A meta-analysis. *International Journal of STEM Education*, 11(1), p. 28.

[46] Kourtesis, P., 2024. A Comprehensive Review of Multimodal XR Applications. *Multimodal Technologies and Interaction*, 8(11), p. 98.

[47] Syed, T. A. et al., 2023. In-Depth Review of Augmented Reality. *Sensors*, 23(1), 146.

[48] Kim, K., Billinghurst, M., Bruder, G., Duh, H. B. and Welch, G. F., 2018. Revisiting Trends in Augmented Reality Research. *IEEE Transactions on Visualization and Computer Graphics*, 24(11), pp. 2947–2962.

[49] Madary, M. and Metzinger, T. K., 2016. Real Virtuality: A Code of Ethical Conduct. *Frontiers in Robotics and AI*, 3, 3.

[50] Cummings, J. J. and Bailenson, J. N., 2015. How Immersive Is Enough? *Media Psychology*, 19(2), pp. 272–309.

[51] Slater, M. and Sanchez-Vives, M. V., 2016. Enhancing our lives with immersive virtual reality. *Frontiers in Robotics and AI*, 3, 74.

[52] Speicher, M., Hall, B. D. and Nebeling, M., 2017. What is mixed reality? *Proceedings of the 2017 CHI Conference on Human Factors in Computing Systems*, 5485–5490.

[53] Kim, K. et al., 2018. Revisiting Trends in Augmented Reality Research. *IEEE Transactions on Visualization and Computer Graphics*, 24(11).

[54] Bailenson, J., 2018. *Experience on Demand: What Virtual Reality Is, How It Works, and What It Can Do*. W. W. Norton & Company.

[55] Shi, W. et al., 2016. Edge Computing: Vision and Challenges. *IEEE Internet of Things Journal*, 3(5), pp. 637–646.

[56] Dionisio, J. D. N., Burns III, W. G. and Gilbert, R., 2013. 3D virtual worlds and the metaverse. *ACM Computing Surveys* (CSUR), 45(3), 34.

[57] Pacchierotti, C. et al., 2017. Wearable Haptic Systems for the Fingertip and the Hand. *IEEE Transactions on Haptics*, 10(4), pp. 580–600.

[58] Culbertson, H., Schorr, S. B. and Okamura, A. M., 2018. Haptics: The present and future of artificial touch sensation. *Annual Review of Control, Robotics, and Autonomous Systems*, 1, 385–409.

[59] Moro, C., Phelps, C. and Redmond, P., 2021. Sustainable integration of immersive technology in higher education: Challenges and recommendations. *Journal of Educational Technology & Society*, 24(2), 50–63.

Chapter 2

Influence and Utilization of Immersive Technologies Across Diverse Industries

Anamika Raj*
Department of Computer Science, Applied College, King Khalid University, Abha, Saudi Arabia

Abstract

Immersive systems have changed industries by realizing new interaction modes and visual experiences and improving learning effects. The entertainment and gaming industries get the most out of immersive technologies since they provide highly engaging simulations of their user bases and dynamic content generation. Virtual Reality is used in surgical, pain, and therapeutic practice, while Augmented Reality is used for real-time diagnosis and patient care. The technologies are adopted in the education sector to promote learning and engage the learners enough to enable them to grasp what is taught. Some applications of AR that aid manufacturing and automotive industries include using AR in designing and modelling products, assembling products, and training workers. Retail and e-commerce incorporate virtual try-on solutions to increase consumer interactions and lower turnover rates. The experiential applications in the tourism sector include virtual site visitation and changing the way of travel planning. In defence, simulations enhance combat training and additional planning. New uses in the real estate business, architecture, and distant working have changed how visualisation and efficiency are approached. Despite all these promises, the following barriers still exist: high development costs, the limitations of the device, and privacy issues. This chapter aims to provide an overview of immersive technologies and their applications in various fields, the strengths and weaknesses of such technologies, and prospects for boosting their adoption in an integrated environment of the digital world.

Keywords: virtual reality, augmented reality, immersive technologies

1. Introduction

The development of AR and VR can be considered a key driver of technological changes that affect industries' means of communication with audiences and the efficiency of their

* Corresponding Author's Email: araj@kku.edu.sa

In: Shaping Tomorrow
Editors: Prithi Samuel, A. Sathya, Balamurugan Balusamy et al.
ISBN: 979-8-90134-076-9

functioning. AR and VR represent two of the most promising and rapidly developing aspects of technologies for interaction with digital objects and application, creating new human experiences as a separate application area in various industries. From improving customer satisfaction in retail shops to replicating critical environments in healthcare and education industries, their use is advancing more rapidly than ever before [1].

It makes them not limited to the gaming and entertainment industry but is used in manufacturing, real estate, tourism, and defense [2]. Field: assembly of products; how it works: In the area of manufacturing, besides objects, best practices are illustrated with reference to the real equipment needed for assembly, which helps in reducing the errors involved. The real estate industry, through VR, lets clients physically tour homes without physically visiting the property from the cosiness of their homes. Likewise, AR is used in the tourism industry to give tourists value-added services like history telling and landmarks [3].

Going to the effects of AR and VR, one of the major areas they are known to have impacted is through the customers. Retail apps with AR technology allow determining how furniture will look in a consumer's house or how specific clothes will fit. Such an approach to engaging the customers not only helps making them more satisfied but also decreases the return ratio and strengthens the customer franchise. Like VR, AR places users into virtual stores or exposes brands in engaging forms creative than conventional advertisements [5].

AR and VR are also increasingly adopted across corporate education and continuing professional development learning [6]. In the medical domain, VR simulations prepare doctors and other caregivers for dexterous procedures without subjecting patients to associated harm. AR surgeries improve the conducted' accuracy, and virtual dissection labs enable the student to dissect the human body virtually.

The integration of AR and VR is not the latest craze in technology, but there is a shift in way people engage with information, the environment, and even people. These technologies help organisations redesign their approaches and achieve improved visualisation, interactivity, and personalisation. AR is a common standard in EKDR for data overlays where businesses need their supply chain or inventory in real-time, and VR is more commonly used for remote teaming, where individuals can work together virtually irrespective of their geographical location [7].

This chapter critically discusses the impact of AR and VR predominantly in numerous industries and proves that they are effectively used as innovation and enhancement tools. This article explores the causes and motivations for their implementation, potential difficulties that may be met, tangible outcomes, and how these technologies affect a business's performance and customer experience. Exploring concrete examples from practice and understanding various industries, we will discover how and in what way Augmented Reality and Virtual Reality are changing the world of work, entertainment, and business.

Every industry's ongoing integration of AR and VR takes development possibilities to the next level. For example, interactive applications of museums and cultural institutions open the use of Augmented Reality in furthering education and entertainment. AR enhances real-life construction projects by providing additional visualization of construction sites, thus improving planning and design execution. Major sports have not been left behind by these technologies, where AR gives fans live statistics while VR provides athletic skills trainers with simulation technologies [8].

In a world that has seen exponential growth in the emergence of new concepts from the technological perspective, AR and VR remain among the most enlightening and groundbreaking concepts [9]. These tools blend imagination incorporating technology, creating a means for people in the future to be consumed by daily experiences. As we progress through their usage and implementations, their impact on defining the industries of tomorrow becomes much more apparent.

2. Technological Foundations of AR/VR

Therefore, Augmented Reality (AR) and Virtual Reality's (VR) transformative ability is built on sound technical existence [10]. These technologies use sophisticated hardware and software systems to develop optimum multi-sensory and multi-modal interactions of real or synthetic worlds.

2.1. Hardware Components

The hardware that forms and constitutes AR and VR systems acts as central supportive structures to deliver immersive experiences. Key components include:

a) Display Devices:
   - Head-Mounted Displays (HMDs): Full immersion VR headsets such as Oculus Rift and HTC Vive, and Augmented Reality headsets such as Microsoft Holo Lens offer the user a first-person view of the virtual environment.
   - Smart Glasses and AR Headsets: Obviously, there are AR-specific devices, such as Magic Leap or Google Glass, that place additional digital information in the real environment.
   - Mobile Devices: Smartphones and tablets also serve as AR devices, and cameras and touch screens are used AR content in ARto deliver AR.

b) Tracking Systems:
   - Motion Tracking: Programmable sensors such as accelerometers, gyroscopes, and magnetometers developed in mobile devices make it possible to achieve precise movement of users.
   - Eye Tracking: Eye-tracking integration to social interfaces is improved by focus point detection.
   - Positional Tracking: Inside-out tracking or external sensors define the user's precise position in physical space.

c) Input Devices:
   - Gloves and full-body feedback let the users function naturally with virtual items.

2.2. Software Frameworks and Algorithms

AR and VR software are as essential as hardware in creating real and fascinating effects [11, 12]. Core components include:

- *Rendering Engines:* Real-time 3D or game engines like Unity and Unreal Engine are responsible for developing and rendering realistic environment simulations. These engines aim at graphics that display realistic-looking images and high performance.
- *AR Software Development Kits (SDKs):* ARKit from Apple Inc., ARCore from Google, and Vuforia for Hollywood are some of the tools that are used to build AR applications. They include image recognition, surface detection, and environment mapping applications.
- *SLAM (Simultaneous Localization and Mapping):* SLAM allows technical AR systems to build and dynamically update their presentation of the real space, which is critical for placing objects in the correct locations and creating a sense of location.
- *AI Integration:* Elements such as object recognition, voice information processing, and existing help for AR/VR applications are devised with artificial intelligence. Users interact with material more naturally because adaptive algorithms receive signals from AI.

2.3. Network and Cloud Services

AR and VR require robust networks to process extensive signal data and deliver optimal interactive experiences. Key aspects include:

- *Edge Computing*: Sit close to the user to enable the processing of data with lower latency than is required for real-time applications such as AR navigation or VR gaming.
- *5G Connectivity*: Fast connectivity and low network delay are ideal for AR/VR content delivery, especially for mobile phones.
- *Cloud Computing*: Cloud platforms provide storage and deployment of AR/VR assets to cater to sharing platforms and scanning.

2.4. Sensor Technologies and Spatial Computing

Today, high-level sensors and spatial computing are embedded into AR and VR to close the gap between real and virtual environments.

- *Depth Sensors*: LiDAR sensors offer precise information on the depth required for three-dimensional mapping and cloning.
- *Environmental Sensors*: Sensors like the light sensors will help react to fluctuations in light and other aspects of real life.

- *Spatial Computing*: Uses both product and software to enable the systems to learn to interact with any 3D realities.

2.5. Human Machine Interface (HMI)

Interactivity is at the core of AR/VR, although the methodology of its definition differs from that of other technologies [13]. Evolutions in HMI facilitate this association by augmenting the easy-to-use controls, gesture recognition, and voice control [14]. Haptic feedback adds another dimension to the experience through which the user can "experience' the texture of what is being touched and the realism of interactions being felt [15].

3. Applications of AR/VR in Healthcare

Virtual Reality (VR) and Augmented Reality (AR) are two innovative technologies that greatly improving various aspects of healthcare. They offer fresh models for learning, assessment, intervention, and the delivery of patient services [16]. Figure 1 illustrates the distribution of AR/VR applications across various industries, highlighting that the education, healthcare, and gaming sectors exhibit the highest adoption rates, followed by manufacturing, retail, and real estate, demonstrating the broad and diversified utilization of immersive technologies in both consumer and enterprise domains. Here are some key applications of AR/VR in healthcare:

- *Medical Training and Education:* Both AR and VR provide compelling training experiences to learners practicing in the medical field. These technologies offer the ability to visualise the structures of anatomy and the ability to simulate surgical experiences with no harm coming to the patient.
- *Surgical Assistance:* AR can help to display demanding information, including the MRI or CT scans, on the patient's body during surgery. This real-time data helps increase surgical treatments' effectiveness because it offers clear guidelines to the surgeons.
- *Telemedicine, Including Consultations and Treatment:* VR can also be applied to remote consultations so that clients and physicians can interact in virtual reality. This is especially important for patients who are based in remote regions or those who have mobility disabilities, so that they do not have to move to get the required medical attention.
- *Enhanced Method of Identifying and Managing Diseases:* AR helps diagnose and treat patients by giving doctors and other caregivers immediate access to patient information and patient records. This makes decisions faster and more accurate when needed most by the patient, hence achieving better results.
- *Physical therapy and rehabilitation:* Healthcare applications of virtual reality thus provide positive engagement and motivation to patients' rehabilitation programs. Most of these virtual exercises can be used to monitor the progress and provide feedback in the recovery process, which enhances the quality of recovery.

- *Emergency Navigation:* AR can also enable medical personnel to assist a patient undergoing some complicated process in an emergency by demonstrating how to do it, for example, the correct way of using a defibrillator or CPR. This can be important in critical situations where a person can save his or her life.
- *Empathy Training for Doctors:* It means that various patients' experiences can be recreated in VR, allowing doctors to at least have an idea of what patients have to deal with. That is why this empathy training may help doctors to become more polite in front of patients and be more compassionate to them.
- *Suppose patients are to adopt healthy behaviors and practices. In that case, they must become active participants in their treatment and care:* AR and VR are effective ways of providing patients with knowledge about their diseases or treatment processes. This enables patients to adopt a personal approach to their health issues and ensures they participate in their treatment process.
- *Occupational Stress and Health Psychology:* VR is applied therapeutically, including the use of post-traumatic stress disorder, anxiety, and depression. It offers the necessary climate within which the patient can deal effectively with the condition, enhancing mental health.
- *Research and Development:* AR and VR technologies are particularly connected to medical research and development. FFDA-approved software allows researchers to perform virtual experiments, view molecular models, and test out new treatments, quickening the process of finding a cure.

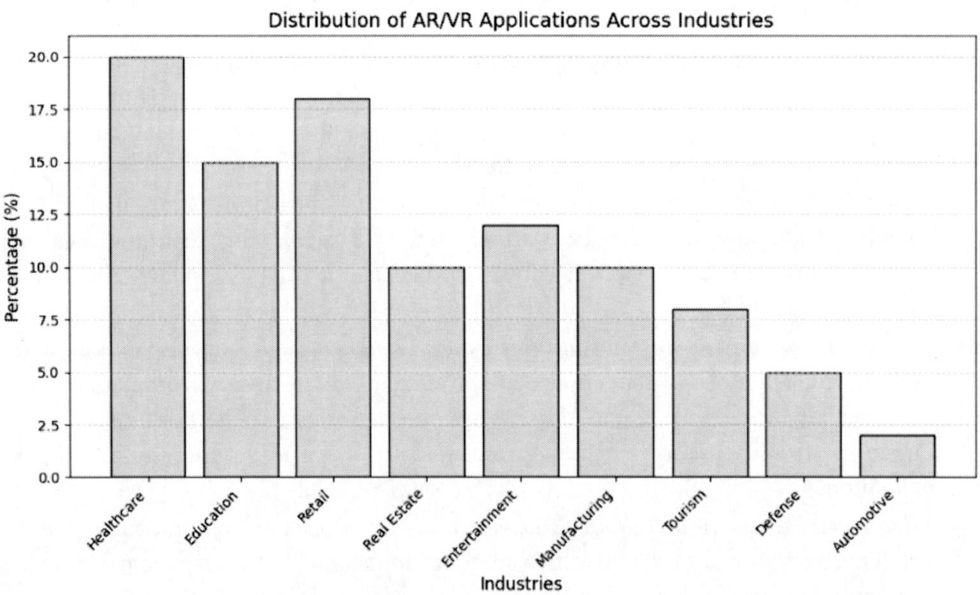

Figure 1. AR/VR Application Distribution by Industry.

- *Pain Management:* AR and VR are included among the non-drug approaches to pain management. Such technologies can also encompass patient care by substituting the patient's environment with a soothing and time-consuming virtual environment to help patients cope with acute and chronic pain. This is especially helpful in operations, physical therapy, and for other patients with ailments such as fibromyalgia.

- *Autism Therapy:* People with autism and other learning disabilities are attending VR to ensure that they interact with others, learn how to communicate, and even deal with their sensitive skin. Such simulations, as discussed here, allow for learning while maintaining all safety and can be made according to the patient's needs.
- *Cognitive Rehabilitation:* Stroke, TBI, or any other cognitively impaired patients can benefit from VR-based cognitive rehabilitation programs. These exercises are fun activities and tasks that foster the affected patient's memory, attention, and problem-solving skills.
- *Preoperative Planning:* AR and VR ensure that surgeons make proper preparations for surgeries, particularly complicated ones. Using precise and elaborate digital images of arteries and veins and other organs inside a patient's body, the surgeons can practice the same surgery, look for different problems they may meet, and be much more accurate finally, resulting in fewer mishaps and improved results.
- *Telemedicine and Tele mentoring:* AR and VR enable the implementation of telemedicine as they use a real and interactive approach to such consultations. It also offers the possibilities of telementoring, where distant and less experienced surgeons can consult their peers during operations or where the senior surgeons control the young ones' movements in operation theatres irrespective of distance.
- *Pharmaceutical Research:* AR and VR have their applications in pharmaceutical research, mainly due to their ability to offer visual and real-life representations of molecules, drug interactions, and the final simulation of clinical trials. These technologies improve the efficiency of drug development since they offer analytical insights that standard methods do not provide.
- *Stress Relief and Relaxation:* It has been estimated that VR environments with meditative purposes effectively treat stress and anxiety in patients. These virtual experiences can be scenic nature, voice-guided meditations, or relaxing music pieces, and they have great value for patients during chemotherapy or other aggressive treatments or with mental illnesses.
- *Geriatric Care:* Technology has the potential to enhance elderly care by supporting cognitive, physical, and social functioning through the use of AR and VR. These technologies can improve the quality of life of older people since they can be used to improveimprove the comfort for awaiting their demise as individuals with restricted mobility or who dwell around game institutions.
- *Phobia Treatment:* Virtual Reality exposure therapy is, therefore, a proper way of handling phobias. With time, the patients are taken through the procedures that cause their fear in a simulated environment so that they can learn how to deal with them. This technique has been applied to other phobias like acrophobia- fear of heights; aerophobia- fear of flying; and speech phobia- fear of speaking in public.
- *Blood Draw Assistance:* AR technology can also help healthcare practitioners search for a vein when drawing a blood sample or inserting an IV line. The current application of AR will use the overlay of vein maps on the patient's skin, increase the success rate, and speed up the procedures without additional discomfort to the patient.

4. AR/VR in Education and Training

Augmented Reality (AR) & Virtual Reality (VR) are now helping people change how education and training are delivered [17]. Such technologies provide the kind of interaction that can significantly improve learning and training processes [18]. The purpose of AR/VR in the field of training and education is given in Table 1. The primary purposes of AR/VR in education and training include:

- *Enhanced Engagement and Retention:* AR and VR effectively design learning interfaces that provide meaningful and attention-capturing experiences to learners. Incorporating actual life situations increases the fun of a student and thus enables them to understand and even remember the information much better.
- *Realistic Simulations:* AR and VR enable the creation of a mimic of real-life operations and settings. This is especially useful where practical experience is paramount, just like in the health sectors, aviation, and manufacturing industries. Students can repeat some procedures and cases in protected conditions with numerous opportunities for carrying out practical exercises without adverse consequences.
- *Remote and Flexible Learning:* AR and VR allow learners to review training materials and practice using simulations from any location and at any time. This is particularly relevant in the 21st century, where learners will likely have different timetables and physical locations. Through AR and VR, remote learning helps to reach more people with education and training.
- *Hands-on Training:* AR adds digital information on top of the physical environment and offers content based on context and features in the environment. This is especially beneficial in the training conducted at the workplace, where the learner can be trained online and immediately coached and mentored. VR places the learner in a virtual environment where they can practice skills and procedures without objects and equipment.
- *Cost Efficiency:* This paper established that using AR and VR in training reduces the time and money required to travel and secure class space and other physical resources. They also reduce the danger of training in dangerous areas, reducing the costs of accidents and injuries.
- *Personalized Learning:* AR and VR can be used in a way that will be more effective for each learner and in accordance with his/her desires. Flexible learning systems can change the level of difficulty/complexity and contents based on the learner's performance in order to deliver the best and most suitable training for each learner.
- *Collaborative Learning:* AR and VR enable learners to interact with other learners and instructors in learning activities. This fosters group cohesion, collaboration, and conflict-solving abilities, which are vital in today's world.
- *Innovative Teaching Methods:* AR and VR make teachers embrace pro-change, follow new change agenda, and integrate new technologies in their teaching. This can, in turn, result in more enriched and interesting classroom practice and a culture of professional learning.

- *Cultural and Historical Exploration:* Examples of how AR and VR can be used to teach history or culture are when learners can be taken to different eras or cultural sites to get a first-hand feeling of the topics under study.
- *Skill Development and Assessment* These technologies can be applied in designing and evaluating specific competencies, including language, technical, and interpersonal competencies.
- *Accessibility*: AR and VR can help to reach persons with disabilities during education and training processes by creating other forms of interaction.
- *Motivation and Reward* Elements embedded in a gamification of AR and VR for learners include carrots, a star, and a bar, indicating increased performance, which makes learning engaging.
- *Environmental Awareness:* Simulation of adverse impacts of climate change, pollution, and the like, which may be used to educate society and encourage people to become responsible for the environment.
- *Creative Expression:* These technologies promote imagination and innovation because students can construct and edit virtual spaces – artistic and design abilities.

Table 1. Training and education purposes of AR/VR

Purpose	Description	Field/Application	Example
Enhanced Engagement	Captures learners' attention and improves retention	General Education	Interactive history lessons
Realistic Simulations	Simulates real-world scenarios for hands-on practice	Healthcare, Aviation	Medical procedure simulations, flight training
Remote and Flexible Learning	Provides access to training materials from anywhere	Corporate Training	Remote sales training, leadership development
Hands-on Training	Offers real-time guidance and feedback in real-world contexts	Manufacturing	Assembly line guidance, equipment maintenance
Cost Efficiency	Reduces the need for physical resources and travel	Various Fields	Virtual classrooms, online workshops
Personalized Learning	Tailors learning experiences to individual needs	Special Education	Adaptive learning systems for students with disabilities
Collaborative Learning	Facilitates interaction and teamwork in virtual environments	Team Training	Virtual team-building exercises
Innovative Teaching Methods	Encourages the adoption of new technologies and teaching approaches	General Education	Incorporating VR in science classes

5. Transformation of Retail, E-Commerce, and Industry 4.0

The integration of AR/VR technologies is reshaping retail, e-commerce, and Industry 4.0 by revolutionizing how businesses engage with consumers and optimize operations [19]. In retail and e-commerce, AR/VR enables highly interactive and personalized shopping experiences. Customers looking to purchase clothes, accessories, or home furniture can benefit from virtual try-ons, which reduce uncertainty and primarily return rates. Holographic shops are likely to give consumers a virtual shopping experience, combining the benefits of online shopping with the sensory appeal of physical shops. The effective use of augmented reality in directions and in-store guidance has already been implemented in retail stores and effectively influences customers' interactions and purchases [20].

In Industry 4.0, AR/VR significantly redesigns manufacturing processes, product design, and workforce training. AR offers another way of displaying prototypes and assembly instructions, thus minimising mistakes. Virtual Reality makes it possible to have rehearsals for training employees for operations on elaborate equipment, with minimal interruptions to actual operations. These technologies also contribute to predictive maintenance by superimposing actual data on physical assets, which reduces maintenance time and boosts productivity. In addition, e-commerce app companies are using Augmented Reality and Virtual Reality to provide highly intelligent and personalized suggestions to customers with the help of artificial intelligence and machine learning. This digital transformation helps to build deeper customer trust and business loyalty and helps analyze the consumer through engagement analytics.

Despite these obstacles and growing adoption rates of AR/VR in these sectors, fundamental problems include high costs and compatibility with devices; however, with the new affordable hardware, cross-platform solutions, and scalable cloud-based architectures, these problems are expected to be solved. Over time, this new technology of AR/VR will pave the way for innovations and efficiency of operations and change the face of consumer buying experiences, putting AR/VR on the frontline to effect changes in retail as well as Industry 4.0. It helps improve competitiveness and brings industries into line with the requirements of a market where digital tools are rapidly gaining popularity.

The architecture of the conceptual framework for AR/VR applications comprises four modules: AR/VR application architecture, input data feed for pre-processing and content generation, rendering and delivery architecture, and outcomes of user engagements [21]. Figure 1 presents the conceptual model of AR/VR systems for Industry 4.0. This framework emphasises the seamless integration of AR/VR technologies with real-time data inputs, efficient processing mechanisms, and scalable distributed platforms to deliver immersive experiences.

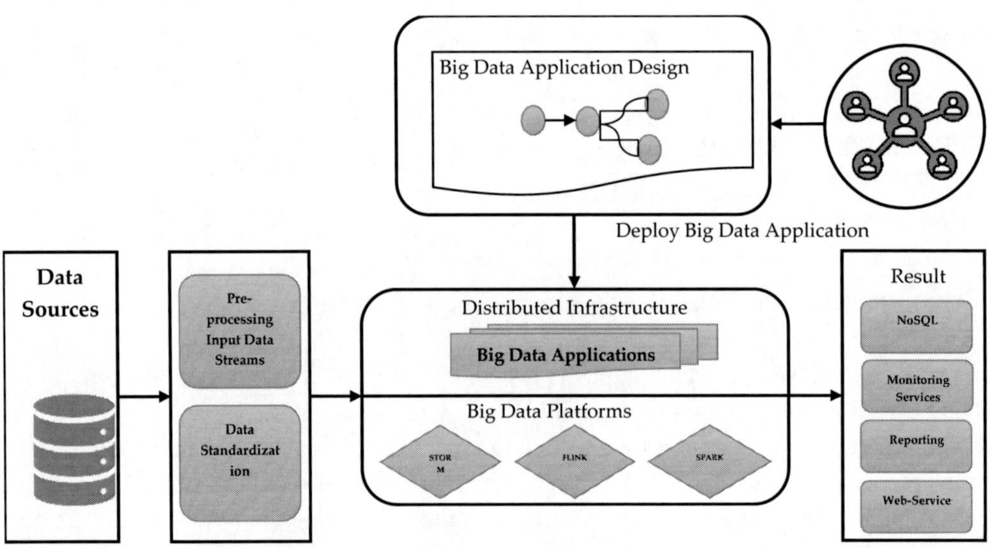

Figure 2. Conceptual framework of big data.

3.1. Big Data Application Design

This module allows system engineers to add support for various visual editors to their AR/VR applications. The developed applications are considered as directed graphs, where vertices represent different functionalities of AR/VR, including the rendering processes, interaction methods, and content generation algorithms. Real-time experiential production occurs at programming junctures and is standardised to handle information from various sources, as depicted in Figure 2. The data sources, including the 3D model, the data from sensors, and real-time analytics, are associated with the respective programming nodes to achieve interoperability in processing and delivery. Figure 2 illustrates the AR/VR Content Development Programming Model to show how all these components work together to form versatile applications.

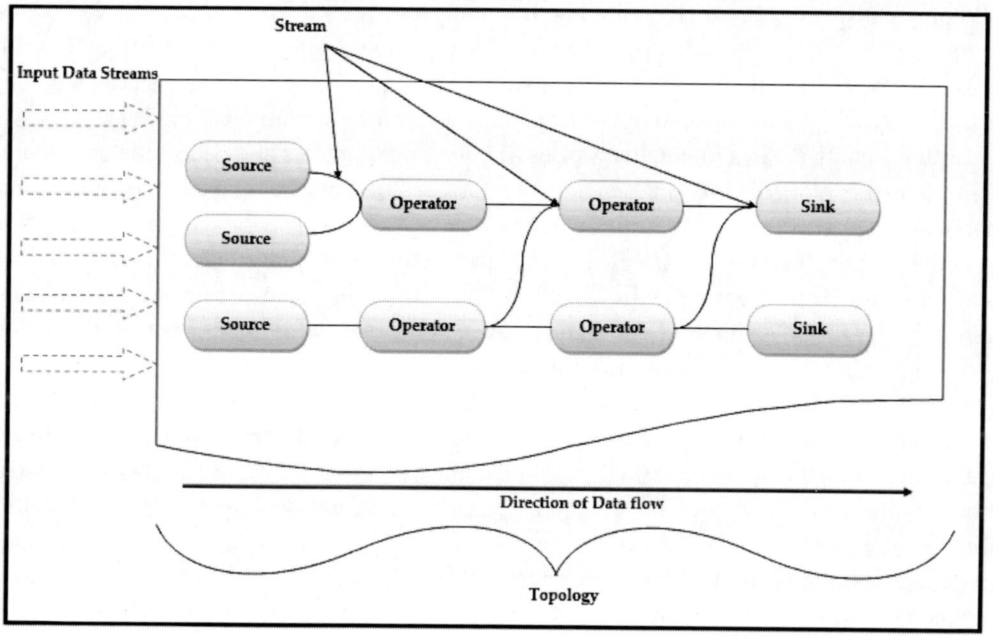

Figure 3. Big data analytics programming model.

Thus, with the help of programming nodes, application logic is created without reference to the internal data and interfaces. A tremendous amount of data sources were collected into the platform to reclaim the related information on the diversified characteristics of a factory—the heterogeneity of the data results in the dissimilar format of the data. Thus, the data format is one of the most significant issues in applying big data analytics in Industry 4.0.

6. Applications in Tourism and Entertainment

The application of Augmented Reality (AR) and Virtual Reality (VR) elements in tourist and recreational facilities has dramatically influenced how people spend their leisure time and have fun. Such technologies are revolutionising conventional interaction methods by providing added dimensions to interaction with increased specificity and comfort. In tourism, with AR/VR, the user is made to have a feel for the different places without having to be physically there. Another application of VR is in preparing potential travellers for some sense of the destination before they decide to visit; Virtual Reality enables people to preview landmarks, museums, and cultural attractions before they finally decide to tour them for real.

AR extends visitors' learning experience by superimposing historical, cultural, or contextual information onto the fundamental physical structures of the sites using smartphones or Augmented Reality glasses. This enriched engagement heightens the knowledge and value of destinations. Further, virtual reality-based virtual tours have become helpful for disabled or older adults who can only imagine visiting some places physically. That is why, nowadays, the term "virtual tourism" is slowly becoming more popular, mainly due to the world's quarantine measures and environmental preservation. It also explicitly understands that through highly realistic VR, people can go for a tourist experience in a natural setting, an ancient archaeological site, or even a city, all without moving an inch – thus saving carbon emissions. The tourism industry is also capturing the use of AR/VR to repeat historical events and enable the user to experience the past era, a stimulating way of learning. AR/VR has dramatically changed storytelling and connecting with the audience in the entertainment industry.

Virtual Reality creates interactive stories as engaging as games and helps viewers become involved in the plot, directly influencing the further content and making the piece more emotional. AR/VR is one of the most developing industries because the gaming industry was one of the pioneers that used AR/VR. It is 360° immersive as it allows players to dive into the games, enabling them to have a realistic experience. AR gaming, also known as location-based gaming, is a form of gaming where features of the real world are augmented by computer-generated graphics, such as in Pokémon GO.

AR/VR has also impacted other valuable events like concerts, theatre, and sports events, live streaming. Virtual Reality enables people to watch events live from their preferred locations while giving them the feeling of sitting in the front row. AR increases on-site activities introduces integrated layers of information, such as scores during a match or live graphics during a show, to the audience. Looking at the case of theme parks and other full-featured attractions, AR/VR is used to build an environment that would help guests interact with a storyline as if they were in fictional or historical settings. They are also being used in museums and other cultural centres to create new, engaging exhibit experiences with art and history. Through VR, a visitor can literally 'walk' right into a picture or an archaeological site in an interactive manner, thereby increasing educational utility and recreation.

With future developments in AR/VR technology, it is believed that haptic feedback, AI, and edge computing will improve the realism and depth of the tourism and entertainment sectors. Issues like high development costs, limited capabilities of the target devices, and a large variety of content are being approached through innovations in both hardware and software that otherwise make these technologies more mainstream. In conclusion, it can be stated that AR/VR is changing the tourism and entertainment industry by bringing innovative solutions that are engaging, interactive, and accessible. These technologies range from virtual tourism and virtual storytelling, which bringbring significant change to people and industries to transform how people learn and experience destinations and stories. The Comprehensive Analysis of AR/VR in Tourism and Entertainment is detailed in Table 2.

Table 2. Comprehensive analysis of AR/VR in tourism and entertainment

Perspective	Inference	Mode of Deployment	Application	Use Case	Advantage
Tourism Experience	AR/VR enhances exploration by providing virtual previews of destinations or enriched on-site experiences.	VR headsets, AR mobile apps, smart glasses	Virtual tours, on-site AR experiences	Virtual exploration of historical landmarks or inaccessible destinations.	Reduces travel planning uncertainties, increases inclusivity, and minimizes environmental impact.
Cultural Engagement	Immersive experiences allow users to explore historical events and cultural narratives interactively.	AR mobile apps, museum installations	AR-based cultural exhibits, VR recreations	Recreating historical events or cultural festivals in VR.	Promotes cultural preservation and fosters deeper audience engagement.
Entertainment Media	AR/VR transforms storytelling by allowing users to interact with real-time content.	VR platforms, AR-enhanced displays	Virtual reality films, interactive storytelling	Immersive cinematic experiences where users play an active role.	Deepens emotional connection with narratives and increases user satisfaction.
Gaming	AR/VR introduces highly engaging gameplay with real-time interaction and realism.	VR gaming consoles, AR mobile platforms	Immersive gaming	AR-based games like Pokémon GO or VR multiplayer games.	Increases player engagement and blends physical and digital interactions.
Live Events	Virtual platforms offer remote participation in concerts, sports, or theatre performances.	VR live-streaming, AR-enabled venues	Virtual concerts, AR-enhanced live performances	Attending concerts remotely with VR or accessing AR statistics during sports events.	Enhances accessibility, offers personalized experiences, and reduces logistical challenges.
Theme Parks	AR/VR creates interactive attractions, enriching user engagement.	On-site VR installations, AR-guided tours	Interactive rides, VR-based storytelling	Experiencing fictional worlds through VR rides or AR-guided adventures.	Increases visitor satisfaction and creates novel entertainment formats.
Museum Interaction	AR/VR makes exhibits dynamic, allowing users to interact with history and art virtually.	AR/VR devices, mobile apps	Virtual museum exhibits, interactive art displays	Walking into a 3D-rendered historical site or exploring a painting interactively.	Enhances educational value and accessibility, attracting diverse audiences.

7. Challenges and Future Prospects in AR/VR Adoption

This section explores the potential and issues related to implementing Augmented Reality (AR) and Virtual Reality (VR) tools across industries. Despite the fact that AR/VR has shown significant opportunities in sectors like healthcare, education, retail, manufacturing, tourism and hospitality, defence, and entertainment and has the capability to bring revolutionary change, its application is still restricted by technical, economic, and operational constraints. The main challenges that must be solved for the OS to become more popular are high development costs, limitations of devices, privacy questionnaires, and reluctance to change. At the same time, the potential of AR/VR in the future can be described as incredible as further 5G and AI technologies, along with edge computing, continue to evolve. The section describes the possibilities of such technologies, such as developing new applications for them, increasing accessibility, and enabling their easy integration into existing systems. By managing current problems and building on upcoming possibilities, AR/VR can open up unimaginable capacities that catalyse economic production and improve client experiences in all fields. The following analysis underlines the general and specific difficulties peculiar to various sectors. It discusses how new tendencies and opportunities can help to eliminate these obstacles and build a unified digital environment. The AR/VR faces numerous challenges in industry that is depicted in Table 3.

Table 3. Diversified challenges in industry

Industry	Challenges	Impact of Challenges	Possible Solutions
Healthcare	High cost of devices, lack of trained personnel, patient data privacy issues.	Limits widespread adoption and efficient utilization in critical applications.	Subsidized hardware, AR/VR training programs, and blockchain for securing patient data.
Education	Limited access to technology in underprivileged regions, high costs, and resistance to change in traditional systems.	Creates inequality in access to AR/VR-based education.	Government-funded initiatives, affordable devices, and awareness campaigns to promote adoption.
Retail & E-Commerce	High development costs, device compatibility issues, and low consumer adoption.	Slows innovation and reduces the competitive advantage of smaller retailers.	Development of cross-platform solutions, reducing hardware costs, and enhancing user-friendly interfaces.
Manufacturing	Complexity in integration with existing systems, high initial investment.	Slows digital transformation and affects operational efficiency.	Modular AR/VR solutions that integrate seamlessly and financial incentives for adoption.
Tourism	Limited availability of immersive content and high hardware costs.	Restricts market reach and innovation in travel planning experiences.	Investment in content creation, partnerships with travel platforms, and affordable AR/VR hardware.
Defence	High costs of simulations, reliance on hardware infrastructure, and cybersecurity risks.	Affects preparedness and increases dependency on traditional methods.	Development of cost-effective simulations and robust cybersecurity frameworks.
Real Estate	Lack of standardization in AR/VR solutions and high device dependency.	Slows adoption among smaller real estate firms.	Creation of industry-wide standards and development of lightweight, affordable solutions.
Entertainment	Device discomfort, short battery life, and lack of content diversity.	Reduces user satisfaction and market retention.	Innovation in lightweight hardware, improved battery technology, and diverse content creation.

AR/VR technology has a promising future and holds the potential to create major changes in numerous fields. AR/VR is currently in the early stages of adoption, but the continuous improvement of enabling technologies like 5G, edge computing, and artificial intelligence (AI) will provide better performance, accessibility, affordability, and efficiency to AR/VR in the future. Combining AR/VR with smart IoT gadgets will also improve the real-time interactivity of industries at a much higher level to create more personalized solutions. The predictions for AR/VR applications in the healthcare sector include accurate surgical operations, disease monitoring, and therapeutic uses. AI-integrated VR training will provide a better and safer medical training environment with high accuracy. For education, future AR/VR platforms will enable learning environments by connecting globally privileged and underprivileged schools and universities through affordable and efficient cloud solutions. Increased use of Augmented Reality and Virtual Reality will be seen across retail and e-commerce spaces with applications such as AI-driven virtual shopping assistants and better virtual fitting experiences. This shift is expected to enhance consumer satisfaction levels and minimize the logistics involved. As a tool of Industry 4.0, the application of AR/VR in manufacturing will continue to grow, with smart factories deploying AR-based maintenance, predictive analytics, and multiuser, virtual workplaces. The dynamics of the tourism industry will advance with the help of the application of AR-aided virtual travel and AI-produced synthetic content, allowing for economically efficient familiarisation with a destination. Military-related operations will harness real-time, data-enriched Augmented Reality modelling and simulation for the enhancement of combat readiness and, at the same time, promote cost-effective and effective modelling and simulation for large operations. Real estate and architecture will continue to extend the use of AR/VR for realistic property tours, shortening the time of project delivery and allowing remote teamwork.

Some critical features, like AR/VR lightweight devices and extended battery life, remove some of the comfort challenges for the users. Also, the democratisation of AR/VR technology through open source or affordable technology will increase the use of AR/VR in small businesses. The integration of blockchain will solve concerns on privacy and security, and make it possible for industries such as the health and finance sectors to deploy AR/VR systems. As the main application of AR/VR, the entertainment industry is expected to generate even more engaging content in virtual concerts, eSports, and interactive movies. The enhancement of haptic will be advantageous in these applications and provide feedback to the users for added interaction. Social AR/VR platforms will be integrated into the metaverse and expected to revolutionise human interaction through collaboration and connection. Despite the current difficulties, AR/VR technologies will continue to gain adoption by technology vendors, academic organisations, and governments. This means that governments and particularly private stakeholders need to come together and set the standards, share the costs, and facilitate the use of immersive technologies. Technology adoption and implementation will need to be accompanied by proper workforce training to capture the full value of AR/VR initiatives and overcome resistance in conservative industries. The total implementation of AR/VR technology does not pertain to an industry-based future but one that frames the human experience. These innovative technologies should be able to address current issues and contribute toward the development of AR/VR as a fundamental framework of the digital environment, which in turn will help start an era of profound economic and social evolution.

Conclusion

Immersive technologies, including Augmented Reality (AR) and Virtual Reality (VR), have become a global phenomenon that has transformed different industries with new interaction modes and visual experiences. These technologies have changed the ways in which entertainment and games are delivered using interactive simulations and dynamic content. Virtual. In contrast, reality helps train surgeons and develop therapies, while with augmented reality, doctors can diagnose patients immediately and treat them. With augmented reality, doctors can diagnose and treat patients immediately. In education, another area that has been boosted through AR/VR is the development of a favourable learning environment and model. In the manufacturing and automotive industries, AR is used for design and modelling, assembly, and training employees. In contrast, retail and e-commerce fields use AR for consumer experience and decreasing return rates for products with virtual fitting. Immersive applications in tourism allow users to visit the sites virtually, changing the way people plan their travel. In defence, departments use VR for training and strategic purposes. Real estate and architecture use AR/VR for visualization and operation optimization. There are some issues – high development costs, limitations of devices, and privacy – that remain to be critical for the large-scale implementation of the technology. It is crucial to remove these barriers if AR/VR must reach its full potential. This means that AR/VR can be developed as the fundamental platform of the integrated digital environment through the support of technology progression, cost-cutting, and ethical concerns.

References

[1] Aquino, S. (2024). *From Research to Service: Exploring AR/VR in the Industrial Context.*

[2] Pujiono, I. P., Asfahani, A. and Rachman, A., 2024. Augmented Reality (AR) and Virtual Reality (VR): Recent Developments and Applications in Various Industries. *Innovative: Journal of Social Science Research*, 4(4), 1679–1690.

[3] Familoni, B. T. and Onyebuchi, N. C., 2024. Augmented and virtual reality in our education: A review. *International Journal of Applied Research in Social Sciences*, 6(4), 642–663.

[4] Le Tan, T. et al., 2024. Researching Influences of Learner Experience on AR/VR Adoption—The Case of Vietnamese Universities. *Journal of Information Technology Education: Research*, 23, 7.

[5] Logeswaran, K. et al., 2024. Unifying Technologies in Industry 4.0: Harnessing the Synergy of IoT, Big Data, Augmented Reality/Virtual Reality, and Blockchain Technologies. *Topics in Artificial Intelligence Applied to Industry* 4.0, 127–147.

[6] Xiao, R., 2024. Human Resource Management Analysis in the AR/VR Industry: A Case Study on Meta Company. *Highlights in Business, Economics and Management*, 24, 462–469.

[7] Bale, A. S. et al., 2024. Augmenting Knowledge Management with Immersive Technologies: Exploring Transformative Use Cases for AR and VR. *2024 International Conference on Advances in Computing, Communication and Applied Informatics (ACCAI). IEEE.*

[8] Sathya, A. and Aruna, A., 2024. Rehabilitation for Parkinson's Disease Using Virtual Reality (VR): Impact and Observational Analysis. In *Navigating the Augmented and Virtual Frontiers in Engineering*. IGI Global, pp. 1–20.

[9] Restas, A. et al., 2024. A Collaborative AR/VR Platform for Social Manufacturing. *Procedia Computer Science*, 237, 733–741.

[10] Enyejo, J. O. et al., 2024. Effect of Augmented Reality (AR) and Virtual Reality (VR) Experiences on Customer Engagement and Purchase Behavior in Retail Stores. *Magna Scientia Advanced Research and Reviews*, 11(2), 132–150.

[11] Oyewole, A. T. et al., 2024. Augmented and virtual reality in financial services: A review of emerging applications. *World Journal of Advanced Research and Reviews*, 21(3), 551–567.

[12] Jeevika Tharini, V. and Vijayarani, S., 2020. Bio-inspired High-Utility Item Framework Based Particle Swarm Optimization Tree Algorithms for Mining High Utility Itemset. In Advances in Computational Intelligence and Informatics: *Proceedings of ICACII 2019* (pp. 265–276). Springer Singapore.

[13] Putawa, R. A. and Sugianto, D., 2024. Exploring User Experience and Immersion Levels in Virtual Reality: A Comprehensive Analysis of Factors and Trends. *International Journal Research on Metaverse*, 1(1), 20–39.

[14] Tharini, V. J. and Shivakumar, B. L., 2024. A Canonical Particle Swarm Optimization (C-PSO) Approach to Identify High Utility Itemset. *Journal of Computational Analysis and Applications* (JoCAAA), 33(5), 507–517.

[15] Zhang, J., Wan Ahmad Jaafar Wan Yahaya, and Sanmugam, M., 2024. The impact of immersive technologies on cultural heritage: A bibliometric study of VR, AR, and MR applications. *Sustainability*, 16(15), 6446.

[16] Sellam, V., Aruna, A., Joseph, A., Rahul, S. and Rahul, A., 2022, May. Optical Character Recognition Using Localization Techniques. In *AIP Conference Proceedings* (Vol. 2463, No. 1). AIP Publishing.

[17] Yung, R. and Khoo-Lattimore, C., 2019. New realities: A systematic literature review on virtual reality and augmented reality in tourism research. *Current Issues in Tourism*, 22(17), 2056–2081.

[18] Samaddar, K. and Mondal, S., 2024. AR and VR-based travel: A responsible practice towards sustainable tourism. *International Journal of Tourism Cities*, 10(1), 105–128.

[19] Aruna, A. and Senthilselvi, A., 2024. A Novel Approach to Enhance Data Integrity in Blockchain Using Cryptographic Hashing. *2024 Second International Conference on Advances in Information Technology* (ICAIT), Vol. 1. IEEE.

[20] Celestin, M. et al., 2024. Exploring the Impact of AR and VR on Enhancing Customer Experiences and Driving Sales in Retail. *International Journal of Interdisciplinary Research in Arts and Humanities,* 9(2), 87–94.

[21] Khan, K., 2024. Advancements and Challenges in 360 Augmented Reality Video Streaming: A Comprehensive Review. *International Journal of Computing*, 13(1), 1–20.

Chapter 3

Optimizing User Experience with Immersive Technologies

L. N. B. Srinivas*
K. Venkatesh†
and G. Sujatha‡
Department of Networking and Communications, College of Engineering and Technology, SRM Institute of Science and Technology, Kattankulathur, Chennai, India

Abstract

Immersive technologies, Virtual Reality, Augmented Reality, and Mixed Reality, are transforming user experiences across all industries. Computer technologies generate dynamic virtual environments that improve user satisfaction and retention and overall user satisfaction. Toto achieve the optimum user experience optimisation in immersive environments, one must be well-versed in human-computer interaction concepts, as well as in the guidelines for usability, and have knowledge of the effect on psychology through immersion. The chapter discusses various approaches to improve the UX outcomes through immersive technology installations. The research takes into account significant factors in UX that include the designing of user-friendly interface models, as well as the use of seamless user interaction, sickness prevention methods, and AI functionalities for adaptation of the experience. The role of haptic feedback, together with spatial audio and eye-tracking, receives analysis for building applications that are realistic and friendly for users. The expanding use of immersive technology within gaming, education, healthcare and retail requires organizations to optimize user experience since this optimizes accessibility and useable design. The chapter explores multiple difficulties that include equipment constraints, ethical dilemmas, and a requirement for standardized design methods. Through modern UX principles and contemporary design approaches, developers and designers can develop interactive experiences that blend effectiveness with user-friendly system usability. The chapter establishes itself as a complete guide for researchers' designers and developers who need insight into evolving immersive UX optimization framework. Professionals gain the ability to build intuitive, inclusive, powerful, and immersive experiences through understanding the discussed principles and methodologies, which transform digital-human interactions.

---

* Corresponding Author's Email: srinival@srmist.edu.in
† Corresponding Author's Email: venkatek2@srmist.edu.in
‡ Corresponding Author's Email: sujathag@srmist.edu.in

In: Shaping Tomorrow
Editors: Prithi Samuel, A. Sathya, Balamurugan Balusamy et al.
ISBN: 979-8-90134-076-9

Keywords: virtual reality (VR), augmented reality (AR), mixed reality (MR), optimizing user experience, artificial intelligence, UX optimization, digital-human

1. Introduction to Immersive Technologies and UX

1.1. Evolution of Immersive Technologies

Immersive technologies have progressed a great distance in the last few decades, transforming how users interact with virtual worlds. Virtual immersion has its roots in the 1960s when the dawn of computer graphics and head-mounted displays laid the ground for the eventual creation of Virtual Reality and Augmented Reality. One of the earliest known attempts at creating an immersive experience was the "Sensorama," created by Morton Heilig in the 1960s. This machine combined stereoscopic 3D vision, sound, vibration, and even scent to produce a multi-sensory experience [1]. During the 1980s and the 1990s, technology enabled more powerful VR systems, particularly for military simulations, flight simulation, and medical applications. VR was invested in by NASA and research centres to improve the simulation and training process. The Oculus Rift, which arrived at the start of the 2010s, revolutionized immersive technology, and VR entered the masses' lives. Similarly, AR gained more traction with the smartphone, where apps such as Pokémon GO and social media AR filters to place objects in the real world became the trend [2]. Now, immersive technologies extend beyond VR and AR, including Mixed Reality (MR) and Extended Reality (XR), bringing the physical and digital worlds together seamlessly. New developments in artificial intelligence (AI), 5G connectivity, and spatial computing power the latest wave of immersive experiences, revolutionizing gaming, healthcare, education, and enterprise use cases.

1.2. Importance of UX in Immersive Environments

User Experience (UX) plays a crucial role in determining the success of immersive technologies. Unlike traditional 2D interfaces, immersive environments demand an intuitive, engaging, and seamless interaction between users and digital elements. Poorly designed experiences can lead to frustration, disorientation, and even physical discomfort, such as motion sickness in VR applications [3]. One of the primary goals of UX in immersive technologies is to create a sense of "presence," where users feel fully absorbed in a virtual or augmented environment. This is achieved through realistic visuals, natural interactions, and responsive system feedback. A well-optimized UX ensures users can navigate and interact with virtual environments effortlessly, reducing cognitive load and enhancing engagement. The immersive UX platform delivers advantages which transcend entertainment activities and video gaming. The healthcare sector alongside other industries utilizes well-designed virtual reality approaches to improve patient rehabilitation systems through specific VR programs and implements augmented reality interfaces for complex surgical operations. Educational VR simulations can build learning effectiveness through user experience design that creates interactive interfaces which make abstract concepts easy to experience [4]. Developer-created immersive experiences obtain practicality while embracing accessibility and delivering user comfort through a focus on usability. A successful follow-up requires multiple fields working together between human psychology, evolution research, and innovative technology with interface design practices.

1.3. Differences between Traditional UX and Immersive UX

Immersive UX mainly vastly differs from typical UX, which mostly revolves around 2D interfaces (think websites and mobile apps), what happens in VR involves three-dimensional environments where users interact with the digital world. Here are some of the significant differences between traditional UX and immersive UX:

- Interaction Model

Conventional UX involves point-and-click or touch interactions with the user traversing graphical user interfaces (GUIs) through the use of the keyboard, mouse, or touchscreen. Conversely, immersive UX performs more dynamically and intuitively by using natural interactions (e.g., hand gesture, voice, and eye-tracking) [5].

- Spatial Awareness and Orientation

Classic UX is the user interacting with information within a fixed boundary on a screen, such as a computer or handheld device display. On the other hand, intuitive UX has a 360-degree space to work with, and the user is required to navigate and operate inside a 3D space. That brings new design challenges, such as spatial mapping, depth perception and field-of-view adjustments.

- Engagement and Being

A traditional UX means information presented in a manner that is easily accessible and processable by the user. However, immersive UX continues by establishing an enriched feeling of user presence that elicits the feeling of the user actually being inside that virtual environment. Virtual reality supplements reality through realistic 3D graphics and sounds, haptic feedback, etc., and enables the user to have a greater immersion level [6].

- Cognitive Load and User Adaptation

Traditional UX uses interaction patterns that everybody is familiar with, like buttons, menus, and scrollbars. In contrast, immersive UX forces the user to learn how to interact in a new way: movement, gesture, and spatial awareness in the real world. This comes with an additional barrier towards learning the application, and designers should focus on creating intuitive onboarding and guidance systems.

- Physical and Psychological Factors

Traditional UX design focuses primarily on cognitive usability and visual appeal. When discussing immersive UX, it's vital to consider physical factors, motion sickness, ergonomics limitations, and other physiological factors that affect how long clients might spend in virtual universes. Realism needs a counterbalance of comfort to avoid tiredness and discomfort [7].

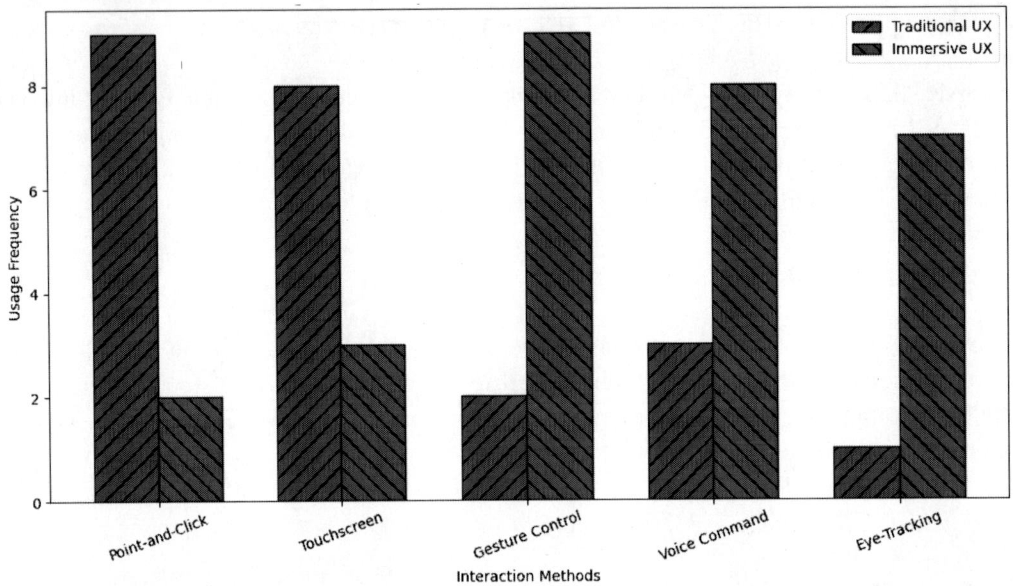

Figure 1. Comparison of interaction models in traditional UX vs. immersive UX.

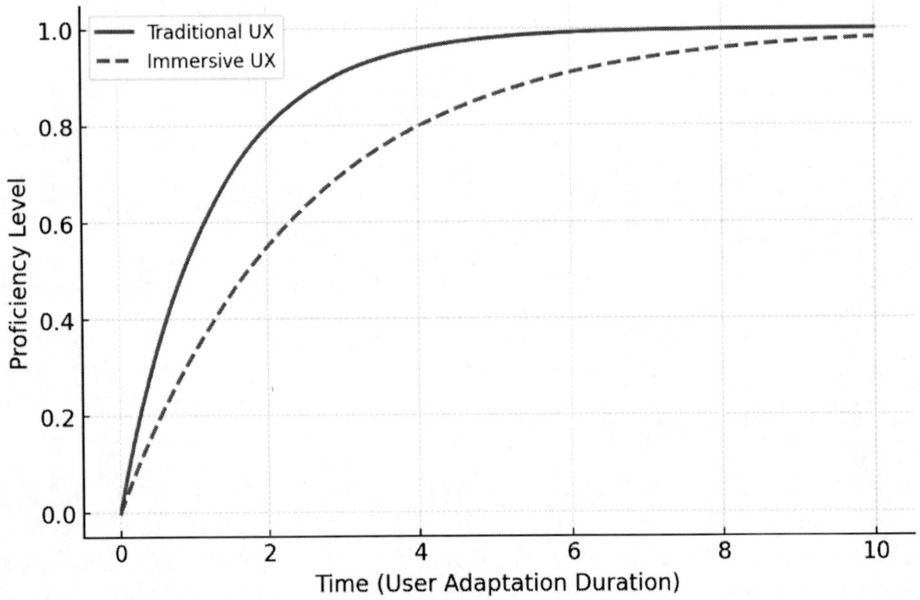

Figure 2. User adaptation and learning curve in traditional UX vs. immersive UX.

Figure 1 depicts the key differences in interaction models between traditional UX and immersive UX. Traditional UX primarily relies on point-and-click or touch-based interactions, where users engage with 2D graphical interfaces through keyboards, mice, or touchscreens. In contrast, immersive UX involves spatial interactions, including hand gestures, voice commands, and eye-tracking, allowing users to engage more naturally with the environment. The graph highlights how immersive UX enhances user engagement and interaction fluidity compared to conventional methods.

Figure 2 depicts how traditional UX stands regarding the user adoption period against the immersive UX adoption period. Traditional UX provides standardized design patterns that enable users to learn interfaces faster to explore them effortlessly. When users embrace immersive UX, they need to understand and learn new tendencies of digital environment interaction through methods like motion tracking and spatial navigation. Immersive UX produces a deep, engaging experience, yet requires greater effort for users to learn its usage before mastering it, as shown in the provided graph.

2. Fundamentals of User Experience in Immersive Environments

2.1. A Fundamental Set of UX Design Principles Exists for Developing VR, AR and MR User Interfaces

Visionary technology User Experiences for Virtual Reality (VR), Augmented Reality (AR) and Mixed Reality (MR) function according to different procedures from classical interface design methods. The main design principle in virtual spaces demands an experience where users feel like they are physically there without leaving their bodies. Creating a realistic presence depends on high-quality visuals combined with realistic spatial audio features with clear interface aniability. A vital characteristic exists between usability and intuitive interface design since this allows users to interact naturally with virtual environments without extra complexity. Interactive systems with intuitive character reduce exposure time and mental strain because they make users perform tasks more fluidly in their virtual environment. The comfort factor, as well as accessibility, are required for immersive UX because poorly designed interfaces may result in sickness as well as harm user comfort. The usability experience becomes better with comfortable ergonomic control sand, adjustable settings, and friendly navigation systems [8]. Realism and feedback systems improve engagement by using haptic responses as well as natural physics and AI that respond to the interaction. Smooth flow of navigation and interaction sequence must be included so that sudden movement or disorientation effects that disrupt the immersive effect are prevented. Picture-based UX guidelines make the designers develop applications that achieve seamless user interface and engagement, as well as accessibility to all.

2.2. Psychological and Cognitive Factors Affecting UX

Immersive technology performance depends directly on human perception abilities, cognitive functions, and psychological reaction to the experience. The ability to understand space relations and depth perception is a critical factor in VR and AR because users need genuine depth cues to handle digital content effectively. The design of depth perception affects comfort as well as clarity, which results in a broken sense of immersion. The degree of user engagement decreases because excessive visual or auditory stimuli create excessive cognitive load and attention management problems [9]. Designers need to strike a proper balance between information density points which they use to steer user attention throughout the system. The user experience undergoes major UX changes due to motion sickness in addition to the challenges of adaptation particularly for applications using VR technology. When visual signals fail to match the signals produced by the vestibular system the body experiences dizziness and nausea. Users can reduce symptoms of motion sickness with stabilizing horizon techniques as well as teleportation movement and high refresh rate maintenance. Experiences with real impact toward engagement typically require emotional and psychological involvement according to research [10]. Engagement deepens when viewers encounter colors plus soundscapes together with interactive storytelling features. The design of immersive applications leads to improved learning effectiveness and improved memory storage thus making VR and AR powerful instruments for educational purposes and training activities. UX designers achieve effective user engagement by comprehending the psychological traits, together with cognitive patterns, to design comfortable experiences for users.

2.3. Measuring UX in Immersive Applications

Evaluating UX in immersive environments requires integrating objective measurement and subjective appraisal. Objective measurement covers task completion rate, measuring the efficiency with which the user manages to complete assigned tasks within a virtual environment, and time on task, measuring the length of time the user spends in an environment. Error rate, which identifies usability issues by detecting incorrect interactions or navigational problems, is also a primary significant measure. Frame stability becomes crucial in VR applications, as low frame rates cause motion sickness and reduce the level of engagement by the user [11]. Besides the objective information, the measurement through the user's subjective experience provides information on the user's comfort and satisfaction level. Self-reporting questionnaires, such as the System Usability Scale (SUS) and the Presence Questionnaire (PQ), assistance in measuring the user's perceived level. Interviews and observational research offer qualitative information on pain points and preferences. Measurement of immersion and presence becomes critical in immersive applications, with the application of the Immersive Tendencies Questionnaire (ITQ) and biometric analysis measuring the level of engagement. Physiological information on the response by the user comes through the application of EEG monitoring and eye-tracking technology, ensuring the fine-tuning of the experiences for maximum comfort. Iterative testing and optimization of the UX are critical techniques in the improvement of immersive applications. Periodic usability testing, A/B testing on interaction methods, and user feedback cycles aid in the refinement of the design decisions and optimization of the overall experience. Applying these measurement methods, the developer manages to create immersive applications that are not only interactive but also highly user-friendly.

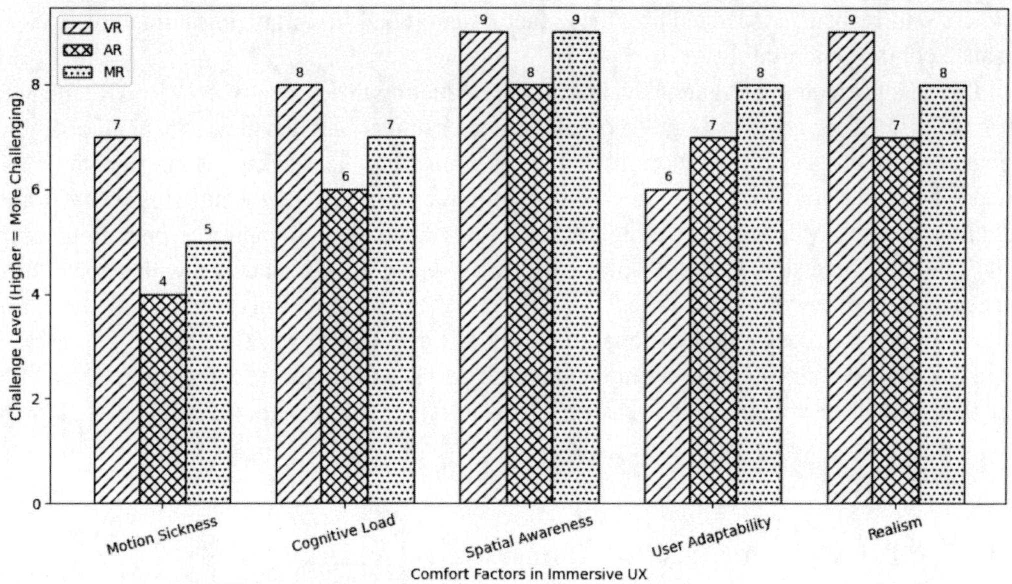

Figure 3. Comparison of UX comfort factors in Virtual Reality (VR), Augmented Reality (AR), and Mixed Reality (MR).

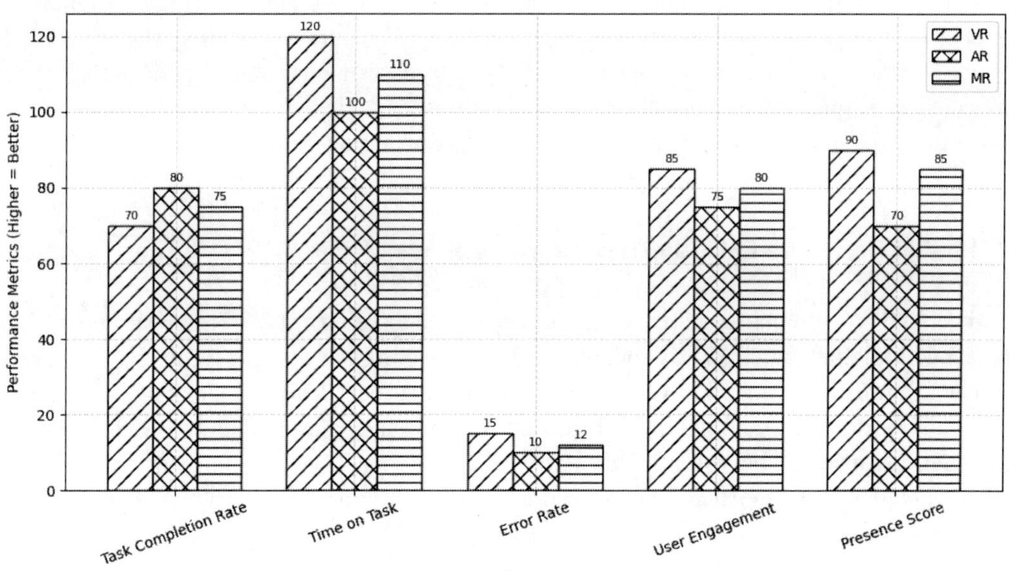

Figure 4. Comparative analysis of UX evaluation metrics.

Figure 3 illustrates the comparison of UX comfort factors in Virtual Reality (VR), Augmented Reality (AR), and Mixed Reality (MR). The graph shows that VR presents the highest challenges in motion sickness and cognitive load due to its fully immersive nature, which can lead to sensory dissonance. AR, which overlays virtual elements onto the real world, reduces these issues but still requires users to manage spatial awareness. MR, blending, but VR and AR aspects still provide a balanced experience and present moderate challenges in motion sickness and realism. Understanding these factors is crucial in optimizing immersive UX to enhance comfort and usability.

The data presented in Figure 4 evaluates UX evaluation metrics between VR, AR, and MR applications. Users achieve higher completion rates under AR as they can handle digital elements in their real-world environment, thus complicating their tasks. VR presents the most extended duration for task completion because its immersive complexity outstrips both AR and VR environments. VR features the highest error rates since hand or controller operations need highly accurate precision, yet AR displays the lowest thanks to its connection with actual world elements. Users show the most engagement during VR experiences because of full enclosure but MR systems strike a middle ground between AR and VR. Under the criteria of presence score that provides a deep sense of immersion, VR reaches the highest score, followed by MR, and then AR. The strength and weakness indicators for immersive technologies help UX designers improve user experiences.

3. Design Principles for Intuitive Immersive Interfaces

The design of natural user experiences with immersive interfaces requires knowledge about human interaction models, human behaviour, and environmental design guidelines. Unlike the traditional 2D interfaces, the immersive technologies Virtual Reality (VR) and Augmented Reality (AR) require spatial awareness, ergonomics, and natural navigation systems. Well-designed immersive interfaces enhance usability, decrease mental stress, and increase user convenience. Higher interaction engagement by the user is obtained when spatial design and navigation guidelines as well as ergonomics optimization are addressed [12].

3.1. Spatial Design and 3D Interface Considerations

In immersive environments, spatial design is a fundamental element that influences how users interact with digital content. The depth and scale which combine with perspective are essential elements for realizing an intuitive and realistic 3D interface design. Users find it easier to understand both their environment and interact with virtual objects when there exists proper spatial arrangement. The essential design principle focuses on keeping proportions and distances realistic [13]. Virtual objects need to follow real-world physical laws together with what users predict to stop disorientation. The necessary elements for successful design involve designers providing clear affordances, which are visual indicators directing users about object functions and the possible methods of interaction. The combination of shadows, textures, and animated effects creates virtual objects that users can more easily identify and interact with. Users need to consider how objects appear in specific locations relative to other objects as their position at different layers. Placing floating menus, dynamic dashboards, and adaptive overlays need to follow ergonomic principles to minimize neck fatigue and cognitive stress. Users maintain efficient immersion interface interaction through careful spatial design, which prevents them from experiencing disorientation or loss [14].

3.2. Navigation and Interaction Design in Immersive Spaces

The essential aspects of virtual and augmented reality user experiences consist of navigation and interaction methods. Immersive environments need different interaction methods because the typical point-and-scroll operations of legacy systems do not apply. The essential VR movement method involves teleportation because it prevents motion sickness through rapid jumps between spots instead of performing continuous motions. Users can select objects through gaze-based navigation by pointing at the items they want to choose, which streamlines their user interactions according to [15]. The usability improves through hand-tracking and gesture-based interactions since users can naturally move their hands to operate virtual objects. The main design principle for AR involves spatial anchoring since it keeps digital elements anchored and stable in real-world environments. The design of user interactions should concentrate on reducing system complexity to bring about higher levels of user engagement. Combining voice commands with hand gestures as input options enhances accessibility and user experience. Virtual interaction becomes more realistic when haptic technologies activate elements like handset vibrations or resistance-based effects. Visual indicators which highlight what users select offer necessary confirmation of intended actions together with animated visual feedback. A system that features properly designed navigation and interaction elements allows users to navigate effortlessly while avoiding confusion during interaction, thus preventing frustration [16].

3.3. Ergonomics and User Comfort in VR/AR Environments

User comfort is a critical factor in designing immersive interfaces. Poor ergonomics leads to fatigue, discomfort, and even health conditions, such as motion sickness or eye strain. One of the primary ergonomics factors to consider is where interactive objects are placed within the comfort region of the user. The interfaces must be positioned at natural viewing angles to prevent excessive neck motion. Text and UI objects need to be scaled correctly to be read without the necessity for eye strain. Another essential factor to consider is avoiding motion sickness during VR experiences. High frame rates (ideally above 90Hz), low latency, and motion stability prevent the conflicts that lead to nausea. Limiting sudden motion of the camera and providing fixed points of reference helps the user maintain their bearings [17]. Hand-based interaction must consider natural arm motion to prevent fatigue. For example, commonly encountered UI objects must be easily accessible for prolonged arm positions for extended durations. In AR, ensuring that virtual overlays do not interfere with critical real-world objects ensures user comfort and safety. Display brightness and contrast, adjustable through user preferences, help further optimize comfort based on lighting conditions. Placing ergonomics as a priority in immersive design, designers develop experiences that are not only compelling but sustainable for long-term use as well [18].

Figure 5 illustrates a comparative analysis of different navigation techniques in immersive environments, evaluating their efficiency and associated motion sickness risks. Teleportation-based movement scores highest in efficiency while maintaining a low risk of motion sickness, making it one of the most user-friendly options. Gaze-based navigation is also highly efficient and minimizes discomfort, making it a preferred method in hands-free applications. Joystick movement, while common, has the highest risk of motion sickness due to continuous motion without physical body movement alignment. Hand-tracking provides a balance between efficiency and user comfort, while voice commands offer an alternative but may lack the precision needed for complex interactions. Designers should choose navigation methods based on the application's goals and user comfort preferences.

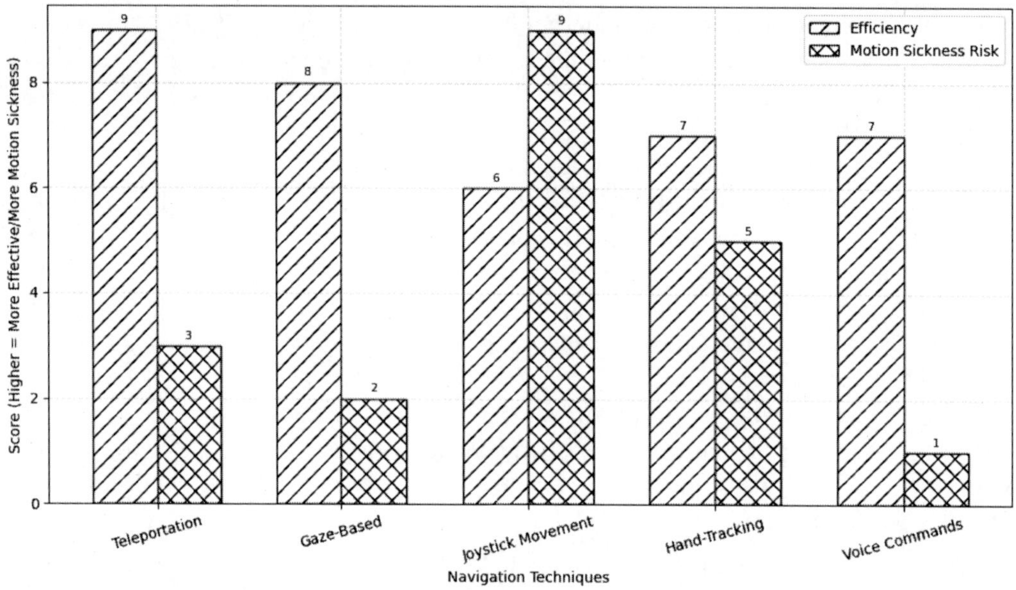

Figure 5. Comparative analysis of different navigation techniques.

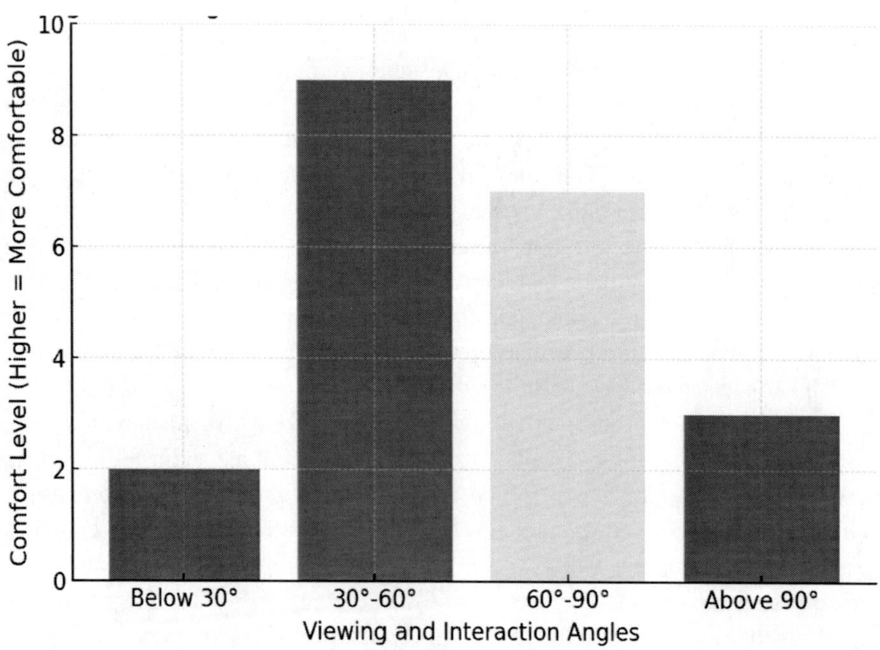

Figure 6. Ergonomic comfort zones in immersive environments.

Figure 6 demonstrates ergonomic comfort zones for immersive environment interactions through the study of user viewing degrees. Figure 6 demonstrates ergonomic comfort zones for immersive environment interactions by studying user viewing degrees and their interaction positions. The user interaction shows its maximum level of comfort in the angle range spanning from 30° to 60° relative to their eye position. The defined range enables users to move their head and arms naturally without facing any physical strain. Users experience moderate comfort when working in the 60°-90° sector but prolonged interaction can tire them out. Interaction at positions under 30 degrees or above 90 degrees provides the lowest ergonomic value because it creates neck and arm strain from abnormal postures. Designers who and develop interfaces within the most comfortable will achieve better usability while keeping users engaged through discomfort-free experiences.

4. Interaction Techniques: Gesture, Voice, and Eye-Tracking

Effective interaction techniques are needed in immersive environments to create intuitive and friction-free user experiences. Unlike the more conventional input devices, including keyboards and touchscreens, immersive technologies rely on more natural interaction techniques, including gesture recognition, voice control, and eye-tracking. These interaction techniques enable the user to interact with the virtual environment in the most natural way possible, with the aim of minimizing friction and maximizing immersion. Each technique has its strengths and limitations, and designers must implement the right, correct, and proper technique in harmony with user demand and technical feasibility [19].

4.1. Gesture-Based Interactions and Their Usability

One of the most intuitive interaction techniques in immersive environments, gestures make it possible to manipulate objects, navigate interfaces, and even communicate through natural hand movement. Gesture interaction leverages motion sensors, depth cameras, and the ability to track hands to interpret the inputs provided by the user. This type of interaction provides a highly interactive experience, as the user can make gestures like grabbing, pointing, and swiping without the need for physical controllers.

A significant advantage of gesture interactions lies in their naturalness, which reduces the cognitive burden associated with learning new input methods. However, problems with usability arise when gestures are not detected consistently or when the gestures require excessive physical strain, leading to fatigue. For more usable gestures, designers need to supply explicit visual and haptic feedback to confirm successful interactions. Additionally, having a set of universally known gestures imposes consistency across applications, making interactions more intuitive to the user. Calibration of the gesture detection system and the supply of fallback input techniques also enhance reliability [20].

4.2. Role of Voice Recognition in Immersive UX

Voice recognition provides immersive environments with a functional hands-free approach to interaction control. Users can control designed interfaces and virtual assistants through their voice while giving commands by using natural language. Virtual reality glasses and augmented reality tasks require this technology to operate properly because physical input is restricted during these interactions. Voice recognition provides users with the benefit of simplifying elaborate user interactions. Users can shorten their input time through direct command speech instead of following multiple menu sequences for navigation. This enhances operational speed and makes their work more effective. People with mobility disabilities find voice input practical for engaging with immersive experiences which enhances accessibility. Voice recognition technology functions optimally when speech processing algorithms work accurately and when the software understands various accents together with different languages and noise environments in the surroundings. Designers should enable systems to learn about users' present conditions and circumstances in their environment for optimized voice command exchanges. Users experience improved feedback clarity when they receive visual and auditory messages which validate their commands. The incorporation of machine learning systems which learn user-specific vocal patterns allows improved recognition accuracy and superior user experience [21].

4.3. Eye-Tracking for Enhancing User Engagement

Eye-tracking technology is an emerging interaction method that allows systems to detect where users are looking, providing valuable insights into attention and engagement. This technology enhances immersive UX by enabling gaze-based navigation, adaptive content rendering, and real-time user behaviour analytics. In VR and AR applications, eye-tracking can replace traditional selection methods by allowing users to interact simply by looking at objects, reducing the need for physical input [22]. The main advantage of eye-tracking systems becomes evident through their capability to enhance rendering performance by utilizing foveated rendering. The rendering method uses high-definition graphics visualization directly in front of users at the expense of minimal detail presentation in edge areas to optimize processing capabilities and system performance. Eye-tracking technology allows adaptive user interface components to shift their positions automatically according to where users look, so their necessary information stays visible, yet unnecessary movements remain eliminated [23].

Although powerful eye-tracking technology exhibits various drawbacks, it requires high accuracy standards, together with calibration precision, and respects privacy requirements. The detection of precise eye positions needs both high-quality sensors and individual user system calibration. User privacy depends on two critical measures, which consist of defending gaze data security and stopping unapproved tracking processes to earn user trust. Eye-tracking technology promotes enhanced user engagement when deployed effectively because it promotes interactive environments which adapt to user behavior.

Figure 7 presents a comparative analysis of three key interaction techniques in immersive environments: gesture recognition, voice commands, and eye-tracking. Voice interaction demonstrates the highest efficiency, as it enables hands-free operation and quick execution of commands. However, its accuracy is slightly lower than eye-tracking due to speech recognition challenges like accents and background noise. Eye-tracking achieves the highest accuracy, as it directly maps user intent to interface responses with minimal effort. While highly engaging, gesture-based interaction shows a moderate efficiency and accuracy score due to recognition limitations and physical constraints. Fatigue levels are highest for gesture interactions, as prolonged hand and arm movements can cause strain, whereas voice and eye-tracking require minimal effort. These insights help in selecting the most suitable interaction method based on application requirements and user needs.

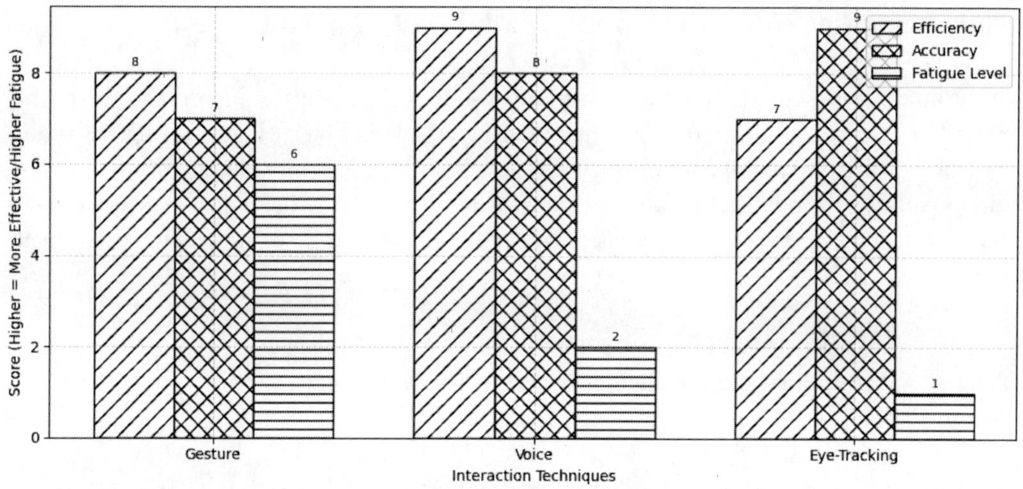

Figure 7. Comparative analysis of three key interaction techniques.

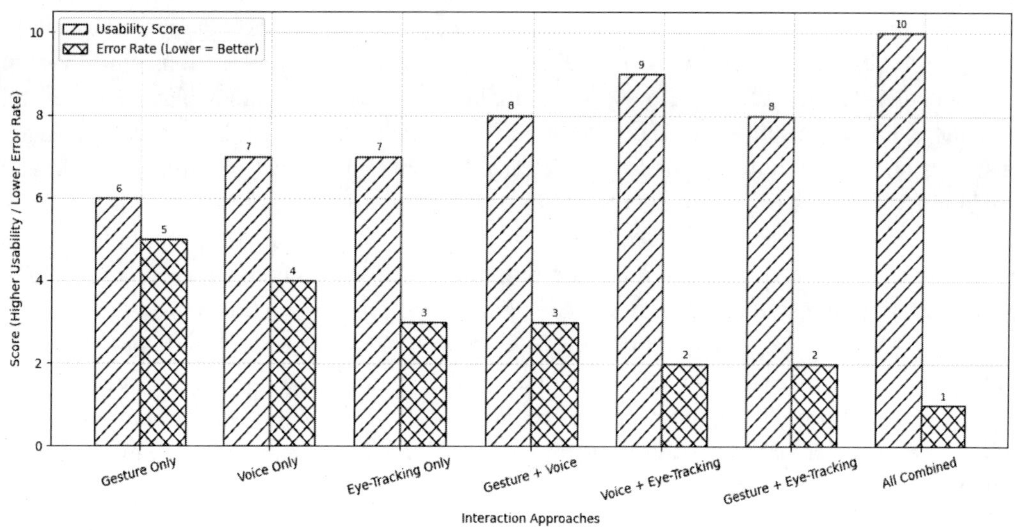

Figure 8. Effectiveness of different multimodal interaction approaches.

Figure 8 compares multimodal interaction techniques in immersive environments based on error rate and usability. In single-mode interaction, as in gesture-only, voice-only, and eye-tracking-only, the usability remains average, but the error rates are higher because each has its limitations. In multimodal interaction with multiple interaction techniques, the usability increases as the error rate lowers. The gesture + voice and voice + eye-tracking techniques perform well, leveraging speech recognition with physical gestures or gaze tracking. The best results are obtained with a fully multimodal system that integrates gesture, voice, and eye-tracking, with the maximum usability and the lowest error rate. This reflects the advantage of multimodal interaction in maximizing the user experience, minimizing the user's fatigue, and enhancing the system responsiveness.

5. Enhancing Realism with Haptics, Spatial Audio, and AI

A truly immersive experience extends beyond visual engagement by incorporating sensory feedback, dynamic soundscapes, and intelligent user interactions. Haptic feedback, spatial audio, and artificial intelligence (AI) work together to enhance realism, making virtual environments feel more lifelike and interactive. By integrating these elements effectively, immersive technologies can provide users with a heightened sense of presence, engagement, and interactivity [24].

5.1. Users Gain Realistic Experiences through the Implementation of Haptic Feedback

Virtual environments become more realistic through haptic feedback which generates touch-based physical sensations for users. Wearable devices including gloves and suits and controllers utilize three force types - vibrations and force feedback and motion resistance to create the sensation. Virtual objects become more realistic because haptic technology enables users to sense these objects, which strengthens their awareness of their interactions with virtual environments. Haptic feedback makes its main contribution to gameplay and virtual simulations because users experience firearms recoil effects alongside object surface contact sensations and virtual impacts during simulations. Virtual haptics systems in medical as well as aviation training settings help users build physical memory skills and boost precision through simulated touch experiences. Researchers in haptic technology created ultrasonic haptics to provide touch-free interaction through air pressure wave transmission instead of needing specialized user equipment [25]. The implementation of haptic feedback systems needs correct calibration because improper settings can lead to distractive discomfort or excessive stimulation. The delivery of feedback should match human-body reactions because this maintains suspension of disbelief in virtual worlds. Proper system integration of haptic technology advances virtual reality absorption because it creates seamless connections between synthetic and organic environments.

5.2. Spatial Audio Design for Immersive Environments

Sound technology is the fundamental factor that generates perceived depth to establish realistic immersive experiences. Spatial audio technology functions as 3D or binaural audio because it applies real-world sound behaviors by transforming directional sounds and distance and loudness parameters in relation to user movement position. The system uses spatial adjustments to match sound output to user movement, whereas standard stereo output distributes sound without adaptation. A properly executed spatial audio design system effectively improves users' capability to understand their surroundings in both AR and VR environments. Due to spatial audio technology, users can determine enemy positions through directional sounds during gaming. Virtual meetings would become more natural through spatial audio because this technology provides voice positioning relative to other participants' physical positions. The application of spatial audio in AR apps enables automatic synchronization with real-world environments and virtual objects, creating a heightened sense of presence [26]. Spatial audio efficiency depends on the proper placement of sounds and responsiveness in real-time. Employing head-tracking technology ensures that the sound dynamically adjusts with the user's motion, creating a sense of reality. Implementing sound occlusion, where objects distort or occlude the sound waves, adds to the feeling of authenticity. The creation of immersive soundscapes enables the developer to extent, significantly enhancing the virtual space's believability.

5.3. AI-Driven Personalization and Adaptive UX

Immersive experiences are directed in analysing user behaviour and dynamically adapting content – the responsibility of artificial intelligence (AI), which plays a transformative role in optimising events. AI-powered personalization: With artificial intelligence making each interaction specific to the user, it can customize content based on the preferences, skill level, and engagement patterns of the user. In VR training scenarios, AI can also reactively change difficulty levels in real-time, serving up everyone's individual challenge that fits with their progress. In gaming and entertainment, AI-powered avatars can react to the emotions and actions of users, leading to more responsive and realistic interactions. Moreover, AI boosts accessibility [27] and has people using voice recognition, gestures to predict movement, and many more that are real-time language translation, thus making an immersive experience for many people. AI-powered adaptive UX can also have predictive capabilities, one of the advantages of AI. AI learns from gaze patterns, reaction times, and movement behaviors to optimize user interfaces due to lower cognitive load and better usability. For instance, an AI-powered VR ecosystem can move interface elements to the user's face as the gaze naturally moves around, reducing unnecessary head turns. Similarly, predictive analytics could recommend relevant content or assistive guidance to enhance engagement and efficiency. To leverage the benefit, AI personalization should be complemented by ethical regulations, especially on data privacy and algorithmic bias. To create fair and inclusive experiences, transparent data usage policies and AI models considering various aspects of diverse user behaviours are needed. Along with haptic and spatial audio technology, AI personalization further, making virtual realms more actionable, adaptive, and realistic than ever.

"The Impact of Haptics, Audio and AI in Virtual Environments" (Figure 9). As we see, the baseline case with no enhancement yields a low immersion score. Spatial audio enhances immersion by offering realistic sound depth, further augmented with haptic feedback for a tactile element when interacting with content. Adaptive & Personalized Engagement: AI-driven UX takes user experience a step further with adaptive interactions and personalized engagement. By combining all three enhancements, Philips immersed users in a more immersive experience by incorporating multisensory inputs, demonstrating the critical role played in creating an immersive experience through the design of multisensory and intelligence elements into the technology.

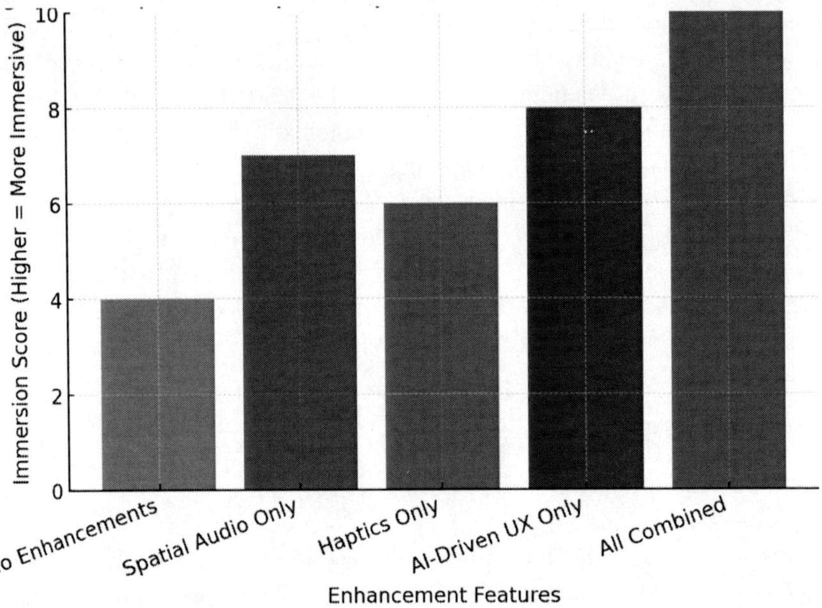

Figure 9. Impact of haptics, spatial audio, and AI on user immersion.

6. Addressing Motion Sickness and User Comfort

Challenges in Immersive Space, such as VR [16], are associated with sickness or negative user experience. Because their vestibular system experiences conflicts between visual sensory input, users often become dizzy, nauseous or fatigued. The key to solving both accessibility issues and reducing the time spent on the user is urgent. In turn, developers who recognize the causes of immersive discomfort and implement the correct design solutions will produce more comfortable virtual experiences.

6.1. Causes and Impact of Motion Sickness in VR

One key reason for the discomfort that occurs after using VR is a conflict between motions that users see while using the tool and signals sent to their bodies about how much they are moving in reality. Always moving through virtual spaces while their bodies remain physically still, their brains can't rectify the discordant sensory signals, creating nausea, vertigo and disorientation. Latency issues create visual lag, which, combined with low frame rates, makes natural motion perception difficult as this disrupts it. The discomfort arises when users experience field-of-view (FoV) dimensions that are too wide or too narrow because it warps their spatial awareness ability. The symptoms of motion sickness worsen when users perform fast movements while using joystick-based navigation since these tools force them through abnormal acceleration patterns. The ability of users to stay focused gets affected by fatigue when they undergo continuous exposure to immersive virtual environments without sufficient rest intervals. Motion sickness management failures will discourage users from adopting immersive technology, resulting in restricted use of these systems in gaming, training, and virtual collaboration scenarios [28].

6.2. Techniques to Minimize Discomfort and Fatigue

Several design techniques can be implemented to minimise discomfort and enhance user experience in VR. Reducing system latency and increasing frame rates to at least 90Hz ensures smoother visuals and prevents motion blur, significantly decreasing nausea. Locomotion methods such as teleportation, where users "jump" between locations rather than moving continuously, help avoid sensory conflicts contributing to sickness. Adjusting the field of view dynamically, a technique known as "tunnelling," can stabilise peripheral vision during movement, making transitions less disorienting. Additionally, minimizing sudden accelerations and rapid rotations allows users to perceive motion more naturally, preventing dizziness. Adding in fixed reference points — such as a virtual cockpit for flight simulators or a stabilized HUD (Heads-Up Display) — helps provide a stable visual anchor that fosters better spatial awareness. They start with some short sessions, and over time, their brain gets used to the new sensory experience, thus overcoming motion sickness.

6.3. Best Practices for User Comfort in Immersive Applications

Beyond motion sickness, comfort in immersive experiences includes ergonomics, personalization, and interface optimization. Comfortable, balanced headsets distribute weight so they don't put strain on the head and neck, making them easier to use for more extended periods. Individual playable settings, like movement speed, rotation type, and suppression of movement blur, enable the user to tailor the experience to fit their preferences. Through supporting fatigue management, periodic reminders to break prevent eyestrain and physical discomfort. Adequate lighting and contrast adjustments ensure visual acuity, reducing mental strain and readability problems. Additionally, proper calibration of the headset and controller and proper tracking eliminate jittery motion, which could cause disorientation without these adjustments. Adopting these best practices, developers are able to create immersive experiences that are user-centric, promoting higher usage and adoption in VR applications [29].

The figure presented in Figure 10 shows different methods that work best to minimize motion sickness for immersive environments. Raising frame rates demonstrates the best success rate because they smooth the visuals to minimize sensory conflicts and eliminate nausea. The method of teleportation enables maximum effectiveness because it minimizes both unnatural acceleration and mismatches between motion perception. Adjusting FoV through vertical tunneling minimizes peripheral vision instability to stop dizziness occurrences. Virtual cockpits with fixed reference points together with HUD elements present stable images which enhances user spatial perception. Users who slowly build their exposure to VR through gradual adaptation allow their brains to develop an ability to handle discomfort that happens during prolonged VR use.

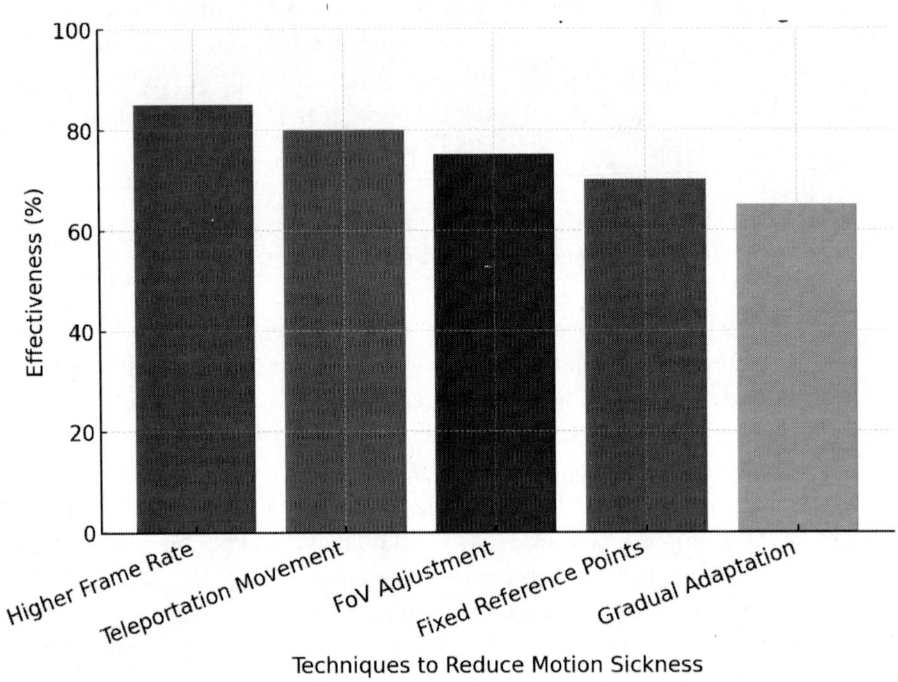

Figure 10. Effectiveness of various techniques in reducing motion sickness.

Conclusion

Immersive technologies described as virtual reality (VR), augmented reality (AR), and mixed reality (MR) have transformed the way users interact with digital worlds. A thorough integration of intuitive interface design, non-intrusive interaction techniques, and user-centric enhancements (haptic feedback, spatial audio, and AI) is necessary to enhance user experience (UX) in these immersive spaces. Through tackling issues such as motion sickness, ergonomics, and real-time adaptability, developers can create immersive applications that are engaging, as well as comfortable and accessible to a wider audience. In this work, research was conducted for UX optimization factors in immersive environments with the spatial organization, intuitive navigation and multimodal interaction methods for example gesture control, voice commands and eye-tracking. Using Haptic Feedback With AI: Coupling haptic feedback with AI-driven personalization to offer individualized touch-tactile experiences leads to enhanced user engagement through naturalistic and dynamic virtual interactions. The optimization process involves three dominant strategies that reduce discomfort through the minimization in latency as well as frame rate optimization and adaptive UX deployment for seamless user engagement. Structural developments in software and hardware technology systems will drive immersive technologies forward with increased interaction capability and realism as well as solution to the issues at the moment. The commitment to creating friendly and accessible systems enables the developer to enhance immersive technology capabilities through new opportunities in gaming, training, healthcare, education, and remote collaboration. The future development of immersive environments calls for user-oriented policies because these standards will create better interfaces and more accessibility for everyone.

References

[1] Fatima, Ishrath, and Kavitha Sooda. "Enhancing Immersive Virtual Reality Product Experiences: Strategies for Graphics Quality, Performance Optimization, and User-Centric Interfaces." In *2023 IEEE Engineering Informatics*, pp. 1-5. IEEE, 2023.

[2] Runsewe, Oluwayemisi, Lucy Anthony Akwawa, Samuel Olaoluwa Folorunsho, and Olajide Soji Osundare. "Optimizing user interface and user experience in financial applications: A review of techniques and technologies." *World Journal of Advanced Research and Reviews* 23, no. 3 (2024): 934-942.

[3] Hutson, James, and Piper Hutson. "Immersive technologies." In *Inclusive smart museums: Engaging neurodiverse audiences and enhancing cultural heritage*, pp. 153-228. Cham: Springer Nature Switzerland, 2024.

[4] Putawa, Rilliandi Arindra, and Dwi Sugianto. "Exploring user experience and immersion levels in virtual reality: A comprehensive analysis of factors and trends." *International Journal Research on Metaverse* 1, no. 1 (2024): 20-39.

[5] Partarakis, Nikolaos, and Xenophon Zabulis. "A review of immersive technologies, knowledge representation, and AI for human-centered digital experiences." *Electronics* 13, no. 2 (2024): 269.

[6] Yang, Qin. "E-commerce User Experience and Interaction Design Under Intelligent Optimization and Virtual Reality Technology." In *International Conference on Frontier Computing*, pp. 180-188. Singapore: Springer Nature Singapore, 2024.

[7] Tao, Li, and Tetyana Honcharenko. "Integrating advanced human-computer interaction and machine learning models for optimizing VR systems in educational and business applications." *Bulletin of the National Technical University «KhPI» A series of "Information and Modeling* (2024): 1-2.

[8] Lysenko, Sergii, and Artem Kachur. "Challenges Towards VR Technology: VR Architecture Optimization." In *2023, the 13th International Conference on Dependable Systems, Services and Technologies (DESSERT)*, pp. 1-9. IEEE, 2023.

[9] Lu, Yao, and Sujit Dey. "JAVRE: a joint asymmetric video rendering and encoding approach to enable optimized cloud mobile 3D virtual immersive user experience." *IEEE Journal on Emerging and Selected Topics in Circuits and Systems* 6, no. 4 (2016): 544-559.

[10] Chandana, B. Hari, Nazeer Shaik, and P. Chitralingappa. "Exploring the frontiers of user experience design: Vr, ar, and the future of interaction." In *2023 International Conference on Computer Science and Emerging Technologies (CSET)*, pp. 1-6. IEEE, 2023.

[11] Wu, Pengjun, Yao Liu, Huijie Chen, Xiaowen Li, and Hui Wang. "VR-empowered interior design: Enhancing efficiency and quality through immersive experiences." *Displays* 86 (2025): 102887.

[12] Smith, John. "Human-computer interaction: Enhancing user experience and productivity." *International Multidisciplinary Journal Of Science, Technology & Business* 1, no. 4 (2022): 1-4.

[13] Yang, Shuran. "*The power of immersive technologies: a sociopsychological analysis of the relationship between immersive environments, storytelling, sentiment, and the impact on user experience*." PhD diss., University_of_Basel, 2023.

[14] Bhaskaran, Vasudev, and Upal Mahbub. "Immersive User Experiences: Trends and Challenges of Using XR Technologies." *Computer Vision* (2024): 260-278.

[15] Zhou, Shuwen, Wenxuan Zheng, Yang Xu, and Yingchia Liu. "Enhancing user experience in VR environments through AI-driven adaptive UI design." *Journal of Artificial Intelligence General Science (JAIGS) ISSN: 3006-4023* 6, no. 1 (2024): 59-82.

[16] Hao, Xiaoyan. "Intelligent User Experience Design in Digital Media Art under Internet of Things Environment." *Informatica* 48, no. 15 (2024).

[17] Sun, Linjing, Boon Giin Lee, Matthew Pike, and Wan-Young Chung. "Optimizing Interface and Interaction Design for Non-immersive VR Firefighting Games: A User Experience Approach." In

International Conference on Intelligent Human Computer Interaction, pp. 344-352. Cham: Springer Nature Switzerland, 2023.

[18] Rossi, Silvia. "*Understanding user interactivity for the next-generation immersive communication: design, optimisation, and behavioural analysis*." PhD diss., UCL (University College London), 2022.

[19] Devi, G. Dharani, Neeraj Kumar, J. Manikandan, and V. Rekha. "Innovative brain tumour detection: Stacked random support vector-based hybrid gazelle coati algorithm." *Biomedical Signal Processing and Control* 101 (2025): 107156.

[20] Manikandan, J., and K. Jayashree. "Enhancing lung nodule classification: a novel CViEBi-CBGWO approach with integrated image preprocessing." *Journal of imaging informatics in medicine* 37, no. 5 (2024): 2108.

[21] Shah, Aishah. "*Evaluating User Interface and User Experience in Immersive Environments–A Comprehensive Evaluation Framework*." PhD diss., School of Electrical Engineering and Computer Sciences (SEECS), NUST, 2023.

[22] Scholz, Joachim, and Andrew N. Smith. "Augmented reality: Designing immersive experiences that maximize consumer engagement." *Business Horizons* 59, no. 2 (2016): 149-161.

[23] Hu, Tao, Qianwen Fu, Lei Chen, and Mengdi Shi. "Optimizing Building Information Modeling System Design Elements for Enhanced User Experience: A Multidimensional Approach." *Traitement du Signal* 41, no. 2 (2024).

[24] Hu, Tao, Qianwen Fu, Lei Chen, and Mengdi Shi. "Optimizing Building Information Modeling System Design Elements for Enhanced User Experience: A Multidimensional Approach." *Traitement du Signal* 41, no. 2 (2024).

[25] Aurelia, Sagaya. "Immersive Technologies: Navigating the Impacts, Challenges, and Opportunities." (2024).

[26] Raza, Ali, Amjad Rehman, Rukhshanda Sehar, Faten S. Alamri, Sarah Alotaibi, Bayan Al Ghofaily, and Tanzila Saba. "Optimized virtual reality design through user immersion level detection with novel feature fusion and explainable artificial intelligence." *PeerJ Computer Science* 10 (2024): e2150.

[27] Luo, Yin, Jun Liu, and Li Zhang. "ARO-CapsNet: A Novel Method for Evaluating User Experience in Immersive VR Furniture Design." *International Journal of Advanced Computer Science & Applications* 15, no. 11 (2024).

[28] Luo, Yin, Jun Liu, and Li Zhang. "ARO-CapsNet: A Novel Method for Evaluating User Experience in Immersive VR Furniture Design." *International Journal of Advanced Computer Science & Applications* 15, no. 11 (2024).

[29] Ma, Jianming, and Xihan Lei. "Exploring the pathways to optimize immersive imaging experiences using AIGC technology." In *2024 7th International Conference on Artificial Intelligence and Big Data (ICAIBD)*, pp. 523-529. IEEE, 2024.

Chapter 4

Barriers to and Prospects for the Adoption of Immersive Technologies

N. Mahendiran[1,*]
A. Sathya[2,†]
Prithi Samuel[3,‡]
Balamurugan Balusamy[4,∥]
and Chithirai Pon Selvan[5,¶]
[1]Sri Ramakrishna College of Arts and Science, Coimbatore, Tamil Nadu, India
[2]Sri Ramachandra Faculty of Engineering and Technology,
Sri Ramachandra Institute of Higher Education and Research, Chennai, India
[3]Department of Computational Intelligence, School of Computing, SRM Institute of Science and Technology, Kattankulathur Campus, Chennai, Tamil Nadu, India
[4]School of Engineering and IT, Manipal Academy of Higher Education, Dubai Campus, Dubai, UAE
[5]School of Science and Engineering, Curtin University Dubai, UAE

Abstract

The use of Virtual Reality (VR), Augmented Reality (AR), and Mixed Reality (MR) is characterised by a complex interaction between opportunities and challenges. Some of the challenges include high cost of implementation, problems with compatibility of devices limited availability of content, and lack of framework. The issues associated with users are privacy invasion, and low levels of digital literacy, which cause limited adoption. Lack of awareness or adequate professional knowledge adds to organizational resistance especially amongst small and medium enterprises. The future for immersive technologies looks bright due to the constant development of 5G connectivity, edge computing, and affordable hardware. They allow for integrated, quality experiences to be made more widely available. Virtual and augmented reality solutions have even more significant opportunities for application in the healthcare sector, education, manufacturing, tele surgeries, Smart classes, and digital twins. To increase inclusiveness, the developed applications must address

[*] Corresponding Author's Email: mahendiran@srcas.ac.in
[†] Corresponding Author's Email: arunachalam.sathya@gmail.com
[‡] Corresponding Author's Email: drprithisamuel@gmail.com
[∥] Corresponding Author's Email: kadavulai@gmail.com
[¶] Corresponding Author's Email: pon.selvan@curtindubai.ac.ae

In: Shaping Tomorrow
Editors: Prithi Samuel, A. Sathya, Balamurugan Balusamy et al.
ISBN: 979-8-90134-076-9

regional and sector requirements. Efforts are needed for development collaborations among policymakers at the government level, technology developers, and the industry leaders to address existing barriers. This chapter explores the opportunities and obstacles of integrating ITs while providing a conceptual roadmap for managing their advantages for various applications to promote their proper and ethical use.

Keywords: immersive technology, connectivity, barrier, prospect, quality, cost, hardware, and software

1. Introduction

Virtual Reality (VR), Augmented Reality (AR) and Mixed Reality (MR), also known as immersive technologies, are one of the biggest and most significant revolutionary steps made in modern computing. These technologies have compelled change in how one engages in content and real space. Due to the interactive nature of these technologies, there is the creation of real and virtual environments, where the user is fully involved. Their uses encompass various sectors such as health, learning institutions, production, media, business, and military sectors in which they are used to improve the functionality, learning, and experience. Immersive technologies come from the notion that one can construct an environment or extend an environment to deliver presence, interaction and even the feeling of the real-time environment. The VR, virtually places a user into fully synthetic environment where they can interact with 3D simulations. AR, on the other hand, augments the physical environment by placing computer-generated graphics on top of the real world, making the real-world experience more interactive with an added value of providing related information.

MR integrates the positive elements of both VR and AR, but allows the interaction between virtual and real objects in real time. All these technologies are based on new developments in such critical areas as hardware, software, and computational paradigms, such as sensors, displays, rendering engines, and machine learning algorithms. The introduction of immersive technologies is not an easy task, as it involves technical, economic, social, and organisational characteristics [1]. This technological research suggests that the availability of powerful and cheap devices, including head-mounted displays, separately or integrated in AR-enabled smartphones, is one of the key reasons why people are adopting VR.

The evolution in processing power, edge computing, and 5G has resolved some significant disadvantages, including latency and connectivity, to allow the delivery of immersive experiences. However, problems such as high initial expenditures, compatibility issues, and data privacy and security issues remain as the main challenges to the implementation of the technology. Various industries have proved that the concepts involving the use of immersive technologies are not mere novelties but create and deliver value to solve practical problems. For example, in the field of medicine it is employed in such areas as surgical simulations, rehabilitation, and mental health treatments that help ensure protected, and controlled spaces for application [2, 3].

In education, using AR-based applications improves on the same by providing interactive content that would otherwise be harder to teach. Both digital twins and MR tools have been used in manufacturing to enhance design sequences and production flows and enable remote productive collaboration. As for the largest category, entertainment has experienced increased engagement in VR gaming and AR live events in providing user-engaging experiences. The successful implementation of these technologies is subject to overcoming several essential issues [4].

Challenges of a technical nature, including the issues of rendering, tracking, and interactivity, are well beyond the capabilities of current desktop computing platforms. Also, a few rules or guidelines for software development specifically for smart devices, along with a compatible and integrated structure between devices and platforms, represent one more challenge. Some of the constraints that characterise this subsector include high equipment cost, software development and maintenance that make it difficult for SMEs and individuals to venture into this subsector.

Another factor is socio-psychological includes visual discomfort caused by HMD, motion sickness, and reluctance to implement new methods. From a management viewpoint, the use of rich technologies depends on awareness, experience, and preparedness to implement the tools into organizational practice [5]. Most businesses, especially those in the old economy, do not possess the technical expertise or support to achieve the full potential of virtual solutions. Moreover, it is critically important to address the issue of data privacy and security in regard to virtual and augmented reality technologies because such systems work with real-time data. Issues of ethical contentiousness, including misapplication, dependency or developing unequal opportunity, likewise require scrutiny.

The barriers that cannot be ignored, but in general, the future of immersive technologies looks very bright [6]. As technology grows, it has made it possible for more and more people to afford these tools, which they can afford to pay for. Immersive technologies have incorporated artificial intelligence (AI) and machine learning to make them more personal and flexible. New opportunities are opened in telemedicine, virtual tourism, and virtual retailing, which revolutionize the industry. In addition, implementing the immersive technologies can be boosted by timely cooperation of all the stakeholders such as government, academic institutions, companies, and technology providers [7].

Governments, therefore, have a critical part to play in funding and shaping the policy environment that, both explicitly and implicitly, supports the development of such ecosystems through regulation and other measures such as standardisation. Social education on how to use these technologies individually, and as organisations and institutions, can assist individuals and institutions in utilising these technologies for the betterment of their organisations and lives. Since the applications are driven by industries, and designed to measure user need, the innovations that come out are realistic, applicable, and can successfully reach out to the users across the population pyramid. In sum, immersive technologies are the shift from traditional approaches to the interaction of man with digital and material reality.

Although there are many barriers to implementing these technologies, it cannot be argued that they offer great possibilities for changing industries and enhancing people's lives [8]. Eliminating all the technical, economic, social and ethical barriers with the help of collective and planned approaches will ensure that the society ensures that the immersive technologies will be an essential part of life. Consequently, this paper aims to understand the challenges and opportunities for immersive technologies to support the development of tactics to unleash their potential [9].

This chapter begins with an Introduction, providing an overview of immersive technologies and their potential across industries. It then explores Barriers and Prospects in the Adoptionof Immersive Technologies, discussing the challenges and opportunities these technologies face.

The chapter delves into the Key Barriers to Adoption, including cost, technical limitations, and user resistance. Following this, it highlights Promising Prospects, focusing on technological advancements and successful applications in various sectors. It then offers Strategies for Overcoming Barriers, proposing solutions for cost reduction, enhanced interoperability, and improved user experience. The chapter proceeds to examine how to Facilitate Widespread Adoption and Future Directions, stressing the importance of ethical considerations and inclusive practices. Finally, it concludes by summarizing the key points and emphasizing the need for collaborative efforts to fully realize the transformative potential of immersive technologies.

2. Barriers and Prospects in the Adoption of Immersive Technologies

Virtual Reality (VR), Augmented Reality (AR), and Mixed Reality (MR) technologies are changing the manner people engage with digital contexts and reality. These technologies have the potential to improve usability, effectiveness, and prospect various industries, like healthcare, education, manufacturing, entertainment, retailing etc. The immersive technologies, although being highly effective, have various limitations for their adoption. On the same note, there are bights insight that indicates that these aforesaid technologies will gradually form a part of human life in the next few years [10].

Challenges of the adoption of immersive technologies are technical, economic, organizational and user related. The use of VR, AR, and MR technologies demands enhanced devices and applications, the creation of which is associated with high costs, implementation, and further support. These financial issues, especially for organisations of small size, pose a problem of access and expansion. Current real-time constraints and computational resources, temporal synchronization, and platform compatibility issues are the main barriers to achieving a well-interconnected, tight integration and good usability. Creating high-quality content and applications makes this problem more difficult and time-consuming for adoption, as it requires professional knowledge and software. Such challenges include a lack of technical know-how, organisational resistance to change, and integration of immersive technologies into the organisational workflow, among others. On the user side, there are psychological factors like virtual reality nausea, unfamiliar interaction devices, and privacy issues which hold back the general adoption. As stated above, these barriers form a complex adoption gap that hinders the diffusion of immersive technologies in industries.

Growth of adopting immersive technologies for learning in equipment, software, and networking, which makes the technology more achievable. New use cases across sectors of healthcare, education, manufacturing, and entertainment reveal the possibilities of its use. For instance, in the health sector, it facilitates enhanced surgical support and patient recovery, while in learning, it promotes engaging education. The advancement in technology, like the availability of affordable standalone VR/AR devices and the adoption of 5G, eliminates constraints like high costs and latency.

The innovations in compatibility across platforms and the usage of open-source tools promote innovation and expand forums for application. Rules and ethical standards that apply to privacy and security issues are gradually strengthening trust that supports integration. Strategic partnerships among technology vendors, industrialists, and governments are a key driver of progress towards creating immersive environments. All these factors combine to place immersive technologies at the centre of the need to transform how users are engaged, innovate the way organisations work and address numerous issues in different fields.

Despite its promise, the adoption of immersive technologies has challenges which include: cost, hardware and software issues, end-user apprehension, and organizational hurdles. However, these obstacles are being mitigated by the continued improvement of technologies and growing appreciation of the possibilities of such technologies [11]. The applications of immersive technologies that address costs, interoperability, and user experience limitations have the capacity to transform many industries and improve people's lives. Cross-sectoral cooperation, methodological harmonization, and extending attention to ethical imperatives will stand at the heart of the emerging adoption of immersive technologies. Based on the current developments of these technologies, there is greater potential for growth and adaption into various applications, which is the road map of these technologies. Different barriers in adoption of immersive technology is given in Table 1.

However, the challenges of applying immersive technologies in organisations can be seen in the absence of skills, knowledge, training, experience, and, therefore, the inability to implement them. Adopting asset-intensive solutions is sometimes disruptive of the current working procedures, which are not well embraced by employees used to the status quo. Furthermore, due to the factors such as the restricted budget, the small and medium enterprises (SMEs) cannot afford resources for training, integrating technologies and further support.

Table 1. Barriers in immersive technology adoption

Barrier	Description	Challenges	Impact on Adoption	Potential Solutions
High Costs of Implementation	Expensive hardware, software, and infrastructure requirements.	High-performance VR/AR devices, computing systems, and specialized expertise.	Limits accessibility, particularly for small businesses and individuals.	Develop affordable devices, leverage cloud-based platforms, and offer financial incentives or subsidies.
Technical Limitations and Lack of Interoperability	Inefficiencies in performance and incompatibility across devices and platforms.	Latency issues, fragmented ecosystems, and insufficient cross-platform standards.	Hampers seamless integration and scalability across industries.	Promote open standards like OpenXR, improve latency with advanced networks (e.g., 5G/6G), and unify APIs.
Content and Application Development Challenges	High complexity and resource requirements for developing immersive applications.	Need for advanced 3D modeling, real-time rendering, and environmental mapping expertise.	Results in a shortage of relevant, engaging content for diverse sectors.	Invest in low-code/no-code platforms, provide training programs, and foster collaboration in content creation.
User Resistance and Psychological Barriers	Physical and psychological discomfort and concerns about privacy/security.	Motion sickness, intimidating interfaces, and apprehension about data collection/misuse.	Reduces user adoption and long-term engagement with immersive technologies.	Design ergonomic devices, develop intuitive interfaces, and establish transparent data protection policies.
Organizational and Institutional Challenges	Hesitancy to invest in immersive technologies due to unclear ROI and cultural resistance.	Lack of expertise, resistance to workflow changes, and limited budgets in small and medium enterprises.	Slows integration into traditional industries and diminishes organizational adoption rates.	Build awareness through ROI demonstrations, provide training programs, and offer grants to support adoption.

3. Promising Prospects

The existing obstacles of immersive technologies show potential for future development due to progress in hardware, software, and networking. Smart standalone VR/AR devices and the advancement in 5G make access easier, and reduced latency improves the real-time expertise [12]. Companies are leveraging VR, AR, and MR technology across industries, ranging from healthcare, education, and manufacturing where, VR is used in management of pain, education and training, AR helps in surgeries and manufacturing, MR for using digital twins for maintenance and productivity. Interoperability has been improved by cooperation between industry participants, evidenced by open-source solutions and clear ethical standards. These advancements make immersive technologies as revolutionary tools with more integration into society. Table 2 presents the promising prospects in the adoption of immersive technologies, emphasizing their expanding applicability across diversified domains.

Table 2. Promising prospects in the adoption of immersive technologies

Aspect	Key Points	Challenges	Proposed Solutions
Technological Advancements	Introduction of affordable standalone VR/AR devices and advancements in 5G and edge computing.	High initial costs for devices, infrastructure dependency, and the need for seamless real-time performance.	Leverage cost-effective hardware, improve network capabilities, and enhance device processing efficiency.
Emerging Applications Across Sectors	Adoption in healthcare, education, and manufacturing with applications like pain management and digital twins.	Sector-specific challenges, limited cross-industry knowledge, and resource constraints.	Develop tailored solutions, encourage cross-sector collaborations, and showcase sector-specific success stories.
Collaboration and Standardization	Efforts towards interoperability through open-source frameworks and ethical data regulations.	Market fragmentation, lack of unified standards, and ethical data handling concerns.	Promote open standards, enforce privacy frameworks, and establish industry consortia for collaboration.
Strategies for Overcoming Barriers	Reducing costs, addressing technical challenges, simplifying content creation, and fostering user adoption.	Resistance due to discomfort, high development costs, and organizational inertia.	Implement training, design ergonomic devices, provide funding, and showcase ROI benefits.

Opening sources and creating different cross-platform development tools can lead to lower costs, spurred further development activity, and contribute to the advancement of immersive technologies. In addition, by developing ethical standards and privacy regulations, anxiety about data safeguard could be resolved and consequently, acceptance will be increased.

4. Strategies for Overcoming Barriers

By opening sources and coming up with various cross-platform development tools, costs might be reduced, research gets further development activity and the improvement of immersive techniques. Moreover, by creating the ethical requirement in addition to the regulating rules of privacy, the worry regarding the safety of data could be averted and therefore, acceptance will be achieved.

4.1. Reducing Implementation Costs

High implementation costs continue to be the key factor that creates barriers the adoption of immersive technologies. To this end, all stakeholders should aim to avail themselves of cheaper hardware and software technologies [13]. One of the main strands of progress in the direction of making VR and AR more accessible is the creation of dedicated VR/AR headsets which do not require a high-performance computer as a base. These devices reduce the perceived risk of consumers and organizations because it does not require expensive hardware setups. Furthermore, they also found that implementing cloud-based, and even more immersive technologies solutions can lower costs. With cloud computing, data processing and storage can be done in real-time, and this eliminates the need to invest in expensive infrastructure to host the applications on the company's premises. Incumbent real-time software vendors such as NVIDIA and Microsoft market. Another good approach is cooperation between software, and final consumers. As a result of such collaborations, the efforts, as well as the costs of development, can be combined, thus giving birth to more effective and industry-specific innovations.

4.2. Addressing Technical Challenges

Some of these are technological constraints that include: high latency, inadequate computational capacity, and lack of compatibility. To overcome these challenges, stakeholders need to focus on the science that needs to be done in these arena. Of these, the more critical are hardware and software where the goal is to achieve the optimization. Technological enhancements such as GPUs, sensors, and display have a very high potential to enhance the performance of immersive systems. 5G and edge computing are also crucial primarily crucial in minimizing the latency as far as real-time interactions are concerned, especially primarily for applications that require high bandwidth data transfer. Another crucial area is the one of interoperability. Standardization across the industry and shared architectural solutions for VR/AR platforms can be developed as open source, to remove barriers to integrating various platforms in different devices and ecosystems. Industry players such as the Khronos Group, through projects like OpenXR, are, however, trying to set up these standards, hence minimising market fragmentation.

4.3. Simplifying Content Development

It is common to find that creation of content for Immersive technologies is capital intensive and calls for a skilled profession, in fields including 3D modeling, real time rendering and Machine learning. This significant, therefore, remains a major barrier which can only be solved by coming up with better and easier-to-use tools and platforms. To name a few, Unity's Visual Scripting and Unreal Engine's Blueprint are the low and no-code building tools that can enable non-technical creators to build engaging content. This simplified the content development process and allows organizations to develop sophisticated applications swiftly. Moreover, the funds provided for training or cooperation with educational establishments may create a learned population equipped to create an immersive experience. Certificates in the fields of industry and practical sessions can enable the specialists to design and implement applications that would be engaging in line with the requirements of different industries.

4.4. Enhancing User Experience and Addressing Resistance

Some of the reasons which explain why users are reluctant to embrace immersive technologies include: discomfort, unfamiliarity, and privacy issues. Solving these problems can only be achieved by addressing the following directions usability and trust. There is a possibility of increasing the comfort of wear and using VR/AR solutions through changes in the design and construction of the devices. New materials for headsets, better tracking devices, and self-adjusting displays can increase comfort and practicality by a great deal. To reduce psychological resistance, the immersive technologies must incorporate, straightforward and easy-to-use interfaces or interfaces that are not complicated. Nontechnology learners can be eased in by simple gesture–based controls, voice controls, and contextual cues. Data security and privacy issues can also be soothed by observing adequate data protection measures. There is a need to have clear and legal working policies on collecting and processing data, primarily for the organizations that work under the GDPR. Making more secure systems that protect user information will go a long way in developing trust and more usage.

4.5. Overcoming Organizational and Institutional Barriers

Immersive technologies in organizations need a culture change and usually need to be embedded in the organisational structures. The leaders also need to explain why some of these technologies are important and that they might even bring some ROI. To this end, it is advisable to propose a phased approach to the implementation of immersive technologies in organizations' processes. The nature of pilot projects and proof-of-concept programmes enables businesses to experiment with applications in controlled settings, evaluate their benefits and optimal strategy before widespread implementation. Other factors include training and upskilling employees, which are also very important factors in the adoption process. To increase the adoption level of immersive tools and applications, organisations should offer practical sessions and materials to educate staff. This process can be further supported by technology providers and consultants who will be able to provide specific solutions and continuous technical help [14].

4.6. Building Collaborative Ecosystems

The present study suggests that technology vendors, academic institutions and policymakers should work together to address the challenges and promote the advancement of immersive technologies. Collaborative ecosystems need to be developed to encourage and support the sharing of knowledge, the coordination of resources and the identification of everyday issues. To increase the gearing up of immersive technologies, PPPs can assist with funding, physical backbone, and research. Special programs and grants may also help in persuading SMEs, existing and emerging, to engage in immersive solutions. In addition, industry associations and other consortia have a critical role to play in the promotion of best practice, generation of standards and the facilitation of collaboration. Some of the organizations that exist to foster growth for the technology include the Augmented Reality for Enterprise Alliance (AREA) and the VR/AR Association.

4.7. Encouraging Cross-Industry Applications

Immersive technologies are not limited to a specific sector; hence, they can be adopted in almost any field, starting from healthcare and education and ending with manufacturing and retail. Some of the best strategies used by analysts are showcasing how their use cases were successful and portraying how others could be similarly effective in the future. For example, presenting the VR example of an application for medical training, the AR example of a shop for the individual shopping experience, and an MR example of tools for using technology in the manufacturing industry for predictive maintenance can all help demonstrate these tools' possibilities. It is crucial to learn from other industry sectors and different case examples to get to know how other organisations managed to apply immersive solutions to their needs. The primary goal of addressing the barriers to the adoption of immersive technologies is that they must be solved integrally, which more often involves the solution of financial, technical, user, and organisational issues. The goal of cost reduction, technical advancement, minimalism in content, user-oriented solutions, and people's combined efforts will help stakeholders get the most out of immersive technologies [15]. Combined with these strategies and the constant progress of advancements and supportive ecosystems, will open up possibilities for further widespread adoption of the said technologies and bring about a change in the industries and immersive technologies as how people interact with digital space.

5. Facilitating Widespread Adoption and Future Directions

Enabling the mass adoption of immersive technologies including VR, AR and MR requires tackling current issues and creating a framework for growth that's sustainable and scalable. That is whywith the further development of these technologies, there is a prospect of redefining the sectors through incorporation into user relations, business processes, and knowledge acquisition. The ideas of key steps and future directions can facilitate this process successfully [16]. Arguably one of the most significant challenges of adopting immersive technologies is making such technologies available to a broader population. Manufacturers and developers must seek to produce affordable commoditised hardware and software with good performance.

Standalone VR headsets, which eliminate the need for expensive external systems, exemplify this approach [17]. The representational heuristic also shows that the costs of the cloud-based platforms for immersive experiences can be lower than those of traditional solutions and thus more accessible. Small companies and educational institutions can afford these solutions that would help make these technologies more widely adopted. To this extent, there is a need for interaction across the different platforms and devices so that immersive technologies will be widely used. It is imperative that standard patterns applicable to the industry be defined, as well as that open-sourced frameworks be used. Some efforts like

OpenXR are made to cover up the compatibility problems and create single development environments for applications to run on different hardware and operating systems. This leads to minimization of market segmentation and offers developers means of creating flexible approaches.

Immersive technologies are only effective if users commit their trust in the technology. Issues of data privacy, security, and ethical usage must be previewed to avoid being met with worst-case scenarios. Organisations require formulating strong measures that will ensure the protection of data, policies that are clear and compliance measures with the law. The regulation of rights to use data gathered in immersive environments, or obtaining the necessary consent from the users, and attempts to introduce secure identity verification systems will promote trust and usage. The main reason is going to be the integration of immersive technologies into various sectors as the primary factor in boosting utilization.

Some industries like healthcare, education, manufacturing, and retail are already finding application of immersive solution for training, visualization and optimization of existing processes. When promoted with success stories and demonstrated values, such patterns can encourage applications in other areas. For instance, AR in retail, VR, and especially MR in medical training and manufacturing predictive maintenance show the versatility of these technologies. Therefore, there is a need to cooperate among key stakeholders such as technology suppliers, industries, policy makers, and academic institutions. For instance, PPPs can give monetary sources, structure and research aid to SMEs. Subsidies and grants offered by the government to companies for the implementation of immersion technology can add more fuel to the fire, which means still faster growth and integration. The potential of immersive technologies is to be found in constant development and synergy of compatible developments like AI, IoT, and blockchain.

Coordinated multimedia AI interactions for immersion, intelligent spaces, and predictive interactions can improve naturally immersive environments. The interaction of IoT with physical and digital environments ensures that data is relayed in real-time to physical worlds, making applications more interactive in real environments. Blockchain technology can solve problems of security of transaction and data, and confidentiality of data, thus creating trust in virtual markets. As 6G networks and edge computing advance, the efficiency of applications involving immersion will be even improved in terms of latency. They shall advance the opportunities for large-scale application of Virtual Reality in various fields such as Smart Cities, Virtual Tourism and Remote working.

To ensure that immersive technologies are more fully adopted by enterprise, a complex and holistic program must be designed with accessibility, interoperability, training, trust, and cross domain application at its core. If these aspects are attended, and based on new developments, immersive technologies can be a part of human life as a permanent component of virtual world influencing industries and changing the way people interact. Key trends of innovation, collaboration, and scalability will define the future of immersive experiences to maximize its ability for global impact [18].

Conclusion

The use of virtual reality (VR), augmented reality (AR), mixed reality (MR) is a revolutionary shift to how people and organizations engage with digital spaces. Although some limitations including high costs of implementation, technology constraints and development of contents persist, the future of these technologies cannot be doubted. With the steady progress in the field of hardware, software, and connections along with attempts to solve the problems of compatibility and standard usage, these issues are being solved gradually and the scope for a more general use is being opened. Promoting cost effectiveness, promoting skills development, and guaranteeing the users' confidence due to the high level of privacy and security are essential in developing strategies for increasing the adoption rate. Moreover, it requires joint efforts of companies, governments, and universities to build an environment that would foster innovation and company's scalability. Broadly adopting immersive technologies across almost every field such as health, learning, production, and sales show that they can bring realistic solutions. In the future, such related developments as artificial intelligence, IoT, and blockchain will only complement each other and contribute to the further development and increased popularity of immersive technologies. In that context, the goals addressing the accessibility, innovation, and the responsible use of immersive technologies may turn these technologies into indispensable tools in people's daily lives, key drivers of change in industries and new paradigms of interaction with digital environments.

References

[1] Riches, S., Taylor, L., Jeyarajaguru, P., Veling, W., & Valmaggia, L. (2024). Virtual reality and immersive technologies to promote workplace wellbeing: a systematic review. *Journal of Mental Health*, *33*(2), 253-273.

[2] Baxter, G., & Hainey, T. (2024). Using immersive technologies to enhance the student learning experience. *Interactive Technology and Smart Education*, *21*(3), 403-425.

[3] Winkler, N. (2024). Breaking Barriers: The Path to Immersive Technologies Adoption in Small and Medium-sized Enterprises.

[4] Tharini, V. J., & Vijayarani, S. (2020). IoT in healthcare: Ecosystem, pillars, design challenges, applications, vulnerabilities, privacy, and security concerns. In *Incorporating the Internet of Things in healthcare applications and wearable devices* (pp. 1-22). IGI Global.

[5] Winkler, N. (2024). *Breaking Barriers: The Path to Immersive Technologies Adoption in Small and Medium-sized Enterprises.*

[6] Subaveerapandiyan, A., Baiju, A., Ahmad, N., Verma, M. K., & Sinha, P. (2024). Exploring metaverse literacy: immersive technologies in library environments. *Journal of Web Librarianship*, *18*(2), 39-63.

[7] Creed, C., Al-Kalbani, M., Theil, A., Sarcar, S., & Williams, I. (2024). Inclusive AR/VR: accessibility barriers for immersive technologies. *Universal Access in the Information Society*, *23*(1), 59-73.

[8] Sathya, A., & Aruna, A. (2024). Rehabilitation for Parkinson's Disease Using Virtual Reality (VR): Impact and Observational Analysis. In *Navigating the Augmented and Virtual Frontiers in Engineering* (pp. 1-20). IGI Global.

[9] Colamatteo, A., Sansone, M., Pagnanelli, M. A., & Bruni, R. (2024). The role of immersive technologies in cultural contexts: future challenges from the literature. *Italian Journal of Marketing*, *2024*(1), 113-142.

[10] Hung, L., Zhao, Y., Lam, M., Ren, H., & Wong, K. L. Y. (2024). Protocol: Facilitators, barriers and impacts to implementing dementia care training for staff in long-term care settings by using fully immersive virtual reality: a scoping review protocol. *BMJ Open*, *14*(5).

[11] Gutierrez-Bucheli, L., Goh, J. T., Rashidi, A., Maxwell, D., Digby, R., Fang, Y., ... & Arashpour, M. (2024). Adopting immersive technologies in construction training: determining educational decision-making criteria through a Delphi technique. *Smart and Sustainable Built Environment.*

[12] Brückner, K., Ehrlinspiel, M., Huneke, S., & Prien, M. H. (2024). *Breaking Barriers: Exploring the Power of Immersive Media as a Strategic Communication Tool in NGOs.*

[13] Puthenpura, V., Hunter, M., & Marks, A. (2024). "*Techquity*" in pediatric, adolescent and young adult oncology: addressing inequities through artificial intelligence and immersive technologies.
[14] Gupta, R., Rathore, B., Biswas, B., Jaiswal, M., & Singh, R. K. (2024). Are we ready for metaverse adoption in the service industry? Theoretically exploring the barriers to successful adoption. *Journal of Retailing and Consumer Services*, *79*, 103882.
[15] Chang, H. Research on Risk Prevention of Digital Technology in Metaverse Education.
[16] Aruna, A., & Sathya, A. (2025). Knowledge and Service Exchange Using Blockchain. In *Blockchain Technology Applications in Knowledge Management* (pp. 335-366). IGI Global Scientific Publishing.
[17] Riches, S., Taylor, L., Jeyarajaguru, P., Veling, W., & Valmaggia, L. (2024). Virtual reality and immersive technologies to promote workplace wellbeing: a systematic review. *Journal of Mental Health*, *33*(2), 253-273.
[18] Partarakis, N., & Zabulis, X. (2024). A review of immersive technologies, knowledge representation, and AI for human-centered digital experiences. *Electronics*, *13*(2), 269.

About the Author

Dr. N. Mahendiran has 15 years of teaching experience. He is currently working as an Assistant Professor in Computer Science at Sri Ramakrishna College of Arts & Science, Coimbatore. His area of specialization is Networking. He has published more than 15 research works at the national and international levels, including journals and books. He is currently guiding 2 research scholars in the field of Data Mining. He is a life member of the International Association of Engineers (IAENG) and the Indian Society for Technical Education (ISTE).

Chapter 5

Educational and Training Innovations Through Immersive Technologies

Mishmala Sushith*
P. Nirmala Priyadharshini†
Afreen Hussain‡
and G. Bharathy Gnanam‖
Department of Information Technology, Adithya Institute of Technology, Kurumbapalayam, SS Kulam, Coimbatore, India

Abstract

The rapid growth of immersive technologies, including Virtual Reality (VR), Augmented Reality (AR), and Mixed Reality (MR), has transformed teaching and learning practices dramatically. AR and VR create rich, interactive, and immersive environments that allow learners to gain, practice, and retain knowledge and skills at higher rates. Immersive learning fosters experiential learning that mimics real-world scenarios to lessen the mental burden while creating a link between theory and practice. Immersive technologies provide scalable, tailored learning opportunities that accommodate varying learning styles in school and university education. Augmented-realityapps can connect the classrooms to the rest of the world, allowing learners to see digital information overlaid on actual things, and VR-based simulation can help learners physically interact with historical events, scientific phenomena, and complex problem-solving scenarios without the risks associated with the real world. In professional training, abusive simulations are also successfully utilized in fields like wellbeing care, aviation and engineering to transfer experiential learning without actual-world dangers — rising competence and security. Moreover, with the help of AI-powered analytics on immersive learning platforms, driving real-time assessment and feedback, teaching methods are optimised to the fullest. Nonetheless, some issues must be solved to fully benefit from immersive learning, such as high implementation costs, accessibility, and the need for specialized content creation. The world of immersive technologies in teaching and learning has undergone a tremendous transformation. This

* Corresponding Author's Email: mishmala@gmail.com
† Corresponding Author's Email: nimipeter88@gmail.com
‡ Corresponding Author's Email: afreenzak@gmail.com
ǁ Corresponding Author's Email: bharathy_gnanam@adithyatech.com

In: Shaping Tomorrow
Editors: Prithi Samuel, A. Sathya, Balamurugan Balusamy et al.
ISBN: 979-8-90134-076-9

chapter examines existing innovations, real-world applications, and pedagogical benefits, as well as future research agendas.

Keywords: virtual reality (VR), augmented reality (AR), mixed reality (MR), AI-driven analytics, immersive technologies, pedagogical benefits, immersive learning

1. Introduction to Immersive Learning Technologies

Electronic learning platforms have transformed learning experiences by integrating advanced digital tools to develop dynamic and interactive learning platforms. The technologies employ simulation techniques through artificial intelligence systems and use mixed-reality technology to connect theoretical learning with practical applications. The experiential learning method employs experiential learning as opposed to the traditional teaching techniques that use passive reception of information. The presence of advanced technology, powerful devices, AI advancements, and the enhancement in internet connectivity enables adaptive learning on an individualized level. Computer-based immersive learning technologies make students more active and aid in the development of their skills through experiential learning in a controlled environment [1].

1.1. Definition and Evolution of Immersive Learning

The methodology improves understanding by stimulating various sensory functions, boosting active learning, and strengthening memory storage. Early flight simulator technology for pilot training isa historical origin of immersive learning practices since it offered a safe learning space for skill development [2]. Modern technological advancements have made virtual and augmented reality accessible through every learning domain and institution. This training method currently serves both medical education and engineering simulations, as well as military practice and corporate workforce development, proving its capacity to function effectively in various educational spaces.

1.2. Three Fundamental Technologies: VR, AR, and MR, and Their Educational Value

Immersive learning takes its direction from three essential technologies, which include Virtual Reality (VR), Augmented Reality (AR) and Mixed Reality (MR). Users enter fully digital domains through virtual reality to discover simulated environments that let them gain practical learning skills in risk-free environments. The benefit of this approach is best observed in medical surgery training because trainees get essential practice experience through simulated procedures without endangering actual patients. AR brings digital content on top of physical objects, improving users' interactions by providing supplemental information [3]. The usefulness of these technologies appears through conventional educational media that utilise AR and interactive museum displays accompanied by instant translation systems. User interaction becomes significantly stronger when MR enables people to work with digital materials inside actual physical spaces. Educational establishments, along with industries, can implement these technologies to supply interactive training programs which strengthen critical thinking while improving problem-solving abilities [4].

1.3. Impact of Immersive Learning on Student Engagement and Knowledge Retention

Immersive learning benefits greatly through increased student involvement, leading students to retain learned material better. Academic learning techniques based on passive knowledge absorption often reduce student interest and weaken information memorization rates. The educational experience gets transformed via immersive learning because it lets students actively interact with simulated environments, enhancing their ability to remember information [5]. According to research, student retention rises better through experiential VR-based simulations than traditional text-based and lecture instructions. Through its interactive design, immersive learning encourages learners to become more curious, thus motivating them to study challenging subjects with interest. These technological solutions enable personalisation by supplying live feedback and tailored educational streams that accommodate unique learning strategies. The developing nature of these technologies will transform education and training methods into more inclusive and efficient learning atmospheres [6].

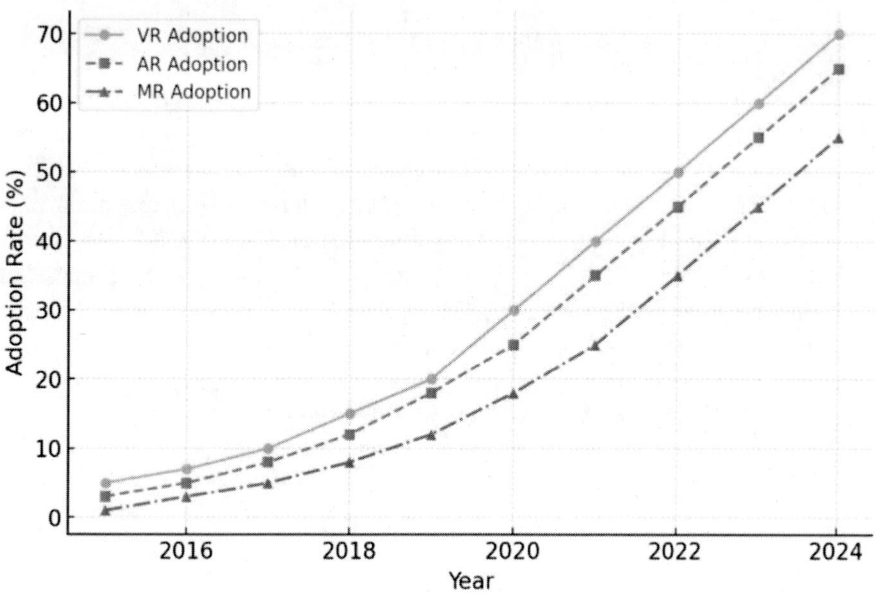

Figure 1. Growth of immersive learning technologies over time.

The line graph in Figure 1 shows the trend in the use of immersive learning technologies (VR, AR, and MR) from 2015 to 2025. The trend shows a steady increase in the use of technology in learning institutions. Virtual Reality (VR) has the most growth, with a projected usage of 70% by the year 2025. Augmented Reality (AR) closely follows, with its advantage in that it easily integrates with the mobile learning platforms. Mixed Reality (MR), though with the lowest usage, shows a steady growth as interactive and hybrid learning experiences are enhanced. The trend shows the increasing utilisation of immersive technologies to enhance engagement, improve knowledge retention, and the acquisition of practical skills in learning and training.

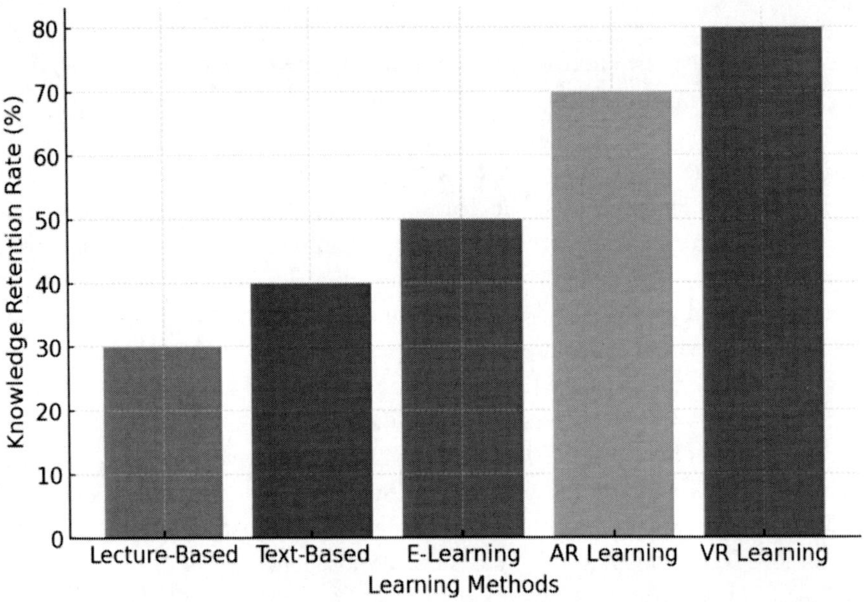

Figure 2. Comparison of Knowledge Retention Rates Across Learning Methods.

Figure 2 compares knowledge retention rates across five different learning methods: lecture-based learning, text-based learning, e-learning, augmented reality (AR) learning, and virtual reality (VR) learning. The bar chart highlights that traditional methods, such as lecture-based learning (30%) and text-based learning (40%), have lower retention rates than technology-enhanced learning approaches. E-learning demonstrates a moderate improvement at 50%, while immersive methods—AR (70%) and VR (80%)—show the highest retention rates. These findings align with cognitive learning theories, which emphasise the benefits of experiential and interactive learning in reinforcing memory retention (Williams & Lee, 2024). The data suggests immersive learning technologies significantly enhance information retention by engaging multiple sensory modalities and fostering active participation.

2. Theoretical Foundations of Immersive Learning

Immersive learning is rooted in various theories emphasising experiential and interactive learning. The success of immersive technologies in learning depends on the principles that enhance engagement, retention, and cognitive processing. By providing interactive and real-world environments, immersive learning facilitates deeper understanding through active engagement rather than passive information consumption [7]. This section covers the dominant learning theories that form the backbone for immersive learning, the information processing factors involved in virtual environments, and the role of presence and interactivity towards better learning outcomes.

2.1. Learning Theories Supporting Immersive Education (Constructivism, Experiential Learning)

Educational theories show close connections with immersive learning because they advocate interactive learning techniques that depend on student experiences. Immersive technologies apply fundamental approaches which enhance student involvement while keeping stored information active during retention time and enhance learning methods. Various educational principles recommend immersive learning due to its virtual environments, which enable students to engage actively instead of just listening to lectures [7]. The following part analyses the dominant learning ideas backing immersive teaching approaches alongside the cognitive processing capabilities of virtual learning platforms, together with fundamental approaches toward developing better educational outcomes through presence and interactive activities.

The teaching method of experiential learning, according to David Kolb, supports immersive education approaches since it encourages educational experiences with direct sensory components. Kolb's learning cycle, which includes concrete experience and reflective observation as well as abstract conceptualisation and active experimentation, matches the format found in numerous immersive learning scenarios. Virtual reality systems allow students to conduct purposeful, realistic training simulations before considering their experiences and using acquired knowledge in actual scenarios. The experiential teaching method enables students to hold information longer than standard lecture-based education techniques [8].

2.2. Cognitive Load and Information Processing in Immersive Environments

The success of immersive learning measures the way students process information digitally and their ability to recall it. Cognitive Load Theory (CLT), created by John Sweller, defines the mental system that manages new information storage in the brain. CLT establishes the distinction between cognitive load as three categories that include the complexity of the information as intrinsic load and irrelevant distractions as extraneous load and planned learning activity as germane load. Design decisions with immersive technologies determine whether or not they raise or reduce the level of cognitive load when implemented [9].

Well-designed immersion technology optimises learning through intuitive and interactive pedagogy that accommodates the students' cognitive capabilities. Cognitive load on the students' side relies on the quality of the learning environment, as excessive stimulus or disconcerting navigational methods, irrelevant information, overwhelms the learners and lowers their learning potential. The guided approach with adaptive levels of complexity and timely performance feedback enables the learners to focus on important information without feeling cognitively overloaded.

2.3. Role of Presence and Interactivity in Effective Learning

Virtual environments rely on presence to enable learners to experience a psychological sensation of physical presence in that simulated environment. A deep sense of presence between learners and virtual learning materials leads to better motivation, emotional involvement, and improved student engagement. A strong immersive experience results from real-time simulations, high-definition visuals, sounds, and interactive inputs that react to user movements. According to research, learners who feel and firmly immersed in virtual environments have better information retention and execute their learned knowledge effectively in actual situations [10]. Users become more effective learners when they experience interactive learning because it shifts them from content consumption to active involvement. The immersive educational landscapes let users handle objects while they navigate through models to gain immediate feedback, which supports experiential learning since traditional school approaches do not provide this experience. Through interactive techniques that include role-playing simulations and gamified mechanics, self-paced, and, learning becomes more engaging and self-paced as well as individualised for each student. The effectiveness of digital learning platforms will improve through the advancements of immersive technologies, which incorporate adaptive interactivity functions and AI-driven personalisation systems [11].

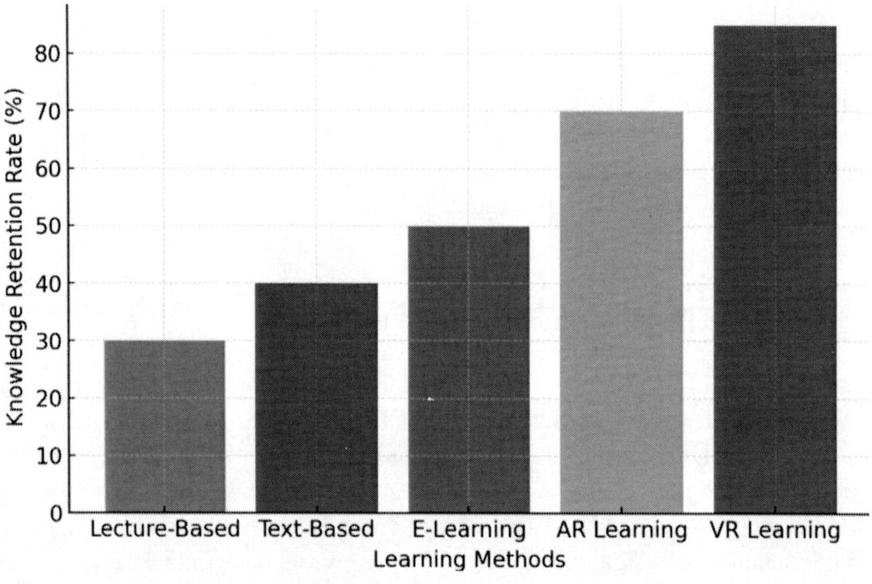

Figure 3. Effect of immersive learning on knowledge retention.

Figure 3 presents a bar chart comparing knowledge retention rates across various learning methods, including traditional and immersive approaches. The data suggests that lecture-based learning has the lowest retention rate (30%), followed by text-based learning (40%). E-learning shows a moderate improvement (50%), while immersive methods such as Augmented Reality (AR) learning (70%) and Virtual Reality (VR) learning (85%) demonstrate significantly higher retention rates. These findings are corroborated by learning theories that emphasise the importance of active engagement in information retention. Passive reception of information, typical in traditional learning, tends to result in lower retention due to its lower interactivity and engagement. In contrast, immersive learning leverages the theories of experiential learning where the learner actively participates in simulated situations, increasing the comprehension of the concepts and retention in long-term memory. The sharp increase in AR and VR-based learning retention rates indicates their success in delivering substantial learning experiences. The provision of simulations in real-world settings, experiential interaction, and timely feedback maximises the cognitive process and reduces forgetting. Therefore, immersive learning technologies are increasingly essential in modern educational and training programs.

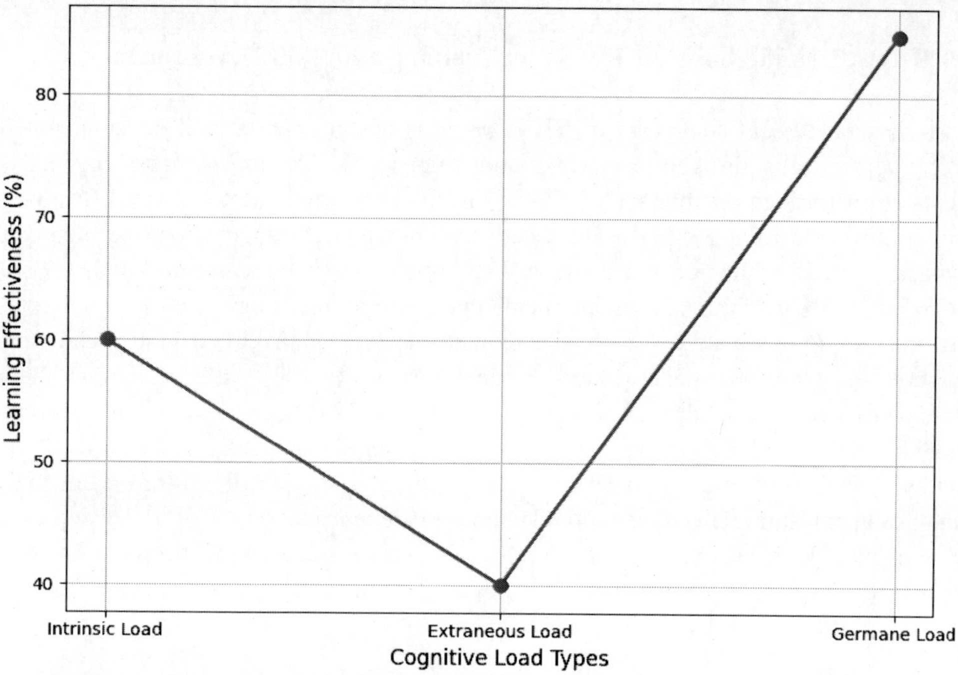

Figure 4. Effectiveness of immersive learning based on cognitive load types.

The effectiveness levels of immersive learning and their association with various cognitive load types appear in Figure 4. The three cognitive load categories, known as Intrinsic Load and Extraneous Load, together with Germane Load, determine learning outcomes in immersive environments. Material complexity as intrinsic load negatively impacts training performance, making the subject matter harder to understand. Extraneous Load causes noise that diverts learners into irrelevant subjects thus harming their focus abilities and reducing learning effectiveness. The learning success depends heavily on the cognitive effort that students utilise to build meaningful connections with instructional content, as represented by Germane Load. Immersive learning reaches its peak effectiveness when learners have minimal distractions and intrinsic factors, so their focus remains on the germane learning aspects. Learners experience enhanced knowledge retention with better engagement because the balanced system focuses them on essential educational material.

3. Virtual Reality (VR) in Education and Training

Virtual Reality has emerged as a powerful force in learning and training, offering interactive, experiential, and immersive learning opportunities. Compared with traditional education, VR enables students to engage with virtual environments that closely resemble real-world situations, facilitating the acquisition of practical skills and knowledge retention. In offering a secure environment for experimentation and exploration, VR is revolutionising the disciplines of STEM learning, medical training, and engineering. While VR has several strengths, problems related to the cost, accessibility, and technical limitations must also be overcome [12].

3.1. VR-Based Simulations for Hands-on Training and Skill Development

The primary significant advantage of VR learning is that it enables skill development with practical applications through real-world simulations. VR has the learning advantage as students learn through an interactive simulation mode as opposed to textbook learning or passive lecturing learning methods. Simulated field training in areas of aerospace engineering, manufacturing, and healthcare makes use of VR technology to aid students in skill development through practising in simulated environments that are risk-free. Flight simulator training for pilots and surgery simulation for physicians take place through virtual reality and surgery simulation for physicians takes place through Virtual Reality platforms before medical professionals work on actual planes or real patients [13]. VR-based simulations also ensure individualised learning through the provision of adjusting to the progress and skill set of the individual. Interactive feedback mechanisms ensure the learner identifies mistakes and masters techniques in real-time. This experiential learning model enhances the skill to solve problems as well as confidence, leading to better real-world performances. As more and more sectors adopt VR for training, the efficiency in skill building through VR will further increase.

3.2. Use of VR in STEM, Medical Training, and Engineering Education

The significance of virtual reality in STEM education grows rapidly since it creates challenging topics easier to understand while being more interactive. The present-day physics and chemistry education allows students to use 3D virtual laboratories to execute online experiments which offer both chemical safety alongside variable modifications. Through this method students gain understanding of concepts in a brand-new interactive environment which helps them develop abstract comprehension. Virtual Reality modifies educational content specifically designed for medical students and medical training programs. Through VR simulations, medical students have the opportunity to develop surgical competence, diagnose patients, and master emergency procedures. Students can obtain practical experience through virtual environments because these platforms offer protective and risk-free spaces to practice skills that they will need to use with real patients. Research evidence demonstrates that medical trainee performance improves through VR-based education since it enhances memory retention while improving their accuracy in procedures and building their self-assurance [14]. The field of engineering integrates VR-based learning environments successfully because of their significant advantages. The development of prototypes along with engineering idea testing and equipment simulation operate successfully in virtual simulations prior to building real-world models. By adding VR technology to curriculum structures educational institutions can offer students powerful hands-on learning through interactive sessions that let them test systems alongside materials and structures.

3.3. Challenges and Limitations of VR in Learning Environments

Advantages notwithstanding, there are some challenges for VR in education that will need to be overcome in order to get the most out of it. High cost of VR hardware and software is one of the main worries. Widespread adoption is hampered by many institutions' inability to afford all the VR headsets, high-performance computers and content development that goes with it.'' The next focus area is accessibility and usability. VR does offer an engaging learning experience, but it might not be the right fit for every student. Virtual reality (VR) headsets offer immersive learning experiences, but they can cause motion sickness or discomfort in some users if used for long durations. Moreover, lag, resolution issues, software compatibility, and other types of technical difficulties during e-learning can obstruct teaching and learning [15]. More importantly, VR content needs careful design and development to offer significant value as a learning environment. Non-immersive and non-interactive VR simulation with poor educational relevance. Teachers are not trained to monastic way to use VR in their teaching methods so that students get the most out of them as possible. Addressing these limitations will require ongoing advancements in VR technology, cost reduction strategies, and better integration into curricula. As VR continues to evolve, it holds the potential to become a standard tool for education and training, offering learners new ways to explore, practice, and master complex subjects [16].

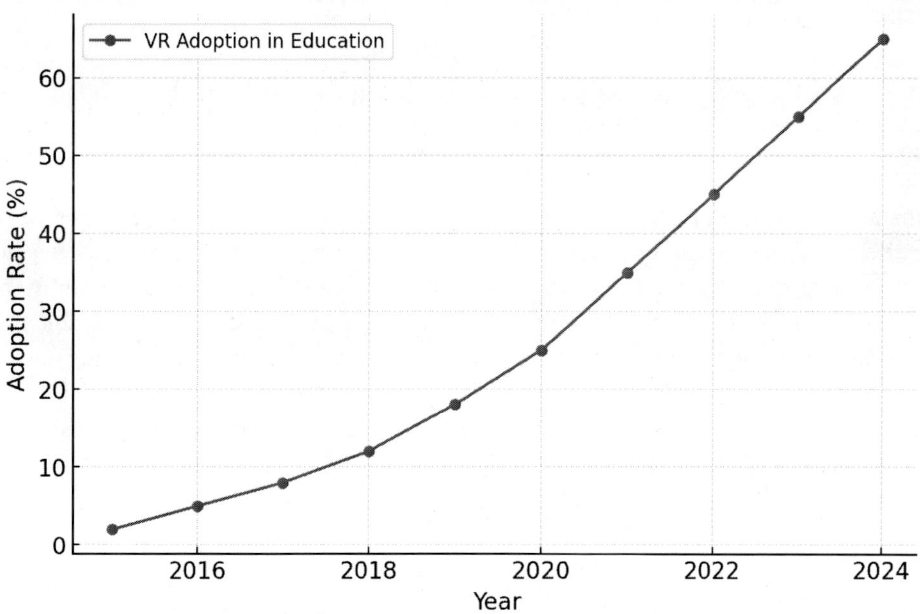

Figure 5. Growth of VR adoption of education over time.

The adoption rates of Virtual Reality (VR) in education show steady growth from 2015 to 2025 as Figure 5 indicates. Public institutions started implementing virtual reality technology at a low rate of 2% in 2015 while it reached a significant adoption level of 65% by 2025. The expanding use derives from two main factors: rising interest in realistic learning methods as well as continual progress in both VR platforms and software capabilities. The post-2020 surge in VR adoption matches the time where technological progress matched with simpler access to

VR equipment. Many educational institutions now quickly progress in incorporating VR-based simulations because industry leaders like STEM education with medical training and engineering. Based on this trend VR will keep transforming education through its interactive engagement in providing effective learning experiences.

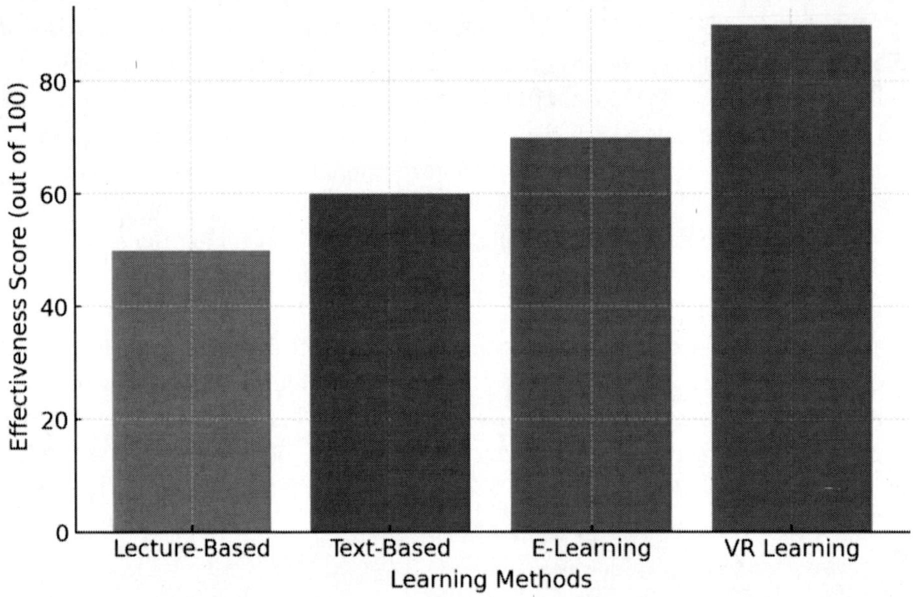

Figure 6. Comparison of learning effectiveness in VR over traditional methods.

The study in Figure 6 examines educational method effectiveness by prioritizing the performance of Virtual Reality (VR) learning. Educators who rely on lectures achieve 50 points on the effectiveness scale, and text-based learning earns 60 points, while e-learning reaches 70 points according to the measurement scale of 100. Research shows that Virtual Reality-based learning demonstrates the greatest effectiveness since it garners a score of 90. The study backs up research which demonstrates how immersive environments enhance learning outcomes because they enable active participation and real-world simulation and experiential learning. The reported high effectiveness of VR learning demonstrates that educational inclusion of VR technology enables more successful skill education together with better conceptual understanding than typical educational approaches.

4. Augmented Reality (AR) and Its Impact on Learning

Augmented Reality (AR) is transforming the learning space by overlaying digital information on the real world, creating interactive and immersive learning opportunities. Unlike Virtual Reality (VR), which fully immerses the user in a virtual environment, AR overlays virtual information on real-world settings, enhancing engagement and comprehension. The application of AR in the educational field transcends disciplines, from classroom teaching to vocational training and professional development. Technical limitations and accessibility are the primary hurdles that must be bridged for the widespread use of AR in educational institutions [17].

4.1. AR-Enhanced Classroom Learning and Interactive Textbooks

Educational spaces undergo fundamental changes because AR technology allows students to access educational objects that boost their learning process. AR-enhanced textbooks include dynamic content features that include 3D models along with animations and real-time simulations for students to view complex concepts in visual ways. The integration of virtual elements via digital overlays with realistic applications and vast information guides students to become interested in subjects like science as well as history and mathematics. AR educational applications enable students to see molecules visually while viewing three-dimensional human body structures and conduct virtual laboratory work without safety risks. The AR site reconstructions, accessible through handheld devices, let students experience historical locations and develop deeper knowledge by allowing them to physically traverse these sites. Students obtain better learning from AR technology because it shows visual explanations of mathematical equations to make complex theories more straightforward to understand. Studies show that the effectiveness of combined AR teaching works because students learn more effectively and gain increased motivation through practical simulations [18].

4.2. AR Applications in Vocational Training and Professional Development

Vocational education receives vital support from AR technology, which simultaneously benefits professional education development. AR simulations for healthcare, manufacturing, and engineering industries give learners safe access to real-time training that replaces actual hands-on experiences. The use of AR allows healthcare trainees and medical practitioners to study detailed three-dimensional human body models along with performing virtual surgery procedures to receive instantaneous feedback. The educational program creates a deep learning environment that strengthens the acquisition of skills and minimises errors while leading to better patient health results. The engineering and manufacturing industry uses AR applications to help personnel build complex equipment, fix problems, and obtain sequential instructions for technical procedures. Interactive training using this method reduces errors and improves productivity levels in high-risk professional settings [19]. Through AR platforms, professional development trains employees directly in their workplace by using real-world simulations to obtain new occupational skills. The features of AR-based learning platforms allow custom building for industry requirements so professionals can learn relevant practical knowledge. Education becomes more efficient when employees learn through a training system combining risk-free interaction, leading to better knowledge retention.

4.3. The Implementation of Augmented Reality Education Requires the Solution of Technical and Accessibility Limitations

Multiple issues need resolution to broadly accept AR education beyond its existing benefits. The high price of AR devices as a major obstacle because educational institutions face financial strain when purchasing smart glasses and tablets. Meritorious development of high-quality AR content presents a substantial and economic barrier that prevents some educational organisations from implementing AR effectively [20]. The successful application of AR-based learning encounters obstacles due to technical limitations in software systems' compatibility and hardware specifications. Various AR applications need robust computing systems and stable internet connection capabilities that cannot always be guaranteed throughout the educational environment. Educational institutions must train their teaching staff to implement AR tools properly while developing strategies that help learners make the most out of their experiences [21]. Researchers and technology developers actively develop heightened accessibility and price-reducing methods for AR technology. Education benefits from improved AR solutions available in the cloud, affordable applications, and better hardware development, which tightens the link between educational technology and students. AR technology will evolve into standard educational equipment that provides customized learning experiences through interactive and stimulating educational interactions according to Figure 7.

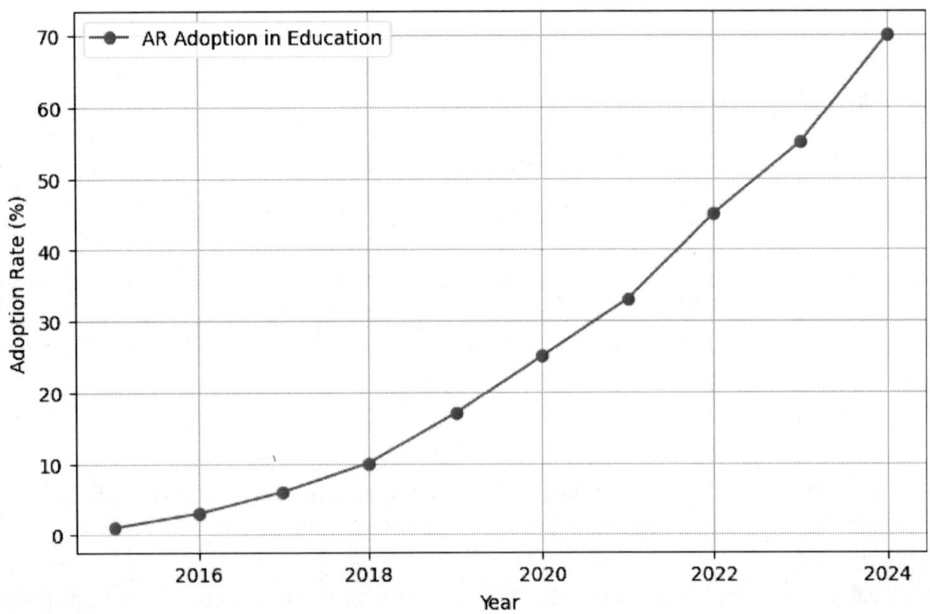

Figure 7. Adoption rate of AR in education over time.

5. Mixed Reality (MR) and Hybrid Learning Environments

Mixed Reality (MR) represents a transformative step in educational technology by blending elements of both Augmented Reality (AR) and Virtual Reality (VR). Unlike AR, which overlays digital content on the real world, or VR, which immerses users in a fully digital space, MR allows users to interact with both physical and virtual environments simultaneously. This hybrid approach creates dynamic learning experiences that enhance engagement, improve knowledge retention, and support collaboration. MR is particularly beneficial for skill-based training, remote education, and personalized learning environments. As technology advances, MR is expected to play an integral role in shaping the future of education [22].

5.1. Enhancing Collaboration and Interaction through MR

One of the most compelling arguments in favor of MR is that it facilitates collaboration among students, even when the students are geographically dispersed. Integrating real-time interaction with virtual aspects, MR enables the engagement of students and instructors in interactive demonstrations, collaborative problem-solving, and interactive discussion sessions. For example, MR-based virtual classrooms enable geographically dispersed students to share a virtual workspace where the students can work on projects, conduct virtual experiments, and engage with 3D models in real-time [23]. The use of MR in professional education and higher learning has also led to more interactive and immersive learning sessions. Engineering students can work in teams to create virtual prototypes, medical students can rehearse collaborative surgeries in a simulated environment, and business students can rehearse decision-making simulations in a more real-world context. MR does not make learning limited to one textbook or even a single monitor, but an interactive and participatory process. This type of engagement has been found to improve the cognitive process as the depth of concept comprehension.

5.2. MR Applications in Practical Skill Training and Remote Learning

The practical educational setting finds MR teaching methods to be particularly beneficial for achieving their objectives. Regulatory organisations give authorisation for utilising MR technology to develop realistic training areas in low-risk educational spaces across healthcare facilities and aviation and industrial programs. They use Medical Reality platforms to study 3D representations of complex anatomical structures, which enables performing surgical exercises without needing cadaver access. Students gain dual advantages from interactor learning experiences because they develop their clinical expertise and increase their professional confidence as they transition to work in patient settings. The aviation industry works with manufacturing to develop MR-powered training simulations for personnel to fix equipment and system failures while advancing their technical knowledge through virtual machinery representations. Trainees benefit from MR because they can undertake realistic tasks that include digital assistance to prepare skills without putting themselves at risk or requiring financial resources. The adoption of MR technology has enabled virtual learning to develop active distant education capabilities. One significant issue with traditional online coursework is how difficult it makes students develop basic practical competence because of minimal practical education. The technology of MR develops full virtual learning spaces that let students connect naturally with both people and digital educational resources through virtual time-based collaboration. Science students perform virtual laboratory experiments while art students build digital sculptures alongside language learners practicing conversations with virtual AI characters. The interactive capabilities of MR enable educators to use it as a vital resource for contemporary teaching [24].

5.3. Future Potential of MR in Personalized Education

MR has great potential as the educational technology is revolutionized in the era of personalized learning. This difference is simply because MR offers personalized learning paths based on each student's pace and progress, unlike the traditional classroom where all students are expected to follow the same curriculum at the same tempo. Moreover, intelligent MR learning systems can monitor student performance, analyze learning patterns and adapt content to ensure students understand the material. In language learning, for instance, an MR app can give a learner real-time feedback on pronunciation and adapt exercises based on their strengths and weaknesses. For example, in STEM education, students with difficulty grasping holistic mathematical concepts can be offered additional interactive visualizations and problem-solving challenges catered to their specific weaknesses. Combining artificial intelligence with MR can make education adaptive and meet the individual needs of each learner [25].

Moreover, as MR devices become more affordable and widely accessible, their integration into mainstream education will continue to expand. Future advancements in 5G, AI-driven MR applications, and lightweight MR headsets will further enhance the capabilities of this technology, making personalized and interactive learning a reality for students worldwide.

6. AI and Data Analytics in Immersive Learning Systems

Artificial Intelligence (AI) and data analytics transform immersive learning through personalized adaptive educational offerings that rely on data-driven insights. AI systems evaluate student activities while making forecasts for educational requirements to deliver customized learning materials thus generating an active educational framework. Real-time student performance details obtained through data analytics enable instructors to make improvements in their instructional strategies. Students achieve better retention rates alongside increased engagement through AI-powered virtual tutoring systems, which combine with real-time feedback systems to create more effective immersive education. AI and data analytics transform educational platforms by delivering smart personalized learning approaches that adapt dynamically to user needs [26].

6.1. AI for Adaptive and Personalized Learning Experiences

AI adaptive learning systems modify the delivery of content according to the specific needs of individual students, providing a more efficient and individualized learning process. Traditional learning tends to be one-size-fits-all, but AI enables real-time personalization through monitoring student progress, learning habits, and levels of understanding. Using machine learning algorithms, AI identifies where a student has difficulty and delivers focused interventions, including more explanation, interactive practice, or customized tests. In Virtual Reality (VR) and Augmented Reality (AR) immersive environments, personalization with AI enhances engagement through dynamic adaptation of the situation to the skill set of the trainee. For example, in medical simulation, AI dynamically adjusts the complexity level in a surgical procedure according to the trainee's performance. Similarly, in language learning, AI dynamically adjusts the conversation level and word suggestions according to the proficiency level. This dynamic adaptation enhances the efficiency of immersive learning, which improves understanding and knowledge retention [27].

6.2. Data-Driven Analytics for Student Performance Assessment

The assessment and performance monitoring of students in immersive learning occurs through the implementation of critical data analytics procedures. Standardized assessments and assignments used in traditional measurement fail to provide an accurate view of student learning progress. Immersive learning systems with built-in data analytics systems monitor student actions while recording student interaction intensity and timespan and compiling complete performance analytics for each student.

Virtual reality-based engineering students receive performance assessments through data analytics that measure their machine assembly proficiency by monitoring errors and timing results. AR analytics tools evaluate student performance during chemical experiments by determining experimental accuracy, which helps adapt learning recommendations. The gathered information allows teachers detect learning deficiencies so they can change approach strategies while directing support to students. Students' future success levels can be predicted through predictive analytics which provides recommendations for necessary interventions to students at risk of falling behind [28].

6.3. Real-Time Feedback and Intelligent Virtual Tutors in Immersive Learning

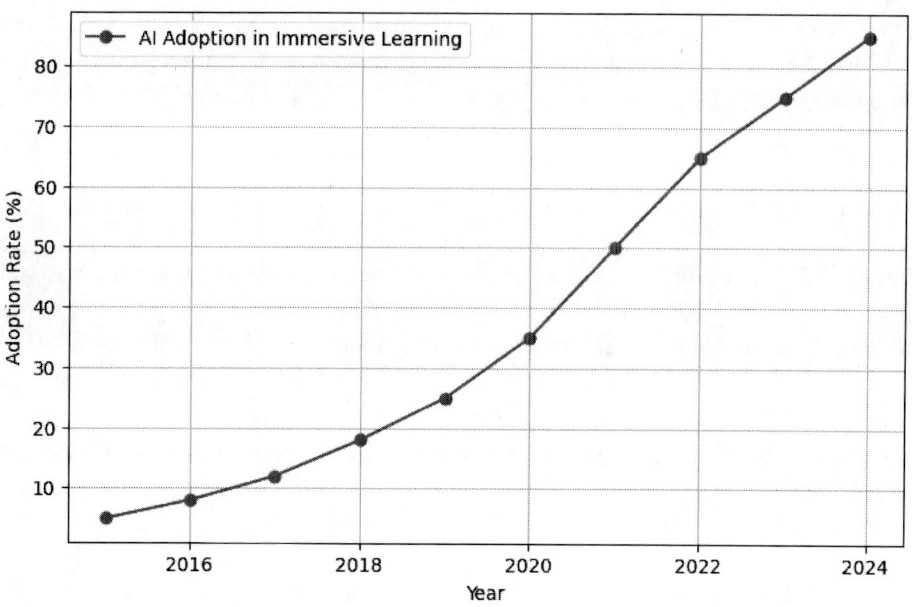

Figure 8. Growth of AI in immersive learning over time.

One of the most significant applications of AI in immersive learning is real-time feedback, which allows students to make adjustments and improve immediately. Unlike traditional learning models, where feedback is provided with a lag, AI-driven immersive environments provide instant feedback based on the interaction of the students. This feature is especially valuable in skill-based learning, where real-time correction can enhance the learning process. AI-enabled intelligent virtual tutors are interactive instructors that guide students through interactive learning experiences. The natural language processing and the techniques based on deep learning are utilized by the AI tutors to respond to the students' queries, explain, and modify the teaching methods in real-time. For example, in a VR-based language learning system, the AI tutor might speak to the student realistically, correcting the grammar and the pronunciation in real-time. Similarly, in an AR-based maths software, the AI tutor might guide the students through, complicated steps to solve maths problems interactively, and it has been shown clearly in Figure 8.

The interaction between real-time feedback and intelligent virtual tutoring leads to a more self-paced and interactive learning process. The students can learn at their own pace, receive individualized instruction, and be directly involved in the learning process. Virtual tutors, as AI technology evolves, will be more advanced, giving a more human-like and efficient learning process.

7. Industry-Specific Applications of Immersive Training

Professional development and learning across industries is changing with Immersive VR and AR learning. We can learn practical skills even in a virtual environment thanks to real-life interactive simulations offered by VR and AR technologies. In medicine, aviation, and business, immersive learning improves knowledge retention and decision-making while minimizing the risks of on-the-job training. VR and AR-based workforce development programs that are industry-integrated are changing the ways of learning, making it more effective and engaging.

7.1. VR and AR in Healthcare: Medical Simulations and Surgical Training

Immersive technologies have become widely used in the healthcare sector for medical training that allows students and professionals to perform complex procedures in a virtual space. VR Medical Simulators enable trainees to engage with vividly replicated 3D maps of human anatomy, carrying out virtual dissections and procedures on patients—without the necessity of real human lives being jeopardized. These simulations create a safe environment for learners to err and practice so they can perfect their techniques before carrying out procedures on real patients in clinical environments.

Programs based on virtual reality surgical training allow medical personnel to conduct virtual procedures based on realistic haptic touch simulation of the surgical tool. The approach has demonstrated helpful in improving surgical precision, error discount, and practitioner confidence. Augmented reality is also included in medical education for live overlays over procedures, allowing doctors to visualise significant structures of patient anatomy. To train professionals effectively without putting real patients at risk, new medical training technology has emerged.

7.2. Aviation and Aerospace: Immersive Flight Simulations

The aviation and aerospace industry has relied upon simulations for its pilot training industry, and the introduction of VR and AR has only added more capabilities to simulation experiences. VR is not a novelty; for flight simulators, it means a whole virtual cockpit simulation, allowing pilots to learn takeoff and landing methods and emergency procedures in the most realistic way possible. The simulations emulate weather patterns, mechanical failures and even air traffic that the pilots might face in a real flight.

AR technology enhances the efficiency of pilots' training by overlaying necessary flight information, navigational data, and safety alerts on a pilot's line of sight. This hands-free operation allows trainees to be led in real-time without focusing their attention on their surroundings. In aerospace engineering, immersive simulation enables technicians to develop and maintain airplane components in a virtual setting, avoiding errors and increasing efficiency. The ability to train pilots and other air personnel in a low-cost, error-free setting has made immersive technologies an essential tool in the aviation field, and it was schematically illustrated in Figure 9.

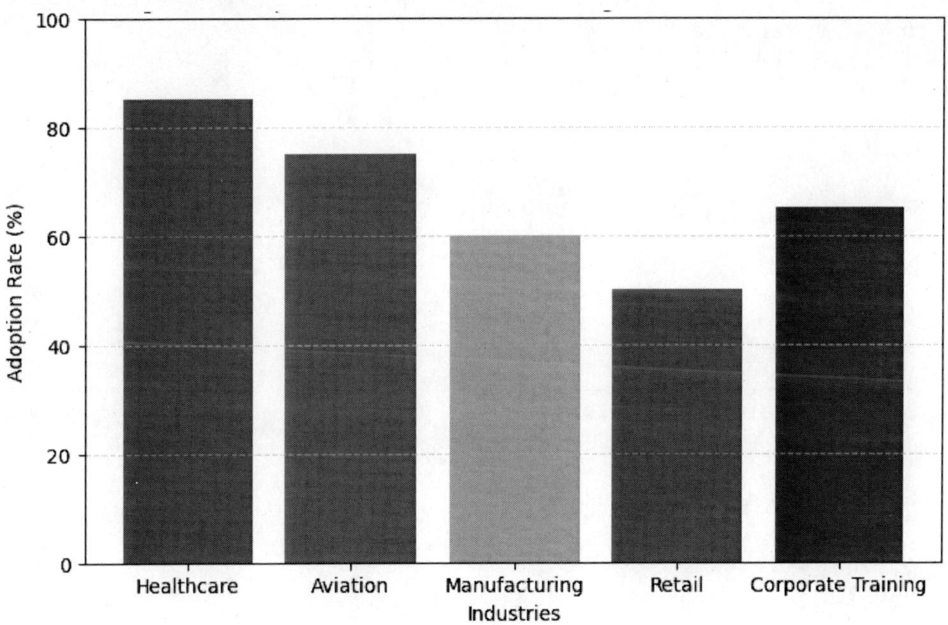

Figure 9. Adoption of immersive technologies in different industries.

7.3. Corporate Training and Workforce Development through Immersive Learning

Beyond healthcare and aviation, immersive learning is increasingly being adopted in corporate training programs to enhance employee development. Companies are leveraging VR and AR to provide realistic, scenario-based training in fields such as customer service, leadership development, safety training, and technical skill acquisition. Employees can engage in interactive role-playing exercises, practice conflict resolution, and receive real-time feedback through AI-driven virtual coaches. Employees can practice hazard response techniques through Virtual Reality workplace safety trainings which let them experience dangerous situations without facing actual risks. Workers use AR applications to receive overlay instructions for machinery assembly, which results in reduced mistakes and enhanced productivity. VR technology serves corporate leadership training by enabling employees to navigate simulated sessions for business negotiations, public speaking, and crisis management practices, as illustrated in Figure 10.

Enhanced interactive learning spaces developed through immersive technologies enhance employee retention while improving workplace tasks. The future of corporate learning will transition toward personal and effective elements thanks to industries that select VR and AR technologies for employee training.

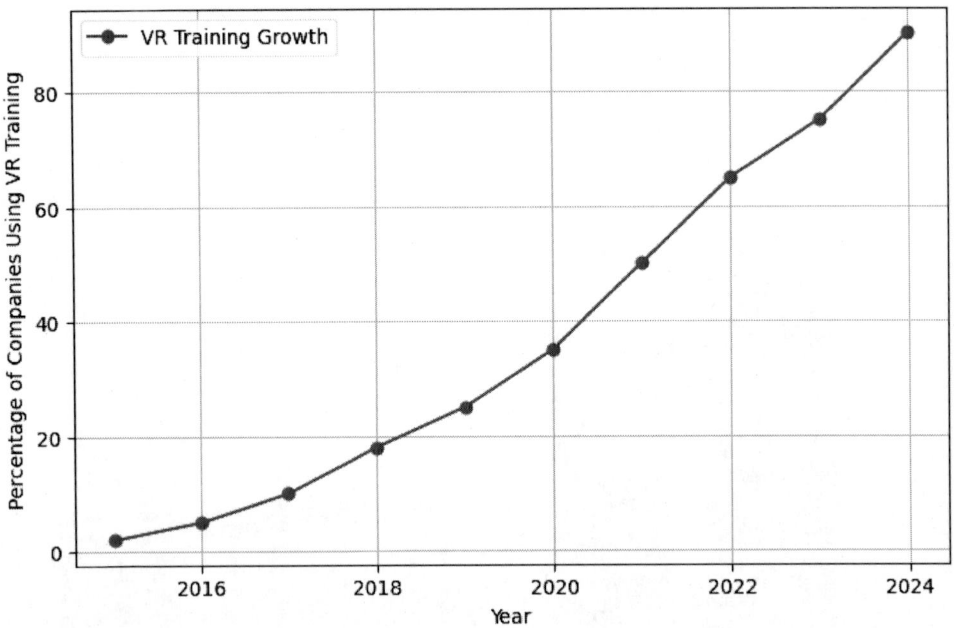

Figure 10. Growth of corporate VR training over time.

Conclusion

Immersive technologies, namely Virtual Reality (VR), Augmented Reality (AR), and Mixed Reality (MR), have revolutionized the pedagogy of teaching and learning, bringing significant value towards enhancing learning experiences. Interactive and immersive environments that are designed through these technologies make the active participation of the learner possible, facilitating the acquisition of knowledge, skill building, and motivation. In professional training as well as in conventional schooling, immersive simulations bridge the gap between the theoretical and the practical, enabling the learner to learn real-world situations in a simulated, safe environment.

Immersive technologies in educational contexts create individualized learning environments with flexible educational content which responds to different student learning needs and uses interactive approaches that capture the attention of all learners. The use of AR applications helps create interactive classroom environments while VR technology enables students to gain immersive hands-on experience of complex historical events. The safety and proficiency of working professionals, especially healthcare providers, aerospace engineers, and medical professionals, become more effective through virtual reality testing replicating real-world environments without safety hazards. Future implementations face obstacles involving expensive barriers to adoption, accommodation doubts, and content development requirements. Distinctive solutions need to be found to achieve the full potential of immersive technologies. Modern AI analysis continues improving while immersive platforms develop exact real-time exam capabilities which enhance learning strategy performance. Immersive learning tool advancement through ongoing research will establish efficient educational and training solutions with better scalability in upcoming years.

References

[1] Onopriienko, Iryna, Kateryna Volodymyrivna Onopriienko, and Salmane Bourekkadi. "*Immersive technologies in adult learning as an innovative marketing tool in the educational market*." (2023).

[2] Sviridova, Ekaterina, Elena Yastrebova, Gulmira Bakirova, and Fayruza Rebrina. "Immersive technologies as an innovative tool to increase academic success and motivation in higher education." In *Frontiers in Education*, vol. 8, p. 1192760. Frontiers Media SA, 2023.

[3] Qu, Zhonglin, Chng Wei Lau, Simeon J. Simoff, Paul J. Kennedy, Quang Vinh Nguyen, and Daniel R. Catchpoole. "Review of innovative immersive technologies for healthcare applications." *Innovations in Digital Health, Diagnostics, and Biomarkers* 2, no. 2022 (2022): 27-39.

[4] Bakhmat, Nataliia, Kateryna Kruty, Hanna Tolchieva, and Tamara Pushkarova. "Modernization of future teachers' professional training: on the role of immersive technologies." *Futurity Education* 2, no. 1 (2022): 28-37.

[5] Manikandan, J., S. Karthik, and L. Naveen. "Effective Identification of Glaucoma using Fusion Deep Learning Approaches." In *2024 International Conference on Electronic Systems and Intelligent Computing (ICESIC)*, pp. 7-11. IEEE, 2024.

[6] Pramanik, Sabyasachi. "Immersive Innovations: Exploring the Use of Virtual and Augmented Reality in Educational Institutions." In *Augmented Reality and the Future of Education Technology*, pp. 66-85. IGI Global, 2024.

[7] Tan, Samson. "Harnessing immersive technologies for innovation in teaching and learnings." In *Learning intelligence: Innovative and digital transformative learning strategies: Cultural and social engineering perspectives*, pp. 305-334. Singapore: Springer Nature Singapore, 2023.

[8] Dick, Ellysse. "The promise of immersive learning." *Information Technology & Innovation Foundation, Washington, DC* (2021).

[9] Savytska, Inna, Olena Tryfonova, Inna Feltsan, Vitalii Alekseiko, and Yaroslav Ahiy. "Immersive technologies in the educational space." *Amazonia Investiga* 13, no. 75 (2024): 343-358.

[10] Bizami, Najwa Amanina, Zaidatun Tasir, and Si Na Kew. "Innovative pedagogical principles and technological tools capabilities for immersive blended learning: a systematic literature review." *Education and Information Technologies* 28, no. 2 (2023): 1373-1425.

[11] Ryan, Grace V., Shauna Callaghan, Anthony Rafferty, Mary F. Higgins, Eleni Mangina, and Fionnuala McAuliffe. "Learning outcomes of immersive technologies in health care student education: systematic review of the literature." *Journal of medical Internet research* 24, no. 2 (2022): e30082.

[12] Jin, Shuaizhen, Jingbin Huang, and Zheng Zhong. "Application of Immersive Technologies in Primary and Secondary Education." *Frontiers of Digital Education* 1, no. 2 (2024): 142-152.

[13] Binytska, Kateryna M., Olha O. Bilyakovska, Oleksandra I. Yankovych, Galyna V. Buchkivska, Olena P. Binytska, Valentyna V. Greskova, Inna P. Ocheretna, Oleksandr Yu Burov, and Svitlana H. Lytvynova. "Implicit potential of immersive technologies implementation in the educational process at

the universities: world experience." In *Proceedings of the symposium on advances in educational technology, aet*. 2020.

[14] Wang, Dan, and Xi Huang. "Transforming education through artificial intelligence and immersive technologies: enhancing learning experiences." *Interactive Learning Environments* (2025): 1-20.

[15] Beck, Dennis. "Augmented and virtual reality in education: Immersive learning research." *Journal of Educational Computing Research* 57, no. 7 (2019): 1619-1625.

[16] Pears, Matthew, Marina Yiasemidou, Mohamed A. Ismail, Domenico Veneziano, and Chandra Shekhar Biyani. "Role of immersive technologies in healthcare education during the COVID-19 epidemic." *Scottish Medical Journal* 65, no. 4 (2020): 112-119.

[17] Rezaei, Ali R. "Applications of immersive technologies in education: A systematic literature review." *Advances in Online Education: A Peer-Reviewed Journal* 2, no. 3 (2024): 232-251.

[18] Manikandan, J., and K. Jayashree. "Enhancing lung nodule classification: a novel CViEBi-CBGWO approach with integrated image preprocessing." *Journal of imaging informatics in medicine* 37, no. 5 (2024): 2108.

[19] Soundarya, N. P., Tarun Kumar, and Harshit Kumar Gupta. "A Framework to Deploy Immersive Technologies for Effective Education." In *International Conference on Business and Technology*, pp. 216-225. Cham: Springer Nature Switzerland, 2024.

[20] Liubchak, Volodymyr O., Yurii O. Zuban, and Artem E. Artyukhov. "Immersive learning technology for ensuring quality education: Ukrainian university case." In *CTE Workshop Proceedings*, vol. 9, pp. 336-354. 2022.

[21] Gnanadurai, Jasmine Beulah, S. Thirumurugan, and V. Vinothina. "Exploring immersive technology in education for smart cities." *Immersive technology in Smart Cities: Augmented and virtual reality in IoT* (2022): 1-25.

[22] Ahmed, Allam, and Michael JD Sutton. "Gamification, serious games, simulations, and immersive learning environments in knowledge management initiatives." *World Journal of Science, Technology and Sustainable Development* 14, no. 2/3 (2017): 78-83.

[23] Kovalchuk, O. I., M. P. Bondarenko, A. G. Okhrey, I. Yu Prybytko, and E. M. Reshetnyk. "Features of using immersive technologies (virtual and augmented reality) in medical education and practice." *Morphologia* 14, no. 3 (2020): 158-164.

[24] Prokhor, Viktoriia, Oleksandra Mrykhina, and Orest Koleshchuk. "Effectiveness of Implementing Immersive Technologies within University Sustainable Development Systems." *Eastern-European Journal of Enterprise Technologies* 131, no. 13 (2024).

[25] Wang, Zheng. "Artificial intelligence in dance education: Using immersive technologies for teaching dance skills." *Technology in Society* 77 (2024): 102579.

[26] Babalola, Akinloluwa, Patrick Manu, Clara Cheung, Akilu Yunusa-Kaltungo, and Paulo Bartolo. "Applications of immersive technologies for occupational safety and health training and education: A systematic review." *Safety science* (2023): 106214.

[27] Koritarov, Todor. "Fostering Learning Innovations in Maritime Education: A Synthesis of Blended, Project-Based, and Immersive Learning Approaches." *German International Journal of Modern Science/Deutsche Internationale Zeitschrift für Zeitgenössische Wissenschaft* 94 (2024): 43-48.

[28] Fornasari, Alberto. "Immersive technologies and innovation in educational contexts: an exploratory investigation at the University of Bari." *Scienze pedagogiche* (2023): 161.

Chapter 6

Strategic Marketing and Branding Through Immersive Technologies

P. Balaji Srikanth[1*]
S. Murugaanandam[1†]
V. Rajaram[1‡]
P. Banu Priya[‖]
and S. Nithiya[2¶]
[1]Department of Networking and Communications, School of Computing,
SRM Institute of Science and Technology, Kattankullathur, Chennai, India
[2]Department of Computing Technologies, School of Computing,
SRM Institute of Science and Technology, Kattankullathur, Chennai, India

Abstract

Strategic marketing and branding experience transformation through immersive digital technologies, which consist of Virtual Reality (VR), Augmented Reality (AR) and Mixed Reality (MR) in the present digital landscape. Immersive technologies generate new business approaches that help companies interact with customers and boost brand experiences and customer retention. The immersive marketing approach goes beyond standard techniques since it enables users to connect emotionally through engaging with products and services in intensely immersive virtual settings. AR enables retail try-outs that improve shopping experiences, but consumers can fully immerse themselves in brand stories through VR capabilities. Integrating Artificial Intelligence (AI) and data analytics further refines these experiences by personalizing content and predicting consumer behavior. This chapter explores the role of immersive technologies in shaping brand narratives, improving customer engagement, and driving sales. It also discusses challenges such as high development costs, technological limitations, and consumer adoption barriers. Additionally, ethical considerations regarding data privacy and user experience will be examined. By understanding the evolving landscape of immersive marketing, businesses

* Corresponding Author's Email: balajis7@srmist.edu.in
† Corresponding Author's Email: murugaas@srmist.edu.in
‡ Corresponding Author's Email: rajaramv@srmist.edu.in
‖ Corresponding Author's Email: Banuprip2@srmist.edu.in
¶ Corresponding Author's Email: nithiyas@srmist.edu.in

In: Shaping Tomorrow
Editors: Prithi Samuel, A. Sathya, Balamurugan Balusamy et al.
ISBN: 979-8-90134-076-9

can develop effective strategies to enhance brand positioning and create compelling consumer experiences.

Keywords: immersive technologies, virtual reality (VR), augmented reality (AR), mixed reality (MR), artificial intelligence (AI), consumer adoption, adoption barriers

1. Introduction to Immersive Technologies in Marketing

The current digital era drives consumer expectation evolution, hence businesses integrate VR, AR, and MR technologies into their marketing strategies for improved brand perception and customer engagement. The consumer engagement aspect of immersive marketing differs from traditional marketing since it enables active brand storytelling interaction that deepens emotional connections. The integration of these technologies enables businesses to display their products through creative formats, allowing, which allow potential customers to handle the products before buying them. Impressive technologies through their virtual try-on features, virtual reality experiences, constructed with augmented reality, together with virtual reality experiences and mixed reality features, allow businesses to reshape their connections with consumers. The advancing nature of these technologies presents an increasingly vital marketing function which lets brands generate novel methods to dominate a competitive market landscape [1].

1.1. Definition and Scope of Immersive Technologies

Digital innovations known as immersive technologies modify human relations with their environment through virtual content integration into real-world activities. The technology generates present-like interactions between users who can interact with digital content in a genuine and hands-on manner. Virtual Reality creates a total digital environment for users to experience. At the same time, while Augmented Reality adds computer-manipulated components onto natural surroundings, enhancing user interaction with physical environments. MR combines virtual and physical elements through real-time integration, allowing users to handle them together [2]. The range of applications from immersive technologies surpasses entertainment and gaming and includes various sectors, from retail to healthcare and education to marketing. Marketers now employ immersive technologies to develop memorable marketing experiences which boost customer engagement while improving purchase decisions. These technologies enable businesses to build interactive product demonstrations, personalized customer journeys, and virtual brand experiences that drive increased consumer involvement and retention [3].

1.2. Differences Between VR, AR, and MR in Marketing

Virtual Reality (VR), Augmented Reality (AR), and Mixed Reality (MR) are distinct yet interconnected technologies that contribute to immersive marketing in unique ways. VR creates a wholly digital environment, isolating users from the real world and immersing them in a computer-generated space where they can explore products, services, or brand narratives in a highly interactive manner. VR is particularly effective for experiential marketing campaigns, allowing brands to transport consumers into virtual showrooms, branded simulations, or engaging storytelling experiences [4]. AR, on the other hand, enhances the real world by overlaying digital elements onto physical surroundings through devices such as smartphones, AR glasses, or tablets. It is commonly used in retail, where consumers can visualize products in their environment before purchasing. AR-driven applications, such as virtual try-ons for fashion and cosmetics, interactive product packaging, and location-based marketing, provide brands with innovative ways to engage customers [5]. MR combines elements of both VR and AR, enabling digital objects to interact with the physical world in real time. Unlike AR, where digital elements are overlaid but do not interact with the real world, MR allows for seamless integration, making it highly useful for applications both digital and physical interaction, such as virtual training or product customisation. Each of these technologies serves a distinct purpose in marketing, and brands strategically choose between them based on their campaign objectives, audience engagement goals, and technological feasibility.

1.3. The Role of Sensory Engagement in Branding

The quality of sensory engagement establishes key elements in branding since it controls how customers understand brands and feel about them and their choices. Visual, along with auditory cues traditionally used in marketing, have advanced with immersive technologies through sensory-enhanced experiences that boost consumer-brand engagement. Multiple senses can be activated through VR, AR and MR systems thus creating enhanced emotional and cognitive consumer responses [6]. Users experience immersive virtual reality scenarios that involve haptic feedback devices which enable them to touch virtual products as well as see and hear them allowing brand events to create stronger memories. AR creates richer real-life engagements by combining visual effects and auditory elements, activating user interest while enhancing their involvement. MR serves as a technological connection between physical objects and virtual digital components which produces dynamic interactions that improve sensory interactions. The power of sensory engagement excels in storytelling since brands can develop stories that consumers can experience as well as see and hear. Brand loyalty increases and consumer recall enhances because immersive technologies enable brands to produce marketing campaigns that deliver comprehensive sensory experiences which create emotional bonds with audiences. Consumer engagement in brands through active participation plays a major role in transforming customer conduct which results in enhanced brand support and larger sales [7].

1.4. Historical Evolution of Immersive Marketing

The rise in technology and changing consumer expectations has influenced the growth of immersive marketing. Marketing methods initially relied on print, broadcast, and television ads, which provided little interaction and engagement. As the advancement in digital technologies, brands started leveraging the internet, social media, and cell phone apps to create more interactive and targeted advertising efforts. The creation of AR and VR towards the latter half of the 20th century and the start of the 21st century marks the turning point in the, as brands began moving beyond traditional media and creating fully immersive experiences. Initial uses of AR, such as the implementation of QR codes and simple digital overlays, provided the background for more advanced AR-driven store experiences, interactive ads, and gamification advertising efforts. VR initially gained traction in the gaming and entertainment fields but soon found its way to the field of marketing, where brands leveraged it for virtual showrooms, branded experiences, and 360-degree stories. The creation of MR further expanded the possibilities by interacting with the physical and the digital in real-time. Today, immersive marketing continues to evolve with the advancement of AI, 5G, and cloud computing, making the technologies more accessible and seamless. As the need for personalization and engagement continues to change, immersive technologies will play an increasingly significant role in the field's future direction, providing brands with new mechanisms to engage and connect with their audiences [8].

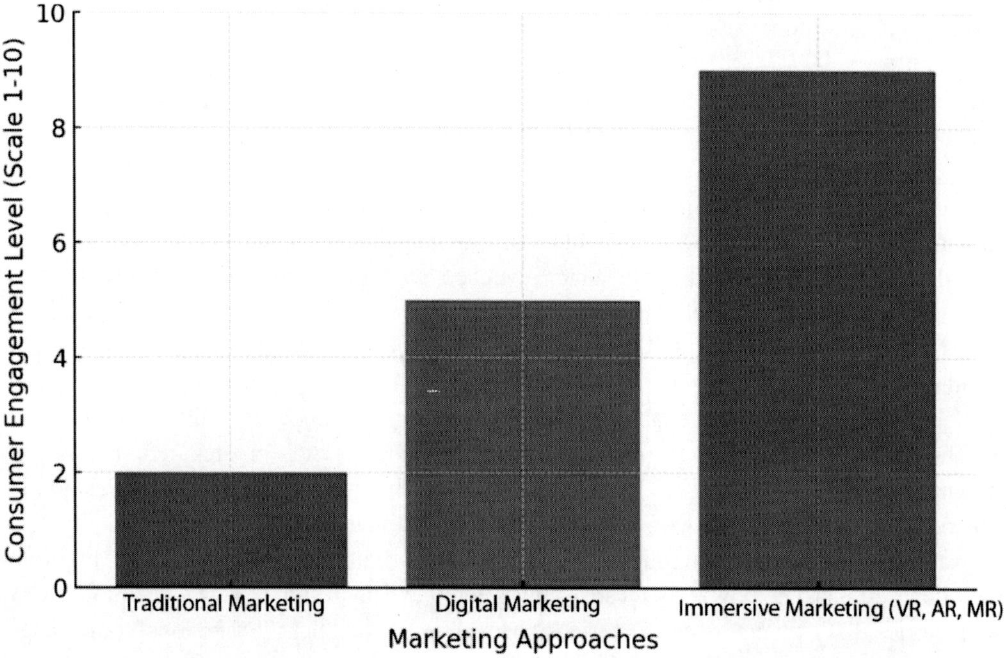

Figure 1. Consumer engagement level across marketing approaches.

The key divergences between Virtual Reality (VR), Augmented Reality (AR) and Mixed Reality (MR) exist according to Figure 1 through their isolation levels, real-world connections and their respective marketing uses. The immersive nature of VR enables it to be an excellent platform for storytelling through physical isolation, thus making it the best option for storytelling-driven campaigns and experiential branding. AR technology allows digital content to overlay on real-world environments, providing, providing excellent impact for interactive advertising, virtual try-on services, and location-specific marketing efforts. MR delivers hybrid experiences that let users touch virtual objects inside real-life environments for customized products and hands-on brand interactions. Brands utilize this analysis to select VR or AR technologies because their engagement goals determine which platform will deliver the depth of consumer interaction they need.

Figure 2 contrasts the degree of consumer interaction in traditional, digital, and immersive marketing. Traditional marketing relies on passive consumption through print and television advertising, whereas digital marketing brings more interaction through social media, websites, and apps. However, immersive marketing surpasses the two by enabling active consumer interaction, creating emotional connections, and enhancing recall for the brand. The graph also indicates the rising trend towards immersive marketing with the progress in technology, making VR, AR, and MR more interactive and accessible. Brands are capturing consumer attention through immersive experiences and capturing consumer attention through immersive experiences and creating more significant brand affinity and higher conversion rates through highly interactive and customised content.

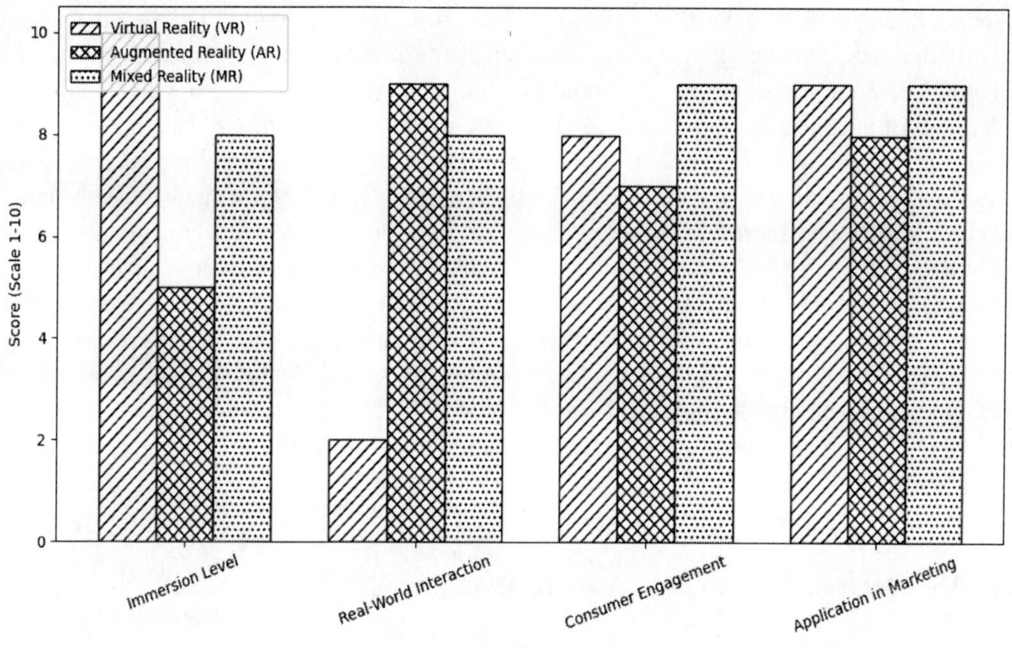

Figure 2. Comparison of VR, AR and MR in marketing.

2. Evolution of Branding and Consumer Engagement

Branding, together with consumer engagement practices, has radically changed since traditional times because of advancing technologies and altering customer demands. During the traditional era of branding a business used logos alongside slogans combined with ads which they displayed on print media and television platforms. In earlier stages of branding, consumer involvement operated from passive roles because brands took complete control of communication while giving little chance for customer interaction. Digital technological advancements transformed branding from static visual communication to interactive experiences, according to [9]. The combination of social media, websites, and mobile applications empowered brands to initiate dialogues with their customers, which advanced their engagement approaches to more specific customer-focused decisions. Branding has reached its latest stage through immersive technologies because consumers now experience brand engagements beyond vision and hearing to immersive participation, strengthening emotional bonds. Businesses wishing to improve their audience relationships apply immersive branding methods that create memorable memorable and expanded brand experiences for consumers [10].

2.1. Traditional vs. Digital Branding Strategies

Through traditional branding methods people controlled their messages and disseminated them through newspapers and radio and placed them on billboards and showed them on television commercials. Widespread brand awareness functions successfully through these strategies although these methods failed to establish actual customer interaction. The brand held an authoritative stance as marketing messages flowed in one direction from the brand to consumers who received these messages. Digital branding brought forward an approach which combined high levels of engagement and interaction between brands and consumers. The internet along with social media transformed branding practices through its power of time-based dialogue and customized marketing and quantitative business decisions. Digital branding enables business-stakeholder interaction through website interactivity and, social media advertising, and email marketing tailored for individual users [11]. Thanks to consumer analytics, businesses can deliver the proper marketing communications to target audiences exactly when they need them, thus improving digital branding performance. Digital branding surpasses usual branding methods by focusing on engagement because it encourages consumers to join brand-related discussions and content sharing and feedback processes. Due to this transformation, brands now operate with heightened flexibility, which enables them to follow customer trends exactly as they develop [12].

2.2. The Shift from Passive to Interactive Marketing

After traditional passive marketing, interactive marketing has become the main transformation in how consumers interact with companies. Traditional marketing involved brands which delivered messages to consumers through television commercials and brochures, yet received no participation from consumers. Consumers maintained little influence on their consumption, while their contact with brands only extended to service requests and purchases. The development of digital platforms and social media networks has made marketing evolve into a two-step interaction between companies and their clientele. Through social media platforms, consumers could participate in brand interactions by posting comments and product reviews while engaging in real-time communications that affected other target customers [13]. The introduction of virtual environments as an update to marketing allows consumers to share real-time experiences with brands through interactive technology. Modern users can participate in product experiences through augmented reality interfaces that let them evaluate attributes before buying or explore branded materials in hands-on ways. Customers become more involved through interactive marketing which strengthens brand loyalty and provides businesses with consumer preference and behavioral data [14].

2.3. Impact of Immersive Technologies on Brand Perception

Immersive technologies have revolutionized brand perception through engaging, memorable, and emotionally impactful experiences. Unlike traditional and digital marketing strategies relying on visual and text-based content, immersive branding allows consumers to interact with a brand through virtual environments, augmented interactions, and mixed-reality applications. More engagement leads to a deeper psychological relationship between brands and consumers [15]. When consumers can walk through a store virtually, virtually try clothes using AR, or participate in a fully immersive VR storytelling activity, their brand perception changes from that of a provider of products or services to that of an experiential brand that enhances their life. Beyond this, immersive experiences create a sense of exclusivity and personalization and make consumers more attached to a brand. Brands that utilize such technologies come across as innovative, forward-thinking, and customer-centric. As immersive branding continues to evolve, businesses that effectively deploy such technologies can differentiate themselves in competitive markets and establish stronger consumer trust and long-term brand loyalty.

2.4. Consumer Behavior in the Age of Immersive Experiences

The consumer behaviour has completely changed with immersive experiences on the rise and the consumers expect interactive, personalized and sensory experiences. Out-of-the-box advertising processes that relied on one-size-fits-all messaging are becoming less effective as consumers of today are looking for experiences tailored to their distinct needs and desires. Immersive technologies allow brands to satisfy these new expectations by allowing the consumer to interact with products and services in its natural condition with much more simplicity and immediate feedbacks. Virtual try-ons, interactive experiences and immersive company storytelling redefining consumer selections by decreasing uncertainty and transferring buyer confidence. Moreover, immersive experiences increase the time consumers spend in their purchase consideration process, consumer tends to explore virtual environments, participate in gamification-based promotional campaigns, and share the experiences in social media. Centre Stage is transformed into Consumer Centre Stage, as consumers change their behaviour, and as a result. Those that know and master through immersive technologies are in better shape to establish more substantial connections with customers, promote excellent customer satisfaction, stimulate brand advocacy within more experience driven excellent customer satisfaction, and stimulate brand advocacy within more experience-driven markets [16].

The change in consumer engagement with traditional digital and immersive brand strategies appears in Figure 3 through a series of lines showing temporal values. The trend shows traditional branding losing consumer interest because it depended on static advertisements as well as print media and television commercials. Consumer engagement levels expanded dramatically with the arrival of digital branding through the interactive website features, social, social networks, and customized contents. The most enormous most significant surge has been observed in immersive branding techniques since they became more popular in recent years. Modern consumers can interact with brands through virtual reality (VR), augmented reality (AR), and mixed reality (MR) platforms to have dynamic experiences with products and services. Immersive branding shows all indicators that it will soon become the leading brand strategy since companies are actively looking for new methods to provide customized experiences.

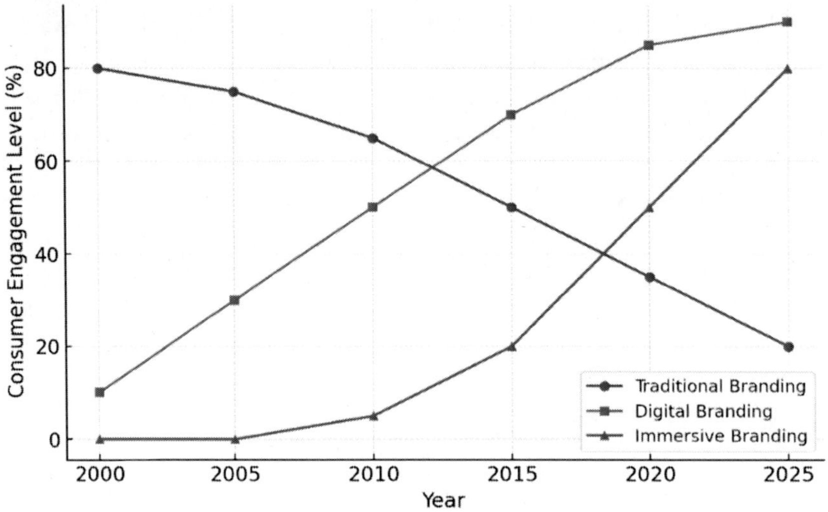

Figure 3. Evolution of Consumer Engagement Across Branding Strategies.

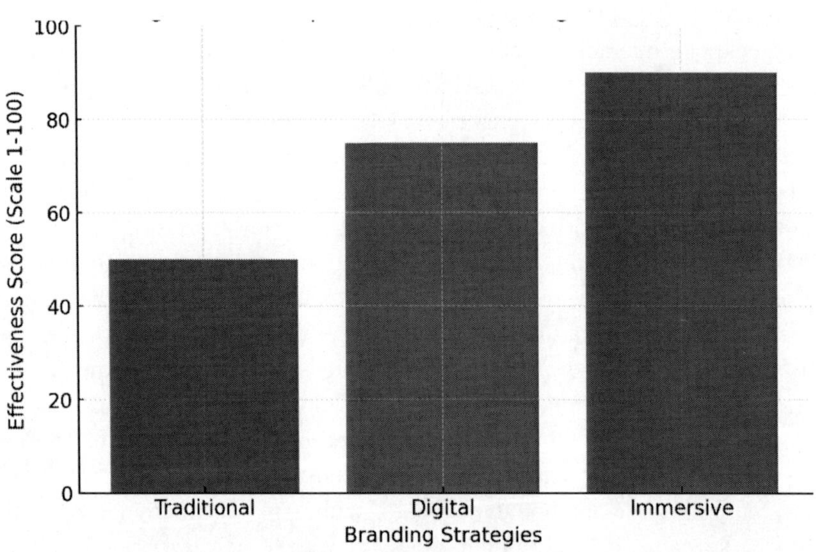

Figure 4. Comparison of Branding Effectiveness.

Using a bar chart to represent the effectiveness of traditional, digital and immersive branding strategies, Figure 4 shows the disparities in the value each approach provides. This effectiveness scale from 1 to 100 indicates how much each approach strikes a consumer's cord and drives your brands engagement goals. The lowest score was for traditional branding, which is characterized by one-way communication with little consumer interaction. Digital branding sees a considerable difference in uses data-driven strategies and interactive platforms to engage audiences more closely. 1. Immersive Branding: Featuring the most interactive, tailored experience, and experiential-based marketing systems to build near connections to consumers.

This comparison highlights the increasing relevance of immersive technologies in branding, showing how brands that are combining VR, AR, and MR can offer more compelling and impactful consumer experiences.

3. Virtual Reality (VR) and Its Role in Brand Storytelling

With Virtual Reality (VR) as a disruptive instrument in brand storytelling, businesses can drive emotions and engage consumers immediately with their story. Unlike traditional advertising methods that depend on passive content consumption, VR enables audiences to enter a brand's world, becoming part of its values, history, and message. Such levels of immersion create a deeper relationship between consumers and brands and more effective storytelling. This provides a way for brands to create memorable experiences with immersive nature, through which brands can not only showcase their products but also connect deeper with users emotionally and increase their brand recall. The interactive nature of this experience is particularly valuable in sectors that can build stories about their offerings, such as tourism, entertainment, real estate, and luxury retail. In traditional media, the consumers read or watched a story. Still, with VR, consumers became a part of the story, which engages the consumers with a presence like never before. Still, with VR, consumers become a part of the story, which engages the consumers with a presence like never before, which is impossible with regular media [17].

3.1. Creating Immersive Brand Experiences with VR

VR provides an unparalleled opportunity for brands to craft immersive experiences that captivate audiences in ways never before possible. Companies can transport consumers to virtual spaces representing their brand identity, whether it is a futuristic showroom, an interactive adventure, or a behind-the-scenes look at their production process. Engaging multiple senses through VR enhances emotional connections, making brand experiences more memorable. Many brands leverage VR to simulate real-world scenarios, allowing consumers to explore products, services, or brand values in a controlled, yet highly interactive setting. For example, automotive companies offer virtual test drives, allowing users to experience their vehicles without visiting a showroom. Similarly, travel and hospitality brands create virtual tours that give potential customers a taste of exotic destinations before booking. These immersive experiences build consumer confidence, reduce uncertainty, and enhance decision-making by providing a tangible sense of the product or service [18].

3.2. VR-Based Product Demonstrations and Showrooms

Marketing professionals use VR to establish virtual product demonstrations and showrooms as one of its primary applications. Before shopping, consumers depended on physical store encounters to check products beforehand. The virtual reality technology allows brands to duplicate retail experiences digitally so customers can access these replicated shopping environments without geographical restrictions. Through virtual reality showrooms people can explore simulated products while gaining full freedom to examine products from various viewpoints together with real-time functionality testing and product customization. The application caters best to the fashion, furniture, and consumer electronics industries because it provides potential buyers with visual and interactive knowledge that drives their purchase choices. The technology of virtual reality showrooms enables both personal customers and business-to-business marketers to display complex products like industrial equipment and architectural concepts to interested clients through immersive displays. Businesses build trust with their customers through VR product previews while also decreasing return rates and improving the interactive nature of their shopping stores [19].

3.3. Psychological Effects of VR in Consumer Engagement

The psychological impact of VR plays a vital role in consumer engagement, as it impacts emotion, perception, and decision-making. VR creates a sense of presence, where the consumer feels that he or she exists within a virtual space, which enhances the emotional richness of brand experiences. Higher engagement leads to better information recall, as the consumer remembers brands that offer interactive and immersive experiences. VR also creates the phenomenon known as embodied cognition, where the consumer equates virtual action with real action, enhancing his or her engagement with the brand. The other psychological impact is the feeling of personalization and uniqueness—if the consumer views VR content, it feels as a custom-made, unique experience, building brand loyalty. VR also reduces anxiety and indecisiveness in buying, as the consumer gets to sample the product before making a buy decision. Brands, through these psychological factors, are able to create deeper and more meaningful relationships with their audiences, leading to higher engagement and conversion rates [20].

3.4. Case Studies: Brands Leveraging VR for Marketing

VR proves its success as a marketing tool through various brand implementations of global companies because it drives better consumer engagement while increasing brand devotion. isable showrooms from IKEA present customers with the ability to both explore and customize furniture using VR technology inside virtual home settings. The interactive format demonstrates to users precisely how their selected products would occupy their personal living areas, leading to enhanced purchase security. Automotive producers like Audi and Volvo made VR test drives available to let customers inspect vehicle specifications in an intensely immersive digital environment. The fashion brands Tommy Hilfiger and Gucci use virtual exhibitions for live runway shows which customers watch remotely from home. Marriott Hotels and other tourism companies use VR to deliver preview tours of their destinations thus generating more travel bookings from customers. These case studies highlight how VR is revolutionizing marketing by offering interactive, engaging, and memorable brand experiences that drive consumer interest and loyalty [21].

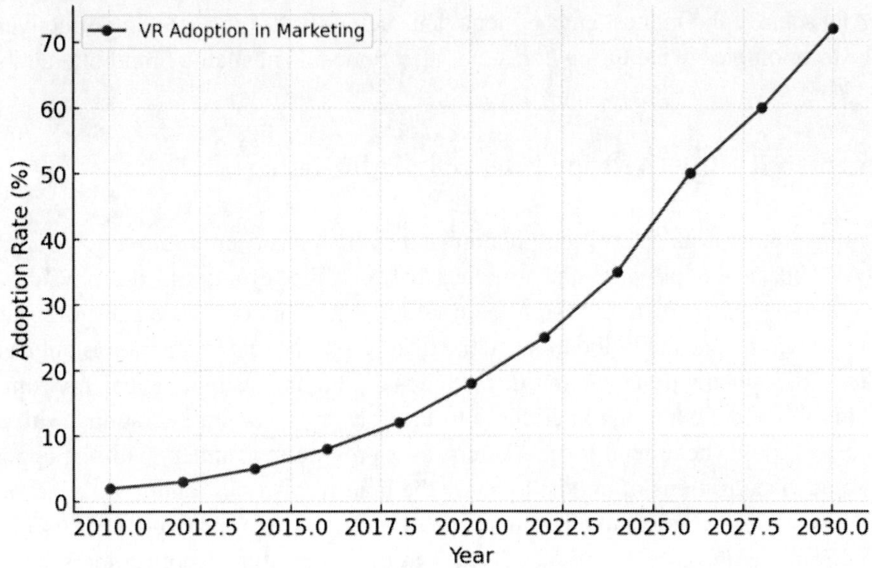

Figure 5. Growth of VR adoption in marketing over time.

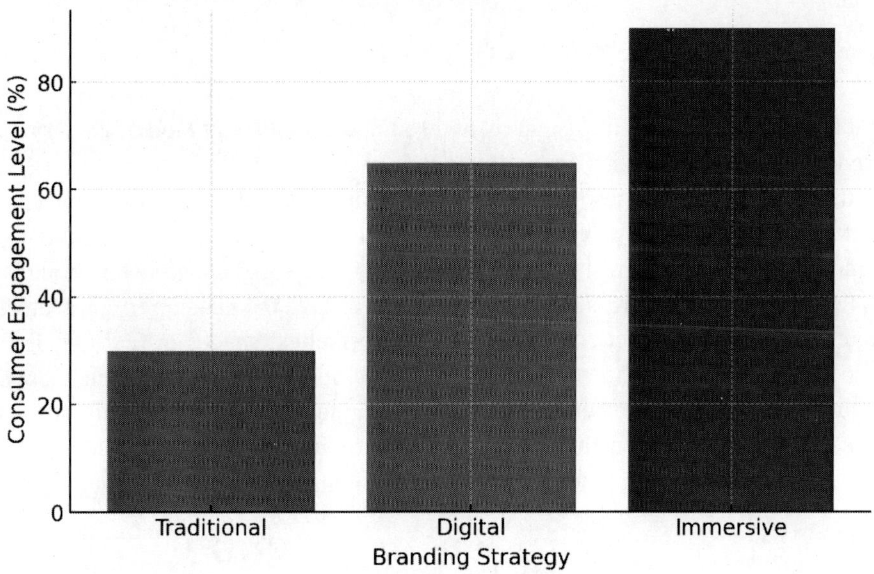

Figure 6. Consumer engagement levels across branding strategies.

This line graph in Figure 5 shows the rise in Virtual Reality (VR) use in marketing from 2010 to 2030. The trend shows a steady growth, with the speed increasing beyond the year 2020. This indicates that as the VR technology has been advancing to make it more affordable and accessible, more and more businesses are using it as a part of their marketing to create immersive consumer experiences.

This bar chart, given in Figure 6, compares consumer engagement levels across three branding strategies: Traditional, Digital, and Immersive. The data indicates that traditional branding methods have the lowest engagement, while immersive branding strategies (such as

VR and AR) achieve the highest engagement. This demonstrates the growing effectiveness of immersive technologies in capturing consumer attention and enhancing brand interactions.

4. Augmented Reality (AR) for Interactive Marketing

Interactive marketing is an interesting phenomenon, which has been improved by Augmented Reality (AR) because it provides the interface between the virtual and the physical world. Marketing through AR is different from the traditional techniques where consumers are only exposed to printed media and billboards and the like, where the real interaction is only a dream. This makes AR an interactional technique that adds digital objects onto actual environment in real time to offer more exciting experiences to the consumers, when interacting with brands. Nowadays, this tool is beneficial for marketers, as it provides consumers with the opportunity to make some visualizations of goods, to study the brands' histories, and to take part in some integrated advertising campaigns. Through such a progressive framework, AR is making a future where marketing is not only about presenting information for customers but for the customers to engage their senses directly in a story branded [22].

4.1. Best Augmented Reality Try-Ons for Retailers

Among all the use cases of AR, the use in retail through the implementation of the virtual fitting method remains one of the most effective. People can employ AR-based apps to assume, for instance, the clothes, accessories, makeup, or even furniture all without having come into contact with them. From Gucci to Nike, brands in fashion have used augmented reality to enable the customers to see how certain shoes or a piece of apparel would appear when bought. Other brands in the beauty niche, such as L'Oréal and Sephora, have the makeup try-on feature using augmented reality that allows clients to try various cosmetics' shades in real life. IKEA and Wayfair in the furniture and home décor have AR applications through which buyers can virtually arrange furniture in their homes to determine the looks and suitability. These applications not only enhance customer satisfaction by reducing uncertainty, but also minimize return rate and hence increase consumer's confidence in buying products online.

4.2. AR-based Gamification for Customer Engagement

Gamification with AR has emerged as a new trend to boost customer engagement. Employing game-like mechanisms in promotional campaigns, brands can create interactive and playful experiences that drive customer engagement. AR-based gamification has been successful in promotional campaigns, scavenger hunts, and reward programs, boosting customer retention and brand recall. Pokémon GO, one of the most popular, has demonstrated the power of AR in evoking consumer interaction and engagement with the physical and digital environment. Brands followed the same trend, designing AR-based treasure hunts where the customer could redeem discounts, rewards, or special products by interacting with AR objects in real-world locations. Fast food chains and beverage brands have also joined the bandwagon of AR gaming by using interactive filters and mini-games in their smartphone apps, rewarding the user with coupons and incentives. This practice creates excitement and emotional associations with the consumer, increasing the likelihood of associating good experiences with a brand [23].

4.3. AR-Powered Advertising and Social Media Integration

Social media has become a major outlet for AR-based advertising, allowing brands to engage with their target audiences in highly interactive ways. For example, Instagram, Snapchat, and TikTok have added AR filters that allow interaction with branded messages, creating a more interactive form of advertising. AR-powered filters and effects allow the user to try out products, alter their appearance, or play with animated brand objects, facilitating organic sharing and virality. This form of interactive advertising not only increases brand visibility but also fosters user-generated content, as the consumer posts their AR-activated experiences on their social network. Brands also employed AR on billboards and print media, where the use of a QR code via a smartphone or other cell phone leads to static images coming alive, with the addition of more information regarding the product or animations. Employing AR as part of advertising and social media campaigns allows brands to break through the traditional advertising noise and create shareable, memorable experiences that drive consumer engagement and brand recognition [24].

4.4. The Role of AR in Personalized Marketing Campaigns

Personalization is a key driving factor behind successful marketing strategies, and AR has hugely augmented brands' abilities to present customized experiences to consumers. Brands can make user-specific suggestions through AR technology based on user behavior, interests, and real-time interactions. For example, AR-powered smart mirrors in retail spaces can suggest clothing based on previous purchases or fashion trends at present, giving a customized shopping experience. Similarly, AR apps can suggest beauty products through facial recognition and machine learning-based analysis based on a person's skin tone and facial structure. Car brands have utilized AR personalization as well by helping users visualize and personalize car setups at point-of-sale and make real-time modifications to colors, features, and accessories. Through AR-enabled personalization of experiences, brands not only increase customer satisfaction but also build stronger emotional connections with their audience as consumers feel that products and services have been customized to their specifications and aspirations.

Consumer interaction by AR marketing strategy (based on the level of consumer interaction, as shown in Figure 7. This bar chart compares consumer engagement levels established by AR marketing strategy, with the following methodology: AR Try-Ons, AR Gamification, AR Advertising, and Personalized AR And the stats show it too; consumers are much more likely to engage with content that caters directly to them, meaning that Personalized AR experiences enjoy the most interactions. AR Try-Ons also drive considerable engagement—especially in the retail and beauty sectors, where customer value lies in being able to visualize purchasing a product. Right behind it is AR Gamification, a proven strategic marketing technique that leverages the AR gamification process to increase engagement through interaction and rewards. AR ads, while effective, are not particularly engaging in terms of interaction levels, which would mean less participation from the consumer. This highlights the increasing importance of AR in marketing and contrasting levels of consumer engagement within different AR implementations.

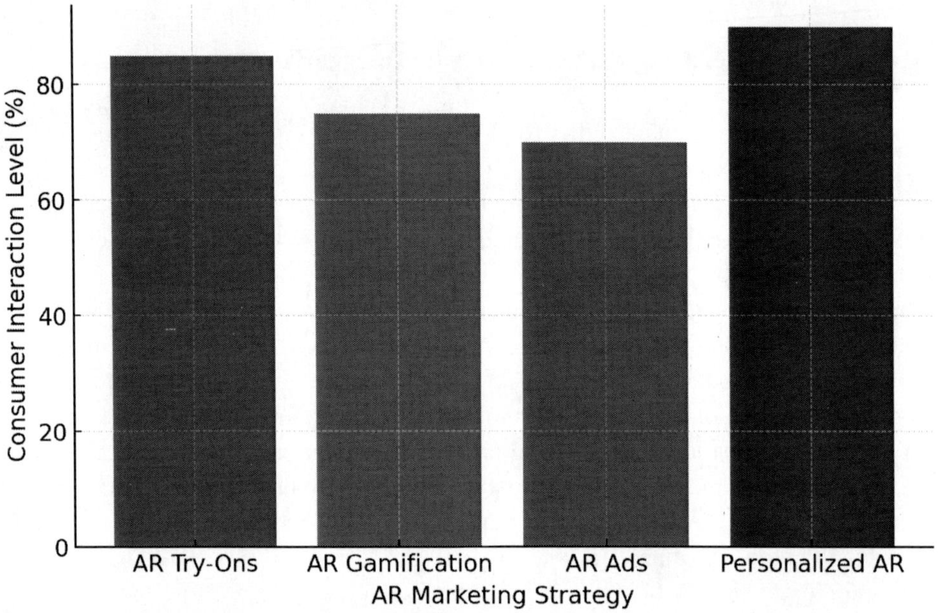

Figure 7. Consumer interaction levels in AR marketing strategies.

5. Mixed Reality (MR) and Hybrid Consumer Experiences

Through Mixed Reality (MR), people experience an interactive merging of physical objects with digital elements, enabling virtual objects to react to real-world elements. Users experience virtual object engagement through Mixed Reality (MR) instead of being fully submerged in Virtual Reality (VR) spaces or viewing Augmented Reality (AR) digital content overlive environments. The adoption of this technology by branding and marketing sectors keeps increasing because companies strive for fresh consumer interaction methods through immersive solutions. Through the combination of AR and VR technology MR generates new possibilities for marketing engagement as well as product interaction and experiential branding thus portraying itself as a vital tool for contemporary marketing operations [25].

5.1. Understanding MR and Its Applications in Branding

MR is revolutionizing the branding methods by making it possible for consumers to engage in digital content much more realistically. Brands are using MR to bring about immersive branded experiences that are beyond passive television commercials. For instance, MR-driven interactive products demonstrations permit consumers to investigate digital replicas of products within a genuine global context for more far-reaching information, and momentum to dispose of to make buys. Retail companies use MR for virtual shopping assistant that gives recommendation and detailed visualization for more interactive and informative shopping experience. Also, MR-based storytelling is changing brand narratives by enabling consumers to enter into interactive brand worlds where they become able to see a company's values, heritage, product development over time in a brand story. As much as engagement lead to higher emotional attachment between brands and customers, results in long term customer loyalty, higher intent to purchase.

5.2. Combining AR and VR for Enhanced Interactivity

Consumers can reach remarkable levels of interaction because MR technology merges AR with VR capabilities. Modern branding techniques utilize this amalgamation to develop cohesive user experiences which connect people between physical environments with digital platforms. Consumers at retail stores with MR technology combine virtual trying on of clothing with physical sample interaction to experience blended shopping. MR showrooms in the automotive industry let potential buyers experience actual vehicles. At the same time, they adjust digital features in real-time by modifying colors and interior selections and choosing accessories through holographic controls. Companies employ MR during trade shows and live events to allow viewers to control virtual product presentations that display extensive product details and functionalities. MR-driven branding strategies that unite AR and VR deliver stronger consumer engagement, building a direct emotional bond between consumers and brand products.

5.3. MR for Product Customization and Virtual Prototyping

Today's demand by consumers for customized products is well-supported by MR technology that serves as a primary solution to such demand. Real-time personalization of products is supported by MR to enable consumers to make modifications to features prior to buying. Customers can see other fabric options and colors and design options that are applied to virtual couches that mimic their home settings in retail applications. Shoe companies allow individuals to customize their products through holographic models in design and material selection and colors schemes prior to making their purchases. The market research industry experiences a substantial impact through MR technology that enables producers and auto businesses to take advantage of virtual prototyping systems to run their operations. Companies create digital prototypes that help verify product features to actual production, thus lowering production costs and delivering higher design precision. Brand satisfaction is more strongly boosted when consumers co-create products through customization at this level due to their ability to match products with their personal preferences.

5.4. Industry Examples: MR in Fashion, Automotive, and Real Estate

MR across industries highlights its adaptability and power in marketing and consumer engagement. In fashion, the likes of Tommy Hilfiger and H&M have tested MR-fuelled fitting rooms that allow customers to try on virtual clothing with personalized styling suggestions. Incorporating both physical and virtual aspects of the shopping experience will provide a more interactive and transparent form of fashion retail. In the automotive sector, MR has transformed the car-buying experience. And the likes of BMW and Audi have begun to offer MR showrooms that allow prospective buyers to view virtual models of vehicles, customize their specifications and interact with digital dashboards ahead of a purchase. This immersive experience will enable customers to visualize their ideal vehicle in a detailed and engaging manner, leading to more informed purchasing decisions. The real estate industry has begun using MR solutions to improve real estate showings for their viewers. Through MR real estate firms enable potential buyers to explore properties virtually while they can modify design elements and see real-time renovation changes in properties. The combination of time savings for customers and sellers through this interactive system also leads to better purchasing decisions due to whole-property visuals. Incorporating MR into modern branding and marketing enables different industry businesses to build innovative methods that attract consumers and boost both sales numbers and lasting brand impressions. Through its perfect integration of digital with physical elements, MR creates advanced interactive marketing standards, leading to active consumer participation in brand stories instead of content consumption.

The plot given in Figure 8 of Mixed Reality (MR) adoption level (fashion, automotive and real estate) from 2015 to 2030 has been demonstrated in Figure 8. Notably, the highest adoption rates are seen in the automotive industry, with the most growth observed after 2020, thanks to car manufacturers increasingly using MR to enable virtual showrooms and digital customisation of vehicles. Hot on its heels comes the fashion industry with MR-based virtual fitting rooms and interactive shopping experiences. The adoption of real estate is gradually increasing, especially as virtual property tours and digital staging solutions continue to expand. This trend supports the idea that MR is progressively being absorbed into industries, providing customers with interactive enterprises and reshaping marketing and sales experiences.

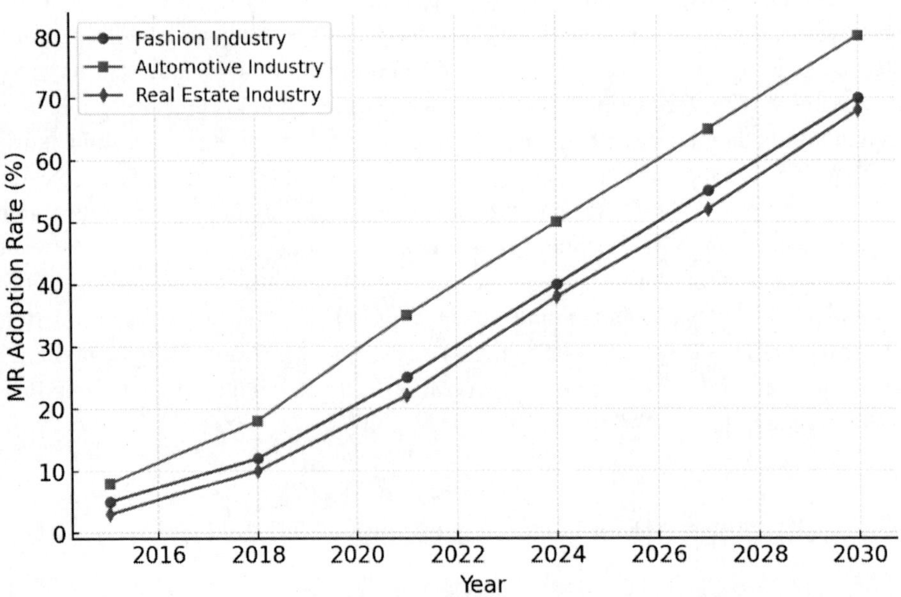

Figure 8. Growth of MR adoption in different industries over time.

6. Artificial Intelligence and Data-Driven Personalization

Artificial intelligence (AI) has revolutionised marketing by enabling brands to offer very customised and immersive experiences to consumers. Through being able to analyse massive amounts of information, AI-based marketing strategies can predict customer needs, forecast tastes, and provide customised content in real time. The integration of AI with immersive technologies such as Virtual Reality (VR), Augmented Reality (AR), and Mixed Reality (MR) has also boosted engagement with consumers through offering interactive, responsive, and dynamic brand experiences. Personalisation through AI enables marketing campaigns to speak to individual consumers and create stronger brand connections while increasing customer satisfaction. As brands continue to embrace AI, marketing is shifting from a one-size-fits-all approach to a data-driven model in which every customer receives exclusively customised interactions based on behavioural information [26].

6.1. AI's Role in Enhancing Immersive Marketing Strategies

AI is bringing intelligent content and automating the engagement with customers, making it a core technology in immersive marketing optimisation which needs extraordinary real-time engagement. Using AI algorithms to understand customer behavior and personalized interests to deliver tailored augmented and virtual experiences. Retail spaces that embrace AR utilize AI technology to recommend items to users based on their purchasing history and browsing behavior: another advance in why retail is becoming more efficient. AI: VR-based storytelling platforms use AI to make the stories dynamic during the execution, and so the experience keeps changing and adapting as per customer organic responses and user engagement metrics. Using AI with immersive technology allows brands to provide seamless personal experiences which help increase customer presence and build relationships with the brand in context of the end user.

6.2. Predictive Analytics for Personalized Consumer Journeys

AI serves as a key optimization driver for immersive marketing through its delivery of intelligent content and its automated customer interactions as well as its improvement of time-sensitive engagement opportunities. Brands use AI algorithms to evaluate how consumers behave and what they prefer so they can develop specific virtual and augmented experiences. The combination of AI algorithms in AR-based retail allows users to receive product recommendations from past launches with their existing browsing records so shopping is more individualized. VR-based storytelling uses AI technology which changes interactive content in real-time while adjusting the experience according to consumer emotional responses and their degree of engagement. AI working with immersive technologies helps brands develop a fully customized brand-customer interaction that encourages stronger consumer commitment to their brands.

6.3. AI-Powered Chatbots and Virtual Assistants in Branding

In branding, AI-assistants and chatbots are vital tools for real-time engagement and customer assistance. While traditional customer service channels tend to have slower response times and limited availability, AI-powered bots can offer instant, 24/7 support, answering users the questions or concerns and guiding the user through their shopping experience. These tech-infused virtual assistants utilize NLP (Natural Language Processing) and Machine Learning to comprehend user intent and respond accordingly. In immersive marketing, AI chatbots are used in VR and AR applications to guide users through their interactive environment. In a virtual shopping environment, for instance, an AI assistant can offer personalized product recommendations and respond to customer queries as they happen. Also, AR-enabled chatbots can help users as they navigate through the virtual try-on process. This ensures that they make informed purchase choices. The use of AI-driven chatbots and virtual assistants considerably improves customer interactions, accelerates buying processes, and fosters better consumer-brand relationships [27].

6.4. Adaptive Marketing: Real-Time Consumer Interaction with AI

Adaptive marketing with AI enables brands to engage with consumers dynamically with content and interactions adjusted to real-time information. AI systems monitor user behavior in real time, environmental factors, and engagement levels to offer customized experiences. For instance, in digital advertising, AI can modify advertisement content based on user demographics, location, and browsing records. In VR-based brand storytelling, AI changes content of narratives to match user emotions to make it more impactful. In AR-based retailing, AI-driven recommendation engines modify product displays based on customer interests and purchasing behavior. This adaptability ensures that marketing campaigns remain relevant and engaging, leading to higher customer satisfaction and brand loyalty. As technology advances with AI, adaptive marketing will continue transforming brand engagement with consumers to produce hyper-personalized, data-driven experiences that drive business growth [28].

A graphic representation depicting the importance of AI applications in immersive marketing appears in Figure 9 through a pie chart. The fundamental component of AI applications consists of predictive analytics since it represents 25% of overall usage which helps companies customize their approach to anticipate behavior patterns. Customer support, along with virtual assistance, receives significant representation from chatbots powered by artificial intelligence technology at 20% in the market. The mentioned adaptive marketing represents an 18% share of AI technology applications across various businesses. The sector of VR/AR personalization takes up 22% of all AI-driven applications because companies utilize AI algorithms to offer customized content experiences to unique users. Brands use real-time interaction as their final AI application comprising 15% of their operation because it allows them to respond immediately to customer needs through adaptable strategies. Proof from the distribution demonstrates AI's essential role in transforming immersive marketing which enhances customer engagement and builds better brand relations.

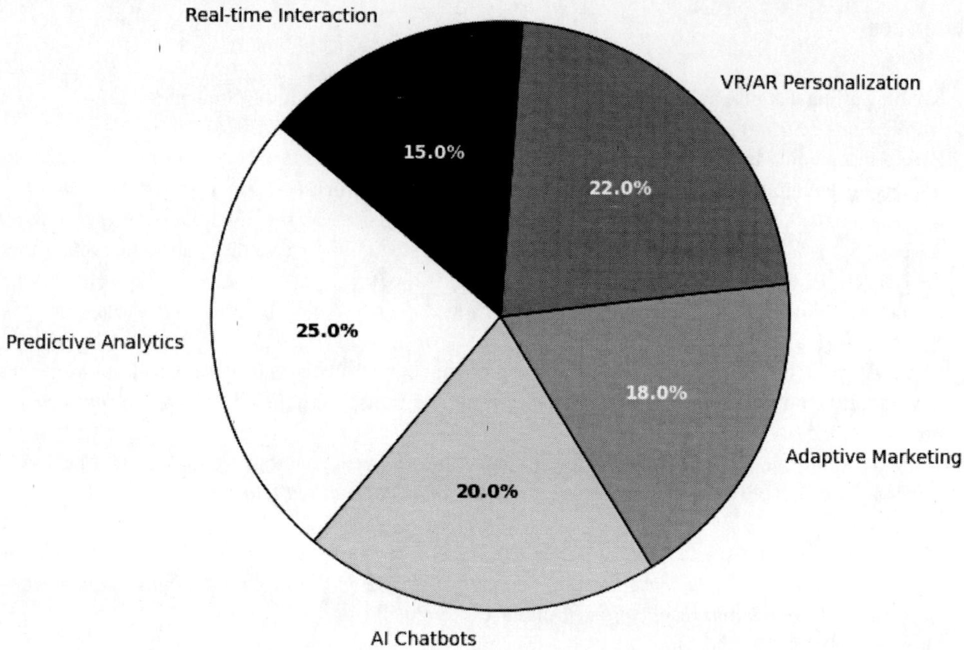

Figure 9. Distribution of AI applications in immersive marketing.

Conclusion

Immersive technologies like Virtual Reality (VR), Augmented Reality (AR), and Mixed Reality (MR) are revolutionizing the landscape of strategic branding and marketing. These technologies offer businesses with unprecedented ways to create interactive, immersive, and highly customized customer experiences. By seamlessly combining physical and digital spaces, immersive marketing practices enhance brand stories, make products more experiential, and build more emotional connections between brands and consumers. As a result, traditional passive approaches to marketing are being replaced quickly with dynamic, interactive experiences that empower consumers to interact with brands in a meaningful way. The integration of Artificial Intelligence systems into marketing allows data-driven customized targeting and leads to real-time engagement with consumers. Artificial Intelligence through chatbots and adaptive strategies with recommendation systems delivers personalized content based on customer behaviors and preferences. AI collaboration with immersive technologies transforms brand relationships with their consumers through highly effective personalized marketing initiatives. Businesses implementing VR, AR or MR technologies must develop strategic approaches that increase brand exposure with better user interactions and stronger customer relationships. The moving forward evolution of immersive marketing presents itself as much more than a simple technical advancement because it means brands now interact differently while building relationships with their consumers. Brands that masterfully combine immersive technologies with AI-powered personalization in their marketing strategies will obtain a competitive edge that will determine future marketing trends in digital experience-based consumer environments.

References

[1] Khalil, Zarjina Tarana, and Areej Ahmed. "Technology-driven Branding Strategies: AI, AR, and VR Applications." *Strategies for Brand Communications and Management* (2024): 214.

[2] Rivera-Pesquera, Martha, Silvia Cacho-Elizondo, and Rafael Duran-Dergal. "Forget-me-not? using immersive technologies in brand-building communication processes: An exploratory study in the Mexican context." *Journal of Creative Communications* 16, no. 3 (2021): 303-313.

[3] Varelas, Sotirios. "Virtual immersive platforms as a strategic innovative destination marketing tool in the COVID-19 era." *Sustainability* 14, no. 19 (2022): 12867.

[4] Pokhodnia, Marika. "*Enhancing Museum Brand Awareness through Immersive Technologies: A Case Study for MHNC-UP*." (2024).

[5] Chen, Chen, and Mike Z. Yao. "Strategic use of immersive media and narrative message in virtual marketing: Understanding the roles of telepresence and transportation." *Psychology & marketing* 39, no. 3 (2022): 524-542.

[6] Ambika, Anupama, Hyunju Shin, and Varsha Jain. "Immersive technologies and consumer behavior: A systematic review of two decades of research." *Australian Journal of Management* 50, no. 1 (2025): 55-79.

[7] Boletsis, Costas, and Amela Karahasanovic. "Immersive technologies in retail: Practices of augmented and virtual reality." In *Proceedings of the 4th International Conference on Computer-Human Interaction Research and Applications*. SciTePress, 2020.

[8] Gopakumar, Sridevi, and Madhava Priya Dananjayan. "Augmented reality in modern marketing: The ultimate solution to engage the digitally overwhelmed, budget-conscious audience?." *Journal of Information Technology Teaching Cases* (2023): 20438869231202712.

[9] Rachmad, Yoesoep Edhie. *The Gimmicks Illusion of Presence: Virtual Reality Marketing Tactics for Immersive Brand Experiences*. Editora Porto Vinho Edição de Livros, Edição Especial 2024, 2024.

[10] Rachmad, Yoesoep Edhie. *Augmented Marketing: Enhancing Brand Experiences with Artificial Intelligence and Augmented Reality*. Karachi Jinnah Kitab Ishaat, Khaas Edition 2024, 2024.

[11] Manikandan, J., and K. G. Harini. "Deep Learning-Based Lung Cancer Detection and Classification with Hybrid Sampling for Imbalanced Data." In *2024 International Conference on Smart Electronics and Communication Systems (ISENSE)*, pp. 1-6. IEEE, 2024.

[12] Alabi, Moses. "*The Strategic Implications of the Metaverse for Brand Building and Customer Experience.*" (2024).

[13] Alanadolya, Alshaimaa Bahgat, Suha Fouad Salemb, Sarabjit Kaur Sidhuc, and Nastaran Richards-Carpenterd. "*Examining Immersive Brand Storytelling in Extended-Reality Arenas*."

[14] de Oliveira, António Sérgio Monteiro. "Measuring the effectiveness of advertising with immersive technologies." PhD diss., Master's thesis]. Copenhagen Business School, 2016.

[15] Scholz, Joachim, and Andrew N. Smith. "Augmented reality: Designing immersive experiences that maximize consumer engagement." *Business Horizons* 59, no. 2 (2016): 149-161.

[16] Adinugroho, Iwan. "Marketing in the Metaverse: Unlocking Opportunities for Brands in Virtual Worlds." *YUME: Journal of Management* 7, no. 2 (2024): 1623-1632.

[17] Leung, Xi Y., Dimitrios Buhalis, and Giampaolo Viglia. "Immersive advertising through co-creation: Lessons from the visitor economy: How to enhance experiential competitiveness with an "attract, convert, and delight" strategy." *Journal of Advertising Research* 64, no. 3 (2024): 319-334.

[18] Hanji, Sanjay V., Nagaraj Navalgund, Savita S. Hanji, P. Mary Jeyanthi, Rajkumar V. Raikar, and Naveen Pol. "Immersive Experiences and Brand Recall in the Metaverse: A Comparative Analysis of Virtual Reality and 3D Interfaces." In *International Conference on Smart Computing and Communication*, pp. 249-259. Singapore: Springer Nature Singapore, 2024.

[19] Manikandan, J., and K. Jayashree. "Enhancing lung nodule classification: a novel CViEBi-CBGWO approach with integrated image preprocessing." *Journal of imaging informatics in medicine* 37, no. 5 (2024): 2108.

[20] Bonetti, Francesca, Eleonora Pantano, Gary Warnaby, and Lee Quinn. "Augmenting reality: Fusing consumers' experiences and interactions with immersive technologies in physical retail settings." *International Journal of Technology Marketing* 13, no. 3-4 (2019): 260-284.

[21] Chakraborty, Uttam, and Santosh Kumar Biswal. "Diffusion of innovation in direct-to-avatar (D2A): A study of immersive communication and branding in the metaverse." *Computers in Human Behavior* 158 (2024): 108318.

[22] Buchanan-Oliver, Margo, Angela Cruz, and Jonathan E. Schroeder. "Shaping the body and technology: Discursive implications for the strategic communication of technological brands." *European Journal of Marketing* 44, no. 5 (2010): 635-652.

[23] de Azevedo Guimarães, Larissa. "*Beyond Reality: The Metaverse as a Strategic Tool for Branding and Marketing Innovation*." Master's thesis, Universidade NOVA de Lisboa (Portugal), 2024.

[24] Brown, William, George Wilson, and Oliver Johnson. "*Understanding Consumer Perceptions of Virtual Reality in Marketing.*" (2024).

[25] Rathore, Bharati. "Metaverse marketing: Novel challenges, opportunities, and strategic approaches." *Eduzone: International Peer Reviewed/Refereed Multidisciplinary Journal* 7, no. 2 (2018): 72-82.

[26] Cross, Karen, Lyndsay Mesjar, Josie Steed, and Yang Jiang. "Immersive innovations for the communication of heritage, handcraft and sustainability." *International Journal of Fashion Design, Technology and Education* 18, no. 1 (2025): 15-25.

[27] Pabla, Harleen, and Harmeen Soch. "Navigating the Metaverse: A Comprehensive Guide to Marketing, Branding, and Innovation." In *Research, Innovation, and Industry Impacts of the Metaverse*, pp. 146-166. IGI Global, 2024.

[28] Zaki, Yasmina, Meng-Shan Wu, and Allam Hamdan. "Exploring the Integration of the Metaverse for Marketing and Branding in Organizational Framework." In *Business Development via AI and Digitalization: Volume 1*, pp. 247-257. Cham: Springer Nature Switzerland, 2024.

Chapter 7

Enhancing Customer Experience Through Immersive Technologies

Balamurugan[1,*]
M. Saravanan[1,†]
A. Vijay Vasanth[1,‡]
M. Suresh Thangakrishnan[2,‖]
and A. R. Nagoor Meeran[3,¶]
[1]Department of Networking and Communications, SRM Institute of Science and Technology, Kattankulathur, Chennai, India
[2]Computer Science and Engineering, Einstein College of Engineering, Tirunelveli, India
[3]UTAS (University of Technology and Applied Science), Shinas, Oman

Abstract

The contemporary digital environment encourages businesses to create new ways to improve customer experience (CX) alongside improved engagement levels. Immersive technology that includes VR, AR, MR, and XR devices transforms customer experience into personalised interactive ones that engage audience interest. With these technologies, brands have new ways through which they can integrate physical spaces with virtual spaces, which enable them to better retain customers' interest than ever before, as well as increase customer loyalty and quality of customer decisions. This section investigates how immersive systems modify customer interaction quality through multiple business sectors including retail and hospitality and healthcare and entertainment. Research considers virtual reality for virtual store development and augmented reality for interactive products before digital components are integrated into real spaces to enhance customer experience. The chapter explains how data analytics platforms and artificial intelligence (AI) create a customised immersive experience through understanding consumer behaviour and taste. The article examines technological barriers, privacy issues, and implementation barriers, followed by proposed solutions to handle these obstacles. The chapter highlights new

* Corresponding Author's Email: pookumbala@gmail.com
† Corresponding Author's Email: Saravanm7@srmist.edu.in
‡ Corresponding Author's Email: a.vijayvasanth@gmail.com
‖ Corresponding Author's Email: suresh.nellai@gmail.com
¶ Corresponding Author's Email: nagoor.meeran@shct.edu.om

In: Shaping Tomorrow
Editors: Prithi Samuel, A. Sathya, Balamurugan Balusamy et al.
ISBN: 979-8-90134-076-9

immersive customer experience trends, including metaverse technology development and innovation in AI-driven virtual assistants and haptic control technology. Immersive technologies allow businesses to develop attractive brand messages while satisfying customers better and achieving market dominance. This chapter delivers an extensive analysis of immersive technologies in customer experience through real examples and market research projections which help businesses implement such innovations successfully.

Keywords: virtual reality (VR), augmented reality (AR), mixed reality (MR), extended reality (XR), artificial intelligence (AI), data analytics

1. Introduction to Immersive Technologies in Customer Experience

Immersive options are revolutionizing business-to-consumer relationships through innovation in new ways that increase customer engagement and individualization and maintain brand confidence. The category consists of VR and AR and MR and XR because they unite digital elements with a focus on bridging gaps among virtual and real-world spaces. Brands establish stronger consumer relationships by embracing immersive experience which offers interactive memorable interactions for solving present marketplace needs. The development of immersive technology platforms exists because of continual artificial intelligence, which together, cloud computing innovations and high-performance graphics processing, produce experiences that affect all business sectors [1].

1.1. Definition and Scope of Immersive Technologies

Digital innovations under immersive technologies merge elements between virtual content and real-world surroundings, or they perform full virtual environment simulations. Wearable virtual reality devices provide complete digital immersion, enabling users to experience virtual spaces as they interact with realistic virtual environments. Bilingual Reality projects digital content on real environments so users can view products interactively with contextual information displayed through smartphones, tablets or AR glasses. MR effectively merges digital and physical realities because it enables users to engage with virtual objects alongside real-world objects at once, thus making it suitable for applications in retail, training, and design-based scenarios. XR functions as a unified label that subsumes various emerging technologies because these digital encounter systems keep merging and developing. Immersive technologies span industries from retail and healthcare to entertainment, real estate, and education because companies use these technologies to engage their customers better while achieving smarter decisions and developing stronger brand attitudes [2].

1.2. Evolution of Customer Experience in the Digital Era

The advancement of digital technology has led to major transformations in customer experience because it has transitioned from conventional personal interaction to modern technology-based personalised encounters. Customers today expect perfectly combined omnichannel interactions that allow them real-time connectivity, personalized guidance, and easy purchasing processes. In the past, customer experience relied on physical store shopping, personal customer service connections and printed materials for advertisements. E-commerce, mobile applications, and social media platforms have changed business engagement by enabling interactions between businesses and consumers through various digital platforms [3]. Competing businesses became more intense, so basic digital access no longer provided enough value to customers. Modern consumers attempted to engage with brands through something that gave them interactive and personalized information and emotionally charged interactions. The escalating consumer demand resulted in immersive technologies becoming popular since these technologies provide digital users with engaging experiences. Companies using VR, AR, and MR technologies help customers experience products and brands in ways previously impossible. AR and MR technologies help customers experience products and brands in previously impossible ways, leading to the subsequent development of customer experience [4].

1.3. The Role of Immersive Technologies in Enhancing Engagement

Tools in immersive technology serve as major drivers for improved customer involvement by creating dynamic and interactive interactions that maintain user focus. Standard marketing methods use passive methods. After all, customers only receive information through advertisements, product descriptions, and customer reviews. Compared to passive customer engagement digital content, active customer participation digital content enables more emotional connections between customers and brands. AR-powered applications let customers preview products in their surroundings, decreasing their buying uncertainties and strengthens their purchasing commitment. Through VR-based experiences, customers journey into virtual domains of brands where they can both inspect products and join virtual events, as well as take part in immersive narrative experiences. MR technology furnishes users with a high level of interactivity because it lets them control virtual digital elements in their actual physical environment, through which they can enhance their product comprehension while making better purchasing decisions. Immersive technologies make customers direct participants throughout their buying process which results in higher levels of interaction and better brand retention [5].

1.4. Multiple Advantages of Immersive CX

Implementing immersive technology in customer experience generates multiple advantageous aspects that help businesses and their customers. Immersive experiences function as an effective business tool to create distinct brand image and sustain customer loyalty while boosting rate of customer conversions. Interactive brand experience allows customers to create emotional connections that drive satisfaction and develop loyal relationships with their audience. The implementation of virtual try-on and interactive product visualization capabilities along with 3D model features and experiential functions decreases customer returns because shoppers gain better information before purchasing. Through immersive methods businesses achieve data collection on how consumers behave and choose which is applied to perfect their marketing approaches and enhance their product range. Immersive technologies create better convenience options along with personalized solutions and improve consumers' confidence when making their buying decisions. Customers gain the ability to examine products in genuine ways through virtual experience from home environments thus bypassing traditional shopping trips to physical stores yet maintaining interactive engagement. The gamification elements integrated into various immersive experiences strengthen user connectivity which simultaneously makes the shopping trip entertaining as well as memorable. Immersive technologies in customer experience strategies by businesses will establish a relationship between brands and consumers that reaches new heights of both personalization and immersion [6].

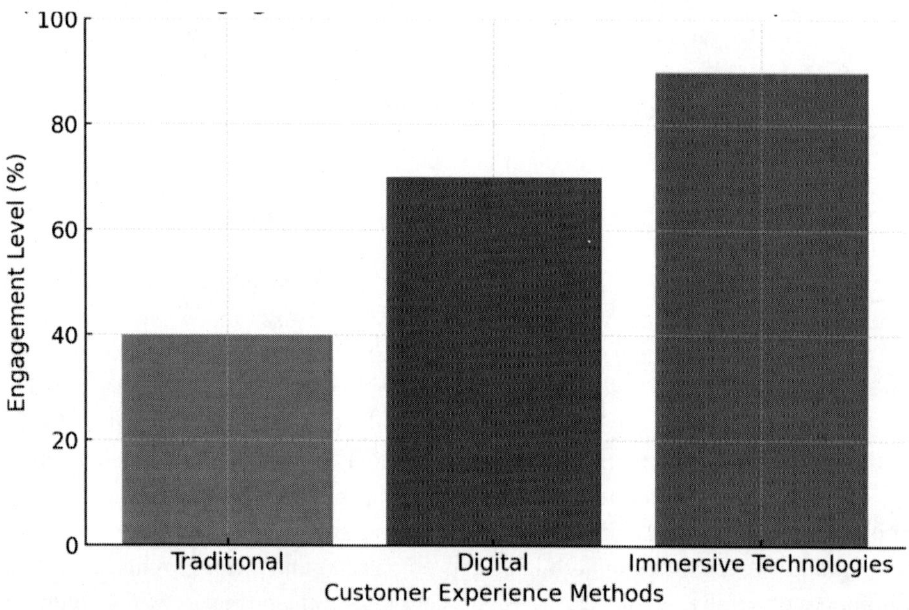

Figure 1. Comparison of engagement level across customer experience methods.

Figure 1 depicts customer engagement ratings between various customer experience approaches. Traditional customer contact methods, such as in-store engagement and advertising, display the lowest customer participation rate because they depend on passive customer involvement. Digital engagement is enhanced through e-commerce websites and mobile apps as they offer interactive user interfaces with personalized suggestions. Customers demonstrate the most extensive engagement through immersive technologies because these systems let them actively explore virtual and augmented environments that increase their brand connection.

Figure 2 depicts how immersive technology excels over digital and traditional channels when it comes to customer satisfaction and conversion rate generation. Customer satisfaction, together with conversion rates, increases when using digital techniques, yet immersive technologies achieve better results than either traditional or digital methods when it comes to customer experiences. Immersive technologies create high satisfaction because customers experience realistic products, which reduces their doubts about buying decisions. The rise in conversion rates demonstrates that customers will finish transactions after using immersive product interactions through VR, AR and MR systems, thus proving their effectiveness for customer engagement strategies.

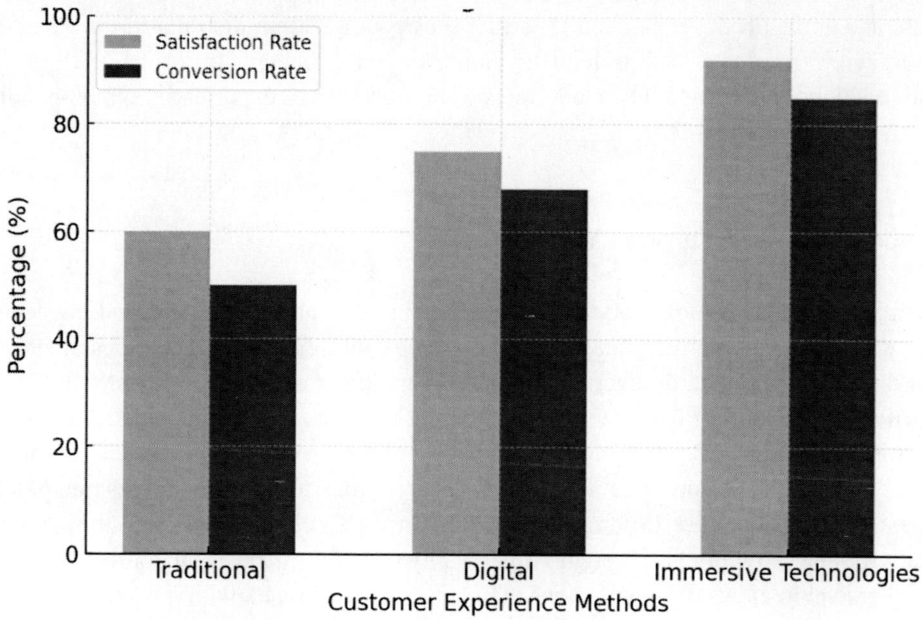

Figure 2. Impact of immersive technologies on customer satisfaction.

2. The Role of Virtual Reality (VR) in Customer Engagement

The modern customer engagement sector transforms Virtual Reality because it provides customers highly interactive experiences that outperform classic digital communications. Customers have access to a complete simulated environment through VR technology, which surpasses the static images, videos, and texts that traditional customer engagement methods use to achieve emotional brand attachment. Companies employ VR technology to build customer experience spaces that allow users to touch products and view services through realistic simulations and fully immerse in brand contents. The transition between passive customer experiences and active involvement led to a total transformation of the customer experience in retail, together with real estate and hospitality, along with entertainment. Consumer expectations advance because VR is a vital tool that improves brand interactions, creating stronger and customized memorable brand connections [7].

2.1. VR-Powered Virtual Shopping and Retail Experiences

Virtual shopping has completely transformed the retail sector because it enables customers to shop from virtual stores without leaving their houses. Users can access virtual retail settings, which display physical store arrangements, allowing them to browse products as well as interact with virtual sales staff and receive immediate shopping support. Virtual shopping environments within e-commerce surpass static product display of traditional e-commerce because customers can view products from any angle and use realistic spatial movements which duplicate actual shopping experiences. Participating customers have online access to VR fitting rooms from fashion brands which let them virtual try clothes before making purchase decisions effectively. Furniture and home décor retailers build virtual showrooms within their platforms which help customers view products within realistic domestic environments prior to buying. Such innovative solutions increase buyer confidence through virtual experiences which results in decreased product returns [8].

2.2. Immersive Brand Through VR

With virtual reality as a tool, storytelling achieves its ultimate worth for brand engagement through delivering interactive engaging brand worlds that deeply immerse customers. The method differs from standard advertising that delivers information since VR storytelling lets users actively engage with brand content by joining the story from its core. Brands produce brand stories through VR technology that offer intense emotional experiences for their audience. The luxury automotive industry enables virtual test drives, which let potential customers feel like they are driving high-performance vehicles even though they have not physically visited showrooms. Through virtual reality technology travel and tourism companies offer immersive previews of! destinations which provide customers with powerful excitement that improves their decision-making abilities. Brands reinforce customers' emotions through interactive virtual spaces that induce long-lasting changes in purchasing behaviour and brand loyalty [9].

2.3. Virtual Platform and Product Demonstrations

Through VR-based virtual platform, businesses now provide customers revolutionary possibilities to deeply examine products by exploring their attributes and operational aspects in real time. Virtual showrooms enable businesses to display products without spatial constraints and operational expenses, allowing them to show unlimited items in an attractive virtual environment. Through virtual reality technology, automotive businesses enable customers to see detailed walkaround tours of their vehicles so customers can explore everything inside and outside the cars without dealership visits. Real estate companies enable property-related investment decisions through VR tours that let potential buyers walk through spaces to see interior design plans and spatial layouts of properties. Technology brands implement VR demonstrations to present new gadgets and electronic devices while enabling customers to interact personally with product design features. This process improves customer interaction and simplifies purchasing decisions through an improved, efficient, and pleasant product evaluation method.

2.4. VR in Customer Service and Support

In customer service, VR delivers substantial changes through innovative methods that boost customer support capabilities. The virtual assistive technologies operated by VR create an interactive experience for customers to handle their questions and get aid more effectively than traditional systems. Business operations utilise VR-based customer support systems that let users conduct simulated real-time encounters with virtual help personnel through virtual environments. Through Virtual Reality technologies, companies achieve better results in their troubleshooting programs, training methods, and new employee onboarding programs. Through virtual reality tutorials, technology companies facilitate the setup of complex software by visually showing customers each step of the process. Healthcare providers use VR customer service tools to enable remote medical sessions where patients have realistic clinical encounters from their homes instead of scheduling physical clinic visits. Businesses implement VR to enhance customer satisfaction while cutting service costs and improving service response speed through innovative support tools [10].

2.5. Case Studies: Successful VR Implementations in CX

Many innovations now use VR technology in their customer experience strategies to show how virtual reality systems help keep and interest consumers. IREKA implemented a VR showroom capability that lets customers design interior spaces through virtual home environments to try and arrange furniture before purchase. The initiation enabled better customer trust in purchasing choices while eliminating the need for physical store exploration. VR marketing from Adidas introduced users to extreme sports experiences from professional athlete perspectives through its innovative platform. The immersive storytelling method dramatically boosted consumer branding relationship while allowing improved customer relationships. Autonomy experienced success in the automotive sector with virtual reality showrooms that allowed customization of models and interior examination and virtual test drives, which better served customers' needs and influenced purchase behaviour. The tourism industry has adopted VR by letting Marriott Hotels enable customers to preview travel destinations virtually before making booking decisions. The mentioned practical uses prove how effective VR systems prove for enhancing customer experiences alongside individualized navigation and brand affiliation [11]. Deploying VR technology toward its evolution will extend its effects on customer experience creation so brands can establish better interactive connections. Businesses can achieve competitive advantage by investing in VR engagement strategies that deliver special and fascinating interactive encounters to customers in today's digital business environment.

Various industrial sectors demonstrated their increasing adoption of Virtual Reality through, Figure 3, to achieve better customer engagement. Virtual reality adoption is most prevalent in real estate since property tours through virtual interfaces have become essential for both buyers and investors. The automotive market closely aligns with the lead group as manufacturers employ VR technology to create virtual showrooms and virtual test drives that transform car purchasing possibilities. Retail operations profoundly incorporate virtual reality for virtual shopping tasks and interactive product presentation features, which enhance customer purchase decisions. The tourism sector, together with the healthcare industry, demonstrates rising adoption of virtual reality technologies to provide immersive vacation previews and virtual medical appointments to users, respectively.

Figure 4 compares customer satisfaction levels before and after VR implementation across different industries. The data establishes that VR substantially improved satisfaction ratings in every evaluation segment. The satisfaction rates remained moderate until companies implemented Virtual Reality technology because of standard service restrictions. The introduction of VR-powered experiences delivered outstanding satisfaction results to customers. VR test drives alongside customized vehicle views resulted in substantial growth of customer confidence in the automotive sector. VR previews and virtual healthcare consultations helped the tourism sector and healthcare services reach higher satisfaction rates by delivering more involved and efficient solutions. The research highlights how VR technology delivers drastic improvements to the experiences customers have in different sectors.

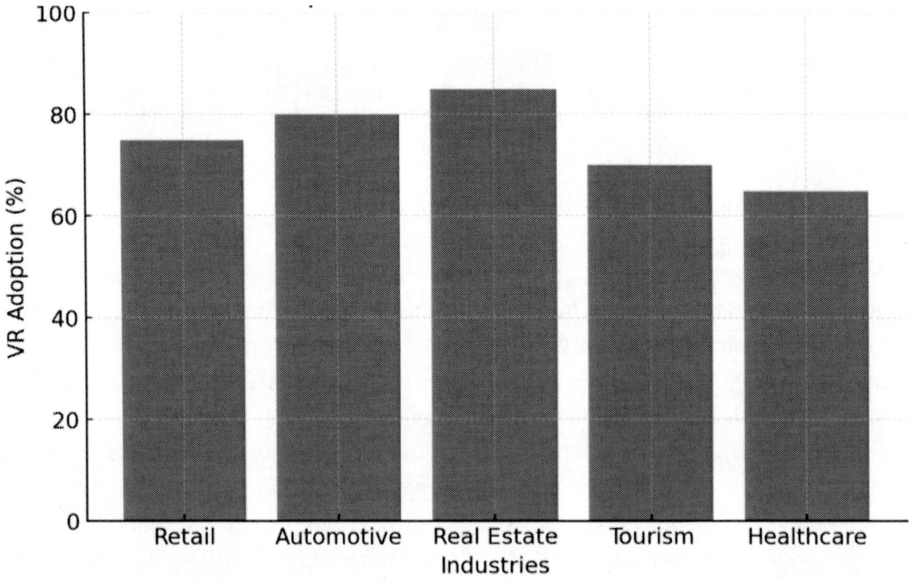

Figure 3. VR adoption across different industries.

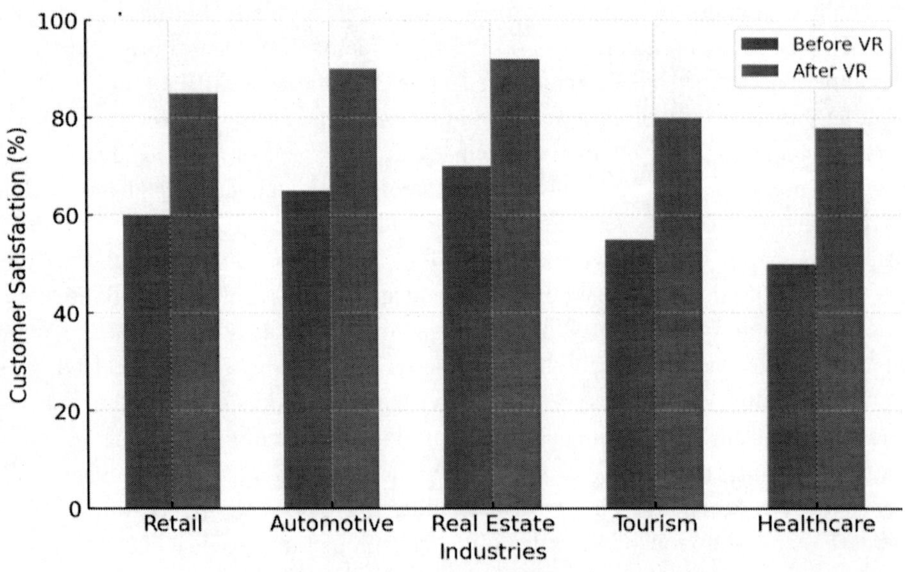

Figure 4. Impact of VR on customer satisfaction across industries.

3. Augmented Reality (AR) and Interactive Product Visualization

Augmented Reality (AR) revolutionized product consumer interactions with its ability to unify physical retail products with virtual digital information. AR enables better visualization by placing digital elements on top of real-world settings that customers can experience. With this technological advancement, customers experience live engagement with virtual product designs as well as highly individualized shopping experience. Retail operations partnered with the e-commerce function to be smarter through AR integration, which enables customers to obtain interactive previews to support better purchasing choices. Customers gain confidence regarding their purchase through in-life visualization because it lets them see how a product would integrate before buying so they feel more connected to brands. AR visualization tools presently dominate industries like fashion, home décor, beauty, and automotive because these sectors depend on product experiences to determine consumer choices [12].

3.1. AR-Driven Virtual Try-Ons for Fashion and Accessories

The adoption of AR-powered virtual try-ons in the fashion industry brought about a fundamental transformation that allows customers to see how clothing, makeup items, and accessories will look on their body before buying anything. Standard online fashion shopping fails to demonstrate how products appear on someone else, resulting in buyer disappointment and high refund levels. Through AR, users gain access to their smartphone camera or AR-mirror technology for on-the-spot, real-time self-assessment of fashion items like clothing, accessories, and sunglasses, along with shoes and makeup. Through AR-powered applications, companies in the fashion and beauty industry allow their consumers to test different styles, colours, and sizes of products virtually without actual ownership. The increase in interactivity through augmented reality systems produces better customer contentment and higher conversion rates because users feel confident about their purchase choices. The fashion and beauty industries have broadly adopted AR because of its personalised shopping capabilities, which have transformed into a leading retail technology.

3.2. AR in Home Décor and Furniture Shopping

Customers now use AR to view furniture options before purchasing them through transformed home décor and furniture shopping experiences. The retail leader IKEA utilizes AR-based applications that let customers virtually place digital furniture throughout their homes to check if the items fit their space and look requirements. Through its IKEA Place app customers can view furniture items using authentic representations of sizes and color options that assist in making better purchasing decisions. Due to this technology, users no longer need to guess about their purchases online or attend showrooms. Customers benefit from a platform that enables them to view various arrangements and simultaneously test different styles while conducting simple option comparisons. Users benefit from AR-based home improvement applications through wall color testings, flooring material selection, and decorative element trials before buying to achieve personalized and satisfying shopping experiences. AR integration with home décor business operations increases customer satisfaction while minimising returns and improving overall consumer happiness [13].

3.3. AR-Enhanced Product Packaging and Information Accessibility

As AR is incorporated into packaging, there are new opportunities for consumers to interact with their products through interactive experiences. Smart packaging solutions use AR technology to give smartphone users access to extra product data and application steps alongside promotional materials upon scanning barcodes. Relevant food brands supply consumers with interactive preparation content flowing from scanned product labels. Using AR by cosmetic companies lets consumers view product ingredients besides application tutorials and sustainability information to build trust through transparent operations. Detailed product information available at once through AR helps customers make better purchases, which results in improved brand devotion and superior shopping interactions. AR-powered packaging has gained traction in the market because it changes consumer interactions with products while strengthening their relations with brands [14].

3.4. AR-Based Gamification and Customer Engagement Strategies

Brands use AR gamification as a major sales approach to connect with customers while improving retail engagement. Companies create business campaigns which use AR technology to attract customer participation and reward discovery while developing brand loyalty. Retailers and marketers use AR-based scavenger hunts, loyalty programs, and interactive advertisements that combine new ways to give shoppers better experiences with memorable memories. Brands employ location-based AR to steer customers to secret discounts inside physical stores while boosting client movement and engagement levels. Through gamified AR, users can discover special content together with limited-time promotional deals of AR elements in product launches. Implementing AR within gamified systems creates customer fascination and deepens brand relationships, leading customers to return and use the platform [15].

3.5. Case Studies: Transformative Effects of AR

Numerous worldwide brands have implemented AR technology into their customer journey plans to show how it affects buyer decision processes. The mobile app of Sephora provides virtual try-on via AR technology that lets users test makeup products before their final purchase. Implementing this new technology resulted in a decline in product returns and better consumer trust in internet shopping. Nike's AR-powered shoe sizing solution enables customers to make accurate online shoe purchases through virtual fit measurements. AR foot analysis provides single-footed users with exact measurements that produce accurate recommendations, thus minimising their frustration about improper sizes. Wayfair utilises an AR visualisation application in their furniture platform to let customers virtually position their home furniture, which generates better conversion numbers and decreases product return rates. The beverage industry uses AR to provide innovative packaging solutions that unlock special content and interactive promotion experiences. One such brand is Coca-Cola. Multiple practical cases show that AR transforms customer behaviours because organizations can use immersive experiences to help customers make better choices and build strong connections that increase engagement levels [16].

The development of AR technology will expand its impact on retail, branding, and customer experience so that these domains can deliver enhanced interactivity with personalised features. Acceptance of AR-driven strategy by companies leads to competitive superiority through the creation of customised shopping roads that boost consumer engagement.

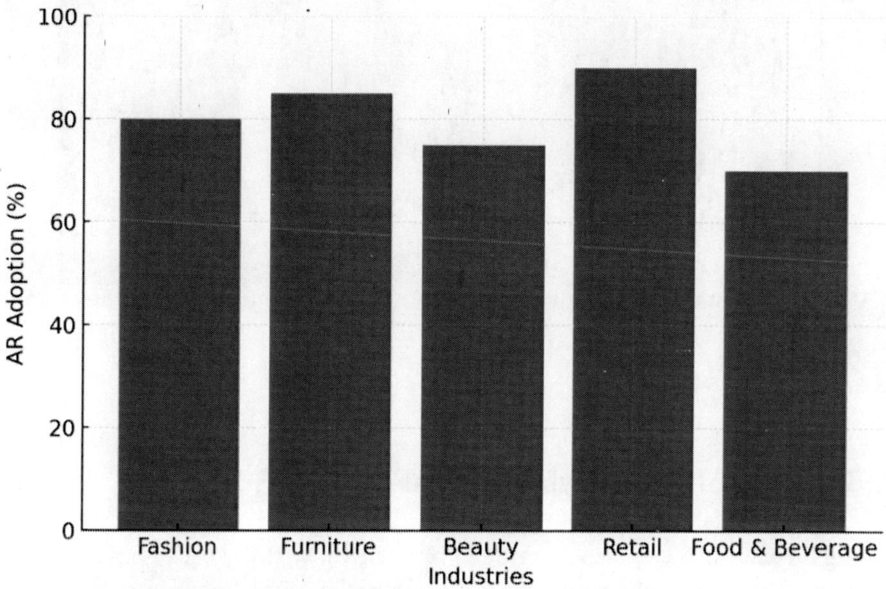

Figure 5. AR adoption across different industries.

Figure 5 explains the deployment of Augmented Reality throughout different business sectors as companies utilise AR to provide improved experiences for their customers. Retailers strive at the forefront in implementing AR solutions because businesses use virtual fittings, interactive product displays, and AR-based indoor store orientation to deliver better shopping experiences. Customers in the furniture industry can now preview home décor items in their home spaces through AR applications during the purchasing process. The fashion and beauty industries explore AR to provide customers with virtual try-on features that let them make buying decisions more confidently.

Industry comparisons in Figure 6 reveal that customer participation grows substantially because businesses deploy AR technology. Customer engagement remained moderate until customers could experience augmented reality because traditional shopping methods created restricted capabilities. Customer interaction increased substantially with AR advances because new AR-powered solutions brought personalised and interactive product exploration capabilities to users. Retail leads all industries in achieving maximum improvement due to AR displays that allowed customers to interact through virtual products during shopping. The furniture and beauty sectors experienced substantial elevation in customer participation because realistic product views and accurate visualizations became available to consumers. Food and beverage companies benefited from AR-enabled packages and gamification techniques, generating heightened customer interest. The collected data proves AR technology boosts customer activation while enhancing business decisions throughout various industrial sectors.

Figure 6. Impact of AR on customer engagement across industries.

4. Mixed Reality (MR) and Hybrid Digital-Physical Experiences

Customers gain enhanced experiences through Mixed Reality (MR) because it unites physical elements with digital components. Users can engage with virtual elements alongside actual objects through Mixed Reality since it is different from Augmented Reality and Virtual Reality. This technology creates better customer interactions through its ability to allow users active engagement with products, services, and brands in the current moment. Businesses leverage MR to offer tailored shopping environments, interactive product demonstrations, and automated solution services that meet modern customer demands. MR technology allows digital information to be superimposed on physical areas, creating stronger customer interactions and better decision-making power for purchasing and reducing purchasing uncertainty. The retail sector, along with automobile and real estate businesses, implements MR technology to develop blended digital-physical interactions within their offerings that redefine customer interactions with products and services [17].

4.1. MR in Enhancing In-Store Shopping with Digital Overlays

Retailers work with MR technology to increase shopping experiences within stores by adding digital virtual elements that instantly show information alongside provided trip advices and display interactive examples to customers. Customers equipped with MR-enabled headsets or smart glasses can access digital content that overlays physical products, allowing them to view various product variations and specifications and receive personalized recommendations. The sensor-shaping fashion market employs MR to show virtual depictions of clothes through different styles, colours and sizes, which avoids traditional physical testing. The shopping journey becomes better when electronics stores allow customers to see realistic 3D model versions of devices while testing their internals and features before buying. Grocery retailers integrate MR-based directions and product detail displays, which enable their customers to search for items and get nutritional data and promotional deals. Combining virtual news overlays with actual retail environments through MR technology produces a unified engaging shopping process that improves customer satisfaction and purchasing choices [18].

4.2. Hands-Free MR Solutions for Retail Staff and Customer Assistance

Retail operations improve due to MR, which provides hands-free solutions to enhance store associate and customer service team functions. Staff members using MR headsets obtain instant inventory information alongside real-time stock status while watching digital assembly instructions for their products. The hands-free system raises operational efficiency while shortening service durations and decreasing dependency on old paper documents as well as screen-based operations. MR-powered virtual assistants boost customer support by delivering dependable troubleshooting services and on-the-spot guidance to helpers. Home improvement stores apply MR solutions to let their staff provide clear visual assembly instructions that enhance customer support services while minimizing errors. Workplaces that use MR as a driver for their logistics solutions see their warehouse workers receive digital overlay guidance for perfect execution of picking and packing tasks. Implementing MR within retail operations enables businesses to achieve improved workflow efficiency and enhance both employee productivity and customer service speed and quality [19].

4.3. MR for Experiential Marketing and Live Demonstrations

The integration of MR technology transformed experiential marketing because brands now produce inventive campaigns that draw their customers deeply. MR brings customers to the forefront of brand stories through interactive experiences, which convert them from audience members to interactive storytellers. Multiple companies leverage MR to operate virtual temporary storefronts allowing their customers to browse digital showrooms featuring life-size virtual products in physical environments. The automotive sector uses MR technology to deliver virtual vehicle demonstrations that let customers examine inner vehicle elements, design exteriors, and perform digital test drives without physical showroom requirements. Products from beauty and skincare companies feature MR mirrors that let users see different makeup combinations and skincare effects instantly as they appear in real life, thus improving personal skincare options while letting users explore products in detailed ways. Brand interactions at live events and trade shows are successful with MR technology because they allow visitors to view product demonstrations on digital displays and view holographic projections and personalized brand messages. MR offers brands an effective method to combine narrative elements with functional interactivity, resulting in effective, compelling marketing experiences [20].

4.4. MR Systems Enhance the Effectiveness of MR Systems

AI creates smarter and context-oriented customer engagements that result from MR integrations with Artificial Intelligence technology. AI-driven MR system analysis includes real-time personalized suggestions based on users' behaviour patterns, preferences, and factors around them. By utilising AI technology, MR headsets in retail environments can identify individual shoppers while gathering their transaction data to create accurate recommendations related to their buying patterns. MI-driven virtual assistants on MR platforms provide individualized purchasing suggestions to consumers via voice commands, comparative options, and individualized discount offers. Through AI-integrated MR systems, furniture retailers allow their customers to see how specific furniture pieces look in their homes by making recommendations based on space, furniture, and natural lighting characteristics. Customers in the automotive sector can benefit from AI-based MR applications that let them test car features and dynamic performance analytics while receiving secure assessments and personalized configuration options. Companies using the union of MR technology and artificial intelligence deliver individualized data-reliant service which improves user retention and satisfaction levels.

4.5. Case Studies: MR in Retail, Automotive, and Real Estate

Numerous industries use MR implementations to build superior customer service platforms and optimize business procedures. The retail sector welcomes Nike and other brands through MR-powered shopping experiences which show 3D products to customers and enable design customization with AI-generated recommendation support. Through integrated MR applications, Lowe's provides customers with guide assistance for DIY projects. Lowe's provides guided assistance for DIY projects, allowing them to connect with interactive installation overlays for simplified access to DIY processes. The automotive industry employs MR technology for virtual showrooms, enabling potential auto mobilists to assess car models through interactive configurations while performing driving simulations before purchasing. The real estate development sector adopted MR technology to provide potential homebuyers with seamless remote property viewing through digitally interactive full-scale displays. Potential homebuyers now apply virtual reality technology to tour digital properties in authentic sizes, where they can change anything and perform real-time renovations to assess properties better. Different case studies confirm how MR has expanded throughout multiple industries by advancing consumer interaction and streamlining choices while generating new combined virtual-real contact approaches [21].

Research and development in MR technology will expand its capabilities to create better and more dynamic consumer interaction options. Organizations applying MR-driven approaches achieve better competition alongside transformative customer-merchant interactions within physical as digital environments.

Analysis from Figure 7 reveals the industries using Mixed Reality (MR) technology with their retail sector alongside automotive, real estate, healthcare, and education institutions. Companies in the automotive industry take the lead role in MR adoption because they use this technology to produce virtual showrooms and create interactive customization tools for their vehicles. The retail sector maintains its position behind automotive because MR enables, together with interactive shopping environments, virtual product try-ons, and advanced AI recommendations. The real estate industry has implemented MR technology substantially for remote property exploration that uses digital renderings shown at actual life scale to prospective buyers. Healthcare, alongside the education sectors, face slower adoption of MR compared to retail and automotive sectors since they integrate this technology to develop superior training and consultation systems, as well as innovative educational tools.

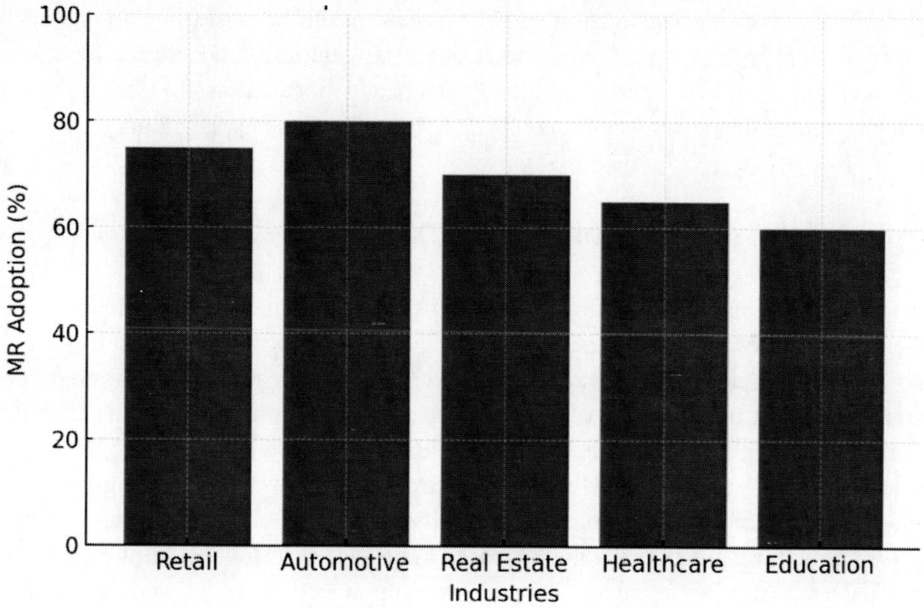

Figure 7. MR adoption across different industries.

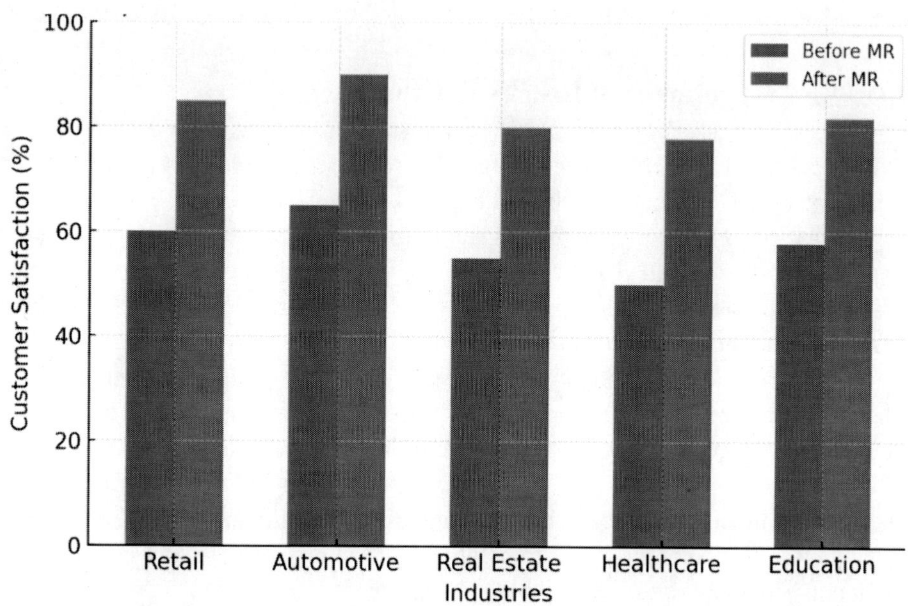

Figure 8. Impact on MR on customer satisfaction across industries.

Customer satisfaction surveys show that industries use the figure 8 to monitor satisfaction changes during MR implementations. Traditional engagement tools resulted in average customer satisfaction before the MRI introduction into the customer experience. An increased customer satisfaction outcome became evident through implementing MR, especially within the automotive and retail sectors. Adopting MR technology provided customers with rich virtual shopping environments, individualised product suggestions, and interactive product shows, strengthening their buying choices. Virtual property tours and visual property tools through MR drove strong satisfaction growth in real estate because they improved buyer confidence during property purchasing decisions. The sectors of healthcare together with education demonstrated better participant involvement and more successful learning processes, which demonstrated the powerful effects of MR to boost customer satisfaction.

5. Personalization and AI in Immersive CX

New customer experiences are developed through personalised interactions. After all, Artificial Intelligence combines with immersive technologies, including Augmented Reality (AR), Virtual Reality (VR), and Mixed Reality (MR). AI technology makes personalized immersive CX possible through modification of content suggestions and user interactions according to everyone's preferences. AI-based technologies within immersive spaces create real-time user interactions to deliver more involved and relevant experience than traditional digital spaces. AI is employed with immersive technology for modifying virtual purchasing systems, designing interactive storytelling procedures, and AI-based assistance features that ensure users receive personalized customer engagement. Brands are empowered with AI and immersive CX solutions for enhancing customer emotions, and building loyal relationships through tailored experiences according to individual users [22].

5.1. AI-Driven Customisation of Immersive Experiences

The ability of AI to create personalized virtual environments depends on its analysis of user data interactions and subsequent simulations of responsive virtual environments. The technology of AR-powered retail allows AI systems to evaluate real-time adjustments of virtual try-on experiences so users can visualize how items fit their bodies according to both shape and past purchases and current personal style. The technology in VR environments functions through AI by transforming digital environments to develop individualized virtual spaces allowing users to experience destinations, training simulations, or entertainment scenarios. AI accomplishments in gaming sectors and entertainment industries adapt gameplay mechanics to match player referrals regarding their ability, emotional reactions, and decision practices. AI systems within MR applications adjust training module complexities according to student performance to create highly optimized educational experiences. The AI-based personalization capabilities boost user involvement, transforming her interactive experiences into more meaningful and beneficial ones [23].

Applying artificial intelligence functions to study consumer actions helps developers forecast what customers will prefer.

Analysing consumer behaviour through data analytics based on AI technology serves as a fundamental method to understand what customers expect and want in immersive environments. The analysis of user virtual product interactions, together with their selection patterns and engagement durations, becomes possible with machine learning algorithms applied by companies. Inaugural tracking devices from AI systems monitor user patterns of visual attention combined with physical movements and spoken directions as well as exploratory motions in AR/VR frameworks to detect emerging patterns of customer interest. The acquired customer behavioural data assists businesses in perfecting their products and optimising virtual storefront product positioning while increasing user satisfaction through behavioural prediction. The VR shopping recommendation system uses AI models to identify customer behaviour patterns just like e-commerce services do to make personalized suggestions. The predictive capabilities enable personalised product presentations for customers, which enhances their conversion ability and satisfaction rates while minimising their decision-making strain.

5.2. AI-Powered Virtual Assistants in AR/VR Environments

AI-based virtual assistance services become essential components of immersive customer experiences through their immediate delivery of guidance and support, together with information access. The combination of AR-based retail and AI-powered assistants enables customers to explore stores with the help of voice or gesture commands to receive product information that can answer their questions. Healthcare professionals can perform patient diagnosis and gain immediate data recommendations by using AI-powered virtual assistants working inside MR environments for patient care. Implementing AI-powered chatbots for customer support delivers enhanced interactive assistance to users in their interactions with virtual reality simulations and augmented reality-based service applications. AI-powered virtual assistants operate with enhanced convenience features, shortened waiting times, and superior user engagement through their ability to deliver appropriate responsive support [24].

5.3. Sentiment Analysis and Emotion Recognition for Adaptive CX

Sentiment analysis and emotion recognition technologies powered by AI give immersive CX improved capabilities to read user emotions so content and interaction mechanisms can adjust accordingly. Money-saving machine learning techniques evaluate human facial movements, vocal loudness, and physiological patterns. At the same time, consumers engage in immersive activities to help companies modify their services in real-time. Devices that use AI technology evaluate user emotions to change gaming scenarios, soundtrack quality, or game difficulty levels to boost player engagement. The emotion recognition system in AR fitting rooms permits retailers to observe customer responses toward their clothing selection, enabling better product recommendation models. Entire training and corporate settings use sentiment analysis from MR applications to change the level of difficulty in training as an approach to deliver customised and efficient learning experiences to their student population. AI emotional analytics delivers adaptable immersive experiences which address personal needs and emotional states, thus generating more interactive and engaging interactions [25].

5.4. Case Studies: Personalisation Strategies with AI and Immersive Tech

Multiple businesses across various industries utilize AI personalization for immersive CX and their customer acquisition and business performance demonstrate success. L'Oréal, among other beauty brands, applies AI-powered AR to build virtual try-on capabilities that help customers find suitable makeup shades based on their facial characteristics and skin tone. Fashion company Gucci serves customers through AI-based AR shopping recommendations of personal clothes styles [26, 27]. The automotive industry joined with artificial intelligence to implement virtual reality technology at Audi showrooms, which tailors exhibition areas to match customer-specific choices, allowing shoppers to interact with vehicle configurations according to their preferences. AI-assisted medical diagnosis through MR technology, which generates individualised treatment plans, enabling healthcare practitioners to use real-time patient data analysis, which generates individualised treatment plans so doctors can make informed decisions. Research in education shows progress from AI-Led VR learning platforms which modify educational material through tracking student interest then delivering better individualized learning methods. The selected case studies demonstrate the increasing importance of AI as an immersive CX delivery method that creates more engaging and intelligent customer interactions for numerous industries [28].

The evolution of AI technologies will lead to further development of personalized customer interactions which businesses will use for improving their immersive experiences. Biological AI integration with immersive technologies helps brands engineer suitable experiences relevant to users' context and emotionally appealing while building prolonged customer loyalty. Companies that apply AI personalization strategies to their immersive digital structures will boost CX performance and transform customer-model brand relationships in today's digital marketplace [29].

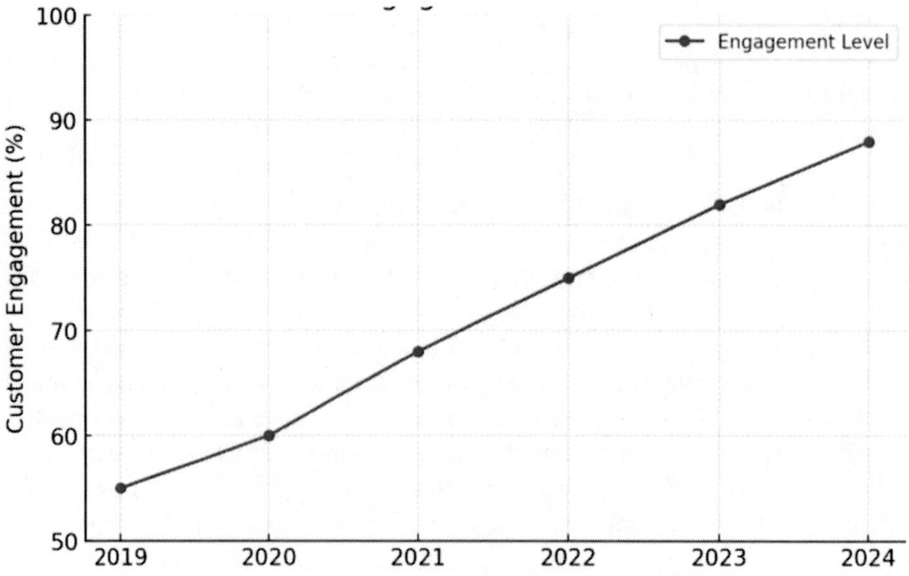

Figure 9. Increase in customer engagement with AI-driven immersive CX.

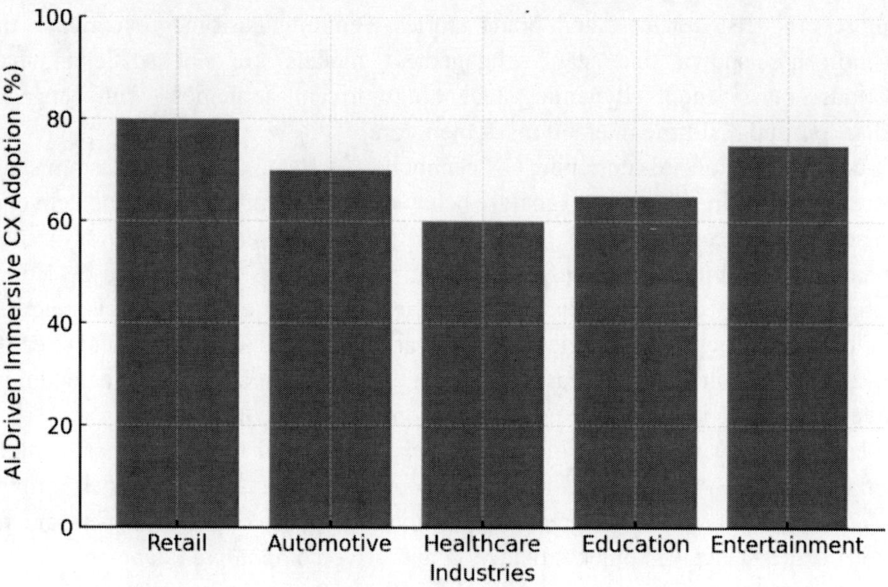

Figure 10. AI-driven Immersive CX adoption across industries.

Figure 9 illustrates the increasing impact of AI-driven immersive technologies on customer engagement over the years. As businesses progressively integrate AI into AR, VR, and MR experiences, customer engagement levels have risen from 55% in 2019 to 88% in 2024. This upward trend highlights how personalized immersive experiences are fostering deeper brand-customer interactions, enhancing satisfaction, and encouraging longer engagement durations. The continuous advancements in AI, including improved sentiment analysis, predictive personalisation, and adaptive virtual assistants, have contributed to this consistent growth in customer engagement across various industries.

Figure 10 presents a comparison of AI-driven immersive CX adoption across different industries. The retail sector leads with the highest adoption rate, as AI-powered AR try-ons and personalized shopping experiences have become mainstream. The entertainment industry follows closely, utilising AI to enhance VR gaming, adaptive storytelling, and interactive experiences. The automotive sector has also embraced AI-driven immersive CX, employing VR-powered showrooms and AI-enhanced virtual assistants for customer engagement. Healthcare and education sectors, while slightly behind, are steadily integrating AI-driven immersive solutions to enhance training simulations, virtual learning, and patient interaction. The widespread adoption of AI-powered immersive technologies underscores their role in transforming customer interactions, making experiences more engaging, relevant, and effective.

Conclusion

Immersive technology, with AI at its core, is transforming customer experience through highly interactive, engaging, and personalized interactions across various domains. The intersection of Virtual Reality (VR), Augmented Reality (AR), and Mixed Reality (MR) has bridged digital and physical spaces, giving consumers more intuitive and interactive ways through which they can explore products, services, and brand stories. Building customer experience through digitalisation has shown that static engagement models are not sufficient; business organisations must adopt dynamic, technology-driven strategies with engagement, personalisation, and real-time interactions at their core.

AI's contribution towards enriching CX cannot be overstated. AI-driven customisation has empowered business organisations to analyse behaviour, predict preferences, and deliver highly personalised experiences within AR, VR, and MR realms. AI-driven virtual assistants have made interactions with customers easier, and sentiment analysis and emotion detection have empowered brands to alter offerings, so that each customer engagement is relevant and effective, practical. These technologies have increased customer satisfaction and strengthened brand loyalty, as customers are increasingly drawn towards organizations that offer unique and immersive experiences tailored to their specifications.

The continued advancement of immersive technologies and AI will further revolutionize customer experience. As hardware becomes more accessible and AI models grow more sophisticated, businesses will have greater opportunities to create seamless, hyper-personalized interactions that enhance customer satisfaction and drive competitive advantage. Companies that embrace immersive CX will set new industry benchmarks and redefine how customers engage with brands in an increasingly digital world. The future of customer experience is immersive, intelligent, and deeply personalized, making it imperative for businesses to integrate these technologies into their long-term strategies.

References

[1] Tom Dieck, M. Claudia, and Dai-in Danny Han. "The role of immersive technology in customer experience management." *Journal of marketing theory and practice* 30, no. 1 (2022): 108-119.

[2] Flavián, Carlos, Iis P. Tussyadiah, and Carlos Orús. "How immersive technologies are redefining the customer journey. Guest editorial." *International Journal of Contemporary Hospitality Management* 36, no. 11 (2024): 3557-3565.

[3] Porancea-Răulea, Andreea. "Improving Customer Satisfaction in the Immersive Experiences Era." *Revista Academiei Fortelor Terestre* 29, no. 4 (2024).

[4] Flavián, Carlos, Sergio Ibáñez-Sánchez, and Carlos Orús. "The impact of virtual, augmented and mixed reality technologies on the customer experience." *Journal of business research* 100 (2019): 547-560.

[5] Hoyer, Wayne D., Mirja Kroschke, Bernd Schmitt, Karsten Kraume, and Venkatesh Shankar. "Transforming the customer experience through new technologies." *Journal of interactive marketing* 51, no. 1 (2020): 57-71.

[6] Uwaoma, Prisca Ugomma, Emmanuel Osamuyimen Eboigbe, Nsisong Louis Eyo-Udo, A. C. Ijiga, S. Kaggwa, and A. I. Daraojimba. "Mixed reality in US retail: A review: Analyzing the immersive shopping experiences, customer engagement, and potential economic implications." *World Journal of Advanced Research and Reviews* 20, no. 3 (2023): 966-981.

[7] Parise, Salvatore, Patricia J. Guinan, and Ron Kafka. "Solving the crisis of immediacy: How digital technology can transform the customer experience." *Business Horizons* 59, no. 4 (2016): 411-420.

[8] Abou-Shouk, Mohamed, Nagwa Zouair, Ayman Abdelhakim, Hany Roshdy, and Marwa Abdel-Jalil. "The effect of immersive technologies on tourist satisfaction and loyalty: the mediating role of customer engagement and customer perceived value." *International Journal of Contemporary Hospitality Management* 36, no. 11 (2024): 3587-3606.

[9] Hwangbo, Hyunwoo, Yang Sok Kim, and Kyung Jin Cha. "Use of the smart store for persuasive marketing and immersive customer experiences: A case study of Korean apparel enterprise." *Mobile Information Systems* 2017, no. 1 (2017): 4738340.

[10] Vergallo, Roberto, and Luca Mainetti. "The role of technology in improving the Customer Experience in the banking sector: A systematic mapping study." *IEEE Access* 10 (2022): 118024-118042.

[11] Hudson, John. "Virtual immersive shopping experiences in metaverse environments: predictive customer analytics, data visualisation algorithms, and smart retailing technologies." *Linguistic and Philosophical Investigations* 21 (2022): 236-251.

[12] Baxter, Gavin, and Thomas Hainey. "Using immersive technologies to enhance the student learning experience." *Interactive Technology and Smart Education* 21, no. 3 (2024): 403-425.

[13] Ambika, Anupama, Hyunju Shin, and Varsha Jain. "Immersive technologies and consumer behavior: A systematic review of two decades of research." *Australian Journal of Management* 50, no. 1 (2025): 55-79.

[14] Oyedokun, Tunde Toyese. "Digitally Enhanced World of Realities: Immersive Technologies and Innovative Business Models." In *AI-Driven Business Model Innovation*, pp. 37-70. IGI Global Scientific Publishing, 2025.

[15] Bonetti, Francesca, Eleonora Pantano, Gary Warnaby, and Lee Quinn. "Augmenting reality: Fusing consumers' experiences and interactions with immersive technologies in physical retail settings." *International Journal of Technology Marketing* 13, no. 3-4 (2019): 260-284.

[16] Rachmawati, Aliviya Kurniya, and Hengki Tornando. "Challenges in Consumer Adaptation to Immersive Technologies: A Comprehensive Literature Review." *eCo-Buss* 7, no. 1 (2024): 317-328.

[17] Devi, G. Dharani, Neeraj Kumar, J. Manikandan, and V. Rekha. "Innovative brain tumor detection: Stacked random support vector-based hybrid gazelle coati algorithm." *Biomedical Signal Processing and Control* 101 (2025): 107156.

[18] Pleyers, Gordy, and Ingrid Poncin. "Non-immersive virtual reality technologies in real estate: How customer experience drives attitudes toward properties and the service provider." *Journal of Retailing and Consumer Services* 57 (2020): 102175.

[19] Nhan, Vo Kim, Ho Tien Dung, and Nguyen Thanh Vu. "A conceptual model for studying the immersive mobile augmented reality application-enhanced experience." *Heliyon* 8, no. 8 (2022).

[20] Manikandan, J., and K. Jayashree. "Enhancing lung nodule classification: a novel CViEBi-CBGWO approach with integrated image preprocessing." *Journal of imaging informatics in medicine* 37, no. 5 (2024): 2108.

[21] Baddam, Parikshith Reddy. "Revolutionizing customer experience through innovative digital marketing approaches." *Global Disclosure of Economics and Business* 11, no. 2 (2022): 71-86.

[22] Sharma, Nidhi, and Divya Mahajan. "Enhancing Customer Experience by Semi-Immersive Virtual Reality in Real Estate Business." In *Multidisciplinary Applications of Extended Reality for Human Experience*, pp. 81-95. IGI Global, 2024.

[23] Razak, Ismail. "Augmented reality marketing: enhancing customer experience through latest technology." *Jurnal Multidisiplin Sahombu* 4, no. 01 (2024): 10-17.

[24] Yadav, Usha, and Sheetal Soni. "An Inferential Analysis of Customer Experience Transformation Through AR VR Immersive and Collaborative Environments." In *International Conference on Artificial-Business Analytics, Quantum and Machine Learning*, pp. 127-139. Singapore: Springer Nature Singapore, 2023.

[25] Orús, Carlos, Sergio Ibáñez-Sánchez, and Carlos Flavián. "Enhancing the customer experience with virtual and augmented reality: The impact of content and device type." *International Journal of Hospitality Management* 98 (2021): 103019.

[26] Scholz, Joachim, and Andrew N. Smith. "Augmented reality: Designing immersive experiences that maximize consumer engagement." *Business Horizons* 59, no. 2 (2016): 149-161.

[27] Rane, Nitin, Saurabh Choudhary, and Jayesh Rane. "Metaverse for enhancing customer loyalty: effective strategies to improve customer relationship, service, engagement, satisfaction, and experience." *Service, Engagement, Satisfaction, and Experience (November 1, 2023)* (2023).

[28] Pantano, Eleonora, Giuseppe Pedeliento, and George Christodoulides. "A strategic framework for technological innovations in support of the customer experience: A focus on luxury retailers." *Journal of Retailing and Consumer Services* 66 (2022): 102959.

[29] Fan, Xiaojun, Xinyu Jiang, and Nianqi Deng. "Immersive technology: A meta-analysis of augmented/virtual reality applications and their impact on tourism experience." *Tourism Management* 91 (2022): 104534.

Chapter 8

Design Methodologies for Immersive Environments

Keerthi Rohan
and J. Jeyalakshmi*
Department of Computer Science and Engineering, Amrita School of Computing,
Amrita Vishwa Vidhyapeetham, Chennai, India

Abstract

Immersive spaces, supported by AR, VR, and MR, are redefining the nature of digital interaction in a wide array of industries such as gaming, healthcare, education, and enterprise sectors. The design and the development of such spaces must be marked by a true multidisciplinary approach combining human-centered design (HCD), spatial computing, cognitive sciences, and real-time interaction methodologies toward creating engaging user experiences. This chapter presents the core design methodologies enhancing immersion, such as iterative prototyping, adaptive user interface design, multimodal interaction techniques, and environmental storytelling. User experience (UX) best practices are defined, stressing essential issues such as motion sickness, cognitive load, interaction complexity, and accessibility. Moreover, we also look at the contributions of artificial intelligence (AI) and machine learning (ML) in personalised adaptive experiences, real-time scene generation, and intelligent virtual agents. Integration with haptic feedback, eye tracking, and spatial audio offers higher realism and interaction fidelity. By applying strong design frameworks with iterative testing, experts will create those immersive systems ready to be behind the development of scalable and intuitive systems for meaningful and seamless interactions between users and virtual environments.

Keywords: artificial intelligence, Augmented Reality, Virtual Reality, Mixed Reality, immersive technology

1. Introduction

Augmented reality (AR), virtual reality (VR), and mixed reality (MR) all fall under the umbrella term immersive technologies. These technologies transform the user experience when

* Corresponding Author's Email: j_jeyalakshmi@ch.amrita.edu

In: Shaping Tomorrow
Editors: Prithi Samuel, A. Sathya, Balamurugan Balusamy et al.
ISBN: 979-8-90134-076-9

integrating with digital content. They intensify the presence, engagement, and interactivity aspects of a product, thereby becoming applicable in diverse fields like gaming, healthcare, education, industrial training, and remote collaboration. Users experience content embedded in digital and physical environments more intuitively and naturally, thus creating spaces for new innovations [1]. The quantitative figures regarding the global adoption of immersive technologies are shown in Figure 1.

Nevertheless, the design process of an immersive experience is more than a technology issue; it entails a systematic approach to user experience (UX) design, cognitive psychology, and real-time system development. Contrasting with their 2D counterparts, immersive environments invoke different ways of navigation, interaction mechanisms, and feedback. Poorly designed experiences can cause motion sickness, cognitive overload, or just loss of interest [2, 3].

Immersive environments are classified into three main categories in Table 1:

Table 1. Classification of immersive environments

Technology	Description
Virtual Reality (VR)	Totally immerses users in a computer-generated environmental experience wherein they are totally divorced from the real world [4]
Augmented Reality (AR)	Value-added experience in the real-world environment through a digital overlay on objects, enabling users to manipulate virtual items within the parameters of a real space [5]
Mixed Reality (MR)	Blending virtual and real, it is the possibility that allows the end user to interact continuously and in real-time with the remaining spatial awareness [6, 7]

These technologies, to achieve their full effect, must follow specific design principles that enable seamless human interactions and mitigate certain usability problems, such as motion sickness, poor depth perception, and confusing controls [8, 9].

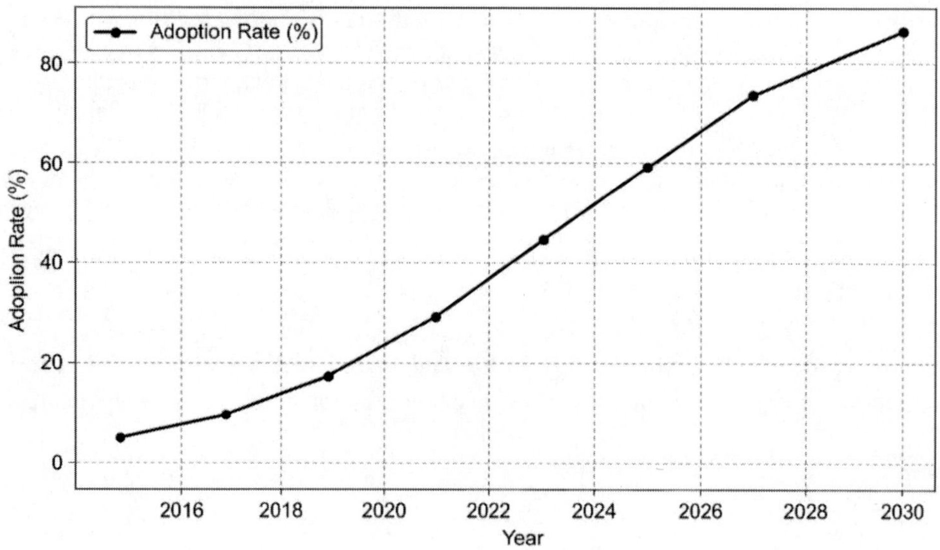

Figure 1. Global adoption of immersive technologies (2015-2030).

The new generation of immersive technologies is not without challenges; indeed, with increasing usage comes a greater need for structured and conscious design methodologies for effective user experiences [10]. The really compelling design difficulties are in the following:

- Motion Discomfort: Latency, low frame rates, or non-natural movement patterns tend to make the user uncomfortable and nauseated [11, 12]
- Cognitive Overload: Flooding users with too much visual/auditory information into the space reduces engagement [13, 14].
- Accessibility: Usability for persons with disabilities-whether visual, auditory, or motor impairments [15, 16].
- User Adaptability: Complying with the nature of the user and experience and thereby designing intuitive interfaces so that users can learn quickly about interaction with the virtual environment [17].

The following sections of this chapter, in Table 2, discuss different design methodologies that will be highly essential in formulating an immersive experience.

Table 2. Design methodologies in immersive experience

Methodology	Focus Area
Human-Centered Design (HCD)	Prioritising user needs and intuitive interactions.
Agile & Iterative Development	Using rapid prototyping and real-time user feedback to refine immersive experiences.
Spatial Computing Principles	Effectively design 3-dimensional interfaces in line with human perception and other ergonomic considerations.
Challenges & Ethical Considerations	Safety, privacy, inclusion, and ethical considerations in immersive environments [18]

These methodologies, therefore, provide the designers and developers with tools to create large, richly engaged immersive experiences that can be readily attuned to the users and their seamless blending of digital spaces into physical contexts [19].

2. Human-Centered Design in Immersive Environments

Human-Centred Design (HCD) is a problem-solving paradigm embracing users' needs, behaviours, and experiences into the design of immersive environments, such as Virtual Reality (VR), Augmented Reality (AR), and Mixed Reality (MR). Unlike traditional software development, multidisciplinary teams that may prioritise the function, the approach of HCD assures immersive experiences that are easy to use, accessible/applicable, and comfortable for anyone.

As it now stands, users of immersive environments are no longer passive observers; rather, they actively participate in the digital space. This change brings in considerations for ergonomics, cognition, and sense, so as to preclude disorientation, fatigue, and frustration. HCD borrows some of its fundamentals from:

- User Centered Design – Understanding user expectations, physical constraints, and interaction patterns [20]

- Iterative Prototyping – Development in a changing process according to repeated real user feedback.
- Accessibility & Inclusivity – Designing for users having diverse needs and capabilities.
- Cognitive Load Management – Designing interactions with natural patterns for interactions bestowed on the user.

2. Key Aspects of Human-Centered Design in Immersive Environments

2.1. Understand User Behaviour and Interaction Patterns

In the design of immersive experiences, there is a necessity to understand how humans move, interact with, and process their environment naturally, especially in the space-altering 3D environments [21]. This entails the following:

- Gaze-based interaction: Making eye tracking yield information about the understanding of where a user's eye is focused on eye-informed guidance for interaction.
- Hand tracking & gesture control: More naturalistic interaction without using controllers.
- Voice commands & speech recognition: Hands-free interaction in AR/VR application scenarios.
- Haptic Feedback & Sensory Integration: Simulates reality touch-based feedback for immersion.

For instance, one type of example is eye-tracking technology used in VR training simulations, so that wherever the user is looking is known. They then ensure that the most critical instructions would be in their FOV without distractions.

2.2. Motion Sickness and Discomfort Reduction

Among the numerous problems posed in immersive environments is motion sickness arising from the difference between visual perception and physical activity [22, 23]. The principles of HCD recommend the following to overcome this challenge:

- Frame Rates Maintain: at least 90+.
- Teleportation-based navigation instead of artificial movement.
- No motion: Stable focal points.
- Allow customizable settings to adjust motion comfort levels.

For example, a VR flight simulator might allow some users to experience dizziness from rapid movements. Some HCD-driven solutions might include allowing the user to set field-of-view (FOV) restrictions to reduce motion sickness [24].

2.3. Spatial UI and Interaction Design

Traditional buttons, 2D menus, or icons work in a very poor and inefficient manner in a 3D immersive environment. A good spatial user interface (SUI) conforms to the following principles:

- Allow Natural Movements: utilise the hands to grab, rotate, or scale objects.
- Adaptive UI Positioning: only position interactive elements within easy reach without blocking the user's vision.
- Minimising Cognitive Load: Avoid cluttering screens and show only the data needed when needed.

Example: In an AR-assisted surgery, an adaptive UI ensures that a surgeon only sees the patient's critical vitals and overlays on the operating field.

3. Agile and Iterative Development for AR, VR, and MR

Immersive technologies, ranging from Augmented Reality (AR), Virtual Reality (VR), and Mixed Reality (MR), need a flexible, self-driven approach for development. In contrast to traditional software applications, where user interfaces and interactivity tend to be entirely standardised, immersive experiences consist of dynamic 3-D environments, real-time rendering, and spatial interactions. It is a process that requires constant refinement.

Agile and iterative development methodologies provide a scaled and flexible framework for the design of such environments. If the principles of such methodologies, such as rapid prototyping, continuous user feedback, and iterative improvements, are followed, issues such as motion sickness, usability challenges, and complex interactions can be caught at an early design stage. Yes, it is all about why Agile development is important for AR, VR, and MR. Immersive, indeed, defines unique propositions to which Waterfall and other traditional methodologies do not lend themselves easily. Some of these include:

- User Interactions That Cannot Be Predicted: Unlike environments that can be controlled with relatively static 2D applications, personifying immersion requires really intuitive, ADAPTIVE user interfaces that are based on movement, gestures, and voice.
- Hardware & Software Limitations: The various devices (e.g., a VR headset, AR glasses, mobile AR, etc.) come equipped with different processing capabilities, display qualities, and tracking accuracy attributes.
- User Comfort & Ergonomics: Motion sickness, cognitive load, and other types of interaction-related fatigue need testing and iteration in the real world.
- Immature Technology Stack: Immersive technologies change rapidly, very frequently integrating new rendering engines, input devices, and methods of spatial computing.

Agile development has flexibility and adaptability because it allows teams to test, adjust, and iterate throughout the development cycle rather than waiting until the product is truly finalized [25].

3. The Agile Process for Immersive Development

Agile consists of short, iterative cycles or sprints wherein a product will have been functional and will be enhanced after user testing. Key stages for Agile development applied to AR/VR/MR include:

3.1. Ideation and Planning

Define user needs and experience goals for immersion. Identify hardware constraints (e.g., VR headsets vs. AR mobile devices). Establish core interaction models (gesture controls, gaze tracking, haptic feedback). Create a storyboard or low-fidelity wireframes to map out the experience. For example, A firefighter's training simulation in a VR environment would likely begin by storyboarding fire scenarios, performing fairly realistic actions associated with those scenarios (i.e., pick up a fire hose), and establishing user goals (for example: safely evacuating the building).

3.2. Rapid Prototyping and Testing

Build low-fidelity prototypes using simple models with placeholder assets. Hold playtesting sessions to see what the user does. Before committing to high-fidelity assets, iteratively improve based on testing. Rapidly prototype using Unity, Unreal Engine, or WebXR [26].

For example, an AR-based museum guide might first use basic object tracking and UI overlays for testing before advanced features like AI-driven voice assistance were added.

3.3. Sprint-Based Development and Iteration

Develop features over 2-4 week sprints aimed at specific goals (for example, enhancing object tracking, refining gesture recognition).

Each iteration should be end-user tested to gather feedback about usability, realism, and comfort level.

Based on motion sickness tests, hand tracking accuracy, and spatial interaction ease, UI/UX should be adapted.

Multiple sprints added haptic feedback, sound design, and AI-based adaptive elements.

Example:

Simple model placement would define the basis for Mixed Reality architecture visualisation, which is likely to start, but over time will be integrated with sharing capabilities and occlusion handling, augmented lighting control in real time, and eventually develop interactive collaboration tools.

3.4. Performance Optimisation and Refinement

Rendering should be ensured to be real-time efficient (60-90 FPS for VR to beat motion sickness). Assets should be optimised, minimising load time while increasing reactivity in AR applications.

Physics would be calibrated to human belief expectations [27].

Flight would have extensive A/B testing with different end users' preferences (i.e., teleportation movement vs. free movement in VR).

4. Challenges in Designing Immersive Environments

Designing immersive environments for Augmented Reality (AR), Virtual Reality (VR), and Mixed Reality (MR) goes beyond software and UI/UX design alone. In contrast to conventional applications, immersive experiences require developers to take into consideration the whole range of human perception, real-time interactivity, spatial awareness, and, of course, user comfort.

Poorly done design may lead to motion sickness, cognitive overload, technical limitations, and usability issues, with the resulting user experience being unintuitive or entirely repugnant. This section deals largely with the major issues related to immersive designing environments, in addition to possible optimistic solutions toward overcoming such barriers [28].

4.1. Motion Sickness and User Comfort

Motion sickness (simulator sickness) is one of the most severe problems that exists in immersive environments, most especially the VR ones. It is caused when the visual and vestibular (inner ear) inputs do not match. When the brain feels as though it is moving (the action is occurring in a visual format) and the body does not act like it is moving, it leads to dizziness, disorientation and nausea.

Some Common Causes of Motion Sickness in AR/VR/MR:

- Low Frame Rates – Lags when moving below 90 FPS can make physical motion seem sluggish.
- Latency Issues – Head or body movements causing a delay in the user's perspective.
- Artificial Locomotion – Using the joystick to move without corresponding body motion.
- Field of View (FOV) & Peripheral Vision Issues – Sudden drastic changes in the degree without smooth transitions irritate the brain.

Ways through which Motion Sickness could be Mitigated:

- High Frame Rates: (90+ FPS in VR, above 60 FPS in AR).
- Use Teleportation-Based Locomotion, Instead of Continuous Movement.
- Includes User-Configurable Comfort Settings like: Snap-Facing, FOV Reduction, Motion Blur Controls.
- Fixed Reference Points to Ground Users (e.g., a stationary cockpit in flight simulators).

Example: In VR driving simulators, inserting an artificial steering wheel as a fixed reference greatly reduces the motion sickness caused, once again, by clearing people's focus [29].

4.2. Interaction Design Challenges

Standard UI elements such as buttons, drop-downs, and menus transfer poorly into immersive environments, prompting designers to create spatial interactions that are seemingly natural but at the same time easy to use.

Some Common Interaction Challenges:

- Gesture & Hand Tracking Issues – Too difficult for users to get correct and reliable gesture recognition.
- Eye-Tracking & Gaze Navigation – Accidental clicks as a result of unintentional gaze on objects.
- 3D Space Floating Menus Obstruct & Become Unreachable - Floating menus in 3D space can become hard to reach without access.

Best Practice Standards in Immersive Environments for Interaction Design:

- Design for Hand and Eye Tracking, Not Just Controllers.
- Hover Vote Selection, with Visual Feedback, Instead of Clicking.
- Allow Voice Commands to Actuate Hands-free Interaction.
- Minimise UI Clutter—Show Only Contextually Relevant Information.

Example: In Microsoft HoloLens AR applications, menus are placed well within easy hand reach instead of being placed very high or too low in space.

4.3. Cognitive Load and Information Overload

Immersive environments may provide too much information and thus become overwhelming. Unlike interfaces on screens, where a user may concentrate on one part of the screen at a time, the totality of immersion usually demands spatial consciousness as well as split attention between different aspects at all times [30].

Cognitive Overload Causes in AR/VR/MR:

- Excessive Visual Clutter – Too many UI elements overwhelm users.
- Navigation Systems that Require Complex Types – Non-intuitive movement and menu systems increase cognitive strain.
- Involuntary Interaction Models – Familiar gestures or movement techniques confuse the user.

Reducing Cognitive Load:

- Progressively Revealing - Show Information Only When Required.
- Employing Audio Cues Instead of Visual Elements.
- Minimalistic and Context-Aware Interfaces.
- Give Users Control over the Flow of Information to their Pace

Example: IRLs in VR training use this methodology wherein only the next required task will be displayed rather than the entire workflow so that they can pay more attention to, and remember, the instruction better.

4.4. Hardware Limitations and Performance Constraints

Immersive experiences demand high processing power, low latencies, and real-time rendering. However, none of these devices is immune to the increasingly complex requirements of a 3D virtual world that runs at high resolutions.

Major Hardware Issues:

- Processing Power and GPU Limitations – High-fidelity VR needs highly efficient GPUs, which none of the mobile AR devices have.
- Battery Life Problems – These are highly power-demanding devices in the case of AR headsets, as well as the standalone ones of VR.
- Limits on Field of View (FOV) and Display – Injection of limited FOV can lessen the feel of immersion.

Optimisation Techniques:

- Level of Details (LOD) Techniques to Reduce Rendering Load.
- Performance Optimise Assets Without Compromising Visual Quality.
- Use Cloud-Based Processing for Complex AR/VR Applications.

Example: Real-time occlusion techniques inject realism without GPU overload for mobile device AR applications.

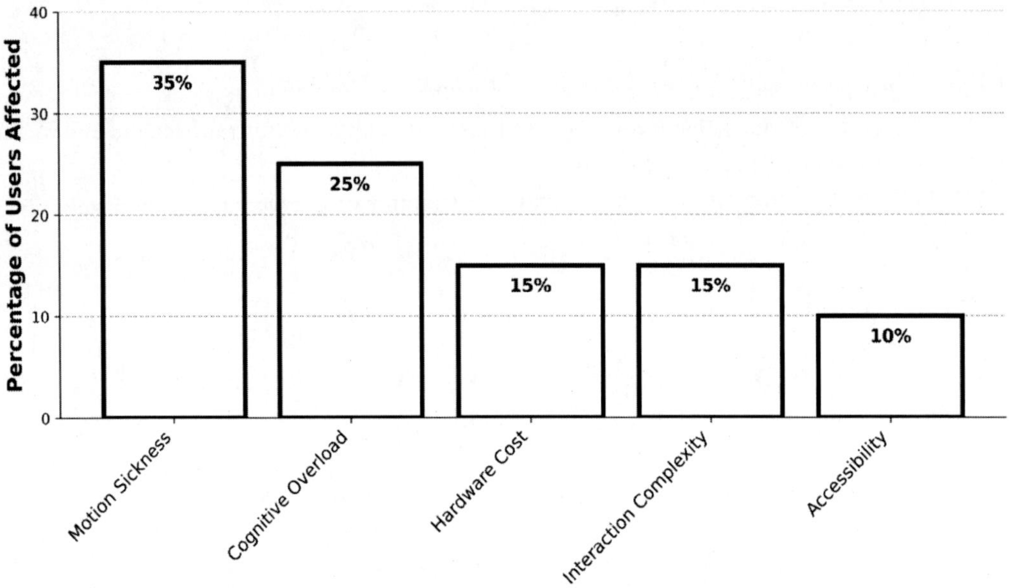

Figure 2. Challenges in immersive design.

5. Ethical and Privacy Concerns in Immersive Environments

Privacy issues arising from data collection by AI sources involve biometric tracking and observation of the user behaviour, which in turn creates serious concern over privacy as it collects personal data, biometrics, and behaviour data. The major challenge of Immersive Design is shown in Figure 2.

Major Privacy and Ethical Issues:

- Eye-Tracking and Gaze Data Collection – Commonly used for advertisement purposes but raises questions on whether it can be consent.
- Real-world Scanning in AR/MR – There is better tracking, hence allowing applications to store user environments.
- Safety in Social VR and Online – This includes harassment and trolling, along with misconduct performed in virtual commons.

Proposed Solutions:

- Full Control for Users about What Data Will Be Collected.
- Transparent Data Policies for Biometric Tracking.
- Stronger Moderation & Reporting Tools in Social VR.

Example: Meta's Horizon Worlds (VR Social Space) has had issues with privacy and introduced stricter personal boundaries into virtual space to protect against harassment.

5. Future Trends and Innovations in Immersive Environments

Extended Reality (XR), including Augmented Reality (AR), Virtual Reality (VR), and Mixed Reality (MR), is pivoting rapidly due to advancements in artificial intelligence (AI), spatial computing, 5G connectivity, and brain-computer interfaces (BCI). This will result in the metamorphosis of immersive experiences, becoming less restricted, more realistic, and increasingly personalised, with applications in healthcare, education, gaming, and enterprise solutions. Newer technologies are maturing to the extent that immersive experiences will now offer a more natural, responsive, and seamless interaction. This section considers some of the major trends and innovations that will shape the coming life of immersive environments. Figure 3 lists the emerging trends in immersive environments.

Artificial Intelligence Allows Personalized Experiences and Adaptive Environments Artificial Intelligence (AI) plays a prominent role in enriching the immersive experience by creating environments that are dynamically responsive to user stimuli, behaviours, emotional state, and preferences. Homepage Innovations in AI for Immersive Environments:

- AI Avatars & Assistants – Realistic NPCs (non-player characters) in VR that react intelligently with user interactions.
- Adaptive Learning Systems – AI-driven VR training that automatically increases or decreases difficulty based on user performance.
- Emotion Recognition & Adaptive UX – AI that changes the experience in real-time by analysing facial expressions, gaze tracking, and body language.

For example, NPCs driven by AI can dynamically respond to users in Meta's Horizon Worlds to ensure even more realistic and engaging social interactions.

5.1. Cloud XR Streaming (AR/VR without the Need for Expensive Hardware)

Cloud XR streaming is fast becoming a new method by which low-cost or no-cost users share high-fidelity immersive content on light devices by cloud processing. One of the biggest roadblocks to mass adoption of the tech: The excessive hardware requirements—high-performance VR headsets and AR glasses—damage all options of essentially new ways of doing things.

So, the cloud XR is a working solution for:

- A low-latency rendering process occurs on the server in the cloud instead of on the local device.
- 5G and Edge Computing reduce latency to allow for real-time streaming.
- Access cloud services directly from mobile devices to enjoy AR/VR without carrying or investing in heavy hardware.

Example: NVIDIA CloudXR allows VR/AR streaming from resource-rich cloud GPUs to lightweight headsets, and high-level experiences become accessible for all.

5.2. Brain-Computer Interface for Neural Interaction

Brain-Computer Interfaces (BCI) give the user the possibility to command an AR/VR environment through neural signals without the use of physical controllers, creating a hands-off and intuitive interaction model.

BCI Deployment in Immersive Environments:

- Mind-Controlled Interfaces – Users navigate in VR environments using brain signals.
- Neural Feedback in Healthcare – BCI-controlled virtual therapy for stroke rehabilitation and mental healthcare.
- Enhanced Accessibility – Immersive experiences created for the use of individuals with movement difficulties.

Example: Neuralink & OpenBCI are working to develop a BCI-controlled VR and AR system to allow its users to drag and drop digital objects using only their thoughts.

5.3. Haptic Feedback and Full-Body Immersion

While visual and auditory feedback in immersive environments have made great strides, touch feedback (haptic feedback) is the next promising frontier. The future of immersive systems will include tactile sensations, force feedback, and perhaps even temperature simulation, providing a fully immersive experience.

Key Innovations in Haptic Technology:

- Haptic Gloves & Suits – Wearables providing realistic touch sensations (e.g., feeling the weight of a virtual object).
- Ultrasonic & Air-Based Haptics – Use of ultrasound waves to provide non-contact feedback.
- Tactile Textures & Material Simulation – Surfaces in VR that feel soft, rough, or slippery as per their respective contexts.

Example: HaptX VR gloves enable users to "feel" virtual objects through the provision of force feedback in their training simulations and gaming.

5.4. Spatial Computing and AR Cloud for Persistent Digital Twins

Spatial computing and AR Cloud technologies enable the creation of AR experiences persisted across time and devices, allowing users to interact with shared digital content in the real world.

Applications of Spatial Computing & AR Cloud:

- Persistent AR Content – AR objects retain their position even after the application is restarted.

- Real-Time 3D Mapping & Navigation – AR-powered smart cities with interactive overlays.
- Enterprise & Industrial Applications – Digital twins of factories and urban environments for real-time monitoring and predictive analyses.

Example: Google's ARCore and Niantic's Lightship ARDK allow persistent AR experiences in which digital objects remain anchored in real-world locations.

5.5. Holographic Communication Enabled by 6G Towards Hyper-Connected Immersive Environments

Though 5G has vastly improved connectivity for AR/VR applications, the advent of 6G, which is slated for 2030, should offer ultra-low latency and near-instantaneous data transfer with AI-powered network optimisations. This will reward hyper-connected immersive experiences that seamlessly blend real and virtual worlds.

Impediments Introduced by 6G to AR/VR/MR:

- Ultra-Reliable Low Latency Communication (URLLC) – Responsiveness, i.e., near-instant for real-time interactions.
- Massive Device Connectivity – Seamless AR overlays on urban infrastructure and IoT devices.

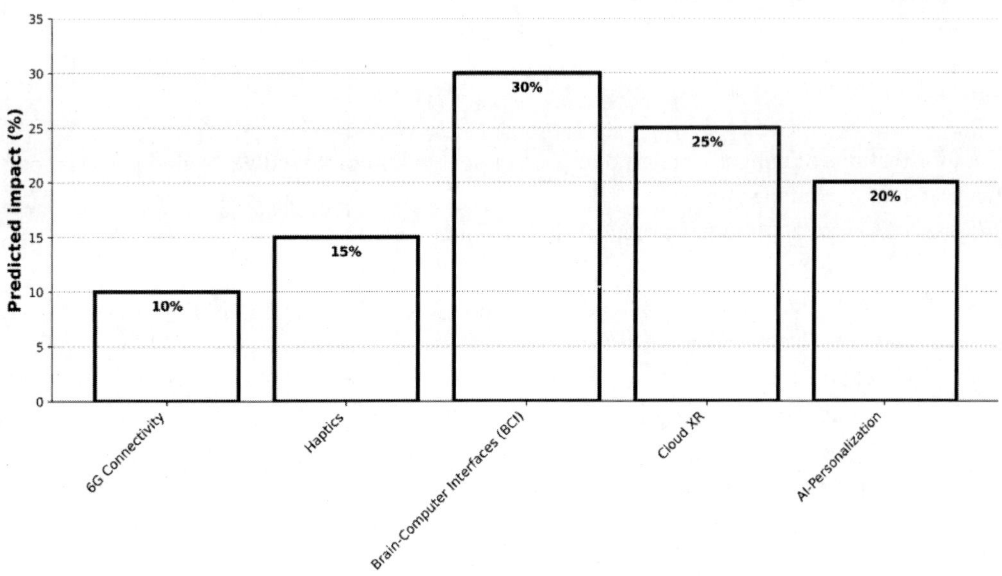

Figure 3. Future trends in AR/VR/MR (2030 Predictions).

Example: 6G will support a holographic form of communication, allowing older persons to have augmented realities of bodily-sized two-way interaction with each other instantaneously.

A Call for Ethical Discussions and the Next Generation of Digital Presence Ethical considerations in privacy, data security, and identity will be prominent as immersive environments grow in realism and global acceptance. Ethical Challenges of Tomorrow's Immersion

- Human & Biometric Privacy – How should issues relating to the storage and usage of eye-tracking data, facial evaluation, and neural data be handled?
- Deepfakes & Theft of Virtual Identity – Protecting avatars and digital entities through some form of regulation against the aforementioned.

6. Ethical Considerations in Immersive Technology

New ethical predicaments come into being with the rise of Augmented Reality (AR), Virtual Reality (VR), and Mixed Reality (MR) technologies concerning privacy and data security, identity in the digital world, accessibility, and personal psychological well-being. The immersive environments capture the user data, which includes very intimate and personal parameters from eye movements and biometric signals to hand gestures, voice patterns, and even neural activity in Brain-Computer Interfaces (BCI) cases. Not properly designed technically and ethically, the technology can lead users to violate their privacy, be manipulated, become addicted, and be excluded from society. This section discusses the main ethical issues posed by these types of immersive environments and proposes ways for their responsible design.

6.1. Risks of Privacy and Data Safety

The major features of ethical concern over immersive technology revolve around personal data collection, storage, and usage.

Types of Data Captured in Immersive Environments:

- Eye Tracking and Gaze Data – Navigation, advertisement, and behaviour analytics
- Hand and Gesture Tracking- Records patterns of movement that could be employed for surveillance.
- Voice and Facial Recognition – All the things so-called "identity hijacking" in biopolymeric tracking.
- Environmental Scanning- (AR/MR) Maps real spaces that have the potential of exposing sensitive spots.

Privacy Issues include:

- Surveillant Users – Actions can be followed against a person without formally consenting to it.
- Monetising Data – Revenue generation due to hyper-targeted advertisements without the consumer knowing is possible through gaze tracking.

- Hacking and Biometric Theft – Through retinal scans, fingerprints, and voice signatures, misappropriation can occur.

Possible Solutions:

- Full Privacy Disclosures – All info generated about the data collected and its treatment should be made known to users.
- Decentralised and Encrypted Data Storage: High-end security against unauthorised access and reduces hacking advantages.
- User-controlled Permissions: The user must be able to opt in and opt out of all the data tracking features.

Example: Data usage by eye-tracking from the Meta Quest headsets for advertising provokes discussion if users should enjoy greater control over the gathered data.

6.2. Digital Identity, Deepfakes and Virtual Manipulation

As immersive environments allow users to create avatars similar to real people, deepfakes and digital twins, ethical issues mainly involve identity theft, fake news, and deception.

Digital Identity Theft Risks:

- Cloning Avatars: Unauthorised duplication of a person's digital likeness for ill purposes.
- Deepfake Manipulation in VR or AR: Using AI-generated voices and faces for scams and misinformation.
- Virtual Impersonation in the Social VR World: Pretending to be someone else for malicious intent.

Potential solutions:

- Avatar cloning prevention will be ensured under a blockchain-based digital identity verification.
- Authenticity guaranteed by the Ethical AI for Deepfake Detection will add up to the equations of social VR interaction.
- Stricter Digital Identity Theft Regulations: Governments and firms should put very strict identity verification protocols in place.

Example: Users impersonating others on VR social platforms like Horizon Worlds or AltspaceVR lead to fraud and harassment.

6.3. Psychological and Behavioural Effects of Immersion

Given the hyperrealism of an immersive environment, it raises a number of concerns regarding the potential psychological impact and addiction and the blurring of lines between the virtual and real.

Major Psychological Risks:

- Overindulgence in VR and dissociation- Spending too much time in virtual spaces translates into social isolation.
- Distorted Reality Perfectionistic: Over-exposure to immersive material tends to lead to inaccurate recall of memories or decreased emotional connection to worldly occurrences.
- Psychological Manipulation in the case of AR Advertising: Integrated advertising with reality may result in failures in discerning between authentic and sponsored content.

Potential Solutions:

- Limits to Usage Time & Digital Well-being Features give incentives for healthy immersive experiences.
- Transparency in AR/VR Advertising: AR ads should be clearly marked to avoid misleading advertising.
- Mental Health Interventions in VR: Use immersive therapy to treat PTSD, phobias, and anxiety.

Example: Cases of users spending over 8 hours a day in virtual worlds have been reported on VRChat as expressed concern about digital addiction and dissociation.

6.4. Ethical Design and Accessibility in Immersive Environments

It is a primary ethical responsibility of developers to guarantee design that is fair, inclusive, and accessible. The great majority of users with disabilities are being discarded from immersion today, resulting from design decisions not made correctly.

Ethical Design Issues:

- Lack of Accessibility Elements: Not many VR apps incorporate screen readers, voice commands, or use adaptive controls.
- AI-driven Avatars: AI-based facial recognition techniques really fail in detecting other ethnicities, genders, and disabilities.
- Affordability Level: Immersive high-end hardware is not meant for most users, which has resulted in digital inequality.

Potential Solutions:

- Inclusive Design Practices - Voice controls, haptic feedback, customizable UI, and colourblind-friendly modes must be included in AR/VR devices.
- Create Lower-Cost XR Devices for More Adoption - Companies developing affordable AR/VR solutions should improve access.
- Bias Testing in AI-based Avatars-training AI on diverse datasets to ensure fair representation.

Example: The user group with limited mobility benefited from the introduction of voice command and gaze-based selection in Microsoft HoloLens.

6.5. Ethical Questions Concerning AI-Created Virtual Beings and NPCs

Most human-like creations are now increasingly becoming artificial intelligence-enabled students whom one may refer to in singular or plural as NPCs, AI avatars, or chatbots. As concern for the well-being of these systems is growing, the ethical dilemmas that surround them are increasingly complex-they usually involve conditions about emotional manipulation, ethical decisions in AI making, and their social impacts. Figure 4 explains the Privacy and Ethical Concerns in Immersive Technology.

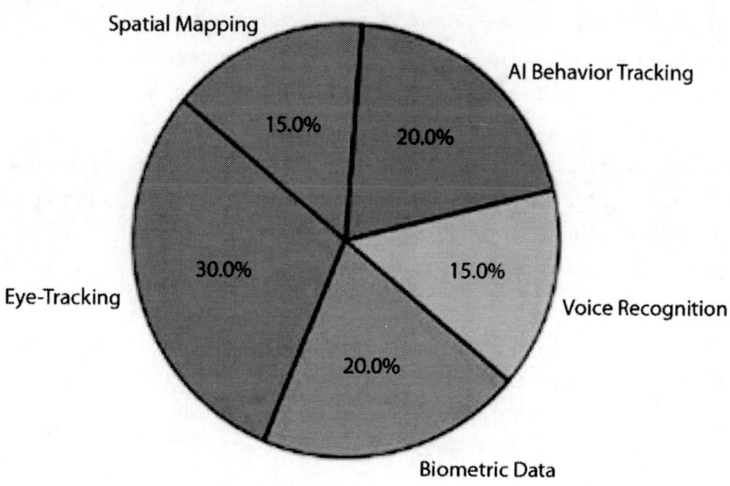

Figure 4. Privacy and Ethical Concerns in Immersive Technology.

The Ethical Issues of Consideration in AI-Driven Virtual Beings:

- Imitation of Emotions in Artificial Intelligence - Some AI avatars emulate the emotions of humans just to direct the user in a particular way.
- Bias in AI-Generated Characters - Stereotypes might be enhanced through AI-driven NPCs.

Conclusion

From interaction to learning, working, and experiencing digital environments, immersive technologies, including Augmented Reality (AR), Virtual Reality (VR), and Mixed Reality (MR), are changing the dynamics in a fast-paced world. They have disrupted industries, including gaming, education, healthcare, industrial training, and remote collaboration. However, their success will depend on structured designs, ethics, and technology.

This chapter has gone through the fundamental design methodologies for the successful development of immersive environments that are engaging and user-friendly. We considered:

- Human-Centered Design (HCD) to ensure accessibility, comfort, and intuitively interactive environments.
- A very Agile and Iterative development method encouraging rapid prototyping and user-driven refinement.
- Challenges in immersive design, including motion sickness, cognitive load, and accessibility.
- Trends and innovations toward AI-driven personalisation, cloud XR streaming, haptic feedback, and Brain-Computer Interface (BCI).
- Ethics, including considerations of data privacy, digital identity, psychological effects, and inclusive design.

There are, however, challenges ahead for developers and researchers to evolve immersive technologies further, with an emphasis on experiences where user well-being, inclusivity, and ethicality take precedence. Innovations coming soon, including 6G networks, an AI-powered adaptive environment, and spatial computing, will continue to create further blurring in the domains of the digital and physical worlds.

Through human-centered design, ethical AI, responsible data collection, and cross-disciplinary collaboration, we can ensure that immersive environments are wonderfully safe, accessible, and transformational for those who engage with them for years to come.

References

[1] Bowman, D., & Hodges, L. (1999). Formalizing the Design, Evaluation, and Application of Interaction Techniques for Immersive Virtual Environments. *J. Vis. Lang. Comput.*, 10, 37-53. https://doi.org/10.1006/jvlc.1998.0111.

[2] Spittle, B., Frutos-Pascual, M., Creed, C., & Williams, I. (2022). A Review of Interaction Techniques for Immersive Environments. *IEEE Transactions on Visualization and Computer Graphics*, 29, 3900-3921. https://doi.org/10.1109/TVCG.2022.3174805.

[3] Yang, B. (2023). Virtual Reality and Augmented Reality for Immersive Learning: A Framework of Education Environment Design. *Int. J. Emerg. Technol. Learn.*, 18, 23-36. https://doi.org/10.3991/ijet.v18i20.44209.

[4] Semerikov, S., Vakaliuk, T., Mintii, I., Hamaniuk, V., Soloviev, V., Bondarenko, O., Nechypurenko, P., Shokaliuk, S., Moiseienko, N., & Shepiliev, D. (2022). Design methodology for immersive educational resources. Educational Dimension. https://doi.org/10.31812/educdim.4716.

[5] Mulders, M., Buchner, J., & Kerres, M. (2020). A Framework for the Use of Immersive Virtual Reality in Learning Environments. *Int. J. Emerg. Technol. Learn.*, 15, 208-224. https://doi.org/10.3991/ijet.v15i24.16615.

[6] Yu, R., Gu, N., Lee, G., & Khan, A. (2022). A Systematic Review of Architectural Design Collaboration in Immersive Virtual Environments. *Designs*. https://doi.org/10.3390/designs6050093.

[7] Hajirasouli, A., Banihashemi, S., Sanders, P., & Rahimian, F. (2023). BIM-enabled virtual reality (VR)-based pedagogical framework in architectural design studios. *Smart and Sustainable Built Environment*. https://doi.org/10.1108/sasbe-07-2022-0149.

[8] Herr, C., Holzer, D., Kaijima, S., Kim, M., Melenbrink, N., & King, N. (2015). *A Real-time Immersive Environment as a Tool for Design.*

[9] Bowman, D., Koller, D., & Hodges, L. (1998). A methodology for the evaluation of travel techniques for immersive virtual environments. Virtual Reality, 3, 120-131. https://doi.org/10.1007/BF01417673.

[10] Heydarian, A., Carneiro, J., Gerber, D., Becerik-Gerber, B., Hayes, T., & Wood, W. (2015). Immersive virtual environments versus physical built environments: A benchmarking study for building design and user-built environment explorations. *Automation in Construction*, 54, 116-126. https://doi.org/10.1016/J.AUTCON.2015.03.020.

[11] Paes, D., Arantes, E., & Irizarry, J. (2017). Immersive environment for improving the understanding of architectural 3D models: Comparing user spatial perception between immersive and traditional virtual reality systems. *Automation in Construction*, 84, 292-303. https://doi.org/10.1016/J.AUTCON.2017.09.016.

[12] Zhang, Y., Liu, H., Kang, S., & Al-Hussein, M. (2020). Virtual reality applications for the built environment: Research trends and opportunities. *Automation in Construction*, 118, 103311. https://doi.org/10.1016/j.autcon.2020.103311.

[13] Kalantari, S., & Neo, J. (2020). Virtual Environments for Design Research: Lessons Learned from use of Fully Immersive Virtual Reality in Interior Design Research. *Journal of Interior Design*, 45, 27 - 42. https://doi.org/10.1111/joid.12171.

[14] Checa, D., & Bustillo, A. (2019). A review of immersive virtual reality serious games to enhance learning and training. *Multimedia Tools and Applications*, 79, 5501 - 5527. https://doi.org/10.1007/s11042-019-08348-9.

[15] Bourgeois-Bougrine, S., Bonnardel, N., Burkhardt, J., Thornhill-Miller, B., Pahlavan, F., Buisine, S., Guegan, J., Pichot, N., & Lubart, T. (2022). Immersive Virtual Environments' Impact on Individual and Collective Creativity. *European Psychologist*. https://doi.org/10.1027/1016-9040/a000481.

[16] Belaroussi, R., Dai, H., González, E., & Gutiérrez, J. (2023). Designing a Large-Scale Immersive Visit in Architecture, Engineering, and Construction. *Applied Sciences*. https://doi.org/10.3390/app13053044.

[17] Vergunova, N., & Blinova, M. (2024). TRENDS OF ARTIFICIAL INTELLIGENCE AND IMMERSIVE DESIGN USE IN THE FORMATION OF ARCHITECTURAL ENVIRONMENT. *Municipal economy of cities*. https://doi.org/10.33042/2522-1809-2024-3-184-59-64.

[18] Al-Suwaidi, M., Agkathidis, A., Haidar, A., & Lombardi, D. (2023). Application of Immersive Technologies in the Early Design Stage in Architecture Education - A Systematic Review. *Architecture and Planning Journal* (APJ). https://doi.org/10.54729/2789-8547.1222.

[19] Sommer, B., Lee, C., Martin, N., & Torrisi, V. (2020). *Immersive Design Engineering*. 1-16. https://doi.org/10.2352/issn.2470-1173.2020.2.sda-265.

[20] Alatta, R., & Freewan, A. (2017). Investigating the Effect of Employing Immersive Virtual Environment on Enhancing Spatial Perception within Design Process. *International Journal of Architectural Research: Archnet-IJAR,* 11, 219-238. https://doi.org/10.26687/ARCHNET-IJAR.V11I2.1258.

[21] Bowman, D. (1998). Interaction Techniques for Immersive Virtual Environments: Design, Evaluation, and Application.

[22] Paes, D., Irizarry, J., & Pujoni, D. (2021). An evidence of cognitive benefits from immersive design review: Comparing three-dimensional perception and presence between immersive and non-immersive virtual environments. *Automation in Construction*, 130, 103849. https://doi.org/10.1016/J.AUTCON.2021.103849.

[23] Pang, J. (2024). Display and Interaction Design of VR Technology in Environmental Design. *Applied Mathematics and Nonlinear Sciences*, 9. https://doi.org/10.2478/amns-2024-1432.

[24] Crolla, K., Song, J., Bunica, A., & Sheikh, A. (2024). Integrating Extended Reality in Architectural Design Studio Teaching and Reviews: Implementing a Participatory Action Research Framework. *Buildings*. https://doi.org/10.3390/buildings14061865.

[25] Akin, S., Ergun, O., Surer, E., & Dino, I. (2020). An immersive performative architectural design tool with daylighting simulations: a building information modeling-based approach. *Engineering, Construction and Architectural Management*. https://doi.org/10.1108/ecam-07-2020-0562.

[26] Cho, M., & Kim, M. (2017). Users' Design Process in Immersive Environments. *Korean Institute of Interior Design Journal*, 26, 64-71. https://doi.org/10.14774/jkiid.2017.26.2.064.

[27] Hamilton, D., McKechnie, J., Edgerton, E., & Wilson, C. (2020). Immersive virtual reality as a pedagogical tool in education: a systematic literature review of quantitative learning outcomes and experimental design. *Journal of Computers in Education*, 8, 1 - 32. https://doi.org/10.1007/s40692-020-00169-2.

[28] Neo, J., Won, A., & Shepley, M. (2021). *Designing Immersive Virtual Environments for Human Behavior Research*. , 2. https://doi.org/10.3389/frvir.2021.603750.

[29] Huang, X. (2018). *Design Globally, Immerse Locally - A Synthetic Design Approach by Integrating Agent Based Modelling with Virtual Reality*.

[30] Xu, B. (2024). Exploration of Visual Communication Design Methods Combining Virtual Reality Technology. *Applied Mathematics and Nonlinear Sciences*, 9. https://doi.org/10.2478/amns-2024-1339.

Chapter 9

Innovations in Collaborative Communication Through Immersive Therapeutic Technologies: Challenges, Ethics, and Future Pathways

Sarita Peddi*
and Geetha Manoharan†
School of Business, SR University, Warangal, Telangana, India

Abstract

Augmented reality, mixed reality, and virtual reality are turning out to be revolutionary in the arena of therapy interventions for mental disorders, but huge lacunas are still there as far as their uses are concerned. This chapter reports a systematic review of empirical research and literature that estimates how immersion technologies can make mental health interventions more robust for anxiety, depression, and PTSD. By employing a mixed-methods strategy, it combines the quantitative clinical trial data and qualitative user experience to show how immersion technologies increase participation and emotional engagement more effectively than control treatments. Examples from findings are its positive use in exposure therapy for phobias and AR's application in augmenting mindfulness work. The conclusion highlights ongoing investment in these technologies, which will enable more individuals underserved to obtain care. Lastly, it promotes combining high-tech digital solutions to improve mental health care, which will be more available and effective for generations to come.

Keywords: augmented reality (AR), virtual reality (VR), mixed reality (MR), mental health, well-being

* Corresponding Author's Email: psakki3@gmail.com
† Corresponding Author's Email: geethamanoharan1988@gmail.com

In: Shaping Tomorrow
Editors: Prithi Samuel, A. Sathya, Balamurugan Balusamy et al.
ISBN: 979-8-90134-076-9

1. Introduction

1.1. Overview of the Mental Health Landscape

Worldwide problems of mental health have now emerged as a public health issue, with a growing rate of incidence for mental illnesses like anxiety, depression, and post-traumatic stress disorder. The WHO states that nearly one out of every eight individuals worldwide have mental health disorders, further exacerbated by the COVID-19 pandemic, which has greatly affected mental health (Maulik et al., 2020). The pandemic has augmented social isolation, economic uncertainty, and health worry, which contribute to the mental health crisis requiring urgent intervention with creative solutions (Panchal et al., 2020).

The growing necessity for effective, available treatments on the mental health front is met with challenges relating to availability, affordability, as well as stigma about traditional modalities of treatment. Such calls demand out-of-the-box thinking as far as available conventional interventions are to cater to that gap, for the time being. Health technology interventions and technology-reliant ones are fast emerging on the horizon as strong avenues that may answer the demands placed under such circumstances.

1.1.1. Importance of Innovative Solutions

The application of new solutions in mental health treatment has several advantages. To start with, it improves accessibility, where individuals can engage with therapeutic resources from their homes. This is highly essential to remote and underserved communities (Sawrika et al., 2022). In addition, technology interventions personalized treatment choices, which are developed according to the individual's needs and preferences, and this is vital in successful mental health treatment (Moggia et al., 2024). Finally, creative solutions can assist in minimizing stigma surrounding mental health treatment by offering anonymous and non-judgmental spaces for individuals to seek help and resources (Vegt et al., 2024).

1.1.2. Introduction to Augmented Reality (AR), Virtual Reality (VR), and Mixed Reality (MR)

Augmented Reality (AR), Virtual Reality (VR), and Mixed Reality (MR) are cutting-edge technologies that have earned themselves a reputation in most fields, including mental health.

1.1.3. Definitions and Differences

Augmented Reality (AR) is the superimposition of computer information on the physical world, hence improving the perception of the user regarding the world around them. Examples are mobile apps that offer guided meditation or mindfulness activities while users engage with their environment (Sweileh et al., 2022).

Virtual Reality (VR) is immersion in a purely virtual environment, generally of headsets to make the subject feel as if they are present in an area that exists digitally. Exposure therapy for anxiety disorders utilised VR to expose subjects to phobias in a controlled environment (Pelucio et al., 2025).

Mixed Reality (MR) draws on elements from both AR and VR, where real and virtual elements co-exist simultaneously and can exchange in real-time. This offers possible application contexts in therapy, such that the user can concurrently engage with real-world and virtual contents (Klein et al., 2024).

1.1.4. Trends in growing Mental Health Interventions

Applications of AR, VR, and MR for mental health treatments are developing extremely fast because of the technological innovations and expanding amounts of accessible research evidence on their effectiveness. The research evidence shows that VR is an effective therapy for anxiety disorders and PTSD since it can be used to immerse in safe environments where exposure therapy and skills acquisition might occur (Andersen et al., 2023). AR apps have also been a promising class of applications that can support mindfulness practice and cognitive behavioural therapy with live support and feedback (Sweileh et al., 2022).

As these technologies continue to improve, so does the potential for a mental health care revolution. They offer unique opportunities to create compelling, interactive, and customized therapeutic experiences that open the door to a new paradigm for mental health care.

2. The Evolution of Technology in Mental Health

2.1. Historical Context

2.1.1. Traditional Mental Health Treatments

History teaches that mental health treatment has dramatically changed over time as human understanding of mental illness and the human mind evolves. Mental health treatment was originally crude and sometimes inhumane. In ancient societies, mental illness was very often attributed to supernatural causes or divine retribution. Therefore, treatments included exorcisms and confinement to asylums (Kee & Lai, 2024).

This was a trend toward humane treatment during the 19th century with the rise of the moral treatment movement. Early reformers such as Philippe Pinel called for gentle care and underlined the importance of a treatment-oriented atmosphere. Asylums became focused on therapy rather than punishment, despite conditions usually being abysmal.

The 20th century introduced psychoanalysis, which made Sigmund Freud's theories popular. During this period, other techniques of psychotherapy were also discovered, such as CBT (Camacho et al., 2021), which was used to replace negative thought patterns. The access to these treatments was, however, very limited and only accessible to people who could afford private therapy or those who lived close to mental health facilities.

2.1.2. Technological Advancements in Mental Health

The latter half of the 20th century brought psychopharmacology into the world of mental health treatment. With this came the drugs antidepressants and anti-psychotics, which slowly started to bring relief to millions of mentally disordered patients (Ridings et al., 2022). However, the rising drug use brought debates regarding the importance of psychotherapy and the dangers of over-medication. Technology gradually increased involvement with the advent of a digital age in mental health care. The late 20th and early 21st centuries introduced therapies using computers and online tools. People would seek the help they needed from either websites or forums; simultaneously, the form of teletherapy in its primitive form came into the system, by which therapists could reach the clients through remote locations (Breslow et al., 2024).

2.2. The Role of Technology Today

2.2.1. Teletherapy and Online Support

Today, technology plays a highly important role in mental health care. Teletherapy, along with other online support services, is accepted by people everywhere in the world (Breslow et al., 2024). Teletherapy enables clients to receive therapy sessions through video conferencing, telephonic calls, or via messaging apps. It really removed the geographical barriers as well as made this service more accessible. the COVID-19 pandemic accelerated the adoption of remote therapy as it has become very hard to continue having regular in-person meetings.

According to research, teletherapy can be as effective as face-to-face therapy for many. It offers convenience, flexibility, and privacy, which is a big advantage for people who might feel stigmatized or uncomfortable seeking help in person. Online platforms also offer various resources, such as self-help tools, educational materials, and community support forums, creating a comprehensive support system for people seeking mental health care (Breslow et al., 2024).

2.2.2. Introduction of Immersive Technologies

Recently, immersive technologies like virtual reality (VR) and augmented reality (AR) have begun to appear within the context of mental health treatment (Smink et al., 2022). The former two offer a different approach to therapy, especially for disorders like anxiety disorders, PTSD, and phobias (Garibay et al., 2021).

For example, in the case of VR exposure therapy, the patient can safely confront his fears in a controlled environment, facilitating desensitization and coping strategies. This method has already shown promising results in the treatment of PTSD, were, under the guidance of a trained professional, patients can safely relive traumatic experiences (Garibay et al., 2021).

The other application is in improving mindfulness and relaxation practices, where it provides an interactive experience to the user for emotional well-being. These technologies are not only engaging users in new ways but also accommodating diverse learning styles, thereby making mental health care more personalized and effective.

2.2.3. The Future of Technology in Mental Health

The future of mental health care is bright with the advent of newer technologies. As the science of technology is progressing, AI is increasingly being used in diagnostics and treatment recommendations, analysing various sources of data to come up with patterns and then suggesting interventions. AI-based chatbots and virtual assistants are also on the horizon, promising instant support and resource availability for those in need. However, there is the issue of ethical dilemmas and concerns. For instance, privacy in terms of security of such data remains a key issue, while the scope for human touch being eclipsed by machines is another. Though it is an aspect where the completion of traditional therapy is also seen as highly relevant (Ramos et al., 2024).

The evolution of technology has changed the landscape of mental health treatment and support. From historical practices rooted in misunderstanding to today's innovative tools and approaches, technology has expanded access and improved outcomes for many individuals. As we move forward, it will be essential to balance technological advancements with ethical considerations and the need for compassionate, human-centered care.

3. Understanding AR, VR, and MR

3.1. Definitions and Key Characteristics

3.1.1. Augmented Reality (AR)

Augmented reality is a way of overlaying digital information, be it images, sounds, videos, or even GPS data, onto real life, adding to a user's perceptions of their environment. It doesn't immerse the user in a fully artificial environment but adds virtual elements to a real-life environment. In other words, AR uses devices like smartphones, tablets, and specialised glasses to experience a world view. The key characteristics of AR include the ability to maintain the user's connection to the physical world while integrating digital content, which allows for interactive and context-aware experiences (Dargan et al., 2023).

AR solutions have experienced a tremendous growth rate in education, healthcare, and mental health. The impact of AR applications in education by improving engagement and retention through immersive (Tewar et al., 2024), interactive learning experiences. In mental health, AR has been used in exposure therapy, where the patient is made to confront his or her fears by layering anxiety-inducing stimuli in a familiar setting.

3.1.2. Virtual Reality (VR)

Virtual Reality (VR), in contrast, provides a completely immersive digital environment, replacing the user's real-world surroundings with a simulated one. Users of VR usually experience it through headsets that provide a 360-degree view of a computer-generated environment along with audio and sometimes haptic feedback, which creates a deep sense of presence. The most characteristic feature of VR is that it can fully immerse a user in a simulated experience, at times isolating the person from the physical world (Soudhamini, 2024).

In therapeutic settings, VR has been used to treat a range of mental health disorders, including PTSD, anxiety disorders, and phobias. According to research, exposure therapy in VR, in which users are exposed to simulated phobias or traumatic memories, can reduce anxiety levels by a considerable margin. For example, VR has been used to treat veterans with PTSD by recreating controlled combat scenarios in a safe environment (Virvou et al., 2023).

3.1.3. Mixed Reality (MR)

Mixed Reality (MR) draws on both two technologies, permitting physical objects and digital contents to intermingle to interact simultaneously in real space. Besides overlaying AR, the MR also involves the element of interaction whereby users deal with the overlays as they would with some part of that world; this usually requires advanced, sophisticated technology; it often resorts to some advanced sensors and screens (Guo et al., 2022).

In clinical applications, MR has been promising for advancing surgical training and medical education. MR can assist professionals in the health care arena to practice skills in an environment that is safe yet controlled by simulating the real-world medical scenarios that are interactive 3D models. MR Applications in rehabilitation therapy are gaining momentum, providing patients with interactive, engaging exercises that aim at motor skills and physical recovery [5].

3.2. Mechanisms of Action

3.2.1. How AR, VR, and MR Differ in Application

Augmented reality (AR) is most used to enrich the view of the real world with less engagement of the viewer in a digital environment. Many applications of AR offer either guidance, information, or entertainment to the user that still maintains their view or consciousness of their surroundings. For example, in mental health practice, AR can be engaged in assisting patients in practicing social skills in settings in which they would see such prompts or feedback in real-time (Talafidaryani et al., 2023).

Virtual Reality (VR) is more immersive, making it suitable for applications where full engagement is required. VR can simulate environments that would be difficult or impossible to reproduce in real life, such as exposing a patient to a traumatic memory in a controlled setting. The immersive nature of VR allows individuals to practice responses to specific situations, thereby honing coping strategies, which are especially effective for phobia treatment.

Mixed Reality (MR) works as a midway point in between AR and VR-allowing user interaction and engagement with a digital layer that interacts naturally with their physical environment. Therapies using MR may take the form of skill learning, where simulated situations involving realistic environments might be carried out by a patient that is physically there. This includes scenarios like physical rehabilitation, where patients can see their movements as both physical and digital avatars interact, enhancing the therapeutic experience (Asiain et al., 2022).

3.2.2. Engagement and Interactivity as Therapeutic Tools

All three technologies incorporate engagement and interactivity as a key part of their makeup, which forms the heart of their therapeutic value. High user engagement through immersion in VR is crucial to the therapy process. In this context, interactive scenarios can simulate stressful situations such as public speaking or social situations and allow users to be safe in dealing with those situations. It not only enhances confidence but also builds ways to handle situations (Freitas et al., 2021).

Similarly, AR is an interaction as it has therapeutic cues or prompts layered in a patient's realistic environment, encouraging participation. As per research, motivation and compliance with carrying out a therapeutic task can be boosted if AR makes the task even more interesting (Sadeghi Milan et al., 2024). Interactive components in gamified apps can enhance user engagement during therapy, thereby making the process less intimidating or daunting.

Mixed Reality elevates interactivity by allowing users to be able to manipulate digital and physical objects with ease. For example, in rehabilitation, MR environments may influence the performance of patients on exercise as they get feedback live. This enhances interaction, thereby bringing better results in terms of performance and rehabilitation efficiency (Sadeghi Milan et al., 2024).

AR, VR, and MR are among the most innovative technological developments in therapeutic practice and further upgrading in treatment and rehabilitation processes toward mental health. Both have peculiar characteristics and purposes and concern the satisfaction of different requirements by incorporating activity and interaction as the cornerstone in further enhancing the effects and impact of each one. Further research and development will be required to bring forth the complete realisation of such technologies in terms of outcome improvement in mental health.

4. Applications for AR and VR in Mental Health

Augmented Reality (AR) and Virtual Reality (VR) (Asiain et al., 2022) have been used to integrate into mental health treatments. They transform the traditionally applied approaches to therapy and significantly enhance the experience of patients dealing with psychological conditions. A review of applications of AR and VR in mental health is presented, especially in relation to the treatment of exposure therapy for PTSD, stress reduction methods, and relaxation techniques together with improving Cognitive Behavioral Therapy (CBT) (Camacho et al., 2021).

4.1. Exposure Therapy

4.1.1. Phobias and Anxiety Disorders

One of the most well-known treatments within psychology for curing phobias and anxiety disorders is known as exposure therapy. Exposure treatment has included slow exposure of the patient under safe control to their feared objects or situations. Through VR and AR, this approach has transformed towards better exposure experience for patients. A virtual world is created where the very things that the patient dreads in real life are replicated, and the fears and phobias are confronted in a safe environment (Freitas et al., 2021).

The VR exposure therapy is effective in treating specific phobias such as acrophobia and spider phobia. The study participants underwent the virtual process of increasingly threatening experiences accompanied by immediate therapist feedback and support. Post-treatment, a statistically significant improvement in the decrease of their anxiety levels, as well as coping strategies, were recorded.

4.1.2. Case Studies and Effectiveness

There are many documented case studies of the effective clinical application of VR exposure therapy. For instance, there is a case report (Gupta et al., 2024) in which the treatment provided to a person with a severe fear of flying was discussed. This is how the therapist progressively exposed the patient to this experience of flying through simulated exposure using a VR session. The exposure ranged from virtual checks-in at the airport all through the actual process of the flight. After all that exposure at the end, the patient had a substantial decrease in anxiety and even went to take a flight without having any fear of flying.

Technology is not only used for controlled exposure but also repeated practice, which is essential in overcoming phobias. A meta-analysis carried out found that VR exposure therapy significantly outperformed traditional exposure therapy with higher patient satisfaction and engagement.

4.2. PTSD Treatment

4.2.1. Immersive Narratives and Re-Consolidation of Memories

Among post-traumatic treatments of serious challenges in mental health intervention is the use of innovative approaches for successful management. VR-based narratives allow patients to revive or relive their own painful experiences in a safe setting, hence allowing their traumatic experiences to undergo memory re-consolidation. Because a patient is immersed, they can be able to cope with their fears before even being guided by a therapist, before these cognitive and emotional integration setbacks, when dealing with trauma.

The efficacy of VR for treating veterans diagnosed with PTSD (Garibay et al., 2021). The patients involved underwent VR simulations that replicated the combat scenario they were involved in, but also exposed to treatment dialogues with avatars, simulating the victims' experiences. In so doing, the outcomes proved to show a high score in terms of symptomatology due to the immersive experience of using VR and the supportive aspects of the therapeutic treatment interaction.

4.2.2. Evidence from Clinical Trials

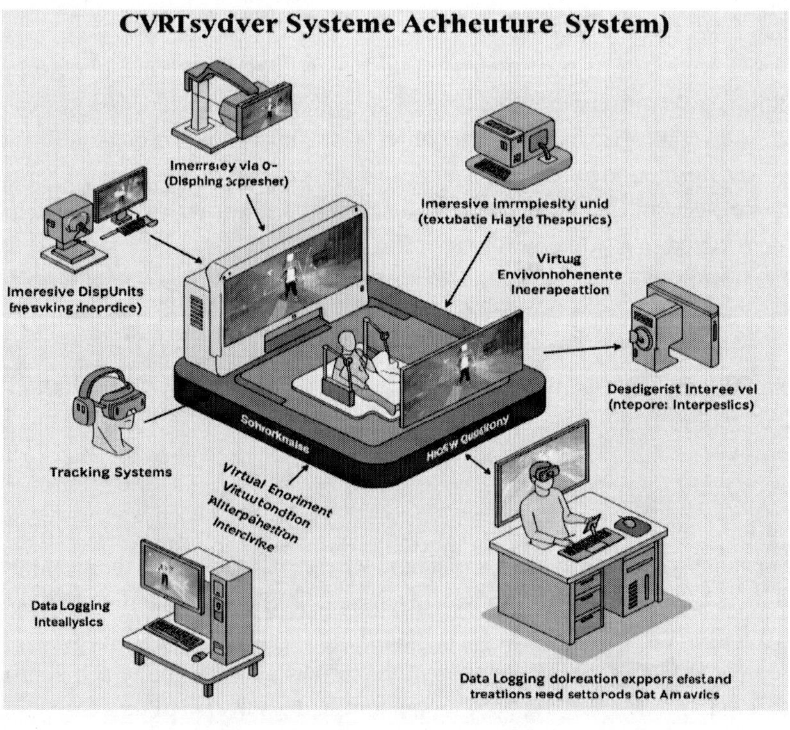

Figure 1. The system architecture of a Collaborative Virtual Reality Therapy (CVRT) system.

The efficacy of VR in the treatment of PTSD has been increasingly supported through clinical trials. All studies on VR-based interventions for PTSD across various populations, including veterans, survivors of sexual assault, and disaster victims. It is concluded that VR interventions yielded significant reductions in PTSD symptoms compared to control groups treated with standard care (Garibay et al., 2021).

Experiments on survivors of sexual assault explored its effect with VR-assisted exposure therapy (Gupta et al., 2024). It was observed that the group under the VR therapy showed improvement more in intrusive thoughts as well as avoidance behaviours, rather than the other groups, and therefore stated the use of VR in healing purposes that has also been applied toward the processing of traumatic memories. Figure 1 illustrates the system architecture of the Collaborative Virtual Reality Therapy (CVRT) system, delineating its core components.

4.3. Stress Reduction and Relaxation Techniques

4.3.1. Virtual Relaxation Environments

Other than exposure therapy, AR and VR have been used to create virtual relaxation settings that assist people in relieving stress and enhancing their mental health. The virtual environment exposes the users to a setting that is both relaxing and aesthetically pleasing. VR can be used to create serene environments like beaches or forests to enable users to practice relaxation techniques, such as deep breathing and guided imagery. This demonstrated that subjects reported a significant reduction in perceived stress scores after participating in short sessions in these virtual environments. Second, the results indicated that habituation to these de-stressing VR experiences may have a greater potential for promoting a sense of empowerment or control in managing stress.

4.3.2. Mindfulness and Meditation Programs

Mindfulness is one of the widely utilised practices in mental health treatment. The implementation of VR has made mindfulness and meditation much easier and more effective to practice. Programs for VR can offer experiences of guided meditation, making users feel transported to very serene environments, allowing a person to focus and concentrate even better. A meta-analysis conducted confirmed that VR mindfulness programs significantly improve participants' scores on mental health, especially about anxiety reduction and overall mood (Andersen et al., 2023).

A classic example is VR-based mindfulness applications tailored for people experiencing chronic stress. This helps users go through an intense experience where they can immerse themselves in mindfulness through calm virtual environments (Gupta et al., 2024). Users with regular use of such software experienced increased relaxation and decreased anxiety.

4.4. Cognitive Behavioural Therapy (CBT) Enhancement

4.4.1. Gamification of Therapeutic Exercises

The introduction of VR and AR in therapies has offered new avenues to innovate therapeutic exercise practices and make them interesting as well as accessible. In fact, the concept of gamification entails adding game mechanics in the intervention, which has worked out to be very effective in increasing patients' motivation and involvement with the treatment. The outcomes of a VR-based CBT program wherein tasks for cognitive restructuring and exposure exercises were gamified. The results indicated that gamification led to higher engagement levels among participants, resulting in more significant therapeutic gains compared to traditional CBT approaches. Participants reported greater enjoyment and motivation, which translated into improved adherence to treatment protocols.

4.4.2. Integration with Virtual Therapists

Other strong AR and VR applications in CBT are virtual therapists. These avatars would be able to give instantaneous, time-sensitive feedback, counselling, and support in such sessions. Studies performed showed that patients speaking with virtual therapists in a VR environment were much more comfortable discussing their issues compared to face-to-face contact interactions (Zeine et al., 2023).

This integration allows for individualized therapeutic experiences for every patient, hence the general effectiveness of the CBT (Brocki et al., (2023, February)) interventions is higher. As virtual therapists may monitor the progress of patients and adjust interventions in a real-time manner, these provide flexibility and responsiveness in a manner that can make therapy outcomes increase.

Applications of AR and VR in mental health are developing rapidly with significant improvements that enhance treatment efficacy for various psychological conditions. From exposure therapy for phobias to PTSD treatment through immersive narratives (Garibay et al., 2021), stress-reduction activities through virtual environments of relaxation, and gamification and virtual therapists to enhance cognitive-behavioral therapy, these technologies offer innovative ways to heighten patient interest and efficacy in therapy sessions. With advancing research, the modality of treatment changed, and AR and VR have the potential to make such treatment more accessible and effective.

5. The Benefits of AR, VR & MR in Mental Health

Integration of augmented reality (AR), virtual reality (VR), and mixed reality (MR) in the realm of mental health will bring revolutionary opportunities for promoting advancements in therapy outcomes. These technologies not only transform the mode of treatment but also solve age-old issues related to access, engagement, and even data management. This paper discusses the benefits of AR, VR, and MR for mental health based on three criteria: accessibility and affordability, engagement and motivation, and data collection and monitoring.

5.1. Accessibility and Affordability

5.1.1. Reaching Underserved Populations

Among the key strengths of AR, VR, and MR, there is accessibility to these services in reaching the disadvantaged population. Mental health services are usually limited because of geographical, financial, or social constraints. They affect the underprivileged communities adversely, and it is via this technology that the gap will be closed in getting remote access to the needed therapeutic interventions, mainly for the people from rural backgrounds or those experiencing stigma over the sessions of therapy.

Therapy sessions could easily be administered to patients with VR-based therapy in remote villages in India. The research showed not only how feasible VR therapy was to be in such settings, but also the high patient satisfaction rate among participants who have previously been unable to access mental health services because of distance. Similarly, in the context of the West, amidst the lingering impact of the COVID-19 pandemic, therapists have widely utilised VR platforms to remotely conduct therapy sessions with clients across the globe to focus on the global reachability of these technologies.

5.1.2. Cost Comparison with Traditional Therapies

Considering cost-effectiveness, AR, VR, and MR interventions must be evaluated about how much more they are as compared to traditional therapies. Although the investment in equipment and software for VR appears to be quite high in the beginning, long-term benefits and savings may be significant. A report by [2] shows that therapy using VR resulted in shorter sessions compared to traditional therapies, and therefore, a lower overall treatment cost for the patients.

Furthermore, the scalability of VR and AR applications in mental health can help to reduce the cost. For instance, once a treatment program for VR is developed, it can be rolled out to hundreds of patients at a time, thereby reducing the per-person cost of therapy. It is especially important in India, where services for mental health are often poorly funded and inaccessible. It also found that the inclusion of VR in existing mental health frameworks could reduce the burden on healthcare systems since therapists could manage larger caseloads effectively.

5.2. Engagement and Motivation

5.2.1. Increased Patient Engagement

One of the significant advantages of using AR, VR, and MR in mental health is that they make patients very engaged. The traditional ways of treatment may sometimes feel static and uninspiring for patients, which may not stimulate them to actively participate in their treatment. In contrast, the AR and VR experience are engaging, holding the patients' attention and making them want to be active in treatment-related exercises (Davies, 2023, September). Patients engaged considerably more in exposure therapy provided by VR than they would in standard exposure therapy. This is because VR technology is immersive, hence letting the patient confront fear in a controlled yet natural situation that increases motivation towards that process.

Furthermore, the gamification features of VR and AR can add more to engagement. In these technologies, the addition of game-like features such as rewards for completion of therapeutic tasks or interactive challenges makes mental health treatment enjoyable and motivating. This is very crucial for young patients or those who may be intimidated or find traditional methods unappealing.

5.2.2. User-Friendly Interfaces and Personalised Experiences

It was the advances of AR and VR that have led the development to more user-friendly interfaces, which have made AR and VR technologies accessible to even a greater population.

Therapeutic mental health applications can have user-friendly designs to engage with users with less technical knowledge, so patients are able to think only of how they might heal rather than thinking of troubleshooting technology problems.

In addition, these technologies help in offering customised experiences of care tailored to the needs of individual patients. For instance, a personalised therapy program through VR may engage different scenarios tailored to respond to a patient's individual fears or challenges. This tailoring not only increases the appropriateness of the therapy experience but also creates an enhanced emotional involvement with care since the patients feel that the treatment is specifically tailored for their needs.

Table 1. Comparative analysis of traditional methods

Feature	Traditional In-Person Therapy	Individual VR Therapy	Individual VR Therapy
Collaborative Interaction	High	Low	High
Spatial Presence	Medium	High	High
Environmental Control	Low	High	High
Remote Accessibility	Low	Medium	High
Cost (Hardware/Software)	Low	Medium	High
Data Collection	Low	Medium	High

Author Source Table 1 provides a comparative overview of CVRT against traditional in-person and individual VR therapy.

5.3. Data Collection and Monitoring

5.3.1. Tracking Progress and Responsiveness

Real-time data collection and analysis by AR, VR, and MR technologies significantly increases the ability to successfully manage mental health. Platforms provide engagement levels, emotional response, and behavioural change tracking to support therapists in tracking patient progression easily (Rashidi et al., 2025). For instance, integrated wearable devices with VR apps may measure physiological responses such as heart rate and sweat and produce objective data that could guide therapists to make alterations to the therapy.

To create an idea of how the data generated by VR therapy sessions can be used by therapists to adjust the treatment protocol based on individual responses by the patient, Cullen et al., (2021) conducted a pilot study in 2023. This would possibly make the interventions more responsive and better overall in terms of effectiveness.

5.3.2. Potential for Continuous Assessment of Mental Health

The use of both AR and VR can radically modify the method over time regarding mental health monitoring. Traditional assessment is usually done by periods of sessions that cannot represent the total mental health condition of a patient. On the other hand, with AR and VR applications that collect data continuously, mental health status is assessed continuously and helps in giving insights into changes in the mental health condition of the patients (Davies, 2023, September).

For example, Carlson's (2023) study highlights the positive aspect that using VR environments during usual follow-ups with patients helps avoid the negative impact of anxiety or depression-related symptoms. The ongoing acquisition of data would help therapists figure out early warning signs about anxiety or depression, hence interventions made prior to the escalation of the symptoms. Such proactive management is especially useful for chronic mental illness, whereby support to the patient is ensured well before any crisis occurs.

It means that the introduction of AR, VR, and MR in mental health treatment has several benefits, like better accessibility and affordability, more engagement by patients, and more advanced data collection. The geographies that had earlier been barriers to access are now broken, and this means that underrepresented groups will be able to access the therapeutic resources meant for their mental health, which equates to fair care. The nature of these interventions becomes even more immersive and game-like, bringing along a higher level of engagement and motivation; data-collecting mechanisms would ensure precise and responsive adjustment to the given treatment. As this knowledge advances, the introduction of AR, VR, and MR into mental health service provision might significantly alter current therapeutic outcomes and mental care service provisions.

6. Challenges and Limitations of AR, VR & MR in Mental Health

As the technologies of Augmented Reality (AR) (Dargan et al., 2023), Virtual Reality (VR) (Asiain et al., 2022), and Mixed Reality (MR) advance in the context of mental health therapy, a host of challenges and limitations arise regarding their implementation. These challenges range from technological barriers to ethical considerations and issues regarding efficacy and acceptance. This paper discusses these challenges in detail, using evidence from recent literature and focusing on insights from both Indian and international contexts.

6.1. Technological Barriers

6.1.1. Equipment Costs and Accessibility

The most significant challenge of the adoption of AR, VR, and MR in mental health is the cost incurred for the necessary equipment. It can be quite expensive to use high-quality VR headsets and AR devices along with their required software for therapeutic purposes. The financial burden imposes limitations on many mental health professionals and patients, particularly in low-resource settings, such as many parts of India (Fuxiong, 2023, January). The initial capital invested in VR systems mostly keeps mental health facilities of India from adopting these technologies. Although the long-run advantages may be worth such an investment, the significant financial outlay at the onset serves as a major turn-off. Even when institutions are willing to invest, they often struggle with ongoing maintenance costs and the need for regular updates of hardware and software to keep pace with technological advancements (Fuxiong, 2023, January).

Furthermore, technical infrastructure still lacks in many rural or underserved areas. These applications of VR and AR need high-speed internet facilities and reliable power supply and sources, which may not be evenly distributed in many regions around the world. In this respect, while the positive impacts of these technologies toward improving mental health treatment exist, their actual application may yet be hindered by many financial and infrastructural burdens.

6.1.2. User Experience Challenges and Motion Sickness

User experience plays a critical role in ensuring that VR and AR interventions work effectively. However, several patients will face problems in using these technologies. A common problem experienced by most users is motion sickness. This occurs in VR, where visual input may conflict with physical movement, making the user uncomfortable. Symptoms of motion sickness may include dizziness, nausea, and even disorientation, which could dissuade patients from using VR therapy.

This was because the design of the virtual environment was one aspect that helped mitigate such problems. The thoughtful choice in design is critical, and this includes frame rates, field of view, and user control mechanisms. Results indicated that environments that prevented rapid movements or allowed a sense of stability to users could minimise the risk of motion sickness. However, this calls for developers to design quality and engaging experiences that also pay attention to the physical comfort of the user, which can be a technical challenge (Gupta et al., 2024).

Moreover, the learning curve of new technologies is often challenging for users, especially older adults or those less familiar with digital interfaces. Initial frustration or discomfort can cause reduced motivation to use therapeutic apps and thereby reduce their overall impact. Therefore, the resolution of user experience issues is essential to enhance acceptance and use of AR, VR, and MR in mental health.

6.2. Ethical Considerations

6.2.1. Privacy Concerns and Data Security

With data collection and analysis of vast amounts of information on users' activities, thoughts, and progression by AR, VR, and MR technologies, it poses serious concerns regarding privacy and security of data (Gupta et al., 2024). Patients remain unaware of how data will be gathered or utilised during their communication with such technologies, thus infringing upon their rights to privacy.

Data protection precautions are not always in effect. In most cases, guidelines may not be clear for mental health practitioners on how patient data gathered using AR and VR apps is stored and treated. Lack of clarity can lead to data compromise or abuse, and this brings massive distress to patients.

To counter such problems, moral guidelines controlling the development and usage of AR and VR for mental health purposes should guarantee patient confidentiality and their right to privacy. Creating transparent data governance policy aided by regulation, such as that in Europe under the GDPR, will be crucial to protect sensitive user information.

6.2.2. Informed Consent and User Autonomy

Informed consent is one of the major ethical issues that pertain more to the new technologies like AR and VR. It demands that the patients are properly informed about the nature of the interventions being presented, including potential risks and benefits. VR and AR applications are, however, complicated, and it becomes difficult for the patients to comprehend the details of what they are consenting to.

Furthermore, the highly immersive nature of such technologies also puts a question mark over user agency. There exists a risk of patients being bullied into using technological interventions or being unable to opt out of experiences that are painful. It is up to mental health practitioners to see to it that the patient is in control of his or her own therapeutic path and has easy avenues to opt out or change their experiences on a comfort scale.

A study of informed consent processes within the context of AR and VR technologies reveals that to maintain patient autonomy, this information should be offered clearly, briefly, and conveniently (Gupta et al., 2024). Also, consent conversations should persist regarding these issues, particularly those related to children and vulnerable populations, to ensure compliance with ethical guidelines.

6.3. Efficacy and Acceptance

6.3.1. Variability in Treatment Effectiveness

While AR and VR hold great promises for enhancing outcomes of treatment for various mental health conditions, there remains considerable heterogeneity in the effectiveness of these interventions. There can be considerable variation in how effective AR and VR interventions are among people because of many factors, such as the type of condition being treated, what technology is being used, and the characteristics of the individual patient.

Meta-analysis (Andersen et al., 2023) detected that while some patients had dramatic improvement in anxiety and PTSD symptoms with VR exposure therapy, others had very little improvement or did not complete treatment because of side effects (Garibay et al., 2021). Such inconsistency could render it difficult to plan treatment for the therapist since they cannot anticipate which of the patients may be responsive to AR and VR treatments. More research and standardised assessments that explore predictors of successful outcomes will make treatment more specific and personal.

6.3.2. Acceptance Among Therapists and Patients

Acceptance among mental health professionals and patients is an important factor in integrating AR and VR in practice. Although interest among therapists to utilise technological advancement in therapy has grown, many still express reluctance about using it due to concerns over the efficacy, dependability, and appropriateness of these interventions (Ridings et al., 2022).

Therapists' acceptance of AR and VR is most often determined by their own familiarity with technology, type of training, and also belief in the efficacy of such interventions. Some structured training programs to improve their technological competence may reduce this concern and enhance acceptance itself.

On the patient's side, while most would be keen on the possibility of VR and AR, some scepticism and mistrust might hinder its acceptance. Some patients might resist the application of technology in the treatment of mental illness because they fear privacy, technology will not work, or negative experiences from past digital interventions (Ridings et al., 2022). Patient education and openness regarding how these technologies function, as well as evidence regarding their effectiveness, are central to building acceptance and facilitating their use.

There is vast application potential in the areas of mental health treatment and therapy with AR, VR, and MR, while there are also various challenges and limitations ahead that must be thoroughly debated. Technical challenges encompass costs of equipment, the user experience, privacy, and ethical matters in AR, VR, and MR, whose solutions must proactively address remedies for successful use. Furthermore, addressing variability in treatment efficacy and striving towards both therapist and patient acceptance levels must be ensured to promote effective integration of these novel technologies into the mental health care system. By research aimed at these challenges and ethical standards, with attention drawn to user requirements, greater future success in the treatment of mental health is to be anticipated.

7. Future Directions in AR, VR and MR for Mental Health

Augmented, Virtual, and Mixed Realities promise to change the landscape of mental health care. With advancements in technology yet to come, there appears to be an increasingly vast room for utilizing such technologies for therapy. Future directions in the applications of AR, VR, and MR for mental health are explored in this chapter by centering on research and development, the implementation into traditional practice, and world opinion toward embracing technology.

7.1. Research and Development

7.1.1. Emerging Technologies and Their Potential

The emerging technologies of AR, VR, and MR continue to unlock new possibilities for the treatment of mental health. From biofeedback devices with VR for enhancing mindfulness practice to AI-based personalization algorithms that alter the therapeutic environment as per the individual's requirements, the potential for innovation is enormous. Emerging technologies, like BCIs, also have the potential to enhance the feeling of immersion and interactivity of therapy.

For example, newer advances of BCI can be used to track in real-time user emotional states and adjust the virtual environment based on that. Such responsiveness can personalise the treatment and make it more responsive to individual reactions, thus making the therapy more effective (Virvou et al., 2023). Additionally, integrating machine learning into such technologies can assist with predictive analytics, whereby clinicians can track risky behaviours and intervene prior to crises occurring.

Another promising line of investigation involves social VR environments, wherein the user can interact with avatars of real or imaginary scenarios. It could thus prove to be highly helpful in conditions such as social anxiety disorder, where exposure to social settings may be mimicked in a controlled virtual environment (Virvou et al., 2023). Research is needed for these interactions' specifics and user experience optimisation, therapeutic outcome assessment across diverse demographics, etc.

7.1.2. Areas for Further Investigation

While there has been a great deal of progress in the application of AR and VR in mental health, many areas need further research. Longitudinal studies would be necessary to determine whether these interventions have a sustained effect on mental health outcomes (Gupta et al.,

2024). Furthermore, there is a need for more robust studies that include diverse populations to better understand how cultural and individual differences influence the effectiveness of immersive interventions.

In addition, further research into the ethical implications of AR and VR technologies is also very important, especially concerning issues of consent, privacy, and data security. Under an understanding of ethical concerns, both from the patient's and provider's perspectives, regulatory frameworks can be crafted to protect user rights with innovation.

Research into user experience and accessibility will also be significant. With the diversity of potential users ranging from various age groups to levels of technological competence, accessible and user-friendly interfaces are a significant challenge. Studies examining usability in settings such as schools, clinics, and homes may enhance adoption rates and effectiveness.

7.2. Integration into Traditional Mental Health Practices

7.2.1. Collaborative Models between Technologists and Mental Health Professionals

The successful implementation of AR, VR, and MR technologies in mental health care depends on the collaboration between technologists and mental health practitioners. Developing collaborative models that integrate technological expertise with clinical insights can ensure that interventions are both innovative and clinically relevant (Tewar et al., 2024).

This partnership may thus make it possible for the development of bespoke VR and AR experiences in congruence with evidence-based therapeutic practices. For instance, closer collaboration with psychologists and psychiatrists will assist developers to better understand the nuances of the different disorders and thus better design interventions that may precisely address therapeutic goals (Mishra et al., 2023). Moreover, technology and healthcare providers can give feedback loops which drive continuous improvement. Thus, based on real-world applications, there may be iterations on enhancements.

7.2.2. Educational Initiatives for Therapists

Educating mental health professionals about the potential benefits and practical applications of AR and VR technologies is important. Preparing therapists to integrate these tools into their practice is crucial to overcome resistance to technological adoption (Pande et al., 2023). Training programs can prepare therapists with the skills necessary for navigating and managing these technologies effectively.

Curricula that combine technology training with traditional therapeutic practices can enable a comprehensive understanding of how to apply these tools in clinical settings (Gupta et al., 2024). Furthermore, continuous professional development opportunities focused on emerging technologies will help mental health practitioners stay updated on the latest advancements, which will, in turn, lead to more innovative and effective therapeutic practices.

The development of awareness among therapists toward ethical issues concerning AR and VR is what will equip them with lessons they can use during treatment. This duality in attention toward ethical considerations, along with developing practical applications, will ensure that integration with technology is done responsibly (Gupta et al., 2024).

7.3. Global Perspectives

7.3.1. Variability in Technology Adoption Across Cultures

The adoption and integration of AR, VR, and MR technologies in mental health care do vary significantly across cultural contexts. Developed countries, having more access to advanced technologies, remain a challenge for low- and middle-income countries regarding infrastructure, financial resources, and cultural acceptance of technology within therapeutic settings (Bansal et al., 2023).

Research by Choudhary et al., (2023) indicates that mental health has cultural perceptions regarding willingness to adopt the new modes of treatment. Countries with a stigma of mental health may encounter barriers in introducing technological interventions. Therefore, it becomes pertinent to match the cultural narrative with the targeted population before the introduction of such technologies. Cultural sensitivity may then promote a better reception of such interventions, augment their effectiveness, and ensure proper integration.

7.3.2. Opportunities for International Collaboration

As we know the global nature of the challenges in mental health, international collaboration is an opportunity to push forward AR, VR, and MR technologies. Collaboration among researchers, clinicians, and developers from different countries could promote knowledge exchange and best practices, thus making more holistic and culturally relevant interventions possible (Virvou et al., 2023).

Further research in collaborative efforts might identify how cultural differences would influence the effectiveness of VR therapies and what adjustments may be necessary for different settings. The joint projects could focus on developing affordable, scalable solutions that reach underserved communities and improve equity in mental health care (Lee et al., 2024).

Moreover, international organisations can play a catalytic role in implementing technological integration in mental health through the provision of research and development grants while ensuring ethical standards. Activities related to the sharing of resources and knowledge through global platforms hasten the implementation of innovative mental health interventions across borders.

Thus, the future of AR, VR, and MR in the psyche seems promising enough due to substantial opportunities for effective enhancement and increasing accessibility of treatment. However, the potential realisation of these innovations will only depend on challenges regarding development and research, measures taken in education, and cultural sensitivity toward the adoption of technology, which, in itself, would call for some coordination between technologists and mental health professionals toward integration into clinical practices. Moreover, a global perspective would make the understanding of how these technologies can be customised to meet diverse cultural needs and lead to improved mental health outcomes around the globe.

Conclusion

Augmented Reality (AR) (Dargan et al., 2023), Virtual Reality (VR) (Asiain et al., 2022), and Mixed Reality (MR) technologies will transform mental health care. These are emerging tools that can transform practices of therapy, enhance patient engagement, and come up with new solutions for solving the most daunting problems of mental health care. Time to identify and tap this potential for betterment in mental health treatment is now.

Summarising the Potential of AR, VR, and MR in Transforming Mental Health Care

Through the applications of AR, VR, and MR, technologies that develop immersed environments help with exposure therapy, interactive experiences, and acquire skills within a safer environment. There are studies indicating that VR intervention allows exposure and processing of fear that significantly reduces symptoms of anxiety disorders, phobias, and PTSD (Virvou et al., 2023). The technologies can further improve conventional therapies by boosting motivation and participation in treatment for patients with mental illness.

For instance, its adoption in CBT (Camacho et al., 2021) has been mentioned to have high prospects of use in various clinical contexts, such as training autistic spectrum disorder patients on social skills and for treating those suffering from severe depression (Virvou et al., 2023). Furthermore, these technologies can be tailored according to a personal treatment plan of every patient with specific needs so that it is possible to achieve better clinical outcomes (Mishra et al., 2023). It would allow people to prepare to cope and build skills in AR and VR through immersive, interactive experiences of real-world challenges.

Call to Action for Stakeholders in Technology and Mental Health

To fully realize the potential of AR, VR, and MR in mental health care, stakeholders, including mental health professionals, technologists, policymakers, and researchers, must collaborate closely. Mental health practitioners must be educated about these technologies and understand their clinical implications to incorporate them effectively into therapeutic practices. Simultaneously, technologists must collaborate with mental health professionals to ensure that the design and implementation of these tools meet the specific needs of practitioners and patients (Tewar et al., 2023).

Policymakers will always be at the core of ensuring an environment that supports and promotes technological innovation in mental health, for instance, funding for research initiatives, development of policies addressing ethical issues, as well as promoting training initiatives among mental health practitioners. It is possible for policymakers across sectors to create and collaborate on frameworks to ensure safe and effective usage, with access to diverse populations (Atkins et al., 2022).

Vision for the Future: Shaping Tomorrow with Innovation in Mental Health

The future vision of mental health care involves the synergy of technology and therapeutic practice that promotes holistic, patient-centered approaches. AR, VR, and MR technologies will advance to a level where they can be used not only to treat mental health disorders but also to build resilience and well-being in people (Gupta et al., 2024).

Looking forward, innovation in mental health care should focus on inclusion and accessibility so that the most advanced technologies get to the people who really need them, mostly the underserved communities. Overcoming barriers to access and adapting interventions to cultural contexts will make the landscape of mental health care much more equitable and responsive to individual needs.

Finally, the incorporation of AR, VR, and MR technologies into mental health care will be an exciting frontier to enhance therapeutic effectiveness and overall patient experience. The time to act is now. With collaborative and thoughtful work toward this vision, stakeholders can reshape the future of mental health treatment and pave the way for a healthier tomorrow.

References

Andersen, N. J., Schwartzman, D., Martinez, C., Cormier, G., & Drapeau, M. (2023). Virtual reality interventions for the treatment of anxiety disorders: A scoping review. *Journal of Behavior Therapy and Experimental Psychiatry*, *81*, 101851.

Asiain, Joaquín, Malena Braun, and Andrés J. Roussos. "Virtual reality as a psychotherapeutic tool: current uses and limitations." *British Journal of Guidance & Counselling* 50, no. 1 (2022): 1-28.

Atkins, R., Johnson, S., Pontes, M. C., Stellmacher, T., Gadaleta, D., Lewis, H., ... & Williams, W. (2022). Socio-demographic and coping correlates and predictors of depressive symptoms among low-income and ethnic minority mothers at-risk. *Clinical Nursing Research*, *31*(1), 100-114.

Breslow, A. S., Lopez, M., Warren, B., Levin, J., Sharma, A., Watnick, D., ... & Bauman, L. J. (2024). Lessons Learned from a Community-led, Pilot Teletherapy Group for Older Women Living with Depression and HIV. *AIDS and Behavior*, *28*(12), 4079-4093.

Brocki, L., Dyer, G. C., Gładka, A., & Chung, N. C. (2023, February). Deep learning mental health dialogue system. In *2023 IEEE International Conference on Big Data and Smart Computing (BigComp)* (pp. 395-398). IEEE.

Camacho, K. S., Page, A. C., & Hooke, G. R. (2021). An exploration of the relationships between patient application of CBT skills and therapeutic outcomes during a two-week CBT treatment. *Psychotherapy Research*, *31*(6), 778-788.

Carlson, Clint G. "Virtual and augmented simulations in mental health." *Current Psychiatry Reports* 25, no. 9 (2023): 365-371.

Cullen, A. J., N. L. Dowling, R. Segrave, J. Morrow, A. Carter, and M. Yücel. "Considerations and practical protocols for using virtual reality in psychological research and practice, as evidenced through exposure-based therapy." *Behavior Research Methods* 53, no. 6 (2021): 2725-2742..

Dargan, Shaveta, Shally Bansal, Munish Kumar, Ajay Mittal, and Krishan Kumar. "Augmented reality: A comprehensive review." *Archives of Computational Methods in Engineering* 30, no. 2 (2023): 1057-1080.

Davies, S. (2023, September). VR and Sensors in Alleviating Loneliness. In *2023 11th International Conference on Affective Computing and Intelligent Interaction Workshops and Demos (ACIIW)* (pp. 1-5). IEEE.

Freitas, J. R. S., Velosa, V. H. S., Abreu, L. T. N., Jardim, R. L., Santos, J. A. V., Peres, B., & Campos, P. F. (2021). Virtual reality exposure treatment in phobias: a systematic review. *Psychiatric Quarterly*, *92*(4), 1685-1710.

Fuxiong, C. (2023, January). A Novel Virtual Reality (VR) based Intelligent Guiding System. In *2023 International Conference on Intelligent Data Communication Technologies and Internet of Things (IDCIoT)* (pp. 294-297). IEEE.

Garibay, E., Ghafoori, B., & Ranney, M. J. (2021). PTSD symptom expression in Latina sexual assault survivors. *The International Journal of Health, Wellness and Society*, *11*(2), 69.

Guo, H. J., Bakdash, J. Z., Marusich, L. R., & Prabhakaran, B. (2022). Augmented reality and mixed reality measurement under different environments: A survey on head-mounted devices. *IEEE Transactions on Instrumentation and Measurement*, *71*, 1-15.

Gupta, Nidhi, Kirti Sharma, Shivam Kumar, and Priyanshu Kumar. "Metaverse-Driven Advances in Immersive VR Experiences for Behaviour Analysis and Skill Development." In *New Business Frontiers in the Metaverse*, pp. 135-154. IGI Global, 2024.

Kee, T., & Lai, A. (2024). Learning motivation and psychological empowerment of socioeconomically disadvantaged learners–an empirical study on inclusive project-based learning during Covid-19. *International Journal of Inclusive Education*, *28*(11), 2438-2457..

Klein, C. S., Hollmann, K., Kühnhausen, J., Alt, A. K., Pascher, A., Seizer, L., ... & Renner, T. J. (2024). Lessons learned from a multimodal sensor-based eHealth approach for treating pediatric obsessive-compulsive disorder. *Frontiers in Digital Health*, *6*, 1384540.

Maulik, Pallab K., Graham Thornicroft, and Shekhar Saxena. "Roadmap to strengthen global mental health systems to tackle the impact of the COVID-19 pandemic." *International Journal of Mental Health Systems* 14 (2020): 1-13.

Moggia, Danilo, Wolfgang Lutz, Eva-Lotta Brakemeier, and Leonard Bickman. "Treatment Personalization and Precision Mental Health Care: Where are we and where do we want to go?." *Administration and Policy in Mental Health and Mental Health Services Research* 51, no. 5 (2024): 611-616.

Panchal, Nirmita, Rabah Kamal, Kendal Orgera, Cynthia Cox, Rachel Garfield, Liz Hamel, and Priya Chidambaram. "The implications of COVID-19 for mental health and substance use." *Kaiser family foundation* 21 (2020): 1-16.

Pelucio, L., Quagliato, L. A., Cardoso, A., Horato, N., & Nardi, A. E. (2025). Could the use of web-based applications assist in neuropsychiatric treatment? An umbrella review. *BMC psychology*, *13*(1), 1-21.

Ramos, G., Hernandez-Ramos, R., Taylor, M., & Schueller, S. M. (2024). State of the science: using digital mental health interventions to extend the impact of psychological services. *Behavior Therapy*.

Rashidi, A., Woon, G. L., Dasandara, M., Bazghaleh, M., & Pasbakhsh, P. (2025). Smart personal protective equipment for intelligent construction safety monitoring. *Smart and Sustainable Built Environment*, *14*(3), 835-858.

Ridings, L. E., Davidson, T. M., Walker, J., Winkelmann, J., Anton, M. T., Espeleta, H. C., ... & Ruggiero, K. J. (2022). Caregivers' and Young Children's Emotional Health Needs After Pediatric Traumatic Injury. *Clinical pediatrics*, *61*(8), 560-569.

Sadeghi Milani, Alireza, Aaron Cecil-Xavier, Avinash Gupta, Joe Cecil, and Shelia Kennison. "A systematic review of human–computer interaction (HCI) research in medical and other engineering fields." *International Journal of Human–Computer Interaction* 40, no. 3 (2024): 515-536.

Sawrikar, Vilas, and Kellie Mote. "Technology acceptance and trust: overlooked considerations in young people's use of digital mental health interventions." *Health Policy and Technology* 11, no. 4 (2022): 100686.

Smink, A. R., van Reijmersdal, E. A., & van Noort, G. (2022). Consumers' use of augmented reality apps: prevalence, user characteristics, and gratifications. *Journal of Advertising*, *51*(1), 85-94.

Soudhamini. (2024). Writing the Virtual: Diverse Modes of Development in Cinematic Virtual Reality. In *Screenwriting for Virtual Reality: Story, Space and Experience* (pp. 233-255). Cham: Springer International Publishing..

Sweileh, Waleed. "Analysis and mapping of scientific literature on virtual and augmented reality technologies used in the context of mental health disorders (1980–2021)." *The Journal of Mental Health Training, Education and Practice* 18, no. 4 (2023): 288-305.

Talafidaryani, Mojtaba, Seyed Mohammad Jafar Jalali, and Sérgio Moro. "Tracing the evolution of digitalisation research in business and management fields: Bibliometric analysis, topic modelling and deep learning trend forecasting." *Journal of Information Science* (2023): 01655515221148365.

Tewari, Shuchita Pant, Richa Misra, Kritika Nagdev, and Himani Sharma. "Role of online health communities in patient compliance: a social support perspective." *Journal of Systems and Information Technology* 26, no. 4 (2024): 562-585.

Vegt, N., Visch, V., Spooren, W., van Rossum, E. F., Evers, A. W., & van Boeijen, A. (2024). Erasing stigmas through storytelling: why interactive storytelling environments could reduce health-related stigmas. *Design for Health*, *8*(1), 46-77.

Virvou, Maria. "Artificial Intelligence and User Experience in reciprocity: Contributions and state of the art." *Intelligent Decision Technologies* 17, no. 1 (2023): 73-125.

Zeine, Foojan, and Nicole Jafari. "Awareness Integration Theory: A Comprehensive Telehealth and Virtual Psychotherapy Tool for the Treatment of Anxiety and Depression." *Annual Review of Cybertherapy and Telemedicine 2023* (2023): 239.

Chapter 10

Security and Privacy Consideration in Immersive Environments

K. Jayashree[1,*]
Vijay Priya[2,†]
R. Babu[3,‡]
B. V. Krishna[4,‖]
and J. Manikandan[5,¶]
[1]Department of Artificial Intelligence and Data Science, Panimalar Engineering College, Chennai, India
[2]Department of Information Technology, Rajalakshmi Engineering College, Chennai, India
[3]Department of Computational Intelligence, School of Computing, SRM Institute of Science and Technology, Kattankulathur Campus, Chennai, India
[4]Department of Computer Science and Engineering, KCG College of Technology, Chennai, India
[5]Department of Information Technology, St. Joseph's College of Engineering, Chennai, India

Abstract

Immersive environments, powered by Virtual Reality (VR), Augmented Reality (AR), and Mixed Reality (MR) technologies, are transforming industries such as gaming, education, healthcare, and remote collaboration. But such environments also pose critical security and privacy concerns due to the massive amount of personal, behavioural, and biometric data they collect. Traditional cybersecurity mechanisms find it difficult to fight against threats such as illicit data access, deepfake tampering, identity spoofing, and real-time tracking vulnerability. This chapter addresses key security and privacy concerns in immersive environments, with emphasis on data protection, secure authentication, and encrypted communications. It addresses novel methods such as Zero-Knowledge Proofs (ZKP), Homomorphic Encryption (HE), Blockchain-driven identity management, Secure Multi-Party Computation (SMPC), and Differential Privacy (DP) for resisting threats. Ethical considerations and policy frameworks such as GDPR, CCPA, and future governance

[*] Corresponding Author's Email: k.jayashri@gmail.com
[†] Corresponding Author's Email: priya.vijay@rajalakshmi.edu.in
[‡] Corresponding Author's Email: babu.rajen17@gmail.com
[‖] Corresponding Author's Email: brahmadesamkrishna71@gmail.com
[¶] Corresponding Author's Email: jmanekandan@gmail.com

In: Shaping Tomorrow
Editors: Prithi Samuel, A. Sathya, Balamurugan Balusamy et al.
ISBN: 979-8-90134-076-9

frameworks for the metaverse are also addressed for their impact on user privacy. The chapter addresses extensively the trade-off between user experience and security and provides recommendations for developing privacy-assuring immersive environments for safety and usability. With the use of novel cryptographic techniques and integrating them with privacy-improving technologies, this research hopes to create a baseline for future research and real-world deployments in secure immersive ecosystems.

Keywords: immersive environments, virtual reality (VR), augmented reality (AR), mixed reality (MR), homomorphic encryption (HE), differential privacy (DP)

1. Introduction to Immersive Environments: VR, AR, and MR

1.1. Understanding Immersive Environments

Immersive environments apply more advanced digital technologies for interactive and engaging experiences, replicating real and fictional environments. The environments are generally driven by Virtual Reality (VR), Augmented Reality (AR), and Mixed Reality (MR) with different levels of digital interaction and fusion with reality. With improvements in high-performance computing, artificial intelligence (AI), and cloud infrastructure, immersive technologies are being applied in industries including video games, education, healthcare, manufacturing, and remote working [1].

1.2. Virtual Reality (Virtual Reality): Complementary Complete Virtual Worlds

Virtual Reality (VR) is a whole-immersion technique, producing a computer-synthesised environment, disconnecting people from the real world. Using head-mounted displays (HMDs), controllers, and space-tracking systems, Virtual Reality offers an interactive experience where individuals can interact and explore computer-synthesised environments [2].

Key Features of VR:

- Complete immersion: The user becomes fully covered in a virtual setting with complete lack of visibility of the real environment.
- 3D spatial interaction: 6 Degrees of Freedom (6DoF) are employed for movement and interaction in VR systems.
- Hardware-dependent: Requires specific headsets including Oculus Rift, HTC Vive, and PlayStation VR.
- Use Cases: Games, training simulations, therapy, architectural visualisation, and virtual tourism.

Despite its benefits, there are also challenges for VR, including motion sickness, expensive hardware, and invasion of privacy because of real-time tracking of the user.

1.3. Augmented Reality (AR): Making the Real World Virtual with Virtual Overlays

Augmented Reality (AR) enhances the real world by overlaying computer data, images, text, and 3D objects onto a live video stream. AR doesn't replace reality, unlike Virtual Reality, and instead enhances the real world with computer data, and therefore is more applicable for real-world use [3].

Key Features of AR:

- Partial immersion: AR superimposes computer graphics on real environments, with the user still being engaged with their environment.
- Device flexibility: Capable of being used on smartphones, smart glasses (e.g., Microsoft HoloLens, Magic Leap, Google ARCore).
- Real-time interaction: The computer's objects immediately respond to real movement.
- Use Cases: retail (try-ons virtually), navigation (Google Maps AR), medical training, industrial design, and marketing.

However, AR also has its security threats, including data privacy, unauthorised access, and vulnerability of real-time location tracking.

1.4. Mixed Reality (MR) and Blending of AR and VR

Mixed Reality (MR) is a more advanced form of immersive technology, combining the best of AR and VR, and allowing real-time interaction between real and digital objects. MR accommodates the user's capacity for interacting with and modifying virtual objects without their perception of space being lost [4].

Key Features of MR:

- Blended digital and real experiences: MR unites digital content and interacts with the real world. Advanced spatial computing: Employs AI-based environment mapping and object identification. Requires specialised devices: MR can be implemented with expensive devices like Microsoft HoloLens and Magic Leap.
- Use Cases: Remote collaboration, medical diagnostics, engineering simulations, and interactive learning. MR bridges the gap between AR and VR and remains costly and hardware-intensive, limiting its widespread adoption.

The comparative examination of VR, AR, and MR puts their differences into context in terms of immersion levels and dependencies on hardware. Figure 1 demonstrates that maximum immersion (10/10) can be achieved with VR, fully engaging people in a computer-simulated environment, and MR (8/10) provides interactive blending of real and virtual environments. AR (5/10) has minimum immersion because, unlike the other two, AR superimposes computer graphics on real environments without fully engaging people in a computer-simulated environment.

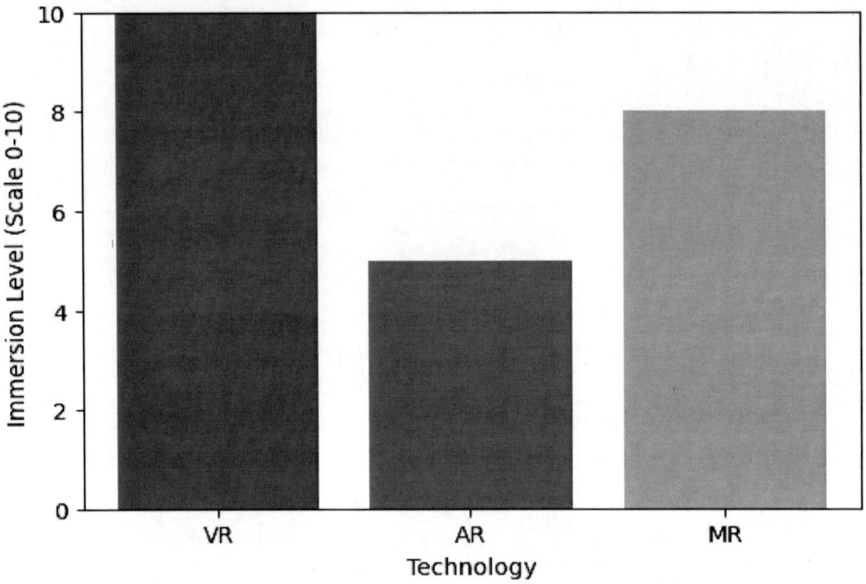

Figure 1. Immersion levels of VR, AR, and MR.

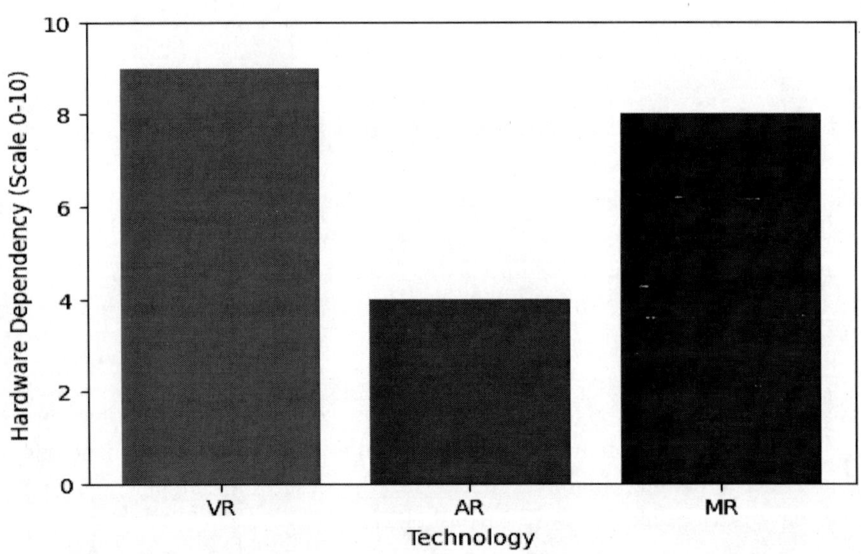

Figure 2. Hardware dependency in VR, AR, and MR.

On the other hand, Figure 2 demonstrates different levels of dependencies on hardware of these technologies. The maximum levels of dependencies on hardware (9/10 and 8/10) are with VR and MR, with their requirements of dedicated headsets, hand controllers, and computer horsepower for smooth performance. AR (4/10) has minimum dependencies on hardware, with its use of commonly available consumer devices such as phones and tabs. The study suggests that, even more immersive, VR has its maximum requirements of extensive hardware and massive computer horsepower, and AR, more convenient, has more useful and applicable purposes with limited people's immersion, and MR, being a middle ground, has its optimal blending of interactivity and requirements on hardware. The differences, therefore, are critical in determining the best utilisation of immersive technologies across industries in terms of accessibility, people's experience, and technical feasibility. Also, with the advancement of immersive environments, their security and privacy will be critical in their safe and ethical utilisation.

2. Key Security Threats in Immersive Experiences

2.1. Unauthorised Data Access and Hacking

Unauthorised data access is a significant vulnerability for immersive environments, where real-time data exchange, networked devices, and cloud storage underlie AR, MR, and VR apps. Threat actors can use network infrastructure vulnerabilities, weak authentication mechanisms, and unpatched code to gain access to private user data without authorisation. The consequence of such breaches can be identity theft, monetary fraud, and exposure of private behavioural and biometric data. Hackers can also gain access to virtual spaces for tampering with content, intellectual property theft, and wiretapping private conversations. Proper encryption, access policies, and regular code updates need to be implemented to limit such threats [5].

2.2. Man-in-the-Middle (MitM) Attacks in AR/VR

MitM attacks are a major challenge in immersive spaces due to wireless connectivity for real-time data sharing. In such attacks, criminals use intercepted communications between the user and the server, and this allows them to tamper with, edit, and even steal data being transmitted. A typical example of this can be when attackers compromise AR apps and insert harmful virtual content into a user's environment, causing tampering and misinformation. Similarly, eavesdropping and injecting false interactions can breach meetings and collaborative sessions in VR. End-to-end encryption (E2EE) of immersive apps, secure communication protocols, and artificial intelligence (AI) for identifying anomalies are major solutions for prevention against such breaches [6].

2.3. Identity Spoofing and Deep Fake Manipulation

Identity spoofing and deepfake manipulation pose serious threats in immersive environments where voice and digital avatar interaction are commonplace. Deepfakes can be produced with the use of AI and can be employed for realistic impersonation of real users, and this can be employed for impersonation, fraud, and deception. This can be of major concern in corporate meetings, Virtual Reality social spaces, and online video games, where trust in the identity of the user is of importance. Deepfake can be used for voice command tampering, evasion of biometric authentication, and disinformation. Deepfake-detecting AI, blockchain identity verification, and multi-factor authentication can reduce such threats [7].

2.4. Denial-of-Service (DoS) Attacks

DoS and Distributed Denial-of-Service (DDoS) attacks can drastically slow down immersive experiences by sending too much traffic to the VR/AR servers, leaving them unfunctional. The consequences of such attacks are greatest for big events in the virtual space, online multiplayer, and corporate use of VR, where real-time interaction is critical. A successful DDoS can lead to delays, disconnections, and even failures, and incur monetary and reputational damages for the service providers. To mitigate this risk, immersive platforms must install traffic filtering, load balancing, and artificial intelligence-based threat identification mechanisms for recognising and repelling suspicious network behaviour [8].

2.5. Exploitation of Sensor and Tracking Data

Immersive technologies rely on a variety of different sensors for hand gestures, gaze, movement, and facial identification. The data can be exploited, however, for profiling, surveillance, and even behaviour prediction for use by cybercriminals. The data can be intercepted for use by unscrupulous actors for the reconstruction of habits, emotional responses, and even biometric data, and this can result in breaches of confidentiality and blackmail. A perfect example of this can be viewed with pilfered eye-tracking data, where a user's unconscious inclinations can be made explicit, leaving them vulnerable to personalised ads and psychological manipulation. Imposing strict data anonymisation, on-site data processing with the use of edge computing, and encrypted data storage can protect consumers from such threats. Social Engineering and Phishing in VR/AR Social engineering and phishing attacks have been enriched with the immersive experience of AR and VR environments, becoming even more deceptive. The attackers can impersonate familiar faces, such as corporate leaders and technical support personnel, and fool individuals into divulging login credentials, money, and other private information. In AR environments, attackers can create deceptive overlays, pushing individuals into hazardous behaviour, such as unauthenticated purchases and clicking on deceptive links. Immerging environments, unlike traditional phishing, also allow attackers to use realistic voice dialogue and computer-synthesised human-like characters, with greater rates of success. The employment of AI-driven behavioural outlier identification, user training, and strict identity checks can reduce such sophisticated attacks [9].

Figure 3 illustrates that unauthenticated access and deepfake identity spoofing pose the biggest threats in immersive environments, with severity levels of 9 and 10, respectively. The two can lead to identity theft, financial fraud, and massive disinformation in online environments. Sensor data compromise also has a high rating (9/10) because immersive devices collect extensive behavioural and biometric data, and hence, they are valuable targets for attackers. Man-in-the-Middle (MitM) attacks, phishing, and DoS attacks also rate very high, and this points towards the need for the use of solid encryption, secure authentication, and anomaly detection systems.

Figure 4 illustrates the occurrence of such attacks, with the greatest being unauthorised data access (30 of 100 incidents) and then phishing and social engineering attacks (25 of 100 incidents). This suggests that, even with higher severity of deepfake spoofing and sensor data exploitation, they are not very frequent when compared with more frequent attack vectors such as unauthorised access and phishing, which are typical of immersive environments. The report points towards pre-emptive security solutions, including AI-driven threat discovery, blockchain identity verification, and real-time cybersecurity monitoring, for securing immersive ecosystems against future threats.

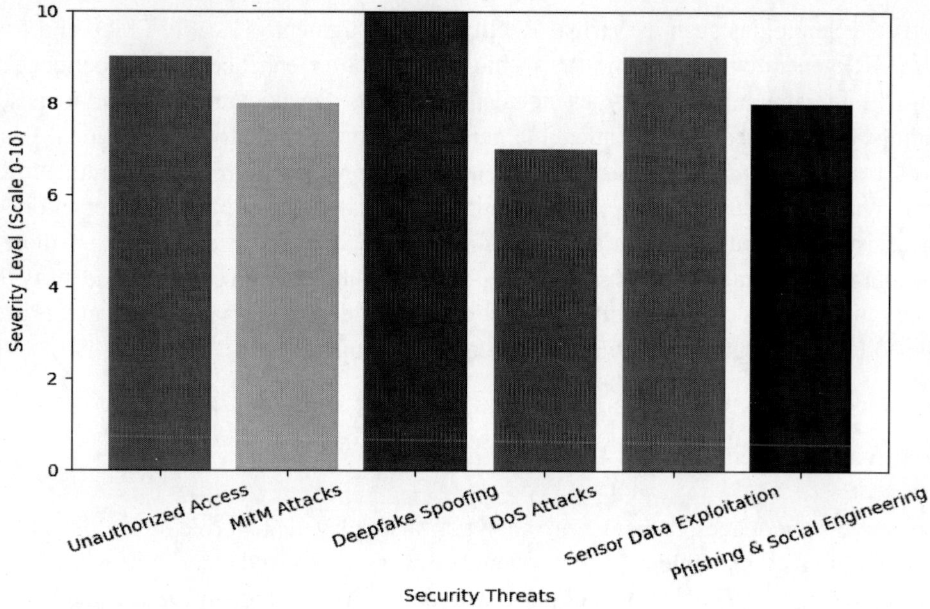

Figure 3. Severity of security threats in immersive environments.

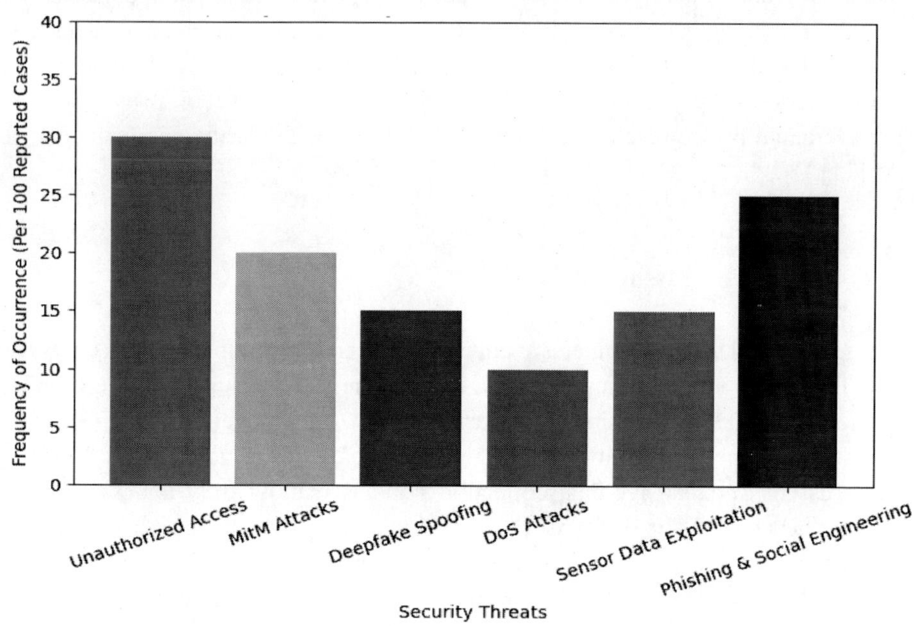

Figure 4. Frequency of security threats in immersive environments.

3. Privacy Risks in Biometric and Behavioural Data Collection

3.1. Types of Biometric Data in Immersive Environments

Immersive technologies such as Virtual Reality (VR), Augmented Reality (AR), and Mixed Reality (MR) generate massive amounts of biometric data for enhanced user experiences and friction-free interaction. The data types include fingerprints, facial identification, iris scans, and voiceprints, and are used for authentication, personalisation, and security. Facial identification monitors user emotion and expression, and iris scans provide high-security authentication systems. The voice data enables voice identification and voice-controlled interaction with virtual assistants. Though such usability-enabling biometric characteristics exist, there are significant privacy-related problems, and access without authorisation can lead to identity theft, illicit surveillance, and biometric fraud. Proper data storage, data encryption, and authorisation for data collection are needed for the prevention of such misuse [10].

3.2. Behavioural Analytics and User Profiling

In immersive experiences, behavioural analytics also play a key role in modifying user experiences based on movement, gaze, and hand gestures. Advanced algorithms learn from the way individuals interact with virtual objects, where they are looking, and where and how they are moving, with the goal of maximizing engagement and recommending more personalized content. But this level of tracking has major privacy dangers, because granular behavioural data can be used for psychological profiling of individuals, revealing unconscious likes, habits, and susceptibilities. The data can be used for behavioural manipulation, personalised ads, and even political influence without explicit user permission. With the use of privacy-preserving analytics, differential privacy techniques, and data policies with clarity, such dangers can be minimised [11].

3.3. Data Ownership and Issues of Consent

One of the biggest challenges of immersive environments is determining who has analysed, the right to own the data captured and analysed. Platform owners, device manufacturers, and third-party apps generally take ownership of data captured and stored, even if consumers generate this data with their behaviour and physiological signals. A large group of consumers inadvertently assent to expansive data collection policies without fully understanding what happens with their data. The lack of clarity brings ethical challenges, especially when immersive platforms sell data from consumers for advertisements and research. Clear mechanisms of consent, data access, and decentralised identity systems can ensure consumers retain rights to their data [12].

Re-Identification Risks Even when data from behaviour and biometrics has been anonymised, there remains a very real risk of re-identification, where data aggregators and attackers can connect anonymous data points with real identities. Gaze behaviours, for instance, can be matched against pre-existing databases with motion tracking patterns, and even typing speeds, to ascertain a user's identity. This can be of major concern for whistleblowers, political activists, and people who want their online lives to be private. The more there has been advancement in big data and artificial intelligence, the higher the risk of being de-anonymised, and hence, there's a need for utilising techniques of data privacy such as federated learning, homomorphic encryption, and k-anonymity in order not to be re-identified [13].

3.4. Third-Party Data Sharing and Surveillance

Many immersive platforms rely on third-party solutions for advertisements, data analytics, and cloud computing, and this has created data sharing and surveillance issues. If behavioural and biometric data are shared with advertisers, consumers can be made targets of profiling, exploitative, and hyper-personalised ads. Governments and intelligence agencies can also use immersive platforms for surveillance on a mass scale, and this creates questions of ethics and laws on user autonomy and online rights. If there are no strict regulations, companies can sell data of their consumers to unknown third-party actors, and individuals can be made subjects of uncontrolled data-related privacy threats [14]. Enforcing stringent data-sharing policies, mechanisms for user opt-out, and regulations can be needed to limit third-party access to individual data. Data Storage and Breach Vulnerabilities: Storing large pools of behavioural and biometric data centrally exposes them to being a very attractive target for data breaches and cyberattacks. If these centralised databases fall into the wrong hands, attackers can access irrevocable, unalterable, and private biometric identifiers. A leaked facial template or iris scan can facilitate attackers impersonating individuals for their lifetime, with remediating being virtually impossible. Poorly encrypted data storage systems and insecure clouds also pose a greater risk of unauthorised access. The use of decentralised data storage solutions, blockchain-technology-driven authentication, and artificial intelligence-driven threat detection can boost security and protect against massive data breaches in immersive environments [15].

Figure 5 illustrates the seriousness of varying privacy issues in immersive environments on a scale of 0-10. The highest risk factor is vulnerability to data breaches (10/10) because behavioural and biometric data are very personal and, if leaked, can lead to irrevocable identity theft. Difficulty with collecting biometric data and data ownership both rate high (9/10) because of the legal and ethical questions of who has access and control of user data. Third-party data sharing (8/10) and behavioural profiling (8/10) are also significant threats because immersive platforms regularly record user behaviour and can share this with advertisers and third-party organisations. The risk of re-identification (7/10) is relatively lower in terms of seriousness, but still significant because anonymised biometric data can regularly be traced back to actual identities.

Figure 6 provides insights into the occurrence of such threats to privacy in immersive environments. The data breaches are highest in occurrence, with 30 of 100 instances, and emphasise the need for rigorous encryption and data decentralisation. The collection of biometric data (25/100 instances) and sharing with third-party actors (18/100 instances) are also prevalent, suggesting the lack of proper user permission mechanisms on of immersive platforms. Behaviour profiling (20/100 instances) occurs with substantial frequency, with companies utilising user data for personalised ads and content. Though data ownership conflicts and re-identification threats are lower in occurrence (15/100 and 10/100 instances, respectively), they still pose substantial threats to privacy. The research suggests the need for strict data regulations, tighter user privacy settings, and more complex cryptographic techniques for securing individual data in immersive environments.

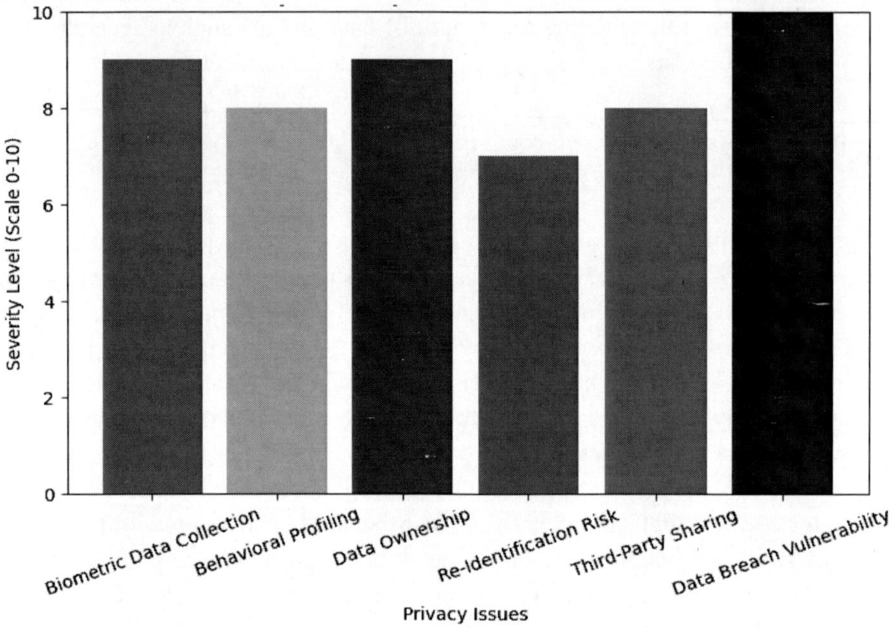

Figure 5. Risk Severity of privacy issues in immersive environments.

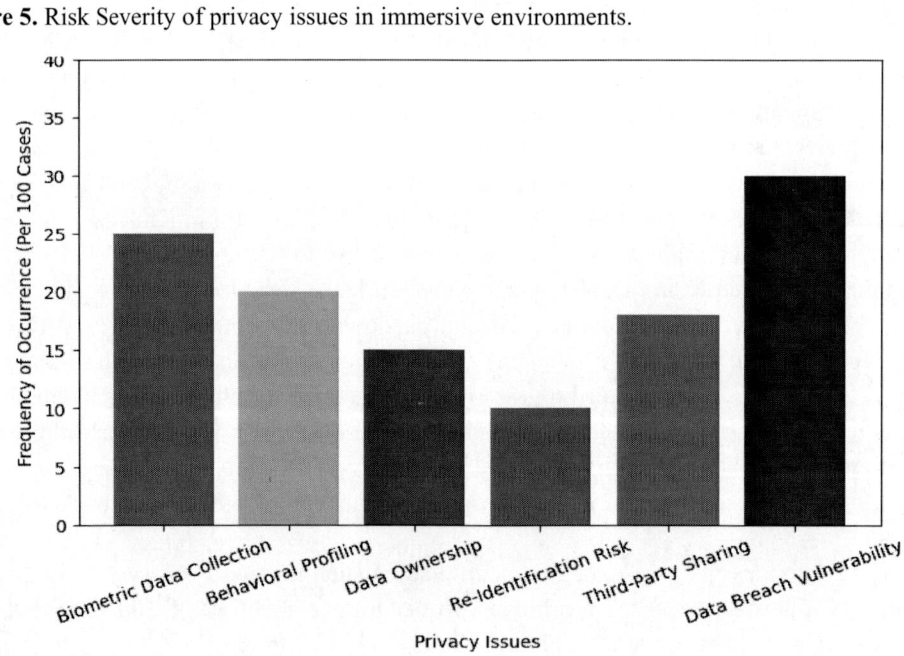

Figure 6. Frequency of privacy issues in immersive environments.

4. Authentication and Identity Management in Virtual Spaces

4.1. Traditional Authentication Methods for AR/VR

Traditional authentication methods in immersive environments rely mainly on password-based systems, widely regarded as insecure and exploitable online. The passwords can be guessed, leaked, and intercepted through phishing, brute force, and data breaches. With individuals interacting with multiple different virtual platforms in AR and VR apps, remembering and entering complex passwords becomes cumbersome, reducing security and usability. The lack of interoperable authentication frameworks between different immersive platforms also contributes to exposure. With the evolution of online threats, single-password authentication becomes outdated, and more rigorous authentication processes must be established for protecting identities online [16].

4.2. Multi-Factor Authentication (MFA) in Virtual Environments

Multi-Factor Authentication (MFA) provides much greater security with more than a single point of verification for access. In immersive environments, MFA can be blended with biometric identification (e.g., facial identification, iris scan), token-based identification (hardware- and software-created single-use passwords), and behavioural identification (capturing movement behaviour and habits). The layered approach reduces the likelihood of access from outside sources even if there has been a breach of one of the factors. Challenges of implementing MFA in VR/AR environments, including smooth user experience without breaking immersion, optimal accuracy of biometric identification, and compatibility of devices between different platforms, need to be addressed [17].

4.3. Decentralised Identity Systems

Decentralised Identity Systems (DIS) are proving to be a secure and privacy-centred solution for immersive environments. A major tenet of DIS, Self-Sovereign Identity (SSI) ensures individuals can be their identity owners and controllers without relying on centralized identity authentication providers. In contrast to holding credentials on a centralised database, SSI uses blockchain and crypto keys to enable individuals to authenticate their identity securely on other virtual platforms. The solution enhances security with the removal of single points of failure, reducing identity theft risk, and with individuals being in complete control of their data. But large-scale adoption of SSI has interoperability, regulatory, and easy-to-implement barriers [18].

4.4. Biometric-Based Authentication

Biometric authentication is one of the strongest and widely used solutions for securing immersive environments. Face, iris, and fingerprint identification are very secure because they authenticate individual physiological traits, and they are difficult to counterfeit and mimic. The means of authentication are of critical importance in VR video games, corporate video conferencing, and AR-driven corporate apps, where access must be guaranteed. But with biometric authentication, there are also data-privacy, data-storage, and data-breach risks of compromising biometric data. Because, unlike passwords, biometric data can't be changed after being broken into, there must be guaranteed data-storage security, data-encryption, and data-regulatory governance for securing people's biometric data [19].

4.5. Voice and Gesture Authentication

Voice and gesture-based authentication methods are picking up pace with advancements in immersive technologies. Voice authentication checks for voice patterns of a user for identification, and therefore, voice authentication becomes a convenient and hands-free way of authentication for use in AR and VR environments. Gesture-based authentication, on the other hand, depends on movement tracking and behavioural observation for recognising individuals on the basis of their personal hand movement, gait, or style of interaction. These forms of authentication foster usability and security, as they rely on real behaviour, which is not easy to impersonate. But they are still in developmental phases and suffer from environmental noise disturbance (for voice authentication), accuracy for different populations of individuals, and resistance against spoofing attacks [20].

4.6. Challenges in identity verification

Ensuring secure identity verification in online spaces is a daunting task due to the growing identity theft, deepfake impersonation, and tampering with avatars. Threat actors can impersonate genuine individuals with the use of AI-synthesised avatars and stolen biometric data, leading to illicit access and fraud. Social VR spaces and corporate use cases of the metaverse must be able to resist identity spoofing and filter between genuine and artificial identities created with the use of artificial intelligence. The utilisation of blockchain-driven digital identity verification, artificial intelligence-driven anomaly detection, and real-time biometric verification can prevent identity spoofing and foster trust in online interactions.

Figure 7 illustrates the relative performance of different methods of authentication in immersive environments. Multi-Factor Authentication (MFA) and biometric authentication rank highest in terms of security (9/10) and therefore are safest against unauthenticated access. Decentralised identity solutions also rank highest (8/10) in terms of security and resistance against cyber-attacks, for not being centralised. But password-based authentication ranks worst (4/10) in terms of security and (3/10) in terms of resistance against cyber-attacks, and therefore there's a need for phasing out single-authentication via passwords from immersive platforms. Gesture-based authentication ranks highest in terms of convenience (9/10) but lower in terms of security (6/10) due to the vulnerability of being spoofed.

Figure 8 depicts adoption rates of various methods of authentication in immersive environments. Authentication with passwords still has wide usage (30%), despite its vulnerability, implying a slow transition towards more secure approaches. There's adoption of MFA (25%), with more layers of security being introduced in immersive environments. There's also an increase in usage of biometric authentication (20%), for corporate purposes and for use on high-security VR systems. The use of decentralised identity solutions (10%), however, remains low, mostly due to interoperability. The use of voice (8%), and of gestures (7%), has low usage, mostly due to accuracy and spoofing. The report indicates more use of decentralised identity systems and of biometrics for more security in virtual environments.

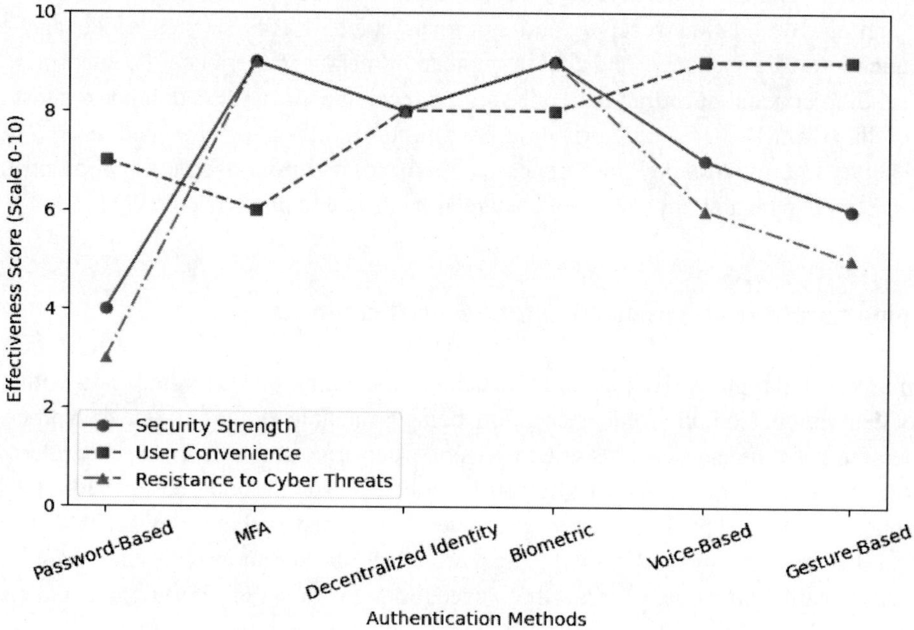

Figure 7. Effectiveness of authentication methods in immersive environments.

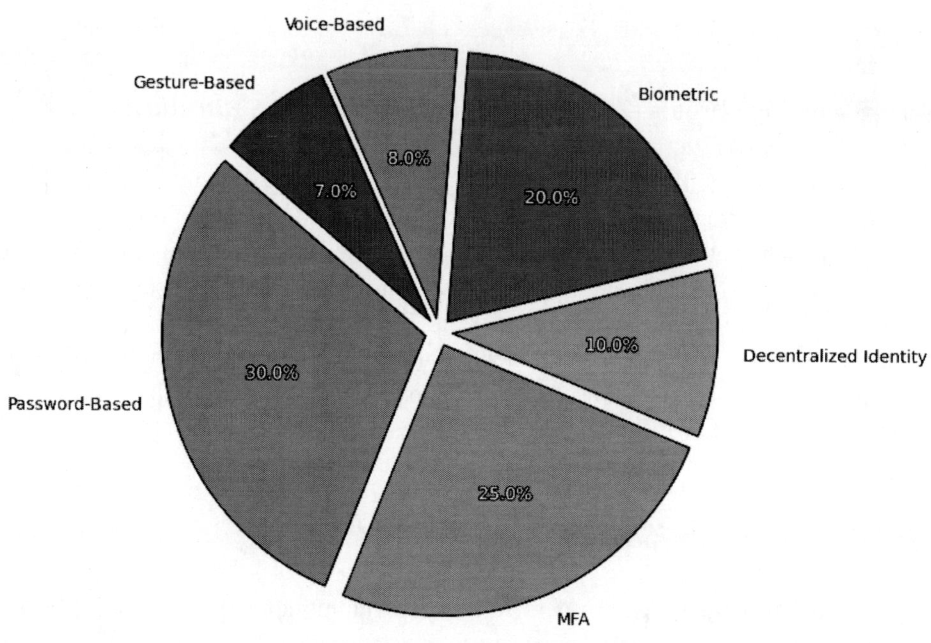

Figure 8. Usage distribution of authentication methods in immersive platforms.

5. Cryptographic Techniques for Securing Immersive Environments

5.1. End-to-End Encryption (E2EE) for AR/VR Communications

End-to-End Encryption (E2EE) is a critical security solution for securing real-time communications and data exchange for AR/VR. E2EE ensures data can be viewed only by the sender and the destination receiver and not intercepted. E2EE secures voice and video communications, file exchange, and chat in-game in immersive experiences by encrypting data on the sending end and decoding data only on the receiving end. E2EE defends against man-in-the-middle (MitM) attacks, and private user communications are guaranteed. But E2EE can be expensive in terms of delay and processor overhead, and optimized encryption protocols need to be implemented, with a trade-off between security and performance [21].

5.2. Homomorphic Encryption (HE) for Secure Processing

Homomorphic Encryption (HE) accommodates computations on encrypted data without its need for decryption. Homomorphic encryption, being a valuable tool for private data processing in immersive environments, ensures safe treatment of sensitive user behaviour, user interaction, and biometric data. An example of this can be considered with cloud-based Virtual Reality (VR) apps, where encrypted user preference can be analysed without exposure of raw data, with usability and confidentiality being maintained. Fully homomorphic encryption (FHE) being computationally costly, real-time execution in AR/VR environments becomes problematic. To achieve this, partially homomorphic encryption (PHE) or levelled homomorphic encryption (LHE) can be used for achieving a performance and security trade-off [22].

5.3. Zero-Knowledge Proofs (ZKP) for Privacy-Preserving Authentication

Zero-Knowledge Proofs (ZKP) present a way of proving identity without divulging personal data. In immersive environments, where there's a demand for confidentiality and anonymity, ZKP provides authentication without divulging sensitive identity and credential data. A user, for example, can authenticate access into a virtual space without disclosing their identity, username, and password. This reduces data leak and identity theft. ZKP finds its optimal use in decentralized metaverse apps, blockchain identity authentication, and safe monetary exchange in virtual spaces. Its complexity and computational overhead, however, limit its use on a large scale in real-time AR/VR.

5.4. Attribute-Based Encryption for Access Control

Attribute-Based Encryption (ABE) refers to a cryptographic approach that provides access rights or denies access rights based on user-defined attributes. It is very useful for use in immersive environments where there are requirements for multi-user interaction, file sharing with security, and access based on roles. A simple example of this can be considered for use in corporate use of VR, where access of an employee can be limited because of job description, department, or security classification. ABE supports granular access, and only legitimate individuals can be allowed access to specific data. Its performance, however, relies on key management performance, and complex policies can incur delays in real-time immersion [23].

5.5. Secure Multi-Party Computation (SMPC) for Data Sharing

Secure Multi-Party Computation (SMPC) accommodates multiple participants in jointly computing a result without sharing their private input. It finds its application in multi-user Virtual Reality (VR) training simulations, collaborative environments, and virtual healthcare, where private data must be securely processed. In a typical use of a VR-driven medical diagnosis tool, physicians from different centers can jointly process data without sharing unprocessed health data. Whilst data confidentiality with SMPC is guaranteed, there exists a heavy computational demand for performance, affecting real-time performance in immersive environments. Optimised SMPC protocols and hybrid crypto approaches can mitigate performance degradation [24].

5.6. Quantum-Resistant Cryptography for Enduring Security

With the rise of quantum computing, traditional methods of encryption (e.g., ECC and RSA) can be breached. Post-quantum cryptography (PQC) and quantum-resistant cryptography are needed for future security in immersive environments. Lattice-based cryptography, hash-based signatures, and code-based crypto schemes are ways of being quantum-resistant. Emergent future use cases, including blockchain-driven metaverse economies and secure exchange of virtual assets, need to use quantum-resistant means of protecting against future dangers. However, PQC techniques are still being researched and must be optimised for AR/VR systems.

Figure 9 depicts a security vs. performance comparison of various techniques. Zero-Knowledge Proof (ZKP) and Quantum-Resistant Cryptography attain maximum security (10/10) and hence are optimal for future-proof identity and authentication with confidentiality preservation. However, their performance (computational) is low (ZKP: 5/10, Quantum-Resistant: 3/10) and must be enhanced for real-time immersive usage. E2EE (security: 8/10, performance: 9/10) and Attribute-Based Encryption (security: 8/10, performance: 7/10) attain balanced security and performance and hence are viable for access and immersive communications. Homomorphic Encryption (HE) and Secure Multi-Party Computation (SMPC) attain higher security with lower performance ratings due to their complexity of calculation.

Figure 10 depicts adoption trends of crypto techniques in immersive environments. E2EE remains the most widespread (30%), being a standard security practice for encrypted data exchange and messaging. ABE (20%) is being implemented more widely for corporate and enterprise VR environments for need-to-know access control. Homomorphic Encryption (15%) and SMPC (15%) are on the increase, mostly for use in healthcare and banking-related VR apps with secure data processing. ZKP (10%) and Quantum-Resistant Cryptography (10%), however, to increase, with more adoption expected when the technology becomes more mature.

The study finds that security and computational performance requirements must be balanced for the use of crypto solutions in immersive environments.

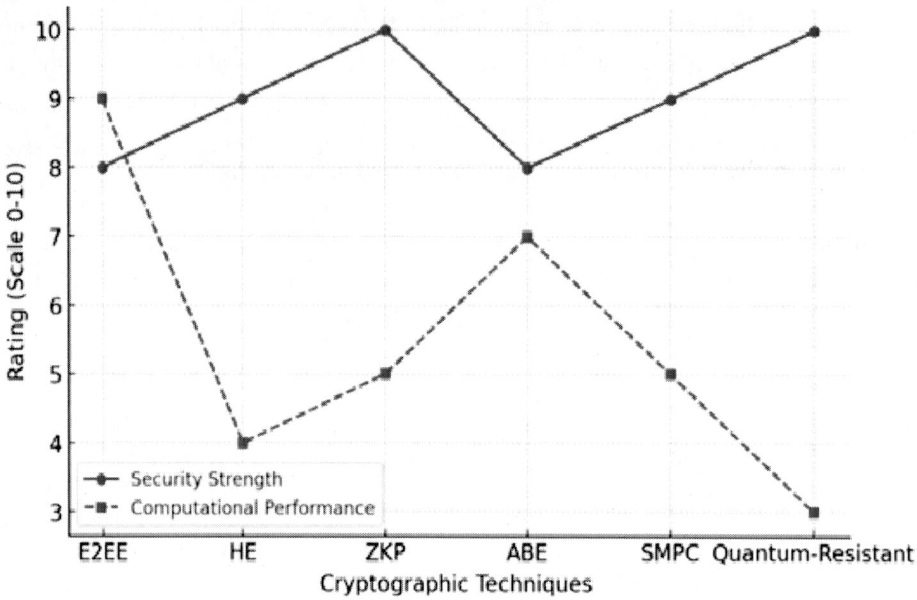

Figure 9. Security vs. performance Trade-off of cryptographic techniques.

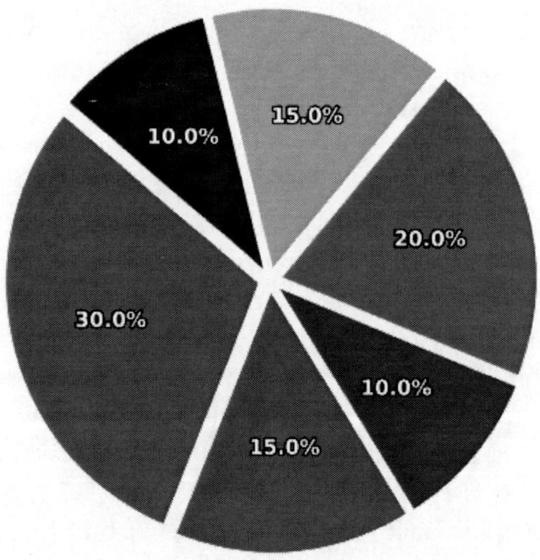

Figure 10. Adoption trends of cryptographic techniques in immersive platforms.

6. Role of AI in Threat Detection and Anomaly Analysis

6.1. AI-Driven Intrusion Detection Systems (IDS)

AI-powered Intrusion Detection Systems (IDS) apply machine learning methods for identifying and reacting against security breaches in AR, MR, and VR environments. The systems regularly check network traffic, user behaviour, and system events for indications of abnormalities, such as probable cyberattacks. Rule-based IDS, however, apply conventional methods, and the systems are not effective against zero-day attacks and evolving threats. The AI-driven IDS, however, apply pattern and anomaly discovery methods for identifying unknown threats, and this enhances security in AR, MR, and VR environments. But AI-driven IDS must be regularly trained on varying datasets for lowering false negatives and false positives, and this ensures accurate identification of threats [25].

6.2. Behavioural Anomaly Detection for AR/VR Environments

AI plays a major contribution towards monitoring user behaviour in immersive environments for identifying suspicious and outlier behaviour. Anomaly behaviour identification relies on machine learning methods for monitoring hand gestures, movement, and eye movement for recognising probable fraud, illicit access, and impersonation of a user's avatar. If, for example, movement of a user becomes unlike their normal way of interacting, then the session can be flagged for additional authentication. But when there's excessive surveillance of user behaviour, then there's a matter of privacy, and therefore there's a need for developing privacy-assuring AI systems able to spot threats without betraying user data.

6.3. Deep Learning for Malware Detection

Deep learning frameworks significantly enhance malware detection in immersive environments with the discovery of new and evolving forms of attacks. Traditional signature-based anti-virus solutions are ineffective against mutating malware, ransomware, and spyware and therefore fail in immersive technologies. Deep learning and neural network-based malware detection frameworks apply convolutional deep networks and neural networks for code structures, execution behaviour, and log file examination of AR/VR apps. The frameworks can find and disable harmful code even before it can compromise user security. Deep learning-driven security solutions, however, require huge training datasets and heavy computational needs, and therefore, are not simple to implement on lightweight AR/VR devices.

6.4. AI-Powered Identity Authentication

AI enhances identity authentication and verification in immersive environments through voice, facial, and biometric authentication. AI identity verification models check real-time voice, facial, and fingerprint data for authentication of user identity, precluding identity spoofing and deepfake impersonation. In immersive environments with multiple users, AI can alert to suspicious logins and apply adaptive authentication based on real-time risk levels. However, AI identity verification systems are biased and, therefore, yield false negatives and false positives for varying populations, and hence, present ethical questions in immersive security.

6.5. Predictive Security Models for Immersive Technology

AI-driven predictive security systems pre-identify potential threats and susceptibilities before they can be exploited. The predictive security systems take historical security data, real-time behaviour of systems, and external threat data and generate preemptive security responses. In immersive environments, potential AR/VR-specific cyber-attacks, such as takeover of virtual space or tampering with sensor data, can be anticipated and preempted. Predictive security, however, must learn continuously from real-time security events and therefore remains data-driven.

6.6. AI Bias and Ethical Issues

AI-driven security systems in immersive environments also present ethical and biased problems affecting security efficacy. Using biased datasets for training can lead to incorrect flagging and ignoring of behaviour, with discriminatory security enforcement. A perfect example of this can be seen with facial recognition for authentication in VR, where accuracy may be lower for certain ethnic populations, with false rejection and greater barriers for verification. There are also privacy problems when large-scale biometric and behavioural data are being analysed with AI models, with possible mass surveillance. To overcome these, there need to be transparent AI models, bias mitigation, and privacy-protecting AI techniques for fair and effective security enforcement.

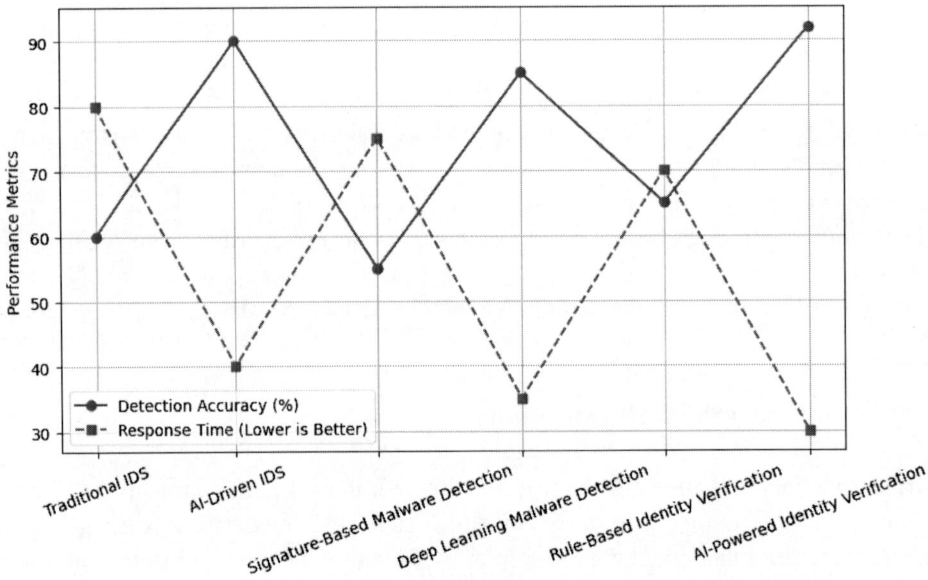

Figure 11. AI-Driven Vs traditional security methods in immersive environments.

The comparison of traditional security methods with AI-driven mechanisms is given in Figure 11, which indicates the key advantages of AI for immersive environments. AI-Driven IDS performs better with higher accuracy (90%) and significantly lower response times, and therefore, is more effective against evolving cyber threats. Deep learning-based malware detection also performs better compared to signature-based because novel variants of malware can be identified without pre-defined signatures. AI-driven identity verification mechanisms, such as facial and biometric identification, attain maximum accuracy (92%) and response times, in contrast with rule-driven authentication mechanisms, which are beset with false positives and delays in verification. Despite these advantages, AI security solutions also present challenges such as bias, privacy, and computational overhead. Traditional methods of security, on the other hand, are deterministic and demand fewer computational assets, but lack adaptation towards new threats in AR, VR, and MR environments. Overall, the graph illustrates that AI-based security solutions present more efficient identification of threats, more rapid response, and more effective authentication mechanisms, and therefore, are more viable for the interactive and dynamic environment of immersive technologies. However, for equitable and ethical AI-based security enforcement, there exists a need for incorporating bias prevention techniques, explainable AI frameworks, and mechanisms for protecting privacy in immersive environments.

7. Ethical Considerations and User Privacy in the Metaverse

7.1. Ethical Dilemmas in Immersive Environments

The rapid growth of the metaverse creates complex ethical questions on surveillance, user consent, and rights in the digital realm. Numerous immersive environments harvest huge amounts of personal, behavioural, and biometric data without explicit knowledge of, and adequate mechanisms for, user consent. Ongoing tracking of user movement, gazing, and behaviour creates a space where people can be under constant surveillance, and there are questions of data ownership and freedom. Also, giving informed consent in such spaces becomes problematic because people may not understand the magnitude of data collection and use, and there are questions of transparency and rights in the digital space.

7.2. Bias in AI-Powered VR/AR Security Systems

AI-driven security systems such as behaviour tracking, facial identification, and automatic threat identification also suffer from algorithmic bias. Imbalanced training data for artificial intelligence systems can lead to disproportionate misclassification of individuals from a particular demographic group, inducing discriminatory access restrictions, incorrect bans, and security misclassifications. Artificial intelligence-driven decision-making can also exacerbate digital disparities, affecting marginalised populations in online spaces. To foster fairness and accountability in artificial intelligence-driven security systems, there needs to be transparent model training, methods of reducing bias, and regular audits against discriminatory enforcement in immersive spaces.

7.3. Psychological and Behavioural Manipulation in Immersive Environments

Immersive environments are very engaging and interactive, and with them, there are also psychological manipulation and addiction-related risks. The metaverse also uses persuasive design techniques, including dopamine-driven feedback loops, gamification mechanisms, and algorithmic content targeting, which can result in compulsive use and changed behavioural habits. Immersive ads and subliminal message methods can also sway user choice without their explicit knowledge, and there are ethical questions surrounding manipulative design. Developers need to take user welfare and ethical UX design into consideration, such that immersive environments don't take advantage of psychological frailties for monetary purposes [26].

7.4. Surveillance and Privacy in the Metaverse

The metaverse depends on big data collection for seamless interaction, and this can be made possible at the cost of user privacy. Advanced tracking methods like eye-tracking, movement tracking, and real-time behavioural observation create a surveillance atmosphere where the user feels monitored. Organisations and third-party actors can reap individual data for personalised advertisements, profiling, and predictive behavioural data, and this raises massive questions of privacy. Balancing security and individual freedom depends on mechanisms for protecting privacy, decentralised identity systems, and strict policy regulations for maintaining user freedom and security.

7.5. Cyberbullying and Harassment in Virtual Worlds

As social experiences in the metaverse become more realistic, harassment, bullying, and online harassment have increased. Compared with other online spaces, immersive experiences are more intimate and real, and hence, harassment in online spaces becomes more psychologically traumatic for victims. The lack of strict policies and content moderation systems means bad actors can abuse such spaces with minimal consequence. To fight against digital safety in immersive spaces, there needs to be strict anti-harassment policies, artificial intelligence content filtering, and safety systems under user control, such as personalised interaction boundaries and real-time abuse report systems. Future Ethical Frameworks for Responsible Immersive Technologies. As immersive environments expand, the establishment of ethical frameworks and governance systems will be paramount for enabling fair and equitable virtual ecosystems. Regulations in the future must be focused on data privacy, digital rights, equitable AI, and algorithmic decision-making disclosure. Ethical design values must facilitate user autonomy, use without exploitative intent, and people-centered governance for the metaverse to be equitable and safe. There must be collaboration between policymaking, developing, and user advocacy communities for defining responsible boundaries, prioritising equity, privacy, and ethical security for immersive technologies [27].

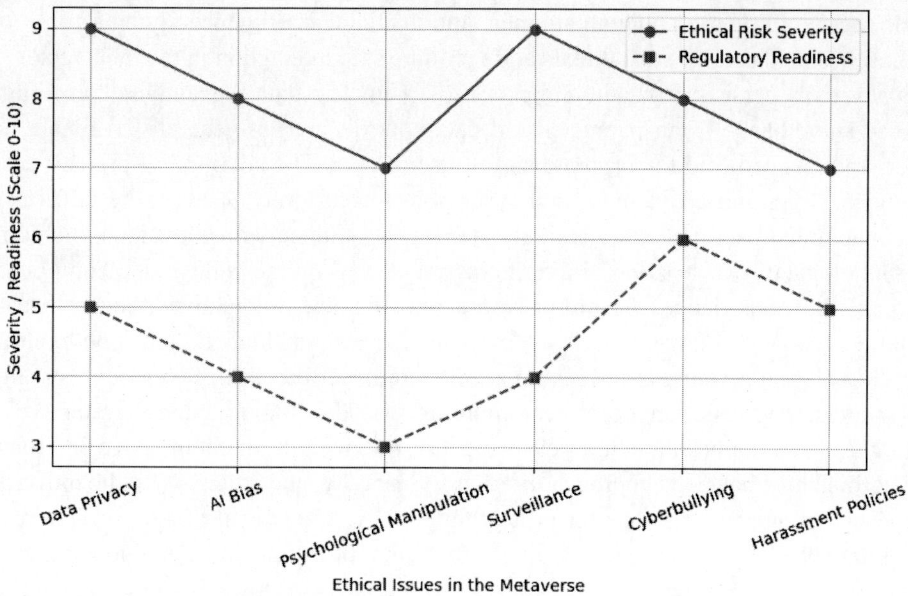

Figure 12. Ethical risks vs. Regulatory readiness in the metaverse.

The line chart given in Figure 12 depicts the gap between ethical risk and regulatory readiness in addressing security and privacy matters related to the metaverse. The scale of risk for data privacy (9/10), surveillance (9/10), and bias in artificial intelligence (8/10) is considerably higher compared with the current level of regulatory preparation (privacy: 5/10, surveillance: 4/10, bias in artificial intelligence: 4/10). Psychological manipulation in immersive environments** also creates a major issue (7/10), and regulations (3/10) lag in terms of protecting against exploitative design. Cyberbullying (8/10) and harassment policies (7/10) are becoming more pressing, and means of their enforcement are still underdevelopment (6/10 and 5/10, respectively).

This disparity between policy and ethical imperatives signals the need for more vigorous policy interventions, responsible AI governance, and user-centered security. With the rise of the metaverse, there must be joint action from policymakers, platform builders, and ethical researchers to ensure equitable, inclusive, and privacy-centred virtual environments prioritising user rights and online flourishing.

Conclusion

The rapid proliferation of immersive technologies, including Virtual Reality (VR), Augmented Reality (AR), and Mixed Reality (MR), has changed the way people interact online, with new means of communication, entertainment, knowledge, and commerce. With these innovations, however, there also emerge significant security, privacy, and ethical concerns, and resolving them becomes paramount for the safety and trust of the online environment. One of the major problems with immersive environments is data security. Unwanted access, Man-in-the-Middle (MitM) attacks, identity spoofing, and data breaches of behavioural and biometric data expose consumers to online threats and breaches of their privacy. Authentication methods with high levels of security, cryptographic techniques, and artificial intelligence systems for anomaly identification shield against such threats and facilitate safe interaction in the metaverse.

Privacy risks persist, about the collection of biometric data, behavioural profiling, and third-party surveillance. Transparencies and data controls are not generally available for the end-user, and this can lead to corporate and ill use of data. The adoption of privacy-enabling technologies, decentralised identity, and strict policy conformity needs to be undertaken in order to shield end-user data and guarantee their rights. Ethical considerations, including AI bias, psychological manipulation, online harassment, and online rights, also complicate the landscape. With experiences becoming more realistic and interactive, there's a call for developing accountable governance systems with fairness, inclusivity, and non-exploitative design. The solution for these issues requires collaborative efforts from developers, researchers, policy makers, and user advocacy communities for developing ethical frameworks for defending user autonomy and online well-being. Overall, the future of immersive environments will be defined by a balanced approach for security, privacy, and ethics. With the utilisation of enhanced cybersecurity, solutions for protecting privacy, and ethical design, we can realise a more equitable and more secure metaverse, with trust, innovation, and valuable connections.

References

[1] De Guzman, Jaybie A., Kanchana Thilakarathna, and Aruna Seneviratne. "Security and privacy approaches in mixed reality: A literature survey." *ACM Computing Surveys (CSUR)* 52, no. 6 (2019): 1-37.

[2] Giaretta, Alberto. "Security and privacy in virtual reality: a literature survey." *Virtual Reality* 29, no. 1 (2024): 10.

[3] Matsui, Tomokazu, Shigetomo Sakuma, Yuki Mishima, Hirohiko Suwa, Keiichi Yasumoto, Tatsuya Amano, and Hirozumi Yamaguchi. "Understanding Privacy Awareness in Immersive Spatial Sharing System." *Sensors & Materials* 36 (2024).

[4] Hine, Emmie, Isadora Neroni Rezende, Huw Roberts, David Wong, Mariarosaria Taddeo, and Luciano Floridi. "Safety and privacy in immersive extended reality: An analysis and policy recommendations." *Digital Society* 3, no. 2 (2024): 33.

[5] Kundu, Ripan Kumar, and Khaza Anuarul Hoque. "Preserving Personal Space: Differentially Private Cybersickness Detection in Immersive Virtual Reality Environments." In *2024 IEEE International Symposium on Mixed and Augmented Reality (ISMAR)*, pp. 11-20. IEEE, 2024.

[6] Di Pietro, Roberto, and Stefano Cresci. "Metaverse: Security and privacy issues." In *2021 third IEEE international conference on trust, privacy and security in intelligent systems and applications (TPS-ISA)*, pp. 281-288. IEEE, 2021.

[7] Viswanathan, Karthik, and Abbas Yazdinejad. "Security considerations for virtual reality systems." *arXiv preprint arXiv:2201.02563* (2022).

[8] Hadan, Hilda, Derrick M. Wang, Lennart E. Nacke, and Leah Zhang-Kennedy. "Privacy in immersive extended reality: Exploring user perceptions, concerns, and coping strategies." In *Proceedings of the CHI Conference on Human Factors in Computing Systems*, pp. 1-24. 2024.

[9] Tukur, Muhammad, Jens Schneider, Mowafa Househ, Ahmed Haruna Dokoro, Usman Idris Ismail, Muhammad Dawaki, and Marco Agus. "The metaverse digital environments: a scoping review of the challenges, privacy and security issues." *Frontiers in big Data* 6 (2023): 1301812.

[10] Kaur, Sukhpreet, Saumya Rajvanshi, and Gurleen Kaur. "Privacy and security concerns with augmented reality/virtual reality: a systematic review." *Augmented Reality and Virtual Reality in Special Education* (2024): 209-231.

[11] Wang, Yuntao, Zhou Su, Ning Zhang, Rui Xing, Dongxiao Liu, Tom H. Luan, and Xuemin Shen. "A survey on metaverse: Fundamentals, security, and privacy." *IEEE Communications Surveys & Tutorials* 25, no. 1 (2022): 319-352.

[12] Lebeck, Kiron, Kimberly Ruth, Tadayoshi Kohno, and Franziska Roesner. "Towards security and privacy for multi-user augmented reality: Foundations with end users." In *2018 IEEE Symposium on Security and Privacy (SP)*, pp. 392-408. IEEE, 2018.

[13] Alkaeed, Mahdi, Adnan Qayyum, and Junaid Qadir. "Privacy preservation in Artificial Intelligence and Extended Reality (AI-XR) metaverses: A survey." *Journal of Network and Computer Applications* (2024): 103989.

[14] Anwar, Muhammad Shahid, Inam Ullah, Shabir Ahmad, Ahyoung Choi, Sadique Ahmad, Jing Wang, and Khursheed Aurangzeb. "Immersive learning and AR/VR-based education: cybersecurity measures and risk management." In *Cybersecurity Management in Education Technologies*, pp. 1-22. CRC Press, 2023.

[15] Iqbal, Muhammad Zahid, Xuanhui Xu, Vivek Nallur, Mark Scanlon, and Abraham G. Campbell. "Security, ethics and privacy issues in the remote extended reality for education." In *Mixed Reality for Education*, pp. 355-380. Singapore: Springer Nature Singapore, 2023.

[16] Wilson, Ethan, Azim Ibragimov, Michael J. Proulx, Sai Deep Tetali, Kevin Butler, and Eakta Jain. "Privacy-Preserving Gaze Data Streaming in Immersive Interactive Virtual Reality: Robustness and User Experience." *IEEE Transactions on Visualization and Computer Graphics* (2024).

[17] Khan, Koffka. "Security Challenges and Solutions in 360-Degree Augmented Reality Video Streaming: A Comprehensive Review."

[18] Guo, Hanyang, Hong-Ning Dai, Xiapu Luo, Zibin Zheng, Gengyang Xu, and Fengliang He. "An Empirical Study on Oculus Virtual Reality Applications: Security and Privacy Perspectives." In *Proceedings of the IEEE/ACM 46th International Conference on Software Engineering*, pp. 1-13. 2024.

[19] George, Ceenu, Mohamed Khamis, Daniel Buschek, and Heinrich Hussmann. "Investigating the third dimension for authentication in immersive virtual reality and in the real world." In *2019 ieee conference on virtual reality and 3d user interfaces (vr)*, pp. 277-285. IEEE, 2019.

[20] Yadav, Akanksha, and KG Neha Reddy. "Virtual Dilemmas: Legal and Ethical Rollercoasters in Immersive Tech Land." In *Multidisciplinary Applications of Extended Reality for Human Experience*, pp. 64-80. IGI Global, 2024.

[21] Saleem, Kashif, Basit Shahzad, Mehmet A. Orgun, Jalal Al-Muhtadi, Joel JPC Rodrigues, and Mohammed Zakariah. "Design and deployment challenges in immersive and wearable technologies." *Behaviour & Information Technology* 36, no. 7 (2017): 687-698.

[22] O'Brolcháin, Fiachra, Tim Jacquemard, David Monaghan, Noel O'Connor, Peter Novitzky, and Bert Gordijn. "The convergence of virtual reality and social networks: threats to privacy and autonomy." *Science and engineering ethics* 22 (2016): 1-29.

[23] Odeleye, Blessing, George Loukas, Ryan Heartfield, Georgia Sakellari, Emmanouil Panaousis, and Fotios Spyridonis. "Virtually secure: A taxonomic assessment of cybersecurity challenges in virtual reality environments." *Computers & Security* 124 (2023): 102951.

[24] Cayir, Derin, Abbas Acar, Riccardo Lazzeretti, Marco Angelini, Mauro Conti, and Selcuk Uluagac. "Augmenting security and privacy in the virtual realm: An analysis of extended reality devices." *IEEE Security & Privacy* (2023).

[25] Abid, Noman. "A Review of Security and Privacy Challenges in Augmented Reality and Virtual Reality Systems with Current Solutions and Future Directions." *Emerging Technologies in AI and Machine Learning*.

[26] Zallio, Matteo, and P. John Clarkson. "Designing the metaverse: A study on inclusion, diversity, equity, accessibility and safety for digital immersive environments." *Telematics and Informatics* 75 (2022): 101909.

[27] O'Hagan, Joseph, Pejman Saeghe, Jan Gugenheimer, Daniel Medeiros, Karola Marky, Mohamed Khamis, and Mark McGill. "Privacy-enhancing technology and everyday augmented reality: Understanding bystanders' varying needs for awareness and consent." *Proceedings of the ACM on Interactive, Mobile, Wearable and Ubiquitous Technologies* 6, no. 4 (2023): 1-35.

Chapter 11

The Role of AR, VR, and MR in Enhancing Emotional Well-Being: Transforming Mental Health Care

Manisha Singh[1,*]
and Sonali Srivastava[2,†]
[1]VIT Business School, VIT Bhopal University, Bhopal, India
[2]Jaypee Business School, Jaypee Institute of Information Technology, Noida, India

Abstract

One in every four individuals is likely to suffer from one or another mental disorder in their lifetime. More than 450 million individuals suffer from mental or neurological disorders globally. Unfortunately, 75% of individuals suffering from mental disorders remain untreated. Furthermore, mental disorders are also a major cause of suicide worldwide. With increasing stress in day-to-day life, the situation is becoming worse day by day. Mental health problems can no longer be treated with traditional modes of treatment, including medication, psychotherapy, and counselling. Hence, innovative treatment approaches are required to address mental health issues efficiently and effectively. Presently, rigorous research work is being carried out to explore the potential of immersive technologies, such as augmented reality, virtual reality, and mixed reality, in improving therapeutic practices. Emotions are an integral part of overall health. They play an important role in our day-to-day decisions, from small purchases to buying a new car or choosing to accept or reject a job offer. Emotional well-being has been defined as a combination of cognitive abilities and lifestyle factors related to psychosocial prosperity. Positive emotions help in broadening vision and shaping one's life; they motivate individuals and help them build their intellectual, social, and physical resources. Apparently, when people experience negative emotions like anger, guilt, and fear, they tend to fix their sights; their actions become focused on a specific goal to improve their situation. Consequently, negative emotions may be appropriate in certain conditions; they should occur sufficiently and cause people to respond in productive ways. The main objective of this study is to investigate the current state of the art of using augmented reality, virtual reality, and mixed reality for enhancing emotional well-being. It is argued that the use of these immersive technologies can facilitate the early treatment of mental health disorders. Furthermore, it can also be applied to health promotion activities. Immersive technologies can be effectively used as a

* Corresponding Author's Email: manishacpri@gmail.com
† Corresponding Author's Email: srivastavasonali1106@gmail.com

In: Shaping Tomorrow
Editors: Prithi Samuel, A. Sathya, Balamurugan Balusamy et al.
ISBN: 979-8-90134-076-9

prevention tool, keeping in mind initiatives such as early identification and early intervention in the prevention pyramid. It can also be used to maintain mental well-being. This study will be helpful for both researchers and practitioners working in the areas of mental health care and immersive technologies.

Keywords: emotional well-being, mental health, healthcare, recovery-oriented practice, technological innovations, digital mental health, AR, VR, MR

1. Introduction

The potential influence of augmented reality, virtual reality, and mixed reality on mental health and emotional well-being support has attracted much attention from researchers and practitioners. Moreover, the advancement of immersive technology is expected to serve as a stimulus to promote the application and acceptance of immersive technology in the mental health domain. By providing a simulated environment, users can benefit from the technology and overcome the limitations of the real environment. The simulated environments invite emotional and behavioural responses from users and help them deal with therapeutic content (Fan et al., 2022). Therefore, the simulated environment benefits users who suffer from emotional and behavioural disorders or wish to enhance particular subjects by delivering appropriate emotion, stress relief, relaxation, education, and performance intervention. Over the last few years, extending the potential application of augmented reality, virtual reality, and mixed reality has attracted the notice of a growing number of researchers. The number of papers studying specific or multiple symptoms of mental disorders is expanding exponentially. Researchers have provided reviews on using augmented reality, virtual reality, and mixed reality in mental health support. Augmented reality, virtual reality, and mixed reality are promising technological tools that enrich the perceived reality of physical presence for a variety of therapeutic and non-therapeutic purposes. Virtual, mixed, and augmented realities partially or completely simulate environments. They elicit emotional, behavioural, and psychological responses from users, providing valuable assistance to those suffering from emotional and behavioural disturbances, igniting therapeutic enthusiasm, and offering powerful new tools for educational and beneficial interventions for enhancing mental and emotional well-being (Soon et al., 2023).

1.1. Background and Rationale

Digital health technologies are transforming mental health care by providing scalable and cost-effective behavioural health care services. Augmented Reality, Virtual Reality, and Mixed Reality show the most potential in using the benefits of three-dimensional visualisation and are gaining increasing attention in fields ranging from psychiatric assessment, psychotherapy, pain management, training healthcare professionals, laboratory studies, and consumer-use applications. This chapter discusses the potential of AR, VR, and MR to address the unmet mental health needs and increase psychological well-being by increasing availability and reducing the barriers to access to high-quality evidence-based care. It focuses on the importance of enhancing emotional well-being as a measure of mental health and key components of psychological and mental well-being, examines the potential of digital health technologies to offer a variety of novel approaches and the potential to enhance the effectiveness of preventive strategies, highlights ethical and practical challenges, and provides examples of initiatives investigating the potential of digital health technologies.

Overall, digital health technologies have the potential to reduce healthcare costs, extend the reach of the current workforce, overcome geographical barriers, reduce the need for specialized training, and create a range of personalized and data-driven experiences. The potential of AR, VR, and MR to contribute to mental health is particularly relevant considering the prevalence and cost of emerging mental health problems, such as anxiety, depression, and substance abuse, and the impact of limited mental health services on multiple populations and social systems. The short-term costs and the uncertain long-term benefits of intervention represent a considerable barrier to more extensive investment in prevention and treatment, and delivering effective care to everyone who needs it could lead to significant economic and social returns. Furthermore, although mental wellness initiatives, psychoeducation programs, and mindfulness services give people the tools to self-manage their mental health, they do not have enough capacity to treat serious mental disorders.

1.2 Scope and Objectives

The scope of this study is centered on promoting the accessibility and acceptability of emerging technologies, particularly in underserved populations, aiming to foster their engagement with augmented reality (AR), virtual reality (VR), mixed reality (MR), and similar technologies. By enhancing individual control, emotional investment, and immersion in both educational and therapeutic settings, the study seeks to improve user experiences. Furthermore, it aims to encourage high-quality empirical and theoretical research that explores the development, applicability, and consequences of these technologies in the realm of mental health. To accomplish these goals, the study will actively invite participation from a diverse array of contributors, including researchers, designers, developers, and practitioners from various fields such as mental health sciences, human-computer interaction, psychology, education, technology-enhanced learning, and psychotherapy, thus fostering a collaborative environment for innovative exploration and application.

Objectives

- To acknowledge how advances in technology and off-the-shelf solutions have reduced environmental barriers and economic constraints hindering AR, VR, MR, and related technologies.
- To explore innovative approaches that utilise these immersive technologies to foster emotional connections, enhance therapeutic experiences, and ultimately improve patient outcomes in mental health care.
- To recognise the shift in the healthcare system towards personalisation, emphasising consumer-patient-centric design of AR, VR, MR, and related technologies and promoting emotional investment in health and wellness technologies.

1.3. Key Definitions

Augmented Reality (AR): AR systems combine real and virtual objects and operate interactively in real time. In AR, the physical and virtual worlds are placed on top of one another. AR integrates digital information and the physical environment (Eswaran & Bahubalendruni, 2022). Virtual Reality (VR): VR is a technology that creates a completely new environment in which a user can live or experience events. In VR, users are separated from the real world and are immersed in a computer-generated virtual world. VR simulates the presence of the user in a virtual environment instead of the real world. Mixed Reality (MR): MR is a combination of AR and VR systems. MR integrates the physical world and the virtual world in real time so that the two can coexist. The key idea behind MR is to make physical and digital objects interact intuitively (Wang et al., 2021).

The three technologies, AR, VR, and MR, are realized by different sensor devices to detect position or motion. Their applications can be diversified over time. In sum, AR technologies enhance users' perceptions and sensations with superimposed computer-generated experiences, VR technologies are more immersive and interactive by isolating people in simulated environments, and MR technologies combine the two experiences to enhance the real world with digital devices to interact with the user (Bhowmik, 2024; Kim et al., 2023).

2. Understanding Emotional Well-Being

The World Health Organization defines health as "a state of complete physical, mental, and social well-being and not merely the absence of disease or infirmity," thereby recognizing the importance of mental health in human well-being. Emotional well-being is the state that characterizes an individual capable of coping adequately with normal life stressors, working productively and fruitfully, and contributing positively to the community (Kim, 2024; Health Organization, 2024). However, most of this understanding has been limited to subjective feelings of happiness, reluctance, life satisfaction, and nurturing social contact. Negative effects have been correlated with a range of mental and physical problems, including poor physical health, emotional disturbances, schizophrenia, personality disorders, cognitive impairments, and substance abuse. Positive emotions play a critical role in helping people with a normal life span to remain resilient, resourceful, and creative in seeking alternative goals, undertaking valued actions, and building durable intimate relationships (Ahrens et al., 2021; Ogunbode et al., 2021).

Emotion is a complex psychological state that represents one's affective judgment and is created by an affective coin. Positive and negative emotions come in many forms, and individual emotions differ in emotional intensity, duration, and level of consciousness. There are several terms for one's state when one uses virtual reality or mixed reality, among which are: immersion, presence, emotional and VR sickness, which are related to but not the same as emotions. Immersion is that which is felt as being vividly 'in' the virtual experience of the virtual world. Presence is used to denote the involvement of the actual space in which one is and the degree of the actual space that is being replaced by the virtual space, which usually occurs when 'in' a VR, and refers to the user's sensation of being present in the virtual world (Kelly et al., 2023).

2.1. Conceptual Framework

Several technological systems have been developed to leverage the impact of these technologies in our daily lives. Many of these systems were commercially applied to entertainment, consumer electronics, and education. The focus of this study is on these technological systems and their applications to human emotion to promote emotional well-being, specifically in mental health care (Kang & Shao, 2023; Steiger et al., 2021). Our investigation into the enabling attributes must be understood through the conceptual framework provided in this section. We next develop the conceptual framework, beginning with the active ingredient for change. Emotion is the active ingredient that can be enhanced to increase personal growth and often plays a key role in mental disorders.

Mental health and mental disorders are classic examples and stark proofs of the importance of understanding the nature of emotions and developing the ability to use them to bring about long-lasting change. The success or failure of mental health care is clearly defined by its focus on emotions. We no longer view mental health care as the practice of focusing on the past, merely discussing problems, or focusing only on the intellect (Konaszewski et al., 2021; Cage et al., 2021). Psychotherapy now considers emotional experiences, emotional expression, emotional comprehension, emotional learning, and emotional enhancement as legitimate means for intervention and promotion.

2.2. Factors Influencing Emotional Well-Being

Emotional well-being is inversely related to the incidence of mental health issues and emotional problems. Be critical in the assessment of the kind and level of emotional factors. Those who age in a community host a range of social, personality, quality of life enhancement, and development. How well you communicate, look at their interests, and those who create a positive atmosphere, an essential part of the trust you depend on, to protect both themselves and others with their level of competence (Flor-Alemany et al., 2022). Negative, not in their control, mentally stop activities, such as thoughts, to be irrational beliefs are activated, their low emotional well-being is limited by hardship. Individuals, an important source of creativity and their physical and mental environmental processes can continue to perform well if they face a high volume of responsibilities. They are the origin of designing and maintaining environmental systems; in other words, they play a primary role. Physical, mental, and emotional needs are met, creating an effective environment. A harmonious lifestyle at work, in turn, will give the highest motivational potential. In discussions about emotional well-being, we talk about a state that deviates from the usual balanced mental state. In other words, emotional well-being, the ability to adapt to the external environment and evaluate the balance with changing circumstances (Huang et al., 2024; Ludviga & Kalvina, 2024) is something in terms of an individual's ability and the name of serious emotional problems do not need, but with a person's production in an acceptable nickname.

3. Mental Health Care Landscape

Mental health is an essential component of a person's well-being, irrespective of age, gender, race, or religion. It determines how an individual handles stress, relates to others, and makes choices. A combination of psychological, general well-being, and emotional well-being gives a person positive and improved mental health. The growth of technology is phenomenal, and it has a major role in shaping almost every field of life. Using the exponential nature of technology in mental health care is essential to address the existing and emerging demand for services. Thus, in the current digital era, the challenge is to formulate and tailor digital mental health intervention tools that could deliver mental health care to meet the demands of people living in an ever-increasingly complex society (Ramos & Chavira, 2022; Di et al., 2021).

The purpose is to provide an overview of various types of pervasive technologies like haptic, AR, VR, and MR, and the role they play in improving the social, emotional, and psychological well-being of individuals. how AR, VR, and MR can help in perceiving the world differently and provide a controlled environment to receive intervention to mould their behaviour effectively is discussed. Virtual reality, augmented reality, and mixed reality all have their roots in the cognitive and motor systems of the brain, where haptic mechanisms play a role that drastically increases the sense of immersion when it is considered in these three realities. These immersive facilities have a long historical path, and it has become a powerful technology, producing strong effects on human psychology (Vairamani2024). For the past 20 to 30 years, several behavioural treatment methodologies have been developed to understand and address the causes of psychological and clinical disorders thoroughly. These modern methodologies facilitate the subject to improve their emotional expressions, socio-behavioural coping strategies to manage stress and anxiety, recover both memory and communication abilities, reintegrate into normal life, and develop personal talents to the maximum (Baragash et al., 2022).

3.1. Challenges and Opportunities

Emotional well-being is considered an integral component of overall health and can be of particular interest in the context of various mental health concerns, such as stress, depression, anxiety, and post-traumatic stress disorder. The transformations that are currently being witnessed in digital health care have enabled health services to extend their reach and impact. However, research in mental health has demonstrated that for digital technologies to be truly effective, they must work in collaboration with existing health systems. Augmented reality, virtual reality, and mixed reality belong to the category of digital health technologies and have, to different extents, promising potential in the context of enhancing emotional well-being, mental health care, and treatment. In the area of mental health care, these innovative areas of research are also progressing. However, research is just starting to scratch the surface (Holt, 2023). As promising as these versatile digital technologies are, they come with their fair share of challenges and often face critiques regarding their real-world implementation. If not developed thoughtfully, these technologies can add to existing mental health care inequalities rather than reducing them. Thus, it becomes important to look beyond the hyped potential of these technologies to adopt a sound ethical and pragmatic approach to their development and monitoring to create a successful synergy, mainly with health industry stakeholders. This chapter provides a reflection on the practical challenges and opportunities for the fusion of augmented reality, virtual reality, and mixed reality in advancing mental health care, referring to lessons from effective emotional well-being applications (Dimitrova & Wiium, 2021).

3.2. Traditional Approaches vs. Technological Interventions

Conventionally, psychological or physical interventions were established to modify behaviour and beliefs, reduce human mental stress and other disorders, and alter mood. The use of AR, VR, and MR technologies reduces the prominence of conventional methods and depicts improvement in the outcomes. Various user-centred applications have been built for enhancing personal well-being through the utilisation of AR, as it overcomes the limitations of conventional approaches. This platform has the potential to facilitate (Usmani et al., 2022; Liu et al., 2022) individuals in recognizing and registering adverse events, emotions, and body sensations, and support their coping endeavours. Similarly, VR presents virtual worlds and scenes that are otherwise not conceivable. It can arouse emotions due to associated pain relief as well as oppose negative feelings and mood alterations.

VR can help people recognise, understand, and manage their feelings, emotions, and thoughts, solve problems, and negotiate troubled relationships in a socially constructive manner. It can motivate and support individuals to initiate, maintain, and engage in positive opportunities that help enhance their future as well as emotional states (Houssein et al., 2022). MR augments one's perception and interaction with the surroundings, and as a result, the AR context is personalized for the individual and can be utilized in a variety of situations. It is integrated into a head-mounted computer supporting Ambient Intelligence technology that enables continuous and context-aware services, which involve the intelligent processing of sensor data that defines an environment (Papadopoulos et al., 2021).

4. Importance of Emotional Well-Being in Mental Health Care

What is the mind? What is its nature? What is its limit? These questions are as old as human civilisation. The subject of the inner mind, consciousness, and emotions remains a mystery. In today's fast and wired world, people are busier than ever, multitasking more than ever, and feeling more overwhelmed and overstimulated than before. In this extreme kind of lifestyle, our emotions can be easily pushed to the extreme as well. This is why greater emotional well-being is becoming the major area of focus in transforming health care. Emotions can, however, be incredibly complex; they have unique and ambiguous characteristics at the same time. They are often experienced and expressed in layers, having cognitive components as well as feeling states, which are often hard to differentiate between the conscious and unconscious. Because of the unique characteristics of emotions, it can be very difficult for a person to reach the ultimate source of their emotional problems (Sonnentag et al., 2023; Ashley et al., 2021; Søvold et al., 2021). Emotions often color and shape people's experiences, affecting their every act of choice. Emotional well-being defines the capacity of people themselves to live in intense and sustainable joy, enthusiasm, peacefulness, love, and pleasure. It is like what ancient humans used to say: "Love your neighbour as well as yourself," where yourself is one of the essential objects in the equation (Graciyal & Viswam, 2021; Sophie et al., 2022).

It is hard to seek good help in coping with emotional challenges because compassion and understanding often are not enough when someone is dealing with severe emotional problems. Training and experience are necessary to help someone who needs expert advice. Emotional well-being is particularly important when it applies to mental health and mental illness, especially in this modern, highly stressful environment. Emotional well-being is difficult to achieve that stress is complicated, and human emotions are complicated as well.

5. Technological Advancements in AR, VR, and MR

Although a variety of technologies have been in use to promote mental, social, and emotional well-being and to improve overall quality of life for many years, there has been an increased focus on utilizing AR, VR, and MR for these purposes recently. This focus is becoming particularly pronounced due to technological advances in computing, sensor hardware, display technology, and network devices for transmitting data. We are now witnessing a rapid reduction in costs and miniaturization of hardware that takes us closer to enabling seamless and appealing AR, VR, and MR experiences even in portable devices without compromising user experiences (Bhowmik, 2024).

AR, VR, and MR applications have been in existence for decades, and their beginnings can be traced back to the early developments of flight simulators. However, significant advancements that enable these applications to become commercially viable as well as to be available for consumer-oriented products are quite recent (Tang et al., 2022). It is well known that personal computers and consumer electronic products often gain wide acceptance only when they bear adequate capabilities of hardware and software that can exploit the computational power of the hardware. That probably explains why AR, VR, and MR are becoming prominent only now. High computational power is essential to generate and update realistic representations of the virtual and real worlds at a user's interest rate; otherwise, the user might suffer from motion sickness and feel nauseated. During the last few years, both the real-time computational power required for AR, VR, and MR and the visual resolutions sufficient for an AR, VR, and MR experience have experienced significant increases (Wang et al., 2021). Consequently, each new and advanced generation of homogeneous consumer electronic products comes with a built-in, ever-increasing capability for rendering ultra-high-pixel-density displays that present realistic high-dynamic-range videos with high audio quality.

5.1. Overview of AR, VR, and MR Technologies

Efforts to define AR, VR, and MR and differentiate them sometimes seem arcane and disproportionately complex. Moreover, actual technologies may display aspects of more than one category. Telling AR, VR, and MR apart is easier when considering these technologies' primary or characteristic features. The physical environment is the primary ingredient in the experience of AR; the physical world is suppressed in VR, while in MR, physicality is reduced. MR is a wider concept that includes AR and VR (Rauschnabel, 2021; Verhulst et al., 2021).

Technology differs both technically and experientially. AR content is superposed onto physical reality. VR content is presented through headsets and reshapes visual experience. MR uses optical see-through HMDs that enable a transparent physical world with digital information superposed on an isolated part of or the whole visual field. Cognitive, emotional, and social experiences are shaped by lived bodies, objects, and space (Wu & Kim, 2022). Consequently, many different aspects and many more elements have to be properly preserved, manipulated, and managed in order not to 'shatter' the telepresence created experientially. Cognitive, emotional, and social knowledge for technology exaltations from various sectors is growing fast, but the problem of capturing enough and appropriate reality embedding factors represents a considerable technical challenge.

5.2. Evolution and Development of AR, VR, and MR in Mental Health Care

AR, VR, and MR have been employed in various fields beyond entertainment and training. Since the mid-1990s, VR tools have been developed for various health care applications, including pain control, PTSD, autism, anxiety, depression, and schizophrenia (Lindner, 2021; Gasmi and Benlamri2022). The development cycle and maturation of AR and MR technologies do not stray much from that of VR, as AR has typically used a headset approach, similar to its VR counterpart, thus drawing on the same hardware construction as VR, albeit possessing different goals, technologies, applications, and audiences (Verhulst et al., 2021).

The evolutionary components common to VR, AR, and MR in mental health care include technological advancement, computer graphics, stereoscopic displays, real-time data processing, human–computer interactions, and clinical or psychological theories. Given these components and previous health care VR developments, it can be anticipated that AR, VR, and MR technologies can bring novel applications and paradigms into the mental health care arena (Usmani et al., 2022; Ma et al., 2021). At present, exposure therapy is the most developed and researched VR mental health application; distractions, pain management, empathy enhancement, physical therapy, and diagnostic purposes also possess significant and specific capabilities. In contrast to VR, AR's unique facial recognition, eye tracking, and limb data overlay capabilities have specific significance for mental health diagnosis and the monitoring/enhancement of empathy. Moreover, AR's widely recognized ability to have a 'real world' context, where the virtual world is overlaid onto the real world, shows promising diagnostic applications that can help clinicians gain a more comprehensive psychological profile of a patient based on their reactions to specific scenarios (Klaib et al., 2021; Jin et al., 2024).

6. Applications for AR, VR, and MR in Mental Health Care

AR, VR, and MR technologies have seen potential applications in transforming the mental health care system dynamically. VR and AR can provide users with a more interactive visual and auditory experience with greater psychological impact. VR intervention could produce a degree of distraction and a reduction or reshaping of awareness, which has been suggested to be effective for pain sensations. VR and AR can enhance self-knowledge through the immersion of the patient in a different and simulated world, providing compassion and promoting interest in treatment and improved patient ease (Usmani et al., 2022; Bansal et al., 2022). The application of VR environments, mainly driven by the unique creation of new and engaging interactive telecommunication environments potentiated by mechanised and animated avatars and features, therefore provides new ways to enhance the rate and reduce the duration of therapeutic engagement by rendering it effective and enjoyable (Cullen et al., 2021). From the analysis of these emerging applications and continued research, design guidelines that define the characteristics of results-driven intelligent interactive AR and VR therapeutic environments for mental health treatments are necessary. Patients with chronic pain and harm in the body can benefit from using AR and VR, which can significantly reduce chronic pain by interfacing with users through multisensory feedback. Virtual restorative environments can provide reduced anaesthesia or medications due to mood and positive mental stimulant actions. Virtual reality and video games, using feedback such as biomedical feedback and virtual reality exposure therapy, can be effective therapy choices. Assistance for MRT training and retention of mental representations in the elderly and children can be obtained, and the user must actively engage in the awareness of an immersive, emotionally engaging AR and VR setting. The majority of VR and AR health studies concentrate on moral education and special needs education. High-value VR that points to mental health programs has protective and healing effects in all kinds of situations and adverse events, particularly in young adolescents. The strength of computer-generated VR, AR, mixed reality, and video games easily elicits high levels of emotional and cognitive reactions from people with various mental disorders who are open to new and adaptable settings. Users are completely immersed in a far more personal therapeutic environment than on a standard phone or face-to-face meeting; an individual health care session with the digital character associated (He et al., 2023) with the consumer is typically preserved. VR and AR therapy make more effective decisions than offline mental health treatments. Therapy future can concentrate on patient needs and patient-initiated minute items, minimise the limitations of psychotherapy, concentrate on successful interactions, and use modern technologies to provide regular and dynamic therapy. Interventions involving intelligent technology, AR and VR, can increase the success and retention rates of current mobile health programs and seem to be the most suitable mental health engagement interventions for the emotionally uncomfortable (Wray et al., 2023). AR and VR applied mental health care services alter mental processes and relieve the burden of psychiatric care, even though the evidence from AR and VR intervention scientific research is still recent.

6.1. Therapeutic Interventions and Treatments

Therapeutic interventions play a central role in ameliorating mental health disorders. Therapists and mental health care providers help individuals identify, understand, and work with their problems. They also help find healthier and more effective ways to cope with life challenges and encourage better mental well-being. Therefore, the use of advanced computer technologies, such as three-dimensional (3D) real and virtual worlds, might play a significant role in transforming patient treatment and mental health care delivery (Haleem et al., 2022; Olawade et al., 2024). By using innovative hardware and evidence-based software, AR, VR, and MR can support a wide range of therapeutic activities and educational programs aimed at improving mental health. The major strength of VR technology in mental health applications is its ability to mimic real-world experiences. VR provides a virtually risk-free environment; the user feels fully immersed in an environment that is perceived as entirely real (Usmani et al., 2022; Ma et al., 2021).

A VR environment can be an authentic alternative when real-world scenarios are extremely costly or impossible. VR allows the instructor to supervise the training repeatedly. VR provides a standard session and accurate assessment. VR can support people who find it challenging to move or are unable to manage more complex or stressful scenarios. Specific cues or feared objects can be removed to trigger less-agitated, harmful responses.

6.2. Virtual Reality Exposure Therapy

Virtual Reality Exposure Therapy (VRET) refers to exposing individuals to the stimuli that trigger their phobias or unpleasant human-computer interaction experiences. This, in turn, allows them, in the presence of a trained clinician, to experience reality without being in those actual triggering situations. Traditionally, it has been reported that using images and video clips will help individuals have control over their situations (Lindner et al., 2021). Researchers, however, point out that it is difficult for individuals to imagine interacting with a trigger using slides; it seldom has a strong impact. On the contrary, virtual reality interfaces have the capability to immerse individuals in a closer analogue of the environment to generate actual responses and reinforcement based on their behavior. This debunks the claim that individuals must imagine their experience. This unique capability of VR is the main advantage that leads to a subsequent report stating that individuals who went through VRET have overcome their phobia (Albakri et al., 2022).

Sense of presence is an important factor in VR exposure therapy; it is a crucial variable, and some researchers argue that it leads to an emotional change in the desired direction. Different types of VR exposure therapy are being utilised today, such as fully immersive VR and augmented reality. It is important to note that different strategies must be employed when VRET is utilised for its treatment. Although AR and VR share similar ideas of exposure, they differ in various significant ways, like the ability to provide exposure to situations. For example, if we consider social phobias, it is much easier to expose a patient to a crowd in VR compared to AR. Moreover, AR experiences the limitations present in GPS technologies and the high cost of the equipment (Lindner, 2021; Torous et al., 2021). The therapist does not face the patient; this also adds to the equipment price, especially when physiological monitoring is required. Providing feedback is a difficulty (Eshuis et al., 2021).

6.3. Mindfulness and Relaxation Applications

Mindfulness applications guide users through relaxation activities that help them become more aware of the present moment and focus on the here and now. Users can choose from meditation, sleep, relaxation, and breathing exercises, as well as body scanning and movement activities such as gentle yoga. The aim of an exemplary application is to guide participants through mindfulness-based activities, helping them learn to control and choose their mental and emotional responses to everyday life situations over time through an engaging, safe, and user-friendly experience. An MR-guided mindfulness application was developed for therapists to teach their clients mindfulness practice and improve the clients' experience by directly immersing them in a guided meditation.

Findings showed that the simplicity of the built-in MR technology allowed therapists to follow existing procedures for teaching clients how to increase their attention to the present moment, choose more adaptive responses to their experiences, and improve their overall functioning by engaging clients with a simulated viewpoint of themselves or for therapists to develop modification options for the MR-guided mindfulness application according to patients' coping abilities and to enable therapists to adapt the MR-guided mindfulness application as required.

7. Augmented Reality (AR) in Mental Health

Augmented Reality (AR) is a technology that superimposes a computer-generated picture on an image in the client's view of the real world, thus offering close cooperation between the two. AR in the gaming industry encourages a lot of public enthusiasm. With a role in mental health, AR has been less thoroughly investigated. After some initial experiments, a company started pioneering this with an app developed for children with autism, where AR is utilised. In autism, the enhancement of social skills is a priority (Cheng & Ebrahimi, 2023; Lan et al., 2023). These improvements are extremely helpful before puberty. A mother and father joined forces to create a groundbreaking AR tool for children with autism. A small cousin displayed great improvements in attention. The video illustrates the outcomes hitting social media for the first time. When alternative therapies have not been making any advancement, the parents of the children are completely exhausted; the outcomes with the app were so encouraging that therapy guidelines began suggesting AR (Torous et al., 2021; Hoang et al., 2022).

With the ageing of society and the increasing prevalence of dementia, there is an urgent need for groundbreaking technology to help people with dementia. Every 170 seconds, a new person is diagnosed, leading to a significant impact on others. It is stated that a large percentage of people in residential care facilities suffer from dementia, and their families constantly feel the burden of being part of the experience of caregiving for someone with this condition. The augmented reality game aims to assist people with early-onset dementia (Qin et al., 2022). The 3D treasure hunt game achieves simulations by visiting historical sites as well as incorporating physical activity for individuals. This game offers an AR trigger table partnered with a tablet. As the image of the participants grows, the printed picture on the pool table generates an AR digital picture on the tablet. Extensive research has also been performed in other dementia care settings, from working games to 3D therapies to simulations and conversation systems.

7.1. Applications in Therapy and Treatment

AR, VR, and MR in Mental Health. This section introduces the latest trends, upcoming research, and significant research related to AR, VR, and MR in the field of mental health care. The term mental health is generally used to describe the state of one's mind and well-being, encompassing emotional, psychological, and social health (Usmani et al., 2022; Holt, 2023). Patients suffering from mental health disorders are unable to lead a healthy lifestyle due to abnormal social behaviour, emotional issues, loss of interest or pleasure, evaluative thinking patterns, and, in severe cases, depression and death. The treatment methods adopted to help patients with these disorders can be costly in terms of finances, energy, appointment schedules, as well as self-esteem.

The serious and beneficial features of the AR therapy application can impact clinical functioning. The successful application of AR in reducing negative symptoms may hold promise for treating differential symptoms, such as goal attainment and social cognitive deficits. The results also represent another successful application of IVA and AR for individuals. Recent games have allowed immersive settings with VR to be perceived as novel and fun, making them more attractive to patients who can benefit from AR (Torous et al., 2021). Previous VR therapy programs used standard desktop monitors, which may not generate environmental cues or promote responsiveness, such as touch or enter gestures. During the VR session, large visible and tangible objects were suitable and comfortable in VR. However, with the extended interactions allowed in VR environments, body tracking has been shown to effectively interact with virtual environments (Haleem et al., 2022).

7.2. Empirical Evidence and Case Studies

Empirical evidence and some indicative case studies demonstrate the promising role of AR, VR, and MR across several mental health cases. The components of AR that can enhance the patients' emotional well-being have been identified, showing that the AR intervention improved the female patients' emotional well-being compared to the control group. In addition, AR has been used to promote the well-being of young patients with craniosynostosis. Similarly, VR has also been proven to be beneficial for many mental health conditions, such as phobias and PTSD (Ma et al., 2021). MR has been applied for the rehabilitation and well-being of stroke survivors, as MR includes physical and emotional well-being improvement opportunities that neither AR nor VR provide (Aderinto et al., 2023).

The AR, VR, and MR demonstrated potential benefits in some applications. These mental health-related AR, VR, MR, and other technologies transform mental health care by creating feasible e-mental health technologies. However, there still exist research gaps. There are of emerging e-mental health technologies due to their written descriptions. However, there is a lack of clear understanding of the specific mental health transformation actions that these e-mental health technologies illustrate (Bansal et al., 2022; Usmani et al., 2022). Moreover, the status of the mental health care transformation actions of these e-mental health technologies has not been fully recognized, and the capability of AR, VR, MR, and other technologies for emotional well-being improvement is vague, which may lead to misunderstandings about the actual role of AR, VR, and MR in enhancing patients' emotional well-being. Also, it is unclear what professionals in the mental health transformation care field could learn from this and why. Consequently, it is unclear how the e-mental health development strategies of the tech world can be constructed, which may lead to inefficient exploitation.

8. Virtual Reality (VR) in Mental Health

Virtual reality (VR) provides patient-centered and personalized options to overcome fears or challenges by creating a sense of coping, bypassing denial or resistance, thereby speeding up the process of improvement and empowerment. VR in mental health focuses on exposure therapy applications, simulating stimuli that evoke traumatic memories. By using a more playful game-based approach, or by giving a user more control over the exercise by altering the stress quotient, the experience can be personalized for every patient (Adeghe et al., 2024). A virtual character can also hold the patient's hand, stand next to them, or provide them with verbal encouragement, reinforcing feelings of trust and security. VR stimuli can creatively take the patient's mind off their mental state. Studies have shown that distraction has beneficial effects on psychological stress. VR can be very useful as a relaxation technique. Retreat and exposure can be controlled in VR to the millimetre and individually.

VR in Mental Health VR's high degree of immersion and the technological possibilities of providing, applying, and simulating stimuli offer great opportunities for a broad range of mental health interventions. Following the advances of new media, VR, and human-computer interaction in these fields, possibilities for treating mental health disorders using new technologies have also increased. Integrating user- and goal-centered design principles into existing VR-based rehabilitation systems will address many unresolved problems in this area. Empirical research can categorically validate the efficacy of therapeutic innovations and has the potential to promote ideas to address clinically significant concerns. VR is well-suited to mental health services and cost-effective mental health interventions. VR simulation provides a beneficial and non-threatening patient environment and opens a fantasy window. The result is a more profound emotional response than traditional treatments (Bantjes et al., 2022). However, the design of new VR systems requires advanced knowledge of the cognitive forcing mechanisms to which our research contributes. These are very limited.

8.1. Therapeutic Applications

Latest digital technologies offer diverse representations of the analogue world. The enhanced capacity to create a feeling of presence for users in a three-dimensional, first-person full-body perspective has attracted particular attention for applications that aim to enhance emotional well-being. In contrast to a more conservative analysis in much of the prior literature, the present contribution goes beyond anxiety and pain reduction to consider a broader range of mental health conditions and proactive personal growth constructs (Paes et al., 2021). The uses of these immersive large-scale virtual environments include cognitive-behavioural therapy, interpersonal and emotional regulation, psychoeducational and motivational interventions. Virtual reality displays have been tested to benefit a broader range of psychological problems, including major depression, post-traumatic stress disorder, attention deficit hyperactivity disorder, and tic disorder (Kaimara et al., 2022).

Augmented reality applications are more recent and less documented than virtual reality uses. They benefit from a wider range of both home and clinical uses, and the development of applications is expected to increase. Benefits for mental well-being include improvements in tremor, mobility, or gait. Because of the relatively small field of factual applications in medicine, the impacts of AR on mental health have not been properly validated up to now. Mixed reality, at the crossroads of the real and the virtual, is also a technology that shows considerable promise for future uses in cognitive medicine. Its development in the medical field is strongly grounded in the extended classical real applications by the introduction of short- and long-term motivation to improve the health of patients (Yeung et al., 2021).

9. Mixed Reality (MR) in Mental Health

Fortunately, in recent years, mixed reality (MR) has provided a new type of mental health treatment to improve mental health and has been a great choice for mental health care and chronic care. Patients with mental disorders have better health outcomes in MR than those without MR. Emotional social presence (ESP) in MR may create situations that are like real-world activities, which may improve patient engagement and treatment outcomes. Emotion recognition, sentiment analysis, and conversation structure are also widely used in MR to understand the state of individuals or groups. Additionally, the therapeutic process can be analysed to understand patient engagement and treatment outcomes. MR therapy can help more people effectively fight mental health stigma and reduce the gap between mental disorders and other treatments. We will establish the data to evaluate the qualifications for further expansion into the MR market (Emmelkamp and Meyerbröker2021; Torous et al., 2021).

9.1. Innovative Uses and Emerging Trends

Health professionals tend to agree that these immersive technologies, given their characteristics, have the potential to promote physiological, cognitive, and affective recovery after different types of diseases and injuries, as well as to reduce and prevent behaviours related to physical symptoms. Despite the hurdles, it is expected that the number of scientific studies on the subject will increase, contributing to the knowledge and evidence that supports the introduction and integration of these resources into the health care cycle. In the field of emotions, several studies have already verified the possibility of using VR to induce specific emotions or to improve the capacity for emotion recognition (Somarathna et al., 2022).

Additionally, most studies developed in the field of mental health also point to positive results in using VR as an extended support in the treatment of anxiety and depression, among other disorders, both at the level of prevention, diagnosis, psychoeducation, and intervention. The results have shown VR to have significant potential for therapeutic purposes. Until recently, these results were due mainly to the technological advances always associated with the prohibition of access or limited access to HMD. It should be noted that patients can use VR themselves, something that is also historically known in the field of CBT-I and the use of affordable and scalable therapies (Emmelkamp and Meyerbröker, 2021). Due to the technological advances associated with the reduction in costs, VR is within everyone's reach. As such, we cannot ignore the fact that properly designed virtual environments can be very expensive tools with a limited impact on users since their development was not guided by well-regulated and systematic research.

9.2. Integration with Existing Interventions

Technological advancements often shift paradigms in existing treatment models. AR, VR, and MR can also be no exception to this. Unlike the previous approach of every new tool and technique replacing previous ones, AR, VR, and MR have the potential to integrate with existing interventions and provide a more comprehensive solution by enhancing therapeutic efficiency (Ma et al., 2021). The visualisation techniques of conventional CBT can be significantly improved by AR, VR, and MR technologies. Similarly, the biofeedback, relaxation, and desensitisation techniques of behaviour therapy can also be transformed with AR 3D environments, smart VR avatars, and MR eye-tracking. Cutting-edge research on AR, VR, and MR is evident for visual exploration, cue exposure, exposure with response prevention, and exposure with discrimination training in anxiety disorder treatment, as well as distraction during injury and wound care. In addition to past trauma therapy, immersive virtual environments that simulate alternative realities to facilitate psychological healing of combat-related post-traumatic stress disorder can be very effective by creating multilayered coping experiences that are rejuvenating for the patient and useful in allowing them the personal space necessary not only for psychological but also for cognitive processing (Tanaka & Vécsei, 2024).

The use of AR, VR, and MR as add-on treatments for inpatients during the psychotic stage can solve ethical issues and cost issues while improving efficacy. It is true that the effect of AR, VR, and MR as adjunctive treatments for patients with severe mental disorders is difficult to obtain. However, AR, VR, and MR are undoubtedly promising methods in post-rehabilitation follow-up. They can be applied in social skills training, cognitive skills training, medication management training, and so on. Through a pleasing and strong image of the self-image and identity of the MR virtual character, the patient can be helped to complete the repair of traumatic memory between the individual and the original object and communicate with family members more smoothly. The social interaction can also be included in VR (Tan et al., 2024). These digital characters may include both real people and virtual humans for use in exposure to social anxiety. If convenient, health care professionals can become virtual companions for patients, guiding them to monitor signs and symptoms with less discomfort and more assertively. Immersive virtual environments can be applied not only to patients without counselling but also to the general population with challenges. For example, a well-placed body action in a particular environment can psychologically heighten accessibility for disabled people, enabling them to develop healthier self-concepts (Choy et al., 2022).

10. Ethical Considerations

In a range of application areas, AR, VR, and MR technologies open many possibilities for new ways of experiencing the world and for putting people into a different 'world.' However, the psychological, emotional, subjective, and behavioural implications of using these devices are far-reaching and have not been fully explored. As applications start to be developed, it is crucial to recognise the dual role that AR, VR, and MR can play in promoting positive health and well-being outcomes on one hand and in posing threats to emotional health and well-being on the other (Choy et al., 2022). To maximize the benefits to mental health, it is important to also address a number of ethical considerations related to the use of these technologies, specifically in mental health and well-being domains. As the most powerful technologies continue to be seized upon by developers and consumers seeking all kinds of advantages and enhancements, it is natural that AR, VR, and MR may also have a strong and lasting impact in the domain of self-image and mental health. The inherent characteristics of technologies may hold potential for negative or harmful outcomes as well as therapeutic and health-promoting ones. It is paramount to identify and explore potential ethical issues and closely consider what new ethical responsibilities arise for technology designers, operators, and researchers. Ultimately, a set of ethical guidelines, practical advice, and best practices should be determined for use by developers, governments, standardisation bodies, insurance companies, health care services, education systems, and end users. The guidelines will consider the real evidence of positive as well as negative emotional health effects, the contexts in which they are employed, why they are used, and the populations, including particularly vulnerable ones, for whom these experiences are important.

10.1. Privacy and Data Security

One of the main concerns stems from the nature of AR, VR, and MR, which heavily depend on acquiring a vast amount of data about a person. Everything we see, feel, or think in the virtual space constitutes data that is generated and continuously shared. The data, once personal images, reactions, thoughts, or emotions were kept private by us. Not anymore. That treasure has been sucked up by data service providers and, therefore, probably passed over to peripheral companies for no other purpose than exploitation, which we also do not have any control over or a say in the decision, thanks to the law or next to nothing regulatory frameworks within which those precious firms are allowed to operate. The massive capacities of AI brains running deep learning algorithms strive for data and dollars (Choy et al., 2022).

In psychiatric and psychological healthcare, patient privacy and data security are even more sensitive issues. Unlike ordinary users, people with psychiatric and psychological issues have a heightened need to protect their personal identifiable information. The advancement of machine learning reveals that even the simplest type of data can be linked to the paradigm of a person, therefore defeating all forms of anonymisation in general use.

10.2. Informed Consent and User Autonomy

AR, VR, and MR experiences, especially when delivered using hardware equipment, can be quite intrusive, particularly when they target and engage cognitive and emotional functions. Behavioural conditioning, from video gaming to social media, has taught both users and providers to take seriously the power of technologies on multiple levels. There is the danger of altering attention, movement, thinking, and mood without explicit intent or permission. This risk has been addressed by growing legislation. In medicine, informed consent is a fundamental right of patients; indeed, it is required by law. How this should be implemented in the case of VR, AR, and MR treatments is still widely debated. The seriousness of the debate reflects the community of scholars, practitioners, and patients regarding the power and scope of these treatments. Several issues regarding how informed consent should be handled need to be addressed. First, who should provide the information regarding these forms of treatment? Second, what and how information should be provided to the patient or user how detailed it has to be? Third, because of the visual, cognitive, and emotional experiences reported by the patient or user of these technologies, VR, AR, MR, and MR-enhanced psychotherapy require proactive informed consent. Given the existing human interaction, algorithms, database searches, and machine learning should also be able to react live to the patient or user (Moy et al., 2021). This contrasts with traditional verbal instructions common in psychotherapy, pharmacotherapy, and, in general, with mental health interventions.

In this case, the informed consent is double-faced: the patient or user needs to be informed of the nature of the intervention and of the existence of the additional "mechanical eye" capable of live action accordingly. The need for a double-faceted informed consent is also taken into consideration in privacy laws and guidelines because healthcare-related data is particularly sensitive. With VR, AR, MR, and mechanical enhancements of standard treatments, the focus shifts from what is perceived and happens during the therapeutic session with the provider to all the remaining time outside of that time window. Not only surveillance cameras but also data mining are examples of systems designed to keep track of what and how we do things in human life. The main difference is that, for patients and users of VR, AR, and MR-enhanced tools, that separation no longer exists. The intrinsic characteristics of the modality "erode the wall" that maintains the difference between the private sphere and the public sphere.

11. Future Directions and Research Agenda

Several potential future directions could contribute to the development and deployment of AR/VR/MR applications and systems for enhancing emotional and mental well-being. These directions are emphasized by deconstructing the issues into areas related to user experience, technological advancements, data and outcome considerations, and additional stakeholder elements such as organisational and policy/governance issues. Additionally, the necessity for interdisciplinary collaboration, consumer and stakeholder engagement research, and the significance of comprehending the full scope of applications of AR/VR/MR technologies for intervention and wellness purposes is highlighted, addressing matters from public speaking anxiety to post-traumatic stress disorder.

User experience enhancement and design are essential to interactions with AR, VR, and MR applications and systems. Although established best practices and design guidelines exist, current application design can be refined by applying insights from earlier applications and studies, taking advantage of new experiences enabled by AR/VR/MR technologies. Such insights will contribute to developing an AR, VR, and MR research agenda focused on enhancing user experience and crucial treatment outcomes. Moreover, involving users in the stages of experience, design, and testing to gather feedback and meaningful input is beneficial, as well as ensuring inclusivity for the largest eligible segment of digital health participants. Evaluation of individual needs, application types, and the requirement for hybrid treatment models that incorporate non-digital health support from family, friends, and professionals should be an integral part of this approach.

11.1. Potential for Scaling Up

The current scope of applications and general research in this area are limited. Very few clinical researchers are utilising these technologies, suggesting that terms like digital psychiatry and digital psychology may need more time to gain widespread acceptance. One significant barrier identified is the lack of technologies for developing ARP and MRP treatments. Filling these technological gaps could enable researchers to advance more rapidly. Research efforts seek to expedite this process and highlight some potential accelerators. The first accelerator involves promoting interdisciplinary exchanges between relevant fields such as medical technology and psychology. Observations indicate that few researchers are incorporating VR into the treatment of psychiatric disorders, despite a considerable number of surveyed psychiatrists believing that VR should be included in treatment offerings. The situation appears consistent for ARP and MRP treatments. Research initiatives aim to facilitate this process by establishing project and educational partnerships focused on such exchanges.

A second accelerator focuses on supporting less robust forms of research by providing necessary infrastructure, thus minimising practical risks. It is widely recognised that clinical science in mental health needs to be validated through practical applications. As larger institutions lean towards evidence-based practices, new therapies in mental health care may only emerge after years of clinical research demonstrating their effectiveness. This presents a dilemma, particularly concerning non-pharmacological novel treatments, as clinical validation requires addressing the operational burdens and infrastructure involved.

Conclusion

Interdisciplinary collaborations are crucial for solving the complex challenges of creating AR, VR, and MR experiences that support mental health. Achieving this requires a thorough understanding of both psychophysiology and emotional experience, as well as human-computer interaction and the creative practices necessary for developing emotional environments. A growing network of AR, VR, and MR enthusiasts trained across multiple disciplines and exposed to empathetic practices could be essential for producing various real-world applications and developing impactful experiences. Increasing numbers of university courses addressing AR, VR, MR, and empathy are nurturing vital skills, yet more efforts are essential to educate AR, VR, and MR developers focused on mental health care. Strong collaborations among diverse scholars and practitioners, including experts in human-computer interaction, computer science, design and gaming, robotics, cognitive neuroscience, emotion research, clinical psychology, general practice, psychiatric specialities, and dramaturgy—will facilitate innovative real-life applications related to mental health. Effective communication, collaboration on technological and ethical solutions, and translating academic knowledge into practical goals are essential components, ensuring that clinicians, caregivers, and patients can benefit from generated knowledge. The status and future directions for AR, VR, and MR represent a necessary initial step in this process.

Research in technology and mental health is rapidly progressing. Given the potential for AR, VR, and MR to enhance emotional experiences, interest is growing in these technologies for developing interventions that build resilience in individuals. When effectively employed, they can critically enhance treatments through powerful psychological processing linked to exposure and sensation-based treatments for phobias and trauma-related disorders. AR, VR, and MR provide novel methods for creating computer-mediated real situations that assist individuals in confronting and managing fear and distress, thereby fostering resilience and emotional well-being. This section has examined various ways AR, VR, and MR can augment treatments and contribute to emotional well-being by advancing experiential characteristics and customisation potential. These technologies combine immersion, imagination, and interaction to forge mechanisms that inspire, educate, engage, and motivate. While they hold the promise of offering tailored experiences for mental health, their applications are currently constrained by balancing challenges, including risks of misuse, lack of guidelines and stakeholder awareness, as well as ethical dilemmas surrounding ownership, security, privacy, psychological reactions, and social value management. These concerns will be addressed in the subsequent chapter, which will delve into the social issues surrounding AR, VR, and MR applications in mental health care.

Advances in technology have the potential to significantly transform mental health care through interventions aimed at promoting emotional awareness, alleviating emotional difficulties, and personalising therapies. Future developments led by researchers, care providers, and individuals facing mental health challenges will help ensure that these technologies meet people's needs. Emerging research focuses on the applicability, specificity, and efficacy of these interventions in enhancing emotional well-being. The mental health community stands on the brink of a digital revolution, with technology spearheading innovative psychological treatments. One approach currently leads the way, while recent developments suggest tremendous potential for improved engagement and learning. With careful preparatory work and rigorous testing, future applications may refine treatment and personalise experiences by harnessing uniquely effective multi-sensory motor linkage properties. Such features have not yet been adequately integrated into current applications. The real-time interactive modulation of heart rate, eye blinks, or pupillary dilation through multi-nodal feedback currently offers a distinctive method for adjusting an individual's arousal and cognitive response in a gradual manner, allowing for incremental exposure to traumatic stimuli. Furthermore, counterbalancing excitement and emotional fatigue is yet to be incorporated in the existing applications of established exposure treatments.

References

Adeghe, E. P., Okolo, C. A., & Ojeyinka, O. T. (2024). A review of the integration of virtual reality in healthcare: implications for patient education and treatment outcomes. *International Journal of Science and Technology Research Archive*, (6), 79–088.

Aderinto, N., Olatunji, G., Abdulbasit, M. O., Edun, M., Aboderin, G., & Egbunu, E. (2023). Exploring the efficacy of virtual reality-based rehabilitation in stroke: a narrative review of current evidence. *Annals of Medicine*, *55*(2), 2285907. doi:10.1080/07853890.2023.2285907.

Ahrens, K. F., Neumann, R. J., Kollmann, B., Plichta, M. M., Lieb, K., Tüscher, O., & Reif, A. (2021). Differential impact of COVID-related lockdown on mental health in Germany. *World Psychiatry: Official Journal of the World Psychiatric Association (WPA)*, *20*(1), 140–141. doi:10.1002/wps.20830.

Albakri, G., Bouaziz, R., Alharthi, W., Kammoun, S., Al-Sarem, M., Saeed, F., & Hadwan, M. (2022). Phobia exposure therapy using virtual and augmented reality: A systematic review. *Applied Sciences (Basel, Switzerland)*, *12*(3), 1672. doi:10.3390/app12031672.

Ashley, C., James, S., Williams, A., Calma, K., Mcinnes, S., Mursa, R., … Halcomb, E. (2021). The psychological well-being of primary healthcare nurses during COVID-19: A qualitative study. *Journal of Advanced Nursing*, *77*(9), 3820–3828. doi:10.1111/jan.14937.

Bansal, G., Rajgopal, K., Chamola, V., Xiong, Z., & Niyato, D. (2022). Healthcare in Metaverse: A Survey on Current Metaverse Applications in Healthcare. *IEEE Access: Practical Innovations, Open Solutions*, *10*, 119914–119946. doi:10.1109/access.2022.3219845.

Bantjes, J., Hunt, X., & Stein, D. J. (2022). Public health approaches to promoting university students' mental health: A global perspective. *Current Psychiatry Reports*, *24*(12), 809–818. doi:10.1007/s11920-022-01387-4.

Baragash, R. S., Aldowah, H., & Ghazal, S. (2022). Virtual and augmented reality applications to improve older adults' quality of life: A systematic mapping review and future directions. *Digital Health*, *8*, 20552076221132099. doi:10.1177/20552076221132099.

Bhowmik, A. K. (2024). Virtual and augmented reality: Human sensory-perceptual requirements and trends for immersive spatial computing experiences. *Journal of the Society for Information Display*, *32*(8), 605–646. doi:10.1002/jsid.2001.

Cage, E., Jones, E., Ryan, G., Hughes, G., & Spanner, L. (2021). Student mental health and transitions into, through and out of university: student and staff perspectives. *Journal of Further and Higher Education*, *45*(8), 1076–1089. doi:10.1080/0309877x.2021.1875203.

Chachignon, P., Le Barbenchon, E., & Dany, L. (2024). Mindfulness research and applications in the context of neoliberalism: A narrative and critical review. *Social and Personality Psychology Compass*, *18*(2). doi:10.1111/spc3.12936.

Cheng, C., & Ebrahimi, O. V. (2023). A meta-analytic review of gamified interventions in mental health enhancement. *Computers in Human Behavior*, *141*(107621), 107621. doi:10.1016/j.chb.2022.107621

Choy, C. S., Cloherty, S. L., Pirogova, E., & Fang, Q. (2023). Virtual reality assisted motor imagery for early post-stroke recovery: A review. *IEEE Reviews in Biomedical Engineering*, *16*, 487–498. doi:10.1109/RBME.2022.3165062.

Cullen, A. J., Dowling, N. L., Segrave, R., Carter, A., & Yücel, M. (2021). Exposure therapy in a virtual environment: Validation in obsessive compulsive disorder. *Journal of Anxiety Disorders*, *80*(102404), 102404. doi:10.1016/j.janxdis.2021.102404.

Di Carlo, F., Sociali, A., Picutti, E., Pettorruso, M., Vellante, F., Verrastro, V., … di Giannantonio, M. (2021). Telepsychiatry and other cutting-edge technologies in COVID-19 pandemic: Bridging the distance in mental health assistance. *International Journal of Clinical Practice*, *75*(1), e13716. doi:10.1111/ijcp.13716.

Dimitrova, R., & Wiium, N. (2021). Handbook of positive youth development: Advancing the next generation of research, policy and practice in global contexts. In *Springer Series on Child and Family Studies* (pp. 3–16). doi:10.1007/978-3-030-70262-5_1.

Emmelkamp, P. M. G., & Meyerbröker, K. (2021). Virtual reality therapy in mental health. *Annual Review of Clinical Psychology*, *17*(1), 495–519. doi:10.1146/annurev-clinpsy-081219-115923.

Eshuis, L. V., van Gelderen, M. J., van Zuiden, M., Nijdam, M. J., Vermetten, E., Olff, M., & Bakker, A. (2021). Efficacy of immersive PTSD treatments: A systematic review of virtual and augmented reality exposure therapy and a meta-analysis of virtual reality exposure therapy. *Journal of Psychiatric Research*, *143*, 516–527. doi:10.1016/j.jpsychires.2020.11.030.

Eswaran, M., & Bahubalendruni, M. V. A. R. (2022). Challenges and opportunities on AR/VR technologies for manufacturing systems in the context of industry 4.0: A state of the art review. *Journal of Manufacturing Systems*, *65*, 260–278. doi:10.1016/j.jmsy.2022.09.016.

Fan, X., Jiang, X., & Deng, N. (2022). Immersive technology: A meta-analysis of augmented/virtual reality applications and their impact on tourism experience. *Tourism Management*, *91*(104534), 104534. doi:10.1016/j.tourman.2022.104534.

Flor-Alemany, M., Baena-García, L., Migueles, J. H., Henriksson, P., Löf, M., & Aparicio, V. A. (2022). Associations of Mediterranean diet with psychological ill-being and well-being throughout the pregnancy course: The GESTAFIT project. *Quality of Life Research: An International Journal of Quality of Life Aspects of Treatment, Care and Rehabilitation*, *31*(9), 2705–2716. doi:10.1007/s11136-022-03121-2.

Gasmi, A., & Benlamri, R. (2022). *Augmented reality, virtual reality and new age technologies demand escalates amid COVID-19. In Novel AI and data science advancements for sustainability in the era of.* 89–111.

Graciyal, D. G., & Viswam, D. (2021). Social media and emotional well-being: Pursuit of happiness or pleasure. *Asia Pacific Media Educator*, *31*(1), 99–115. doi:10.1177/1326365x211003737.

Haleem, A., Javaid, M., Pratap Singh, R., & Suman, R. (2022). Medical 4.0 technologies for healthcare: Features, capabilities, and applications. *Internet of Things and Cyber-Physical Systems*, *2*, 12–30. doi:10.1016/j.iotcps.2022.04.001.

He, M., Wen, Y., Qiu, Q., Sheng, G., Wei, Y., Wang, Z., & Hu, Y. (2023). The effects and gender-related differences of guided forest therapy program on physiological and psychological health of graduating college students. *International Journal of Geoheritage and Parks*. doi:10.1016/j.ijgeop.2023.07.003.

Health Organization, W. (2024). *Working for a brighter, healthier future: how WHO improves health and promotes well-being for the world's adolescents*.

Hoang, D. M., Pham, P. T., Bach, T. Q., Ngo, A. T. L., Nguyen, Q. T., Phan, T. T. K., … Nguyen, L. T. (2022). Stem cell-based therapy for human diseases. *Signal Transduction and Targeted Therapy*, *7*(1), 272. doi:10.1038/s41392-022-01134-4.

Holt, S. (2023). Virtual reality, augmented reality and mixed reality: For astronaut mental health; and space tourism, education and outreach. *Acta Astronautica*, *203*, 436–446. doi:10.1016/j.actaastro.2022.12.016.

Houssein, E. H., Hammad, A., & Ali, A. A. (2022). Human emotion recognition from EEG-based brain–computer interface using machine learning: a comprehensive review. *Neural Computing & Applications*, *34*(15), 12527–12557. doi:10.1007/s00521-022-07292-4.

Huang, F., Wang, Y., & Zhang, H. (2024). Modelling generative AI acceptance, perceived teachers' enthusiasm and self-efficacy to English as a foreign language learners' well-being in the digital era. *European Journal of Education*, *59*(4). doi:10.1111/ejed.12770.

Jin, X., Chai, S., Tang, J., Zhou, X., & Wang, K. (2024). Eye-Tracking in AR/VR: A Technological Review and Future Directions. *IEEE Open Journal on Immersive Displays*.

Kaimara, P., Oikonomou, A., & Deliyannis, I. (2022). Could virtual reality applications pose real risks to children and adolescents? A systematic review of ethical issues and concerns. *Virtual Reality*, *26*(2), 697–735. doi:10.1007/s10055-021-00563-w.

Kang, W., & Shao, B. (2023). The impact of voice assistants' intelligent attributes on consumer well-being: Findings from PLS-SEM and fsQCA. *Journal of Retailing and Consumer Services*, *70*(103130), 103130. doi:10.1016/j.jretconser.2022.103130.

Kelly, N. J., Hallam, J., & Bignell, S. (2024). Correction to: Using interpretative phenomenological analysis to gain a qualitative understanding of presence in virtual reality. *Virtual Reality*, *28*(1). doi:10.1007/s10055-024-00940-1.

Kim, J. H., Kim, M., Park, M., & Yoo, J. (2023). *Immersive interactive technologies and virtual shopping experiences: Differences in consumer perceptions between augmented reality (AR) and virtual reality (VR). Telematics and Informatics*.

Kim, S. (2024). *World Health Organization quality of life (WHOQOL) assessment. Encyclopedia of quality of life and well-being research.*

Klaib, A. F., Alsrehin, N. O., Melhem, W. Y., Bashtawi, H. O., & Magableh, A. A. (2021). Eye tracking algorithms, techniques, tools, and applications with an emphasis on machine learning and Internet of Things technologies. *Expert Systems with Applications*, *166*(114037), 114037. doi:10.1016/j.eswa.2020.114037.

Konaszewski, K., Niesiobędzka, M., & Surzykiewicz, J. (2021). Resilience and mental health among juveniles: role of strategies for coping with stress. *Health and Quality of Life Outcomes*, *19*(1), 58. doi:10.1186/s12955-021-01701-3.

Lan, L., Sikov, J., Lejeune, J., Ji, C., Brown, H., Bullock, K., & Spencer, A. E. (2023). A systematic review of using virtual and augmented reality for the diagnosis and treatment of psychotic disorders. *Current Treatment Options in Psychiatry*, *10*(2), 1–21. doi:10.1007/s40501-023-00287-5.

Lindner, P. (2021). Better, virtually: The past, present, and future of virtual reality cognitive behavior therapy. *International Journal of Cognitive Therapy*, *14*(1), 23–46. doi:10.1007/s41811-020-00090-7.

Lindner, P., Dagöö, J., Hamilton, W., Miloff, A., Andersson, G., Schill, A., & Carlbring, P. (2021). Virtual Reality exposure therapy for public speaking anxiety in routine care: a single-subject effectiveness trial. *Cognitive Behaviour Therapy*, *50*(1), 67–87. doi:10.1080/16506073.2020.1795240.

Liu, Z., Ren, L., Xiao, C., Zhang, K., & Demian, P. (2022). Virtual reality aided therapy towards health 4.0: A two-decade bibliometric analysis. *International Journal of Environmental Research and Public Health*, *19*(3), 1525. doi:10.3390/ijerph19031525.

Ludviga, I., & Kalvina, A. (2023). Organizational agility during crisis: Do employees' perceptions of public sector organizations' strategic agility foster employees' work engagement and well-being? *Employee Responsibilities and Rights Journal*. doi:10.1007/s10672-023-09442-9.

Ma, L., Mor, S., Anderson, P. L., Baños, R. M., Botella, C., Bouchard, S., … Carlbring, P. (2021). Integrating virtual realities and psychotherapy: SWOT analysis on VR and MR based treatments of anxiety and stress-related disorders. *Cognitive Behaviour Therapy*, *50*(6), 509–526. doi:10.1080/16506073.2021.1939410.

Moy, M. L., Wayne, P. M., Litrownik, D., Beach, D., Klings, E. S., Davis, R. B., … Yeh, G. Y. (2021). Long-term Exercise After Pulmonary Rehabilitation (LEAP): a pilot randomised controlled trial of Tai Chi in COPD. *ERJ Open Research*, *7*(3), 00025–02021. doi:10.1183/23120541.00025-2021.

Ogunbode, C. A., Pallesen, S., Böhm, G., Doran, R., Bhullar, N., Aquino, S., … Lomas, M. J. (2023). Negative emotions about climate change are related to insomnia symptoms and mental health: Cross-sectional evidence from 25 countries. *Current Psychology (New Brunswick, N.J.)*, *42*(2), 845–854. doi:10.1007/s12144-021-01385-4.

Olawade, D. B., Wada, O. Z., Odetayo, A., David-Olawade, A. C., Asaolu, F., & Eberhardt, J. (2024). Enhancing mental health with Artificial Intelligence: Current trends and future prospects. *Journal of Medicine, Surgery, and Public Health*, *3*(100099), 100099. doi:10.1016/j.glmedi.2024.100099.

Paes, D., Irizarry, J., & Pujoni, D. (2021). ... *cognitive benefits from immersive design review: Comparing three-dimensional perception and presence between immersive and non-immersive virtual environments*.

Papadopoulos, T., Evangelidis, K., Kaskalis, T. H., Evangelidis, G., & Sylaiou, S. (2021). Interactions in augmented and mixed reality: An overview. *Applied Sciences (Basel, Switzerland)*, *11*(18), 8752. doi:10.3390/app11188752.

Qin, W., Li, F., Jia, L., Wang, Q., Li, Y., Wei, Y., … Jia, J. (2022). Phosphorylated Tau 181 serum levels predict Alzheimer's disease in the preclinical stage. *Frontiers in Aging Neuroscience*, *14*, 900773. doi:10.3389/fnagi.2022.900773.

Ramos, G., & Chavira, D. A. (2022). Use of technology to provide mental health care for racial and ethnic minorities: Evidence, promise, and challenges. *Cognitive and Behavioral Practice*, *29*(1), 15–40. doi:10.1016/j.cbpra.2019.10.004.

Rauschnabel, P. A. (2021). Augmented reality is eating the real-world! The substitution of physical products by holograms. *International Journal of Information Management*, *57*(102279), 102279. doi:10.1016/j.ijinfomgt.2020.102279.

Somarathna, R., Bednarz, T., & Mohammadi, G. (2022). Virtual reality for emotion elicitation-a review. *IEEE Transactions on Affective Computing*.

Sonnentag, S., Tay, L., & Nesher Shoshan, H. (2023). A review on health and well-being at work: More than stressors and strains. *Personnel Psychology*, *76*(2), 473–510. doi:10.1111/peps.12572

Soon, P.-S., Lim, W. M., & Gaur, S. S. (2023). The role of emotions in augmented reality. *Psychology & Marketing*. doi:10.1002/mar.21884.

Sophie, V., Sara, C., Jellen, T. J., & Lieven, A. (2022). The role of 'peace of mind'and 'meaningfulness' as psychological concepts in explaining subjective well-being. *Journal of Happiness Studies*.

Steiger, M., Bharucha, T. J., Venkatagiri, S., Riedl, M. J., & Lease, M. (2021). The psychological well-being of content moderators: the emotional labor of commercial moderation and avenues for improving support. In *Proceedings of the 2021 CHI conference on human factors in computing systems* (pp. 1–14).

Søvold, L. E., Naslund, J. A., Kousoulis, A. A., Saxena, S., Qoronfleh, M. W., Grobler, C., & Münter, L. (2021). Prioritizing the mental health and well-being of healthcare workers: An urgent global public health priority. *Frontiers in Public Health*, *9*, 679397. doi:10.3389/fpubh.2021.679397.

Tan, X., Wang, K., Sun, W., Li, X., Wang, W., & Tian, F. (2024). A review of recent advances in cognitive-motor dual-tasking for Parkinson's disease rehabilitation. *Sensors (Basel, Switzerland)*, *24*(19), 6353. doi:10.3390/s24196353.

Tanaka, M., & Vécsei, L. (2024). From lab to life: Exploring cutting-edge models for neurological and psychiatric disorders. *Biomedicines*, *12*(3), 613. doi:10.3390/biomedicines12030613.

Tang, Y. M., Chau, K. Y., Kwok, A. P. K., Zhu, T., & Ma, X. (2022). A systematic review of immersive technology applications for medical practice and education-trends, application areas, recipients, teaching contents, evaluation methods, and performance. *Educational Research Review*, *35*.

Torous, J., Bucci, S., Bell, I. H., Kessing, L. V., Faurholt-Jepsen, M., Whelan, P., … Firth, J. (2021). The growing field of digital psychiatry: current evidence and the future of apps, social media, chatbots, and virtual reality. *World Psychiatry: Official Journal of the World Psychiatric Association (WPA)*, *20*(3), 318–335. doi:10.1002/wps.20883.

Usmani, S. S., Sharath, M., & Mehendale, M. (2022). Future of mental health in the metaverse. *General Psychiatry*, *35*(4), e100825. doi:10.1136/gpsych-2022-100825.

Vairamani, A. D. (2024). *Enhancing social skills development through augmented reality (AR) and virtual reality (VR) in special education. Augmented Reality and Virtual Reality in Special Education*. 65–89.

Verhulst, I., Woods, A., Whittaker, L., Bennett, J., & Dalton, P. (2021). Do VR and AR versions of an immersive cultural experience engender different user experiences? *Computers in Human Behavior*, *125*(106951), 106951. doi:10.1016/j.chb.2021.106951.

Wang, P., Bai, X., Billinghurst, M., Zhang, S., Zhang, X., Wang, S., … Ji, H. (2021). AR/MR remote collaboration on physical tasks: A review. *Robotics and Computer-Integrated Manufacturing*, *72*(102071), 102071. doi:10.1016/j.rcim.2020.102071.

Wray, T. B., Kemp, J. J., & Larsen, M. A. (2023). Virtual reality (VR) treatments for anxiety disorders are unambiguously successful, so why are so few therapists using it? Barriers to adoption and potential solutions. *Cognitive Behaviour Therapy*, *52*(6), 603–624. doi:10.1080/16506073.2023.2229017.

Wu, Y. F., & Kim, E. Y. (2022). Users' perceptions of technological features in augmented reality (AR) and virtual reality (VR) in fashion retailing: A qualitative content analysis. *Mobile Information Systems*, *2022*, 1–13. doi:10.1155/2022/3080280.

Yeung, A. W. K., Tosevska, A., Klager, E., Eibensteiner, F., Laxar, D., Stoyanov, J., … Willschke, H. (2021). Virtual and augmented reality applications in medicine: Analysis of the scientific literature. *Journal of Medical Internet Research*, *23*(2), e25499. doi:10.2196/25499.

Chapter 12

Integration of Immersive Technologies with the Internet of Things (IoT) and Artificial Intelligence (AI)

A. Aruna[1,*]
A. Sathya[2,†]
and V. Jeevika Tharini[3,‡]

[1]Department of Artificial Intelligence and Machine Learning,
[2]Department of Artificial Intelligence and Data Analytics,
[3]Department of Computer Science,
Sri Ramachandra Faculty of Engineering and Technology,
Sri Ramachandra Institute of Higher Education and Research, Chennai, Tamil Nadu, India

Abstract

The continuous enhancement of Virtual Reality (VR), Augmented Reality (AR), and Mixed Reality (MR) in association with the Internet of Things (IoT) and Artificial Intelligence (AI) is revolutionising the digital environment in various fields. This chapter discusses each of these innovative technologies and focuses on how they are integrated to revolutionise healthcare, education, manufacturing, and cities. IoT enables real-time data collection, AI enables data analysis and decision making at faster rates, and immersive technologies are used to render a clear interface for the data. In the health care domain, AR depicts real-time IoT sensor data in surgeries accompanied by AI diagnosis data. Manufacturing has challenges like smart machinery with AR/VR training and IoT-based predictive maintenance empowered by AI. As with immersive educational tools, adaptive learning environments are managed by AI, while IoT is used for monitoring. Smart city and urban planning use MR platforms to evaluate IoT data, including traffic flow and natural disasters. This chapter also discusses challenges such as data privacy, latency, and computational complexity that are discussed alongside the solutions like edge computing and blockchain security. Pursuant to use cases and promising integration opportunities with IoT and AI, the chapter offered a brief on the interactions and potential development of extending immersive technology into the new generation of intelligent interaction systems.

[*] Corresponding Author's Email: arunaarulmani@gmail.com
[†] Corresponding Author's Email: arunachalam.sathya@gmail.com
[‡] Corresponding Author's Email: Jeevi153gv@gmail.com

In: Shaping Tomorrow
Editors: Prithi Samuel, A. Sathya, Balamurugan Balusamy et al.
ISBN: 979-8-90134-076-9

Keywords: virtual reality (VR), augmented reality (AR), mixed reality (MR), internet of things (IoT), artificial intelligence (AI), immersive technologies, smart healthcare, AI-powered diagnosis, IoT sensor data

1. Introduction to Immersive Technologies, IoT, and AI

The full-featured technologies, IoT, and AI provide opportunities for the radical modification of numerous sectors of activity and the change of the ways of interaction with the digital environment [1]. These technologies are not mutually exclusive but are rapidly integrating, creating new solutions that make processes more effective, precise, and easy to use in various industries, including medicine, industry, education, trade, entertainment, and smart regions. This convergence is producing smart systems which can perform real-time decision making, predictive analysis and improved user interactions [2].

Virtual Reality (VR), Augmented Reality (AR) and Mixed Reality (MR) technologies are reshaping the experience of an individual with content. These technologies produce ecological contexts that are highly interactive and rich in sensory modalities that enrich human experiences. While in VR, the user is completely placed in a virtual environment, in AR, additional information is placed on top of the physical environment surrounding the user [3]. While MR is a blend of both, for users to be able to physically manipulate objects in the real environment in real time. These developments are introducing enhanced interaction possibilities in many sectors, including well-being, knowledge, and entertainment.

Virtual Reality (VR) establishes complete computer-simulated environments that users can enter, perform, and navigate within with the help of equipped devices that include headsets, controllers, and motion trackers [4]. The VR experience is fully synthesised, making users interact with fictitious situations as if they were real. According to the field of its application, VR is used in training, rehabilitation and therapy and pain relief in the medical field. In education, VR is an exciting way of learning that can take students through different eras or even create an environment in which certain scientific principles may be observed [5].

The VR users are placed in a completely artificial environment, with AR information placed in the actual physical environment, making the interaction with it much richer. AR is implemented in various fields through the use of devices like smartphones, tablets, and AR glasses, whereby in retail, customers are able to see the products in their own premises without physically having to place the products in the house and in health sector whereby surgeons are able to see real-time information as they perform their operations [6]. Given the fact that using AR makes it possible to add more information about the real world, it can be considered both a great medium for entertainment purposes and a useful tool in studying and working on different projects [7].

MR is a transition between VR and AR wherein real and virtual objects are integrated and interactively combined. While AR only adds some information on top of the real environment, MR allows digital objects to respond to environmental changes in real-time. MR generates interactive, real-world environments where the user can physically move things virtually and at the same time perceive objects/ reality in his/her environment [8].

MR is employed in industries like manufacturing, where mock training is conducted in systems that mimic actual processes and tools in an organisation, and people get a feel of the machinery and environment before touching them [9]. IoT is an interconnected web of physical objects embedded with technologies that enable them to send and receive data through the internet [10]. IoT is as versatile as it is extensive in terms of application and reaches across numerous sectors, making it an already colossal network where items, buildings, and structures, even people, are fitted with sensors and software and the like to log and relay information [11]. This connectivity lets devices be monitored, controlled and optimised from the central control point, making IoT a key component in a smart environment [12].

Artificial Intelligence (AI) is the ability of a computer system to imitate those mental processes which enable humans to learn as well as solve problems [13]. It covers a broad area across the various technologies, such as ML (Machine Learning), DL (Deep Learning), and NLP (Natural Language Processing) among which are finding their ways into integration with other technologies such as IoT and immersive technology to foster the development of intelligent systems that are autonomous in nature [14]. Artificial intelligence, a wider concept, includes machine learning as a practice of feeding data into a system and making it learn and predict without coding. In the health care industry, it applies in imaging analysis for disease detection, while in the retail industry, it applies to the recommendation systems for customisation, and in the retail industry, it applies to the recommendation systems for customised shopping. The AI and ML are illustrated in Figure 1.

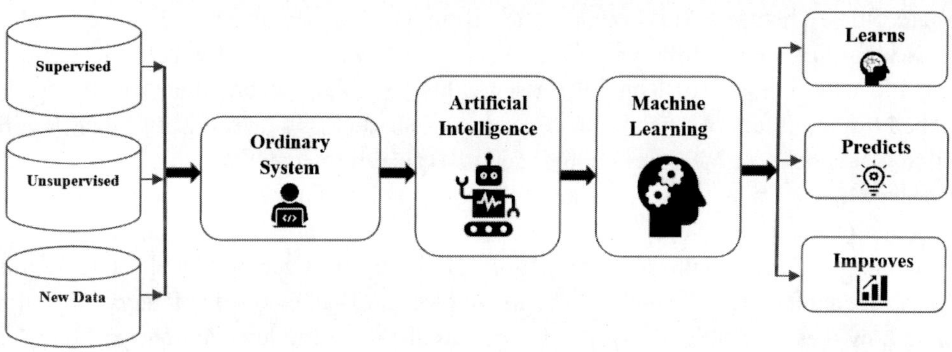

Figure 1. Integration of AI and ML.

Natural Language Processing, another branch of AI, enables the machine to read and process natural language; it supports tools such as chatbots, virtual assistants, and sentiment analysis tools. The combination of AI with IoT allows for better decision making by augmenting real-time data from smart gadgets, improving such sectors as manufacturing and health care. There are so many industries that have embraced the use of autonomous systems, powered by AI, among them being automotive industry, whereby self-driven cars use IoT sensors and AI algorithms to make decisions of how to drive, and manufacturing industries where AI driven robots make decisions on their own when doing stuffs like assembling products and maintaining equipment's. Such improvements are revolutionising many sectors, providing higher productivity, precision, and self-governing systems. The combination of immersive technologies, IoT, and AI forms a unique combination that gives a new dimension of interaction and real-time decision making, as well as intelligent decision making across various sectors [15].

When these improvements in technology are integrated, it will be possible for an intelligent system to work with the human end-users effectively, as well as be able to adapt to any change within the environment. Virtual Reality (VR) and Augmented Reality (AR) with Mixed Reality (MR) are effective in representing data visualisation and interactive interfaces. IoT connects devices and sensors, allowing for real-time data collection and monitoring, while AI analyses this data to drive decisions, predictions, and automation.

The combination of these immersive technologies allows for creating systems that are capable of both reacting to the inputs now they are received and being able to update that reaction to become more effective in the future. For instance, in health care, applications of AI along with IoT can assist in creating tailored treatment plans depending on the current information and information supported by immersed technologies can help to create virtual training for medical staff. AI IoT systems can enhance production lines in manufacturing industries in real-time and use analytical data to detect and avoid equipment breakdowns. This blend of immersive technologies, IoT and AI will usher in the new age of various industry segments like healthcare, manufacturing, education, and smart city solutions to build smart and autonomous systems that either augment or reinvent efficiency, productivity, and user experience.

The integration of immersive technologies, IoT, and AI is progressing at a very rapid pace and is changing the course of society. of these technologies provide a smarter, connected and 'active' environment in areas like health care, manufacturing, education, retail, entertainment and smart cities. Therefore, it is only a matter of time before new technologies are developed which will further optimise the processes, leading to lower costs and which will ultimately making life even better [16]. Nevertheless, as the generative technologies in question are developed further, issues of data protection, security, sharing, and merging arise that should be solved to make these technologies popular and effective. Immersive technologies, IoT and AI are aspects which are sure to show remarkable growth in future for research as well as practical implementation across the fields.

This chapter begins with an Introduction, providing an overview of the integration of immersive technologies, IoT, and AI. The Technological Framework for Integration follows, detailing how these technologies work together. Real-World Implementations and Use Cases explore practical applications across industries. The Applications of Immersive Technologies, IoT, and AI section highlights specific examples in healthcare, manufacturing, education, and more. Technological Challenges and Solutions discusses key issues such as data privacy and computational complexity, along with potential solutions. Prospects and Research Opportunities outline future research areas. The chapter concludes with a Conclusion and Recommendations, offering insights into the continued development and implementation of these technologies.

2. Technological Framework for Integration

The technological framework for integration refers to the way the technologies in the different organisations are integrated to support the achievement of strategic goals [17].

The combination of immersive technologies, IoT, and AI is indeed the next generation innovation, as it combines the best of the latest technologies to create a new platform that allows interactivity, automation, and data intelligence in various fields. To achieve this synergy, there is a need for strong technological support. They are complex and consist of numerous integrated layers and components that must function in concert to deliver the sustained operational, capacity and flexibility required in this framework. In the following section, there is a detailed analysis of the major components of the concept.

2.1. Data Acquisition Layer

The data acquisition layer is the primary layer in the entire integration framework shown in Figure 2 above. Smart objects with sensors collect data from the physical world at every given time. These devices measure various physical characteristics including temperature, humidity, motion, pressure and many others, converting real-world events into electrical signals. To achieve this, the following data is essential to design and develop appropriate and realistic immersive experiences.

For instance, in a smart home, IoT sensors may capture room temperature and use this information to change virtual representations in Augmented Reality-based home control systems. The detail of this data defines the subsequent layers in the framework.

2.2. Connection and Communication Standards

Data exchange between IoT devices, AI systems and immersive platforms has to be efficient. There are other protocols like MQTT, CoAP and AMQP that allow real-time and small data exchange. Moreover, realisations in the 5G network guarantee low latency, which is relevant for applications, for example, VR gaming and AR surgery.

Another way in which edge computing is central to reducing latency is by processing data closer to the source. The use of edge computing offers to offset reliance on centralised cloud systems as a way of improving the interactions of integrated systems.

2.3. AI-Driven Data Processing

After that, IoT devices help to gather data, and AI systems help to process, analyse, and provide conclusions. Automatic learning tools classify, estimate, and decide based on the data analysis known as pattern recognition. For instance, even in the industrial environment, AI can identify which equipment is likely to fail, based on its sensor record, to perform preventive maintenance.

NLP and computer vision are the other components that add to the system. NLP allows voice-controlled interactions while computer vision allows interpretation of visual data for objects, gestures and changes in the environment. Such capabilities add value to the user experience in immersive environments because interactions are facilitated and enhanced by AI.

2.4. Immersive Interface Design

Augmented Reality (AR), Virtual Reality (VR), and Mixed Reality (MR) are the top layer of the presented framework since they are directly connected to the user. AR adds digital information on top of the physical environment and offers the user relevant information about the surroundings. VR provides fully fake environments for users to engage with and interface with AI-created situations. MR integrates both methods, where the user to interface with actual and computer-generated objects at the same time.

For example, the use of AR in a retail store can place information about the product, customer feedback, and recommendations on the physical store's aisles. These interfaces therefore must be comfortable, easily accessible and easy to use to encourage wider use of the technology.

2.5. Middleware and Integration Platforms

About middleware platforms, they are intermediaries that provide interfaces and services between IoT devices, AIs and immersive solutions. These platforms perform activities like protocol conversion, data acquisition and API mediated integration. They also offer development tools and frameworks that allow a developer to create and launch integrated applications quickly.

Unity and Unreal Engine. Unreal Engine, as a game engine and IoT middleware such as ThingWorx and AWS IoT Core, gives developers the means to design and implement applications that use real-world data and AI.

2.6. Security and Privacy Framework

Overlaying technologies such as IoT and AI into immersive technologies poses a new set of security and privacy risks. The framework should contain sufficient safeguards that shall minimise vulnerability to intruder access and cybercrimes. That is, encryption protocols, Blockchain technology, and Artificial Intelligence-based threat detection systems are some of the facets.

For instance, Blockchain can offer a decentralised means of trust for IoT devices, which will guarantee data genuineness. Using artificial intelligence, it is possible to detect any irregularity in traffic and indicate a possible violation of security. Users' privacy also should not be compromised, which means user data should be anonymised where possible and made accessible only to people who really have to work with it.

2.7. Scalability Interoperability

With more IoT devices and immersive applications being developed, the issue of scalability is emerging as one of the most important. The technologies such as cloud computing resources, containers, Docker and orchestration, such as Kubernetes, are making the systems capable of scaling up or down according to the present demand.

Interoperability is as important because it means that different vendors' devices and platforms can be connected. Standardisation, open APIs used by parties in the ecosystem, bring together uniformity and implementation of global standards, keeping competition from fragmenting the ecosystem.

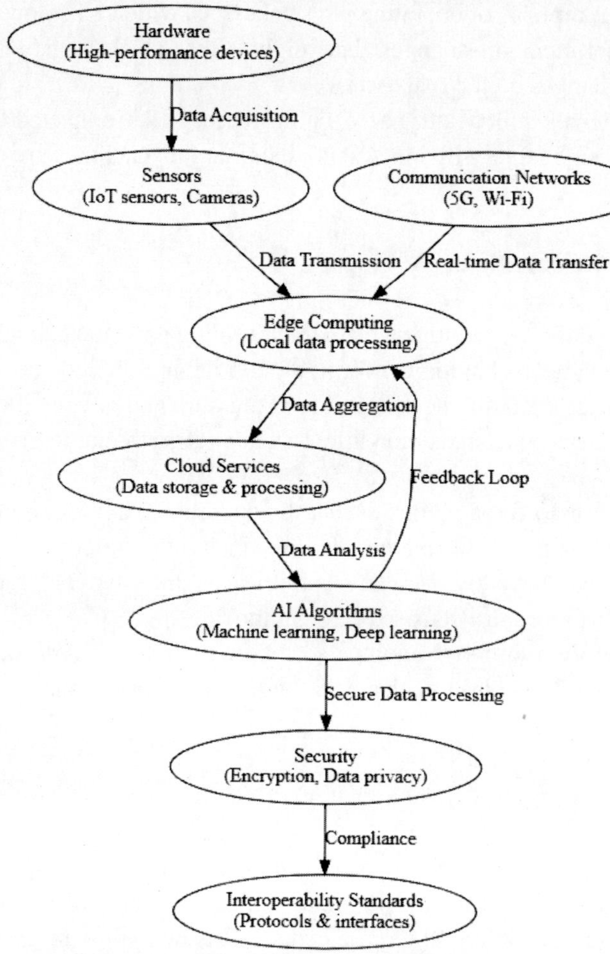

Figure 2. Technological Framework for Integration of Immersive Technologies, IoT, and AI.

3. Real-World Implementations and Use Case

The use cases of applying immersive technologies together with IoT and AI are revolutionizing industries and improving outcomes and user experiences. Further, we provide specific real-world examples and applications by domain.

3.1. Smart Manufacturing

Successively, in the context of the manufacturing segment, IoT combined with AI and immersion has given rise to Industry 4.0. Machinery IoT sensors include temperature sensors, vibration sensors, and operational efficiency sensors. AI uses this data to forecast possible failures, to schedule the maintenance accordingly.

Employees wearing AR headsets can see real-time augmented reality information, including data on the performance of the machinery and how to repair it. Digital twins refer to the electronic avatars or replicas of operating physical assets, which allow operators to conduct simulations or to experiment on changes that might affect production without necessarily having to make such changes on the real assets.

For instance, Siemens's built MindSphere platform uses IoT, Connected Intelligent Minds, AI, and AR to optimise the factory by minimising the time the machines are out of order.

3.2. Healthcare and Telemedicine

In healthcare, IoT and Artificial Intelligence are transforming patient care and training through the integration of immersive technologies. Wearable IoT devices include devices that measure physiological parameters, including heart rate, blood pressure and oxygen levels. AI processes this data to look for patterns that signal conditions such as arrhythmia, to give early signals for treatment.

AR can be of great help for surgeons during the operations, having in mind that they can place some important data on the patient's body, including blood vessels and tumours. Computer programs can currently simulate surgeries as the student practices, especially because learning is done through VR-based training modules.

For instance, AccuVein employs augmented reality assisted by Artificial Intelligence to provide more visibility of the veins to enhance the Intravenous insertions.

3.3. Smart Cities

The IoT networks of smart cities focus on traffic control and patterns, energy usage, and security. AI algorithms control the traffic signal timings efficiently, minimise wastage of energy and estimate the infrastructural requirements. AR is one of the immersive technologies that offers citizens and city planners an opportunity to see data in real-time.

For instance, augmented reality navigation applications can show traffic jams, parking spaces and timetables of public transportation in a user's view. In Singapore, the Smart Nation project incorporates IoT, AI, and AR to enhance the quality of life of people in cities.

3.4. Retail and E-Commerce

The Internet of Things devices are used in the retail industry to monitor stocks and consumers' behaviour. AI targets shopping experiences based on the past and present shopping habits of the client. There are several benefits to this kind of experience, and incorporating immersive technologies adds to this experience by allowing try-ons and visualisation.

For example, the IKEA app, based on AR, enables users to see how furniture will look in their houses. Users' choices are suggested by AI algorithms, and IoT sensors monitor store traffic patterns to improve store design.

In Figure 3, there is a depiction of the real-world application of immersive technologies broken down by sector, and the level of implementation for each sector [18].

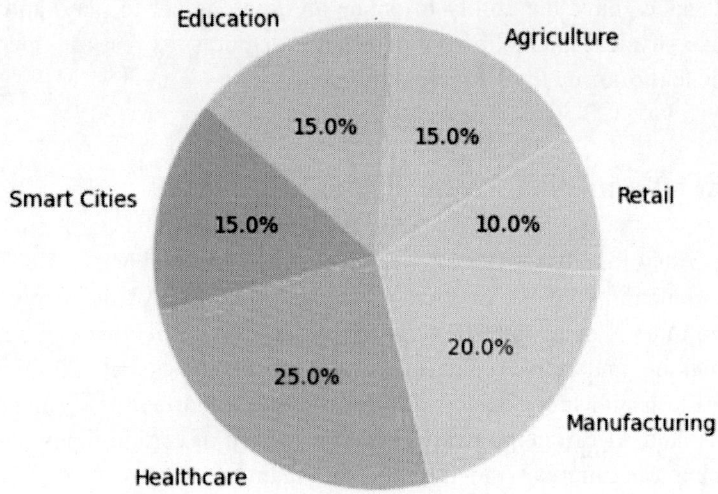

Figure 3. Distribution of Real-world Implementation by Industry.

3.5. Training and Education

Integrating immersive technologies with IoT and AI revolutionises training and education by enhancing the process with interactive and personalised learning environments. Participant interaction with the IoT is recorded through sensors, including eye tracking and response time. AI makes the content relevant depending on the performance of the students to make learning effective.

This makes use of VR simulations, allowing for realistic scenarios for hands-on training. For instance, pilots employ Virtual Reality flight simulators that mimic cockpit situations, and IoT gadgets to measure stress, determine preparedness.

3.6. Agriculture and Smart Farming

Smart devices used in agriculture include sensors that check moisture content, nutrients and weather. AI then uses this data to give recommendations on when to water or apply fertilisers, for example. AR applications provide fields with data overlays, which enable farmers to make better decisions.

For instance, the technology giant John Deere uses IoT, AI and AR to help farmers maximise crop yields and avoid resource misuse.

3.7. Entertainment and Gaming

The entertainment industry is now using the concepts of immersive technologies, IoT, and AI to deliver personalised experiences. IoT sensors in gaming controllers record data on motion and pressure in real time, and AI adjusts the game based on the player's actions.

VR and AR games have the ability to create an environment to play, and IoT-enabled wearables increase physical interactions. For instance, haptic suits that are operated through IoT give users feedback during the VR gaming experience.

4. Applications of Immersive Technologies, IoT, and AI

Applications of Virtual Reality (VR), Augmented Reality (AR) and Mixed Reality (MR) and when used in conjunction with the Internet of Things (IoT) and Artificial Intelligence (AI), bring about a revolution in many industries. These technologies provide real-time engagement, smart decision-making, and realistic data interaction, enhancing operation, training, and use. For example, in the healthcare industry, AR can project important assessment information during operations, and AI can help towards the anticipation of certain illnesses. For VR and AR, manufacturing can improve the training and maintenance processes, and IoT smart machinery can improve productivity. AI and IoT also help in modifying environments in learning institutions and the MR platform in urban and disaster management in smart cities. These combined technologies bring new opportunities, enhancing the performance of industries as well as making industries personal and flexible in terms of the needs. The diversified applications are described in Table 1.

The application of immersive technologies, IoT and AI creates great benefits in many industries through increasing effectiveness and decision-making and providing better user experiences. Although these technologies present a concept of uncharted possibilities, issues such as data privacy, integration, and scalability must come to the fore. With this progressive change in industries, AI, IoT, and immersive technologies will continue to transform sectors such as healthcare, manufacturing, education, and urban planning to become more sustainable, safe, and effective.

5. Technological Challenges and Solutions

The integration of VR, AR, MR, IoT, and AI brings about several technological complexities that require implementation for the various domains [19]. One main issue unaddressed is data protection and privacy, given that augmented reality, virtual reality, and IoT produce massive volumes of information, much of which is confidential.

- Blockchain provides the solution by enabling secure and immutable storage of the data, and homomorphic encryption allows the data to be computed on without revealing the data. There are several problems that become paramount in real-time applications, including latency in AR-guided surgeries or IoT used in manufacturing. They are using edge computing to work data nearer to its origin and the use of enhanced communication networks, 5G and 6G, which guarantee minimal latency.
- The high computational cost of immersive and AI systems necessitates application-level lightweight AI models alongside hardware support such as GPUs & TPUs. Multiple system integration with the old setup is a recurring problem in both the

manufacturing industry and city design. These risks can be managed by a hybrid of old and modern frameworks that include the gradual migration ones.

- AR/VR devices and IoT hardware are costly, which acts as a key constraint to the market. Inclusiveness of these technologies can be enhanced by cloud-based immersive solutions and affordable and sustainable manufacturing technologies.
- The runtime exception and energy consumption occur in IoT devices, especially for remote areas deployment. Energy conservation measures, along with the use of renewable energy, especially solar energy, could be identified as some of the best practices. The development of content for the immersive environment continues to be rather resource-demanding. It is also possible to employ AI tools for the creation of interactive AR/VR content as well as collaborative frameworks within open-source platforms.
- The scalability and user adaptability are of the same importance level. Scalability of the models is improved through distributed AI and a modular IoT application architecture, whereas acceptance is ensured by the integration of easy-to-use interfaces and user training programs. It is crucial to have strong and effective AI auditing for ethical issues addressing bias, as well as heterogeneous data fusion that needs a standard IoT protocol and various datasets for making fair and interoperable decisions for these transforming systems.

The key technologies – VR, AR, MR, IoT, and AI – present new challenges that must be overcome to achieve real-time interoperability in multiple application fields. Privacy and data security are still important, while blockchain and homomorphic encryption offer solutions. Since latency is problematic in real-time applications, it is solved with the help of edge computing, as well as advanced connection networks, including 5G and 6G. These impose high computational costs, therefore, require lean models and implementation tools such as GPUs and TPUs. Issues observed in extending new systems over the existing structures can be managed effectively using the hybrid structure and phased implementations. Challenges that are unique to AR/VR devices and IoT hardware include high costs, which can only be overcome by affordable manufacturing and cloud-based immersive solutions. Energy issues, particularly with IoT-based systems located in hard-to-reach regions, can be addressed using solar energy.

6. Prospects and Research Opportunities

A combination of Virtual Reality (VR), Augmented Reality (AR), Mixed Reality (MR), Internet of Things (IoT) and Artificial Intelligence (AI) suggests the potential of enormous changes in several fields. When combined, these technologies deliver the highest level of interactivity, real-time data visualisation, and, therefore, decision-making possibilities for intelligent systems in the healthcare, manufacturing, educational, and smart city industries. Some are better diagnostic tools, such as AI surgery, Augmented Reality surgery overlays, and IoT wearables for individual patient treatment plans. Future research may lie in applying interventions in simulators and real-time connected sensors in telemedicine and remote surgeries.

Table 1. Applications of immersive technology

Field & Application	Technology Involved	Use Case	Benefits	Description
Healthcare - AR-assisted surgery	AR, AI, IoT	Real-time overlay of diagnostic data	Enhanced precision and better outcomes	Augmented Reality assists surgeons by overlaying critical information like scans, AI-driven diagnostics, and patient data during surgeries, improving accuracy and reducing errors.
Healthcare - AI-based diagnostics	AI	AI algorithms for analyzing medical images or symptoms	Faster, more accurate diagnoses	AI models analyze medical data and images to assist doctors in diagnosing diseases more accurately and efficiently, reducing human error.
Manufacturing - Predictive maintenance	IoT, AI	Real-time monitoring of equipment health	Reduced downtime and cost savings	IoT sensors collect real-time data on machinery performance, and AI analyzes this data to predict and prevent potential equipment failures before they occur.
Manufacturing - AR/VR-based training	AR, VR	Employee training through immersive simulations	Cost-effective training and reduced human error	AR/VR technologies are used to simulate factory environments for employee training, enhancing hands-on skills without physical risks or costs.
Education - Adaptive learning environments	AI, AR, IoT	Personalized learning experiences	Improved student engagement and outcomes	AI and AR work together to create dynamic, adaptive learning environments tailored to students' needs, enhancing engagement and retention of knowledge.
Education - Virtual classrooms and remote education	VR, AI, IoT	Real-time interaction and collaborative learning	Enhanced accessibility and inclusivity	VR-based classrooms provide immersive learning experiences, enabling remote students to interact in a virtual environment, breaking geographical barriers.
Smart Cities - Traffic and resource optimization	MR, IoT, AI	Real-time traffic monitoring and planning	Enhanced traffic flow and resource use	Mixed Reality helps visualize IoT data on traffic flow, optimizing city resources in real-time, improving urban mobility, and reducing congestion.
Smart Cities - Disaster management and prediction	AI, IoT	Real-time data for natural disaster monitoring	Faster response and disaster prevention	AI algorithms analyze IoT sensor data to predict and mitigate the impact of natural disasters like earthquakes, floods, and wildfires, enabling proactive response.
Agriculture - Precision farming	IoT, AI, AR	Monitoring crop health and soil quality	Optimized resource usage and yield	IoT sensors collect environmental and soil data, while AI analyzes it to optimize irrigation, fertilizer use, and pest control, enhancing agricultural productivity.
Agriculture - AR-guided pest control	AR, IoT	Real-time pest monitoring and guidance	Improved accuracy in pest control	AR guides farmers in real-time to identify pest threats and apply targeted control methods, reducing pesticide use and enhancing crop yield.
Retail - Virtual try-ons and immersive shopping	AR, AI, IoT	Immersive product try-ons and recommendations	Personalized shopping experience	AR enables customers to try on clothes or accessories virtually, improving the shopping experience while AI personalizes product suggestions based on preferences.
Retail - AI-powered inventory management	AI, IoT	Smart inventory tracking and restocking	Improved stock management and reduced waste	AI and IoT sensors monitor inventory levels in real-time, automating stock replenishment, reducing waste, and ensuring product availability.

Field & Application	Technology Involved	Use Case	Benefits	Description
Retail - MR-based customer feedback collection	MR, IoT	Real-time customer feedback and product customization	Enhanced customer experience	MR technology allows customers to interact with digital representations of products, providing instant feedback, improving product development and customer satisfaction.
Defense - VR simulations for soldier training	VR, AI	Immersive simulations for military training	Cost-effective, realistic training scenarios	VR creates realistic combat and mission simulations for soldiers, allowing them to experience and react to high-risk scenarios without actual danger.
Defense - AI-powered threat detection	AI, IoT	Real-time monitoring of potential threats	Increased security and reduced response time	AI analyzes data from IoT sensors to detect potential threats, enabling faster responses to security risks.
Defense - Immersive battlefield simulations	VR, AI	Realistic training environments for military strategy	Enhanced mission preparedness and safety	VR creates interactive battlefield environments where soldiers can practice strategies, improving tactical decision-making in real scenarios.
Entertainment - Immersive storytelling experiences	VR, AR	Personalized, interactive VR/AR storytelling	Engaging and customizable user experience	VR and AR create immersive stories that adapt to user choices, allowing for highly engaging, personalized narrative experiences.
Entertainment - AI-driven interactive gaming platforms	AI, MR	Dynamic, user-driven game scenarios	Highly personalized gaming experience	AI adapts the gameplay based on user preferences, enabling personalized and interactive gaming environments.
Entertainment - IoT-enabled dynamic content creation	IoT, AI, 6G	Real-time content updates based on user interaction	More immersive, interactive content	IoT sensors and AI algorithms collect and process real-time data, dynamically altering entertainment content, enhancing the user experience in real-time.

Table 2. Comprehensive analysis on research opportunities

Field	Research Opportunities	Key Challenges	Potential Solutions	Future Prospects
Healthcare	- AI-assisted diagnostic tools integrated with AR for real-time data overlays.	Data privacy and latency issues.	Edge computing and blockchain for secure data.	Fully autonomous healthcare systems with real-time global access.
	- IoT-enabled wearable devices for continuous monitoring and personalized treatment.	Limited device battery life and data integration.	Energy-efficient IoT devices.	AI-driven predictive diagnostics and global telemedicine.
	- VR-based rehabilitation programs and therapy simulations.	Patient adaptability to VR systems.	Improved user-friendly VR hardware.	Expanding VR therapy for mental health and physical recovery.
Manufacturing	- Predictive maintenance using AI and IoT for real-time failure prevention.	High computational demands.	Lightweight AI models and decentralized systems.	Fully automated smart factories with self-optimization.
	- VR/AR-based workforce training and simulation environments.	High cost of hardware and training.	Scalable and affordable training systems.	Workforce upskilling with AR/VR across industries.
	- Smart machinery optimization with autonomous IoT-based analytics.	Integration of legacy systems.	Hybrid systems supporting legacy and IoT devices.	Universal standards for Industry 4.0.
Education	- Adaptive AI-powered learning environments using AR/VR tools.	Lack of widespread adoption.	Government-backed adoption policies.	Personalized global learning environments accessible to all.
	- Development of virtual classrooms for remote and inclusive education.	Limited infrastructure in remote areas.	Low-cost immersive technologies.	Bridging global education gaps with immersive tech.
	- IoT for monitoring student engagement and environment optimization.	Privacy concerns in monitoring.	Encrypted and anonymized data collection.	Data-driven adaptive classrooms.
Smart Cities	- MR platforms for visualizing and optimizing IoT traffic and resource data.	Real-time data processing latency.	5G and edge computing integration.	Fully autonomous smart city ecosystems.
	- AI-powered disaster prediction and management using real-time IoT feeds.	Handling massive, heterogeneous data.	AI-optimized data fusion techniques.	Predictive citywide disaster management systems.
	- Urban planning with immersive simulations and predictive modeling.	High computational requirements.	Scalable cloud and edge systems.	Sustainable, AI-driven urban expansion models.
Agriculture	- AI-based IoT solutions for precision farming and crop health monitoring.	Connectivity issues in rural areas.	IoT with satellite-based networks.	Increased crop yield with minimal resource wastage.
	- AR applications for real-time farm analytics and pest control guidance.	Lack of skilled personnel.	AR-based training modules.	Fully automated precision farming.
	- Integration of immersive tools for training in modern farming techniques.	High cost of AR/VR devices.	Affordable and durable immersive tools.	Rural empowerment through advanced farming knowledge.
Retail	- Virtual try-ons and immersive shopping experiences using AR/VR.	User accessibility and cost.	Cloud-based AR/VR applications.	Personalized retail experiences across digital platforms.
	- AI-driven IoT for personalized customer recommendations and inventory management.	Data privacy concerns.	Blockchain for secure transactions.	Autonomous inventory and customer experience optimization.

Field	Research Opportunities	Key Challenges	Potential Solutions	Future Prospects
	- Mixed reality environments for product design and customer feedback collection.	Scalability for small businesses.	Open-source MR tools.	Democratization of immersive technologies in retail.
Defense	- VR simulations for soldier training and mission rehearsals.	Realistic scenario modeling.	Advanced AI-powered simulators.	Immersive real-world training scenarios with minimal cost.
	- AI-powered threat detection integrated with real-time IoT sensors.	High false-positive rates.	Enhanced AI accuracy using diverse training data.	Real-time, proactive threat neutralization systems.
	- Immersive battlefield simulations for strategy development.	High hardware and software demands.	Distributed simulation environments.	Collaborative, real-time strategy modeling across agencies.
Entertainment	- Development of immersive storytelling experiences in VR/AR.	Content development complexity.	AI-assisted storytelling tools.	Fully immersive, personalized entertainment experiences.
	- Integration of AI-driven personalization in MR-based gaming platforms.	High cost of adoption for users.	Subscription-based models for accessibility.	AI-generated interactive gaming environments.
	- IoT-enabled feedback systems for dynamic content generation.	Real-time data processing challenges.	AI and 6G-enabled dynamic content creation.	Entertainment ecosystems driven by real-time user interaction.

In the same regard, the manufacturing domain presents a chance to improve smart factory performance with the help of AI IoT analytics, and extensive usage of VR simulations of the working environment for training employees. Research can on the further development of autonomous systems accompanied by the ability to predict and prevent failures of equipment in a real-time manner. Education and urban planning can also be seen as having great opportunities. The use of AR/VR tools in line with advanced learning tools that use artificial intelligence can deliver an adaptive learning environment. IoT data in urban planning can be visualised by MR platforms to analyse resource distribution and disaster influence. Future studies may examine the deployment of AI and VR for predictive urban modelling, and therefore, modelling and, therefore, promote sustainable urban growth. Thus, there are still problems that should be solved, including data privacy, high computational demand and latency issues.

There is research potential in exploring new solutions such as low-latency edge computing for latency-sensitive applications, low-footprint AI models that can run in resource-scarce environments, and a blockchain platform for data sharing. Ethical issues or user acceptance of these technologies could also be embraced in an interdisciplinary study. New and emerging technologies such as quantum computing and 6G networks extend the ability of IoT-AI-immersive systems. Further investigation of the two schemes can lead to ultra-low latency, high throughput, and efficient data processing, making these intelligent systems more reliable, easy to scale, and extendible to various areas. The Comprehensive Analysis on Research Opportunities are detailed in Table 2.

The integration of VR, AR, MR, IoT and AI is promising for many sectors as it provides means for improving real-time data analysis and visualisation, intelligent decision making and providing interaction capabilities. The industry that is bound to benefit most from such opportunities is the healthcare industry, where items like AI-diagnosis, IoT watch-like devices, and virtual reality-based synthetic mimics of therapeutic processes are expected. The future possibilities covered in this work include future autonomous global healthcare systems and predictive diagnostics based on IoT and AI. In manufacturing, these technologies facilitate predictive maintenance, augmented and virtual reality workforce training, smart optimisation, and other issues such as computational complexity and integration with legacy systems.

Education will transform through an adaptive learning environment and virtual classroom through AI and IoT, as education for all and focused education across the globe. Smart cities and urbanisation employ MR platforms and AI for disaster response, traffic flow, and green city solutions. Agriculture can use AIoT in smart farming, AR for analysis, and immersive solutions for training farmers with better resource utilisation and improved yield. Current issues that are likely to emerge are the issue of privacy of data, delays, and high computational complexity, which can be solved by the use of blockchain, edge computing, and lightweight AI models. Prospects are moral issues, users willing to adapt their lifestyle for a greener environment, and the use of quantum computers and future generation mobile networks such as 6G for building highly reliable and easily scalable systems. Further collaboration between fields guarantees that progress will be made and that new opportunities will be revealed in many fields.

Conclusion and Recommendations

The integration of Virtual Reality (VR), Augmented Reality (AR), and Mixed Reality (MR) with the Internet of Things (IoT) and Artificial Intelligence (AI) is reshaping diverse domains through the creation of intelligent interaction systems. This convergence facilitates real-time data acquisition via IoT, rapid data analysis and decision-making through AI, and user-friendly visualisation enabled by immersive technologies. Some of the use cases include AR surgeries; AI-enabled diagnosis, among others. Like other industries, manufacturing also benefits from such things as predictive maintenance, smart machinery, and AR/VR-based training of employees. IoT is employed by the learning management systems with adaptive AI by learning; MR assists smart city planning by traffic organising and natural disaster management. The issues such as data privacy, latency and computational complexity have remained as key challenges even with the new innovations. Such problems need to be solved using edge computing to minimise latency, blockchain to enhance data security, and computational resources. More future work should be devoted to the improvement of the interoperability and the scalability of these technologies across domains. More research on different lightweight and decentralised architectures of IoT-AI-immersive systems is advised to make the development and the applications cheaper and accessible. Industry collaborations can go even further to foster innovation. This transformative synergy defines a formidable frontier for intelligent systems, hence the need to apply ethical and secure approaches in all applications.

References

[1] Eagleson, Roy, et al., "Clinical trainee performance on task-based AR/VR-guided surgical simulation is correlated with their 3D image spatial reasoning scores." *Healthcare Technology Letters* 11.2-3 (2024): 117-125.

[2] Kaswan, Kuldeep Singh, et al., "AI-Based AR/VR Models in Biomedical Sustainable Industry 4.0." *Computational Intelligence in Bioprinting* (2024): 53-78.

[3] Wut, Tai Ming, and Mei-Lan Peggy Ng. "Virtual reality and augmented reality of tourism research: a review and research agenda." *Journal of Quality Assurance in Hospitality & Tourism* (2024): 1-24.

[4] Sathya, A., and A. Aruna. "Rehabilitation for Parkinson's Disease Using Virtual Reality (VR): Impact and Observational Analysis." Navigating the Augmented and Virtual Frontiers in Engineering. *IGI Global*, 2024. 1-20.

[5] Jeevika Tharini, V., & Vijayarani, S. (2020). Bio-inspired High-Utility Item Framework based Particle Swarm Optimization Tree Algorithms for Mining High Utility Itemset. In *Advances in Computational Intelligence and Informatics: Proceedings of ICACII 2019* (pp. 265-276). Springer Singapore.

[6] Tharini, V. J., & Shivakumar, B. L. (2024). A Canonical Particle Swarm Optimization (C-PSO) Approach to Identify High Utility Itemset. *Journal of Computational Analysis and Applications* (JoCAAA), 33(05), 507-517.

[7] Gao, Hui, Alain Yee Loong Chong, and Haijun Bao. "Metaverse: literature review, synthesis and future research agenda." *Journal of Computer Information Systems* 64.4 (2024): 533-553.

[8] Sellam, V., Aruna, A., Joseph, A., Rahul, S., & Rahul, A. (2022, May). Optical character recognition using localization techniques. In *AIP Conference Proceedings* (Vol. 2463, No. 1). AIP Publishing.

[9] Yung, Ryan, and Catheryn Khoo-Lattimore. "New realities: a systematic literature review on virtual reality and augmented reality in tourism research." *Current issues in tourism* 22.17 (2019): 2056-2081.

[10] Samaddar, Kaushik, and Sanjana Mondal. "AR and VR-based travel: A responsible practice towards sustainable tourism." *International Journal of Tourism Cities 10*.1 (2024): 105-128.

[11] Aruna, A., and A. Senthilselvi. "A Novel Approach to Enhance Data Integrity in Blockchain using Cryptographic Hashing." *2024 Second International Conference on Advances in Information Technology* (ICAIT). Vol. 1. IEEE, 2024.

[12] Arora, Manpreet. "Virtual Reality in Education: Analyzing the Literature and Bibliometric State of Knowledge." *Transforming Education with Virtual Reality* (2024): 379-402.

[13] Paulsen, Lucas, Susanne Dau, and Jacob Davidsen. "Designing for collaborative learning in immersive virtual reality: a systematic literature review." *Virtual Reality* 28.1 (2024): 63.

[14] Zhou, Zhongyun, Zidie Chen, and Xiao-Ling Jin. "A review of the literature on the metaverse: definition, technologies, and user behaviors." *Internet Research* 34.1 (2024): 129-148.

[15] Monla, Ziad, et al., "Indicators Specification for Maturity Evaluation of BIM-Based VR/AR Systems Using ISO/IEC 15939 Standard." *International Conference on Extended Reality*. Cham: Springer Nature Switzerland, 2024.

[16] Sudiarno, Adithya, et al., "Investigating the Future Study Area on VR Technology Implementation in Safety Training: A Systematic Literature Review." *Journal of Safety Science and Resilience* (2024).

[17] Arif, Yunifa Miftachul, et al., "A Systematic Literature Review of Serious Games for Physical Education: Technologies, Implementations, and Evaluations." *Global Innovations in Physical Education and Health* (2025): 1-36.

[18] Hassan, Lobna. "*Accessibility of Educational Games and Game-Based Approaches to People with Learning and Physical Disabilities: A Systematic Literature Review.*" (2024).

[19] Suryodiningrat, Satrio Pradono, Arief Ramadhan, and Tsukasa Hirashima. "The Elements of Every Metaverse Types: A Systematic Literature Review." *TEM Journal* 13.1 (2024).

Chapter 13

Inclusive Design and Accessibility in Immersive Environments

G. Tamilmani[1,*]
M. Anousouya Devi[2,†]
P. Saranya[2,‡]
R. Usharani[3,‖]
and S. Sageengrana[4,¶]

[1]Department of Computational Intelligence, SRM Institute of science and technology, Kattankulathur, Tamil Nadu, India
[2]Department of Computational Intelligence, SRMIST, Kattankulathur, Tamil Nadu, India
[3]Department of Computational Intelligence, Faculty of Engineering and Technology, School of Computing, SRM Institute of Science and Technology, Kattankulathur, Tamil Nadu, India
[4]Department of Computational Intelligence, SRM Institute of Science and Technology, Kattankulathur, Tamil Nadu, India

Abstract

Offering immersive spaces with accessible and inclusive design remains pivotal in the assurance of equal access to all users with diverse abilities. Mass uptake of virtual reality (VR), augmented reality (AR) and mixed reality (MR) in various industries calls for immediate barrios to accessibility issues. Inclusive design foundations for immersive spaces are subjected to examination through user-centred frameworks which espouse accommodating user needs. The examination offers disability-related problems associated with visuallimitations, and cognitive disability while demonstrating technologies for overcoming such barriers. The examination includes a discussion on assistive technologies as well as adaptive interfaces and inclusive content creation strategies for accessibility enhancement. The writing highlights regulatory requirements as well as industry ethical standards, along with best practices to achieve immersive content accessibility. Applying AI-facilitated customization strategies alongside inclusive design principles enables

* Corresponding Author's Email: tamilmag@srmist.edu.in
† Corresponding Author's Email: anousoum@srmist.edu.in
‡ Corresponding Author's Email: saranyap4@srmist.edu.in
‖ Corresponding Author's Email: usharanr2@srmist.edu.in
¶ Corresponding Author's Email: sageengranadhas@gmail.com

In: Shaping Tomorrow
Editors: Prithi Samuel, A. Sathya, Balamurugan Balusamy et al.
ISBN: 979-8-90134-076-9

immersive spaces to be rendered more accessible and interactive to users. The chapter offers industry examples as well as future trends that demonstrate successful implementations of inclusive immersive experiences. The research evaluates design practices as well as accessibility standards while exploring user engagement practices to promote knowledge on fair digital interface practices.

Keywords: virtual reality (VR), augmented reality (AR), mixed reality (MR), cognitive impairments, AI-driven customization

1. Introduction

Extended Reality (XR) which encompasses Virtual, Augmented, and Mixed Reality is speeding up in the classroom, clinics, factories, museums, and public services where accessibility and inclusion is becoming a first-order design issue and not a concern of an add-on. Distinguishing between immersive systems and web and mobile interaction is the embodiment of interaction, which is spatial, real time, and embodied; consequently, the barriers tend to multiply, encompassing the visual (poor contrast, small letters, flickering details), auditory (no captions or spatial clues), motor (subtle controller actions, fixed heights of reaches) and cognitive (bandwidth usage, intricate navigation) and vestibular (cybersickness) subsystems. However, the XR also has its own benefits of inclusion with multimodal redundancy (spatial audio, haptics, gaze-driven prompts, scalable user interface, customizable locomotion, and, more and more, AI-assisted personalization that can acquire and use the preferences of a user (e.g., high-contrast themes, simplified scenes, caption positioning, interaction pace, etc.) without infringing upon privacy and control. This chapter explores the principles towards inclusive design of immersive spaces with a user-centred, disability-conscious approach, considering both visual and cognitive design, and accounting motor and vestibular intersections; surveys assistive technologies (audio description in XR, spatial captioning, haptic cues), adaptive interfaces, and inclusive content strategies; and frames practice in terms of regulatory standards and ethical guidelines, and regards compliance as the minimum standard on equitable experience. We describe the approach to assessing the accessibility in XR, which combines both the comfort/cybersickness and task indicators with the approach to the participatory and scenario-based research, and we summarize the industry examples that can exemplify the successful and scalable implementations. By doing so, we would add a barrier-to-response taxonomy, a practical checklist to inclusive immersive content, and a realistic framework to AI-driven customization, which holds that an inclusive design and responsible AI used concurrently can make immersive spaces more accessible, interactive, and empowering to different users in school, family, community, and workplace settings.

2. Understanding Inclusive Design in Immersive Environments

The main objective of inclusive design for immersive experiences is to make digital interactions usable by everyone regardless of the nature of their disabilities. Virtual reality (VR), augmented reality (AR), and mixed reality (MR) technologies continue to dominate the market, so the main element of ethical and user-centred design is accessibility by everyone. The provision for a wide variety of users becomes a main benefit of inclusive design since flexible interfaces lead to increased usability by all groups of users including users with disabilities. A design process that considers various user requirements from the beginning of development incorporates accessibility into the system rather than waiting too long. Interactive digital users benefit from inclusive design integration in virtual worlds that facilitates equal use and breaks down barriers to toolkit access [1].

2.1. Principles of Inclusive Design in Digital Spaces

Core principles of an inclusive digital environment involve flexibility and empowerment of users within design specifications. Electronic experiences under this principle should be usable by everyone, including people with diverse abilities, without the requirement of additional adaptations or modifications. Flexible use design involves the provision of diverse modes of interaction, such as gestures, voice, and accessory hardware devices, to meet the diverse needs of individual users in accessing virtual content. Redesigning simple features improve navigation through virtual environments by reducing cognitive disorientation and facilitating learning. The principle of perceptible information requires content to be provided in text along with audio and visual cues, which enables diverse ability levels to efficiently utilise and access the system. Design features that reduce unintended actions are an integral component of tolerance for error systems, which enables immersive experiences to be more user-friendly and prevents frustration. Users find digital environments comfortable that low physical effort eliminates both mental stress and repetitive input actions, which may hinder accessibility. Adoption of these core principles leads to immersive environment development which gives priority to user requirements for diverse audience participation [2].

2.2. Importance of Accessibility in Virtual and Augmented Realities

In order to create usable immersive experiences, such as in virtual and augmented reality, the pathway to these experiences must be accessible to users of varying ability levels. These technologies are barriers, preventing people with disabilities from being able to participate in education, work, entertainment and social exchanges — proper accessibility passes are needed, otherwise. The biggest issue with implementing user interfaces in VR and AR is making the technology accessible to people with visual impairments. The state of the art for current immersive applications relies mainly on visual interface elements, which become increasingly complex for low vision users and blind users to process. This disconnect can be resolved by introducing screen-reading technology with verbal control systems along with haptic response performance capabilities. Not only those who need visual access, but users with hearing disabilities also need equal access to an aural experience. With real-time captioning and sign language avatars, spatial audio can be set [3], enabling users to undertake immersive activities.

Immersive spaces are particularly afflicted by the threat of PWD due to such spaces needing users to perform hand gestures and head-tracking movements [51]. Combining eye-tracking with flexible controls, interface solutions that allow those with mobility difficulties to move around virtual environments without interference. Severe cognitive accessibility challenges affect people with autism or dyslexia and other related neurodiverse situations. The users with cognitive impairments will be assisted by virtual worlds which have simple navigational routes along with reduced/guided complex stimuli mixed with structured operation of information presentation rules. Eventually, when they integrate all major accessibility specifications into immersive technology tools, a vast majority of users will not be excluded from the benefits of such systems serving educational and rehabilitative and social connection needs [4].

2.3. Role of User Experience (UX) in Inclusive Immersive Systems

User experience (UX) is one of the main pillars for the design of inclusive immersive systems, focusing on human perception in interaction with, and navigation of, digital objects and environments. A good UX layout makes immersive systems user-friendly, attractive, and accessible to users with diverse needs. In inclusive design approaches, UX focuses on designing interfaces that you can operate easily. There should be intuitive navigational systems alongside personalised means of interaction that keep primary functions uncomplicated. Heatmap performance is especially relevant with regard to user comfort and motivation over extended periods in immersive system use. These personalisation tools enable users to create their educational experiences [5] as users can choose the text used for display and the guiding text during voice-commanded navigation and environment design.

UX in immersive systems requires essential elements, which include feedback and the ability for fast responses. Live feedback signals displayed audibly or through visuals and touch assistance help users better identify their system actions as well as maintain error-free operations. People who have disabilities require immediate and clear system feedback to operate the product efficiently. Reaching an accessible design in immersive systems depends heavily on testing accessibility and conducting research involving users. The integration and refinement of accessibility features depends on testing usability with different user groups that contain people who have disabilities. Empathy-driven design stands as the essential element of inclusive UX because designers are motivated to understand the experiences which diverse users encounter with their disabilities. Incorporation of accessibility into UX design enables immersive systems to produce meaningful experiences for all, resulting in an improved digital landscape for inclusiveness [6].

The presented Figure 1 compares usability rating levels between immersive systems that implement inclusive design and those that do not. The metrics system consists of four evaluation factors, which rate ease of navigation alongside user engagement, as well as accessibility features and error tolerance levels using a scale from 1 to 10. All categories receive higher scores in systems featuring inclusive design, according to Figure 1, when compared to systems without inclusive features. The biggest distinction exists in accessibility features, which demonstrate immersive systems specifically designed for inclusivity deliver a better accessibility experience to users. Higher ratings for error tolerance emphasise the need to develop systems that reduce accidental activities because they make user interactions more fluid for people with disabilities. Using this evidence, we validate that inclusive system development beginning at the early immersive stage creates better usability solutions for diverse users.

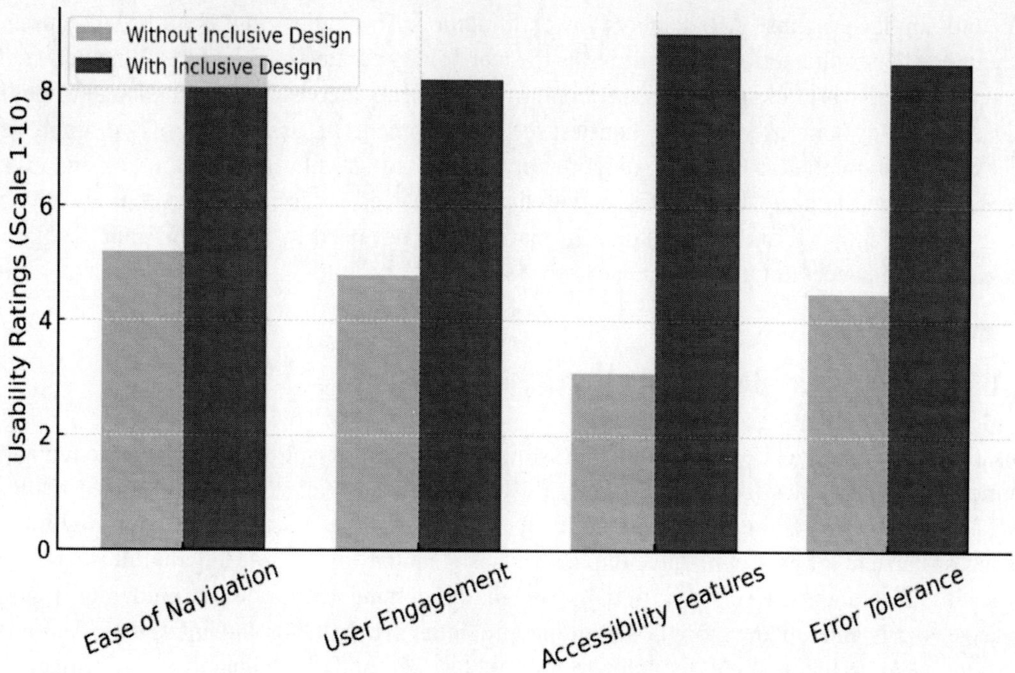

Figure 1. Comparison of usability rating in immersive systems.

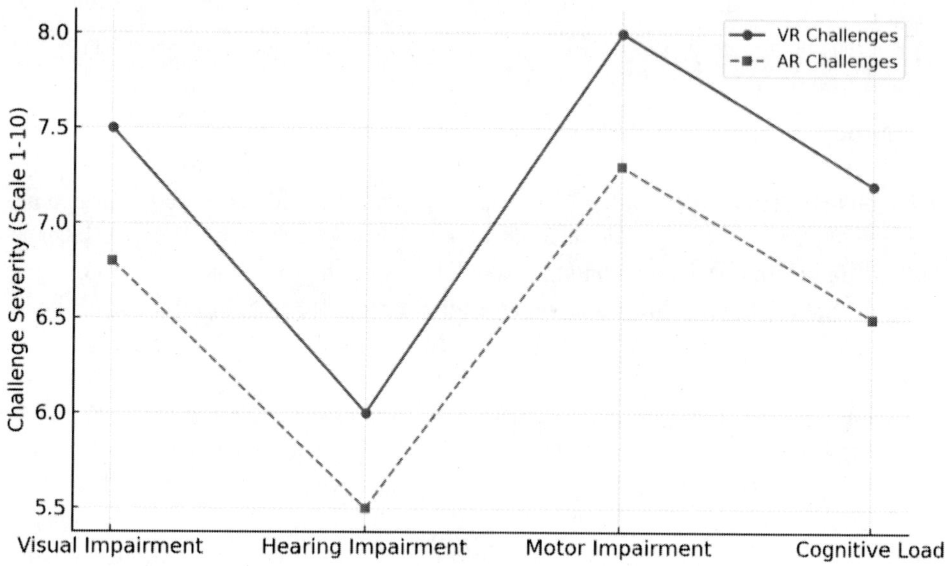

Figure 2. Comparison of accessibility challenges in VR and AR.

Through Figure 2, the research examines the levels of accessibility problems that users face when using both virtual reality (VR) and augmented reality (AR) platforms regarding visual impairment, hearing impairment, motor impairment and cognitive load. Figure 2 illustrates how VR creates more serious difficulties than AR, especially in control limitations and mental workload demands. The high degree of movement necessity and engrossing nature of VR create too much cognitive processing challenge for its users, likely leading to this difference between

VR and similar systems. AR displays lower limitations in challenging areas because users experience better interaction possibilities as the technology creates seamless blending between virtual and real-world elements. Visual impairment presents a considerable challenge to both VR and AR system use, which justifies the development of assistive tools to improve accessibility through screen reader functionality, high-contrast interface design, and adaptive display configuration capabilities. Users with disabilities need accessibility-driven innovations to be brought into VR and AR systems so that they do not need to face significant usability problems when accessing these immersive systems.

3. Barriers to Accessibility in VR, AR, and MR

Disabled users experience significant accessibility hurdles in trying to access interactive and immersive technologies like virtual reality (VR), augmented reality (AR), and mixed reality (MR). The systems relying on visual, auditory, and motor-based features present a multitude of access barriers for users who have impairments, so that they are unable to gain full advantage of such environments. Users who have problems processing lengthy or intimidating digital interfaces can end up developing cognitive problems when using the interfaces. Various barriers need to be tackled to achieve full inclusivity and user equality on immersive technological platforms. Developers who identify and understand issues of visual, auditory, motor, and cognitive accessibility can create accessible immersive environments that work for everyone [7].

3.1. Visual Impairments and the Challenges of Virtual Interfaces

Immersive environments pose challenges for the visually impaired, as those environments are heavily screen-based and focused on visual feedback. Thus, when using VR experiences, users with low vision or blindness face challenges understanding the depth and motion of space as well as the spatial relations. Unfortunately, cross-platform projects fail to utilise enhanced AR content, which is inaccessible to users who do not have these kinds of rendered experiences at their disposal. The results discussed in paper [8] show that users with visual impairments had more difficulties in navigating those interfaces that do not provide touch feedback. To solve the existing problems and make the technology accessible as intended, developers must implement accessibility elements such as screen readers, voice guidance and high-contrast modes to enhance visibility. Spatial audio, paired with haptic feedback, acts as an alternative communication pathway to convey important information, thus making VR more accessible to vision-impaired users. Deployment of immersive technology solutions makes them more accessible for individuals with visual disabilities.

3.2. Auditory Limitations and the Need for Adaptive Audio Solutions

Many virtual reality, AR, and MR systems use positional sound directions to offer their users situational insight and interactive alert signals. Thus, auditory access must remain a top immersive technology consideration. Individuals with hearing impairments cannot detect the necessary audio cues, which results in problems with dialogue comprehension, along with difficulties in using sound alerts and interactive elements. The use of traditional subtitles turns out to be insufficient in dynamic virtual environments since multiple sound sources and proper spatial position-related cues remain essential for a compelling user experience. The developers should integrate adaptive audio features, which include real-time captioning as well as sign language avatars and visual sound indicators that convert auditory signals into alternative formats [9]. Users can personalize their audio settings to enhance hearing by modifying sound frequencies as well as voice amplification and essential sound filtering for different levels of hearing impediments. Immersive environments which incorporate these features guarantee users with auditory disabilities will find accessible digital experiences without any form of exclusion [10].

3.3. Motor and Mobility Issues in Interaction with Immersive Technologies

Users with motor dysfunctions experience major difficulties when using VR, AR, and MR systems because these technologies need precise body movements for motion tracking, hand gestures, and controller utilisation. Users who experience limitations in mobility or deal with paralysis or muscular disorders cannot perform complex physical actions needed to experience many immersive experiences, which require reaching, grabbing, and moving within spatial boundaries. Users with dexterity problems face a barrier to virtual environment navigation because standard input tools fail to fit their needs [11]. Brain-computer interfaces (BCIs) offer a means of interacting with digital environments by relying on neural signals so that physical movement is no longer a prerequisite for interacting with the digital environment. Versatile input systems that produce realistic user interactions for people who require varying degrees of mobility assistance need to be developed so as not to exclude them from modern digital systems [12].

3.4. Cognitive Load and Usability Challenges for Neurodivergent Users

Immersive design usually ignores cognitive accessibility, which represents a vital component for enabling a comfortable digital experience interaction between neurodivergent users. People with autism, ADHD, and dyslexia typically struggle with sensorial overload and complex menus and fast information processing during VR, AR, or MR-based participation. These highly immersive systems generate sensory overload that makes users struggle to concentrate and effectively process instructions as described in [13]. User accessibility requires development efforts that create basic interfaces and organised navigation schemes, together with customizable content displays that offer stimulus control functionalities for individuals. Reasonable usability comes from guided tutorial systems together with adjustable text options and toolsets that promote focus. Step-by-step instructions combined with options for managing distractions enhance the usability experience of neurodivergent people. Developers who focus on cognitive accessibility during immersive design developments will produce digital settings that support users with various cognitive requirements while improving their comfort level [14].

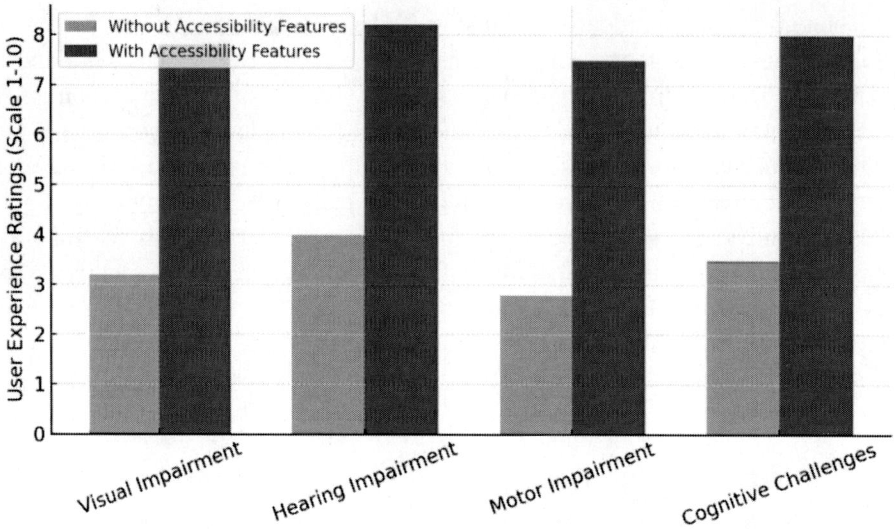

Figure 3. Comparison of user experience with and without accessibility features.

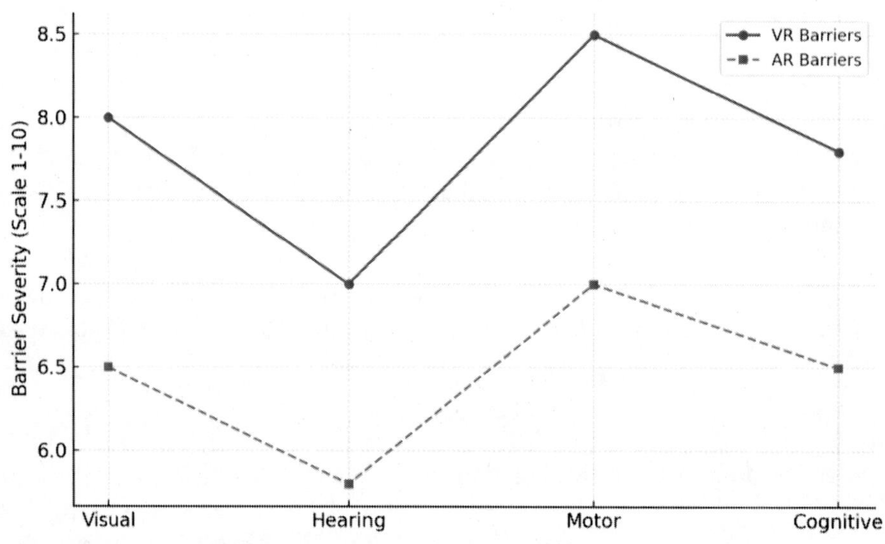

Figure 4. Comparison of accessibility barriers in VR and AR.

User ratings on immersive environments receive direct comparison through Figure 3 from environments featuring accessibility features between disability categories of vision, hearing, motor function and cognition. The data in Figure 3 indicates that user experience rates drop significantly when there are no accessibility features present because disabled users encounter accessibility barriers. The immersive environment presents the most challenge to users with motor and visual impairments because such environments require extensive physical and visual interaction for functionality. The ratings improve substantially with integrations of accessible features that include screen readers, together with voice navigation, adaptive controllers, and cognitive-friendly UI modifications. Blending existing solutions accomplishes powerful usability improvements for immersive worlds that create access for diverse sets of users.

The accessibility barriers in virtual reality (VR) and augmented reality (AR) systems differ based on visual and hearing obstacles and physical movement and mental process restrictions, according to Figure 4. Data from Figure 4 indicates that VR systems produce more accessibility obstacles than AR systems, except in cases involving motor and cognitive limitations, which present the largest differences between the two technologies. VR is faced with accessibility issues as its users with neurodivergent conditions struggle to cope with its full-body movement system in combination with controller controls and deep immersion experiences. AR offers lower levels of severity in its operations because it enables users to interact within real-world scenarios by integrating digital content. Visual impairments require innovative assistive solutions for VR and AR systems because both platforms create hurdles for users with impaired vision. The necessary solutions should incorporate haptic feedback systems and improved auditory instructions. The analysis demonstrates why accessibility needs to be customised specifically for each immersive technology since this approach supports the ongoing development of VR and AR systems that work for people with different requirements.

4. Assistive Technologies and Adaptive Interfaces

Modern assistive technologies have created opportunities for all users with various needs to interact with immersive environments. The interaction methods used in virtual reality (VR), along with mixed reality (MR), primarily depend on visual, auditory, and motor-based functions but exist as barriers for people with impairments. Survey-based interfaces create physical and cognitive barriers for interactions between users in the digital environment. Different accessibility innovations that include screen readers, along with haptic feedback, AI-driven voice assistants, brain-computer interfaces (BCIs), and multisensory feedback systems have been instrumental in bringing improved accessibility across platforms. Immersive experiences through technology bridge disability needs by providing accessibility to people with visual disabilities, alongside auditory disabilities and motor disabilities, combined with cognitive challenges [15].

4.1. Visually Impaired Users

Immersive technologies prove hard to operate by visually impaired users since their interface demands both graphical comprehension and spatial orientation abilities. Access to information through virtual and augmented environments is now possible for users through screen readers, which convert texts displayed on screens into speech or braille outputs. These readers support integration with AR applications, so users receive instant descriptions about objects that improve their spatial understanding. Auditory solutions represent only one part of accessibility enhancement for visually impaired users because haptic feedback remains crucial for improving user experience. Through combinations of force-based cues together with vibrations, haptic feedback provides users with a means to detect spatial information and enables operations with virtual items, and helps users navigate with better precision. When haptic technology joins forces with screen readers, both visually impaired people and their immersive environment experience enhanced performance [16].

4.2. AI-Powered Voice Assistants and Real-Time Subtitling for AR/VR

Artificial intelligence (AI) has transformed accessibility in immersive environments as it allows for real-time interaction in addition to adaptive functionality. Users benefit from AI assistants which operate without hands and offer navigation support, together with answers to their questions and step-by-step VR and AR guidance. Users benefit from voice assistants that process vocal instructions, thus providing simplified command experiences that help those who need extra help with manual controls or view-based interfaces. The essential character of real-time subtitling supports users with hearing disabilities because it transforms spoken information directly into readable text for them. The automatic captioning in virtual spaces powered by AI-driven speech recognition allows individuals with hearing disability to participate in conversations while following instructions without facing any communication obstacles. When developers integrate AI technology into immersive platforms, they establish systems which meet various user needs effectively, thus improving accessibility alongside usability [17].

4.3. Brain-Computer Interfaces (BCI) and Gesture Recognition for Motor-Impaired Users

Immersive environments pose challenges to users with motor impairments because they need physical movement followed by manual input to function properly. Users gain the ability to operate digital systems through neural signals with the help of brain-computer interfaces (BCIs). The hardware systems convert neurological patterns into operating commands, thus allowing people with severe movement restrictions to move within simulated spaces while operating digital content and sending messages through digital channels. Accessibility benefits from gesture recognition technology since it enables users to execute operations through reduced physical investments. System interfaces with motion tracking capability identify natural head and face signals and eye actions to serve as input for users who cannot manage standard controller devices. Since BCIs and gesture recognition were incorporated into VR and AR systems, they provide disability-friendly access to immersive content which previously disabled individuals could not experience [18].

4.4. Multisensory Feedback Mechanisms for Enhanced User Experience

A fully inclusive immersive experience needs multisensory feedback devices which work for individuals with different disabilities. Users receive detailed informational feedback through the combination of visual elements with both auditory and haptic and even olfactory feedback components. The combination of visual alerts and haptic vibrations serves users with hearing impairments to notify them about important events, and spatial audio with tactile cues is available to users with visual disabilities for navigation purposes. Complex light effects combined with ambient temperatures and scent-based feedback create an immersive experience, providing increased accessibility benefits to all. Developers who integrate various sensory inputs create full-immersive designs for Universal Accessibility purposes while making accessibility a central aspect of their user interface development process [19].

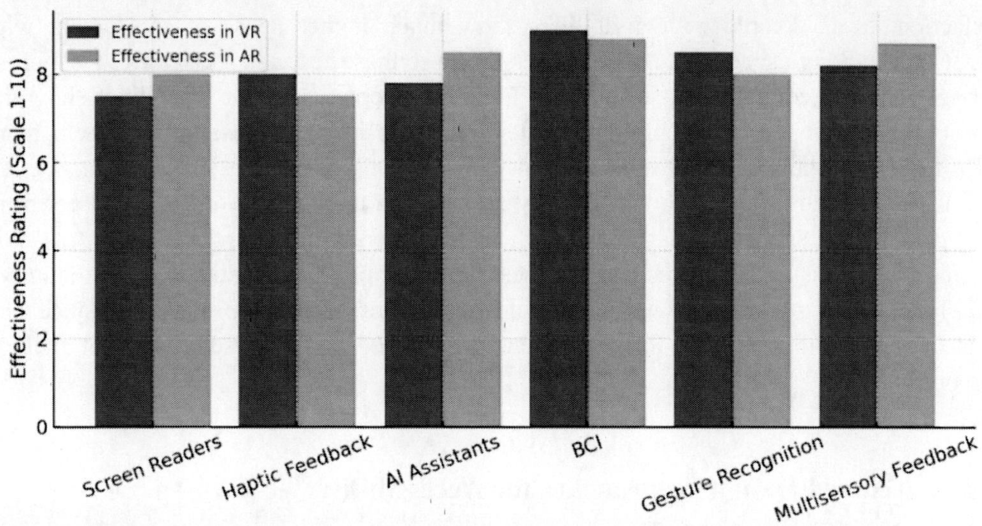

Figure 5. Comparison of assistive technologies in VR and AR.

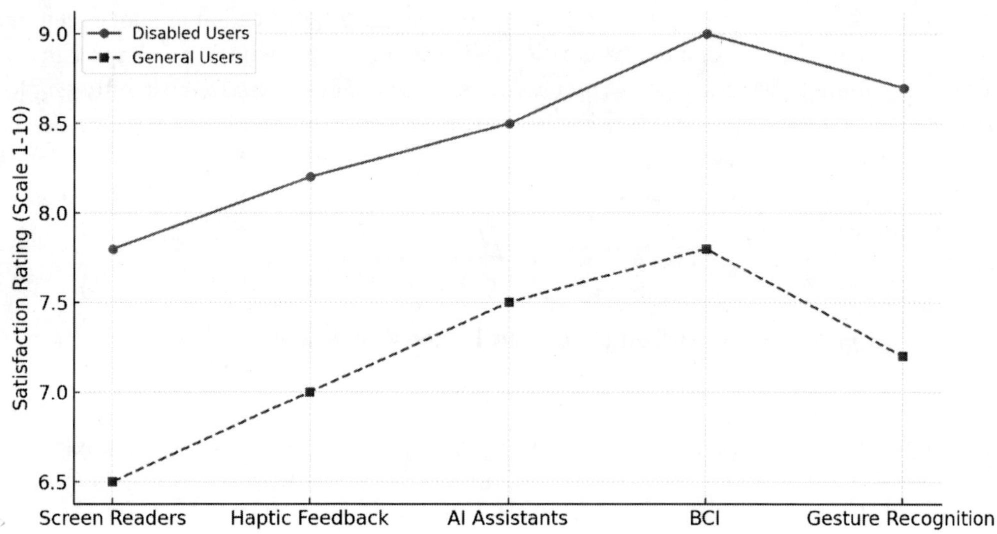

Figure 6. User satisfaction with accessibility features in immersive environments.

Figure 5 depicts how assistive technology tools perform against one another in virtual reality (VR) and augmented reality (AR) environments. Brain-computer interfaces (BCI), along with gesture recognition systems, achieve maximum effectiveness ratings because they let disabled users easily navigate digital environments, as shown in Figure 5. The combination of AI voice assistants and real-time subtitling functions excellently in augmented reality because they enable operational freedom and enhanced accessibility for people who have hearing difficulties. Users experience better haptic and screen reader efficiency in AR systems because they can access real-world environmental context, despite these technologies working equally well in both VR and AR. Assistive technologies generally enhance both VR and AR systems, but their performance level depends on how much interaction is needed between systems.

Figure 6 shows disabled users and general users rate the accessibility features for satisfaction levels. People with disabilities show much higher levels of satisfaction with assistive technology aspects than normal users because these features specifically respond to their accessibility requirements, as shown in Figure 6. People who have disabilities show the highest satisfaction level with brain-computer interfaces because these systems help them regain motor function. General users demonstrate relatively moderate levels of satisfaction towards these features, although they usually do not need them for involvement. Users from both groups show significant satisfaction when they interact with haptic feedback and AI-powered voice assistance features because these solutions provide benefits to a wide range of users. The analysis demonstrates why accessible innovations should have top priority since they establish key building blocks for virtual and augmented software solutions that include everyone.

5. User-Centred Design Approaches for Accessibility

The creation of accessible immersive environments needs a user-centred design method which puts forth different requirements of disabled individuals as its primary focus. Creation of accessible VR and AR experiences is an outcome of developers' dedication to human-centred models in combination with design participation and customisation options, and comprehensive trials of accessibility. The development process of user-centred design performs iterative cycles that connect designers directly with users for technology evolution based on genuine needs. The design approach provides greater usability and inclusion functionality to immersive systems which support users with different senses and physical capability requirements in digital environments [20].

5.1. Human-Centered Interaction Models in Immersive Spaces

Immersive technologies designed through human-centered models base their decisions on users to meet the diverse accessibility needs of all users. Users who depend on vision, mobility, and auditory feedback will encounter barriers to using VR, AR and MR platforms because these platforms usually operate via these three interaction modes. Adaptive interaction models allow individuals with diverse abilities to interact with virtual environments through alternative communication means like gaze-tracking and voice commands with haptic feedback. Multiple input techniques, which unite both vision-based and sound and touch signals, create adaptive user interfaces. Developers who apply human-centered design principles make immersive environments that both users and all viewers can navigate easily and access readily.

5.2. Participatory Design: Involving People with Disabilities in Development

The design of accessible immersive environments is achieved through participatory design if it entails the continuous participation of users with disabilities. Developers acquire specific accessibility insight into user needs when they include participants with different requirements from the design development process's early stages. The co-development process guarantees accessibility as a fundamental element of design, instead of an afterthought after the process is complete. Accessibility standards for immersive technologies can be achieved through usability testing alongside feedback loops and co-creation workshops. Persons with disabilities participating in development activities lead to innovative solutions that more closely mirror users' real-world experiences and are more effective and efficient [21].

5.3. Personalisation and Adaptive User Interfaces for Diverse Needs

The absence of customised user interface features enables users to access immersive environments with substantial ease. Interface customisation features let users customise elements through features that enable modification of size options and contrast levels. Customisation features let users customise elements through features that enable modification of size options and contrast levels. Customisation features let users customise elements through features that enable modification of size options and contrast levels, together with voice-controlled navigation. Modern adaptive systems utilise artificial intelligence in automatically adapting interfaces to individual user preferences combined with behaviour patterns so that users with disabilities experience the best experience. System accessibility allows users who need motor controls to make use of gestures while those who need visual assistance programs gain access to text-to-speech features. Through the features of personalisation, users gain immersive experience control, which causes their interfaces to adapt to personal needs instead of insisting on standard interface conformity.

5.4. Assessment and Testing Methods Should be Implemented for Accessible Immersive Environments

The evaluation process of immersive technologies should include thorough testing for accessibility as a part of creating inclusive systems. The Web Content Accessibility Guidelines (WCAG), together with other standardised frameworks, function as fundamental assessment tools which aid in digital accessibility examination. Tests with users who have disabilities allow the discovery of accessibility barriers that facilitate the development of new interaction models for enhanced accessibility standards. The detection of standard issues by automated testing tools should be combined with practical assessments involving various groups of users to identify refined challenges. Some of the metrics for success in accessibility include user satisfaction ratings and cognitive load testing, in addition to measurement of task completion by users. Developers who repeat testing phases and experience refinement will generate virtual environments that serve innovative purposes while remaining inclusive to all users [22].

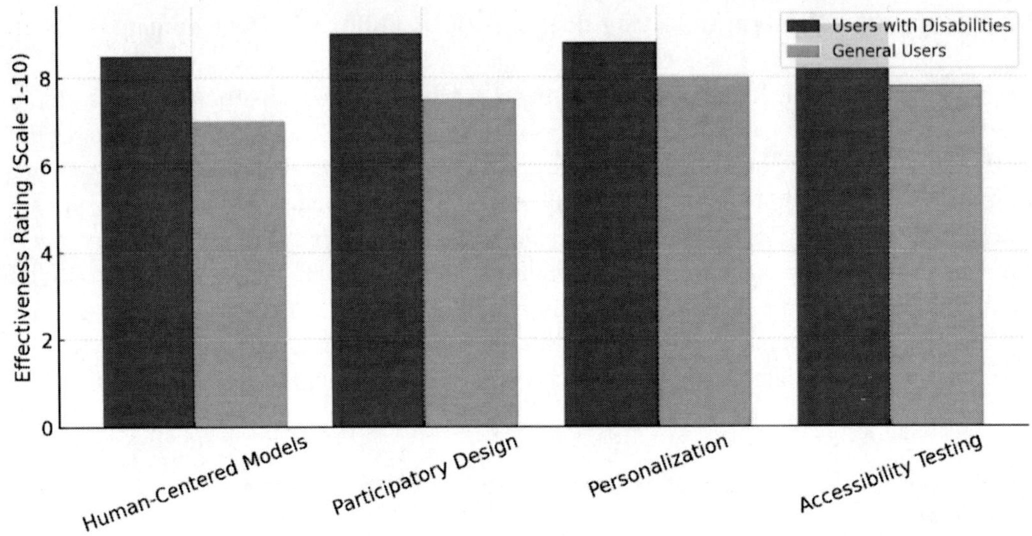

Figure 7. Comparison of user-centred design approaches.

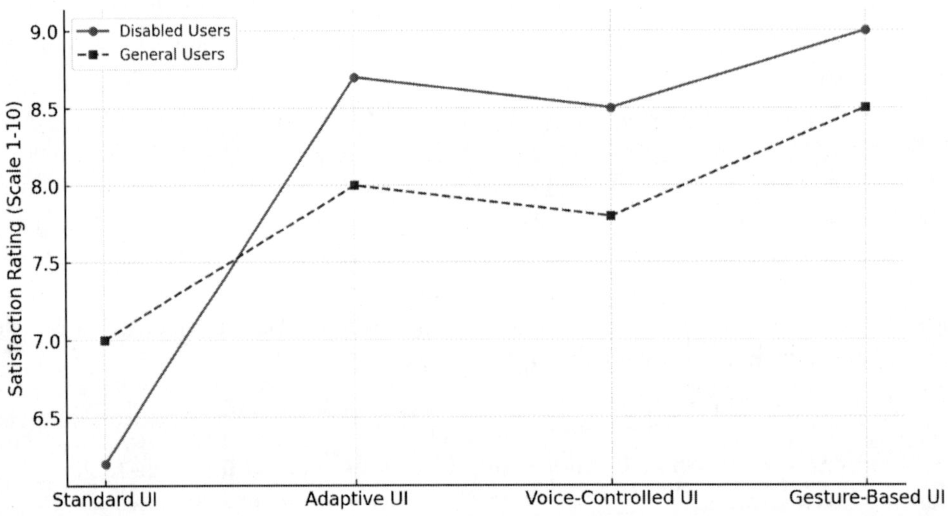

Figure 8. User satisfaction with personalised vs standard interfaces.

Figure 7 demonstrates which user-centred design approaches in immersive environments work best according to users with disabilities and those without disabilities. Accessibility testing, along with participatory design, gets the most positive feedback from people with disabilities because these approaches ensure inclusive environments (Figure 7). The effectiveness of human-centred models and personalisation, human-centred models and personalisation, is very strong when combined with specific interaction methods designed for disabled users. General users perceive accessibility features differently from those with disabilities since accessibility needs do not affect them as intensely. The analysis shows how User-Centred Design principles should be utilised during the developmental process to establish completely accessible immersive environments.

Figure 8 shows user feedback about interface satisfaction, whereby standard interfaces and adaptive interfaces compete against each other. Figure 8 shows that adaptive and gesture-based interfaces deliver maximum satisfaction to users with disabilities because adaptive interfaces offer intuitive, accessible options. The effectiveness of voice-controlled interfaces stands particularly high for users who have motor impairments. Disabled users show lower satisfaction levels toward standard user interfaces because standard interfaces must be improved through adaptive customisation. Users without disabilities express satisfaction at a similar level for all user interfaces, yet they find gesture-based interfaces alongside customizable designs the most gratifying. Researchers have concluded that intuitive interfaces that address diverse needs remain essential to improve accessibility and user satisfaction in virtual worlds.

6. Regulatory Standards and Ethical Considerations

The implementation of accessibility in immersive technologies should follow international standards, together with ethical frameworks that aim at inclusive design. It becomes crucial to create guidelines which will ensure proper development of accessible digital environments while maintaining ethics in VR, AR, and MR technologies since they progress into daily life. Several regulatory requirements and ethical standards combined with accessibility guidelines guide the development of immersive technologies designed for individuals with disabilities. The assurance of user data protection and security must remain a top priority because assistive applications need to prevent unintended risks and data breaches. Companies that link immersive technology development with regulatory requirements and ethical standards produce digital experiences that fulfil inclusivity and legal compliance [23].

6.1. Global Accessibility Standards for Immersive Technologies (WCAG, ADA)

Several worldwide specifications exist for digital platform accessibility, which include rules pertaining to immersive technologies. The Web Content Accessibility Guidelines (WCAG) offers complete recommendations to enhance web content accessibility, yet multiple principles directly translate into making virtual reality and augmented reality environments more accessible. The WCAG enables developers to produce digital environments through its four core principles, which include perceivability, operability, understandability, and robustness, and that work for people with disabilities. The Americans with Disabilities Act (ADA) requires physical and digital spaces to remain accessible, which ensures that virtual environments maintain no barriers toward people with disabilities. The European Accessibility Act and the Accessible Canada Act, together with other standards, promote the necessity of accessible immersive experiences. Developers who follow these guidelines will produce VR and AR applications that both serve numerous user needs and satisfy legal accessibility standards.

6.2. Ethical Implications of Inclusive and Exclusive Design

However, for example, the reason why accessibility is one of the legal requirements due to these immersive technologies results in ethical consequences that determine the technology, measure the benefit of this technology, along with integrating digital inequality and social community, which is nested in social networks. The implementation of inclusive design facilitates full access to immersive experiences for people with disabilities, enabling full social participation and equal opportunity usage for all. The practice of limiting design access to specific users who have disabilities leads to digital segregation that blocks their opportunities to use the system. The ethical principles behind immersive environment design require creators to develop them with inclusivity features that address user experience, usability, fairness, and technological innovation longevity. Developers need to serve diverse users by joining disabled groups in application development and preventing immersive tools from sustaining marginalization. Through ethical design practices, people experience better access to and maintain responsible innovation of emerging technologies [24].

6.3. Privacy and Security Concerns in Assistive AR/VR Applications

Assistive technologies incorporated into AR and VR systems create privacy as well as security dilemmas that developers must resolve with proper attention. Accessibility tools based on AI voice assistants, together with brain-computer interfaces and gesture recognition systems, require personal data collection for delivering customised assistance. Modern data storage requires handling personal information that triggers worries about improper access and safeguarding of protected content. End-user navigation through AI voice assistant-based accessibility solutions coupled with brain-computer interfaces and gesture recognition systems requires the collection of personal data to assist in a personalised manner. User privacy requires developers to implement encryption technologies as well as clear data policies and privacy management tools enabled by users. User trust, together with data security requirements of GDPR and CCPA laws, forms the foundation for developing accessible assistive AR/VR applications [25].

6.4. Legal Frameworks for Accessibility Compliance in Immersive Media

Multiple regulatory laws exist for ensuring compliance of accessibility standards within immersive media. The ADA, alongside similar accessibility requirements in the United States, demands that digital platforms, which include VR and AR applications, become accessible for all individuals with disabilities. The European Accessibility Act requires technology providers to develop digital services that will accommodate and remain accessible for all individuals irrespective of their disabilities. The U.S. Rehabilitation Act Section 508 requires federal agencies to create accessible electronic and information technology, which directly influences the development of immersive tools that serve educational and government services. The implementation of legal regulations mandates accessibility to be an essential consideration during immersive technology development. Companies that do not follow these laws risk both legal proceedings and negative impact on their reputation, as well as financial consequences.

Organisations reduce legal exposure through the development process inclusion of legal compliance standards, which enables them to build immersive environments that welcome all users [26].

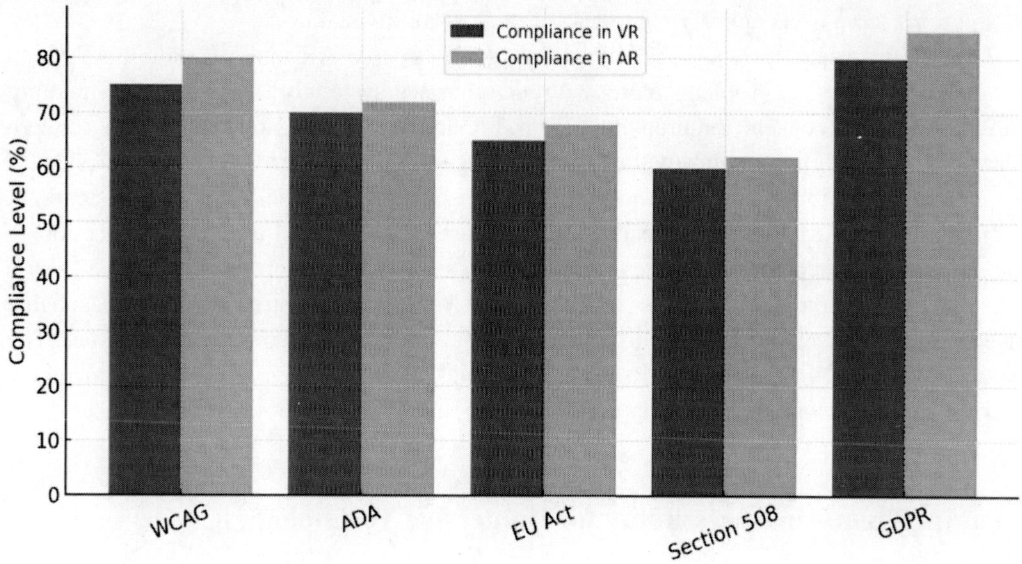

Figure 9. Comparison of accessibility compliance in VR and AR.

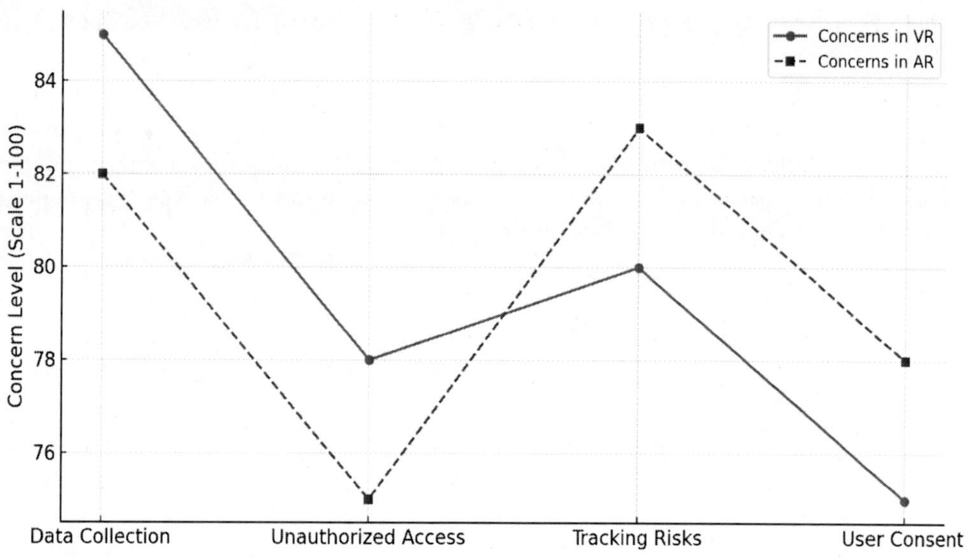

Figure 10. Privacy concerns in assistive AR/VR applications.

Figure 9 compares the compliance levels of various global accessibility standards in virtual reality (VR) and augmented reality (AR). GDPR achieves the highest compliance among different frameworks because it maintains strict rules about protecting data, as shown in Figure 9. WCAG and ADA maintain high compliance standards specifically for AR applications because digital environments can easily follow existing web accessibility standards. Immersive technologies show lower levels of compliance with the European Accessibility Act and Section 508 because these standards identify accessibility requirements which these platforms need to address. The analysis shows the importance of maintaining ongoing work to integrate immersive media technologies with current accessibility rules, which will make sure VR and AR solutions serve users entirely regardless of their disability status.

Figure 10 presents privacy challenges linked to assistive AR and VR solutions, which include data acquisition problems along with unauthorised system breaches and user tracking threats, as well as consent requirements. Both VR and AR demonstrate maximum concern regarding data collection, according to Figure 10, because immersive systems need substantial user data for accessibility customisation. The risks associated with tracking activities stand out prominently in AR applications because location data is used in real-time. The protection of data receiving unauthorised access demands strong encryption protocols and safe authentication standards due to its significance. User consent issues generate reasonable privacy concerns, even though they display less intense concerns than other privacy issues. The research illustrates that assistive AR/VR technologies increase accessibility but need robust security features as well as regulatory compliance to protect the privacy and data of users.

7. Future Trends in Accessibility for Immersive Technologies

Research developers and policymakers who focus on immersive engineering need to make accessibility enhancements a primary priority because these technologies are advancing. Future directions in accessibility pledge themselves to expanding inclusivity based on three major technological advances that include cognitive adaptation technologies and the application of digital twins and sophisticated assistive device design. Collaboration with industry and proper policy directions are the key enablers for the development of an inclusive virtual, augmented, and mixed reality environment of the future. Immersive technologies achieve equality of opportunities when accessibility innovation becomes a priority because they operate independently of a user's physical or cognitive abilities.

7.1. The Rise of Neuro-Inclusive VR and Cognitive Adaptation Technologies

Virtual Reality technology with neuro-inclusivity elements represents a revolutionary framework to support people with autism, along with those with ADHD or dyslexia. Users experience challenges when using traditional VR environments because they encounter sensory overload and complex navigation, together with overwhelming stimuli. The development of cognitive adaptation technologies brings about real-time user-based modifications. The combination of adaptable sensor choices alongside personalised content delivery, along with adaptive learning zones through AI systems, supports users to have better immersive sessions. VR spaces for neuro-inclusive users possess three fundamental characteristics that involve guided navigation, organised interaction, and attention modulation systems for enhancing cognitive accessibility. The advancement of these technologies will make them necessary in developing VR platforms which accommodate users with different cognitive abilities [27].

7.2. Integration of Digital Twins for Personalised Accessibility Solutions

Immersive technology accessibility gets valuable improvements through the development of digital twins, which duplicate real-world environments. The development of tailor-made virtual models enables programmers to execute user behaviour simulations, which they use to tailor experiences specifically for individual requirements. Through digital twin technology users with disabilities get to preview virtual spaces before actual physical contact thus making accessibility planning more effective and decreasing their uncertainty about the way the real space operates. Healthcare facilities use digital twins to develop therapeutic environments which match the specific needs of individual patients' mobility conditions. These systems enable blind people to discover public areas through protected routes. The incorporation of AI systems and real-time data analytics within digital twins has been demonstrated to enhance their usefulness for accessibility solutions through personalised user experiences [28].

7.3. Advancements in Wearable and Assistive XR Devices

The next generation of wearable extended reality (XR) devices is set to bring a revolutionary change toward accessibility in virtual worlds. Developers have started creating smart glasses combined with brain-computer interfaces (BCIs) and haptic feedback wearables for offering users with disabilities uninterrupted interfacing capabilities. Eye-tracking wearables enable people with limited motor abilities to move through VR and AR domains using their gaze demands while haptic glove devices deliver instant tactile sensations to individuals who need vision assistance. The artificial intelligence in wearables enables them to detect both hand movements along with verbal instructions, thus providing users who have physical disabilities with enhanced command options. The advancement of these technologies sets wearable extensions of XR devices to become central elements in creating accessible immersive activities which adapt to different accessibility requirements [29].

7.4. The Role of Policy and Industry Collaboration in Promoting Inclusive Design

To achieve accessibility within immersive technologies, close working relationships between policymakers, industry leaders, and advocacy groups are required. The development of inclusive XR requires developers to follow guidelines from the Web Content Accessibility Guidelines (WCAG) and Americans with Disabilities Act (ADA), while industries must actively participate to tackle new challenges. The establishment of standards for inclusive design in XR environments happens through consolidated efforts between tech companies and government agencies working alongside disability organizations. The advancement of accessibility innovation receives support through encouragements for developers to implement open-source accessibility toolkits and universal design principles. Corporate responsibility programs stimulate funding for research and development of inclusive technologies through their investment efforts. Future digital participation of all users becomes possible through combined efforts between policy execution and industry mutual support for immersive technologies.

Conclusion

Inclusive design combined with accessibility represents a critical necessity for establishing equal usage of virtual, augmented, and mixed reality systems by everyone, including disabled users. The analysis in this book chapter explained basic inclusive design concepts with special focus on immersive space accessibility and UX techniques used to involve different audience types. The major technological advancements in VR, AR, and MR systems have not eliminated existing accessibility problems, which especially affect users with visual, auditory, motor and cognitive impairments. Resolving these problems depends on the deployment of assistive technologies and adaptive interfaces, both through adhering to user-centred design practices and through putting usability and personalisation, both through adhering to user-centred design practices and through putting usability, personalisation, and engagement first. Immersion development needs to follow ethical principles together with global regulatory standards like WCAG, ADA, and GDPR for achieving compliance targets. User security, along with privacy, needs to be protected for people who use assistive applications to stop unpredictable risks from happening. Immersive technologies will adopt three emerging accessibility trends: neuro-inclusive VR and digital twins that create customised accessibility features and new wearables. All parties, including government representatives, along with both businesses and disability advocacy organisations, need to work together to create full accessibility guidelines through encouraging inclusive design practices. Implementing accessibility through the core development process of immersive technology enables the industry to enhance user experiences for everyone regardless of their abilities. Complete digital inclusion necessitates constant study in parallel with leading-edge technological advancement and boundless dedication to equity. A sustained emphasis on accessibility during immersive environment development will preserve their inclusivity and make them accessible to all user groups.

References

[1] Crabb, Michael, Daniel Clarke, Husam Alwaer, Michael Heron, and Richard Laing. "Inclusive design for immersive spaces." *The design journal* 22, no. sup1 (2019): 2105-2118.

[2] Creed, Chris, Maadh Al-Kalbani, Arthur Theil, Sayan Sarcar, and Ian Williams. "Inclusive AR/VR: accessibility barriers for immersive technologies." *Universal Access in the Information Society* 23, no. 1 (2024): 59-73.

[3] Zallio, Matteo, and P. John Clarkson. "Designing the metaverse: A study on inclusion, diversity, equity, accessibility and safety for digital immersive environments." *Telematics and Informatics* 75 (2022): 101909.

[4] Dudley, John, Lulu Yin, Vanja Garaj, and Per Ola Kristensson. "Inclusive Immersion: a review of efforts to improve accessibility in virtual reality, augmented reality and the metaverse." *Virtual Reality* 27, no. 4 (2023): 2989-3020.

[5] Lach, Ewa, Iwona Benek, Krzysztof Zalewski, Przemysław Skurowski, Agata Kocur, Aleksandra Kotula, Małgorzata Macura, Zbigniew Pamuła, Mikołaj Stankiewicz, and Tomasz Wyrobek. "Immersive virtual reality for assisting in inclusive architectural design." In *Man-Machine Interactions 6: 6th International Conference on Man-Machine Interactions, ICMMI 2019, Cracow, Poland, October 2-3, 2019*, pp. 23-33. Springer International Publishing, 2020.

[6] Tavares, Daniela Cardoso, Renan Guarese, Jean Felipe P. Cheiran, and Mauro Ricardo da S. Teófilo. "Immersive Technologies: challenges of the inclusive design in times of natural hazards and climate

change." In *Anais Estendidos do XXVI Simpósio de Realidade Virtual e Aumentada (SVR Estendido 2024)*, pp. 78-81. Sociedade Brasileira de Computacao-SB, 2024.

[7] Yin, L., J. J. Dudley, V. Garaj, and P. O. Kristensson. "Inclusivity requirements for immersive content consumption in virtual and augmented reality." In *Cambridge Workshop on Universal Access and Assistive Technology*, pp. 13-21. Cham: Springer International Publishing, 2023.

[8] Hutson, James, and Piper Hutson. "Immersive technologies." In *Inclusive smart museums: Engaging neurodiverse audiences and enhancing cultural heritage*, pp. 153-228. Cham: Springer Nature Switzerland, 2024.

[9] Connor, Joshue, Shadi Abou-Zahra, Mario Covarrubias Rodriguez, and Beatrice Aruanno. "Xr accessibility–learning from the past and addressing real user needs for inclusive immersive environments: Introduction to the special thematic session." In *Computers Helping People with Special Needs: 17th International Conference, ICCHP 2020, Lecco, Italy, September 9–11, 2020, Proceedings, Part I 17*, pp. 117-122. Springer International Publishing, 2020.

[10] Montagud, Mario, Pilar Orero, and Sergi Fernández. "Immersive media and accessibility: hand in hand to the future." *ITU Journal: ICT Discoveries* 3, no. 1 (2020): 1-8.

[11] Ryskeldiev, Bektur, Yoichi Ochiai, Koki Kusano, Jie Li, Yamen Saraiji, Kai Kunze, Mark Billinghurst, Suranga Nanayakkara, Yusuke Sugano, and Tatsuya Honda. "Immersive inclusivity at CHI: design and creation of inclusive user interactions through immersive media." In *Extended Abstracts of the 2021 CHI Conference on Human Factors in Computing Systems*, pp. 1-4. 2021.

[12] Kim, Jeonghyeon, Jung-Hoon Ahn, and Youngwon Kim. "Immersive Interaction for Inclusive Virtual Reality Navigation: Enhancing Accessibility for Socially Underprivileged Users." *Electronics* 14, no. 5 (2025): 1046.

[13] Saca, Pamela. "Designing Accessible Immersive Learning Experiences." *Journal of Technology-Integrated Lessons and Teaching* 2, no. 1 (2023): 78-87.

[14] Figueroa Jacinto, Rosemarie, and Elizabeth Kappler. "A discussion on accessibility, inclusivity, cultural design considerations, and health & safety advisories for virtual reality head mounted displays." In *Proceedings of the Human Factors and Ergonomics Society Annual Meeting*, vol. 66, no. 1, pp. 1706-1710. Sage CA: Los Angeles, CA: SAGE Publications, 2022.

[15] Siddiqi, Majaz M. "Future of digital education: inclusive, immersive, equitable." *MediaSpace: DME Media Journal of Communication* 5, no. 01 (2024): 8-24.

[16] Nebeling, Michael, Mika Oki, Mirko Gelsomini, Gillian R. Hayes, Mark Billinghurst, Kenji Suzuki, and Roland Graf. "Designing inclusive future augmented realities." In *Extended Abstracts of the CHI Conference on Human Factors in Computing Systems*, pp. 1-6. 2024.

[17] Devi, G. Dharani, Neeraj Kumar, J. Manikandan, and V. Rekha. "Innovative brain tumor detection: Stacked random support vector-based hybrid gazelle coati algorithm." *Biomedical Signal Processing and Control* 101 (2025): 107156.

[18] Shah, Yesha. "*Immersive Accessibility: Enhancing Virtual Reality Interactions Through Intuitive Hand Gestures, Inclusive Design and Gamified Onboarding Strategies*." Master's thesis, New York University Tandon School of Engineering, 2024.

[19] Johnson, Athanasius. "Virtual Reality as a Catalyst in Advancing Inclusive Design for Social and Cultural Sustainability in Architecture." (2023).

[20] Zallio, Matteo, and Peter Clarkson. "Inclusive Metaverse. How businesses can maximize opportunities to deliver an accessible, inclusive, safe Metaverse that guarantees equity and diversity." (2022).

[21] Manikandan, J., and K. Jayashree. "Enhancing lung nodule classification: a novel CViEBi-CBGWO approach with integrated image preprocessing." *Journal of imaging informatics in medicine* 37, no. 5 (2024): 2108.

[22] Campitiello, Lucia, Aldo Caldarelli, Michele Domenico Todino, Pio Alfredo Di Tore, Stefano Di Tore, and Amelia Lecce. "Maximising accessibility in museum education through virtual reality: an inclusive perspective." *Giornale Italiano di Educazione alla Salute, Sport e Didattica Inclusiva* 6 (2022): 1-12.

[23] Guillen, Georgina, Henrietta Jylhä, and Lobna Hassan. "The role sound plays in games: a thematic literature study on immersion, inclusivity and accessibility in game sound research." In *Proceedings of the 24th International Academic Mindtrek Conference*, pp. 12-20. 2021.

[24] Dombrowski, Matt, Peter A. Smith, Albert Manero, and John Sparkman. "Designing inclusive virtual reality experiences." In *International Conference on Human-Computer Interaction*, pp. 33-43. Cham: Springer International Publishing, 2019.

[25] Geerts, David, Radu-Daniel Vatavu, Alisa Burova, Vinoba Vinayagamoorthy, Martez Mott, Michael Crabb, and Kathrin Gerling. "Challenges in designing inclusive immersive technologies." In *Proceedings of the 20th International Conference on Mobile and Ubiquitous Multimedia*, pp. 182-185. 2021.

[26] Wood, Denise. "The design of inclusive curricula for multi-user virtual environments: A framework for developers and educators." *EAI Endorsed Transactions on e-Learning* 1, no. 1 (2011).

[27] Zallio, Matteo, Sam Waller, Camelia Chivaran, and P. John Clarkson. "Visual Accessibility and Inclusion. An Exploratory Study to Understand Visual Accessibility in the Built Environment." (2021).

[28] Radogna, Donatella, Antonio Vasapollo, and Franco Fraccastoro. "Architectures for immersive performances in the green, digital and inclusive transition." *VITRUVIO-International Journal of Architectural Technology and Sustainability* 9, no. 1 (2024): 96-113.

[29] Creed, Chris, Maadh Al-Kalbani, Arthur Theil, Sayan Sarcar, and Ian Williams. "Inclusive augmented and virtual reality: A research agenda." *International Journal of Human–Computer Interaction* 40, no. 20 (2024): 6200-6219.

Chapter 14

Sustainability and Environmental Considerations in Immersive Technologies

J. Shobana[1,*]
K. Senthil Kumar[2,†]
A. M. J. Muthukumaran[2,‡]
Vijayalakshmi Kaliyaperumal[3,‖]
and K. M. Umamaheswari[2,¶]

[1]Department of DSBS, SRM Institute of Science and Technologies, Kattankulathur, India
[2]Department of Computing Technologies, SRM Institute of Science and Technologies, Kattankulathur, India
[3]Department of CINTEL, SRM Institute of Science and Technologies, Kattankulathur, India

Abstract

Immersive technologies consisting of VR, AR, and MR have reshaped several business sectors while improving interaction with users, teaching methods, and operational processes. The speed at which such technologies enter the market exposes serious issues about their sustainability, together with their environmental consequences. The manufacturing process, which includes deployment and disposal of immersive technology hardware products, generates electronic waste along with energy usage and carbon pollution, therefore requires the adoption of sustainable practices in its lifecycle. The environmental effects of immersive technology are analysed along with methods to control their effects through hardware optimisation combined with waste management controls and cloud services that lower consumption levels. The debate considers how immersive technologies attain sustainability through environmental lessons learned virtually and physical demands lessened in tourism while enabling remote work. This chapter gives a full picture of sustainable issues and opportunities in immersive technologies through the identification of key points which must be developed with responsible strategies for guaranteeing environmental benefits.

---

[*] Corresponding Author's Email: shobanaj1@srmist.edu.in
[†] Corresponding Author's Email: senthilk3@srmist.edu.in
[‡] Corresponding Author's Email: muthua@srmist.edu.in
[‖] Corresponding Author's Email: vijalak@srmist.edu.in
[¶] Corresponding Author's Email: umamahek@srmist.edu.in

In: Shaping Tomorrow
Editors: Prithi Samuel, A. Sathya, Balamurugan Balusamy et al.
ISBN: 979-8-90134-076-9

Keywords: immersive technologies, virtual reality (VR), augmented reality (AR), mixed reality (MR), e-waste management, cloud services, remote work

1. Introduction to Immersive Technologies and Their Growth

Virtual worlds today allow users to interact with virtual worlds through immersive systems that convert physical/virtual world boundaries to seamless transitions. These developments enable users to experience extremely interactive multisensory experiences that improve applications in entertainment, education, healthcare, manufacturing, and numerous other sectors. The heightened technological innovations in computing power, artificial intelligence, and high-performance networks catalysed the development of low-cost immersive technologies powered by effective systems. Immersive technologies have emerged as central to industrial adoption while driving digital transformations and developing new business models while transforming the way humans interact with their environments in numerous sectors [1].

1.1. Definition and Classification of Immersive Technologies (VR, AR, MR)

Immersive technologies are digital technologies that create highly realistic interactive experiences for a wide range of applications. The fundamental building blocks of immersive technologies are Virtual Reality (VR), Augmented Reality (AR) and Mixed Reality (MR) that present different methods of integrating digital content with current reality. A fully immersive experience is obtained from VR technology as it completely immerses users in computer-generated virtual worlds to interact with digital objects and environmental elements. Users experience virtual-world presence through special hardware that detects head movement, which enables VR applications to represent major tools for gaming via head-mounted displays (HMDs). They also serve as training and therapy tools [2].

AR enables users to view virtual content that overlays on their actual surroundings because this technology maintains their real-world environment perception. AR through smartphones, smart glasses, and AR headsets adds digital information to normal reality that enhances people's present experiences in their environment. This technology functions in retail businesses as well as educational and industrial sectors because real-time digital augmentation helps boost work efficiency and user involvement throughout both sectors.

MR delivers an enhanced digital and physical fusion through technologies that let users connect easily between virtual and actual objects. The main difference between AR and MR exists in the fact that AR provides static real-world view overlays with digital content, whereas MR enables dynamic digital interaction within a physical space. Spatial computing makes it possible for digital content to detect physical environment modifications and develop such hybrid spaces that permit users to work with physical objects alongside virtual objects. MR continues to gain popularity among designers and engineers because it provides immersive collaboration that improves visualization and problem-solving quality for architecture and engineering practice as well as workplace design [3].

1.2. The Adoption Patterns of Immersive Technology and Its Maderisation in Various Industrial Sectors

Immersive technologies have expanded across all industries at a steep pace because consumers want more, technological upgrades allow it, and 5G networks now support this development. The entertainment industry and gaming have been in the lead in embracing VR and AR for developing interactive and immersive content. Digital entertainment has transitioned to virtual concerts and immersive stories along with metaverse platforms as users now engage in shared virtual spaces instead of consuming traditional media. Immersive technologies have achieved major penetration points within both educational and training systems beyond entertainment purposes. The approach to learning undergoes transformation because virtual simulations give students the opportunity to explore complex matters firsthand. Medical personnel perform surgical training via VR equipment, and enterprise organisations implement AR systems which improve employee performance. Immersive technologies now offer educational establishments and professional organisations an effective instrument for advancing educational progress to their potential to develop realistic training environments with no physical barriers [4].

Immersive technologies bring transformative changes to healthcare services as a leading sector of application. Through virtual reality-based treatment, healthcare professionals cure mental disorders by delivering controlled exposure therapy through secure digital environments for their anxiety and post-traumatic stress disorder (PTSD) patients. Medical procedures are advantaged by AR technology since surgeons are given accurate navigation guidance through real-time patient data visualization overlays during complicated procedures [4]. Healthcare applications offer enhanced patient outcomes while revolutionizing healthcare service distributions. AR and MR technologies currently help the industrial sector execute better manufacturing, as well as maintenance and logistics operations. AR-equipped smart glasses provide workers with real-time visual directions for complex machinery assembly operations, which leads to superior results and faster production times. Through MR technology, engineers can work together in virtual design spaces before starting production since it provides tools for collaborative product development. The developments in these technologies improve operational efficiency to the extent of minimising resource waste, which makes them essential tools for Industry 4.0 [5].

Retail businesses and e-commerce companies use immersive technology to strengthen their customer interactions. Customers can use AR-powered virtual try-on to examine products such as apparel and decorative items through digital previews before buying. These solutions connect the digital and physical shopping worlds. Brand loyalty and satisfaction increase when brands embrace virtual reality showrooms alongside immersive marketing efforts that craft personalized interactive shopping experiences.

Immersive technology advancements will lead to their adoption across many industries thus defining how people will interact digitally in the future. The collective power of artificial intelligence, cloud computing, and extended reality (XR) technology enables developers to create advanced, scalable applications that support immersive experiences. The promising development of immersive systems offers both exciting possibilities and important challenges based on sustainability and ethics frameworks and worldwide access to the technology. The advancement and utilisation of immersive technology are heavily dependent on overcoming critical challenges to successfully ensure its responsible application in the future [6].

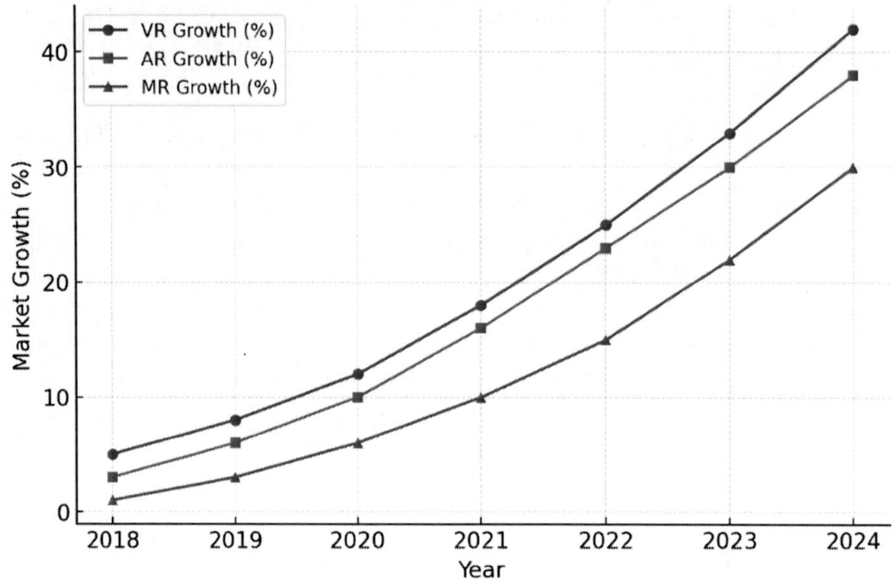

Figure 1. Growth trends of immersive technologies.

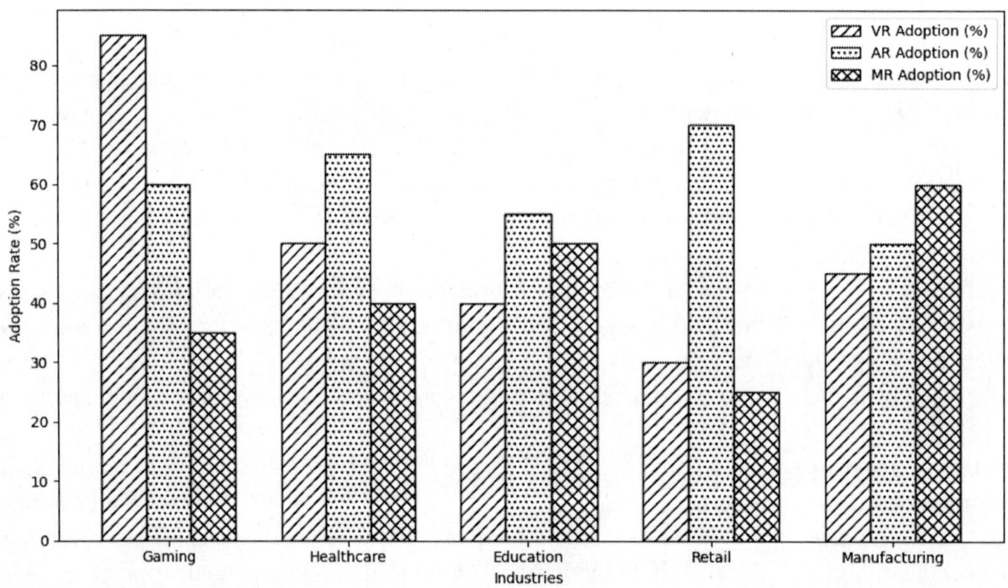

Figure 2. Industry-wise adoption of immersive technologies.

According to Figure 1, the market expansion of Virtual Reality (VR), Augmented Reality (AR), and Mixed Reality (MR) continues from 2018 through 2024. All three technologies show increasing market growth, yet VR maintains the top position, followed by AR and then MR. Research shows AR adoption is increasing because it appears in mobile applications, retail solutions, and enterprise platforms, while MR adoption grows steadily because it serves industrial and collaborative needs.

Figure 2 demonstrates how different industries plan to use immersive technologies across the forthcoming year due to their individual business preferences. Virtual reality achieves the most widespread adoption within the gaming industry to the extent of 85%, making interactive entertainment its primary domain. AR technology finds wide acceptance across retail and healthcare because it supports improved customer interactions and medical picture visualization at levels exceeding 70% and 65%. Manufacturing companies and educational institutions actively use MR because its interactive properties make it possible to deliver real-world experiences through computer-generated interfaces for training and collaborative design processes. Immersive technology solutions are flexible because the industry-specific market trends show how they will evolve to benefit different sectors in the future.

2. Environmental Impact of Immersive Technologies

Higher adoption of immersive technology systems includes noteworthy industry advancements, though it produces ecological concerns in environmental sustainability. Immersive device manufacturing processes, together with their operational needs and end-of-life waste management, generate excessive energy usage, electronic garbage, and carbon pollution. The increasing demand for Virtual Reality (VR), Augmented Reality (AR), and Mixed Reality (MR) technologies requires thorough evaluation of their environmental impact because new measures to reduce their adverse effects must be developed. The evaluation of environmental effects from immersive technology is essential to support ecological innovation, together with preventing technological advancement which results in environmental damage [7].

2.1. Energy Consumption in Immersive Systems

The large energy consumption in these immersive technology systems is on account of high-performance hardware coupled with deeply computational tasks. Virtual reality headsets, augmented reality smart eyeglasses, and mixed-reality devices require high processing resources to render complex images and respond immediately to user inputs. These contain processors and fast refresh-rate displays, and the electronics work requires a constant power supply. Separate base stations need a particular location, power and even several USB ports, while multiple base stations have certain areas of overlap that can be a barrier for consumers trying to help larger environments [8]. The software base of immersive experiences cooperates with the hardware machinery to output energy consumption. VR and AR applications are largely reliant on cloud computing with data centers for both real-time data processing and cloud-based rendering. These data centers are operational 24/7 because they consume significant amounts of electricity to be compute efficient and for cooling systems. The energy needed to be reduced to minimise environmental impact by offering cloud solutions for the adoption of immersive technology into cloud-based applications.

Long hours of use of immersive technology systems, times a lot of devices, times a lot of devices, translates into a substantial energy consumption. Now, various business operations utilise VR technology for virtual meetings, along with training sessions and simulations, which in turn contribute to never-ending growth in operational power consumption. Mainstream immersive applications require the development of energy-efficient hardware, software optimisation, and the connection of renewable energy resources to data centres to result in lower power requirements of these technologies [9].

2.2. Electronic Waste and Lifecycle Assessment of Hardware

Rapid advancement in immersive technology drives manufacturers to replace their products frequently, thus causing the rapid growth of electronic waste (e-waste). The constant technological improvements of displays, processing strength, and tracking features shorten the operational lifetime of VR and AR devices. The progression of newer, more efficient versions of products makes business and consumer markets choose them through device replacements, thus creating electronic waste disposal problems. eco-unfriendly conditions emerge from improper waste disposal of expired headsets and sensors along with controllers plus other peripheral devices [10]. Immersive technology products consist mainly of intricate substances like metals from the rare earth group and plastics, together with lithium-ion battery packs that present strong challenges for recycling. The extraction routines combined with materials processing operations create environmental destruction by using big amounts of energy and water resources. Electronic component discarding without proper measures can trigger hazardous materials to pollute soil and water ecosystems. The increasing amount of disposed immersive devices creates an environmental menace unless we develop appropriate recycling and waste management systems [11].

The production phase of immersive technology hardware systems creates major environmental repercussions based on findings from lifecycle assessment (LCA) analysis. Energy usage during raw materials extraction and circuit board fabrication, together with display component construction, creates environmental stress by releasing pollutants. The e-waste problem can be reduced when technology keeps running longer due to modular designs, repairable components, and upgradeable hardware features. Immersive technology manufacturers should adopt circular economy principles, while take-back programs will allow for sustainable practices to develop within this industry.

2.3. Carbon Footprint of Manufacturing and Distribution

Immersive technology production, together with material transportation, creates total environmental impact throughout its production cycle. The entire production sequence of VR and AR devices includes obtaining raw materials from extraction, followed by component manufacturing through assembly steps, and delivery transportation. The manufacturing cycle and worldwide supply chain logistics operations together produce environmental emissions, where factory operations create the largest pollution impact [12]. Immersive technology manufacturing creates a large carbon footprint because its semiconductor fabrication and display panel production were developed using high energy demands. The production of high-resolution OLED and LCD screens needed for VR and AR headsets occurs in specialised facilities which demand excessive energy consumption. High-end motion-tracking sensors and processors together with haptic feedback components require complex manufacturing systems which produce environmental influence [13].

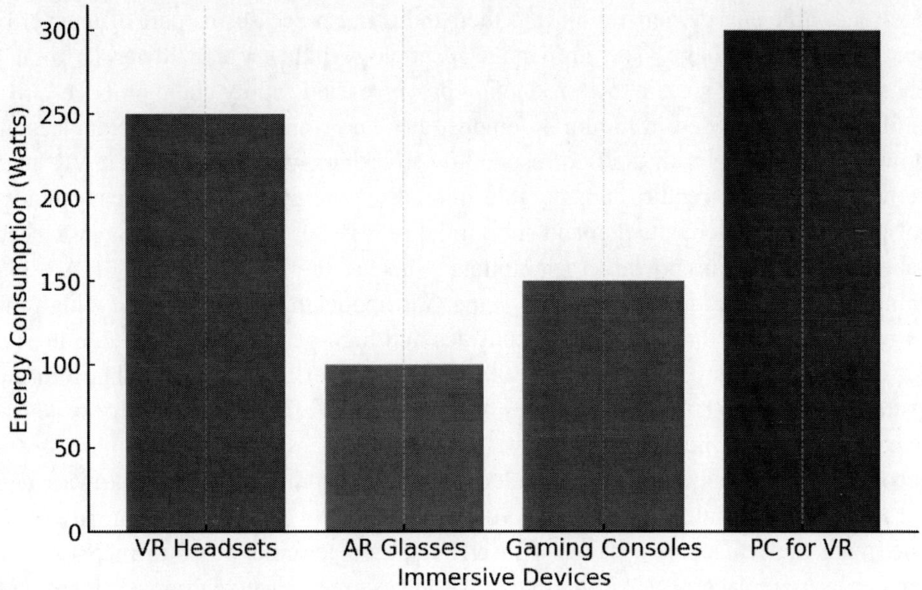

Figure 3. Energy consumption of immersive devices.

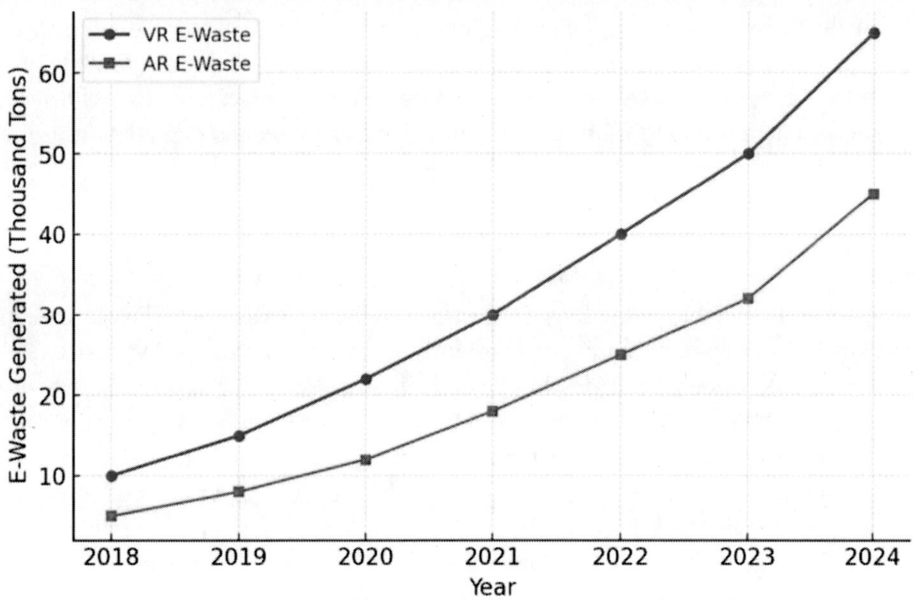

Figure 4. E-waste generation from immersive technologies.

The process of distributing and logistics management creates additional carbon emissions that impact immersive technology. The global distribution of VR and AR devices through aeroplane and maritime, along with land transportation, emits large amounts of carbon dioxide because these devices are produced in separate regions. These devices have packaging containers made of plastic material with non-recyclable components, which produce excessive environmental impacts during distribution [14]. Companies should adopt sustainable sourcing and use recycled materials in hardware production and optimise their distribution logistics to limit emissions. Companies should leverage their resources to fund carbon offset projects and integrate renewable energy generation into their industrial processes as part of their effort to limit environmental damage. The immersive technology industry can lower its total CO2 emissions by prioritising sustainable production processes and supply chain practices.

An illustration provided in Figure 3 demonstrates how various immersive devices utilize their power supply along with their corresponding environmental consequences. VR headsets together with AR glasses require considerable amounts of energy since their advanced displays and real-time tracking elements demand substantial processing power. High-end VR headsets draw about 250 watts in power consumption, whereas the energy usage of AR glasses containing mobile integration reaches 100 watts. VR applications tend to have a high impact on energy consumption through gaming consoles and high-performance PCs due to the fact that VR-compatible PCs consume up to 300 watts of power. Additionally, this information demonstrates that immersive technologies require energy-efficient hardware systems and optimized software to achieve reduced power requirements.

According to Figure 4, the amount of electronic waste from VR and AR hardware devices shows a steady growth pattern from 2018 through to 2024. The demand for immersive devices, combined with the replacement habits of users, causes electronic waste to increase through frequent hardware replacement. VR hardware waste has experienced a dramatic increase from 10 thousand tons in 2018 to an estimated 65 thousand tons in 2024 because VR devices, along with their controllers and sensors, have short lifecycles. The increase in AR hardware waste amounts to 40 thousand tons as the technological development of AR smart glasses and wearable devices continues from 2018 until 2024. Immersive technology waste patterns underscore the necessity to create eco-friendly production processes coupled with recycling schemes and sustainable materials in order to minimize environmental degradation.

3. Sustainable Hardware and Design Innovations

Quick progress in immersive technology production has fueled hardware part requirements, yet raised sustainability issues together with environmental consequences. Hardware sustainability and new sustainable design strategies for devices increase in importance as Virtual Reality (VR), Augmented Reality (AR) and Mixed Reality (MR) technology develop more rapidly. Concerned manufacturers in liaison with researchers design eco-friendly products that integrate power-saving components and modular design principles as well as cycle economy practices to establish a future sustainable immersive technology ecosystem. Innovation has two main purposes: increasing device survival duration while decreasing electronic waste alongside minimizing emissions produced during manufacturing and disposal stages [15].

3.1. Eco-Friendly Materials and Energy-Efficient Components

The immersive hardware industry now utilizes environmentally friendly production materials since businesses want to replace their unsustainable products with safer creations. Technological developments in immersive hardware involve incorporating three main sustainable materials, such as degradable polymers with recycled plastics containing plant-based composites, which reduce environmental strain. These sustainable materials replace conventional petroleum-based plastics since they represent major sources of electronic waste while polluting the environment. Manufacturers examine ways of removing toxic substances such as lead and mercury from circuit boards and displays because they aim to create safer methods for recycling and disposing of immersive devices [16]. The essential aspect of sustainable hardware design includes energy efficiency as one of its fundamental priorities. Immersive electronic devices need high-performance processors as well as high-quality displays and motion sensors, but these need tremendous amounts of electric power. Chipset technology innovation, as well as adaptive refresh rate displays, makes power consumption less with no impact on system performance. Solid-state batteries, as well as power-efficient lithium-ion alternatives, have enhanced the sustainability of AR and MR portable devices through battery technology innovation. The environmental footprint of immersive technology can decrease when renewable sources of energy take part in device manufacturing and power-efficient charging solutions are promoted for their use [17].

3.2. Modular and Upgradable Device Design to Reduce Waste

The brief lifespan of immersive technology equipment generates increasing amounts of discarded electronic materials because users tend to switch between old and new versions. The implementation of modular platforms together with upgradable features stands as one of the best practices to address this problem. Users can easily upgrade their VR or AR headsets through independent component replacement since they need not throw away the device to acquire new functionality. This design strategy decreases both waste generation from outdated technology and offers consumers better affordability and customizable features in their products [18]. Businesses benefit from modular constructions through their promotion of sustainable manufacturing practices because device components can be recycled for use in later product developments. The market now witnesses companies working on detachable hardware components which let users improve their products without creating disposable electronic waste. The durability of immersive devices depends heavily on upgradable firmware and software because these solutions let users access better performance through software instead of requiring new hardware. The adoption of modular system design in immersive technology reduces environmental impact to allow both innovation growth and long-term product usefulness.

3.3. The Implementation of Recycling and Circular Economy Approaches

In order to lower its environmental footprint, the sustainable operation of immersive technology requires direct application of recycling and circular economy processes. The circular economy establishes one-loop systems through material reduction, followed by reuse, and recycling practices to minimise wastage and resource consumption. Immersive technology requires device design with interchangeable parts and take-back systems that enable the public to properly dispose of equipment. More companies now dedicate funds to recycling programs aimed at retrieving valuable materials from previous models of virtual and augmented reality devices. A recycling program that welcomes consumers to submit their outdated devices leads to proper waste diversion from landfills and facilitates the recovery of recyclable hardware materials. Manufacturers decreasing their raw material resource requirements through strategic adoption of refurbished parts in their devices leads to lower environmental emissions related to plant operations. The development of biodegradable electronic components represents a current exploration to reduce the permanent environmental consequences of disposed immersive technology equipment [19].

The creation of a sustainable immersive technology ecosystem requires a union between technology companies, policymakers, and consumers. We must push against this trend by mandating strict e-waste regulations, with incentives for circular economy (resource recovery and reuse) models, coupled with ongoing, sustained campaigns for green manufacturing practices from both governments and regulatory authorities. Not only do you make your purchase smart by choosing sustainable products, but as a consumer, you are also responsible for participating in recycling initiatives. Sustainable design practices in immersive technology hardware development will become essential when the technology advances, since they provide solutions for minimising environmental damage. The industry will remain committed, ensuring that all technology advances serve global sustainability goals using eco-friendly materials and circular economy methods, as well as modular designs and energy-efficient components. The innovations of immersive technology simultaneously benefit both the environment and establish lasting value for businesses and consumers to achieve sustainability in the immersive technology future.

The evolving energy efficiency of immersive devices tracks downward in Figure 5 through a six-year period starting from 2018 while documenting reduced power usage of both VR and AR hardware systems. Since 2018, the initial 300 watts of power consumption by Virtual Reality headsets decreased to about 180 watts by 2024. The energy consumption profile of Augmented Reality devices showed similar savings throughout this period because it declined from 150 watts to 90 watts. The research demonstrates that manufacturing companies put emphasis on environmental responsibility through the creation of energy-efficient devices which match existing performance levels.

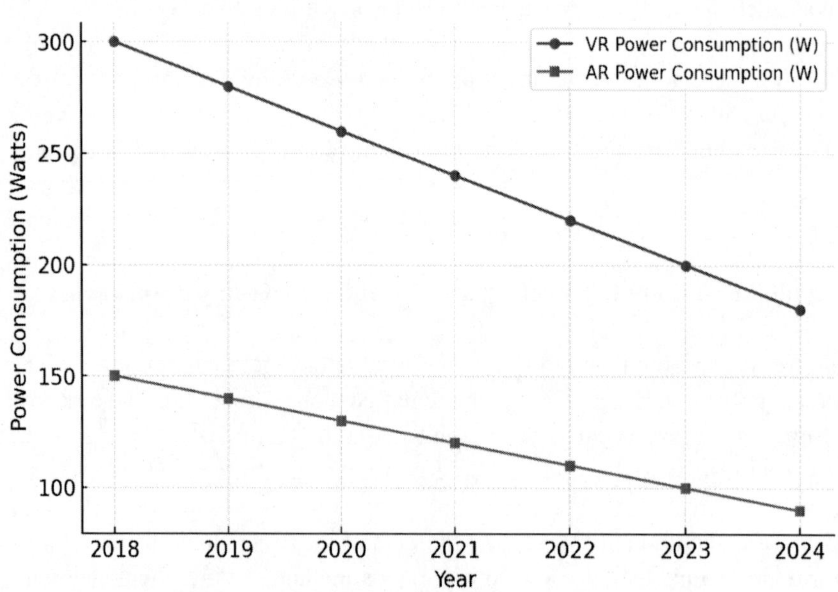

Figure 5. Energy efficiency improvement in immersive devices.

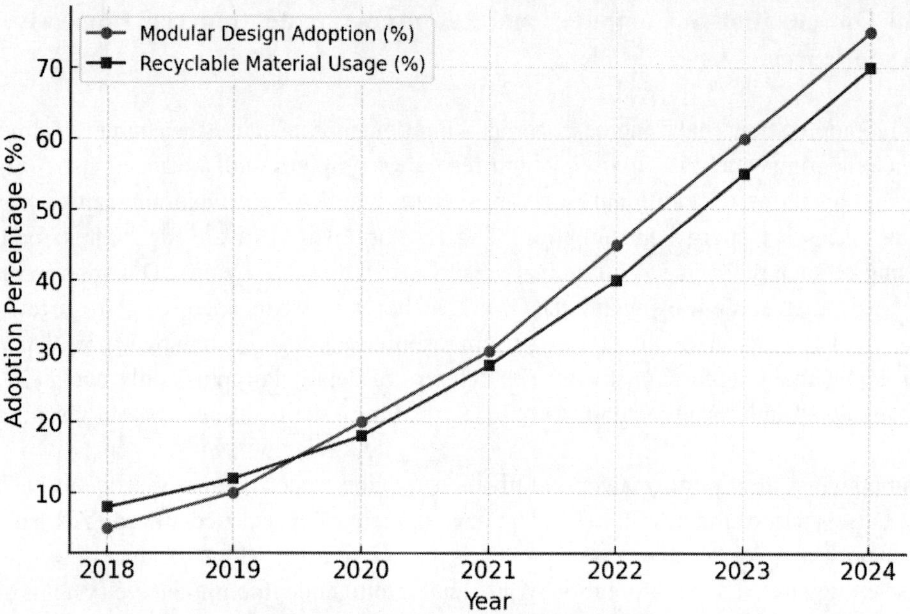

Figure 6. Growth of modular and recyclable hardware in immersive devices.

The adoption rates for modular and recyclable hardware components in immersive technology platforms have steadily risen according to Figure 6 from 2018 until 2024. Information shows that the use of modular devices expanded remarkably from an initial 5% in 2018 to reach 75% by 2024. The industry now places increased emphasis on stretching device lifecycles with substitute replaceable components to lower the amount of electronic waste. The incorporation of reusable elements in immersive electronic devices experienced an expansion from 8% to 70% between 2018 and 2024 on the trajectory of sustainable industrial production. The rising percentage points to a sustainable trend in the industry because materials go through recycling cycles instead of disposal to decrease the environmental effects of immersive tech.

4. Energy Efficiency and Green Computing in Immersive Systems

The fast growth of immersive technologies has created greater computing needs, which require efficient power management systems. Sustainable operations depend on energy efficiency because Virtual Reality (VR), Augmented Reality (AR), and Mixed Reality (MR) systems need major processing power to achieve high-quality simulation experiences. Green computing directs hardware optimisation to minimise resource usage and decrease power needs, and increases operational efficiency at the same time without compromising required performance standards for immersion applications. The immersive technology industry will reduce its environmental impact by using enhanced computational procedures, implementing cloud and edge computing, and establishing sustainable data centre practices [20].

4.1. The Optimization of Computational Resources Creates Superior Immersive User Experiences

Immersive applications have increased processing demands because they require immediate real-time rendering capability involving high-resolution graphics with advanced visualizations. The current operation of traditional hardware systems reaches their maximum capacity, which generates excessive energy consumption. The resolution of software algorithms for better processing efficiency forms a solution that preserves performance quality. Dynamic resolution scaling and other computing techniques work in harmony with adaptive refresh rates and foveated rendering, dynamically scaling system resources up and down in real-time, depending on user engagement and area of focus. The delivery of detailed graphics only occurs in user-viewed areas through these methods to reduce processing demands and uphold visual clarity [21].

Immersive system performance optimization requires specific energy-efficient hardware components as part of the key strategy. The development of specialised VR and AR hardware proceeds with a focus on low-power processing architectures, which produce less heat and decrease energy use. The incorporation of artificial intelligence into immersive systems allows predictive computing mechanisms that analyze user actions to lower system computing operations and decrease processing redundancies. The energy-saving optimisations boost both energy efficiency and portable immersive devices' battery life, therefore making these devices more sustainable for more extensive usage.

4.2. Role of Cloud Computing and Edge Computing in Reducing Energy Usage

The handling of resource-intensive rendering along with AI-based interactions on cloud servers enables VR and AR devices to decrease their power consumption, thus increasing their energy efficiency. The delivery of cloud-based rendered content requires less system processing power from devices, thus reducing power usage while supporting compact energy-efficient hardware [22]. Energy efficiency is improved through edge computing because data processing takes place nearer to end-users, thereby minimising the requirement to maintain a continual cloud server connection. The method of local processing improves application power efficiency by both decreasing data transmission and reducing latency. The distribution of computation across various edge nodes results in efficient delivery of immersive experiences with reduced network congestion, along with energy cost reduction. The hybrid system that integrates edge computing with cloud services creates a better computational infrastructure to ensure high performance without causing damage to the environment.

4.3. Sustainable Data Centers for Immersive Content Hosting

The need is to develop sustainable cloud data centres that can be built quickly and have the capability to process loads of immersive content. The substantial datasets handled by VR and AR applications must be processed through data centres that need large quantities of energy for computing operations, equipment cooling, and facility upkeep. Modern industry leaders build green data centres through investment in data centres that generate power from wind energy, solar power, and hydroelectric power. Data centres become environmentally friendly through renewable energy adoption for the transition from traditional energy systems to maintain their ability to support the growing needs of immersive technology. New data center cooling technologies serve sustainability through their efforts to decrease the excessive energy usage needed to regulate temperatures. Utilisation of top-level cooling devices with liquid cooling and free-air cooling coupled with AI-based temperature control achieves the highest utilisation of energy for operating efficiency. Data centres that follow circular economy principles take advantage of waste heat produced by servers by converting it into heat for local building heating or industrial processes. Energy-efficient immersive technology infrastructure becomes possible through these initiatives, which serve dual purposes of sustainability objectives [23]. Future development of immersive technologies depends on implementing energy-efficient practices together with green computing strategies, which lower their ecological impact. The immersive technology industry can establish a green system by streamlining computational capability and cloud/edge networks to build green technology infrastructures that support innovation while adhering to environmental protection.

Figure 7 represents the upcoming decline in immersive system energy use from 2018 to 2024 through cloud and edge computing implementation. The power requirements of traditional local processing decreased from its original value of 400 watts in 2018 to reach approximately 230 watts in 2024. The pace of energy consumption decline was faster for cloud and edge solutions because these systems shift processing operations into remote distributed servers from 300 watts to 120 watts throughout the 2018-2024 timeline. The technological advancement of optimised computational resource management tools has proven successful in lowering power requirements, which makes immersive technologies more energy-efficient because of cloud and edge solutions.

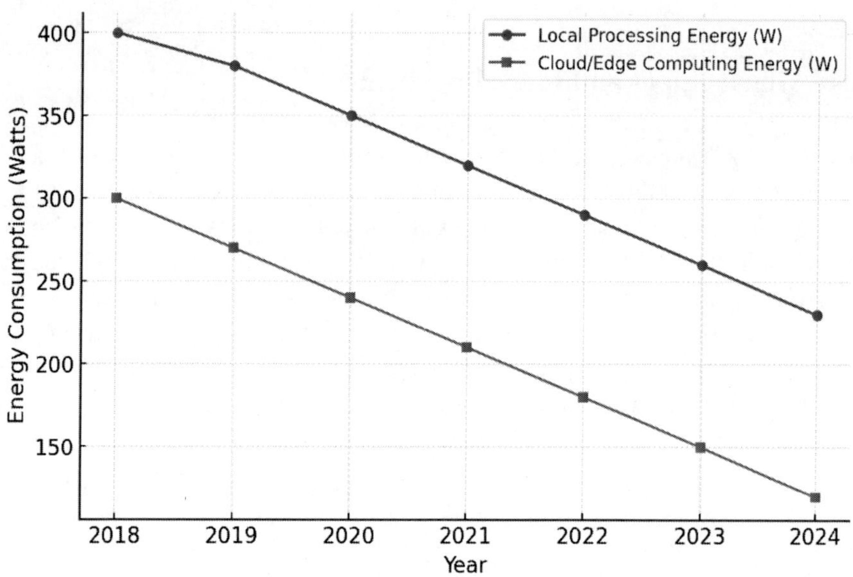

Figure 7. Energy consumption reduction via cloud & edge computing.

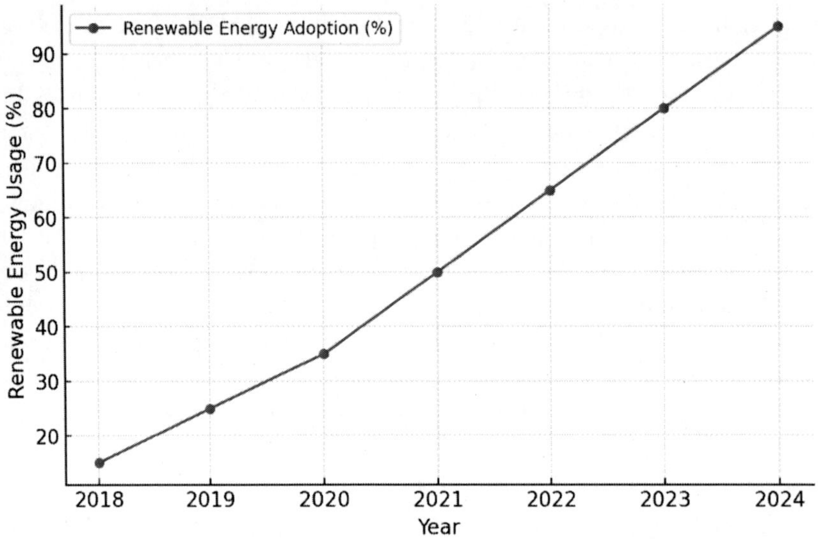

Figure 8. Growth of renewable energy in data centres.

The graphic in Figure 8 illustrates the rising trend of renewable energy usage for data centers which handle immersive content processing. Organisations have steadily increased their renewable energy adoption in data centre operations, which reached 95% during 2024. The data centre industry advances its sustainability commitment through powering facilities by solar power and wind energy, together with hydroelectric components. The transition toward green energy solutions for immersive technology infrastructure cuts down its carbon emissions while conforming to worldwide sustainability goals, which protect the environment from the increasing demand for high-performance computing systems.

5. E-Waste Management and Recycling Strategies

The increasing use of immersive technologies, including Virtual Reality (VR), Mixed Reality (MR), and Augmented Reality (AR), creates more electronic waste, also known as E-Waste, thus generating sustainability and proper disposal concerns. Immersive hardware components consisting of sophisticated materials found in head-mounted displays and sensors with controllers and computing units create major difficulties for recycling and disposal systems. Proper waste management strategies must exist to handle obsolete and damaged immersive devices since poor management leads to environmental damage and resource shortages. A solution for this problem necessitates three layers of intervention, starting with better recycling processes and continuing with laws alongside business-led support for circular economy systems [24].

5.1. Challenges in Recycling Immersive Technology Hardware

To recycle immersive technology hardware successfully, one must overcome the multiple complexities inherent to its component design. The combination of materials in immersive devices, which includes plastic, metal, glass and electronic circuitry, creates challenges for separating the materials during recycling. The rarity of certain metals mixed with lithium-ion batteries and exclusive coatings creates processing difficulties when trying to extract and reuse these components. Modern immersive devices are engineered with durability and small size in mind, so their hardware components function tightly together, which makes their dismantling complicated for recycling operations. Standardised recycling procedures remain unavailable for the processing of immersive devices and technologies. The recycling methods for VR and AR devices remain under development because these devices entered the market after mobile phones and computers, yet manufacturing their recycling procedures faces obstacles. Typical recycling centres lack the proper equipment needed to handle these specific devices, which reduces their ability to recover materials correctly. When VR and AR devices are discarded improperly, the dangerous materials like lead, cadmium and mercury in their components become major environmental problems because they contaminate the environment [25].

The quick progression of immersive technology makes recycling efforts progressively more difficult to manage. Shorter product life spans resulting from new hardware versions with elevated features along with increased specifications cause users to replace devices more often. The regular product updates by consumers and businesses create discarded immersive devices that end up as electronic waste. Flooding electronic waste problems occurs because there are inadequate systems for collecting discarded devices and restoring them for future use.

5.2. Policies and Regulations for Responsible Disposal

Legislative organizations and government institutions create policies which deal with the environmental consequences of discarded immersive technology devices. Extended Producer Responsibility (EPR) regulations adopted by numerous countries force producers to handle their product end-of-life management responsibilities. A requirement of these policies forces companies to design waste collection systems and recycling activities for their outdated or damaged immersive devices to prevent landfill disposal. EPR regulations exist alongside new e-waste regulations that determine the correct methods for managing dangerous substances in immersive technology products. Several regions now enforce restrictions against landfill waste management of electronic waste, which forces businesses together with consumers toward established recycling facilities [26]. The government together with awareness campaigns work to teach people proper methods of e-waste disposal. The proper disposal rate decreases substantially when consumers submit their old immersive devices to certified recycling centers through trade-in programs. Policymakers create a durable waste management system for immersive technology through the use of recycling regulations combined with consumer participation schemes.

5.3. Industry Initiatives for Extended Product Life Cycles

The industry is working on creating lifespan extension strategies that will decrease environmental damage caused by immersive technology devices. Essential to immersive technology waste management is modular and upgradable device design since this approach lets users replace or enhance their components instead of throwing away complete systems.

Manufacturers can minimize future waste output when they develop hardware systems that easily accept technological progress over time. The industry shows increasing interest in dilation and sales programs. The industry currently adopts programs which reconstruct returned products by fixing defective components to provide affordable secondhand devices to customers. The practice supports two important benefits through its dual purpose of e-waste reduction and lower prices for immersive technology. The availability of hardware leasing services together with subscription-based immersive device access supports device reuse which decreases the need for frequent replacements and disposal processes [27].

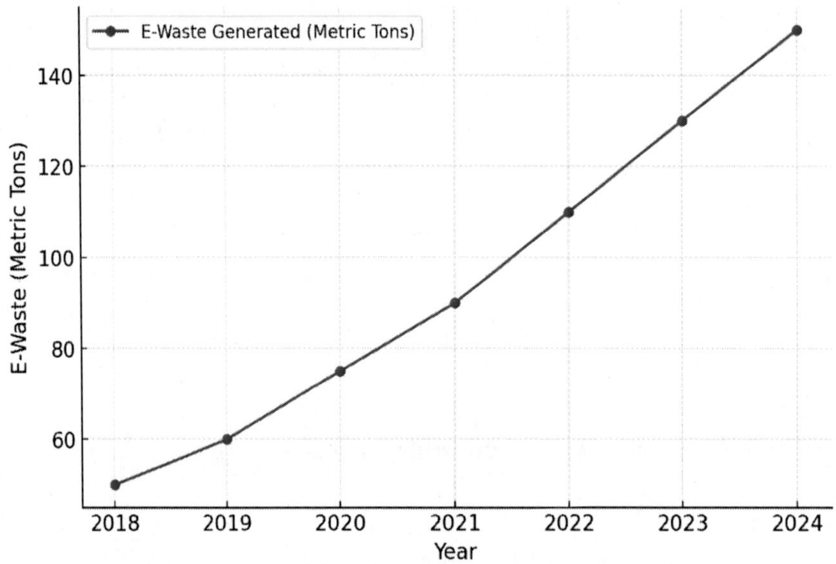

Figure 9. Increase in E-Waste from immersive technology.

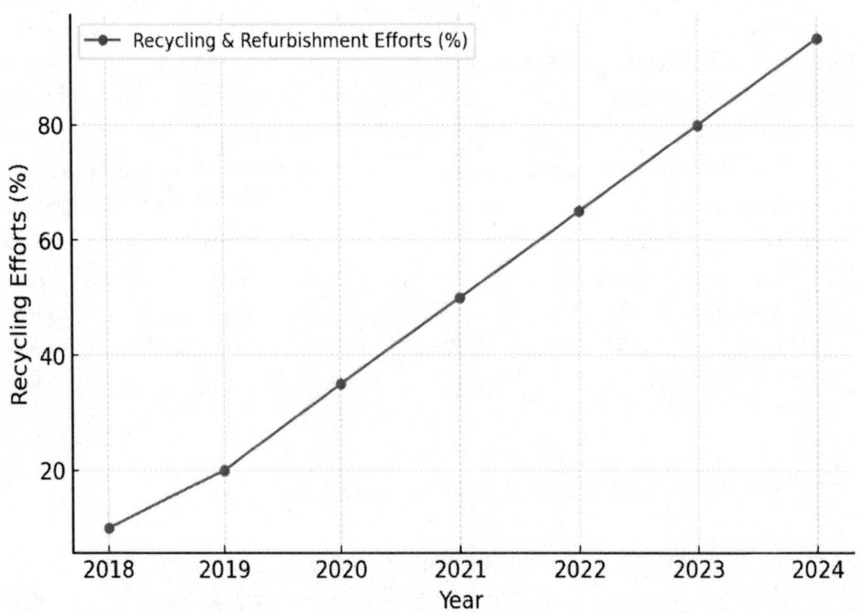

Figure 10. Growth of recycling and refurbishment initiatives.

Technology development stands as a fundamental component which enables manufacturers to create sustainable hardware products. The production of immersive devices uses new biodegradable and recyclable materials, which scientists, along with manufacturers, research to substitute conventional plastic and metal components. The combination of bio-based polymers together with sustainable metal alloys substantially minimizes the environmental impact in both manufacturing and disposing of hardware products. Discard management has improved because new recycling methods simplify the recovery of valuable materials from recycled immersive devices to build a more circular waste management system.

Take-back programs represent a crucial initiative from the industry that stimulates users to return their previous devices because it results in reduced costs on new acquisitions. Users can participate in these programs to have their old equipment processed correctly as an alternative to unnecessarily disposing of it in landfills. Various major technology companies now work with certified waste handling organizations to care for electronic waste as they show dedication to sustainable environmental practices. Immersive technologies create dual advantages and difficulties for sustainable waste disposal due to their growing popularity. The correct handling of immersive technology hardware during recycling requires government regulations, together with technological improvements from producers, and informed public priorities. The immersive technology sector will minimize its electronic waste production by establishing responsible disposal guidelines together with sustainable product development and circular economy methodology promotion. Immersive computing relies on advances in proper recycling system development and material retrieval techniques to achieve sustainability in the upcoming years.

Between 2018 and 2024, a growing amount of immersive technology hardware will become E-Waste; see Figure 9. According to Virtual Reality (VR), Augmented Reality (AR), and Mixed Reality (MR), the adoption of devices has increased, and so has the disposal of outdated or non-functional hardware. Data shows a constant rise of E-Waste, indicated from 50 metric tons in 2018, predicted to be around 150 metric tons by 2024. This trend further highlights the challenge of dealing with electronic waste, as immersive devices typically contain complex materials that are both difficult to recycle and harm the environment, such as rare metals, plastic composites, and electronics. In the absence of appropriate recycling procedures, this waste poses a major sustainability challenge.

The response to the growing amount of e-waste shows well in the growth of recycling and refurbishment in the same timeframe (see Figure 10). An estimated 95% of recycling and refurbishment efforts have increased from 10% since 2018, with across-industry commitment to responsibly managed disposal practices. To counter the environmental footprint of immersive technology hardware, companies and regulatory organisations have put forth measures including long-life cycle product initiatives, refurbishment centres, and material recovery strategies. It shows a growing movement towards more circular economy models, whereby devices are built with easier disassembly, reusing components and "proper" recycling in mind, hopefully averting the rapid growth of immersive tech from turning into an equally rapid rise in e-waste.

6. Role of Immersive Technologies in Promoting Sustainability

New immersive technologies like Virtual Reality (VR), Augmented Reality (AR), and Mixed Reality (MR) have introduced transformational solutions to various industries in their fast development. These technologies go beyond entertainment and training uses to support sustainability initiatives in a variety of sectors. Immersive technologies offer new solutions to minimise environmental effects, improve resource productivity, and provide a better understanding of sustainability challenges. The future sustainability potential is enhanced through virtual collaboration and digital twin optimization of urban planning and environmental education enabled by immersive technologies [28].

6.1. Virtual Collaboration and Remote Work Reducing Carbon Footprint

The main benefit of immersive technologies for sustainability comes from lowering environmental emissions resulting from travel between business locations and managing office spaces. The standard practice of business meetings, along with conferences and training sessions, demanded substantial travel that produced elevated carbon dioxide emissions from air and ground transportation methods. By utilising VR-based virtual collaboration platforms, people, along with teams, can conduct realistic interactive meetings from different locations without requiring actual physical attendance. Submission of personal information data allows businesses to run virtual conference solutions that convert teams into avatar-based entities which interact in shared metaverses while providing actual meeting sensations without actual travel requirements. Digital realities enable remote work operations better than before, so teams eliminate their need to visit physical office spaces each day. Due to their virtual capabilities, employers can give remote staff accessories which help them view data together and handle 3D structures while conducting real-time virtual tasks with co-workers who remain physically separated. Remote collaboration through virtual spaces boosts productivity levels while lowering energy usage in business structures, thus decreasing office building electricity demands for heat, cooling, and illumination. The increasing use of telepresence solutions leads businesses toward sustainable operations, which keep communication channels seamless, combined with operational efficiency.

6.2. Digital Twin Technology for Sustainable Urban Planning

Digital twin technology supports sustainable planning when used for urban resource management as well as urban design through virtual environments. Digital twins are virtual copies of physical spaces that are fed data from actual information using AI and 3D visualization software. Software programs enable urban planners, architects, and policymakers to develop virtual models of cities, buildings, and infrastructure before undertaking actual real-life construction choices. The implementation of digital twins enables multiple simulation tests that enhance energy conservation efficiency, traffic movement, and environmental protection, resulting in better sustainable urban growth. City planners analyse virtual environment models with digital twins to study how green infrastructure elements impact their surroundings. With systematic data analyses of energy consumption as well as waste generation and water usage, city planners create cities that optimise sustainability and reduce the use of resources. Urban systems become more manageable through digital twin technology because it detects environmental weaknesses such as heat islands and flood-prone areas, which allows for the prevention of environmental crises. The method delivers waste reduction and efficient land allocation, which produces sustainable cities for enduring development.

Digital twin technology finds applications in industrial areas where it boosts operational performance as well as minimises material losses. The use of digital twins by factories and production facilities allows them to track energy usage and enhance their manufacturing operations for fewer material waste occurrences. Organisations that merge real-time information with virtual simulation systems obtain the power to create production methods that both protect the environment and improve operational performance.

6.3. VR-Based Environmental Education and Awareness Programs

Immersive technologies are effective in creating motivational learning interactions that form a strong, stimulating framework for environmental education and awareness. The vast majority of approaches to sustainability education still rely on the likes of textbooks, lectures, and passive media, which are unable to accurately convey the value of environmental webinars or to truly engage with students. Students gain better knowledge regarding sustainability by seeing environmental challenges through VR-based education programs since these programs enable users to feel the issues directly. Using VR simulation environments, it is possible to visualize climate change effects, including deforestation and pollution. Through a virtual rainforest experience, virtual reality technology allows users to witness firsthand the illegal logging of rainforest trees, while another simulation exposes marine life consequences from plastic pollution, and the viewer is immersed in virtual ocean scenarios. The emotional responses triggered by looking into an immersive environment end up boosting individual consciousness towards environmental deeds, thus leading to sustainable behaviour choices.

Environmental awareness campaigns utilize VR technology at both the mass scale and at the individual education level. Conservation groups and agencies join forces to make VR experiences that introduce users to the ecological issues and then show ways to sustain the world. Interactive climate change models paired with VR-based wildlife conservation are equally offered alongside these virtual tours of renewable energy facilities, making for active learning opportunities that help pivot users to protecting the planet. Through the combination of emotions along with experiential power that exists in immersive technologies, organisations create meaningful behavioural changes toward sustainability.

Conclusion

The adoption of immersive technologies throughout modern production fields creates environmental boundary conditions yet provides valuable solutions for sustainability. Modern solutions derived from Virtual Reality (VR) technology, Augmented Reality (AR), and Mixed Reality (MR) platforms are now being used as effective tools to mitigate environmental challenges and enhance resource management while revolutionising human-computer interaction. These technologies are becoming more popular, although their environmental impact demands both sustainability goals and user interaction strategies, which should be developed for future usage. Immersive technologies achieve sustainability by helping users decrease their travel requirements as well as lessen resource utilization needs. Virtual collaboration and remote work platforms developed through VR and AR technologies have resulted in major reductions of carbon emissions linked to transportation and office utility consumption. These technologies allow users to experience realistic computer-generated environments without needing their actual physical presence, so they aid the development of sustainable workplace environments. Digital twin technology adoption within urban planning applications and industrial uses creates more efficient energy utilisation, together with decreased waste generation and better infrastructure systems. Through virtual environment simulation, digital twins allow policymakers and engineers, as well as business operators, to make actionable decisions which reduce environmental damage.

The adoption of immersive technologies generates environmental difficulties because they require high energy usage and produce large amounts of electronic waste (E-Waste). Virtual Reality and Augmented Reality applications require high-performance computing processing in real-time, which induces growing energy consumption, releasing carbon. Immersive technology devices become obsolete quickly, which creates large quantities of E-Waste because outdated devices often contain complex elements that cannot be recycled. Multiple solutions need implementation to tackle these problems by developing more energy-saving hardware while deploying sustainable computing methods and advanced recycling techniques.

References

[1] Spina, Sara. "*Tools based on immersive technologies for supporting decision making to achieve sustainability and resilience in Small and Medium Enterprises*." Bachelor's thesis, Universitat Politècnica de Catalunya, 2024.

[2] Soliman, Monica, Johanna Peetz, and Mariya Davydenko. "The impact of immersive technology on nature relatedness and pro-environmental behavior." *Journal of Media Psychology* (2017).

[3] Khanal, Krishna. "Crafting Sustainable Brand Narratives Through Immersive Technologies: The Role of Virtual Reality (VR) and Augmented Reality (AR)." In *Compelling Storytelling Narratives for Sustainable Branding*, pp. 134-144. IGI Global, 2024.

[4] Pfeiffer, Jella, Jonas Fegert, Anke Greif-Winzrieth, Greta Hoffmann, and Christian Peukert. "Can immersive systems help address sustainability goals? insights from research in information systems." *Market Engineering: Insights from Two Decades of Research on Markets and Information* (2021): 135-150.

[5] Negi, Sunder Kala. "Exploring the impact of virtual reality and augmented reality technologies in sustainability education on green energy and sustainability behavioral change: A qualitative analysis." *Procedia Computer Science* 236 (2024): 550-557.

[6] Hutson, James, and Piper Hutson. "Immersive technologies." In *Inclusive smart museums: Engaging neurodiverse audiences and enhancing cultural heritage*, pp. 153-228. Cham: Springer Nature Switzerland, 2024.

[7] Podolskaya, Tatiana, Saulesh Kalenova, Eugenia Vasyuta, Natalia Bryukhanova, and Denis Ushakov. "Immersive technologies as a tool for increasing sustainability and environmental friendliness of tourism activities." In *BIO Web of Conferences*, vol. 116, p. 07046. EDP Sciences, 2024.

[8] Sofiadin, Aidrina. "Application of Immersive Technologies towards Sustainability in Higher Education: a Case Study." *IADIS International Journal on WWW/Internet* 21, no. 1 (2023).

[9] Nikolić, Dragana, and Jennifer Whyte. "Visualizing a new sustainable world: Toward the next generation of virtual reality in the built environment." *Buildings* 11, no. 11 (2021): 546.

[10] Wittmann, Maximilian, Philip Cash, Milton Mariani, Anja Maier, and John Paulin Hansen. "Sustaining behaviour change through immersive technologies: Trends, perspectives, and approaches." *Proceedings of the Design Society* 1 (2021): 2891-2900.

[11] Aurelia, Sagaya. "Immersive Technologies: Navigating the Impacts, Challenges, and Opportunities." (2024).

[12] Al-Emran, Mostafa. "Beyond technology acceptance: Development and evaluation of technology-environmental, economic, and social sustainability theory." *Technology in Society* 75 (2023): 102383.

[13] dos Santos Foguel, Flávio Henrique, and Evandro Luiz Lopes. "*Smart and Immersive Education and Education for Sustainable Development: Possibilities for Integration based on the Sustainable Development Goals (SDGs)*." (2024).

[14] Alkhwaldi, Abeer F. "Investigating the social sustainability of immersive virtual technologies in higher educational institutions: students' perceptions toward metaverse technology." *Sustainability* 16, no. 2 (2024): 934.

[15] Rubio-Tamayo, Jose Luis, Manuel Gertrudix Barrio, and Francisco García García. "Immersive environments and virtual reality: Systematic review and advances in communication, interaction and simulation." *Multimodal technologies and interaction* 1, no. 4 (2017): 21.

[16] Spallazzo, Davide, and Mauro Ceconello. "Defining immersion and immersive technologies." *Design International* (2024): 11-36.

[17] Yang, Eunsil. "Implications of immersive technologies in healthcare sector and its built environment." *Frontiers in Medical Technology* 5 (2023): 1184925.

[18] Yang, Yibo, Shahrul Nazmi Sannusi, and Ammar Redza Ahmad Rizal. "Exploring the role of immersive media technologies in environmental communication: A case study of underwater earth projects." *Environmental Communication* (2024): 1-17.

[19] Stacchiotti, Eleonora. "Imagining Sustainable Futures: The Transformative Potential of Green Immersive Virtual Reality Experiences." *AN-ICON. Studies in Environmental Images [ISSN 2785-7433]* 3, no. I (2024): 74-99.

[20] Ismael, Dalya. "Immersive visualization in infrastructure planning: Enhancing long-term resilience and sustainability." *Energy Efficiency* 17, no. 7 (2024): 83.

[21] Sekhar, K. Ch, Rahul Bhagwan Ingle, E. Afreen Banu, Moti Lal Rinawa, M. Mohan Prasad, and S. Boopathi. "Integrating VR and AR for Enhanced Production Systems: Immersive Technologies in Smart Manufacturing." In *Human-Machine Collaboration and Emotional Intelligence in Industry 5.0*, pp. 90-112. IGI Global, 2024.

[22] Lin, Hsin Mei. "Exploring Creative Narration with Immersive Sustainability in Mixed Reality." *Available at SSRN 4789288*.

[23] Allam, Zaheer, Ayyoob Sharifi, Simon Elias Bibri, David Sydney Jones, and John Krogstie. "The metaverse as a virtual form of smart cities: Opportunities and challenges for environmental, economic, and social sustainability in urban futures." *Smart Cities* 5, no. 3 (2022): 771-801.

[24] Manikandan, J., and K. Jayashree. "Enhancing lung nodule classification: a novel CViEBi-CBGWO approach with integrated image preprocessing." *Journal of imaging informatics in medicine* 37, no. 5 (2024): 2108.

[25] Miranda, José Corraliza. "Immersive technologies: new ways to visualise a possible future world." In *Handbook of Social Impact Assessment and Management*, pp. 517-530. Edward Elgar Publishing, 2024.

[26] MacDowell, Paula. "Teachers designing immersive learning experiences for environmental and sustainability education." In *Immersive education: Designing for learning*, pp. 171-186. Cham: Springer International Publishing, 2023.

[27] Magni, Domitilla, Rossana Piccolo, Veronica Scuotto, Armando Papa, and Manlio Del Giudice. "Immersive Technologies and smart Cities in ASEAN: discovering the future innovation challenges." In *Handbook of Research on Disruptive Innovation and Digital Transformation in Asia*, pp. 50-70. IGI global, 2021.

[28] Devi, G. Dharani, Neeraj Kumar, J. Manikandan, and V. Rekha. "Innovative brain tumor detection: Stacked random support vector-based hybrid gazelle coati algorithm." *Biomedical Signal Processing and Control* 101 (2025): 107156.

Chapter 15

Economic and Market Dynamics in Immersive Environments

M. Anousouya Devi[1,*]
G. Tamilmani[1,†]
P. Saranya[1,‡]
R. Usharani[2,‖]
and S. Uma[3,¶]
[1]Department of Computational Intelligence, SRM Institute of science and technology, Kattankulathur, India
[2]Department of Computational Intelligence, Faculty of Engineering and Technology, School of Computing, SRM Institute of Science and Technology, Kattankulathur, India
[3]Department of CSE, Rajalakshmi Institute of Technology, Kuthambakkam, India

Abstract

New technologies built around Virtual Reality (VR) (Augmented Reality (AR) and Mixed Reality (MR)) are transforming economic systems while reshaping market operations in all sectors of the industry. These technologies, joined with Web3, artificial intelligence, and blockchain services, form elaborate online communities that push against conventional market practices and user relationships. Bringing metaverse tech with it, other immersive platforms, and new economic systems were born, fueled by decentralised financial services and virtual ownership combined with perfect digital engagement. Immersion-based environments drive essential economic changes which affect online business dynamics and enhance employee effectiveness and market evolutionary processes. The conversation examines the ways in which firms are using immersive realities to enhance customer relationships and create new sources of revenue and superior operating outcomes. The research investigates the ways in which decentralized finance (DeFi) and non-fungible tokens (NFTs) create self-sustaining digital economies that reside within virtual spaces. Consumer behavioural patterns in immersive spaces are subject to significant mind and conductive changes that impact current marketing strategies and shopping purchasing

* Corresponding Author's Email: anousoum@srmist.edu.in
† Corresponding Author's Email: tamilmag@srmist.edu.in
‡ Corresponding Author's Email: saranyap4@srmist.edu.in
‖ Corresponding Author's Email: usharanr2@srmist.edu.in
¶ Corresponding Author's Email: uma.s@ritchennai.edu.in

In: Shaping Tomorrow
Editors: Prithi Samuel, A. Sathya, Balamurugan Balusamy et al.
ISBN: 979-8-90134-076-9

decisions. Companies integrating Artificial Intelligence personalisation pieces with spatial computing solutions can design optimised, realistic virtual brand experiences that increase levels of customer loyalty as well as redesign shopping spaces. Virtualisation of real estate markets, as well as education and healthcare systems, offers business opportunities and regulatory challenges that must be reviewed. The study examines modern workforce changes which occur in immersive economic environments. Organisations must adjust their employment systems and productivity methods because of the rising popularity of virtual offices, AI collaboration platforms, and training programs in the metaverse. The new shift elevates important questions regarding job loss, essential skills, and access to the economy that demand deliberate public strategies and programs to elevate employees' skills.

Keywords: virtual reality (VR), augmented reality (AR), and mixed reality (MR), decentralized finance (DeFi) and non-fungible tokens (NFTs)

1. Introduction to Immersive Environments

Digital platforms that are referred to as immersive environments create virtual or augmented environments through which one can feel present and engage in depth. A blend of Virtual Reality (VR), Augmented Reality (AR), and Mixed Reality (MR) technology makes these environments run behind sophisticated digital platforms that have transformed the process of consuming digital content. An immersive environment functions by making digital enhancements that boost user engagement after it duplicates real-life scenarios. With the help of a natural ecosystem, an immersive environment enables users to interact with digitalised content based on their assumptions about spatial computing technologies, along with their respective gestures and the real-time output [1]. The digital revolution has generated innovative economic frameworks together with business prospects and social bonding methods which reshape worldwide industries. Modern-day companies, as well as developers, dedicate their resources to creating better immersive platforms that drive digital interfaces towards immersive three-dimensional engagements. Numerous entities are quicker to embrace these environments because immersive technologies now play an essential role in developing the future digital economy and impact sectors like education, healthcare, retail, and entertainment [2].

1.1. Definition and Evolution of Immersive Technologies (VR, AR, MR)

Immersive technologies have come a long way since their inception, from simple visualisations to extremely advanced digital environments with perfect fusion of physical and virtual. Virtual Reality (VR) is an all-encompassing experience that surrounds you with a computer-generated environment where you can manipulate digital objects and explore thematic environments using a virtual reality (VR) head-mounted display (HMD), as well as motion controllers [3]. VR has been widely adopted in gaming, training simulation and medical applications for many users, bringing them realistic and engaging experiences. In contrast to this, Augmented Reality (AR) is something that enhances the real environment, adding digital content on top of the live scene viewable to the wearer of AR spectacles or people looking at smartphone and tablet screens. This technology has been found to be of significant use in industries of retail, navigation & education to provide users with interactive information without having its connection to its immediate surroundings severed. Mixed Reality (MR) brings together the aspects of both VR and AR, where users can interact with virtual and real objects in real time. AR, which is simply just overlays digital content, but MR actually lets users manipulate and interact as if the virtual aspects were all part of the real-world environment. Improved computing power, AI and sensor hardware have triggered the emergence of immersive technology, enabling those individual experiences to become more realistic, responsive and accessible to everyone. Low-cost VR headset prices, inclusion of AR in smartphones and availability of MR platforms such as Microsoft HoloLens have driven mainstream adoption of these and the emergence of new types of digital interaction and economic models [4].

1.2. Integration with Web3, Blockchain, and AI

This joint immersion raises the digital economies of the Web3 blockchain, as well as the artificial intelligence (AI) platforms from the old web, to creating new interactive experiences in the virtual world. Web3 functions as the next development step of internet technology, which enables decentralised financial transactions with end-user control. Web3 enables users to engage in transactions without centralized control and allows them to fully own digital assets with transparent governance features. The core function of blockchain technology in virtual environments involves safe transaction processing which enables users to manage virtual assets and take part in decentralized financial activities together with trust-free monetary exchanges. NFTs have sped up the adoption of immersive experiences because users can now purchase digital assets such as virtual properties, artwork, and game items. Artificial Intelligence enhances these spaces with machine learning abilities that create automatic services, content creation, and customised user experience. AI virtual support, coupled with generative design capabilities and real-time behavioural analysis, creates dynamic responsive virtual environments. Companies use AI to analyze the way users engage within virtual spaces while creating tailor-made marketing strategies to develop enhanced interaction between clients and companies. Immersive spaces are the primary economic innovation driver based on their transformative effect on digital assets exchange and business model strategies [5].

1.3. The Rise of the Metaverse and Its Economic Significance

The merger of virtual reality (VR) with web3, blockchain, and AI is revolutionising electronic economies and reinterpreting the user experience of the virtual space. Web3 is the next phase of the internet, which includes decentralization, user power and financial operations based on blockchain. In contrast to conventional models based on the centring of platforms, Web3 gives power to decentralised user-to-user behaviour and digital asset ownership, also rendering visible governance structures [6]. Blockchain is essential to facilitate secure and verifiable transactions in immersive environments in such a way that users are enabled to trade virtual assets, participate in DeFi, and engage in trustless economic transactions. With the emergence of non-fungible tokens (NFTs), the immersive experience movement has got even more fuel added to it and now users can buy, sell and trade digital goods, including virtual real estate, art or in-game assets. AI live enriches them via clever automation, programmable content creation, and automated user experiences. AI-driven virtual assistants, generative design tools and real-time observation of behaviour further allow for more dynamic and interactive immersive experiences [7]. Business graphs use AI to analyse users' behaviour inside virtual places, campaign performance improvement, and personalised interactions to raise customer engagement's satisfaction. The confluence of these technologies not only changes the way that we create and exchange digital assets, but it also rethinks the history of business, since the immersive environments are such a driver of innovation in the economic future.

2. Market Trends and Consumer Behaviour in Immersive Environments

The development of immersive experiences has started a basic transformation of consumer trends, which results in industry market modification in numerous business sectors. Virtual and Augmented Reality technologies, along with Mixed Reality, offer convenient access to customers who form stronger brand relationships through new approaches that transcend traditional online interfaces. People can discover virtual shops through immersive systems while trying out products as 3D models before buying and communicating with AI assistants that adapt buying experiences. The emerging technological innovations influence consumer actions in every function in such a way that they are engaged with digital activities, which leads to attaining personalised brand interactions. The changing consumer shopping experiences are creating new marketing approaches in businesses while reshaping how purchasers make their buying decisions. These days, organizations are investing in interactive brand experiences that also generate consumer loyalty as well as induce product buying through innovative audience engagement models [8].

2.1. Shifts in Consumer Engagement and Purchasing Patterns

With the help of modern immersive technologies, consumers have been engaged and transformed into an interactive platform which helps to deliver personalised opportunities for shopping. Shoppers experience products virtually through immersive environments before buying because traditional e-commerce shows them only static product listings. Through AR applications, consumers can see how furniture would fit in their home while they also have access to virtual dress-up options for clothing and real-time cosmetic viewing. Interaction tools provide enhanced trust in consumers' actions and minimise various levels of uncertainty, paving the way to enable major conversion rates. The virtual reality-based shopping malls alongside virtual marketplaces create a sustainable alternative to standard e-commerce shopping by allowing users to experience digital stores and get help from sales staff with access to exclusive product events in realistic settings [9].

Consumers adjust their buying behaviour because of modern technical breakthroughs in the market. People recognise growing value in digital assets, including virtual fashion, NFT-based collectables and metaverse real estate, because these digital items express their identity and help them create a digital lifestyle. Gen Z, along with millennials, lead the way toward this purchasing shift through their asset investments for gaming avatar appearances, along with social media presentations and digital life expression. The adoption of blockchain technology through cryptocurrencies allows users to buy products across various virtual platforms smoothly while bypassing conventional financial institutions. Firms are moulding consumer buying patterns with subscription models, microtransactions, and token reward systems to maintain engaged platform participation. Brands must restructure their models to capitalise on emerging marketplace patterns with marketing strategies prioritising individualised customer interaction and decentralised payment technology [10].

2.2. Immersive Branding, Marketing, and Advertising Strategies

The movement towards immersive experiences has companies reevaluate branding and also marketing approaches so that consumers can engage in a lot of meaningful and interactive ways. The old methods of traditional advertising, old static images and to-the-point slogan ones are getting outdated in an era of what the consumer is demanding, a dynamic, participatory, experiential necessity, not just some static image or some to-the-point slogan. Immersive marketing uses VR, AR and MR to supply very interactive experiences with Brands for attention-grabbing conversations and arousing actions with your audience. For example, luxury fashion brands are creating digital showrooms wherein customers can browse through virtual collections in an environment that is realistic to life, and in the case of cars, the companies are offering VR test drives that allow people to search through vehicles prior to going on to a showroom floor [11].

Advertising in immersive spaces is too changing to suit the principles of spatial computing or interactive advertising. To name, in the metaverse, the brands redeemed in concerts and virtual sports events and in virtual gaming tournaments, embedding their products in a seamless user experience. AI-fuelled virtual influencers, with whom consumers chat now, are increasingly playing a role in immersive branding, suggesting products and providing one-to-one storytelling that connects to their audience. At the same time, however, enterprises are also exploring blockchain-based marketing initiatives for tokenised loyalty programs and NFT-based brand collaborations to build deeper connections with consumers as well. These innovations are upending the brand-customer relationship, changing from one-way communication to a two-way participation model that boosts brand loyalty and customer retention [12].

2.3. Psychological and Behavioural Aspects of Virtual Consumerism

Consumer behaviour undergoes a radical transformation while shopping in shell-inspired environments because shell structures affect how they process mental aspects of their shopping choice. Through their virtual surroundings, customers bond more deeply with online stores in their shopping experience compared to conventional web shopping. Customers usually partake in real brand emotions while feeling products in a very real manner that compels them to make impulse brand-specific purchases. Customers become strongly motivated to shop as they get rewards also obtain exclusive access to program benefits and game events. Brands must construct interactive online formats that support player engagement activities since our natural behavioural pattern shows that people gravitate toward investing more time with any brand [13]. Fashion influences form the basis through which customers participate in virtual shopping. Improving purchasing behavior occurs when virtual domain users seek advice about purchases both during social interactions and the process of seeking recommendations from other participants. Word-of-mouth marketing and brand advocacy result from grassroots promotional efforts because metaverse-based social commerce and virtual events make marketing by means of organic brand advocacy possible. By analyzing consumer patterns AI and ML algorithms enable companies to recommend products that fit individual customers' tastes. The algorithm designs one-of-its-type recommendations that enhance shopping quality and indicate to customers that brands know them, which increases brand trust. Long-term effects of digital immersion harm our minds and generate significant ethical issues regarding digital dependency while compromising our personal data and enabling marketers to influence us. Companies should incorporate ethics in developing such immersive technology to uphold open and helpful services to their customers [14].

The shift of consumer behavior to the digital space appears to present both opportunities for business growth and challenges to overcome. Here, as they search for tactile, customized products that deliver an emotional load, companies must co-opt the business processes to suit customers. Such Immersive technology tools help companies create better images of their brands while also establishing strong customer connections, which leads them to economic excellence in the current digital marketplace.

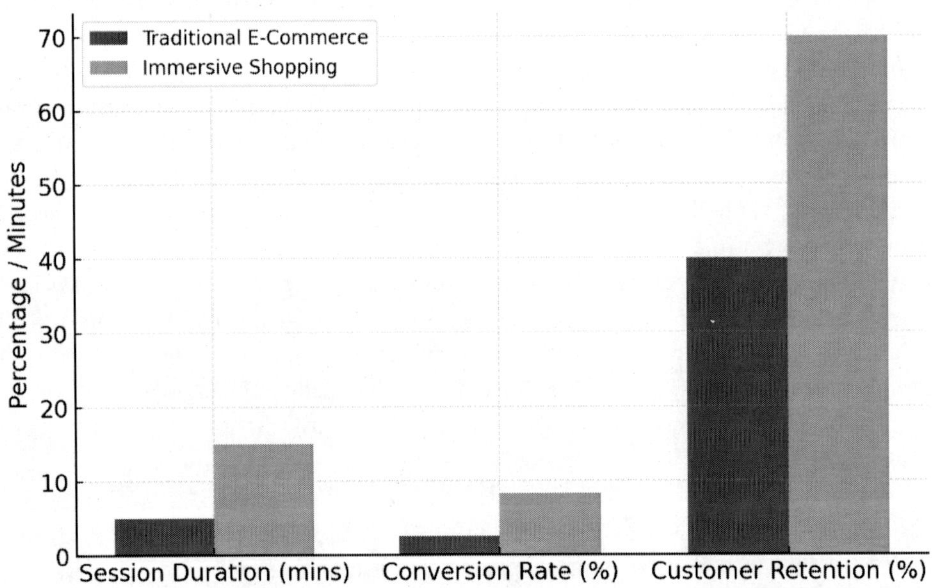

Figure 1. Comparison of traditional E-commerce vs Immersive shopping engagement.

Figure 1 presents a comparison of consumer involvement between ordinary e-commerce stores and shopping contexts that use immersive technology. The graph displays metrics which include session duration, conversion rate, and customer retention. Immersive shopping exceeds traditional online retail in terms of performance, according to the data points. VR/AR-based shopping platforms enable customers to easily interact with products for extended times, which lengthens their sessions by three times. The purchase probability expressed through conversion rate rose remarkably from 2.5% in regular e-commerce to 8.2% in immersive shopping environments since interactive modes drive increased purchase motivation. People tend to maintain their continued use of platforms that deliver immersive experiences because the immersive features generate higher retention rates between 70% and 40% (source – CROVITS report).

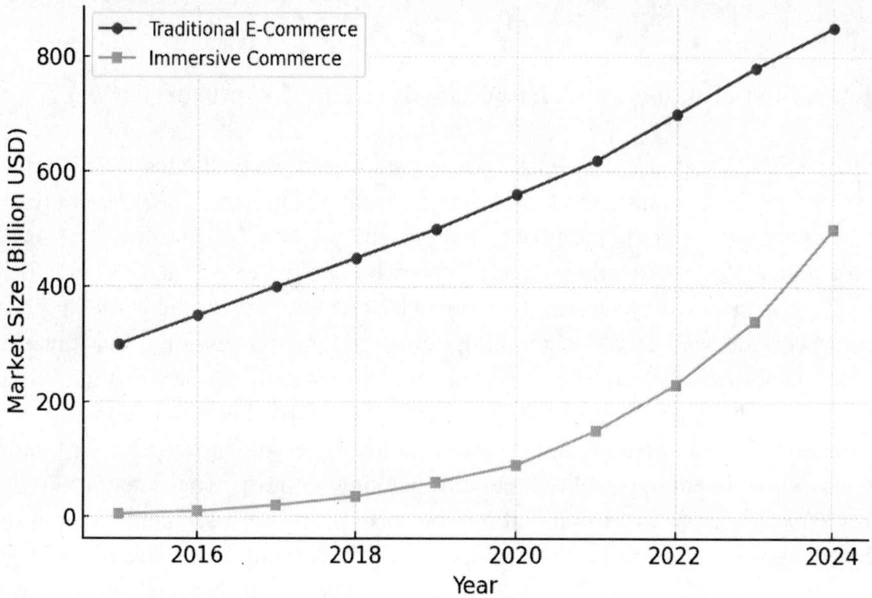

Figure 2. Market growth of immersive commerce vs traditional E-commerce.

Figure 2 shows how immersive commerce markets exceed traditional e-commerce development from 2010 to the present. The traditional e-commerce sector maintained constant growth while reaching a substantial $850 billion USD in revenue by 2025 because customers continued to shop online. The immersive commerce sector shows exponential growth despite its small initial market value of $5 billion in 2015 because it is expected to reach $500 billion by 2025. The rapid market growth results from technological development in VR, AR, and blockchain alongside growing consumer interest in interactive shopping. The steep growth pattern of the immersive commerce sector demonstrates its rising dominance over future market trends by possibly replacing traditional e-commerce business models. The adoption in the metaverse marketplace with virtual product test capabilities and AI-based customization features enhances this trend while promising businesses that incorporate immersive tech achieve huge competitive gains in the emerging digital marketplace.

3. Digital Economies and Virtual Marketplaces

Immersive ecosystems are creating new classes of digital economies beyond legacy markets. Within these virtual spaces, individuals not only consume content, but also create, trade and monetize digital resources. As the transition moves away from owning physical stuff to owning virtual stuff—and mainly due to technology like the blockchain—the way value is created and exchanged in these virtual worlds is also changing. For one, they're global, have low barriers to entry and function independently from large central institutions. This allows users to purchase and sell virtual goods, offer services, or invest in virtual real estate." Returning to normal online areas where users are subject to restrictions on their data and digital items, virtual marketplaces extend real ownership, transparency, and integration across different platforms. All of this contributes to a more inclusive, decentralized economic future [15].

3.1. Tokenization of Assets and Virtual Goods (NFTs, Cryptocurrencies)

Virtual economies function on tokenizing since such an idea facilitates blockchain-secured ownership of digital assets throughout multiple immersive platforms. The physical features and digital factors are made into digital tokens that permit easy conclusion of transactions through the system that offers verification tracking. Non-Fungible Tokens demonstrate ownership transformation because they create permanent ownership registration for digital assets, including artwork, as well as virtual clothing items, in-game possessions, and musical works. The process of duplication stops when NFTs introduce ownership features to digital files, which establishes their value through unique ownership in these virtual worlds. The main transaction method within virtual marketplaces functions with cryptocurrencies for undertaking transactions while operating without central banking entities. The integration of digital currencies remains active in virtual settings because users can use them to acquire virtual properties along with restricted access to decentralized communities. Token implementation enables efficiency growth in marketplaces while providing digital artists with financial value conversion abilities that lead to virtual economy employment opportunities [16].

3.2. Decentralized Finance (DeFi) and Economic Transactions in Immersive Spaces

Decentralized Finance, or DeFi by its name, is a novel approach to finance that removes intermediaries and allows individuals to engage in peer-to-peer finance via smart contracts. DeFi is like the underlying infrastructure to carry out economic activities in an immersive world that are done autonomously, transparently and without borders. Users can lend, borrow, invest and trade digital assets in these spaces via platforms often built as decentralised applications, or dApps, that users access within the metaverse. The combining of DeFi with immersive spaces enables virtual economies to become "self-perpetuating" in that users could operate their finances without any traditional form of banking or payments processing. DeFi is not just a way to do transactions; it enables the creation of virtual financial institutions, tokenised governance, and decentralised insurance in the digital world. Plus, DeFi protocols also allow creators, developers, and entrepreneurs to raise funds through token sales or decentralised crowdfunding, thus democratising economic opportunities. Given the inevitable progression of asimmersive spaces, it is anticipated that DeFi will continue to have an important and defining place within these worlds, as they increasingly become spaces of exchange and commerce [17].

3.3. Case Studies of Virtual Economies in Gaming, Real Estate, and E-Commerce

Many sectors have already capitalised on virtual economies' potential, with gaming, real estate, and e-commerce at the lead. In gaming, such platforms as Decentral and The Sandbox have built immersive virtual economies in which users can buy land, create content, and earn income through token-based operations. Such games grant a degree of economic agency not common in regular video games, enabling people to become digital entrepreneurs in the system. Users buy virtual land, cultivate in-game assets, and trade NFTs for characters, tools, or experiences, earning real-world money in the process. In virtual real estate, digital property is more significant. Users buy land in virtual metaverses, construct properties, and sublease areas for events, advertisements, or shops. Virtual properties have become an expensive investment, with some parcels selling for hundreds of thousands in cash. Businesses also buy land to maintain a foothold in virtual worlds, using immersive brand experiences, customer engagement activations that replicate their physical businesses [18].

In the realm of e-commerce, immersive environments offer a reimagined retail experience where customers interact with products in 3D, receive personalised assistance, and complete purchases using digital currencies. Brands are setting up virtual stores that allow consumers to explore product lines in lifelike detail, try on digital versions of clothing or accessories, and access exclusive digital merchandise. These case studies highlight the growing legitimacy and economic value of virtual marketplaces, demonstrating how immersive environments are not merely entertainment spaces but thriving digital ecosystems with real economic impact [19].

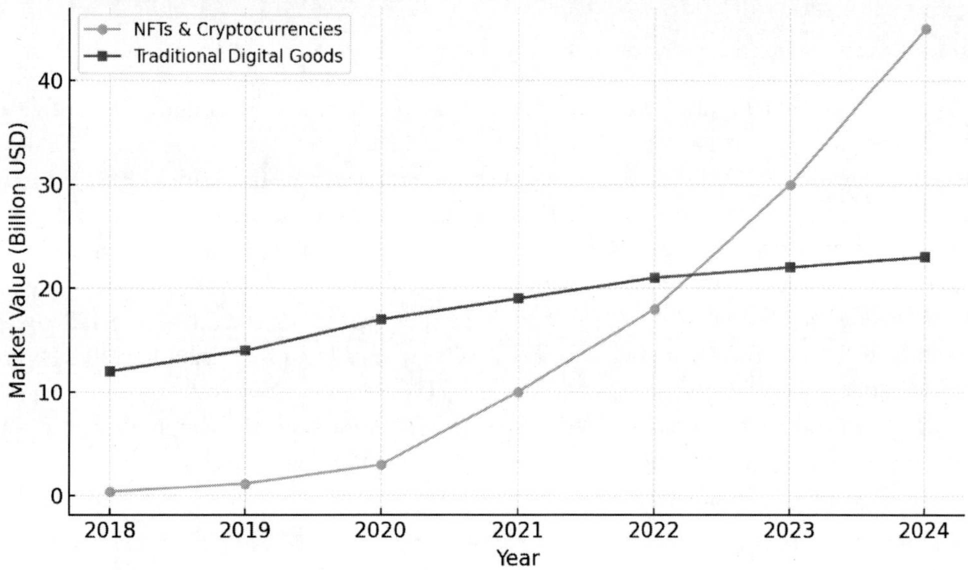

Figure 3. Market growth: NFTs & Crypto vs Traditional digital goods.

The graph given in Figure 3 compares the market growth of NFTs and cryptocurrencies with that of traditional digital goods from 2018 to 2025. While traditional digital goods—such as digital music, e-books, and app store purchases—have shown steady growth, the market for NFTs and cryptocurrencies has experienced an explosive trajectory. In 2018, the NFT and crypto market was relatively insignificant compared to traditional digital goods, but by 2025, it is projected to surpass $45 billion, nearly doubling the size of traditional digital goods. This sharp incline reflects increasing public adoption, institutional investment, and integration into immersive platforms, particularly in the areas of digital art, collectables, and in-game assets.

The graph underscores a shift in consumer value perception, where ownership, uniqueness, and decentralisation are gaining importance over mere access and functionality.

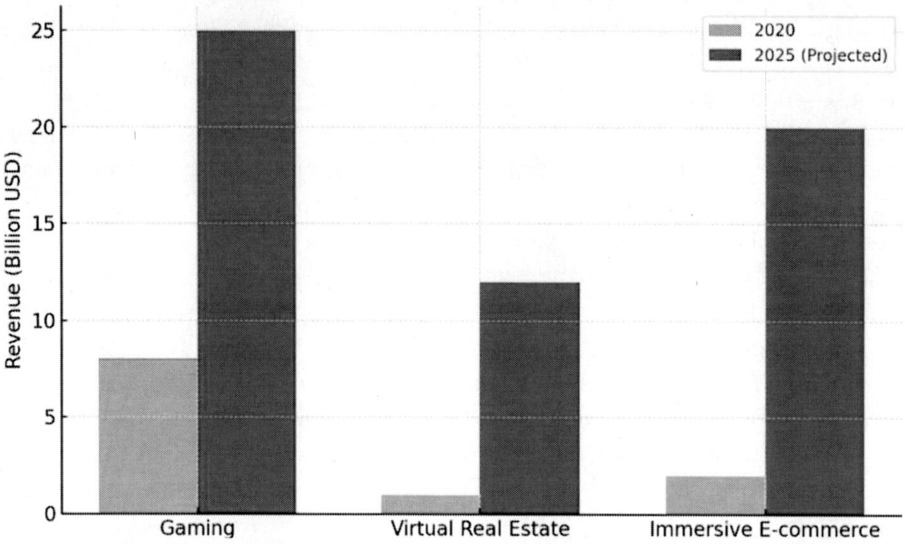

Figure 4. Revenue comparison of virtual economy sectors: 2020 vs 2025.

The graph given in Figure 4 presents a comparison of revenue across three sectors of virtual economies—gaming, virtual real estate, and immersive e-commerce—between 2020 and projected values for 2025. In 2020, gaming already held a substantial lead with $8 billion in revenue, reflecting its maturity and existing digital economies. However, by 2025, it is projected to more than triple to $25 billion. Virtual property, an emerging field in 2020 with revenues totalling just $1 billion, is going to balloon to $12 billion, capturing the trend towards buying, leasing, and monetising virtual land in gaming platforms such as The Sandbox and Decentraland. Immersive e-commerce is also likely to leap from $2 billion to $20 billion as more consumers and businesses participate in 3D shopping spaces that offer real-time personalization and interactive virtual stores. As such, these analogies highlight that immersive spaces aren't simply tech gadgets but economically disruptive ecosystems that are remaking value creation and digital trade.

4. Business Models and Revenue Streams

Consequently, immersive environments have spawned novel business models and monetization approaches that exploit the interactive, persistent, and hyper engaging properties of virtual environments. With such models, users can derive long-term value from the experience, while generating continuous income for the developers and platform holders. Established notions — especially around subscription and advertising — are being changed in these contexts, so businesses are innovating formats to be more interactive and dynamic, specific to the needs of the virtual, augmented and mixed reality (VR, AR and MR) ecosystems. Models like these are revolutionizing the way revenue is generated in businesses [20].

4.1. Subscription-Based, Freemium, and Transaction-Based Models

Immersive environments mostly use subscription-based, freemium, and transaction-based models. Services and content libraries are available under subscriptions that charge users for ongoing access through regular fees. You see this business model in virtual education platforms, fitness apps, and collaboration tools. It gives developers some financial stability to keep improving their content and services. Users can access basic features for free through freemium models but pay for extra features like specialised content, customisation options, or advanced tools. This approach helps boost overall adoption and keeps users engaged, which brings in revenue. Transaction-based systems are common in decentralized areas and metaverse platforms, letting users buy things like NFTs, virtual clothing, and event tickets. Microtransactions help platforms earn money from user-generated economies and real-time activities, which strengthens an economy based on teamwork between developers and users [21].

4.2. Virtual Real Estate and Monetization of Digital Spaces

Virtual property is now at the centre of monetisation in immersive spaces, making virtual digital land a high-value asset. Users in virtual spaces such as Decentraland, The Sandbox, or Spatial can buy parcels of ground, which can be built upon to create stores, galleries, offices, or event spaces. Virtual land is not simply space represented but an economic holding that can be sold, leased, or utilised for hosting monetised experiences. As an example, brands create virtual flagship stores or branded experiences to connect with consumers in new ways, while artists may create art galleries or performance venues to display and sell NFTs. Platforms use the scarce economics applied in physical real estate to generate competitive prices as well as offers for speculation. Monetisation is not limited to ownership—ad placement on virtual billboards, ticketing for virtual events, and leasing storefronts in high-traffic areas are all potentially profitable in these spatial economies. This is indicative of digital visibility and influence now having solid economic value in virtual spaces [22].

4.3. Impact of Immersive Experiences on Traditional Industries (Retail, Education, Healthcare)

Immersive technologies are truly disrupting various industries by changing the way services are being rendered and experiences are being designed. In retail, customers can walk around products in 3D, virtually try on clothes, and practice conversing with sales robots, with much better product visualization and customer satisfaction results. This improves experiences with online shopping and merges the online and offline shopping worlds. Virtual reality is transforming education through immersive simulations, virtual classrooms, and interactive training environments that provide learners with increased engagement, accessibility, and retention. Science, history, or engineering concepts can all be experienced firsthand, creating a more inclusive and experiential method of education. In healthcare, immersive technologies are being used for therapy, surgical training, and patient rehabilitation. VR-based exposure therapy has shown success in treating phobias and PTSD, while AR assists in real-time surgery guidance. These applications signify that immersive environments are not just augmenting traditional industries—they are redefining their core methodologies, creating new standards for interaction, personalization, and efficiency [23].

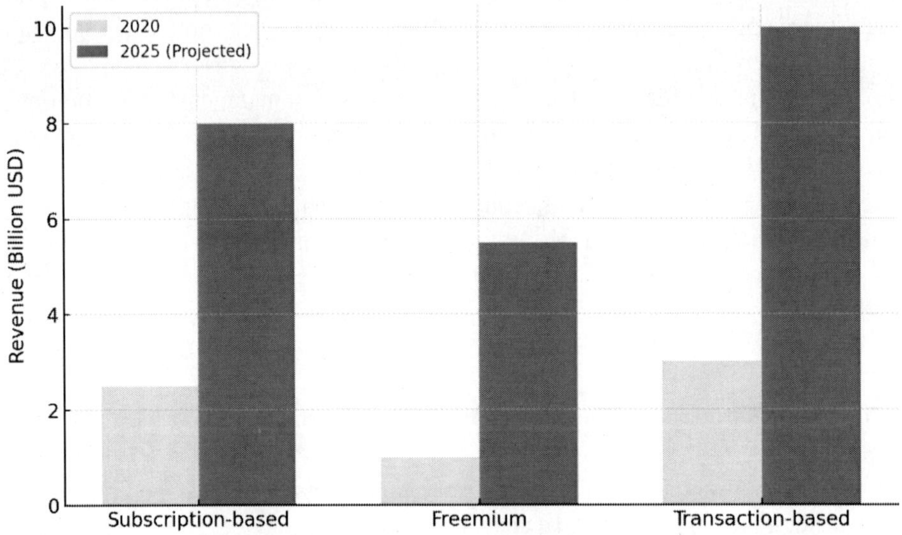

Figure 5. Revenue by business model in immersive environments.

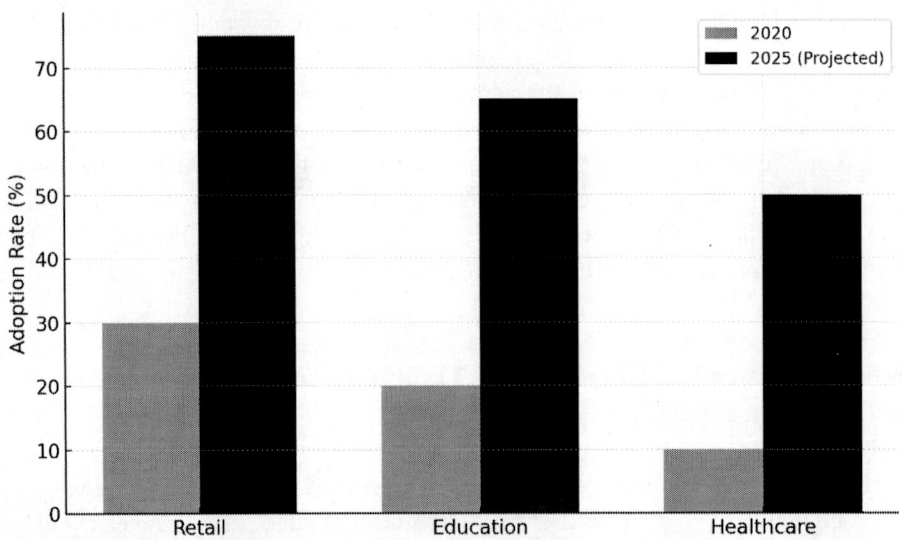

Figure 6. Immersive technology adoption by industry.

The graph given in Figure 5 presents a comparative view of the revenue generated by different business models—subscription-based, freemium, and transaction-based—in immersive environments for the years 2020 and projected values for 2025. In 2020, transaction-based models held the lead with approximately $3 billion in revenue, driven by microtransactions in gaming and NFT purchases. Subscription-based models followed at $2.5 billion, reflecting the early traction of VR fitness, learning platforms, and content libraries.

Freemium models trailed at $1 billion but showed potential due to wide accessibility and gradual monetization. By 2025, projections indicate a significant revenue surge across all models, with transaction-based models expected to reach $10 billion, fuelled by increased adoption of decentralized assets and immersive commerce. Subscription-based models are projected to grow to $8 billion as more users seek continuous access to premium content and services. Freemium models are forecasted to more than triple, reaching $5.5 billion, capitalising on broader user bases and in-app purchases. This trend suggests a growing user willingness to engage financially within immersive ecosystems, especially where personalisation and interactivity are emphasised.

The graph given in Figure 6 highlights the adoption rates of immersive technologies across three major industries—retail, education, and healthcare—comparing data from 2020 with projections for 2025. In 2020, retail led adoption at 30%, primarily due to virtual try-ons, augmented product visualisation, and immersive marketing campaigns. Education had a 20% adoption rate, driven by early-stage virtual classrooms and training modules. Healthcare lagged at 10%, reflecting cautious integration for specialised applications like surgical simulations or VR therapy. Adoption is anticipated to increase dramatically in all three verticals by 2025. In retail, it is projected to reach 75%, with immersive shopping, virtual stores with branding, and customer engagement tools going mainstream. Education is anticipated to hit 65%, as immersive platforms for learning by doing become vital for remote and experiential learning. In healthcare, adoption is projected to grow to 50%, driven by VR-based therapy, medical training, and patient education tools. These percentages point to a watershed moment when immersive tech shifts from being experimental to being vital to traditional sectors, unlocking innovation and new channels for revenue.

5. Supply Chain and Workforce Transformation

Immersive spaces are beginning to transform supply chains and the training, management and deployment of the workforce in a way that has never been done before. Virtual, augmented, and mixed reality applications for enterprise systems are enabling the automation of logistics and increasing operational efficiency and altering the nature of employee relations. These changes are not superficial or at the periphery, but rather, it is a transformation of the old work processes, turning them into new digitalised, decentralised, and more adaptive processes. Greater coordination and agility, along with improved collaboration between humans and computers along the value chain from raw material sourcing to final mile delivery, become the norm as more industries adopt metaverse-based and AI-driven systems. Also, the reconfiguration of workspace, ways of learning, and automation is not only increasing productivity but also training workers to be more useful in roles in digital economies [24].

5.1. Virtual Collaboration and Remote Work in Metaverse-Driven Industries

The rise of immersive tech has really changed how workplaces operate. Now, folks can collaborate in shared virtual spaces, no matter their location. Industries focused on the metaverse are using VR and AR to create digital work environments that can match or even enhance real-life office interactions. In these spaces, people use avatars, participate in brainstorming sessions, give presentations, and hold design reviews, all within a 3D setting. This change makes remote work a lot more engaging and helps teams connect and make decisions better, even when they're far apart. Unlike typical video calls, metaverse platforms offer spatial awareness, natural gestures, and visual cues, making remote conversations feel more genuine. Fields like architecture, engineering, product design, and creative media are benefiting a lot from these immersive workspaces, where complex ideas can be visualized and developed together in a lively digital environment [25].

5.2. Immersive Training and Education for Workforce Development

Creating a memorable, participatory, and personalized learning experience and one that can be scaled quantitatively — these immersive technologies are changing the way we train professionals, giving them the ability to feel and do while remaining safe. In virtual simulations, workers can bring real-world situations into a virtual space to practice some of the most critical skills without the costs and associated risks of physical environments. For example, in fields such as manufacturing, aviation and healthcare, they can practice procedures to manage equipment, respond to emergencies or duplicate surgical workflow in an immersive environment, giving them the experience and confidence in advance before they move to the real thing. They are commonly combined with gamified features, feedback systems, and personalized learning paths, making the learning process even more engaging and motivational [26]. Further, immersive training platforms assist organisations in reducing downtime, decreasing onboarding expenses, and ensuring uniform delivery of knowledge across global teams. As a result, workforce development focuses increasingly on what companies want, favouring hands-on, scenario-based education over college classroom lecture. Figure 7 Workplace Collaboration Tools Change 2020-2025.

5.3. AI-Driven Automation and Productivity in Virtual Environments

The basic automation features of immersive environments stem from artificial intelligence functionality. The new intelligent operational era arises because AI gives computers foresight while providing intelligent avatar assistance for administrative work. Virtual production plants-powered AI systems incorporate digital twin spaces to verify live data for equipment failure prediction and production planning optimization as well as inventory management. These capabilities allow organizations to establish reaction-based solutions to changes which help reduce operational performance barriers. Virtual collaboration environments that use AI tools offer meeting transcription services, together with design enhancement suggestions, alongside workflow administration functions, which produce superior productivity outcomes. Immersive AI platforms provide individualised user experiences due to a mix between behaviour-based analytical systems, along with AI-driven learning solutions and service delivery models and systems for consumer engagement [27]. AI evolution will follow an integrative progression which will produce a unified system that unites human ideas with artificial processing capability for promoting innovation throughout development processes. The development of immersive training compared to AI automation takes place across multiple industrial sectors, as illustrated in Figure 8.

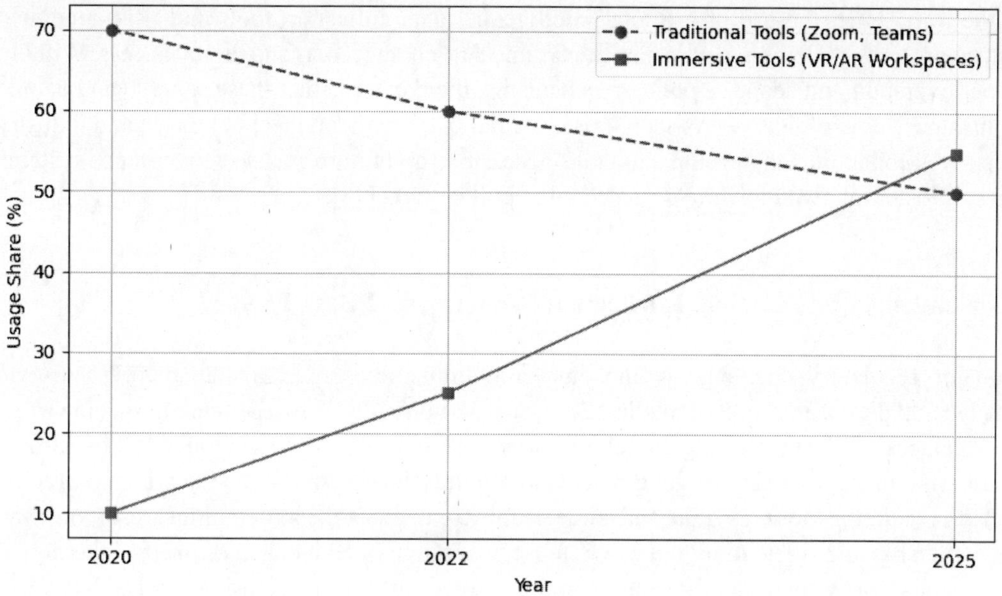

Figure 7. Shift in workplace collaboration tools (2020-2025).

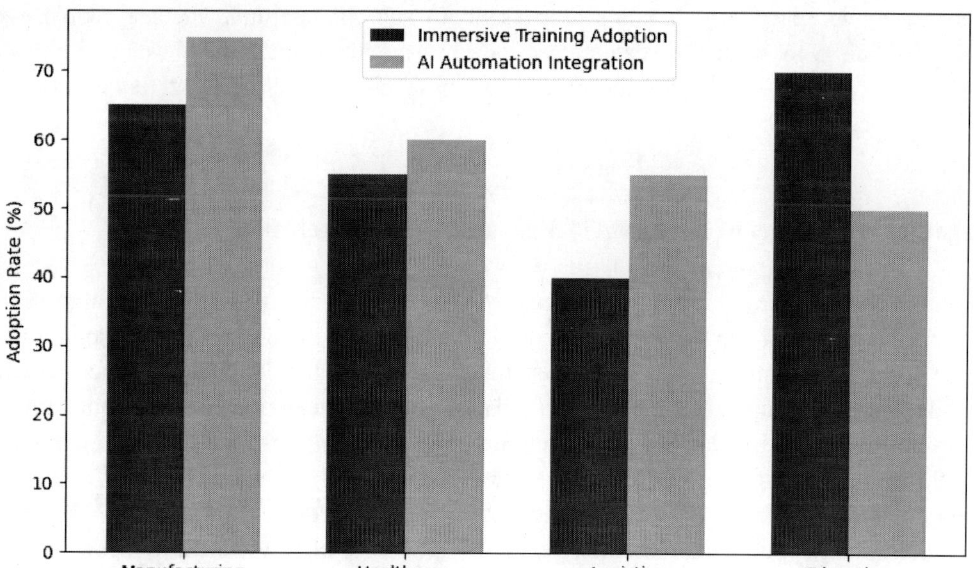

Figure 8. Immersive training vs AI automation across industries.

6. Regulatory and Ethical Considerations

The rapid evolution of immersive technologies and their integration into daily economic enactments is intensifying regulatory and ethical concerns as a headline driver. As immersive environments — such as the metaverse and other extended reality (XR) platforms — are populating the digital landscape, their decentralized and borderless characteristics challenge existing legal systems that were constructed on physical entities and jurisdictional transactions. At the same time, the use of artificial intelligence, data collection tools and user-generated content presents challenging ethical issues around surveillance, bias and digital access. Without proper oversight and adaptive policy mechanisms, the danger is that these spaces can become exclusionary or exploitative. As such, it is essential that regulators, technologists, and industry executives collaborate to develop equitable, accessible, and future-focused governance systems that can foster innovation while preserving the public good [28].

6.1. Challenges in Taxation, Intellectual Property, and Data Privacy

A major regulatory challenge in the emerging immersive environments revolves around taxation and the enforcement of intellectual property rights (IP). When people transact in virtual marketplaces — like purchasing digital land or NFTs — that often goes unnoticed by traditional banks. That makes it tricky for governments to monitor those activities and tax them correctly, and as a result, they lose revenue, and some people try to cheat the system. Plus, resolving who has ownership and rights to digital assets presents a range of IP challenges itself. Take digital art, avatars, or virtual goods; they can be copied or misused easily, especially when decentralized systems don't have standard copyright enforcement. Then there's the data privacy issue. Immersive platforms gather tons of user data, from biometric info to behaviour and how users interact in space, which raises worries about surveillance and whether people even consent to that. A lot of current data protection laws just don't cut it for these new types of personal info, so we really need to come up with specific guidelines that fit the world of immersive tech [29].

6.2. Ethical Concerns Related to AI, Bias, and Digital Exclusion

Concerns over the ethics of immersive spaces are tied closely to the uses of A.I. and algorithms. Some XR platforms rely on AI for content curation, moderation of behaviour, or personalisation of user experience. Unfortunately, these systems are not immune to the biases of their creators or the data they draw upon and thus can help discriminatory interactions within virtual worlds. This might be related to a lack of representation of specific cultures or genders, biased avatar personalization options, or prejudiced personalized content suggestions. Plus, immersive technologies can increase the digital divide. Also, prohibitively expensive VR headsets or peripherals, lack of internet access, or limited digital literacy can isolate individuals/communities, rendering them excluded from fully participating in this virtual economy. The exclusion also continues to exacerbate prevalent social inequities and thus the democratizing potential of the immersive technology. It follows that ethical design should incorporate accessibility, inclusivity and fairness as a central concern in order to ensure that technological advancement is not achieved through the sacrifice of the vulnerable [30].

6.3. Policy Recommendations for Sustainable and Fair Market Growth

In response to these complex challenges, sound and visionary policy is needed. Governments should establish new tax frameworks to consider digital assets and international cross-border virtual trading in a clear, accurate, and fair way within the decentralised financial system. Intellectual property law must be overhauled to define ownership and use rights for digitally created material explicitly, and formatted for enforcement in immersive contexts. Biometric data as well as spatial data must also fall under data protection law to force transparency in data collection, as well as transferring control of personal data to users. Ethically, public-private partnerships can support the development of non-biased AI as well as universal ethical guidelines for XR creators. Investments in infrastructure as well as future education can also bridge digital divides, allowing for wider access to immersive spaces. By encouraging responsible innovation, accessible access and responsive governance, such policy interventions can offer an interim sustainable as well as equitable basis for economic activity in immersive digital spaces.

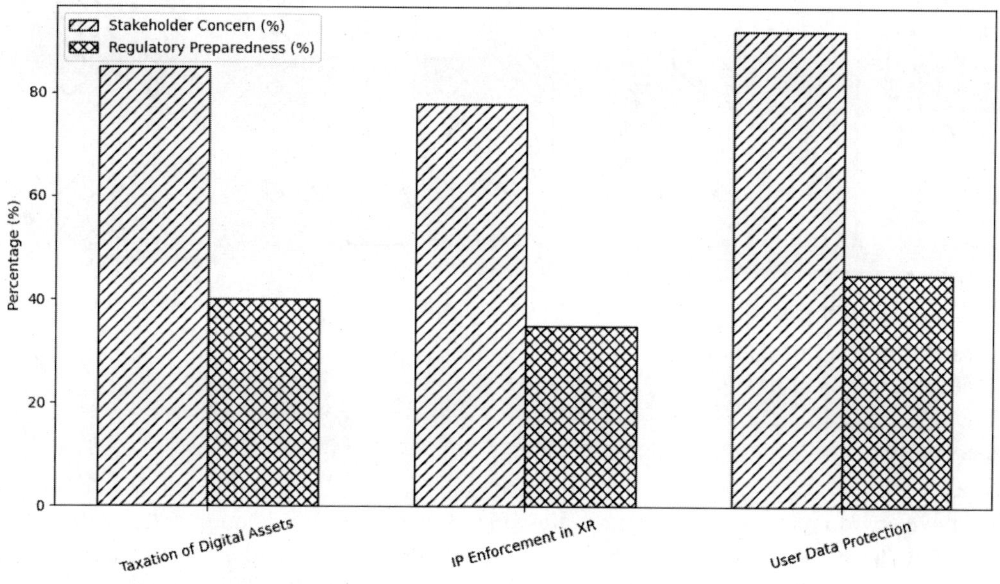

Figure 9. Concerns vs regulatory readiness in immersive ecosystems/

The graph given in Figure 9 compares stakeholder concerns against current regulatory preparedness in three key areas: taxation of digital assets, enforcement of intellectual property (IP) in immersive environments, and user data protection. Most stakeholders expressed high concern—85% for digital taxation, 78% for IP enforcement, and 92% for user data privacy—indicating widespread apprehension about the risks posed by immersive technologies. However, when asked about the adequacy of existing laws and frameworks, only 40%, 35%, and 45% respectively, believed current regulations were sufficient. This stark contrast reveals a significant gap between the pace of technological adoption and the development of corresponding regulatory frameworks. It emphasises the urgent need for lawmakers to prioritise immersive technologies in policy agendas, ensuring a balanced and proactive approach to innovation and consumer protection. On the other hand, the graph given in Figure 10 shows projected rates of digital inclusion and exclusion across different global regions by 2025. North America leads in immersive technology accessibility with 75% of its population expected to be included, followed by Europe (70%) and Asia-Pacific (65%). By comparison, areas such as Africa and Latin America have high levels of digital exclusion, with 65% in Africa and 50% in Latin America likely to have no access. These statistics emphasise disparity in immersive technology adoption based on variance in infrastructures, affordability, and digital knowledge. This disparity enhances the requirements for worldwide cooperation in investment, policy, and learning to make immersive ecosystems accessible to all populations, not simply in economically developed areas.

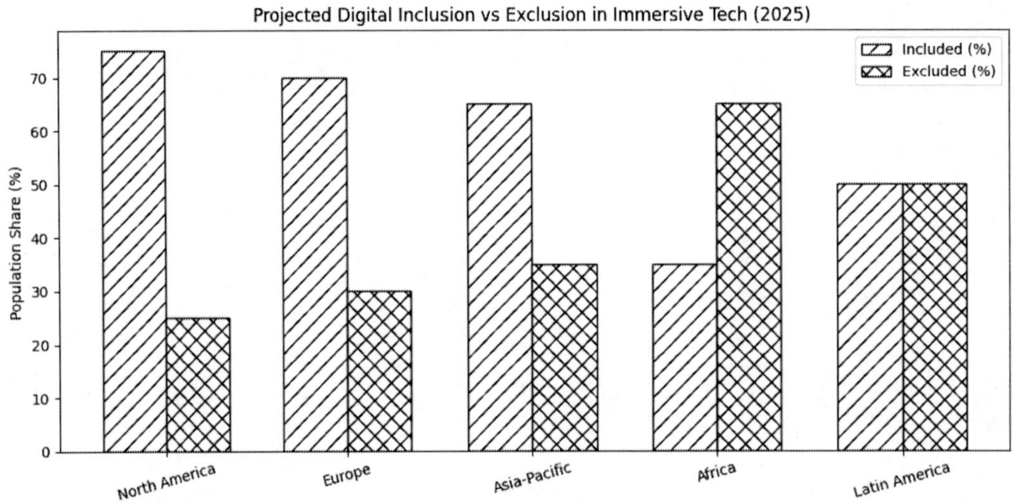

Figure 10. Projected digital inclusion vs exclusion in immersive technology.

Conclusion

Immersive environments born from innovation in virtual reality (VR) + augmented reality (AR) + mixed reality (MR) + artificial intelligence (AI) + blockchain + Web3 tech re-engineering world economic infrastructure. Emerging economies in online space are being born both as an outcome of recent consumer behaviour and the behaviour of marketing and new digital mechanisms and markets of incomes. These environments give companies a level of flexibility and customisation options and system performance, as with anything else, that they connect people through with tools that had been thought of as future customisation options and system performance, as with anything else, that they connect people through with tools that had been thought of as future settings. New economies in terms of immersive systems raise complex questions which impact governance on virtual operations as well as ethics and diverse populations' participation. The requirement to create positive policy models and moral design processes arises because of privacy invasion and intellectual property disputes, as well as algorithm bias, to demand openness, fairness and assurance of accessibility rules. Universal virtual tech access requires infrastructure For All as well as digital education systems to prevent further social class divides. Immersive room will shape their economic and market destiny by means of technology advancements, alongside responsible management and united global views and strategic planning. Immersive surroundings will bring about an egalitarian digital economy with fluid parity when guard's opportunities combined with inclusivity allow for creative development.

References

[1] Durojaye, Abiodun, Amin Kolahdooz, Abdullah Nawaz, and Ata Jahangir Moshayedi. "Immersive horizons: exploring the transformative power of virtual reality across economic sectors." *EAI Endorsed Trans. AI Robot* 2 (2023): e6.

[2] Onopriienko, Iryna, Kateryna Volodymyrivna Onopriienko, and Salmane Bourekkadi. "*Immersive technologies in adult learning as an innovative marketing tool in the educational market.*" (2023).

[3] Uwaoma, Prisca Ugomma, Emmanuel Osamuyimen Eboigbe, Nsisong Louis Eyo-Udo, A. C. Ijiga, S. Kaggwa, and A. I. Daraojimba. "Mixed reality in US retail: A review: Analyzing the immersive shopping experiences, customer engagement, and potential economic implications." *World Journal of Advanced Research and Reviews* 20, no. 3 (2023): 966-981.

[4] Zhao, Xinyang, Xuefang Xie, and Zhuyun Song. "Cultural and economic dynamics of digital immersive art in China's creative industries." *International Journal of Cultural Policy* (2025): 1-13.

[5] Hsiao, Shih-Hui, Yen-Yao Wang, and Tony LJ Lin. "The impact of low-immersion virtual reality on product sales: Insights from the real estate industry." *Decision Support Systems* 178 (2024): 114131.

[6] Heggde, Githa S., Santosh Kumar Patra, and Rasananda Panda. *Immersive Technology and Experiences*. 2023.

[7] Fazio, Gioacchino, Stefano Fricano, and Claudio Pirrone. "Evolutionary Game Dynamics Applied to Strategic Adoption of Immersive Technologies in Cultural Heritage and Tourism." *arXiv preprint arXiv:2409.06720* (2024).

[8] Rachmawati, Aliviya Kurniya, and Hengki Tornando. "Challenges in Consumer Adaptation to Immersive Technologies: A Comprehensive Literature Review." *eCo-Buss* 7, no. 1 (2024): 317-328.

[9] Bennett, James, and Amanda Murphy. "Skills for immersive experience creation." *StoryFutures Academy, London* (2020).

[10] Spina, Sara. "Tools based on immersive technologies for supporting decision making to achieve sustainability and resilience in Small and Medium Enterprises." Bachelor's thesis, Universitat Politècnica de Catalunya, 2024.

[11] Turi, Abeba N. "Metaverse—the immersive 3D virtual world's innovation diffusion in the financial sector." In *Financial technologies and DeFi: a revisit to the digital finance revolution*, pp. 3-28. Cham: Springer International Publishing, 2023.

[12] Kumar, S. Vinoth, Vishnu Kumar Kaliappan, A. Suresh, B. Suresh Kumar, and S. V. Manikanthan. "Safety for Digital Immersive Environments and Social Economic Dynamics Based on Designing the Metaverse." In *Human-Centered Approaches in Industry 5.0: Human-Machine Interaction, Virtual Reality Training, and Customer Sentiment Analysis*, pp. 281-309. IGI Global Scientific Publishing, 2024.

[13] Singh, Bhupinder, and Christian Kaunert. "Innovative Business Models in Digital and Virtual Reality for the Gig Economy: Space-Age Sustainable Development Projecting Smart Business Practices." In *Business Transformation in the Era of Digital Disruption*, pp. 127-156. IGI Global, 2025.

[14] Allam, Zaheer, Ayyoob Sharifi, Simon Elias Bibri, David Sydney Jones, and John Krogstie. "The metaverse as a virtual form of smart cities: Opportunities and challenges for environmental, economic, and social sustainability in urban futures." *Smart Cities* 5, no. 3 (2022): 771-801.

[15] Prokhor, Viktoriia, Oleksandra Mrykhina, and Orest Koleshchuk. "Effectiveness of Implementing Immersive Technologies within University Sustainable Development Systems." *Eastern-European Journal of Enterprise Technologies* 131, no. 13 (2024).

[16] Tom Dieck, M. Claudia, and Dai-in Danny Han. "The role of immersive technology in customer experience management." *Journal of marketing theory and practice* 30, no. 1 (2022): 108-119.

[17] Rubio-Tamayo, Jose Luis, Manuel Gertrudix Barrio, and Francisco García García. "Immersive environments and virtual reality: Systematic review and advances in communication, interaction and simulation." *Multimodal technologies and interaction* 1, no. 4 (2017): 21.

[18] Han, Dai-In Danny, Malu Boerwinkel, Mata Haggis-Burridge, and Frans Melissen. "Deconstructing immersion in the experience economy framework for immersive dining experiences through mixed reality." *Foods* 11, no. 23 (2022): 3780.

[19] Oyewole, Adedoyin Tolulope, Omotayo Bukola Adeoye, Wilhelmina Afua Addy, Chinwe Chinazo Okoye, Onyeka Chrisanctus Ofodile, and Chinonye Esther Ugochukwu. "Augmented and virtual reality in financial services: A review of emerging applications." *World Journal of Advanced Research and Reviews* 21, no. 3 (2024): 551-567.

[20] Chatterjee, Sheshadri, Tomas Kliestik, Zuzana Rowland, and Martin Bugaj. "Immersive collaborative business process and extended reality-driven industrial metaverse technologies for economic value co-creation in 3D digital twin factories." *Oeconomia Copernicana* 2025, no. 16 (2025): 125-161.

[21] Popp, József, and Adela-Claudia Cuţitoi. "Immersive visualization systems, spatial simulation and environment mapping algorithms, and decision intelligence and modeling tools in the web3-powered metaverse world." *Journal of Self-Governance and Management Economics* 10, no. 3 (2022): 56-72.

[22] Li, Qianrong, and Dan Cao. "Reviving Ecological Environments: Strategies for AI and VR Applications in Immersive Cultural Exhibitions." In *SHS Web of Conferences*, vol. 183, p. 01010. EDP Sciences, 2024.

[23] Artyukhova, Nadiia. "Box approach for immersive marketing of educational services in the context of educational reforms1." *Studia commercialia Bratislavensia*: 147.

[24] Leung, Xi Y., Dimitrios Buhalis, and Giampaolo Viglia. "Immersive advertising through co-creation: Lessons from the visitor economy: How to enhance experiential competitiveness with an "attract, convert, and delight" strategy." *Journal of Advertising Research* 64, no. 3 (2024): 319-334.

[25] Hussain, Zahid, Arman Khan, and Aftab Ali. "The impact of user-generated content, social interactions and virtual economies on metaverse environments." *Journal of Sustainable Economics* 1, no. 2 (2023): 34-44.

[26] Yang, Shuran. "*The power of immersive technologies: a sociopsychological analysis of the relationship between immersive environments, storytelling, sentiment, and the impact on user experience*." PhD diss., University_of_Basel, 2023.

[27] Sidhu, Manjit S., Sara Mousakhani, Chen K. Lee, and Kirandeep K. Sidhu. "Educational impact of Metaverse learning environment for engineering mechanics dynamics." *Computer Applications in Engineering Education* 32, no. 5 (2024): e22772.

[28] Warburton, Steven. "Second Life in higher education: Assessing the potential for and the barriers to deploying virtual worlds in learning and teaching." *British journal of educational technology* 40, no. 3 (2009): 414-426.

[29] Naik, Meena, Raymond Barbosa, and Alex Swartsel. "Immersive Learning & XR Technology Skills and Careers: Where the Future of Work Meets Economic Opportunity." *Jobs for the Future* (2023).

[30] Valaskova, Katarina, Marek Vochozka, and George Lăzăroiu. "Immersive 3D technologies, spatial computing and visual perception algorithms, and event modeling and forecasting tools on blockchain-based metaverse platforms." *Analysis and Metaphysics* 21 (2022): 74-90.

Chapter 16

Legal Framework and Ethical Challenges in Patenting AR/VR Innovations in Healthcare Under the Indian Patent Act, 1970

Helen P. Azyu*
and Avishek Chakraborty
School of Law, Christ (Deemed to be University), Bangalore, Karnataka, India

Abstract

Augmented reality (AR) and virtual reality (VR) are gradually becoming significant to various industries, such as gaming, education, industrial design sectors, and healthcare. Even though augmented and virtual reality breakthroughs have already revolutionised healthcare by enhancing diagnosis, treatment, medical education, training and rehabilitation, granting patents to these technologies-imposed challenges when it comes to legal and moral concerns. Section 3(k) of the Patents Act 1970 forbids patenting software-driven discoveries and therapy-oriented applications. Such a legal constraint could be challenging for augmented reality and virtual reality technologies in healthcare, as it mostly depends on algorithmic procedures and therapeutic functions to develop breakthroughs. Other challenges could be section 3(b) of the Patents Act of 1970, which prohibits inventions that are contrary to public order or morality or cause harm to the environment, as ethics and morality play a crucial role in patenting AR/VR healthcare technology. The primary purpose of patent law is to encourage inventions, but it can cause medical care by creating a monopoly and allowing limited access to society. Patenting AR/VR technologies is essential to address moral and ethical concerns, as patenting these technologies in healthcare will promote inequality in patient care. The purpose of the present article is to analyse the ambiguity of the patentability of AR/VR technology in healthcare under the Patents Act of 1970 while addressing moral values with references to the principles of ethics. The paper further examines secondary data on patent grants on biomedical devices that integrate AR/VR across medical disciplines.

Keywords: augmented reality, virtual reality, patent law, moral challenges, healthcare industry, innovation, technologies, biomedical, healthcare technology, India

---

* Corresponding Author's Email: helen.azyu@res.christuniversity.in

In: Shaping Tomorrow
Editors: Prithi Samuel, A. Sathya, Balamurugan Balusamy et al.
ISBN: 979-8-90134-076-9

1. Introduction

Healthcare facilities are being revolutionized more efficiently through augmented reality (AR) and virtual reality (VR) educational methodologies. These tools efficiently enable treatment procedures, diagnostics, education, and all other aspects of patient care. Medical technologies virtually enable both healthcare providers and patients to have better outcomes. VR produces a fictional surrounding, while AR produces layers of virtual data overlaid in the real world; both are highly and increasingly applied in medicine. AR allows medical students and trainees to see complex body structures and conduct procedures on the human body by projecting images onto models or even people. In practice, AR can be used to illustrate the location of specific body parts on a model to clarify anatomical relationships. VR provides total involvement in the activity of interest, making it possible to train for surgery and emergencies in a virtual environment. These technologies eliminate the usage of cadavers and human sources for educational practice, thus promoting safety and ethics.

Nevertheless, patenting AR/VR technology in healthcare faces challenges regarding novelty and inventive steps. AR/VR might be a medical marvellous that revolutionizes healthcare. Patenting AR/VR technologies in healthcare pose complex legal, technical, and moral challenges. In India, these are accentuated because of the conditions imposed by the patent law and realities in healthcare sectors. AR/VR technologies depend on algorithms to function digitally as software that influences the nature and methods of diagnostics, surgeries, and medical training purposes. However, sub-section (k) of section 3 of the Patents Act 1970 software per se is barred from patentability, creating a legal barrier for innovators seeking protection for AR/VR technologies. Moreover, section 3(b) of the Act excludes patents for inventions contrary to public order, morality or environment, thus producing a moral and ethical concern for such technologies, especially regarding data privacy, informed consent, and equitable access. These public interest-based legal exclusions ultimately conflict with the incentive to innovate AR/VR healthcare applications that can change patient care. Patenting AR/VR in health could also lead to conserving monopolies and limiting access to specific patients. A subtle set of legal standards, advanced technology, and moral obligations must be resolved through more research and collaboration among experts in this field.

This technology has been masked by uncertainty as patents play a decisive role in innovation and investing in high-end technology, which could even boost the economy. Many countries have granted patent protection for AR/VR. The granted patent protects the invention in the territory where a patent was obtained.[1] This paper aims to analyse the law and moral concerns regarding patenting in AR/VR inventions and explore the implications of AR/VR healthcare growth in India. This paper will also examine India's legal framework on AR/VR technologies in healthcare and data analysis on the patent application and patent grant on AR/VR healthcare.

[1] Yetisen, Ali K., and Lisa R. Volpatti. "Patent protection and licensing in microfluidics." *Lab on a Chip* 14, no. 13 (2014): 2217-25.

2. The Usefulness of AR/VR Technologies in Healthcare

According to Muñoz-Saavedra, "*In today's society, most technological advancements are made daily, most of which directly affect human life.*"[2] AR and VR are some of the best examples of technology development that have significantly impacted medicine. AR and VR have been found effective for medical and educational purposes. These technologies hold promises for the healthcare industry and even for the pharmaceutical industry. It greatly enhances patient outcomes. For instance, medical purposes like healthcare centres are used for medical training, diagnosis, rehabilitation, and even therapy.[3] These technologies are increasingly being used to promote the healthcare industry and pharmaceutical companies to discover miracles for patients.

2.1. Use of AR/VR for Medical Education

With the help of AR and VR, medical training and education has become more accessible. The trainers can virtually see the human anatomy, thus gaining an all-round view simulating real-life therapies. AR provides opportunities for practical learning, like virtual 3D patients, so medical students can visualize and exercise the surgical procedures before diving into real surgery. Using VR, a more accurate simulation that feels like the actual surgery can be programmed, enabling trainees to do surgeries in real-time.[4] It can transform into an immersive experience in which success is rewarded, and analysing data can be utilised to focus targeted knowledge. For instance, John Hopkins Medical Simulation Centre uses VR for training purposes.[5] The training focuses on resuscitation, allergy, postsurgical treatment, acute-care management, and paediatric life-threatening training. The institute embarked on various VR research with medical and nursing trainees in practical situations that can accommodate many learners.[6]

Though contemporary medical pedagogics and activities show adequate medical and health experts, gaps are still there for development in efficient and effective surgical skills training, as there is a lack of direct care and treatment occasionally. Although clinical internships greatly enhance applied skills, inadequate hands-on training sometimes detracts from facilitating the mastery of these techniques. AR/VR simulators could bridge this gap, becoming more refined and real.[7] The studies conducted at the South Carolina University School of Medicine with a cardiopulmonary patent simulator known as Harvey (an extremely advanced manikin) found that the students trained on the simulator for cardiac examination skills did better on exams.[8]

---

[2] Saavedra, Augmented and virtual reality evolution, 320.

[3] Bottani, Eleonora, and Giuseppe Vignali. "Augmented reality technology in the manufacturing industry: A review of the last decade." *Iise Transactions* 51, no. 3 (2019): 284-310.

[4] Bala, Rajni, and Rajni Saini. "A Study of AR and VR in the Real World." In *Applications of Neuromarketing in the Metaverse*, pp. 271-290. IGI Global, 2023.

[5] Horowitz, Brian. "Medical schools and healthcare institutions are implementing AR, VR and XR training to enable repeatable immersive surgical simulations that bring valuable practice". Health Tech, 15 December 2022. https://healthtechmagazine.net/article/2022/12/ar-vr-medical-training-2023-perfcon.

[6] Guillot, Craig. "The Kaiser Permanente Bernard J. Tyson School of Medicine's Anatomy Resource Center uses technology to aid in teaching about the human body".Health Tech, 23 November 2021. https://healthtechmagazine.net/article/2021/11/qa-dr-jose-m-barral-using-virtual-tools-anatomy-education.

[77] Fisher, Rebecca , Suewan Kim, and Prokar Dasgupta. "The Future of Surgery". *Digital Surgery* (2021): 419-427.

[8] *Ibid.*

The Anatomage table (which features different sizes of the human body) is a virtual tool representing the visualization of the human head, neck, chest, abdomen, pelvis, joints, etc. This platform provides a teaching mechanism for medical students and trainees.[9] It helps a medical professional grasp and learn quickly. Besides, it allows physicians to study and share their preoperative explanations with their patients by showing the virtual blueprint, which may enhance their awareness of their postoperative state.[10] VR surgery simulation can also help doctors to practice their surgery before operating. This practice can increase the possibility of success in the surgical field. For knee arthroscopy, VR has developed a system that simulates knee cap replacement surgery and allows surgeons to practice administering anaesthesia for the procedures appropriately.[11]

2.2. AR and VR in Patient Care and Treatment

For patients who have fear and anxiety, VR technology can be effective for the treatment, including treatment for acrophobia, claustrophobia, and social anxiety, using exposure therapy. Limbix VR technology is used for treating patients who have phobias of high buildings and spiders.[12] To assist children with Autism, Stanford University developed the Autism Glass Project using Google Glass AR technology.[13] For patients who went through arms or leg amputation, AR technology assists in seeing their phantom arms or legs, the portions the amputee has lost. A virtual arm appears on the screen when the patient moves their amputated arm. The virtual arms on the screen will emerge in the same motion, which can help amputees ease their pain.[14]

3. Legal and Regulatory Considerations: Application of AR/VR in Healthcare

Intellectual property law protects idea expression and other intangible notions. In the new economy of the digital age, these protections have become important for intangible essentials. AR combines virtual and actual items to create a 3D world. The applications and technology of AR require different types of Intellectual Property, such as patents, copyrights, and

---

[9] Barsom, Esther Z., Maurits Graafland, and Marlies P. Schijven. "Systematic review on the effectiveness of augmented reality applications in medical training." *Surgical endoscopy* 30 (2016): 4174-4183.

[10] Fluet, Gerard, Alma Merians, Jigna Patel, Anita Van Wingerden, Qinyin Qiu, Matthew Yarossi, Eugene Tunik, Sergei Adamovich, and Supriya Massood. "Virtual reality-augmented rehabilitation for patients in sub-acute phase post stroke: a feasibility study." In *Proc. 10th Intl Conf. Disability, Virtual Reality & Associated Technologies*, pp. 2-4. 2014.

[11] Lee, S., J. Lee, A. Lee, N. Park, S. Song, A. Seo, H. Lee, J-I. Kim, and K. Eom. "Augmented reality intravenous injection simulator-based 3D medical imaging for veterinary medicine." *The Veterinary Journal* 196, no. 2 (2013): 197-202.

[12] Bush, Jimmy. "Viability of virtual reality exposure therapy as a treatment alternative." *Computers in Human Behavior* 24, no. 3 (2008): 1032-1040.

[13] Miloff, Alexander, Philip Lindner, William Hamilton, Lena Reuterskiöld, Gerhard Andersson, and Per Carlbring. "Single-session gamified virtual reality exposure therapy for spider phobia vs. traditional exposure therapy: study protocol for a randomized controlled non-inferiority trial." *Trials* 17 (2016): 1-8.

[14] Osumi, M., A. Ichinose, M. Sumitani, N. Wake, Y. Sano, A. Yozu, S. Kumagaya, Y. Kuniyoshi, and S. Morioka. "Restoring movement representation and alleviating phantom limb pain through short-term neurorehabilitation with a virtual reality system." *European journal of pain* 21, no. 1 (2017): 140-147

trademark rights. However, this paper will discuss only patent law in the light of AR/VR innovation in the healthcare sector. Technologies involving AR/VR provide significant benefits and solutions for the healthcare sector, such as medical training, diagnostic procedures, and patient care. The AR helps in medical training through virtual treatments and learning experiences. Inpatient care is transformed through immersion therapy, with the assistance of visualisation of the complex data of the medicines.[15]

Section 3 of the Patents Act of 1970 lists non-patentable criteria. If an invention falls under the ambit of this provision, the invention will not be able to grant a patent. AR/VR innovation, to qualify for patent protection, has to be new, have inventive steps, and be able to have industrial applications. AR/VR technologies present issues as they involve software algorithms or business methods. Section 3(k) of the Act states that "*a mathematical or business method or a computer program per se algorithms are not patentable*."[16] Despite this provision, patents can still file for AR/VR innovation under Patent law if they satisfy the 'technical advance' requirement. For instance, AR/VR technology, as integrated technology in medical devices such as simulators for surgeries or even diagnostic tools, can qualify for patents where they can establish tangible technical advancements or solve any technical problem. The Indian Patent Office (IPO) has clarified that the combination of software and hardware to improve hardware functionality does not fall under the exclusion of section 3(k) of the Act. This means inventors can claim protection for AR/VR healthcare technologies that provide practical and technical solutions.

3.1. Nature of Patentable Invention

The Patents Act defines patentable invention extensively. Accordingly, if the invention is new and has usefulness, machines, manufacture, etc, it is necessary to note that if any inventions do not fall under the categories mentioned above, such inventions are excluded from patenting. However, any improvement or variation of known procedures, production, or arrangement that is beneficial can be patented. The patent system gives exclusive rights that vary among countries as stipulated by their own national laws and international treaties. The patentable subject matter is generally accepted to qualify for a patent on an invention. The novelty, non-obviousness, and suitability for industrial/valuable applications are all considered patentable.

- Subject Matter of a Patent: To get patented, it must fulfil the criteria of being a patentable subject matter described under the provisions of law relating to patents in the country where the application is filed. The patent subject matter of many countries provides inventions that are excluded from patentability.[17] The patent rules and regulations on the national legislation or the international treaties vary from jurisdiction to jurisdiction. Parker Flook vs Flook, the United States SC decided that

---

[15] Ortiz-Catalan, Max, Rannveig A. Guðmundsdóttir, Morten B. Kristoffersen, Alejandra Zepeda-Echavarria, Kerstin Caine-Winterberger, Katarzyna Kulbacka-Ortiz, Cathrine Widehammar et al. "Phantom motor execution facilitated by machine learning and augmented reality as treatment for phantom limb pain: a single group, clinical trial in patients with chronic intractable phantom limb pain." *The Lancet* 388, no. 10062 (2016): 2885-2894.

[16] Section 3(k) of the Patents Act 1970.

[17] Allen, Lynne. "The Patentability of Computer Programs: Merrill Lynch's Patent for a Financial Services System." *Ind. LJ* 59 (1983): 633.

"any invention which is from the existing only if it uses a mathematical algorithm which implements novelty and non-obviousness can be eligible for a patent. The algorithm per se can also be measured as if it were a part of the existing invention." In Gottschalk v Benson, the U.S Supreme Court decided that "if a process directly claims to a numerical algorithm cannot claim for patent as the patent would anticipate the mathematical formula, which is not under the criteria for patentability."

- Novelty/New: Novelty is the backbone of patent law, as a patent is granted only on an invention that is novel or new and not previously available in the public domain. It demands that the subject matter sought to be patented should not fall under the category of "prior art," which includes everything known, made, or used publicly before a patent application's filing date or priority date.[18] This novelty test involves comparing the claimed invention against existing technologies or publications. In case the invention is identical, or a sole prior art fully discloses its features, it fails the novelty test. AR/VR technologies revolutionized the healthcare sector, offering novel solutions for medical training, patient care, surgery, and therapy. Patenting such AR/VR healthcare inventions depends upon complying with novelty and other norms, like inventive steps and usefulness.

The living anatomical structure overlaid by AR-based systems provided in the operating room or the immersive medical training via the VR platform are some examples of innovative solutions for this field. And because these inventions have to show something the field never knew, they would certainly pass the novelty test to be considered.

- Inventive steps and Non-obviousness: Non-obviousness, also known as inventive steps, is a primary patentability requirement. Non-obviousness is a quality in patent law describing something that is not readily apparent.[19] To get a patent, an innovation must not be obvious to someone skilled in a relevant field. In healthcare, revolutionary solutions introduced by AR/VR usually challenge the boundaries of an inventive step assessment. Some applications include surgical planning, real-time medical imaging, rehabilitation, and training simulations. To patent AR/VR healthcare inventions, one has to prove that the inventions go beyond obvious developments in these domains. Whilst patentable non-obviousness criteria are the same across jurisdictions, the assessment of non-obviousness differs by nation. The goal of the non-obviousness is to prevent patenting inventions that only result through "normal product design and development."[20]
- Usefulness and Industrial Application: One of the most essential criteria for patenting an innovation is its utility and industrial application. The industrial applicability requirement ensures that an invention can be produced or used within an industry.[21] The product must have the capacity to be reproduced and to have at least one definite application within an industry to meet this criterion.[22] The process should show

---

[18] WIPO. "What Is a Patent?" https://www.wipo.int/patents/en/.
[19] Legal information institute. https://www.law.cornell.edu/wex/nonobviousness.
[20] Williams, D. M., and T. K. Bandopadhyaya. "An Analysis of Obviousness Standard in Patent Law-US And Indian Perspective." *Rajiv Gandhi School of Intellectual Property Law, IIT-Kharagpur, India* (2009).
[21] Section 2(1)(ac) of the Indian Patents Act 1970.
[22] Kankanala, Kalyan C. *FUN IP: Fundamentals of intellectual property*. Literators Publishing, 2012.

practical usability in the industrial environment to meet the requirements of this criterion. Uncertain, vague, speculative, or non-specific uses do not qualify as valid applications. Moreover, trivial or lacking credibility for either a product or process use will not pass the industrial applicability threshold.[23]

3.2. Patent Protection in AR/VR

Due to the fast-paced technology, protecting those inventions has become crucial for every invention. The key challenge faced by the innovator/inventor is the lack of proper guidelines and regulations that can assess which inventions would serve the society at large and which inventions are contrary to public order or morality or could harm living organisms. In 2021, the U.S. saw a significant number of AR/VR technologies getting patents, with China leading in granting patents on these technologies.[24] In the US, patent protection is governed by flexible laws that offer more leeway than the more stringent conditions set by Indian patent laws. United States patent law takes an explanatory approach by stating what can be patented, enhancing the legal protection for innovation. However, Indian patent law imposed non-patentable subject matter. The process of patenting AR/VR involves certain criteria. The patent application can be rejected if this technology does not fall within the criteria mentioned in section 3 of the Act. The evolving nature of AR/VR technologies and the rise of patent grants from other countries would be challenging for the Indian patent system. With the slow pace, the legal framework for AR/VR patents in India is still evolving, as there is still a lack of proper provisions to govern these advanced technologies. The existing law that can be administered is under Intellectual Property Law, including those related to Copyrights, Patents, and Trademarks. Under the Indian Patent Act, to meet the requirement for patent protection, AR/VR must fulfil three essential criteria, which are novelty, non-obviousness, and industrial application, which have already been mentioned above.

These requirements form the foundation of patent law and are such that only genuine inventions useful and implementable in AR/VR technologies receive protection. However, due to the technical and multifaceted nature of AR/VR innovations, these criteria are often not satisfied in drafting. The specification should be well drafted to prove that patent claims are novelty, have inventive steps, and have industrial applicability in healthcare scenarios. In addition, Indian patentability innovations include "*discovering new properties, new uses for existing substances, mathematical or business methods, computer programs, and algorithms.*"[25] The eligibility of AR/VR technology to claim patent protection in India can be subject to software patentability. The Patent 2002 amendment clarified that "computer programs per se" are not patentable. Sec 3(k) excludes some computer programs from being treated as inventions, though computer programs themselves are not inventions. Computer

---

[23] Kalyan C. Kankanala. "Patentability requirements in India". BananaIP September 2019 https://www.bananaip.com/patentability-requirements-in-india/

[24] Srikanth Jandhyala, Karthik Kumar, Rajeev Gupta. "Augmented Reality/Virtual Reality Patent Prosecution updated: 2021 Q4 Prosecution Statistics". Finnegan, April 2022. https://www.finnegan.com/en/insights/blogs/prosecution-first/augmented-realityvirtual-reality-patent-prosecution-update-2021-q4-prosecution-statistics.html.

[25] Section 3(k) of the Indian Patents Act, 1970.

programs and their industrial applications in technology are patentable inventions. Computer programs combined with hardware are also patentable.

4. Patent Granted on AR/VR Technologies in Healthcare: Data Analysis

According to the World Intellectual Property Organization (WIPO), patent applications for virtual reality were classified according to technical/functional components and application areas. The emerging innovation area in AR and VR technologies in health care underlines their intersection with advanced computing applications in the medical field. No data is available to specify the distinct patent applications and grants concerning AR/VR in the healthcare sector. However, the European Patent Office and IPO have published data regarding patent applications and grants in medical technology, computer technology, Biomedical, and pharmaceuticals. AR/VR technology could fall under medical and computer technology.

The table below provides the top companies in the AR/VR field. They relate to CPCs (Cooperative Patent Classifications) and keyword-based searches to extract top companies (assignees) operating in the subject domain. Table 1 illustrates the top companies with the maximum number of worldwide patents in the AR/VR field. (Data extracted from Sagacious Elevate.com).[26]

Table 1. Top companies in the AR/VR field

Sl. No	Name of the Top Companies in the AR/VR Field	No. of patent Grant
1	Samsung	4330
2	LG Electronics	2580
3	Sony	2568
4	Microsoft	2310
5	Facebook/Meta	1740
6	Apple	1229
7	Google	1160
8	Epson	676
9	Magic Leap	620

Based on the above data, a competitive landscape is dominated by major technology companies and their commitment to innovation in these immersive technologies. In the above sector, Samsung takes the lead with an impressive 4,330 patents, showing its strong emphasis on AR/VR as part of its broader technological portfolio. Samsung's patents mainly concentrate on display technologies, head-mounted devices, and software frameworks, thus leading to hardware integration for immersive experiences. 2580 patents have closely followed LG Electronics, while Sony's patents stand at 2568. LG's strengths lie in its display and sensor technology advancements, which are key for AR/VR. Sony concentrates on games, besides its immersive media, on top of its AR/VR-related product lines, such as the PlayStation VR. The above have gained substantial niches that ride on their strengths from the consumer electronics sector.

[26] Amit Kuman, Pallavi Sinha. "Augmented and virtual reality innovations and patent trends". Sagacious. https://sagaciousresearch.com/blog/augmented-virtual-reality-innovations-and-patent-trends/.

Microsoft is a massive company with 2310 patents, mainly focusing on business and healthcare solutions for AR/VR. Mixed reality innovation exemplifies wide applications, which can be found in HoloLens- in medical training, aiding surgery or designing industrial design. Its strength is that its patents reveal that Microsoft has developed a fully integrated AR/VR. Meta (formerly Facebook), with 1740 patents in hand, is one of the leaders in VR, not least because it acquired Oculus. Meta has patents in areas of social experiences in immersive environments, VR hardware, and apps for the metaverse; healthcare-related VR solutions to support therapy and mental health are also in demand and growing.

Apple and Google also play a crucial role in AR/VR and lead with 1229 and 1160 patents, respectively. Their applications are more of a broad ecosystem of user-friendly and visually integrated gadgets like headsets. As it targets mass adoption, Google has been targeting and perfecting the software and data integration for VR platforms like Google Cardboard or augmented reality tools. For instance, the specialised players, such as Epson and Magic Leap, hold 676 and 620 patents, respectively. While Epson primarily targets AR display technologies that function in various industrial applications and medical equipment, Magic Leap is a tech powerhouse emphasising broader usage in creating an environment for a better and augmented spatial experience (Data extracted from the *U.S Food & Drug Administration website*). Table 2 summarizes the FDA-classified medical devices incorporating AR/VR technologies across various medical disciplines.

Table 2. Medical device incorporate AR/VR across medical disciplines according to FDA

Sl. No	Name of the Medical Device Incorporate AR/VR Across Medical Disciplines	Number of Medical Devices Incorporate AR/VR Across Medical Disciplines
1	Radiology	28
2	Orthopaedic	25
3	Physical Medicine	6
4	Ophthalmic	3
5	Cardiovascular	2
6	Ear, Nose, & Throat	2
7	Neurology	2
8	General and Plastic Surgery	1
	Total	69

The above table on medical devices with AR/VR technology across various medical fields shows an increasing acceptance of these technologies in healthcare. The results show that Radiology leads with 28 devices, showing how AR/VR can enhance medical imaging and diagnostic accuracy. The above table indicates that AR/VR has transformed and helped doctors to practice or prepare their surgery using simulation through augmented or in 3D settings, thus making it easily accessible and able to study complex anatomical data just like in real-time. Orthopaedic application is the second highest with 25 devices, and they are commonly used in pre-surgical planning, steering in Orthopaedic procedures and rehabilitation. This helps in improving surgical outcomes by visualizing bones and joints.

Furthermore, VR-based rehabilitation programs are increasingly used to assist patients in regaining mobility through entertaining and gamified physical therapy activities. Physical medicine uses six devices in rehabilitation and therapy. Virtual reality environments can mimic real-world conditions. Patients can, therefore, train their motor skills and cognitive processes in a controlled environment. This method is helpful for post-stroke rehabilitation, pain management, and mobility difficulties. Ophthalmic devices show an increasing usage of AR/VR in eye care. It uses those technologies to formulate new diagnostic tools, simulate surgical procedures, and educate patients. For instance, AR headsets help ophthalmologist perform complex procedures by projecting necessary information into their visual field.

Cardiovascular, neurology and ear, nose & throat (ENT) applications are less prominent with two devices each. AR/VR technology is being researched in cardiovascular care for surgical planning and training, and 3D heart representations are being used to enhance procedural precision. In neurology, VR environments are used in neurorehabilitation and cognitive treatment, and in AR, one can see brain parts during surgery. ENT applications apply AR to enhance the visualization of complex anatomical regions in surgical procedures, such as sinus surgery. General and plastic surgery have only one device, meaning AR/VR is still developing in these specialities. The two technologies will change the game of surgical planning because they allow surgeons to view and manipulate 3D models of a patient's anatomy before they make the final surgical intervention.

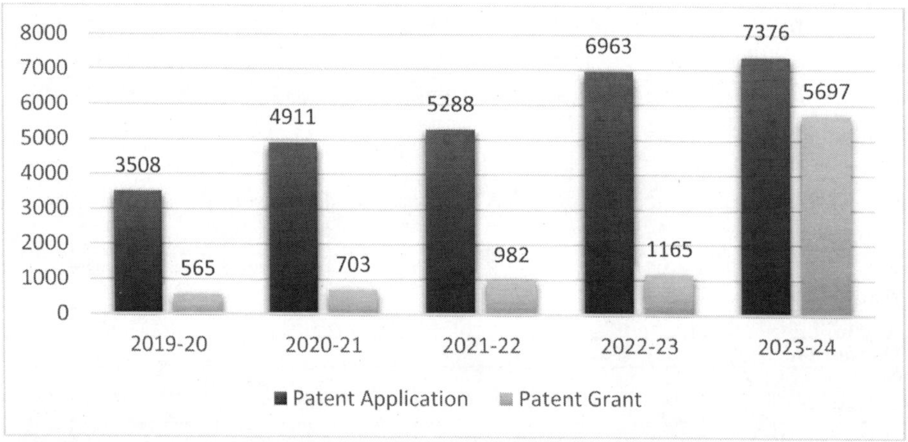

Figure 1. Biomedical Patent filed and granted in India from 2019- 20 to 2023-24 (IPO Website).

Figure 1 shows that the Biomedical patent filed in India from 2015 to 2022 to 2023-24 expresses a distinct pattern. The patent filing rates gradually increased from 2019 to 2024. There are 3508 patent applications filed and 565 patent grants in 2019-2020. In 2020-2021, it slightly increased with 4911 patent applications and 703 patent grants. This indicates that interest in biomedical science was growing and continued. According to Figure 1 above, patent applications and grants have grown marginally every financial year. The highest peak was 7376 patent applications and 5697 patent grants in the last financial year of 2023-2024.

5. Patenting AR/VR Healthcare Innovations: Moral and Ethical Challenge

The disadvantages for the users of VR can be divided into three, i.e., data gathering, inference, physical injury, and manipulation of the immersive experience.[27] VR systems utilise haptic,

[27] Adams, Devon, Alseny Bah, Catherine Barwulor, Nureli Musaby, Kadeem Pitkin, and Elissa M. Redmiles. "Ethics emerging: the story of privacy and security perceptions in virtual reality." In *Fourteenth Symposium on Usable Privacy and Security (SOUPS 2018)*, pp. 427-442. 2018.

audio, and video input to diagnose medical conditions, enhance simulation, and maximise revenues.[28] Many headsets are always on, so data collection is conducted without the user's knowledge and could be marketed to others or exposed to known vulnerabilities. Thus, affecting the quality and cost of advertised good services of AR/VR technology in healthcare. Moreover, health professionals should be familiar with three key concepts that provide video sides a basis for many current ethical principles. The concepts are respect for persons, beneficence, and fairness. At this point, it is expected to refer to Beauchamp and Childress' principles of ethics.

5.1. Principle of Autonomy

The essential idea in medical ethics that requires practitioners to respect individuals' rights to make informed healthcare decisions is the principle of autonomy. Considering the unique nature of AR/VR in healthcare, this principle becomes even more essential. AR/VR healthcare technologies could be sensitive. At some point, patients must give up their rights to collect their data for research or marketing. To tackle this issue, patients must obtain informed consent to help them understand the advantages and disadvantages of collecting their data for medical research. For instance, in VR-based therapy for mental health disorders, i.e., anxiety or post-traumatic stress disorder, patients should be informed of possible consequences such as emotional discomfort. Such open communication is essential to enable the patient to make their own decisions regarding their participation.[29] Some researchers have highlighted the necessity of clearly communicating VR technology's imaginative and exploratory character to avoid creating an unfulfilled expectation or mistaken impression. VR exposure therapy for phobias needs to be designed to gradually expose patients to fearful stimuli without overwhelming them. Ethical rules should disapprove the usage of AR/VR technology in ways that improperly use people's vulnerabilities or impair their decision-making power.[30]

Moreover, ethical use and patient data protection regarding autonomy in AR/VR come into play. It often collects sensitive personal information of biometric data and behaviour. The institute must maintain its patients' rights while collecting, storing, and using the data. Transparency must play a huge role in dealing with patients' data, and consent must be required to use it. To do so, legislative frameworks such as the General Data Protection Regulation and Health Insurance Portability and Accountability Act must safeguard patients' personal.[31]

---

[28] Rizzo, Albert, Jarrell Pair, Peter J. McNerney, Ernie Eastlund, Brian Manson, Jon Gratch, Randy Hill, and Bill Swartout. "Development of a VR therapy application for Iraq war military personnel with PTSD." *Studies in health technology and informatics* 111 (2005): 407-413.

[29] Kim, Hyeon-Young, and Eun-Young Kim. "Effects of medical education program using virtual reality: a systematic review and meta-analysis." *International Journal of Environmental Research and Public Health* 20, no. 5 (2023): 3895.

[30] Seymour-Walsh, A., Weber, A., Bell, A. "The ethical considerations of immersive technology in healthcare." Advances in Medical Ethics (2021).

[31] Sugiura, Atsushi, Toshihiro Kitama, Masahiro Toyoura, and Xiaoyang Mao. "The use of augmented reality technology in medical museums." *Teaching Anatomy: A Practical Guide* (2020): 337-347.

5.2. Principle of Beneficence

The concept of beneficence, which focuses on doing good to persons and preventing harm, is paramount in healthcare ethics. Beneficence must be applied in AR/VR technologies to help improve patient outcomes and ethically yet effectively enhance medical training and healthcare concerns.

AR and VR technology in healthcare has significantly improved patient care by diagnosing complicated diseases and using new types of therapies, which also have very successful results for rehabilitation. For example, using VR simulation, a patient can feel less pain for people who suffer from chronic pain by providing an immersive alteration to reduce the pain. Various research studies have proven that virtual reality therapies in managing pain can reduce pain scores substantially with no need for extra drugs, thereby reducing side effects and maximizing general welfare.[32] AR and VR technology best represent the beneficence principle by improving patient results through non-invasive methods. For mental health treatment, such as exposure therapy for anxiety disorders, PTSD, and phobias, VR can help by creating a safe virtual environment that can relax the anxiety under supervision. This has proven to reduce symptoms considerably while increasing the quality of life for most affected persons. [33]VR, in giving an individualised, effective treatment to a patient, enhances mental well-being and emotional condition among patients. This practice respects the ethical requirement of putting the interests of such a patient first.

The principle of beneficence aims to do good for society. AR and VR technology could help minimise risks and improve safety for the patient. AR allows surgeons to examine the inner structure of human anatomy more clearly during procedures, leading to fewer complications. Likewise, VR-based simulations allow surgeons to rehearse high-risk surgery without endangering actual patients. AR/VR healthcare technologies adhere to the principle of beneficence by easing dangers for their patient and enhancing safety.[34]

5.3. Principle of Nonmaleficence

Nonmaleficence, or do no harm, is a fundamental principle in medical ethics. It mandates that healthcare providers reduce risks and avoid acts that may cause damage to the patient. This concept is particularly significant in using AR/VR in healthcare, as these technologies are novel and sophisticated. AR and VR healthcare technologies are available to minimise the physical and psychological risk for patients with motion sickness. VR occurs under the designation "cyber sickness," mainly dizziness, nausea and fatigue symptoms or simply visual strain when there has been an extended period of exposure to VR, and confusion sometimes. To achieve nonmaleficence, health professionals must limit the time to carry out VR, individualize the experience to specific patients, and ensure proper device calibration. The second danger of

---

[32] Garrett, Bernie, et al. "A rapid evidence assessment of immersive virtual reality as an adjunct therapy in acute pain management in clinical practice." *The Clinical journal of pain* 30.12 (2014): 1089-1098.

[33] Freeman, Daniel, Sarah Reeve, Abi Robinson, Anke Ehlers, David Clark, Bernhard Spanlang, and Mel Slater. "Virtual reality in the assessment, understanding, and treatment of mental health disorders." *Psychological medicine* 47, no. 14 (2017): 2393-2400.

[34] McMenamin, Paul G., Michelle R. Quayle, Colin R. McHenry, and Justin W. Adams. "The production of anatomical teaching resources using three-dimensional (3D) printing technology." *Anatomical sciences education* 7, no. 6 (2014): 479-486.

psychological types, like triggering anxiety or emotional discomfort in immersive settings, also has to be minimised, especially in susceptible populations like patients diagnosed with PTSD or those who are suffering from phobias.

AR and VR experiences would lead to significant engagements, but poorly designed applications will likely cause harm. For example, under extreme or traumatic events in VR simulation, the condition might deteriorate for the patient in question instead. Developers need, therefore, to collaborate with healthcare experts to ensure these simulations are well-designed based on evidence and in concomitance with therapeutic intentions. Continuous patient monitoring and feedback are crucial for improving these experiences and avoiding damage.[35] For instance, the high price of technologies can reduce their reachability and accessibility to marginalised people. This exacerbates the prevailing healthcare inequities. Nonmaleficence requires action to have the technology reach patients across all social classes. This would involve fighting for policies that promote equitable distribution and help vulnerable populations surmount financial obstacles.[36]

5.4. Principle of Justice

The principle of justice in AR/VR healthcare is the fair distribution of resources, equal access to new technologies, and impartial medical decision-making. As AR/VR provide new healthcare, the ethical application of the principle of justice ensures that AR/VR healthcare should be able to provide equal access to all the patients who require this technology without worsening the present situation. Although AR/VR healthcare technologies have great potential in medicine, their affordability remains challenging due to the high cost of infrastructure and the accessibility to patients who do not have health insurance or who are from backwards classes. For these patients, there will be challenges in accessing these technologies. In this matter, the Patent system plays a crucial role in granting AR/VR healthcare technologies.

Moreover, the principle of Justice obliges to be allotted according to medical need and potential effect rather than capability to pay.[37] For example, VR therapy for chronic pain or rehabilitation should be made available to patients who benefit the most rather than the institutions with more financial resources. Therefore, AR/VR technology in healthcare should be guided by transparency and ethical frameworks.

Conclusion and Suggestion

AR and VR have transformed the medical landscape by bringing innovations in diagnosis, treatment, medical education, and the involvement of patients in the medical process. Patenting these technologies would raise substantial legal and ethical dilemmas. Innovation growth

---

[35] Bell, I. H., et al. "Virtual reality as a clinical tool in mental health research and practice." *npj Digital Medicine* 3, Article 142 (2020).

[36] AlGerafi, Mohammed AM, Yueliang Zhou, Mohamed Oubibi, and Tommy Tanu Wijaya. "Unlocking the potential: A comprehensive evaluation of augmented reality and virtual reality in education." Electronic*s* 12, no. 18 (2023): 3953.

[37] Ray, Sougat, Shabeena Tawar, Neha Singh, and Gurpreet Singh. "Transition toward Technological Transformation: Challenges of Implementing Virtual Reality and Augmented Reality in the Health Sector." Journal of Marine Medical Society 26, no. 2 (2024): 161-164.

should maintain equilibrium with the moral problems solved to support the responsible development of AR/VR health technologies. Under the Patents Act, inventions must meet three criteria to protect them: novelty, non-obviousness, and industrial usefulness. AR/VR technologies generally meet these criteria because they are cutting-edge and valuable in practice. However, the intangible and algorithm-driven elements create uncertainty regarding protection under the Patents Act 1970. Section 3(k) of the Act frequently questions whether these AR/VR innovations would be patentable since the provision prohibits "mathematical or business methods or computer programs" per se from being patented.

AR/VR technologies that tie together with healthcare applications, the question would then arise as to whether the software-driven features of their technologies are merely algorithms or technological innovations with practical advantages. By looking into the patentable subject matter, under novelty, AR/VR qualified for the patent invention as AR/VR inventions in healthcare are new and novel; under non-obviousness, AR/VR might not be qualified as AR/VR in healthcare is evident for people who are expert in the field of this technologies, under industrial application AR/VR invention in healthcare have industrial application for medical education, treatment therapy for patients who have a phobia, for surgery preparation by scanning patient's whole body or part of the body and so on.

The present Indian patent requires an update on the features of new technologies with international standards. The significant legal challenges have been related to public health regulations and accessibility. Section 3(b) of the Patents Act of 1970 provides that patents are barred from inventions which could often involve public order or morality. This provision is vital in the light of AR/VR healthcare technologies, which could have raised concerns about protecting data, equal access, or abuse of power. For instance, VR healthcare treatment and AR-based surgical or medical training equipment must be carefully evaluated to protect patients and healthcare inequalities. A standard protocol for reviewing AR/VR technology patent applications is required to address these concerns and ensure public confidence.

Patenting healthcare-related inventions goes beyond mere compliance with the current law. By granting a patent on healthcare technology, the patent holder will be given exclusive rights for over 20 years. These patented inventions will prevent access from others. Preventing others from accessing treatment or not being able to afford the treatment could violate the principle of justice and the fundamental requirement for healthcare. New forms of balancing between the patent holder's right and the public objectives of universal healthcare access are required, which include forced licensing or open-source models. It has been argued that any inventions related to healthcare should not be patented, and they should be in the hands of the government so that society at large will enjoy them at a reasonable price. This could be ideal for everyone; however, it might be a nightmare for the inventors who have spent hours, money and resources, on their invention and could have lost motivation to improve or invent new technology that could benefit human beings. It is significant for the policymaker to establish a framework that will encourage innovation without being skewed toward the monopolisation of AR/VR technology at the cost of public health.

Moreover, AR/VR technology in healthcare creates issues concerning data privacy and informed consent. The granting of the technology has to satisfy moral and legal conditions concerned with data protection. Such harmonisation needs to be created between intellectual property authorities, healthcare regulators, and organisations on data protection to offer all-around rules in patenting AR/VR inventions. Legal and moral obligations require a diversified approach to finding a solution instead of leaving it open for interpretation by the court; explicit provisions and details need to be added to the Act. The Patents Act 1970 should be revised explicitly, recognise AR/VR technology as unique, and have separate provisions that include all the possible inventions that could come shortly. Such advocacy from governments, businesses, and health practitioners could standardise and harmonise guidelines on patenting emerging healthcare technology systems for AR/VR.

In conclusion, patenting AR/VR technologies in health care under the Indian Patents Act 1970 is challenging but working on stimulating inventions while sustaining moral values is essential. So far, India has managed to dispel these technologies' legal uncertainties and ethical quandaries. However, better implementation of intellectual property rights is required for upcoming technologies.

References

AlGerafi, Mohammed AM, Yueliang Zhou, Mohamed Oubibi, and Tommy Tanu Wijaya. "Unlocking the potential: A comprehensive evaluation of augmented and virtual reality in education." *Electronics* 12, no. 18 (2023): 3953.

Allen, Lynne. "The Patentability of Computer Programs: Merrill Lynch's Patent for a Financial Services System." *Ind. LJ* 59 (1983): 633.

Amit Kuman, Pallavi Sinha. "Augmented and virtual reality innovations and patent trends." Sagacious. https://sagaciousresearch.com/blog/augmented-virtual-reality-innovations-and-patent-trends/.

Bala, Rajni, and Rajni Saini. "A Study of AR and VR in the Real World." In *Applications of Neuromarketing in the Metaverse*, pp. 271-290. *IGI Global*, 2023.

Barsom, Esther Z., Maurits Graafland, and Marlies P. Schijven. "Systematic review on the effectiveness of augmented reality applications in medical training." *Surgical endoscopy* 30 (2016): 4174-4183.

Bell, I. H., et al., "Virtual reality as a clinical tool in mental health research and practice." npj Digital Medicine 3, Article 142 (2020).

Bottani, Eleonora, and Giuseppe Vignali. "Augmented reality technology in the manufacturing industry: A review of the last decade." *Iise Transactions* 51, no. 3 (2019): 284-310.

Bush, Jimmy. "Viability of virtual reality exposure therapy as a treatment alternative." *Computers in Human Behavior* 24, no. 3 (2008): 1032-1040.

Bye, Kent, Diane Hosfelt, Sam Chase, Matt Miesnieks, and Taylor Beck. "The ethical and privacy implications of mixed reality." In *ACM SIGGRAPH 2019 Panels*, pp. 1-2. 2019.

Cobb, Sue VG, Sarah Nichols, Amanda Ramsey, and John R. Wilson. "Virtual reality-induced symptoms and effects (VRISE)." *Presence: Teleoperators & Virtual Environments* 8, no. 2 (1999): 169-186.

Devon, Adams, Alseny Bah, Catherine Barwulor, Nureli Musaby, Kadeem Pitkin. "Ethics emerging: The story of privacy and security perceptions in virtual reality." In *Fourteenth Symposium on Usable Privacy and Security (SOUPS 2018)*, pp. 427-442. 2018.

Duan, X., Liu, X., Deng, J. "Equitable access to healthcare technologies: Challenges and solutions for AR/VR." *Global Health Journal*. (2020).

Fisher, Rebecca A., Suewan Kim, and Prokar Dasgupta. "The Future of Surgery." *Digital Surgery* (2021): 419-427.

Fluet, Gerard, Alma Merians, Jigna Patel, Anita Van Wingerden, Qinyin Qiu, Matthew Yarossi, Eugene Tunik, Sergei Adamovich, and Supriya Massood. "Virtual reality-augmented rehabilitation for patients in sub-acute phase post-stroke: a feasibility study." In *Proc. 10th Intl Conf. Disability, Virtual Reality & Associated Technologies*, pp. 2-4. 2014.

Freeman, Daniel, Sarah Reeve, Abi Robinson, Anke Ehlers, David Clark, Bernhard Spanlang, and Mel Slater. "Virtual reality in the assessment, understanding, and treatment of mental health disorders." *Psychological Medicine* 47, no. 14 (2017): 2393-2400.

Garrett, Bernie, et al., "A rapid evidence assessment of immersive virtual reality as an adjunct therapy in acute pain management in clinical practice." *The Clinical journal of pain* 30.12 (2014): 1089-1098.

Gottschalk v Benson (1972) 409 U.S. 63 (1972).

Guillot, Craig. "The Kaiser Permanente Bernard J. Tyson School of Medicine's Anatomy Resource Center uses technology to aid in teaching about the human body." *Health Tech*, 23 November 2021. https://healthtechmagazine.net/article/2021/11/qa-dr-jose-m-barral-using-virtual-tools-anatomy-education

Hoffman, Hunter, Gloria Chamber, Walter Meyer, Lisa Arceneaux, William Russel, Eric Seibel, Todd Richard, Sam R Sharar, David R Patterson. "Virtual reality as a bridge to equitable healthcare access." *Journal of Telemedicine and e-Health*.2021

Horowitz, Brian. " Medical schools and healthcare institutions are implementing AR, VR and XR training to enable repeatable immersive surgical simulations that bring valuable practice." *Health Tech*, 15 December 2022. https://healthtechmagazine.net/article/2022/12/ar-vr-medical-training-2023-perfcon.

Hsieh, Min-Chai, and Jia-Jin Lee. "Preliminary study of VR and AR applications in medical and healthcare education." *J Nurs Health Stud* 3, no. 1 (2018): 1.

J.D. Houvener. "Patenting in Virtual (VR) and Augmented (AR) Reality." *Bold Patent*, February 2023 https://boldip.com/blog/patenting-in-virtual-vr-and-augmented-ar-reality/.

Kale, P. "Patents in the metaverse: an analysis of scope and challenges." *Industry and Higher Education* 39, no. 2 (2024): 155–167.

Kalyan C. Kankanala. "*Patentability requirements in India*." BananaIP September 2019 https://www.bananaip.com/patentability-requirements-in-india/.

Kankanala, Kalyan C. *FUN IP: Fundamentals of intellectual property*. Literators Publishing, 2012.

Kern, Donna H., Arch G. Mainous III, Maura Carey, and Anne Beddingfield. "Simulation-based teaching to improve cardiovascular exam skills performance among third-year medical students." *Teaching and Learning in Medicine* 23, no. 1 (2011): 15-20.

Kim, Hyeon-Young, and Eun-Young Kim. "Effects of medical education program using virtual reality: a systematic review and meta-analysis." *International Journal of Environmental Research and Public Health* 20, 5 (2023): 3895.

Kourtesis, Panagiotis. "A Comprehensive Review of Multimodal XR Applications, Risks, and Ethical Challenges in the Metaverse." *Multimodal Technologies and Interaction* 8, no. 11 (2024): 98.

Kuhail, Mohammad Amin, Jose Berengueres, Fatma Taher, and Mariam Al Kuwaiti. "Advances, Applications and the Future of Haptic Technology." (2024).

Lee, S., J. Lee, A. Lee, N. Park, S. Song, A. Seo, H. Lee, J-I. Kim, and K. Eom. "Augmented reality intravenous injection simulator based 3D medical imaging for veterinary medicine." *The Veterinary Journal* 196, no. 2 (2013): 197-202.

Legal information institute. https://www.law.cornell.edu/wex/nonobviousness.

Liu, Kai, Weiwei Zhang, Wei Li, Ting Wang, and Yanxue Zheng. "Effectiveness of virtual reality in nursing education: a systematic review and meta-analysis." *BMC Medical Education* 23, no. 1 (2023): 710.

McMenamin, Paul G., Michelle R. Quayle, Colin R. McHenry, and Justin W. Adams. "The production of anatomical teaching resources using three-dimensional (3D) printing technology." *Anatomical sciences education* 7, no. 6 (2014): 479-486.

Miloff, Alexander, Philip Lindner, William Hamilton, Lena Reuterskiöld, Gerhard Andersson, and Per Carlbring. "Single-session gamified virtual reality exposure therapy for spider phobia vs. traditional exposure therapy: study protocol for a randomized controlled non-inferiority trial." *Trials* 17 (2016): 1-8.

Nagesh H Karale. "A comparative analysis of patent grant processes in India and the United States." Ipleaders, September 2023. https://blog.ipleaders.in/a-comparative-analysis-of-patent-grant-processes-in-india-and-the-united-states/

Nicholson, Daren T., Colin Chalk, W. Robert J. Funnell, and Sam J. Daniel. "Can virtual reality improve anatomy education? A randomised controlled study of a computer-generated three-dimensional anatomical ear model." *Medical education* 40, no. 11 (2006): 1081-1087.

O'Brolcháin, Fiachra, Tim Jacquemard, David Monaghan, Noel O'Connor, Peter Novitzky, and Bert Gordijn. "The convergence of virtual reality and social networks: threats to privacy and autonomy." *Science and engineering ethics* 22 (2016): 1-29.

Olver, Ian, Susan Dodds, Jeremy Kenner, Ian Kerridge, Kevin McGovern, Eleanor Milligan, Robin Mortimer, and Australian Health Ethics Committee of the National Health and Medical Research Council. "Ethical considerations relating to healthcare resource allocation decisions." Internal Medicine Journal 49, no. 11 (2019): 1364-1367.

Ortiz-Catalan, Max, Rannveig A. Guðmundsdóttir, Morten B. Kristoffersen, Alejandra Zepeda-Echavarria, Kerstin Caine-Winterberger, Katarzyna Kulbacka-Ortiz, Cathrine Widehammar et al., "Phantom motor execution facilitated by machine learning and augmented reality as treatment for phantom limb pain: a single group, clinical trial in patients with chronic intractable phantom limb pain." *The Lancet* 388, no. 10062 (2016): 2885-2894.

Osumi, M., A. Ichinose, M. Sumitani, N. Wake, Y. Sano, A. Yozu, S. Kumagaya, Y. Kuniyoshi, and S. Morioka. "Restoring movement representation and alleviating phantom limb pain through short-term neurorehabilitation with a virtual reality system." *European Journal of Pain* 21, no. 1 (2017): 140-147

Parker v Flook (1978) 437 U.S 584.

Ray, Sougat, Shabeena Tawar, Neha Singh, and Gurpreet Singh. "Transition toward Technological Transformation: Challenges of Implementing Virtual Reality and Augmented Reality in the Health Sector." Journal of Marine Medical Society 26, no. 2 (2024): 161-164.

Rizzo, Albert, Jarrell Pair, Peter J. McNerney, Ernie Eastlund, Brian Manson, Jon Gratch, Randy Hill, and Bill Swartout. "Development of a VR therapy application for Iraq war military personnel with PTSD." *Studies in health technology and informatics* 111 (2005): 407-413.

Saavedra, Augmented and virtual reality evolution, 320.

Sagacious https://sagaciousresearch.com/blog/augmented-virtual-reality-innovations-and-patent-trends/#Intellectual_Property_Landscape_in_AR_and_VR.

Sailesh Patel. "Protecting intellectual property in Augmented Reality." IP Watch Dog, May 2022. https://ipwatchdog.com/2022/05/31/protecting-intellectual-property-augmented-reality/id=149227/.

Section 2(1)(ac) of the Indian Patents Act 1970.

Section 3(k) of the Indian Patents Act, 1970.

Seymour-Walsh, A., Weber, A., Bell, A. "The ethical considerations of immersive technology in healthcare." *Advances in Medical Ethics (2021).*

Shivang Khandelwal, Muskaan Mandhyan and Aryan Jain. "India: Seeing Is Believing: The Future of IP in AR/VR." Mondaq, March 2023. https://www.mondaq.com/india/patent/1299888/seeing-is-believing-the-future-of-ip-in-arvr

Srikanth Jandhyala, Karthik Kumar, Rajeev Gupta. "Augmented Reality/Virtual Reality Patent Prosecution updated: 2021 Q4 Prosecution Statistics." Finnegan, April 2022. https://www.finnegan.com/en/insights/blogs/prosecution-first/augmented-realityvirtual-reality-patent-prosecution-update-2021-q4-prosecution-statistics.html.

Student, ASiT Medical, Daniel Baker, Praveena Deekonda, James Glasbey, Gemma Humm, Helen Mohan, Deirdre Nally et al., "Core content of the medical school surgical curriculum: Consensus report from the association of surgeons in training (ASIT)." *International Journal of Surgery* 84 (2020): 186-193.

Sugiura, Atsushi, Toshihiro Kitama, Masahiro Toyoura, and Xiaoyang Mao. "The use of augmented reality technology in medical museums." *Teaching Anatomy: A Practical Guide* (2020): 337-347.

U.S Food & Drugs Administration. https://www.fda.gov/medical-devices/digital-health-center-excellence/augmented-reality-and-virtual-reality-medical-devices.

Voss, Catalin, Peter Washington, Nick Haber, Aaron Kline, Jena Daniels, Azar Fazel, Titas De et al., "Superpower glass: delivering unobtrusive real-time social cues in wearable systems." In *Proceedings of the 2016 ACM International Joint Conference on Pervasive and Ubiquitous Computing: Adjunct*, pp. 1218-1226. 2016.

Weeks, Sharon R., Victoria C. Anderson-Barnes, and Jack W. Tsao. "Phantom limb pain: theories and therapies." *The Neurologist* 16, no. 5 (2010): 277-286.

Williams, D. M., and T. K. Bandyopadhyay. "An Analysis of Obviousness Standard in Patent Law-US And Indian Perspective." *Rajiv Gandhi School of Intellectual Property Law, IIT-Kharagpur, India* (2009).

WIPO. "What Is a Patent?" https://www.wipo.int/patents/en/.

Yetisen, Ali K., and Lisa R. Volpatti. "Patent protection and licensing in microfluidics." *Lab on a Chip* 14, no. 13 (2014): 2217-2225.

Chapter 17

Exergaming Implications in Various Fields of Rehabilitation: A Novel Approach to Physiotherapy

P. Ajith Kumar[*]
and T. Senthil Kumar[†]
Sri Ramachandra Faculty of Physiotherapy, SRIHER(DU), Chennai, India

Abstract

Exergaming, a combination of exercise and gaming utilised synchronously with an evolving innovation known as immersive technology, which includes virtual reality (VR) and augmented reality (AR). Incorporating the personalised rehabilitation depending on current trends, which enhances people's attention and interest in participation, yields a better functional result. Utilising the virtual reality (VR) and augmented reality (AR) with 3-dimensional animations, multiple spatial audio-visual cues and real-time feedback, as well as recreating a customised environment, is anticipated to increase people's interest in participation towards exercise-based rehabilitation. Immersive technological applications in many elements of rehabilitation assist patients' recovery from physical injuries, such as cerebrovascular insults, Parkinson's disease, orthopaedic injuries, other chronic illnesses and cardiopulmonary problems by replicating the real-life events and movement patterns during rehabilitation. Implementation of immersive technology to facilitate patients with cognitive impairments, such as traumatic brain injuries or neurological disorders, neurodegenerative diseases, by creating immersive interactive environments that stimulate cognitive functions of the brain. Immersive experiences can distract patients from experiencing the pain, especially chronic pain, and shall reduce discomfort during Virtual / Augmented reality-based therapy. It would be intuitive methods of rehabilitation with the benefits of immersive technology in the field of rehabilitation that would enhance the patient's engagement and encourage them to have higher adherence. Immersive technology allows therapists to personalise Exer-gaming programs to each patient's individual requirements. Addressing the problems and development of real-time feedback and modification of games depending on the symptoms may improve the effective implementation and outcome during rehabilitation. Remote rehabilitation using virtual or augmented reality is required to be implemented and introduced to provide easy access for patients with disabilities and chronic complications or injuries in rural or unsupervised

[*] Corresponding Author's Email: ajithkumarp@sriramachandra.edu.in
[†] Corresponding Author's Email: senthilkumar.t@sriramachandra.edu.in

In: Shaping Tomorrow
Editors: Prithi Samuel, A. Sathya, Balamurugan Balusamy et al.
ISBN: 979-8-90134-076-9

areas. Limitations and challenges in implementing the immersive technology include economic, feasibility, safety and reliability aspects. But still, some of the domains remain unexplored with technological advancements in implementations of VR/AR towards health care. Which would be the Artificial Intelligence (AI) that aids in breaking down the barrier of decision-making for therapists during the diagnosis and treatment. This chapter offered a brief of emphasising AR and VR transforming the future of rehabilitation into promising scenarios by bringing the enhanced clinical outcomes following rehabilitation.

Keywords: exergaming, virtual-rehabilitation, tele-rehabilitation, tele-monitoring, remote-rehabilitation, immersive technology, physical rehabilitation, virtual physiotherapy, tele-medicine

1. Introduction

This chapter provides basic utility and contribution of Virtual Reality (VR) and Augmented Reality (AR) in the field of rehabilitation. The Virtual Reality (VR) in the field of rehabilitation is a strategic approach towards patients' recovery by offering a simulated environment under a controlled, safe and sophisticated facility. Similarly, Augmented Reality (AR) involves virtual objects in achieving the project's focal scenarios, depending on the required order of bodily movements. Such advanced innovation would create a higher impact towards patients' adherence and therapeutic outcomes (Burdea 2000). Virtual Reality (VR) and Augmented Reality (AR) may contribute to expected movement patterns for the patients depending on the underlying medical condition of the patient. With an immersive experience and real-time feedback, patients participating in rehabilitation can get trained with reflective learning. Evidence suggests that "exergaming" in the field of rehabilitation by implementing movement sensors for effective monitoring would be an alternate source for routine rehabilitation protocols. The Clinical application of such technology varies widely, including orthopaedics, neurological, cardiovascular, paediatrics, geriatrics and sports injury-related rehabilitation. As the world faced the tragedy due to the pandemic led by COVID-19, it resulted in social isolation, which taught us to live utilising the virtual world. Henceforth VR and AR affirms to home based telerehabilitation for the patient facing inconvenience or requires assistance in reaching to centre or having inconvenience to participate in traditional method of rehabilitation (Bamodu and Ye, n.d.). The benefits expected in implementing such technology in the field of rehabilitation include,

1) Safety and Immersiveness
2) Recreating the impossible or challenging situations
3) Versatility of practising environment
4) Encourages active participation
5) Motivates and builds confidence among participants
6) Reduces stress and enhances progress in performance
7) Prevents or reduces dropout rates

Depending on the severity of the underlying medical condition and the functional recovery of the patient, various kinds of exergaming methods can be adopted. Upon the utility of hardware screens, Exergaming is classified into semi-immersive (Figure 7), which involves projections or large screens of visual experiences adopting 3D virtual spaces, for example: shooting a basketball with a simulation screen. Fully immersive type would include use of devices, such as wearables, such as head-mounted devices (VR headset), and other wearable devices that simulate real-life scenarios with realism, for example, Cognitive and Balance training utilising the VR Headset. Non-immersive type would involve the use of simple video game consoles and computer screens, for example: shooting games on a computer (Naqvi et al., 2024).

2. Principles of Virtual Reality (VR) and Augmented Reality (AR) in Rehabilitation

According to the World Health Organisation, Rehabilitation is defined as "a set of interventions designed to optimise functioning and reduce disability in individuals with health conditions in interaction with their environment" (Reference section 15). Rehabilitation is widely practised for all the disabilities that patients encounter after any underlying medical conditions, which might include physical, cognitive, developmental, sensory and intellectual factors. Across the globe, disability rights movements initiated the "Convention on the Rights of Persons with Disabilities," which was adopted by the United Nations on 3rd May 2008, to preserve the rights and dignity of persons with disabilities. Communication using verbal cues or tactile cues acts as a major source of elements during the conventional rehabilitation (Reference section 16). to implement such an effective communication medium in the VR or AR-based rehabilitation for the physical therapists, it may be challenging. According to the "Convention in the Rights of Persons with Disabilities" Article 2: Communication includes languages, display of text, Braille, tactile communication, large print, accessible multimedia as well as written, audio, plain-language, human-reader and augmentative and alternative modes, means and formats of communication, including accessible information and communication technology." Henceforth, the immersive technologies such as VR or AR themselves act as effective communication between patient and physical therapists (Cao 2016).

2.1. Hardware Components for Immersive Experience in Rehabilitation

Based on the underlying problem due to medical illness, the disability of the people varies, and the requirements of hardware components during practice are unique.

1) Head-mounted devices – VR Headset for balance training (Figure 1)
2) Motion sensors – Improving the joint range of motion
3) Haptic feedback devices – alerting response for positional variations (Figure 2)
4) VR treadmills – Endurance training (Figure 3b)

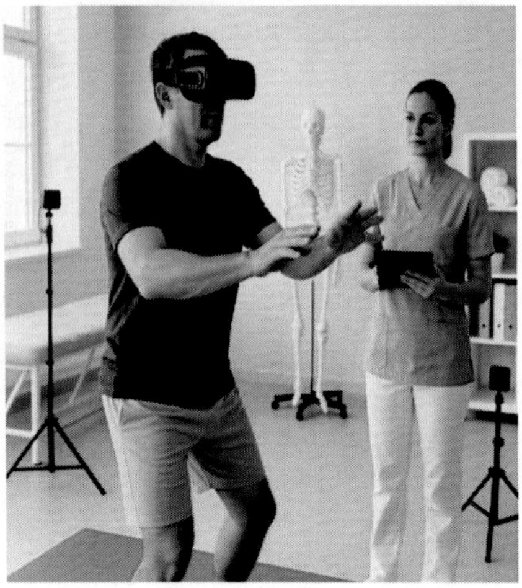

Figure 1. Wearable head mounted devise- VR Headsets (Conceptual Visualization).

Figure 2. Wearable Haptic sensor used as feedback. (Conceptual Visualization).

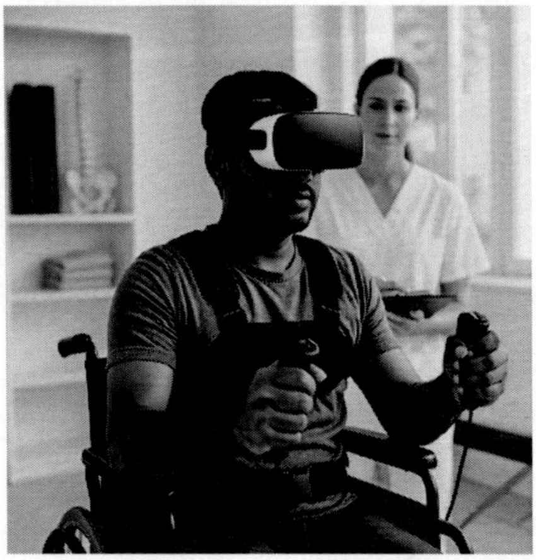

Figure 3a. VR using handheld sensors (Conceptual Visualization).

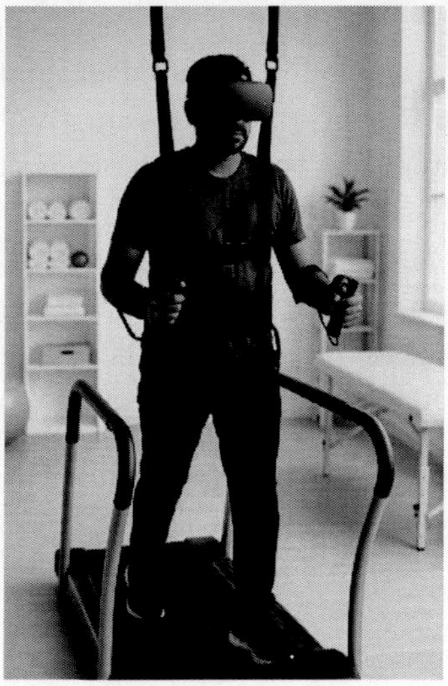

Figure 3b. VR treadmill with handheld device for Exergaming (Conceptual Visualization).

The Anticipated experience with VR or AR-based rehabilitation as a major component would be immersiveness with maximum involvement, and interaction with real-time feedback, also the customisation, depending on the expected outcomes.

2.2. Software Components for Immersive Experience in Rehabilitation

The Program that simulates a realistic environment for effective implementation of practices depends on the underlying disability. Programs like various games that can simulate balance and coordination for those people suffering from neurological diseases like Parkinson's disease, cerebral palsy, spinal cord injuries and cerebrovascular accidents can be practised and managed with such a model of rehabilitation. People who suffer from musculoskeletal weakness may require an advanced level of treatment which are managed with endurance and strength training. Participants are provided with activities such as throwing a ball to reach a target / gait training at a set speed, which might enhance the participants' endurance and strength. Participants who require cardiovascular endurance are classified into submaximal, maximal and supramaximal exercise training with such immersive technology. Activities such as VR treadmill, Aerobic exercises can be prescribed to enhance cardiovascular endurance. Games that enhance the agility, speed, performance and power of participants with gaming software programs like drills, football, basketball, and shooting a ball at targets are indicated for participants who have had sports injuries. Software program that encourages participants to effectively concentrate on reaction time are indicated for sports players.

2.3. Indications for Virtual Reality (VR) and Augmented Reality (AR) Aided Rehabilitation

This chapter primarily focuses on physical rehabilitation and the disabilities of mobility components due to underlying medical conditions. Rehabilitation is a diverse term which also includes auditory and speech rehabilitation, de-addiction rehabilitation, and vision rehabilitation, which was not covered in this chapter. Rehabilitation with physical disabilities due to underlying medical illness based on various bodily systems, such as Neurological, orthopaedic, Cardiovascular, pulmonary, obstetric and gynaecological conditions, is essential for recovery. Depending on the pathology of the underlying bodily system, different disability symptoms and elicited clinical features would lead to an altered quality of life for an individual. For example, People who suffer from underlying neurological disease have symptoms that vary from those with cardiovascular disease. Henceforth, the rehabilitation procedure and exercise prescription are modified based on the management required for symptoms or clinical features of the disease.

Physical Disabilities can be broadly stated as follows,

1) Mobility impairments
2) Vision impairments
3) Speech and auditory impairments

(Behavioural impairments would be considered as psychosocial alterations).

Focus of rehabilitation for physical disability or mobility impairments requires an exercise-based rehabilitation protocol specific to symptoms experienced by the patients. Exergaming must be prescribed depending on the symptom's specificity and underlying pathology. The modification feature of exergaming in accordance with disease symptoms is an important feature for the implementation of virtual rehabilitation for achieving effective outcomes.

3. Methods of Implementing Virtual Reality (VR) and Augmented Reality (AR) in Rehabilitation

3.1. Neurological Rehabilitation

Patients with either progressive neurological disease or acute neurological insults tend to develop symptoms that would be limiting the motor control, balance, coordination and mobility. Traditionally, it is managed using a typical rehabilitation setup (Figure 4). Depending on the area of involvement and nature of the disease, the symptoms are going to vary widely. Virtual reality-based rehabilitation posses advantages by creating an option for participants to practice repetitive tasks endlessly, which would be core components for improving any neurological symptoms. Neurological disorders, including amyotrophic lateral sclerosis, spinal cord injury, cerebrovascular accidents, Parkinson's disease, traumatic brain injury, Guillain-Barré syndrome, peripheral nerve injury, cerebral palsy, muscular dystrophy, and motor neuron disease, require extensive rehabilitation (Kwon, Park, and Koh 2023) (Feng H et al., 2017).

Debilitating physical mobility symptoms of include,

1) Muscle weakness
2) Tremor
3) Spasticity
4) Rigidity

5) Postural deformity
6) Chorea
7) Visuospatial disorder
8) Clonus
9) Reduced reaction time
10) Impaired gait pattern
11) Ataxia
12) Apraxia
13) Dyskinesia

Figure 4. Traditional physical therapy rehabilitation center.

3.2. Orthopaedical Rehabilitation

Musculoskeletal disorders are a wide spectrum of conditions that have acute symptoms which would restrict people's activity of daily living. The orthopaedical conditions indicated for rehabilitation include post-traumatic injuries, post-orthopaedic surgeries – total knee and hip arthroplasty, muscle injuries, nerve lesions, ligament injuries, compression radiculopathy, chronic low back pain, neck pain, osteoarthritis of the knee and hip joints, and periarthritis of the shoulders. The use of Virtual reality rehabilitation in pain modulation has been evident, but managing conditions with defective arthrokinematics requires expertise. Patients, due to senile nature or during their post-operative recovery period they are trained to ambulate independently, utilising either walking sticks or Quadri-pod walker (Figure 5). The virtual reality-based management for the above-mentioned conditions using exercise modulation is fully possible after the initial recovery in post-operative status. Figure 6 conceptually visualizes rehabilitation using Virtual Reality (VR) for wheelchair-dependent patients, illustrating an immersive therapeutic environment designed to enhance mobility, coordination, and cognitive engagement through simulated movement experiences. Similarly, Figure 7 depicts a semi-immersive car simulation game, conceptualized for patients with impaired reaction time or upper limb dysfunction, providing an interactive rehabilitation platform that facilitates motor skill recovery and neurocognitive training.

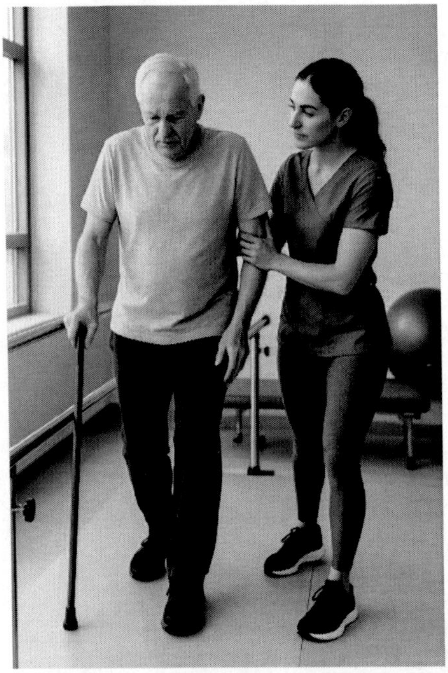

Figure 5. Rehabilitation of patient dependant on walking stick (Conceptual Visualization).

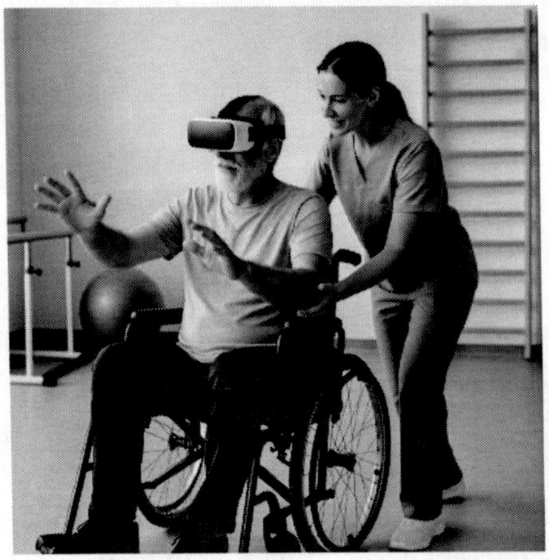

Figure 6. Rehabilitation using VR for patient dependant on wheelchair (Conceptual Visualization).

Figure 7. Semi-immersive car game – for a patient with impaired reaction time or to improve upper limb functions (Conceptual Visualisation).

3.3. Cardiopulmonary Rehabilitation

Cardiovascular disease and pulmonological disease are an array of conditions that are necessarily handled by an expert in the field of cardiopulmonary physiotherapy. Cardiovascular conditions such as coronary artery disease, valve diseases, heart failure, postoperative CABG and valve disorders, conservatively managed myocardial infarction, and percutaneous coronary intervention have a potential risk of possessing altered vasovagal response. It requires exercise prescription based on a thorough assessment of the patient. Patient with cardiovascular incidents is delicately managed after assessment of their vital response, exercise tolerance after getting enrolled for cardiac rehabilitation. The cardiac rehabilitation is defined as "the coordinated sum of activities required to influence favourably the underlying cause of cardiovascular disease as well as to provide the best possible physical, mental, and social conditions so that the patients may by their own efforts preserve or resume optimal functioning in their community and through improved health behaviour, slow or reverse progression of disease." *(Guidelines of cardiac rehabilitation: BACPR 2012).*

The term "Pulmonary Rehabilitation is a comprehensive intervention based on through assessment followed by patient-tailored therapies that include but are not limited to exercise training, education, and behaviour change designed to improve the physical and psychological condition of people with chronic respiratory disease and to promote the long-term adherence to health-enhancing behaviours" as per official guidelines of European Thoracic Society (Spruit et al., 2013). Pulmonological conditions include obstructive lung diseases, restrictive lung diseases, post-pneumonia syndromes, and thoracic deformities, which also have similar vital variability responses as those of the cardiovascular diseases. Major symptoms that are elicited for both patients would be shortness of breath. Optimal level of exercise training can only be prescribed after thorough assessment of their exercise response with their vital parameters. Henceforth, the utility of virtual reality among such patient is limited at their acute stage. Once they are in phase I acute hospital set-up, the full potential benefits of VR and AR can be utilised only during phase II (post-discharge). But still, that may require additional hardware or a medium to monitor their vitals during the course of exercise (Penn et al., 2018).

4. An Effective Tele-Rehabilitation with Tele-Monitoring

Patients enrolled for Rehabilitation are prone to developing varying vital responses irrespective of the associated conditions during the acute stage. Patient enrolled on cardiopulmonary rehabilitation are required to be monitored at a remote set-up due to their vulnerability. Unlike other rehabilitations, which may not require continuous monitoring or supervision once the patient masters the exercises, in cardiopulmonary rehabilitation, the patient requires continuous monitoring and supervision during the exercises. Therefore, there is a lacuna for the hardware source that monitors vitals and sends data to the physical therapists or medical professionals, which can be interpreted and stored for future exercise modifications for the patients. Vital parameters such as Heart Rate, Oxygen Saturation, Respiratory Rate, and Blood Pressure are measured during exercise and post-exercise for the exercise response. Hardware that may contain a sensor to capture all those vitals mentioned above is necessary during the exercise procedure for understanding the exercise tolerance of the patients. Wearables with an automated measurement unit for the above-mentioned vitals are becoming mandatory elements to practice VR and AR-based rehabilitation at a remote set-up securely and safely to prevent adverse events.

Figure 8 conceptually illustrates a wearable band designed to measure heart rate and oxygen saturation, enabling continuous physiological monitoring through integrated biosensors. Figure 9 demonstrates the remote monitoring of vital parameters using a pulse oximeter, emphasizing real-time data transmission for telemedical assessment. Figure 10 depicts the measurement of blood pressure in a remote setup, showcasing the role of connected medical devices in decentralized healthcare delivery. Finally, Figure 11 presents paediatric rehabilitation using a VR headset and handheld sensors, highlighting the integration of immersive technologies to enhance motor coordination, engagement, and therapy outcomes in child rehabilitation contexts.

Figure 8. Wearables band to measure heart rate and oxygen saturation (Conceptual Visualization).

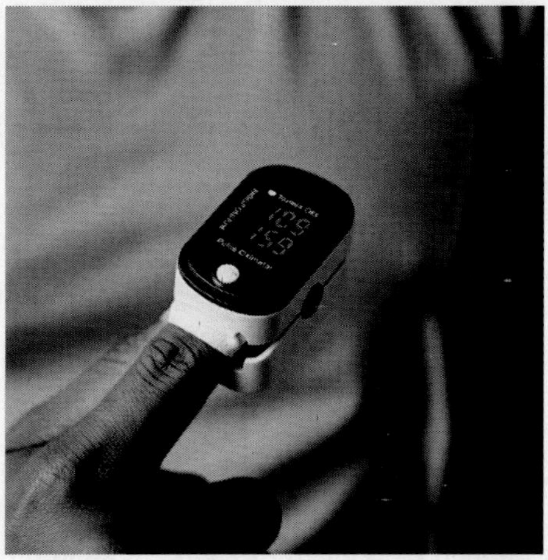

Figure 9. Remote monitoring of vitals using pulse oximeter (Conceptual Visualization).

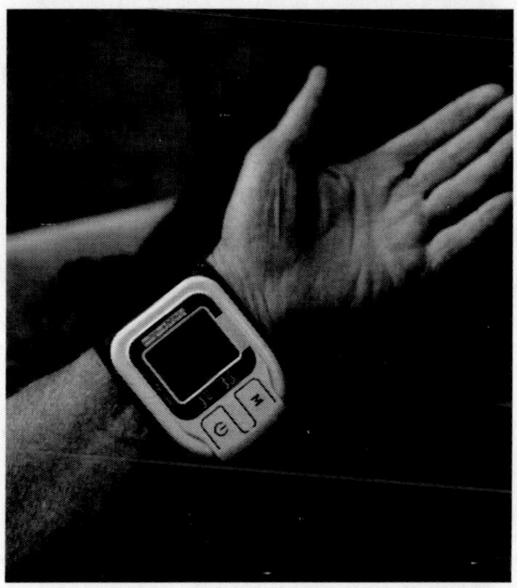

Figure 10. Measurement of blood pressure at remote setup.

Figure 11. Paediatric child rehabilitation using VR headset and handheld sensors.

5. Results of Literature Review

As an emerging field of rehabilitation, telerehabilitation has limited evidence supporting the protocol of management. On a Thorough analysis, we found some evidence that supports the virtual rehabilitation. A survey among physical therapists concluded that the awareness about the implementation of telerehabilitation based on virtual reality and augmented reality for neurological conditions is higher when compared with musculoskeletal conditions and cardiopulmonary conditions. Awareness was very low about the implementation of such telerehabilitation for obstetrics and gynaecological conditions (Joshi & Musale, n.d.). A trial proved to have a significant improvement in balance and gait for patients with Parkinson's disease by implementing Virtual Rehabilitation. This study primarily focused on the balance and gait, since those were major impairments that patients with Parkinson's disease encounter, which requires higher attention to prevent disabilities and improve their independence in activities of daily living (Lv and Guo, 2022).

The case report of hand rehabilitation using the virtual reality hand rehabilitation protocol among stroke patients' group of 4 showed greater improvement after 18 sessions of rehabilitation in their lateral grip, palmar grip and grip strength. However, they are concluding with the point that the patient was engaged effectively with the virtual environment (Tsoupikova et al., n.d.). A Pilot Trial among 5 patients also proved to be more feasible with improved outcomes among the participants. A systematic review reported that virtual cardiac rehabilitation among coronary artery bypass grafting patients improved with functional capacity and psychosocial motive. They are suggesting that implementing such Augmented and Virtual Rehabilitation in cardiovascular patients is promising and has future implications in the field of rehabilitation.

Neurorehabilitation, the VR-based rehabilitation for patients with Parkinson's disease or cerebrovascular insults, is potentially improving symptoms and showing increased interest due to its fun nature, task-oriented training, multi-sensory feedback provisions and high immersiveness, but even with all its potential benefits, it still has conflicts such as high economic constraints. A Meta-analysis also proves that Virtual rehabilitation is effective among patients with Parkinson's disease in improving their balance, and they also suggest that the safety concerns are mandatory, as it must be practised within a secure environment (Kwon, Park, and Koh 2023) (Feng et al., 2019). A Review by Wasim Fathima Shah also suggests that virtual reality emerges as a potential advancement in managing the disease with physical disabilities. This provides an immersive experience to participants, which facilitates increased interest by recreating the environment that suits the management based on the conditions, paving the way for a bright future towards a virtual rehabilitation regimen (Fathima Shah, n.d.).

6. Discussion

Augmented Reality and Virtual Reality in the field of rehabilitation are evolving due to outstanding clinical outcomes and their effective reduction of symptoms with enhanced participation. Participants are actively involved in exercise-based management, engaging them towards the rapid recovery from the symptoms of underlying medical conditions. The literature suggests that participants are showing more interest towards rehabilitation using virtual reality and augmented reality than traditional methods of rehabilitation, due to their feasibility and fun nature. But considering the cost of availing the virtual reality and augmented reality devices by an individual, such a level of futuristic technology must be commercialised to become economically cheaper. The rehabilitation field must adapt to such evolving technology completely for implementing the exercises positively, which enhances speedy recovery for patients and will be one of the futuristic approaches. Such innovation acts as a phenomenal field for the researcher for newer discoveries in terms of advanced hardware like sensors and gadgets, as well as software programs.

Software should be designed in a way that it engages the patient to get involved in an activity that must improve their limiting factors due to medical condition, as well as assist in the identification of undiagnosed limitations by patients. Assessment of the patient's problem, especially the arthrokinematics and biomechanical aspects, is challenging for physical therapists due to the individuality of the patient's problem, especially the arthrokinematics and biomechanical aspects. Standardisation using such advanced technology and Artificial Intelligence (AI) synchronisation would be a phenomenal approach in diagnosing the medical condition associated with physical disabilities. Sports injuries are initially managed with medical management, followed by physical therapy, which helps the player attain full confidence to perform in future games. Whereas recurrent injuries or recurrence of the same injury can result if the player is found with residual weakness of injured muscles after complete recovery. When left undiagnosed even after the course of treatment, that may increase the risk of re-injuring the same site. In order to prevent such scenarios, it is mandatory to diagnose the underlying pathology, with the use of virtual reality or augmented reality, synchronised with AI, which may help reveal such undiagnosed pathologies.

In the field of neurological rehabilitation, for upper motor neuron disease, repetitive movements are a key factor towards neuroplasticity for patients with underlying disease symptoms. Neurological disease symptoms take a longer time to manage due to higher central lesions. Re-education program through which the neuroplasticity is anticipated, but such an immersive experience would be more ideal in creating interest for the participants from getting used to the repeated movements and for understanding the movement more easily. Standardised repetitive movement in neurorehabilitation is an important aspect of improving the movement deficits of the patients. The repeated movement pattern without asynchrony will create new neural pathways and muscle memory, enhancing the neuroplasticity. Gait abnormalities are a unique feature of neurological conditions that vary from individual to individual in terms of the underlying weakness. Identification of the abnormal gait patterns and management of Children with developmental disorders requires enabling selective focal training, which creates more focus and increases concentration for the child to adhere (Tsoupikova et al., 2015).

Musculoskeletal physiotherapy, the virtual reality and augmented reality aids in identification of pain site, due to the complex nature of the muscle pathology such as tendinitis, discitis, neuritis. The peripheralization and centralization of the symptoms are features of disc pathologies in the spinal segments. Identification of the underlying pathology in spinal segments is more challenging to discriminate from skeletal tissues/connective tissues, and neural tissues. Joints of the spine follow the same pattern of pain that is associated with discitis or musculoskeletal pain. Such similarity in pain pattern makes the diagnosis difficult, resulting in poor outcomes. Management of such pathology initially follows the standard protocol as per guidelines, whereas exercise-based management can be practised using virtual reality and augmented reality after the initial treatment with standard physiotherapy modalities or skills performed by a physiotherapy expert. Diagnosis using Artificial Intelligence in the field of orthopaedic rehabilitation would be challenging and still requires larger practice for reliable outcomes because of its complex nature.

Cardiopulmonary Physiotherapy is a delicate approach towards patients after cardiac incidents or respiratory diseases. Due to their high vulnerability and frailty, there is a higher attention towards cardiac monitoring of patients during standard physiotherapy care. The use of virtual reality and augmented reality in the terms of phase II rehabilitation at their remote set up or centres is fully possible, because of its standard exercise protocol depending on the individual patient's exercise capacity. Phase I cardiac or pulmonary rehabilitation (In-hospital phase) requires expert supervision for preventing unexpected outcomes. As the patients' exercise tolerance is calculated in a quantifiable way, the exercise prescription is calculated in terms of metabolic equivalents or VO2 max. Henceforth, the prescribed exercises can be practised safely at a remote setup, if the patient is aware of the clinical conditions. Measurement of the vital parameters during the exercise sessions and post-exercise sessions is mandatory for identifying their response to exercises. The hardware unit or wearables that monitor vitals during the exercise sessions or give feedback would be an ideal measure for practising the exercise among patients with cardiopulmonary disease populations using VR and AR. The patient with urinary incontinence benefits from using the VR and AR in terms of controlling the detrusor muscles. The use of VR and AR in the field of gynaecological or obstetric rehabilitation is increasing nowadays, though it has been limited due to certain psychological concerns.

Conclusion

Head-mounted devices or standard displays are anticipated to create a more immersive experience among the participants during the exercise rehabilitation. More sources of exergaming are to be created in future with reference to varying aspects of symptoms associated with underlying medical pathologies for the implementation of exercise-based rehabilitation. Literature currently is lagging with evidence supporting that exercise-based rehabilitation is effective among patients in larger population trials. The exergaming at home by implementation for patients after cardiopulmonary events requires more attention in terms of safety. The feasibility of implementing the VR and AR is evidently higher whereas the economic cost for availing the VR headset is slowly declining. Making it more economical and commercially available in rural areas across the globe may benefit the population seeking rehabilitation.

References

Bamodu, Oluleke, and Xuming Ye. n.d. "*Virtual Reality and Virtual Reality System Components*."

bErGMaNN, Jeannine, carmen KrEWEr, petra bauEr, alexander KoENiG, robert riENEr, and friedemann MÜllEr. 2017. "*Virtual Reality to Augment Robot-Assisted Gait Training in Non-Ambulatory Patients with a Subacute Stroke: A Pilot Randomized Controlled Trial*" 54 (3). https://doi.org/10.23736/s1973.

Burdea, G. 2000. "Virtual Rehabilitation - Benefits and Challenges."

Cao, Shi. 2016. "Virtual Reality Applications in Rehabilitation." In *Lecture Notes in Computer Science (Including Subseries Lecture Notes in Artificial Intelligence and Lecture Notes in Bioinformatics)*, 9731:3–10. Springer Verlag. https://doi.org/10.1007/978-3-319-39510-4_1.

Fathima Shah, Wasim. n.d. "Digital Dimensions of Healing: A Comprehensive Review of VR in Physical Therapy." *International Journal of Computer Engineering and Technology (IJCET)* 14 (3): 23–33. https://doi.org/10.17605/OSF.IO/UCVDZ.

Feng, Hao, Cuiyun Li, Jiayu Liu, Liang Wang, Jing Ma, Guanglei Li, Lu Gan, Xiaoying Shang, and Zhixuan Wu. 2019. "Virtual Reality Rehabilitation versus Conventional Physical Therapy for Improving Balance and Gait in Parkinson's Disease Patients: A Randomized Controlled Trial." *Medical Science Monitor* 25:4186–92. https://doi.org/10.12659/MSM.916455.

Joshi, Ms Gargi, and Rima Musale. n.d. "Awareness, Knowledge and Attitude About Virtual Reality and Augmented Reality in Physiotherapy Practice Among Physiotherapists." www.ijfmr.com.

Kwon, Sun Ho, Jae Kyung Park, and Young Ho Koh. 2023. "A Systematic Review and Meta-Analysis on the Effect of Virtual Reality-Based Rehabilitation for People with Parkinson's Disease." *Journal of NeuroEngineering and Rehabilitation*. BioMed Central Ltd. https://doi.org/10.1186/s12984-023-01219-3.

Lv, Zhihan, and Jinkang Guo. 2022. "Virtual Reality Neurorehabilitation." *International Journal of Mental Health Promotion*. Tech Science Press. https://doi.org/10.32604/IJMHP.2022.019829.

Naqvi, Waqar M, Ifat Naqvi, Gaurav V Mishra, and Vishnu Vardhan. 2024. "The Dual Importance of Virtual Reality Usability in Rehabilitation: A Focus on Therapists and Patients." *Cureus*, March. https://doi.org/10.7759/cureus.56724.

Penn, I-Wen, Eric Chuang, Tien-Yow Chuang, and Chen-Ya Yang. 2018. "Effects of Virtual-Reality-Augmented Cardiopulmonary Rehabilitation Programs for Patients with Cardiovascular Diseases: A Systemic Review." *Neuropsychiatry* 08 (05). https://doi.org/10.4172/neuropsychiatry.1000499.

Spruit, Martijn A., Sally J. Singh, Chris Garvey, Richard Zu Wallack, Linda Nici, Carolyn Rochester, Kylie Hill, et al., 2013. "An Official American Thoracic Society/European Respiratory Society Statement: Key Concepts and Advances in Pulmonary Rehabilitation." *American Journal of Respiratory and Critical Care Medicine* 188 (8). https://doi.org/10.1164/rccm.201309-1634ST.

Tsoupikova, Daria, Nikolay Stoykov, Derek Kamper, and Randy Vick. n.d. "*Virtual Reality Environment Assisting Post Stroke Hand Rehabilitation: Case Report.*"

Tsoupikova, Daria, Nikolay S. Stoykov, Molly Corrigan, Kelly Thielbar, Randy Vick, Yu Li, Kristen Triandafilou, Fabian Preuss, and Derek Kamper. 2015. "Virtual Immersion for Post-Stroke Hand Rehabilitation Therapy." *Annals of Biomedical Engineering* 43 (2): 467–77. https://doi.org/10.1007/s10439-014-1218-y.

www.who.int/news-room/fact-sheets/detail/rehabilitation.

www.ohchr.org/en/instruments-mechanisms/instruments/convention-rights-persons-disabilities.

Chapter 18

Reforming Distance Education: Empowering Remote and Rural Learning Through Innovative Immersive Technologies

R. Hepzibah Gnana Sinthiya[1,*]
and Janice Sandra David[2,†]

[1]Department of Commerce, Voorhees College, Vellore, India
[2]Department of English, Auxilium College, Vellore, India

Abstract

The purpose of this research is to explore the effects of virtual reality (VR), augmented reality (AR), and interactive simulation in increasing engagement and learning achievement, as well as knowledge grasp, among distance education learning students in remote and rural areas. By reviewing previous work that adopted the Technology Acceptance Model (TAM), the Self-Determination Theory (SDT), and the Cognitive Load Theory (CLT), this study explores whether using Immersive Technologies (IT) can improve learning experiences and engagement levels by motivating and reducing cognitive stress. The present research work followed a quantitative research approach, and data were gathered through a structured questionnaire from students who were pursuing collegiate education in the North Arcot district of Tamil Nadu, India. Data were collected through purposive and snowball sampling, where 306 usable responses were received. In testing the study hypotheses,' Partial Least Squares -Structural Equation Modelling' (PLS-SEM) was used for the analysis. The study reveals that the adoption of immersive technologies in distance learning mode enhances students' engagement, better results, and formidable digital competencies. The implication of this research depicts that the incorporation of IT into distance education opens possibilities for redesigning the learning experience, making education more accessible, and narrowing the gap between those learners in urban centres and those in remote rural areas in the future use of IT in education.

Keywords: immersive technologies, distance education, knowledge retention, student engagement, student satisfaction, learning outcomes, technical difficulties, technical support and training

---

* Corresponding Author's Email: Sinthiyasweety92@gmail.com
† Corresponding Author's Email: sandy.david94@gmail.com

In: Shaping Tomorrow
Editors: Prithi Samuel, A. Sathya, Balamurugan Balusamy et al.
ISBN: 979-8-90134-076-9

1. Introduction

The field of education has transformed and has made significant changes in the evolution of technological advancements in the 21st-century learning environment. In this context, many institutions and educators are rethinking traditional approaches. According to Kuhail et al., (2022), there has been a shift in the process of learning due to technological enhancement and the craving of students striving for flexibility in learning. Online learning has become useful in view of replacing the traditional classroom learning, most especially for students who are in remote areas of a country or state where they are denied easy access to quality educational resources. This system of learning carries the advantage of learning from any part of the world, thus breaking barriers of learning due to region (Bizami, Tasir, and Kew 2023a). Nevertheless, distance education gives numerous benefits, and at the same time, a plethora of challenges arise in participation, communication and learning experience. The use of 'Virtual Reality' (VR), 'Augmented Reality' (AR) and 'Mixed Reality' (MR) in distance education has the possibility of solving the above-mentioned challenges and improving the teaching and learning outcomes for students in remote and rural areas (Irons, Jung, and Keel 2002). VR technologies enhance learner interactivity and content appeal, making it less complicated to grasp concepts by using a realistic approach. By integrating these innovative tools, the educators will be position to deliver the education in a way that will foster high engagement of the learners, particularly those who feel that they cannot acquire more knowledge. It would also make students feel apathetic in distance education (Baxter and Hainey 2024a). However, the ability to put theory into practice is a major challenge in distance education, which can be achieved using immersive learning technologies. For example, through VR, students can replicate a lab or go on a field trip and have a practical session that is impossible for students in rural and remote areas to complete in another state or country (Ntaba & Jantjies 2019). This not only improves understanding but also develops cognitive skills that help in problem solving, which gives importance in the modern and competitive world of employment opportunities. By adopting immersive technologies (IT), educators can build a more integrated and contextual approach to learning that would help students to be well aligned with real-life situations (Childs et al., 2024).

Moreover, awareness and adoption of IT are still limited and very often these technologies are unfamiliar, especially in rural or remote settings. This then brings about issues such as many educators and institutions would not possess resources, training or even knowledge in how to accurately integrate these technologies into their teaching (Irons, Jung, and Keel 2002). In addition, there can be problems at the object level, for example, insufficient availability of Internet connection and devices that do not allow for the effective use of immersive technologies in those areas (Bizami et al., 2023a). Hence, an effort has to be made not only to sell meta-visions but also to equip the end users, that is, educators and students, with the fitting tools and training. To effectively reform distance education, it is essential to foster a culture of innovation and adaptability among educators and institutions. This involves not only integrating IT into the curriculum but also encouraging educators to experiment with new teaching methodologies that leverage these tools (Levy 2014). To utilize IT effectively, professional development programs and workshops can play a pivotal role in equipping educators with the skills and knowledge needed. Additionally, collaboration between academic institutions, technology providers, and local communities can help to create tailored solutions that address the specific needs and hindrances faced by remote and rural learners (Carella &

Melazzini 2023). Furthermore, it is mandatory to mention the ethical and social consequences of applying the IT in the education process (Al-Abdullah and Hassan, 2023). Main concerns towards embracing these advancements include data privacy, accessibility, as well as the digital divide, which must be dealt with in order to get all the learners to benefit from it (Costa, de Mello Santos, and de OLIVEIRA 2022). Educational leaders and policymakers need public policies that can support the use of the technologies in a manner that will not exclude any learner in the technological society (Swargiary, 2024).

Therefore, this paper will explore the impact of IT on the transformation of distance learning, especially for the marginalised remote and rural students. Thus, learning about the modern status of distance education, the contributions of emerging technologies, and the obstacles to their implementation, the present study aims to lay emphasis on the necessity of embracing innovations to develop viable possibilities for distance education for all. Hence, enabling remote and rural education with immersive technologies can help to overcome the gap, create awareness, and build a bridge to society. From this point, this study aims at developing immersive technology to foster further research by the academic community and to drive positive change where not only distance education is available but also augmented with the opportunities for learners that the immersive technologies provide.

After reviewing various literature, the study explored the theories that fit the research gap. Theories such as 'Technology Acceptance Model' (TAM), 'Self-Determination Theory' (SDT), and 'Cognitive Load Theory' (CLT) were considered. By integrating these theories, this study identified the variables that fill the research gap. The effectiveness of IT such as AR, VR and MR in distance learning is measured using the outcomes of the learners, such as 'Student Engagement (SE), Knowledge Retention (KR), Learning Outcomes (LR), Student Satisfaction (SS).' The accessibility to these resources is not easy, and using these technologies requires basic training for the remote and rural area students. The learners might face challenges in using this technology as they might lack skills in accessing the equipment. Hence, 'Accessibility to Resources (ATR), Technical Training and Support (TTS) and Technical difficulties (TD)' are kept as mediating variables to analyse the impact of using IT. The research questions are framed to fill the research gap, which are as follows:

RQ1. Does the use of IT impact SE, KR, LO and SS in distance learning for remote and rural students?

RQ2. Do potentially foreseen advantages and barriers, such as ATR, TST, and TD, have an impact on SE, KR, LO and SS on the adoption of IT in rural distance education?

RQ3. Do ART, TST and TD act as a mediating variable between IT and SE, KR, LO, and SS?

A conceptual framework was established using the research questions and the hypothesis was proposed in order to analyse the relationship between the variables. 'PLS-SEM' (Partial least square-structural equation modelling) analysis is used to test the relationship between the variables, and the interpretations were drawn out of it. The findings of this study will help to guide interventions for enhancing general usability and efficiency of IT-based applications in rural learning environments, which may have the added benefit of narrowing the rural-urban education gap.

This research paper is organised as follows: Section 2 bundles up the previous articles and the linked theories which paved the way to identify the research gap. The variables were found to fill the gap using the literature. The hypotheses were established in order to find the relationship between the variables. The analysis part is given in section 3, where the proposed hypotheses were tested using PLS-SEM analysis, and the interpretations were drawn according to the results. In section 4, discussions were made by giving justifications for the derived results. The practical and theoretical implications were given in section 5, followed by the conclusion, limitations and future scope in section 6.

2. Literature Review

This section delves deeply into the various literatures, theories and articles that were studied previously, which cater to identify the research gap, and the variables were derived. The hypotheses were established, and a conceptual framework was developed to identify the impact of IT on the learning process of distance education in remote and rural areas.

2.1. Immersive Technology (IT) in Distance Education

The IT, such as VR, AR and MR, are disrupting traditional methods of distance education by creating the physical and virtual learning environments nexus (Liubchak, Zuban, and Artyukhov 2022). These remarkable technologies offer real possibilities of learners being able to attend classroom teaching and learning physically, conduct experiments, or experience scenarios of history or scientific legendary places and related simulations while physically being somewhere else (North, 2014). Through concrete ideas and dealing with functional knowledge and competencies favourably, immersive technologies overcome several shortcomings of traditional Distance Education: solitude, inattention, and the absence of manipulative practice (Abdraimova, Zh, and Zhorabaev 2020). Studies show that the possibility of using immersive technology is expansive enough and can be adopted in teaching and learning contexts. While trying to deliver quality education using IT, it not only increases the learning experience but also enhances the students' digital learning skills, which helps to enhance their digital knowledge in future (Fernandes et al., 2023). As tools for enhancing learning and preparing learners with relevant digital skills, IT offer the potential of revolutionising future distance education and learning, through increasing accessibility, effectiveness and engagement (Semerikov et al., 2021).

2.2. Theories and Their Integration

Using the theories of TAM, SDT and CLT, a conceptual framework was developed from which the relationship between the variables was tested using the proposed hypothesis. TAM, introduced by Davis (1989), was used to investigate the adoption of IT in distance education. In this context, the variable IT affect students 'Perceived Usefulness (PU) and Perceived Ease of Use (PEU), which are the basic constructs under TAM (P. Silva, 2015). PU is evident in SE, LO, KR and SS as it provides practical experience and realistic interactions to the learners. On the other hand, the PEU component is affected by other mediating factors such as ATR, TST, and TD, which act to shape the student's perception towards the use of immersive tools (Mustafa and Garcia, 2021). As a result, it improves students cognitive ability that predispose them to positively engage with technology enhanced students' cognitive ability that predisposes them to positively engage with technology-enhanced learning, which results in better academic performance for students pursuing their courses in distance learning (Lai, 2017).

The SDT emphasises the necessity of encouraging mental stability and autonomy in learning settings. SDT also explains that students will study harder when they feel competent and have the independence to study (Gunasekare, 2016). The IT complements the engagement by providing interactive and stimulating environments which can be tailored, among other things, to a range of learning styles and make students feel that people around them consider them valuable. When the IT are coupled with ATR using technical assistance and gaining adequate training, it can go a long way in enhancing KR and overall, LO (M. N. Silva et al., 2014). Nonetheless, Deci et al., (2017) suggest several reservations with these tools stating that organisational technology infrastructure presents several challenges in SE with these Technologies, including TD that limit their application and the lack of strength in supporting necessary structures to counter these difficulties. When the IT is thoroughly designed to effectively embed the features of the system in line with the distinct elements of SDT as proposed in this study, the online distance learning can yield improvement in academic performance as well as SS using IT (R. M. Ryan and Deci 2024).

According to CLT, the cognitive effort is the key factor on which learning outcomes depend. Hence, CLT can be deemed the most important theoretical foundation of integrating ITs into learning (Sweller 2011). These technologies include VR and AR, which can greatly improve SE through the use of real interfaces. However, their effectiveness rests on moderating the cognitive load to enhance KR and LO without burdensomeness (Plass, Moreno, and Brünken 2010). At this point, there is a need for sufficient provision of such ATR as well as the need to provide TST and training to avoid TD arising since it affects the ability of the students and educators to use these tools efficiently (Schnotz & Kürschner 2007). Moreover, it directly relates to the challenge of enhancing SS because well-supported and accessible learning platforms contribute to making the educational experience more favourable. Thus, by aligning CLT principles to IT, the educators will be able to enhance academic achievement and long-term performance (Kirschner et al., 2018).

Integrating TAM, SDT, and CLT sheds light on the importance of user-friendly technologies that reduce the mental stress, which boosts the PEU and PU, which also satisfy the cognitive needs for autonomy, competence, and relatedness. Thus, according to the theories mentioned above, both technology adoption and subsequent continuous usage can be properly explained and motivated to support usability and intrinsic motivation.

2.3. Accessibility to Resources (ATR)

The use of IT leads to a proper, interesting and understandable environment for learning, thus improving the learning process results. Dede (2009), contends that realistic scenarios enable students to practice situated learning, making choices in controlled environments. This approach also enhances the view and involvement of students, but at the same time also allows for coverage of other aspects which may not be so possible in conventional classrooms, like acquisition of knowledge from specialists, and to put practicality in real life. In addition, while incorporating immersive environments, the students can work with the available digital materials through an enhanced, real-life manner. Different studies reveal that students who have learnt using immersive technologies show better understanding, KR and a more positive attitude than the students following traditional learning techniques (De Freitas et al., 2010). This implies that using IT learners are exposed to experiences which are not easily provided within the classroom, as various resources are limited. The use of IT in several sectors has enabled the ATR that can otherwise only be accessed, limited by location or funding. Say, for example, in the case of healthcare, simulations let virtual patients be experienced, which resources might not be easily accessible to the learners in their own institutions. This democratization of training resources is especially helpful for institutions in regions that are not very well served, as far as quality of training material is concerned (Kneebone et al., 2010).

Moreover, by using such technologies, it is possible to solve the problem of remote work by providing people from different locations with access to the necessary resources and knowledgeable specialists. This can be especially applicable to industries like engineering and architecture, where actual data can be placed on top of physical designs, allowing employees to coordinate their work regardless of the distance between them (Baxter & Hainey 2024b). Such capabilities also facilitate resource utilization because they cut across conventional policies of cooperation and exchange of information. Implications of the literature reveal that the use of IT affects ATR in different domains. In learning experiences, resource availability and inclusiveness IT are revolutionising the manner in which information and training are accessed and utilised (Beckem and Watkins, 2012). Hence, the following hypothesis is proposed:

H1 - IT has a positive impact on ATR.

2.4. Technical Support and Training (TST)

Applications of AR, VR, and MR, collectively referred to as IT, have seen a rapid increase in recent years, and they are considered a highly effective tool for developing the technological reinforcement and training processes in many spheres (Bizami, Tasir, and Kew 2023b). Ali (2022) focuses on analysing the effects of IT on the accomplishment of training and development initiatives, on the strength of skills being taught and learned, and on the quantity and quality of support offered to the users in learning environments, whether academic or corporate. Emerging trends in training methodologies have indicated that the application of IT to training has had a noticeable positive impact towards the effectiveness of training since it delivers realistic environments where learners can emulate situations that they are being trained for. Wu et al., (2021) state that through IT, learners can participate in situated learning to acquire new skills in contexts that are real in day-to-day activities but without the set-associated dangers. This way not only makes people more focused but also helps them remember more by applying the knowledge.

Kneebone et al., (2010) show that benefitting from simulation training can be an advantage over conventional training approaches. For example, research has shown that participants in VR training have a better level of performance in endosurgery over those who undertook traditional training. This implies that through this kind of learning it is possible to develop better practice solutions by exposing learners to solutions within a safe environment. Since the acquisition of technical skills is paramount in workplace performance, skill acquisition and transfer became paramount to meeting clients' needs. Skill acquisition and transfer are one of the main benefits that accrue from the use of IT in training. The reason is that learners get time to practice specific tasks as is usually expected within a given skills training program (De Freitas et al., 2010). Chang (2022) shows how AR is applied in educational games, which give the learners an opportunity to practice what they learn in real life, hence improving their mastery of the concepts. It may lead to real gains in confidence and competence where the experience is repeated in such environments. Studies have found that people who use lessons that are as close to practical problems are favourable when it comes to applying skills as they are reciprocal to real life. This transferability is very desirable in areas such as health, aviation, and engineering, where the skills to be applied are crucial in high-risk settings (Partarakis and Zabulis, 2024). Technological support is also provided through IT, and similarly, the collaboration among the outsiders also gets facilitated. This capability not only enhances the efficiency of training but also decreases errors and provides the users with the support they need without leaving their workplace (Sinthiya & Kulothungan, 2021). By considering this the current study depicts the following hypothesis:

H2 - IT has a positive impact on TST.

2.5. Technical Difficulties (TD)

Preedip Balaji & Kumar (2011) focused on examining the technical challenges within IT, including the obstacles to adopting the technology, ease of use problems, and training, as well as operational concerns. One of the primary technical challenges in implementing IT is its implementation cost. The implementation of various forms of immersive systems likely necessitates investments in acquired hardware, software, and networks. Khamis et al., (2024) state that although completed simulations aid in increasing the efficiency of the training programs, the costs are very high at initial stages of instituting the techniques, which cannot be affordable by many organisations, especially those in the healthcare sector, where the funding is normally chocked. This financial factor can thus hinder the acquisition of enhanced training aids, especially by less endowed institutions or those in the developing world. Furthermore, these can be complex and present operational risks that are very hard to overcome because of enhanced functionality of IT systems (Serrano-Ausejo and Mårell-Olsson, 2024). The adoption of VR and AR technologies in organizational practices may sometimes demand expertise in relation to the application of adopted technologies, which may be scarce within organizations. Thus, the technical complexity of immersive systems leads, on a frequent basis, to many users getting frustrated due to the difficulty in learning technical aspects for operating and maintaining such systems. The incorporation of this complexity may reduce the amount of flexibility that can be offered by IT especially in organizations that require constant learning and quick changes in the process (Zhao, Alexander, and Truell 2014).

Fitrianto & Saif (2024) argue that user experience is rather an essential component in the attainment of immersion. They have noted that sometimes, problems arising from technical gadgetry like hardware and software can pose a major influence about the level of user engagement and satisfaction. These technical issues show that, despite the idea that learners are highly technically skilled, these technical challenges can result in negative learner experiences and, hence, affect training (Sinthiya, 2024). The technical challenges raise important concerns over the training and overall functioning of training and operations. It gets worse when users face some technical problems when using the product or set, hence limiting their interaction and acquiring new knowledge (Hepzibah 2023). Gonzálvez et al., (2021) study revealed that technical issues hamper learning motivation and self-confidence in learners everywhere, but particularly in critical concentration including healthcare and aviation. This may lead to a lack of the intended learning goals and may have a poor effect on job performance. Moreover, there may be issues of scaling up IT solutions as they experience technical problems in their implementation in organizations. If users encounter problems often, there will be little confidence in the technology, hence little value to invest in or expand on immersive training solutions (Carpentieri et al., 2022). Lees-Smith (2024) further opined that answering technical challenges is important, inasmuch as creating a culture of innovation and improvement within organisations. Zhang (2019) shows that there is great potential in adopting and incorporating immersive technology in training and operation, but it is coupled with various technical challenges. Challenges to the implementation of immersive technology, concerns about the user experience in an immersive environment, and the potential impact on training require consideration of key factors when implementing the technology. Therefore, by taking this factor into account, the study puts forth the following hypothesis:

H3 - IT has a positive impact on TD.

2.6. Student Engagement (SE)

SE has been defined as a tripartite concept, which comprises the student's participation at behavioural, emotional and cognitive levels. Fredricks et al., (2004) stated that engagement depends on factors such as classroom environment, companionship, and peer interaction. Skinner et al., (2008) revealed that the impact of traditional face-to-face configurations shows that there is a positive relationship between the teacher, students and constructive feedback, which plays a significant role in promoting engagement. However, engagement in online synchronous and asynchronous learning contexts presented the need for a reconsideration of these engagement strategies. According to Alqurashi (2019), the interactions in several online environments are more focused on performance and tricky management, lacking proper concern with proper instructional behaviour recognition. Such gap requires a fresh perspective and application of technology to increase engagement.

The concept of IT in learning environments has been eyed as a possible solution in order to capture students' attention. Studies show that, when it comes to education, both AR and VR produce more engaging learning experiences than conventional approaches (Antonaci, Klemke, and Specht 2019). These technologies are also 'rich' in specific ways, for example, in their capacity to provide a realistic reproduction of real situations and to support interaction and peer learning that is crucial for SE. Detyna & Koch (2023) stress that both AR and VR technologies should only help to support the process of education and not solely depend on it. Particularly, the effective adoption of these technologies crucially depends on understanding sound, evidence-based pedagogy to support these technologies to supplement conventional teaching practices. Saito et al., (2024) also highlighted the need to engage students in the design of teaching environments. The implementation of those technologies by the students themselves can promote better education delivery since the students' engagement will be high in the development process of those technologies. An evaluation of diverse engagement models recommends that to increase the chances for active student participation, it is necessary to identify the students' needs and desires (Freeman et al., 2017). Furthermore, due to COVID-19, the growing use of digital learning tools in education has led to reconsideration of how technology can support learning in fully online and traditional blended learning environments. This has created a need for teacher training programs and schools to continuously transform and prioritize their interventions for using IT in their teaching processes. Therefore, by reviewing various previous literature, it shows that there is plenty of evidence for engagement in traditional approaches, but the new chances that come with using IT remain unexplored, particularly in distance learning. This calls for research that will aim to identify effective instructional paradigms that can embrace these technologies together with students' insights in the development process so that they can foster engagement as required. Hence, this study puts forth the following hypothesis.

H4 - IT has a direct significant effect on SE.

2.7. Knowledge Retention (KR)

Education using VR and AR technologies has been discussed in recent years. Zhang (2019) states that IT technologies can significantly improve students' memory of knowledge and their overall performance, by delivering practice-based learning processes. Shwedeh et al., (2024) propose a review on the impact of virtual environment on the educational process and the powers of VR and AR in improving students' memorisation in comparison with traditional two-dimensional media. The study focuses on the use of IT in vocational learning, focusing on the advances in terms of engagement, motivation and learning. Two groups of participants were involved: one for examining VR applied to a motorcycle labelling task, and the other for a tablet 2D interface. This fact proved the hypothesis stating that the experience of learning in the immersive environment is more effective than the traditional one. The scores of the KR and recall were higher in the VR group. The study also mentions general advantages of using IT in a learning environment which can radically change many approaches to teaching and enhance students' experience, performance and KR.

Huang et al., (2019) state that learning environments can take advantage of the perception of an experience in specific virtual environments that tap into learners' desire to learn and promote better retention. This is in consonance with Partarakis & Zabulis (2024), who opine that with the use of the immersive media, learning becomes more engaging. KR concept is therefore core to the success of immersive technologies when students learn more, especially when they can participate in the learning process (Baxter and Hainey 2024b). For instance, through the use of AR technologies, it becomes possible for a student to manipulate real and virtual objects by either touching, seeing, or referring to them while learning or trying to grasp complex ideas. This is most effective, especially in STEM (science, technology, engineering, and math) learning, where students need to work through the models they solve (Chittaro and Buttussi 2015). Shwedeh et al., (2024) undertook a study on AR apps in Learning Geometry education and found that students who were taught using the AR apps had better KR and recall than the conventional teaching approaches. It substantially enhances KR among students by providing interactive and engaging learning experiences. Each of the ITs elicits several psychological processes that enhance KR. Huang et al., (2019) found that these technologies give a multimedia form of learning in which a student receives both an auditory and visual form, which is believed to assist in memory retention. As a result of the adoption of AR and VR in the classroom, not only does the engagement increase, but also the understanding of the concept, meaning that the information will be easier to master and remember longer down the line, which leads to KR. According to Onopriienko et al., (2023), the effective implementation of immersive technologies in education significantly depends on the adoption of proper pedagogy. Appropriate technology implementation strategies are critical in realising the maximum impact from these technologies. Bagher (2020) delineate that utilising IT, such as VR and AR, in the learning environment positively influences the learning outcome. As a learning engagement tool, IT enables students' activity-based learning and promotes cognitive activity, which embodies a radical paradigm shift in pedagogy. Hence, the study depicts the following hypothesis:

H5 - IT has a direct significant effect on KR.

2.8. Learning Outcomes (LO)

The application of IT in learning environments has lately attracted a lot of interest, especially in the field of learning. Virtual learning environment and AR ensure people get to experience a much more entertaining way of pursuing knowledge as opposed to conventional lessons. The use of IT in learning is the most widely known as an advantage which brings active participation and motivation of students, which leads to remarkable LO (Baxter and Hainey 2024b). Suh & Prophet (2018), proposed that immersive environments enable students to learn content in a more engaging and durable way. According to Kuhail, ElSayary, et al., (2022), this kind of learning environment gives an emotional dimension, ultimately providing individuals with motivation for study. Likewise, in the study of the use of IT by Hamilton et al., (2021) discovered that students considered that IT are more enjoyable than the traditional approach of learning, where students' satisfaction level, as well as their interest and perceived usefulness levels of these tools, support the argument that LO in education is possible. The ability of VR and AR to immerse the user, the training has also been associated with better LO. Works under discussion prove that when learners interact with the content in three-dimensional environments, their LO are better. For instance, Dengel & Mägdefrau (2018), pointed out that some of the participants in their study believed that immersive technologies enhance memorization, especially regarding abstract concepts society can depict in a visual-spatial format. This is in line with cogent theories which press for multi-sensory ways of learning that are effective in concretizing memory enhancement that leads to positive output. This makes it easier to create an involved class and to achieve full concentration among students. G. V Ryan et al., (2022) observed that the virtual objects' affordances of interacting with them, or simulation, motivate the students to take an active role in learning. Besides, this practical approach brings valuable problem-solving features and thinking processes, where such practices can mimic actual-life situations in which learners are offered lessons on how specific concepts and theories work in practice, which provides better LO. Therefore, this study puts forth the following hypothesis:

H6 - IT has a direct significant effect on KR.

2.9. Students' Satisfaction (SS)

Many researchers have noted that employing IT helps to enhance students' interest levels, which increases satisfaction. Goode et al., (2024) state that students who used the VR environments are more tuned, interested and satisfied to learn than those who used the traditional modes of learning. A primary fact is that the benefits of IT have revealed the aspect of SS, because of the opportunity to solve several tasks at the same time. Park & Kim (2022) show that through the use of IT, students gain a better understanding, which enables learning outcomes, hence results in SS. Goode, Roche, Wilson, Zh et al., (2024) in their meta-analysis explained that technological experiences of students using VR and AR boosted their performance than learning in regular classrooms. By having an improvement in the academic results, there is also an improvement in the perception of the learning experience. One must underscore the fact that IT offers students the chance to apply theory in practice, which obviously leads to SS. For instance, medical students who employed the use of VR simulators in practising surgery found higher satisfaction levels, stating that the VR environment was realistic (Chang 2022). Therefore, for learning applications, it is not only helpful but also provides preparation for real-life situations, which will improve SS as a whole after learning all aspects of education. Although there are some issues in using IT in education. They said that problematic experiences, including technical difficulties on machines and compatibility of different software, reduce the learning process (Yun & Min, 2023). Goode et al., (2023) pointed out that students also complained of many technical challenges that made their frustrations high and reduced their satisfaction level. IT offers a great potential for enhancing teaching, but its availability may significantly differ across institutions, resulting in disparity of the student experience. Park & Kim (2022) highlighted the work, stressing that due to poverty, students from poor backgrounds may not have access to the required technology. Thus, they can only receive less accessibility and be less satisfied with their learning.

Baxter & Hainey (2024b) revealed that students who experience difficulties when accessing immersive environments had lower satisfaction rates, which means the necessity of training. In more general cases, some of the students may be deprived of normal satisfaction due to feelings of intimidation or despondency-feelings while facing new technologies. Hence, the study propounds the following hypothesis:

H7 - IT has a direct significant effect on SS.

The hypothetical relationship between the mediating variables and the dependent variables was tested using the following hypotheses:

H8 - ATR has a positive impact on SE
H9 - ATR has a positive impact on KR
H10 - ATR has a positive impact on LO
H11 - ATR has a positive impact on SS
H12 - TST has a positive impact on SE
H13 - TST has a positive impact on KR

H14 - TST has a positive impact on LO
H15 - TST has a positive impact on SS
H16 - TD has a positive impact on SE
H17 - TD has a positive impact on KR
H18 - TD has a positive impact on LO
H19 - TD has a positive impact on SS

To analyse the impact of using IT through the mediating variables the following hypotheses were proposed

H20 - IT has a significant effect on SE when ATR mediates
H21 - IT has a significant effect on SE when TST mediates
H22 - IT has a significant effect on SE when TD mediates
H23 - IT has a significant effect on KR when ATR mediates
H24 - IT has a significant effect on KR when TST mediates
H25 - IT has a significant effect on KR when TD mediates
H26 - IT has a significant effect on LO when ATR mediates
H27 - IT has a significant effect on LO when TST mediates
H28 - IT has a significant effect on LO when TD mediates
H29 - IT has a significant effect on SS when ATR mediates
H30 - IT has a significant effect on SS when TST mediates
H31 - IT has a significant effect on SS when TD mediates.

The following conceptual model shown in Figure 1 depicts the hypothetical relationship between the variables.

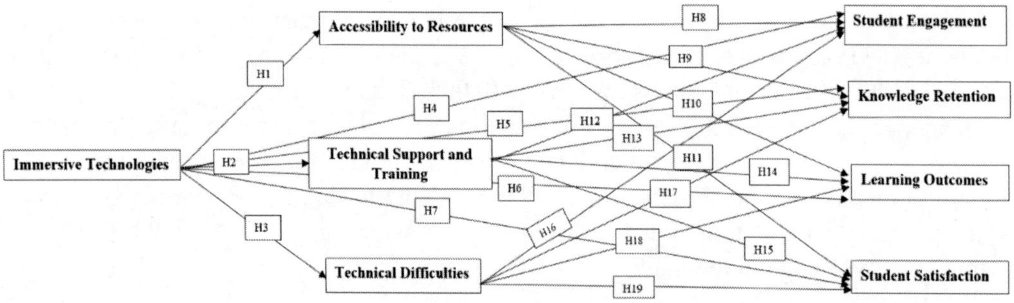

Figure 1. Conceptual framework.

3. Methodology

To achieve the objective, a quantitative research methodology is implemented in this study. The quantitative method is used as it provides the results without any bias, and the association among the variables can be revealed accurately (Davies & Palmer, 2022). The data collection was done using a structured questionnaire, where the scales and instruments were adapted from previous literature. The data collection was made from the students who are pursuing collegiate education in distance learning mode, particularly from the rural and remote areas of the North

Arcot district of Tamil Nadu, India, which includes Tiruvannamalai, Vellore, Tirupattur and Ranipet districts. There are more than 50 colleges and universities that offer various courses in distance education mode (Shiksha, 2024). Purposive sampling and the snowball sampling technique were used for the process of collecting data.

3.1. Measurements and Instruments

Various articles and research papers were collected from the scholarly journals and websites such as Web of Science, Scopus, Elsevier, Taylor and Francis and so on, using the keywords distance education, IT, KR, ATR and the other variables that were previously mentioned. The instruments and the measurement of the scales were adapted from various authors. Each variable was measured using a "5-point scale" (5-strongly agree to 1-strongly disagree). The variables IT was adapted from Baxter & Hainey (2024a), KR from Chittaro & Buttussi (2015), SS from Kuhail, ElSayary, et al., (2022), LO and SE from Ntaba & Jantjies, (2019), ATR from Bizami et al., (2023a), TST from Kuhail, ElSayary, et al., (2022) and TD from Childs et al., (2024).

3.2. Procedures and Participants

Firstly, the researcher gathered the information regarding the colleges and universities that offer distance education in the North Arcot districts from the database of the collegiate education website. Then, the Coordinators of distance education were approached personally to get formal permission to collect the data and to obtain the details of the students. Nearly 35 colleges and universities were approached to address the concern. In most cases, the questionnaire was forwarded through the in-charge directly to the students. Students of all the fields, such as arts and science, medical, engineering, polytechnics, agriculture, etc, are included in the process of data collection. A pilot test was conducted by sending the questionnaire to 25 students, which resulted in minor changes in the questionnaire, such as clarity and the structure of questions being altered. The questionnaire was collected through both online and offline modes. A structured questionnaire was given to the respective coordinators of distance education to collect the data from the students who are accessible directly, and the link to the questionnaire was also sent via WhatsApp to reach out to the students quickly and easily. The in-charges were also asked to pass the questionnaire to their peers working in other colleges and universities to get the questionnaire filled. A total of 313 questionnaires were received back, out of which 7 questionnaires were rejected as it is incomplete and found to be unfit for the analysis. Hence, 306 respondents were used for the purpose of analysis. The adequacy of sample size is checked using 'Kaiser-Meyer-Olkin' (KMO) measure, where the value 0.87 was derived which shows high adequacy value that leads to sufficient reliability and validity of the variables (Z. Zhang et al., 2024).

The data was collected from 67% of male students and 33% of female students. 53% of them are below 18 years old, 35% of them are between 18 and 25, and 12% are above 25 years old. It is revealed that 57.3% of the students are doing bachelor's degrees through distance education, 23.5% of them are pursuing diplomas through distance education, and 19.2% of them are doing master's degrees through distance education.

3.3. Data Analysis

3.3.1. Assessment of Measurement Model

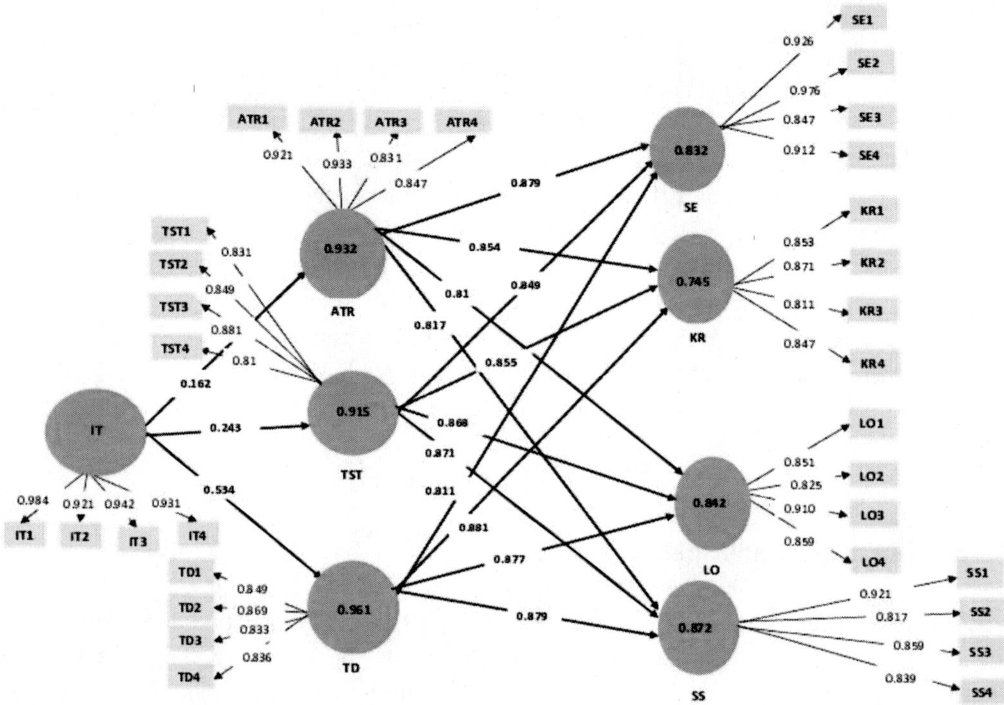

Source: PLS SEM.

Figure 2. Measurement model.

The framework and the hypothesis are tested using the 'PLS-SEM' statistical tool. This statistical tool is used since it has the capacity of analysing numerous variables that are involved in complex models, and both the reflective and formative measurement models can be analysed using 'PLS-SEM' (Ringle et al., 2023). According to Chin et al., (2008), the 'measurement model' was analysed as per figure 2 and secondly, the structural model was evaluated to test the relationship between the variables as shown in Figure 3. The 'reliability' of the model is measured using 'CV (Convergent validity) and AVE (Average Variance Extracted),' and the 'validity' is analysed using 'CA (Cronbach's alpha) and CR (composite reliability).' From Table 1, it is evident that the constructed model is both reliable and valid as it satisfies the thumb rule stated by Sarstedt et al., (2021), i.e., CV > 0.05, AVE > 0.50, CA > 0.80 and CR > 0.70.

3.3.2. Discriminant Validity

To calibrate the discriminant validity, the 'HTMT (Heterotrait-Monotrait ratio)' ratio was used. The correlation between the variables is determined by this ratio. The value of the square root values should be less than 0.90, as suggested by Lowry & Gaskin (2014). The table 2 values satisfy the thumb rule as the maximum square root value is 0.891 (TST <-> LO) (which is less than 0.90. Hence, it determines the discriminant validity.

Table 1. Validity and reliability

	Factor loading	CA	CR	AVE
Immersive Technology (IT)				
IT1	0.984	0.932	0.930	0.811
IT2	0.921			
IT3	0.942			
IT4	0.931			
Accessibility to Resources (ATR)				
ATR1	0.921	0.912	0.912	0.827
ATR 2	0.933			
ATR 3	0.831			
ATR 4	0.847			
Technical Training and Support (TTS)				
TST1	0.831	0.952	0.949	0.815
TST 2	0.849			
TST 3	0.881			
TST 4	0.811			
Technical difficulties (TD)				
TD1	0.849	0.939	0.940	0.826
TD2	0.869			
TD3	0.833			
TD4	0.836			
Student Engagement (SE)				
SE1	0.926			
SE2	0.976	0.959	0.960	0.841
SE3	0.847			
SE4	0.912			
		Knowledge Retention (KR)		
KR1	0.853			
KR2	0.871	0.923	0.924	
KR3	0.811			0.836
KR4	0.847			
		Learning outcome (LO)		
LO1	0.851	0.911	0.912	
LO2	0.825			0.822
LO3	0.910			
LO4	0.859			
		Student Satisfaction (SS)		
SS1	0.921	0.951	0.952	
SS2	0.817			0.847
SS3	0.859			
SS4	0.839			

Source: Author's calculation.

Table 2. HTMT

	Heterotrait-monotrait ratio (HTMT)
IT <-> SE	0.841
IT <-> KR	0.812
IT <-> LO	0.724
IT<-> SS	0.857
IT<-> ATR	0.796
IT <-> TST	0.739
IT <-> TD	0.809
ATR<-> SE	0.845

Table 2. (Continued)

	Heterotrait-monotrait ratio (HTMT)
ATR<-> KR	0.735
ATR<-> LO	0.799
ATR <-> SS	0.841
ATR <-> TST	0.854
ATR<-> TD	0.871
TST<-> SE	0.798
TST <-> KR	0.770
TST <-> LO	0.891
TST <-> SS	0.872
TST <-> TD	0.811
TD<-> SE	0.890
TD <-> KR	0.863
TD <-> LO	0.848
TD <-> SS	0.731
SE <-> KR	0.765
SE<-> LO	0.705
SE <-> SS	0.851
KR<-> LO	0.890
KR<-> SS	0.853
LO <-> SS	0.740

Source: Authors calculation.

3.3.3. Evaluation of Structural Model

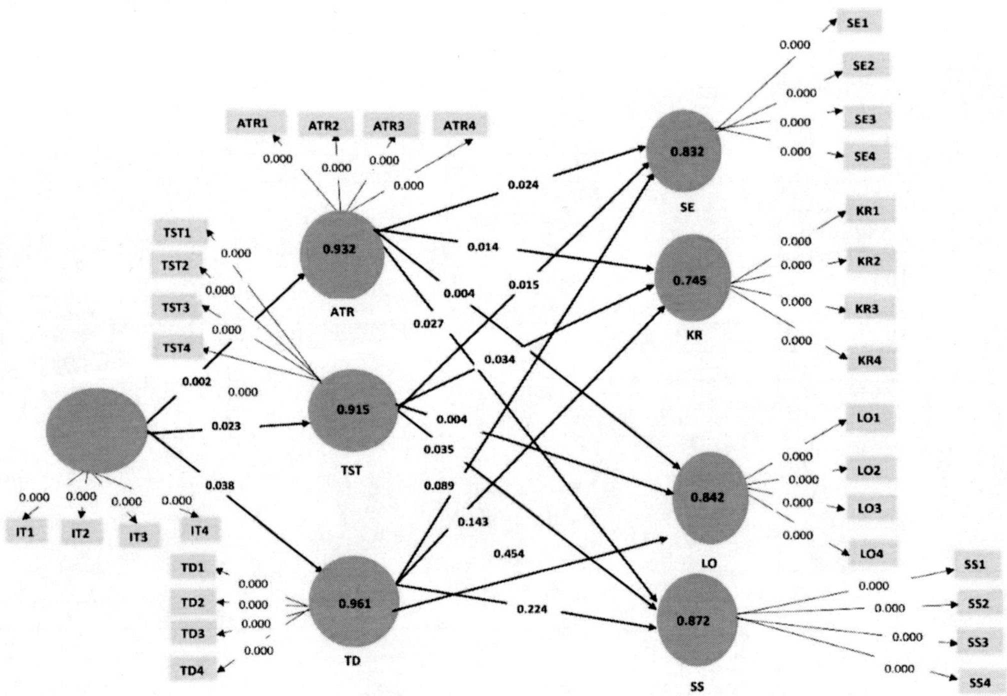

Source: PLS SEM.

Figure 3. Structural model.

3.3.4. Collinearity Assessment

As per Hair et al., (2021), the structural model may face collinearity and multicollinearity issues, which lead to methodological and interpretational challenges, when there is a strong correlation between two indicators. Hence, the variance inflation factor test is used to sort out the collinearity issues. The VIF values should be below 5 to rule out the issue of collinearity. Table 3 (inner values) and Table 4 (outer values) clearly state that there are no collinearity issues in the model as it satisfies the thumb rule.

Table 3. Inner values

	VIF
IT -> SE	2.152
IT-> KR	1.543
IT -> LO	1.789
IT-> SS	1.226
IT-> ATR	1.345
IT -> TST	2.353
IT-> TD	1.126
ATR-> SE	1.257
ATR -> KR	1.141
ATR -> LO	2.453
ATR -> SS	1.326
TST-> SE	1.657
TST -> KR	1.780
TST -> LO	2.334
TST -> SS	1.566
TD-> SE	2.543
TD -> KR	1.981
TD -> LO	1.542
TD -> SS	1.226

Source: Authors calculation.

Table 4. Outer values

IT1	1.431
IT2	3.048
IT3	2.940
IT4	1.851
ATR1	3.477
ATR2	1.540
ATR3	3.443
ATR4	1.742
TST1	3.965
TST2	2.275
TST3	4.376
TST4	2.180
TD1	4.543
TD2	3.983
TD3	3.004
TD4	4.178
SE1	3.643
SE2	2.541
SE3	3.090
SE4	3.987

Table 4. (Continued)

KR1	4.248
KR2	2.493
KR3	2.347
KR4	2.450
LO1	2.731
LO2	3.345
LO3	4.217
LO4	3.540
SS1	3.412
SS2	3.576
SS3	4.351
SS4	2.132

Source: Authors calculation.

3.3.5. Coefficient of Determination (R Square)

By bootstrapping 5000 samples, the 'explanatory power' of the suggested model was also estimated using R^2 statistics (coefficient of determination). The value of R-squared determines the variance of the 'endogenous variable,' which is explained by 'exogenous variables.' The thumb rule values of R square are '0.25(weak), 0.50 (moderate), and 0.75 (significant)' proposed by Hair Jr et al., (2017). All the constructs of R-squared values are above 0.75, which states that the variables are significant from the table 5 below. Moreover, using the blindfolding sampling method, the 'Q-square' values were determined to assess the predictive relevance. The values of 'Q square' must be higher than "0," as per F. Hair Jr et al., (2014). The Q-square values of the Table 5 below satisfy the thumb rule.

Table 5. Predictive relevance and R-squared

Construct	R^2	Q^2
SE	0.832	0.790
KR	0.745	0.681
LO	0.842	0.756
SS	0.872	0.779
ATR	0.932	0.856
TST	0.915	0.882
TD	0.961	0.843

Source: Authors calculation.

The model fit is measured using 'SRMR (Standardized Root Mean Square Residual)' and 'NFI (Normalized Fit Index)' as suggested by Sarstedt et al., (2022). When the values of 'SRMR' is <0.08 and the values of 'NFI' is nearer to 0.9, the model is said to be a good fit. The following Table 6 depicts that the model fits well since it satisfies the thumb rule.

Table 6. Model fit

SRMR	0.069
NFI	0.814

Source: Authors calculation.

The significance of the proposed framework is tested using the 'bootstrapping technique' (Hair et al., 2017). The table below portrays the path outcome of the SEM model. The relationship between the variables is said to be significant when the values of p are less than 0.05.

Table 7. Hypothesises

Hypothesis		B	SD	T stat	P values	Hypothesis Supported
H1	IT>ATR	0.553	0.012	46.083	0.000	YES
H2	IT > TST	0.627	0.071	8.831	0.000	YES
H3	IT > TD	0.540	0.057	9.474	0.000	YES
H4	IT > SE	0.436	0.084	5.190	0.000	YES
H5	IT > KR	0.467	0.079	5.911	0.000	YES
H6	IT > LO	0.302	0.063	4.794	0.005	YES
H7	IT> SS	0.739	0.039	18.949	0.000	YES
H8	ATR > SE	0.432	0.058	7.448	0.000	YES
H9	ATR> KR	0.496	0.067	7.403	0.000	YES
H10	ATR >LO	0.211	0.056	3.768	0.001	YES
H11	ATR> SS	0.267	0.041	6.512	0.000	YES
H12	TST > SE	0.436	0.054	8.074	0.000	YES
H13	TST> KR	0.467	0.079	5.911	0.000	YES
H14	TST> LO	0.302	0.063	4.794	0.000	YES
H15	TST> SS	0.739	0.049	15.082	0.000	YES
H16	TD > SE	0.032	0.188	0.170	0.865	NO
H17	TD> KR	0.096	0.127	0.756	0.450	NO
H18	TD >LO	0.101	0.106	0.953	0.342	NO
H19	TD> SS	0.047	0.093	0.505	0.614	NO
H20	IT >ATR> SE	0.356	0.02	17.800	0.000	YES
H21	IT > TST>SE	0.567	0.064	8.859	0.000	YES
H22	IT > TD>SE	0.112	0.084	1.333	0.185	NO
H23	IT >ATR> KR	0.336	0.057	5.895	0.000	YES
H24	IT > TST>KR	0.357	0.035	10.200	0.000	YES
H25	IT > TD>KR	0.052	0.087	0.598	0.075	NO
H26	IT >ATR> LO	0.426	0.059	7.220	0.000	YES
H27	IT > TST>LO	0.512	0.053	9.660	0.000	YES
H28	IT > TD>LO	0.102	0.089	1.146	0.254	NO
H29	IT >ATR> SS	0.436	0.043	10.140	0.000	YES
H30	IT > TST>SS	0.377	0.071	5.310	0.000	YES
H31	IT > TD>SS	0.021	0.083	0.253	0.800	NO

Source: Author's calculation.

The relationship between the variables is shown in Table 7 above. 'H1 (β = 0.553, SD = 0.012, t = 46.083, p = 0.000), H2 (β = 0.627, SD = 0.071, t = 8.831, p = 0.000), H3 (β = 0.540, SD = 0.057, t = 9.474, p = 0.000),' are supported, stating that IT has significant influence on ATR, TST and TD. The t-statistics and the p values of H1, H2, and H3 indicate that IT has an effect on the mediating variables (ATR, TST and TD). As per a study conducted by Savytska et al., (2024) in order to explore the impact of IT in the educational sector, it is found that IT plays a vital role in collecting study materials, which helps to attain high pass results. Similarly, Sun (2024) conducted a study to explore the technical glitches and the difficulties faced by the students when IT is used. The study revealed that proper training and support help the students to overcome the challenges when IT is used. This supports our study's findings that IT has an impact on ATR, TST and TD. 'H4 (β = 0.436, SD = 0.084, t = 5.190, p = 0.000), H5 (β = 0.467,

SD = 0.079, t = 5.911, p = 0.000), H6 (β = 0.302, SD = 0.063, t = 4.794, p = 0.005), and H7 (β = 0.739, SD = 0.039, t = 18.949, p = 0.000)' are supported. This reveals that IT has a strong positive direct influence on SE, KR, LO and SS. Garlinska et al., (2023) confirm this finding, mentioning that the use of IT keeps the students engaged and helps the students to retain knowledge that leads to LO. Therefore, the pass percentage of the students increases that leads to success factor and SS. ' H8 (β = 0.432, SD = 0.058, t = 7.448, p = 0.000), H9 (β = 0.496, SD = 0.067, t = 7.403, p = 0.000), H10 (β = 0.211, SD = 0.056, t = 3.768, p = 0.001), H11 (β = 0.267, SD = 0.041, t = 6.512, p = 0.000), H12 (β = 0.436, SD = 0.054, t = 8.074, p = 0.000), H13 (β = 0.467, SD = 0.079, t = 5.911,p = 0.000), H14 (β=0.302, SD=0.063, t=4.794, p=0.000), H15 (β = 0.739, SD = 0.049, t = 15.082, p = 0.000)' are supported as the p values of "H8, H9, H10, H11, H12, H13, H14 and H15," satisfy the threshold value of $p < 0.05$. Whereas, 'H16: TD > SE (β = 0.032, SD = 0.188, t = 0.170, p = 0.865), H17: TD > KR (β = 0.096, SD = 0.127, t = 0.756, p = 0.450), H18: TD > LO (β = 0.101, SD = 0.106, t = 0.953, p = 0.342), H19: TD > SS (β = 0.047, SD = 0.093, t = 0.505, p = 0.614)' are rejected since the p value does not satisfy the thumb rule. Therefore, the relationship between the mediating variables and the dependent variables are positive for the ATR, TST and SE, KR, LO and SS. For the variables TD and SE, KR, LO and SS there is a negative impact which clearly depicts that TD has negative influence that leads the student's dissatisfaction where they face problem in achieving the knowledge. This finding is supported by Kaur et al., (2022), stating that availability of resources and proper training helps the students to be engaged, attentive and to gain knowledge but TD brings irritability that leads of lack of concentration among the students. The indirect relationship among the variables were tested using the proposed 'H20 (β = 0.356, SD = 0.020, t = 17.800, p = 0.000), H21 (β = 0.567, SD = 0.064, t = 8.859, p = 0.000), H23 (β = 0.336, SD = 0.057, t = 5.895, p = 0.000), H24 (β = 0.357, SD = 0.035, t = 10.200, p = 0.000), H26 (β = 0.426, SD = 0.059, t = 7.220, p = 0.000), H27 (β = 0.512, SD = 0.053, t = 9.660, p = 0.000), H29 (β = 0.436, SD = 0.043, t = 10.140, p = 0.000), H30 (β = 0.377, SD = 0.071, t = 5.310, p = 0.000),' which shows significant results. Whereas 'H22 (β = 0.112, SD = 0.084, t = 1.333, p = 0.185), H25 (β = 0.052, SD = 0.087, t = 0.598, p = 0.075), H28 (β = 0.102, SD = 0.089, t = 1.146, p = 0.254) and H31 (β = 0.021, SD = 0.083, t = 0.253, p = 0.800)' are insignificant as the p values are greater than 0.05. To explain, the mediating factors such ATR and TST shows positive significant indirect effect between IT and SE, KR, LO and SS but TD shows insignificant indirect effect between IT and SE, KR, LO and SS. This clearly depicts that in distance learning mode students lack satisfaction, lack knowledge and not able to give proper results when they face technical challenge while using IT. This finding is supported by Serrano-Ausejo & Mårell-Olsson (2024), in his study when exploring the challenges face by students in online learning.

4. Discussion

This study sheds light on the impact of IT on improving learning facilities for students in distance education, especially in rural and remote regions. The quantitative study employing the PLS-SEM statistical technique has yielded both positive and negative impacts on the proposed hypotheses. As per the results of 'H1, H2, H3, H4, H5, H6, H7' it is clear that there is a positive influence of IT on different facets of education including ATR, TST, TD, SE, KR, LO and SS. Lee et al., (2021) stress that not only does the IT training increase students interest, but that there are clear student achievement gains in retention of content that will help them do well on exams. The conclusion of this research supports such claims, showing that learners who receive proper support when using IT in their learning activities tend to benefit from the technology by attaining positive learning performances. To test the relationship between the mediating variable and the factors of successive digital learning, the results of 'H8, H9, H10, H11, H12, H13, H14, H15, H16, H17, H18, H19' were analysed. The results show a positive relationship between ATR, TST and SE, KR, LO and SS and a negative relationship between TD and SE, KR, LO and SS. This indicates that IT is not only a boon, but almost mandatory to support distance education students' learning environments. The use of IT in learning Impact often has contributed positively to SE, KR, LO, and SS because of offering participation and interest. Calvet et al., (2019) opined that there is a need to adopt VR and AR as the advancement in these technologies can provide students with educational experiences which make them understand and assimilate the contents taught with more ease. The indirect relationship between the variables was also tested using the 'H20, H21, H22, H23, H24, H25, H26, H27, H28, H29, H30 and H31,' where the results clearly depict there is positive impact between the variables IT and SE, KR, LO and SS when ATR and TST mediates. In contracts, there is a negative impact between the variables IT, SE, KR, LO and SS when TD mediates. These findings therefore suggest that there is a need for educational institutions, especially in rural and remote areas, to properly equip themselves with the necessary IT resources, without any last-minute technical glitches and by providing training programs to the individuals most likely to use these resources in their workplaces. This way, the educational gap can be filled, which is frequently seen in distance learning in remote and rural areas. Immersive technologies do not just improve the experience of learning but enable students to equip themselves, which is essential in a world dominated by technology, and they can potentially bring dramatic changes in distance education, enhancing the ability for all learners to learn deeply, efficiently and enjoyably (Savytska et al., 2024).

5. Theoretical Implications

The findings of this current study propose important implications for the theoretical propositions concerning the application of IT in distance learning, especially relying on excitation techniques like VR and AR. Consequently, the research findings show a positive relationship of PEU and PU of IT that has an impact on SE and LO. This weight from the TAM theory postulates that when students ascertain that a certain technology is easy to use and beneficial, their usage of that technology is enhanced (Scherer, Siddiq, and Tondeur 2019). The results obtained in this study support the conclusions made by Venkatesh et al., (2007) that the positive experiences with the IT increase the educational benefit. The findings also shed the light that appropriate training and usage of technology improve the student's perceived competence and autonomy which makes them part of SDT. Kusurkar et al., (2011) suggest that the satisfaction of the psychological needs will better engagement and motivation. The findings showing an increased trend of IT and SS supports the proposition of SDT in a learning environment because support received from the students enhances their depth of engagement with content. The results reveal that by using IT, it is possible to moderate the cognitive load and enhance the KR and LO. This goes a long way in supporting Sweller (2011), position that the elimination of all unnecessary cognitive load improves the efficiency of learning. The outcomes of the present research support the idea that it is easier and more effective to grasp information when interacting with content within immersive environments, consistent with Mayer (2008). The findings of the study show that the implementation of IT draws students into participation and interaction while learning as envisaged by the CLT. IT caused significant changes in student learning and relations, including increased likability and student LO, which may indicate that these technologies foster contextual learning that results from students' interactions and exploration (Brown, Metz, and Campione 2013). This is supported by Jonassen & Carr (2020), assertion that technology can support constructivist learning environments that are rich in the use of IT. According to findings of the study, the integration of IT increases social presence in online learning environments and has a corresponding positive impact on the SE and SS. This finding concords with the works of Jézégou (2010), who stressed the role of interaction in learning. Positive association between IT and SE indicates that using technologies such as gamification the students feel that they are part of a group that is learning together which is an aspect that is key in online course effectiveness (Hoffmann et al., 2011).

5.1. Practical Implications

The incorporation of ITs like VR and AR systems to distance education brings opportunities for students attending from remote and rural areas since they encounter constraints in accessing upright educational materials (Li, Fang, and Jiang 2022). Another area in which the benefits of VR are striking is virtual scientific laboratories. For example, today, there is a possibility to immerse students who study in remote areas, where actual physical science labs are not available, into complex experiments with the help of platforms like Labster (Erven H. Mosqueda 2023). Besides offering them practical experience, it also builds their knowledge on some academic concepts which are usually hard to understand when taught using conventional textbooks. This way, students' interest in STEM fields would deepen when solving something with the help of interactive simulations like the study of chemical reactions or the law of physics (Falloon, 2019). Apart from the computerized laboratories, there are even greater prospects for using AR in providing students with effective learning outside classrooms. For instance, when using AR tools, instructors can organise virtual tours of historical sites or museums which are perhaps stationary far away. Tools such as Google Expeditions enable students to travel from a class to the Great Wall of China or from a class to the Louvre without leaving the classroom, while learning at the same time is more engaging (Bosmos et al., 2023). Different kinds of learning are most effective in the present interactive learning experiences since the learners can touch and manipulate representations of actual objects and information. Immersive platforms would also help in improving collaboration among students to a very large extent. Software such as Engage and Alt space VR foster a group meeting platform on which students who are from different geographical locations can meet for group projects. At the same time, it builds an effective model of the actual classroom setting as well as improves students' collaboration and mutual communication, which are crucial in the present world. Time-to-time interaction in a 3D space also allows sharing of most essential resources, joint generation of ideas as well as proposing solutions to problems, and therefore enhances students' learning (Alcala, D'Achille, and Bruckman 2023). For these technologies to be used appropriately, trainers must support educators to ensure they use these technologies appropriately. Professionals can design VR simulations through which teachers can rehearse the application of immersive tools under sandbox conditions. For instance, a training program could be a classroom emulation, and the trainers can allow educators to practice various teaching practices and see the results immediately. The practical interaction assists educators in gaining confidence and expertise in the use of technological tools for learning with positive impacts on their students through improved delivery of teaching services (Samaniego Erazo, Esteve-González, and Vaca 2015). However, desirable behaviours can also be rewarded intentionally by using gamification strategies which will enhance students' motivation. Classcraft is an example of how present-day learning platforms incorporate game elements and guidelines in which students gain points and enhance their ability to perform activities and work in teams. The use of such an approach might be more effective in rural areas since other traditional techniques might not be as effective for the students. That is why if learning is treated as a game, educators will be able to stimulate activity to carry out lessons. Other factors that should be afforded priority in the integration of IT are also a matter of accessibility and interactivity (Rivera-Trigueros & Sánchez-Pérez 2020). AR applications allow enhancing students communication experience with real-time translations or subtitles for non-English speaking students or deaf students. For instance, when learning tools such as Google Translate are incorporated with AR, there will be equality in the sense that every learner will be able to be taught accordingly, regardless of their learning disability or origin. This way, each learner has a chance to be engaged in full-blown educational endeavours (Geng, 2024). Finally, IT enable the idea of project-based learning that responds to real-life challenges within students' environment. For example, students can apply VR technology to solve urban planning situations that would enable them to develop solutions to local environmental issues. Besides improving analytical and practical thinking, it contributes to students' responsibility and their willingness to change the world for the better (Radianti et al., 2020).

Conclusion

The adaptation of IT, including VR and AR, in distance education settings promises a revolution in teaching and learning challenges faced by remote and rural learners. These technologies can help connect students from disadvantaged social backgrounds to other learning systems via virtual laboratory equipment, field trips and group learning. The presentation of subject matter in a way that the learner is fully engaged and able to interact with it extends beyond mere recall, comprehension, and critique, but also develops the problem-solving skills required by today's society. Also, development and successful implementation of these technologies necessitate dedication and support for education professional development and making sure they are ready for new technologically enhanced methodologies. By promoting an approach towards innovation and flexibility in the learning processes, the institutions can help their teachers to properly use IT to help their students. Furthermore, challenges of access and equity must also be considered so that all learner, regardless of their disability, economic disadvantage or from a minority background, among others, can effectively benefit from these developments.

Limitations and Future Scope

This current study is subject to certain limitations. Firstly, the study mainly concentrates on the existing literature concerning the use of IT in distance education, which may not identify all the issues arising in actual environments. Secondly, generalisation of the results could be slightly impaired due to the relatively small sample size and the homogeneity of the participants. Furthermore, the study could fail to address the issue of differential technological skills among students, which determines their interaction and performance. Lastly, the fast-growing application of technology presents a threat to the reliability of the research findings since it is almost certain that new methods and tools will be developed in the process of conducting the research. Further research should focus on carrying out practical investigations on the extant uses and impacts of IT in various learning environments to inform learning in the current and even in future contexts, especially in remote and rural settings. Furthermore, expansion of studies into how such approaches in learning as offered by the IT affect the students' interest, their ability to assimilate knowledge, and their performance levels will give further insight into the merits of such technological applications in learning.

References

Abdraimova, E T, Shoibekova A Zh, and K B Zhorabaev. 2020. "Immersive Technologies in a Higher School in the Modern Digital Reality." *Евразийский Союз Ученых*, no. 10-1 (79): 49–52.

Al-Abdullah, Ammar, and Leila Hassan. 2023. "Factors Determining the Success and Failure of EdTech Initiatives in Rural Academic Institutions." *AI, IoT and the Fourth Industrial Revolution Review* 13 (7): 47–60.

Alcala, Katrina, Anthony D'Achille, and Amy Bruckman. 2023. "The Stage and the Theatre: AltspaceVR and Its Relationship to Discord." *Proceedings of the ACM on Human-Computer Interaction* 7 (April): 1–21. https://doi.org/10.1145/3579529.

Ali, Shehbaz. 2022. "The Effectiveness of Immersive Technologies for Future Professional Education." *Futurity Education* 2 (2): 14–22.

Alqurashi, Emtinan. 2019. "Predicting Student Satisfaction and Perceived Learning within Online Learning Environments." *Distance Education* 40 (1): 133–48.

Antonaci, Alessandra, Roland Klemke, and Marcus Specht. 2019. "The Effects of Gamification in Online Learning Environments: A Systematic Literature Review." In *Informatics*, 6:32. MDPI.

Bagher, Mahda M. 2020. "Immersive vr and Embodied Learning: The Role of Embodied Affordances in the Long-Term Retention of Semantic Knowledge." In *2020 Ieee Conference on Virtual Reality and 3d User Interfaces Abstracts and Workshops (Vrw)*, 537–38. IEEE.

Baxter, Gavin, and Thomas Hainey. 2024a. "Using Immersive Technologies to Enhance the Student Learning Experience." *Interactive Technology and Smart Education* 21 (3): 403–25. https://doi.org/10.1108/ITSE-05-2023-0078.

———. 2024b. "Using Immersive Technologies to Enhance the Student Learning Experience." *Interactive Technology and Smart Education* 21 (3): 403–25.

Beckem, John M, and Michael Watkins. 2012. "Bringing Life to Learning: Immersive Experiential Learning Simulations for Online and Blended Courses." *Journal of Asynchronous Learning Networks* 16 (5): 61–70.

Bizami, Najwa Amanina, Zaidatun Tasir, and Si Na Kew. 2023a. *Innovative Pedagogical Principles and Technological Tools Capabilities for Immersive Blended Learning: A Systematic Literature Review. Education and Information Technologies*. Vol. 28. Springer US. https://doi.org/10.1007/s10639-022-11243-w.

———. 2023b. "Innovative Pedagogical Principles and Technological Tools Capabilities for Immersive Blended Learning: A Systematic Literature Review." *Education and Information Technologies* 28 (2): 1373–1425.

Bosmos, Fotios, Alexandros T. Tzallas, Markos G. Tsipouras, Evripidis Glavas, and Nikolaos Giannakeas. 2023. "Virtual and Augmented Experience in Virtual Learning Tours †." *Information (Switzerland)* 14 (5): 1–16. https://doi.org/10.3390/info14050294.

Brown, Ann L, Kathleen E Metz, and Joseph C Campione. 2013. "Social Interaction and Individual Understanding in a Community of Learners: The Influence of Piaget and Vygotsky." In *Piaget Vygotsky*, 145–70. Psychology Press.

Calvet, Laura, Pierre Bourdin, and Ferran Prados. 2019. "Immersive Technologies in Higher Education: Applications, Challenges, and Good Practices." In *Proceedings of the 2019 3rd International Conference on Education and E-Learning*, 95–99.

Carella, G, and M Melazzini. 2023. "Teaching Design in a Fully Remote Environment: Challenges and Changes in the Pedagogical Approach during the Covid-19 Pandemic." *ICERI2023 Proceedings*, 3985–90.

Carpentieri, Renato, Maria Elena Iannoni, Martina Curto, Mario Biagiarelli, Giulia Listanti, Maria Paola Andraos, Beatrice Mantovani, Carla Farulla, Simona Pelaccia, and Giuseppe Grosso. 2022. "School Refusal Behavior: Role of Personality Styles, Social Functioning, and Psychiatric Symptoms in a Sample of Adolescent Help-Seekers." *Clinical Neuropsychiatry* 19 (1): 20.

Chang, Chu-Ling. 2022. "Effect of Immersive Virtual Reality on Post-Baccalaureate Nursing Students' in-Dwelling Urinary Catheter Skill and Learning Satisfaction." In *Healthcare*, 10:1473. MDPI.

Childs, Elizabeth, Ferzam Mohammad, Logan Stevens, Hugo Burbelo, Amanuel Awoke, Nicholas Rewkowski, and Dinesh Manocha. 2024. "An Overview of Enhancing Distance Learning Through Emerging Augmented and Virtual Reality Technologies." *IEEE Transactions on Visualization and Computer Graphics* 30 (8): 4480–96. https://doi.org/10.1109/TVCG.2023.3264577.

Chin, Wynne W., Robert A. Peterson, and Steven P. Brown. 2008. "Structural Equation Modeling in Marketing: Some Practical Reminders." *Journal of Marketing Theory and Practice* 16 (4): 287–98. https://doi.org/10.2753/MTP1069-6679160402.

Chittaro, Luca, and Fabio Buttussi. 2015. "Assessing Knowledge Retention of an Immersive Serious Game vs. a Traditional Education Method in Aviation Safety." *IEEE Transactions on Visualization and Computer Graphics* 21 (4): 529–38.

Costa, Ana Carolina Ferreira, Vitor Homem de Mello Santos, and Otávio José de OLIVEIRA. 2022. "Towards the Revolution and Democratization of Education: A Framework to Overcome Challenges and Explore Opportunities through Industry 4.0." *Informatics in Education* 21 (1): 1–32.

Davies, Christine, and Stephen Palmer. n.d. "A Quick Guide to Quantitative Research in the Social Sciences A Quick Guide to Quantitative Research in the Social Sciences Acknowledgements I Am Very Grateful for the Support and Suggestions of Colleagues Including Professor."

Deci, Edward L, Anja H Olafsen, and Richard M Ryan. 2017. "Self-Determination Theory in Work Organizations: The State of a Science." *Annual Review of Organizational Psychology and Organizational Behavior* 4 (1): 19–43.

Dede, Chris. 2009. "Immersive Interfaces for Engagement and Learning." *Science* 323 (5910): 66–69.

Dengel, Andreas, and Jutta Mägdefrau. 2018. "Immersive Learning Explored: Subjective and Objective Factors Influencing Learning Outcomes in Immersive Educational Virtual Environments." In *2018 IEEE International Conference on Teaching, Assessment, and Learning for Engineering (TALE)*, 608–15. IEEE.

Detyna, Michael, and Marta Koch. 2023. "An Overview of Student Perceptions of Hybrid Flexible Learning at a London HEI." *Journal of Interactive Media in Education* 2023 (1).

Erven H. Mosqueda, Clint. 2023. "Effect of Utilizing Interactive Virtual Lab on Students Performance in Physics." *International Journal of Advanced Research* 11 (05): 1718–41. https://doi.org/10.21474/ijar01/17041.

Falloon, Garry. 2019. "Using Simulations to Teach Young Students Science Concepts: An Experiential Learning Theoretical Analysis." *Computers and Education* 135 (March): 138–59. https://doi.org/10.1016/j.compedu.2019.03.001.

Fernandes, Filipe Arantes, Claudia Susie Camargo Rodrigues, Eldânae Nogueira Teixeira, and Cláudia M L Werner. 2023. "Immersive Learning Frameworks: A Systematic Literature Review." *IEEE Transactions on Learning Technologies* 16 (5): 736–47.

Fitrianto, Ibnu, and Ali Saif. 2024. "The Role of Virtual Reality in Enhancing Experiential Learning: A Comparative Study of Traditional and Immersive Learning Environments." *International Journal of Post Axial: Futuristic Teaching and Learning*, 97–110.

Fredricks, Jennifer A, Phyllis C Blumenfeld, and Alison H Paris. 2004. "School Engagement: Potential of the Concept, State of the Evidence." *Review of Educational Research* 74 (1): 59–109.

Freeman, Daniel, Sarah Reeve, Abi Robinson, Anke Ehlers, David Clark, Bernhard Spanlang, and Mel Slater. 2017. "Virtual Reality in the Assessment, Understanding, and Treatment of Mental Health Disorders." *Psychological Medicine* 47 (14): 2393–2400.

Freitas, Sara De, Genaro Rebolledo-Mendez, Fotis Liarokapis, George Magoulas, and Alexandra Poulovassilis. 2010. "Learning as Immersive Experiences: Using the Four-dimensional Framework for Designing and Evaluating Immersive Learning Experiences in a Virtual World." *British Journal of Educational Technology* 41 (1): 69–85.

Garlinska, Magdalena, Magdalena Osial, Klaudia Proniewska, and Agnieszka Pregowska. 2023. "The Influence of Emerging Technologies on Distance Education." *Electronics* 12 (7): 1550.

Geng, Xiaolong. 2024. "Enhancing Translation Education Through Augmented Reality (AR):" *International Journal of Web-Based Learning and Teaching Technologies* 19 (January): 1–22. https://doi.org/10.4018/IJWLTT.361651.

Gnana Sinthiya, R. Hepzibah, and Kishore Kulothungan. 2021. "IMPACT OF DIGITAL RUMOURS IN AN ACUTE EVENT (With Reference to WhatsApp Users)." *Towards Excellence* 13 (1): 113–25. https://doi.org/10.37867/te130111.

Gonzálvez, Carolina, Ricardo Sanmartín, María Vicent, and José Manuel García-Fernández. 2021. "Exploring Different Types of School Refusers through Latent Profile Analysis and School-Related Stress Associations." *Science Progress* 104 (3): 00368504211029464.

Goode, Elizabeth, Thomas Roche, Erica Wilson, and John McKenzie. 2023. "An Exploratory Study of Student Satisfaction in the Southern Cross Model." *Southern Cross University Scholarship of Learning and Teaching Paper*, no. 7.

Goode, Elizabeth, Thomas Roche, Erica Wilson, and John W McKenzie. 2024. "Student Perceptions of Immersive Block Learning: An Exploratory Study of Student Satisfaction in the Southern Cross Model." *Journal of Further and Higher Education* 48 (2): 153–67.

Goode, Elizabeth, Thomas Roche, Erica Wilson, Jacky Zhang, and John W McKenzie. 2024. "The Success, Satisfaction and Experiences of International Students in an Immersive Block Model." *Journal of University Teaching & Learning Practice* 21 (2): 8.

Gunasekare, ULTP. 2016. "Self Determination Theory (SDT): A Review on SDT as a Complementary Theory of Motivation." *Kelaniya Journal of Human Resource Management* 11 (1).

Hair, Joseph F., G. Tomas Hult, Christian Ringle, and Marko Sarstedt. 2017. *A Primer on Partial Least Squares Structural Equation Modeling (PLS-SEM) - Joseph F. Hair, Jr., G. Tomas M. Hult, Christian Ringle, Marko Sarstedt. Sage.*

Hair, Joseph F, Marko Sarstedt, Christian M Ringle, and Siegfried P Gudergan. 2021. *Advanced Issues in Partial Least Squares Structural Equation Modeling (PLS-SEM)*. saGe publications.

Hair Jr, Joseph F, Marko Sarstedt, Christian M Ringle, and Siegfried P Gudergan. 2017. *Advanced Issues in Partial Least Squares Structural Equation Modeling*. saGe publications.

Hair F. Jr, Joe, Marko Sarstedt, Lucas Hopkins, and Volker G. Kuppelwieser. 2014. "Partial Least Squares Structural Equation Modeling (PLS-SEM) An Emerging Tool in Business Research." *European Business Review* 26 (2): 106–21.

Hamilton, David, Jim McKechnie, Edward Edgerton, and Claire Wilson. 2021. "Immersive Virtual Reality as a Pedagogical Tool in Education: A Systematic Literature Review of Quantitative Learning Outcomes and Experimental Design." *Journal of Computers in Education* 8 (1): 1–32.

Hepzibah, Gnana S. 2023. "'Fake News Viruses on the Deformation Trial: A Look At the Lawsuit Between Johnny Depp and Amber Heard.'" *Humanities and Social Science Studies* 12 (1): 97–104. https://www.researchgate.net/profile/R-Hepzibah-Sinthiya/publication/370105383_FAKE_NEWS_

VIRUSES_ON_THE_DEFORMATION_TRIAL_A_LOOK_AT_THE_LAWSUIT_BETWEEN_JOHNNY_DEPP_AND_AMBER_HEARD/links/643f96e939aa471a524af087/FAKE-NEWS-VIRUSES-ON-THE-DEFORMATION-TRIAL-A.

Hoffmann, Thomas J, Mark N Kvale, Stephanie E Hesselson, Yiping Zhan, Christine Aquino, Yang Cao, Simon Cawley, Elaine Chung, Sheryl Connell, and Jasmin Eshragh. 2011. "Next Generation Genome-Wide Association Tool: Design and Coverage of a High-Throughput European-Optimized SNP Array." *Genomics* 98 (2): 79–89.

Huang, Kuo-Ting, Christopher Ball, Jessica Francis, Rabindra Ratan, Josephine Boumis, and Joseph Fordham. 2019. "Augmented versus Virtual Reality in Education: An Exploratory Study Examining Science Knowledge Retention When Using Augmented Reality/Virtual Reality Mobile Applications." *Cyberpsychology, Behavior, and Social Networking* 22 (2): 105–10.

Irons, Larry R., Donald J. Jung, and Robert O. Keel. 2002. "Interactivity in Distance Learning: The Digital Divide and Student Satisfaction." *Educational Technology and Society* 5 (3): 175–88.

Jézégou, Annie. 2010. "Community of Inquiry in E-Learning: A Critical Analysis of Garrison and Anderson Model." *Journal of Distance Education/Revue de l'Education à Distance* 24 (3): 1–18.

Jonassen, David H, and Chad S Carr. 2020. "Mindtools: Affording Multiple Knowledge Representations for Learning." In *Computers as Cognitive Tools*, 165–96. Routledge.

Kaur, Deepti Prit, Amit Kumar, Rubina Dutta, and Shivani Malhotra. 2022. "The Role of Interactive and Immersive Technologies in Higher Education: A Survey." *Journal of Engineering Education Transformations* 36 (2): 79–86.

Khamis, Huzani, Moh Khairudin Khairudin, Azrul Hazri Jantan, Nuur Alifah Roslan, and Lili Nurliyana Abdullah. 2024. "A Systematic Review of Adapting Immersive Technology in Enhancing Teaching and Learning for Students in Higher Education." *Journal of Advanced Research in Applied Sciences and Engineering Technology*, 130–45.

Kirschner, Paul A, John Sweller, Femke Kirschner, and Jimmy Zambrano R. 2018. "From Cognitive Load Theory to Collaborative Cognitive Load Theory." *International Journal of Computer-Supported Collaborative Learning* 13: 213–33.

Kneebone, Roger, Sonal Arora, Dominic King, Fernando Bello, Nick Sevdalis, Eva Kassab, Raj Aggarwal, Ara Darzi, and Debra Nestel. 2010. "Distributed Simulation–Accessible Immersive Training." *Medical Teacher* 32 (1): 65–70.

Kuhail, Mohammad Amin, Areej Elsayary, Shahbano Farooq, and Ahlam Alghamdi. 2022. "Exploring Immersive Learning Experiences: A Survey." *Informatics* 9 (4). https://doi.org/10.3390/informatics9040075.

Kuhail, Mohammad Amin, Areej ElSayary, Shahbano Farooq, and Ahlam Alghamdi. 2022. "Exploring Immersive Learning Experiences: A Survey." In *Informatics*, 9:75. MDPI.

Kusurkar, Rashmi A, Gerda Croiset, and Olle Th J Ten Cate. 2011. "Twelve Tips to Stimulate Intrinsic Motivation in Students through Autonomy-Supportive Classroom Teaching Derived from Self-Determination Theory." *Medical Teacher* 33 (12): 978–82.

Lai, Poey Chin. 2017. "The Literature Review of Technology Adoption Models and Theories for the Novelty Technology." *JISTEM-Journal of Information Systems and Technology Management* 14 (1): 21–38.

Lee, Joongjae, Jaeheung Surh, Wooseong Choi, and Bumjae You. 2021. "Immersive Virtual-Reality-Based Streaming Distance Education System for Solar Dynamics Observatory: A Case Study." *Applied Sciences* 11 (19): 8932.

Lees-Smith, Hannah. 2024. "An Appreciative Inquiry into How Primary and Secondary Schools Support Emotionally Based School Avoidance." University of Sheffield.

Levy, Karen E C. 2014. "The Automation of Compliance: Techno-Legal Regulation in the United States Trucking Industry." Princeton University.

Li, Pengfei, Zelong Fang, and Tan Jiang. 2022. "Research Into Improved Distance Learning Using VR Technology." *Frontiers in Education* 7 (February): 1–14. https://doi.org/10.3389/feduc.2022.757874.

Liubchak, Volodymyr O, Yurii O Zuban, and Artem E Artyukhov. 2022. "Immersive Learning Technology for Ensuring Quality Education: Ukrainian University Case." In *CTE Workshop Proceedings*, 9:336–54.

Lowry, Paul Benjamin, and James Gaskin. 2014. "Partial Least Squares (PLS) Structural Equation Modeling (SEM) for Building and Testing Behavioral Causal Theory: When to Choose It and How to Use It." *IEEE Transactions on Professional Communication* 57 (2): 123–46.

Mayer, Richard E. 2008. "Applying the Science of Learning: Evidence-Based Principles for the Design of Multimedia Instruction." *American Psychologist* 63 (8): 760.

Mustafa, Abdulsalam Salihu, and Manuel B Garcia. 2021. "Theories Integrated with Technology Acceptance Model (TAM) in Online Learning Acceptance and Continuance Intention: A Systematic Review." In *2021 1st Conference on Online Teaching for Mobile Education (OT4ME)*, 68–72. IEEE.

North, Max M. 2014. "Distance Learning Immersive Environments: Sense of Presence Exploration." *Journal of Visual Languages & Computing* 25 (6): 1040–41.

Ntaba, Afika, and Mmaki Jantjies. 2019. "Open Distance Learning and Immersive Technologies: A Literature Analysis." *16th International Conference on Cognition and Exploratory Learning in Digital Age, CELDA 2019*, no. Celda: 51–60. https://doi.org/10.33965/celda2019_2019111007.

Onopriienko, Iryna, Kateryna Volodymyrivna Onopriienko, and Salmane Bourekkadi. 2023. "Immersive Technologies in Adult Learning as an Innovative Marketing Tool in the Educational Market."

Park, So Young, and Jung-Hee Kim. 2022. "Instructional Design and Educational Satisfaction for Virtual Environment Simulation in Undergraduate Nursing Education: The Mediating Effect of Learning Immersion." *BMC Medical Education* 22 (1): 673.

Partarakis, Nikolaos, and Xenophon Zabulis. 2024. "A Review of Immersive Technologies, Knowledge Representation, and AI for Human-Centered Digital Experiences." *Electronics* 13 (2): 269.

Plass, Jan L, Roxana Moreno, and Roland Brünken. 2010. "*Cognitive Load Theory*."

Preedip Balaji, B., and Vinit Kumar. 2011. "Use of Web Technology in Providing Information Services by South Indian Technological Universities as Displayed on Library Websites." *Library Hi Tech* 29 (3): 470–95. https://doi.org/10.1108/07378831111174431.

Radianti, Jaziar, Tim A. Majchrzak, Jennifer Fromm, and Isabell Wohlgenannt. 2020. "A Systematic Review of Immersive Virtual Reality Applications for Higher Education: Design Elements, Lessons Learned, and Research Agenda." *Computers and Education* 147 (July 2019): 103778. https://doi.org/10.1016/j.compedu.2019.103778.

Ringle, Christian M., Marko Sarstedt, Noemi Sinkovics, and Rudolf R. Sinkovics. 2023. "A Perspective on Using Partial Least Squares Structural Equation Modelling in Data Articles." *Data in Brief* 48 (June). https://doi.org/10.1016/j.dib.2023.109074.

Rivera-Trigueros, Irene, and Maria Del Mar Sánchez-Pérez. 2020. "Classcraft as a Resource to Implement Gamification in English-Medium Instruction." *Teacher Training for English-Medium Instruction in Higher Education*, no. May: 356–71. https://doi.org/10.4018/978-1-7998-2318-6.ch017.

Ryan, Grace V, Shauna Callaghan, Anthony Rafferty, Mary F Higgins, Eleni Mangina, and Fionnuala McAuliffe. 2022. "Learning Outcomes of Immersive Technologies in Health Care Student Education: Systematic Review of the Literature." *Journal of Medical Internet Research* 24 (2): e30082.

Ryan, Richard M, and Edward L Deci. 2024. "Self-Determination Theory." In *Encyclopedia of Quality of Life and Well-Being Research*, 6229–35. Springer.

Saito, Eisuke, Jennifer Mansfield, and Richard O'Donovan. 2024. "Information Economics of Teaching: A Transactional Perspective on Pedagogical Reasoning to Provide a Typology of Pedagogical Equilibrium." *Interactive Learning Environments* 32 (1): 20–33.

Samaniego Erazo, Gonzalo Nicolay, Vanessa Esteve-González, and Byron Vaca. 2015. "Teaching and Learning in Digital Worlds: Strategies and Issues in Higher Education." In , 129–36.

Sarstedt, Marko, Christian M. Ringle, and Joseph F. Hair. 2021. *Partial Least Squares Structural Equation Modeling. Handbook of Market Research.* Cham: Springer International Publishing. https://doi.org/10.1007/978-3-319-57413-4_15.

———. 2022. "Partial Least Squares Structural Equation Modeling." In *Handbook of Market Research*, edited by Christian Homburg, Martin Klarmann, and Arnd Vomberg, 587–632. Cham: Springer International Publishing. https://doi.org/10.1007/978-3-319-57413-4_15.

Savytska, Inna, Olena Tryfonova, Inna Feltsan, Vitalii Alekseiko, and Yaroslav Ahiy. 2024. "Immersive Technologies in the Educational Space." *Amazonia Investiga* 13 (75): 343–58.

Scherer, Ronny, Fazilat Siddiq, and Jo Tondeur. 2019. "The Technology Acceptance Model (TAM): A Meta-Analytic Structural Equation Modeling Approach to Explaining Teachers' Adoption of Digital Technology in Education." *Computers & Education* 128: 13–35.

Schnotz, Wolfgang, and Christian Kürschner. 2007. "A Reconsideration of Cognitive Load Theory." *Educational Psychology Review* 19: 469–508.

Semerikov, Serhiy O, Tetiana A Vakaliuk, Iryna S Mintii, Vita A Hamaniuk, Vladimir N Soloviev, Olga V Bondarenko, Pavlo P Nechypurenko, Svitlana V Shokaliuk, Natalia V Moiseienko, and Dmytro S Shepiliev. 2021. "Immersive E-Learning Resources: Design Methods." In *Digital Humanities Workshop*, 37–47.

Serrano-Ausejo, Elisa, and Eva Mårell-Olsson. 2024. "Opportunities and Challenges of Using Immersive Technologies to Support Students' Spatial Ability and 21st-Century Skills in K-12 Education." *Education and Information Technologies* 29 (5): 5571–97.

"Shiksha." n.d. https://www.shiksha.com/colleges/tamil-nadu-2.

Shwedeh, Fanar, Ahmad Aburayya, Ogbolu Gbemisola, and Ayotunde Adetola Adelaja. 2024. "Assessing the Role of Augmented Reality in Enhancing Employee Operational Engagement and Knowledge Retention in UAE Business Training." *Global Knowledge, Memory and Communication.*

Silva, Marlene N, Marta M Marques, and Pedro J Teixeira. 2014. "Testing Theory in Practice: The Example of Self-Determination Theory-Based Interventions." *European Health Psychologist* 16 (5): 171–80.

Silva, Patrícia. 2015. "Davis' Technology Acceptance Model (TAM)(1989)." *Information Seeking Behavior and Technology Adoption: Theories and Trends*, 205–19.

Sinthiya, R Hepzibah Gnana. 2024. "*A Study on Reliability of News Shared in Social Media Platforms (With Reference to Whatsapp Users*)" 1 (1).

Skinner, Ellen, Carrie Furrer, Gwen Marchand, and Thomas Kindermann. 2008. "Engagement and Disaffection in the Classroom: Part of a Larger Motivational Dynamic?" *Journal of Educational Psychology* 100 (4): 765.

Suh, Ayoung, and Jane Prophet. 2018. "The State of Immersive Technology Research: A Literature Analysis." *Computers in Human Behavior* 86: 77–90. https://doi.org/10.1016/j.chb.2018.04.019.

Sun, Wei. 2024. "Immersive Technology in Education and Its Essential Characteristics." *Рекомендовано До Друку Рішенням Вченої Ради ПАНО Ім. МВ Остроградського (Протокол № 6 Від 25 Жовтня 2024 Року)*, 155.

Swargiary, Khritish. 2024. *ICT Revolutionizing Education.* GOOGLE.

Sweller, John. 2011. "Cognitive Load Theory." In *Psychology of Learning and Motivation*, 55:37–76. Elsevier.

Venkatesh, Viswanath, Fred Davis, and Michael G Morris. 2007. "Dead or Alive? The Development, Trajectory and Future of Technology Adoption Research." *The Development, Trajectory and Future of Technology Adoption Research (April 27, 2007). Venkatesh, V., Davis, FD, and Morris, MG "Dead or Alive*, 267–86.

Wu, C H, Y M Tang, Y P Tsang, and K Y Chau. 2021. "Immersive Learning Design for Technology Education: A Soft Systems Methodology." *Frontiers in Psychology* 12: 745295.

Yun, Soonyoung, and Shinhong Min. 2023. "A Study on Learning Immersion, Online Class Satisfaction, and Perceived Academic Achievement of Flip-Learning Online Classes." *Journal of Survey in Fisheries Sciences* 10 (4S): 432–41.

Zhang, Jun. 2019. "*Immersive Virtual Reality Training to Enhance Procedural Knowledge Retention.*" Purdue University.

Zhang, Zhang, Thosporn Sangsawang, Kitipoom Vipahasna, and Matee Pigultong. 2024. "A Mixed-Methods Data Approach Integrating Importance-Performance Analysis (IPA) and Kaiser-Meyer-Olkin (KMO) in Applied Talent Cultivation." *Journal of Applied Data Sciences* 5 (1): 256–67.

Zhao, Jensen J, Melody W Alexander, and Allen D Truell. 2014. "Immersive Learning of Real-World Problems and Solutions: An Innovative Approach to Attracting Students to Computer Information Systems Programs." *Issues in Information Systems* 15 (1).

Index

E

F

G

H

I

J

K

L

T

U

V

W